Classical Literature
and Its Times

VOLUME **8**

World
Literature and
Its Times

Classical Literature and Its Times

Profiles of Notable Literary Works and the
Historical Events That Influenced Them

Joyce Moss

THOMSON
GALE

Detroit • New York • San Francisco • New Haven, Conn. • Waterville, Maine • London • Munich

THOMSON

GALE

Classical Literature and Its Times
Profiles of Notable Literary Works and the Historical Events That Influenced Them
World Literature and Its Times, Volume 8

Joyce Moss

Product Manager
Meggin Condino

Editorial
Michael L. LaBlanc, Ira Mark Milne

Permissions
Margaret Chamberlain-Gaston,
Susan J. Rudolph

Imaging and Multimedia
Lezlie Light, Dan Newell, Christine O'Bryan

Image Acquisition
Denay Wilding

Manufacturing
Rita Wimberley

Library of Congress Control Number: 2006905345

Printed in the United States of America
10 9 8 7 6 5 4 3 2 1

Contents

General Preface

The world at the dawn of the twenty-first century is a shrinking sphere. Innovative modes of transmission make communication from one continent to another virtually instantaneous, quickening the development of an increasingly global society, heightening the urgency of the need for mutual understanding. At the foundation of *World Literature and Its Times* is the belief that within a people's literature are keys to their perspectives, their emotions, and the formative events that have brought them to the present point. Taking a deep as well as a broad view, the series spans works from the ancient past to the present in the additional belief that the literature of every age contains insights into universal struggles that have continued to plague humankind in different guises.

As manifested in their literary works, societies experience phenomena that are in some respects universal and in other respects tied to a particular time and place. Homer's *The Odyssey,* an epic of ancient Greece set about 1200 BCE, Cervantes's *Don Quixote,* a Spanish novel set about 1600 CE, and James Joyce's *Ulysses,* an Irish novel set around 1900 all center on individual men wandering to or through their home ground. Yet a close look at the works and their historical contexts reveals differences tied to the times and places of these tales. Likewise, Aristophanes *Lysistrata* (ancient Athens) and Julia Alverez's *In the Time of the Butterflies* (twentieth-century Dominican Republic) deal with women's responses to political events in ways that depend on the stories' settings.

World Literature and Its Times regards both fiction and nonfiction as rich mediums for recognizing the differences as well as the similarities among people and societies. In its view, full understanding of a literary work demands attention to events and attitudes of both the period in which the work takes place and the one in which it is written. The series therefore contextualizes a given play, poem, history, biography, essay, speech, dialogue, letter, novel, or short story within both these periods. Each volume in the series covers more than 40 literary works, which together span a mix of centuries and genres in a distinct part of the world. The literature itself guides the discussion in the entries, with its contents determining which historical issues—social, political, psychological, economic, and/or cultural—are treated. Each entry discusses the pertinent issues apart from the literary work, making connections to it when merited and promoting comparisons between literary portrayals and historical accounts. A separate section of the entry devotes close attention to the literary work itself, ensuring knowledge of the work's contents and helping readers extract various historical understandings from it.

Of course, the function of literature is not necessarily to represent history accurately. Nevertheless, the images and ideas promoted by a powerful work—be it Dante Alighieri's *Divine Comedy* (Italian), José Hernandez's *The Gaucho Martín Fierro* (Argentine), or William Shakespeare's *Macbeth* (English)—leave impressions commonly taken to be historical. In taking literature as fact, one risks acquiring mistaken understandings. In his comedy *Clouds*, Aristophanes lampoons the philosopher Socrates so effectively that another ancient writer, Plato, blames the play for conveying a fatally false impression (in one of his own writings, the dialogue known as the *Apology*).

On the other hand, literary works can broaden our understanding of history. They are able to convey more than the cut-and-dried record by portraying events in a way that captures the fears and challenges of a period or draws attention to inner motivations and marginal populations commonly left out of standard histories. Many works in this series—from Plutarch's *Parallel Lives* (ancient Greece and Rome), to Nelson Mandela's "The Rivonia Trial Speech" (mid-twentieth century South Africa)—draw attention to neglected facets of human existence in their day. Often, the characters and ideas in such works defy stereotypes, from Josephus's *The Jewish War* (set in ancient Palestine), to Friar Bartolomé de las Casas's *A Short Account of the Destruction of the Indies* (mid-1500s Latin America), to Chinua Achebe's *Things Fall Apart* (mid-1900s Nigeria). Other works counter stereotypes by depicting a society as complex, as comprised of multiple views and practices (e.g., Najib Mahfuz's *Miramar*, set in Alexandria, Egypt, in 1967).

Even nonfiction must be anchored in its place and time to derive its full value. In the *Politics*, Aristotle identifies the ideal government by surveying those that exist in his day. In eighteenth-century Mexico, in her letter "Reply to Sor Philothea," Sor Juana Inés de la Cruz defends her right to study religious and secular texts in light of the rights accorded to women in New Spain at the time. A third entry, Frantz Fanon's *The Wretched of the Earth* considers the appeal of violence in response to the ravages wreaked on the colonized by their colonizers in mid-twentieth-century Algeria.

The task of reconstructing the historical context of a literary work can be problematic. An author may be writing about events for which we have little information because they happened in the ancient past or there are few historical accounts. Other works may feature legendary heroes who defy placement into a strict time slot (for example, the warrior Achilles in the *Iliad* or the heroic queen of *The Arabian Nights*). In these cases, *World Literature and Its Times* provides legendary background, places a work in the most legitimate period scholarship has ascertained, and arms readers with the latest relevant information

to inform their understanding of a literary text. Still other works are problematic because they present events out of chronological order, as Carlos Fuentes does in *The Death of Artemio Cruz*. In such a case, to promote understanding, the series unscrambles the plot, providing a linear rendering of events along with the associated historical information. All these strategies enable the series to clarify the relationship between fact and fiction, both of which are shown to provide insight into a people and their heritage. As always, the series does so with a warm appreciation for the beauty of a literary work independent of the related historical facts, but also in the belief that ultimate regard is shown for a work by placing it in the context of pertinent events.

Beyond this underlying belief, *World Literature and Its Times* is founded on the notion that a command of world literature bolsters knowledge of the writings produced by one's own society. Long before the present century, writers from different locations influenced one another through trends and strategies in their literatures. Scholars speculate that in the first thousand years BCE, people of the Near East may have helped inspire Greek tales about the origin of the gods. Later Homer, a Greek writer, influenced the Roman poet Virgil who, in turn, influenced the Italian poet Dante across centuries and societies. In our own postcolonial age, such cross-fertilization has quickened. Latin American literature, having been influenced by Spanish trends, itself influences Chinese writers of the present. Likewise, Africa's literary traditions have affected and been affected by France's, and the same holds true for the writings of India and Great Britain. This type of commingling promises only to multiply as knowledge of literary works expands in our increasingly global, ever more technological society, In the process, world literature and its landmark texts gain added significance, attaining new potential to facilitate understanding not only of others but also of ourselves.

The Selection of Literary Works

The works covered in *Classical Literatures and Its Times* have been carefully selected by professors in the field at the universities listed in the Acknowledgements. Keeping the literature-history connection in mind, the development team chose titles for inclusion based on a combination of factors: how frequently a literary work is studied, how closely it is tied to pivotal historical events, how instrumental it is to the development of a genre, how strong and enduring its appeal has been to readers in and out of the society that produced it, and how well it conforms to the ancient conception of a classic as relayed in the Introduction to this volume. Careful attention has also been paid to covering a number of works that feature female, underclass, and minority characters and that raise issues pertaining to these populations. There are, of course, many more valuable ancient Greek and Roman works than could be covered in one volume. The inclusion of the selected works at the expense of others has been made with the above-detailed concerns in mind.

Format and Arrangement of Entries

The volumes in *World Literature and Its Times* are arranged geographically. Within each volume, the collection of entries is arranged alphabetically by title of the literary work. Each entry is organized as follows:

1. **Introduction**—provides identifying information in three parts:

   The literary work—specifies genre of a work, where and when the work is set, the language in which it was written, and the time of writing or first publication.

   Synopsis—summarizes the storyline or contents of the work.

   Introductory paragraph—introduces the literary work in relation to what is known about the author's life and larger corpus of writings.

2. **Events in History at the Time the Literary Work Takes Place**—describes social and political events that relate to the plot or contents of the literary work. The section may discuss background information as well as relevant events during the period in which the work is set. The subsections in this section vary, depending on the particular literary work. In general, the section takes a deductive approach, starting with events in history and telescoping inward to events or issues in the literary work.

3. **The Literary Work in Focus**—summarizes the plot or contents of the literary work, describes ways in which it illuminates history, and identifies sources that helped inspire the work. This section also places the work in literary context, showing its relation to other works. The section starts with a detailed plot or contents summary, followed by a subsection on an aspect of the work that illuminates our understanding of events or attitudes of the period. A third subsection discusses the author's sources and the literary context of the work. This subsection takes an inductive approach, starting with the literary work and broadening outward to events in history.

4. **Events in History at the Time the Literary Work Was Written**—describes social, political, and/or literary events in the author's lifetime related to the plot or contents. Also discussed are reactions to the work, if known, and its impact on later works.

5. **For More Information**—provides a list of all sources that have been cited as well as sources for further reading about the issues or personalities highlighted in the entry.

If a literary work is set and written in the same time period, sections 2 and 4 of the entry on that work ("Events in History at the Time the Literary Work Takes Place" and "Events in History at the Time the Literary Work Was Written") are combined into the single section "Events in History at the Time of the Literary Work."

Additional Features

Relevant primary-source material appears where appropriate in the text and in sidebars. Other sidebars provide historical details or anecdotes that amplify issues raised and promote understanding of the temporal context. At the front of a volume is a set of timelines that presents a historical overview of the society or societies featured in the volume. These timelines are correlated to the literary works treated in the volume. As appropriate, the entries themselves include briefer timelines to summarize intricate periods of history. Graphics are added as needed to clarify information. Finally, the entries contain relevant illustrations of people, places, and events. Given the dearth of images of ancient writers that have survived from antiquity, those reproduced in *Classical Literature and Its Times* are sometimes fanciful creations of later generations.

Comments and Suggestions

Your comments on this series and suggestions for future editions are welcome. Please write: Editors, *World Literature and Its Times,* Thomson Gale, 27500 Drake Road, Farmington Hills, Michigan 48331-3535.

Acknowledgments

lassical Literature and Its Times, the eighth volume of *World Literature and Its Times,* is a collaborative effort that progressed through several stages of development, each monitored by outstanding experts in ancient Greek and Roman literature and history. A special thank you goes to Professor Robert Gurval of the University of California at Los Angeles for overseeing each stage of the development process, from its inception to the final revisions. Warm gratitude is also extended to Professor Mortimer Chambers of the University of California of Los Angeles for furnishing repeated guidance on points of ancient history and to Seán Easton of Arizona State University for contributing his subject-matter expertise to the editorial process and laying the foundation for the Introduction to this volume.

For their incisive selection of the literary works to cover in this volume as well as the English translations on which to base the entries on these works, the editor extends deep appreciation to the following professors:

Robert Gurval, University of California at Los Angeles, Department of Classics

Jeffrey Henderson, Boston University, Department of Classical Studies

Steven Lattimore, University of California at Los Angeles, Emeritus, Department of Classics

Jo-Ann Shelton, University of California at Santa Barbara, Department of Classics

Stephen Scully, Boston University, Department of Classical Studies

William Thalmann, University of Southern California, Department of Classics

Pamela Vaughn, San Francisco State University, Department of Classics

Sincere gratitude is extended to the following professors for their careful review of the entries to insure accuracy and completeness of information:

Mortimer Chambers, University of California at Los Angeles, Department of History

Dorota Dutsch, University of California at Santa Barbara, Department of Classics

Seán Easton, Arizona State University, Department of Languages and Literatures

Vincent Farenga, University of Southern California, Department of Classics

Kristopher Fletcher, University of California at Los Angeles, Department of Classics

Ron Gallucci, University of California at Santa Barbara, Department of Classics

Ellen Greene, University of Oklahoma, Department of Classics and Letters

Robert Gurval, University of California at Los Angeles, Department of Classics

Michael Haslam, University of California at Los Angeles, Department of Classics

Jeffrey Henderson, Boston University, Department of Classical Studies

Acknowledgments

Moshe Lazar, University of Southern California, Department of Comparative Literature

Steven Lattimore, Emeritus, University of California at Los Angeles, Department of Classics

Edwin McCann, University of Southern California, School of Philosophy

Daniel McLean, University of California at Los Angeles, Department of Classics

Alex Nice, Reed College, Department of History

Stephen Scully, Boston University, Department of Classical Studies

Jo-Ann Shelton, University of California at Santa Barbara, Department of Classics

William Thalmann, University of Southern California, Department of Classics

For their painstaking research and composition, the editor thanks the writers whose names appear at the end of the entries they have contributed. A complete listing follows:

Robert D. Aguirre, Associate Professor, Wayne State University

Matthew Brosamer, Associate Professor, Mount St. Mary's College, Los Angeles

Kathryn Chew, Assistant Professor, California State University, Long Beach

Dorota Dutsch, Assistant Professor, University of California at Santa Barbara

Seán Easton, Visiting Assistant Professor, Arizona State University

Jennifer Eyl, Ph.D. Candidate, Brown University

Larry S. Ferrario, Associate Professor, California State University, Dominguez Hills

Kristopher Fletcher, Lecturer, University of California at Los Angeles

Lisa Granados, B.A., University of California at Los Angeles; professional writer

Martin Griffin, Visiting Assistant Professor, Claremont College

Ian Halbert, Ph.D. Candidate, Boston University

Despina Korovessis, M.A., Fordham University; professional writer

Michael Lovano, Assistant Professor, St. Norbert College

Pamela S. Loy, Ph.D., University of California at Santa Barbara; professional writer

Christine M. Maisto, Ph.D. Candidate, University of California at Santa Barbara

Diane R. Mannone, M.A. candidate, California State University, Dominguez Hills; professional writer

Christina Nation, M. A., Pepperdine University, Secondary Teacher, Santa Monica High School

Alex Nice, Assistant Professor, Reed College

Frank Russell, Associate Professor, Transylvania College

Michael L. Satlow, Associate Professor, Brown University

Kelli E. Stanley, Ph.D. Candidate, San Francisco State University

Franco Trivigno, Ph.D. Candidate, Boston University

Colin Wells, M.A., Oxford University; professional writer

A final note of gratitude is extended to Michael L. LaBlanc of Thomson Gale for his careful coordination of content, both text and illustration, and to Anne Leach, who indexed the volume with great sensitivity to readers. Lastly the editor thanks the editing and proofreading team of Moss Publishing, including Lisa Granados, Pamela S. Loy, Diane R. Mannone, Joyce Moss, Danielle E. Price, Monica Riordan, and Lorraine Valestuk, for their careful refinement of the contents through the volume's successive stages. An additional thank you goes to Lisa Granados for her invaluable assistance in organizational management.

Introduction

In all of literature, it has often been said, there are no more than a few basic tales, and humanity keeps repeating them through the ages with vigor as if they were new. A philosopher might identify them as human versus human, human versus nature, and human versus self; a writer mindful of character (human or nonhuman) might otherwise identify them as the tales of the conquering hero and the damsel in distress. Either way, they lie wrapped in the literature of the ancient Greeks and Romans who were among the first to relay them. Consider, for example, the conquering hero of Virgil's *Aeneid*, a man born of a mortal prince (Anchises) and a goddess (Aphrodite), who battles other characters, nature, and himself in a poem that has long been regarded as the pre-eminent epic of Rome.

Ancient Greek and Roman literature does more than tell stories, however. It enlightens, informs, and attempts to improve, making itself vital in the evolution of human affairs. "Roman," his dead father counsels Aeneas on a journey through the underworld, "remember by your strength to rule / Earth's peoples—for your arts are to be these: / To pacify, to impose the rule of law, / To spare the conquered, battle down the proud" (*Aeneid*, 6.1151-54). With these lines, Virgil clarifies for his ancient audience Rome's place in the collection of peoples living on the rim of the Mediterranean Sea, from the southern coast of Europe to the Middle East, to the northern coast of Africa.

Rome's was a world that boasted cultures older than that of the Romans, and of more rarefied accomplishment. In literature, Greece had already forged genres that did more than tell stories. As shown by the lines from the *Aeneid*, it was a primary function of literature in this Greco-Roman world to offer a significant comment on the relationship between an individual or community and the wider realm of existence, and in a way that retained value over time. Out of this conception came the birth of the literary classic.

The impulse that literature should serve such a purpose existed from the beginning of Greek literature through the generation of its Roman counterpart. The first Greek works were epics, narrative poems about the deeds of gods, heroes, and men, including Homer's *Iliad* and *Odyssey* (which emphasized heroic themes) and Hesiod's *Theogony* and *Works and Days* (which emphasized the transmission of knowledge). Composed in the eighth and possibly the seventh century BCE, the four epics are written incarnations of rich oral traditions perpetuated in Greece. This was the Archaic Age, when society consisted of separate communities of Greeks, or *Hellenes* as they had always called themselves. Despite the prevalence of these separate communities, the four epics convey a sense of shared norms and beliefs, as well as a drive toward a common culture. The very circulation of the poems reflected and promoted this drive, as did the origin in the eighth century BCE of such pan-Hellenic institutions as the Olympic games and the Oracle of Delphi.

Meanwhile, true to the richness that literature afforded from the start, the epics treated an emerging, somewhat contrary phenomenon among the peoples of ancient Greece: the growth of their local communities into independent city-states, along with a preoccupation with a hero's relationship to his particular city-state.

Archaic Greek poetry conveyed the harsh beauty of battle and the gentler beauty of family loyalties. Other conceptions of beauty surfaced in antiquity as well:

Fragment 31 (originally numbered 16)
Some say an army on horseback,
some say on foot, and some say ships
are the most beautiful things
On this black earth,

> but I say

It is whatever you love.

These lines are by Sappho, a female Greek poet of the seventh century BCE who wrote not *epic* but *lyric* verse. Composed in various meters and performed to the accompaniment of a dancing chorus, lyric broadened the range of themes, perspectives, and styles in written verse.

The meters of lyric became part of tragic drama in fifth-century BCE Athens, figuring in the songs of the chorus. By the end of the fifth century BCE, popular opinion had decided on the three greatest tragedy writers: Aeschylus, Sophocles, and Euripides. Seven of their plays are featured in this volume (Aeschylus' *Agamemnon*, *The Libation Bearers*, and *The Eumenides*; Sophocles' *Oedipus the King*, *Antigone,* and *Oedipus at Colonus*; and Euripides' *Medea*). In antiquity, as today, these seven were among the tragic "classics"; they not only entertained but also commented in enduring ways on a character's or community's relationship to wider existence. Meanwhile, the tragedies provided some insights into the beliefs and practices of the ancient Greeks. How many more insights could have been gleaned from the rest of their plays had a greater number survived? The seven featured here are but a fraction of the total output of these three dramatists. Altogether they wrote close to 300 plays, roughly 30 of which remain in existence today.

Prose is a younger form of writing than epic or lyric verse. The first great prose genre for the Greeks is historiography, which emerged in the fifth century BCE in Athens through the work of Herodotus. Much like epic, Herodotus's *Histories* engaged in cultural education. But his narrative, unlike epic, showed concern for verifying and sifting through contradictory interpretations of information. Herodotus took as his subject the Greco-Persian Wars of 490 and 480 BCE, and prior events that had contributed to them. Using prose, he adapted Homer's poetic scheme of a monumental narrative of pan-Hellenic heroism to rational inquiry. It was a type of inquiry inherited from the vibrant intellectual center of Miletus in Asia Minor.

For the fifth-century BCE historian Thucydides, the Trojan and Persian Wars paled in importance next to the *Peloponnesian War,* a domestic struggle between Sparta and Athens that consumed all of Greece for decades. At one point in his history, Thucydides uses the third-person, referring to himself as "he" to create an impression of objective reporting, a method adopted in the next century by Xenophon, whose *Persian Expedition* recounts his own participation in an ill-fated military campaign.

By the fifth century BCE, Homeric epic had emerged in written form as a pan-Greek cultural text full of basic principles on how life ought to be lived—what courage means, what constitutes a sound relationship to the gods, and so forth. Socratic philosophy, as it unfolds in the writings of Plato in the fourth century BCE, challenges this view, arguing that familiarity with poetic literature does not make one wise. Plato developed the genre of philosophical dialogue, depicting Socrates as he debates and develops ideas among a group of speakers who are sometimes hostile, sometimes supportive. Wisdom, argues the Socrates of Plato's *Apology*, can be pursued only through constant self-examination and critical inquiry into the nature of virtue. In his dialogue *The Republic*, Plato has Socrates banish the poets from the ideal state he conceives, on the grounds that poetry falsifies by its very nature while poets themselves are deeply ignorant of their subject matter. It follows that a state's poets—Homer included—should not be trusted to shape the minds of the people. The only exception, according to Plato's dialogue, is for poets who sing praises of the state. It is the philosophers, the *Republic* argues, who should rule a state, since they devote their lives to knowledge of truth.

In Plato's view, one of the most destructive influences on the public's impression of Socrates was Aristophanes (whose career spanned the fifth to the fourth century BCE). Aristophanes leaves to posterity the only surviving works of Old Comedy, including the *Clouds,* a play that typecasts Socrates as a highly eccentric inquirer after the secrets of the natural world and a thinker with dangerous ideas who absurdly worships clouds as deities. The power of literature to shape public opinion is at full flourish in this Old Comedy. It furthermore shows that while the genre featured outlandish characters and crude sexuality, it also lampooned prominent men and addressed real-life issues of the day. Female characters appear in Old Comedy too. Among the surviving plays of Aristophanes, the genre's foremost poet-playwright, is *Lysistrata*, a comedy featuring women who take a highly aggressive stance in political affairs. The plot of this imaginative Old Comedy is nothing less than a hilariously effective scheme, planned and executed by the women of Athens and Sparta, to end the Peloponnesian War. Their behavior is so atypical of real-life women at the time that the characters must have seemed utterly fantastical to ancient audiences.

From the late fifth century BCE, the themes and style of comedy changed, finally ushering in another distinct form, New Comedy (late fourth to mid-third century BCE). Private and family matters take precedence in New Comedy, along with both love, which invariably triumphs, and problems born of prejudice and misunderstanding. Among the most notable of the New Comedy playwrights was Menander, whose Greek plots were adapted for Roman audiences by Plautus and by Terence (third and second centuries BCE).

Plautus and Terence provide our earliest complete works in Latin (the language of Rome) that survive today. Typically at issue in a Plautus play is a youth's desire for a young woman, blocked at first by social custom or, as in *The Braggart Soldier*, by a rival. Social barriers are acknowledged in the course of these plays, but not challenged. The later comedies of Terence go further, using the same brand of plot to dwell on ethical questions (in *The Brothers,* the right to marry a partner of one's own choosing) and on subtle issues of one's moral integrity.

In the first century BCE, the poet Catullus strove to adapt lyric poetry, introduced by the Greeks, into a Latin form. In his *Carmina*, Catullus gives love and its emotional consequences a new centrality for Rome, also refashioning the type of language used in esteemed verse. Part of a revolutionary movement of Roman poets at the time, Catullus became a founding voice of the genre known as Latin lyric.

Like Catullus, Lucretius built on the Greek legacy. Only Lucretius used the language of epic verse to conceive his masterpiece—*On the Nature of the Universe* (otherwise known as *On the Nature of Things*). The poem imparts the ideas of the Greek philosopher Epicurus, teaching that the highest good is the absence of pain. Aggravating emotions, even those thought pleasurable or desirable, such as passionate love or political ambition, are to be avoided. Apparently Lucretius inherited from Epicurus, and Plato before him, the aversion of "truth-seeking philosophy" to what was regarded as falsifying, emotionally manipulative poetry. Yet Lucretius uses poetic form to relay Epicurean ideas, among them, a scientific explanation of the atoms of existence. Conveying philosophy in verse, the work appears to be a paradox attempting to resolve itself.

In the 50s BCE, the decade of Catullus and Lucretius, various prose genres also found champions in Rome. In the tradition of Plato, Cicero composed his own *Republic*, making real-life Romans, rather than Socrates, the speakers in his dialogue. As a remedy for an ailing state, Cicero prescribes not an imaginary ideal, as Plato does. but a return to an earlier, "better" age of Roman government. In historical writing, Julius Caesar spent the 50s BCE in Gaul, governing the province for Rome and waging war against neighboring peoples. Keen to keep his name and version of events in public view while away from Rome, he wrote *Commentaries on the Gallic War*, annual reports in which he refers to himself in the third person, adopting an air of objectivity, as others before him had. Like most Roman political and social climbers, Caesar craved not only the material riches but also the public honors that normally came with military conquest. He showed a common lust for status that surfaced in politically ambitious Romans and that Lucretius had already exposed and condemned in *On the Nature of the Universe*. After Caesar's victories in Gaul, this lust would thrust Rome into bloody civil war.

Virgil and Horace, influenced by Lucretius, used poetry to challenge the drive for wealth, property, and public honors. Virgil set his first published volume, the *Eclogues* (c. 40 BCE), in a pastoral landscape representative of communities of rural Italy that were first endangered, then encroached upon by harsh political realities. Horace, like Catullus before him, sought to revive Greek lyric in the Latin language. To this end, Horace adapted different styles to create poetry for a Rome that was no longer beset by civil strife and that, despite any appearances to the contrary, was no longer a republic. The resulting *Odes* at times addressed political subjects, but more often Horace blended public and private matters in poems that could boast a rich variety of themes.

Horace wrote during the formative years of a new regime, when Rome was under the rule of its first emperor, the grandnephew of and successor to Julius Caesar—Augustus (63 BCE–14 CE). Augustus, who saw the advantages of sponsoring literary works to help define his political achievements, built two libraries near his home for Greek and Latin literature, respectively. Supportive in return, Virgil and Horace produced poems that celebrated the achievements of the emerging Augustan regime (the end of civil strife, domestic peace, and military conquest). But these verses were not unqualified songs of praise, for they at the same time disclosed an anxiety over the future.

The various genres flourished in imperial Rome. In poetry, love elegy soared in the hands of Propertius and Tibullus, then expired after Ovid created verse on erotic love (see *Roman Elegy* and *Art of Love*). Along with Virgil, Ovid also shaped Roman verse by creating grand epic poetry. A worthy parallel to Homer's *Odyssey,* Virgil's *Aeneid* treats the lofty story of a survivor of the Trojan War—only from the other side of the conflict, the Trojan camp. Virgil takes as his starting point the well-established belief that Aeneas is an ancestor of Augustus's own clan, making the poem relevant to a picture of Roman history as an evolution that culminates in the reign of Augustus. Ovid's *Metamorphoses* is an epic with no less a theme than the history of the universe, envisioned as a clever, sometimes frightening pageant of transformation from the creation of the world down to where all classical stories cannot but help but go—the present-day of Augustan Rome.

The next century saw the growth of satire, which the Romans, not the Greeks, developed into a separate genre (according to the ancient teacher Quintilian). Sometimes good-humored, sometimes biting, Roman satire generally used verse to expose the follies of people and their pursuits. The earliest Roman to create satire (Gaius Lucilius) wrote in the second century BCE. Now, in the second century CE, Juvenal honed the genre. His *Satires,* composed in the same meter as epic poetry (dactylic hexameter), became a type of protest literature centered on public and private morality. Adopting the persona of an outraged citizen, his speaker lambasted perceived social evils, from corruption among the elite members of Roman society, to the flawed wives of Rome, to its ailing system of patron-client relationships.

Prose genres thrived in imperial Rome too. Taking up historiography were Livy and Tacitus.

Written in rich, flowing style, *From the Founding of the City* is a mammoth history of Rome, from its mythic origins to Livy's own early first century CE. Tacitus followed in the second century with *Annals of Imperial Rome,* an account of the first five emperors written in a style bristling with short barbed comments that reveal terrible truths, lifting the fog of lies and fears that prevailed under earlier rulers. Between Livy and Tacitus came Flavius Josephus, a Jewish historian who had participated in his people's revolt from Roman rule under the emperor Nero. A minority voice that manages to make itself heard, Josephus recounts the history of the revolt from a standpoint sympathetic to the Jews.

An offshoot of historical writing, biographical writing made notable progress in the second century. Plutarch, a Greek under Roman rule, helped forge a Greco-Roman synthesis by pairing the lives of illustrious men, one Greek and one Roman, and relaying their deeds in ways that reveal the nature or character of a man behind his actions. Suetonius, a secretary on the imperial staff, profiled the first dozen Caesars of Rome, sharing sordid details of their private lives, which gave readers a voyeuristic sense of peering into an otherwise hidden realm of Roman society. A few hundred years later, still under Roman rule, Augustine wrote an autobiographical work, his *Confessions.* Composed in the fifth century, well after Christianity had been adopted as the official religion of the Roman Empire, *Confessions* is a first-person account of Augstine's spiritual development. Departing from the traditional emphasis on public life with its achievements and failures, *Confessions* links spiritual self-scrutiny to a sensitivity to psychological issues that had surfaced earlier, in the biographies of Plutarch and Suetonius.

Augustine's spiritual search was a natural successor to a moral introspection conducted for centuries in Rome. Already in the 60s CE Seneca had written a series of essays masquerading as *Moral Letters* to a friend on a wide range of topics, from false friendship, to treatment of slaves, to virtue. The use of literature as a vehicle for moral, spiritual, and philosophical growth would continue beyond Augustine in the fourth century to Boethius in the sixth century, just after Roman rule had collapsed in the West. Thrown into prison by the Goths and then executed, Boethius wrote *The Consolation of Philosophy,* distinguishing himself as the last major voice in the West to write philosophy in Latin from the perspective of someone schooled in Greek.

A latecomer, the novel, the most popular form in modern Western literature, did not fit easily into the mix of ancient genres. The form was either scorned or ignored by critics in antiquity, yet, judging by the numerous fragments found since, novels seem to have been enormously popular then too. While fragments are plentiful, only a few ancient tales of lengthy prose fiction still exist today. In Latin, the two main texts are Petronius's *Satyricon* (first century CE) and Apuleius's *The Golden Ass* (second century CE): the first exists only in fragments; the second survives complete. In Greek, five novels survive complete, culminating with *An Ethiopian Story* by Heliodorus (fourth century CE). Each of the texts named here shows a fascination with life on the margins of social existence. Apparently even in antiquity, the novel fixed on the lives of commoners and/or outsiders. The *Satyricon* follows some ne'er-do-wells comically in search of their next dinner, meanwhile revealing much about social customs of the era, especially when an ex-slave, whose background drives him to absurd extravagances, hosts a lavish dinner party. In seriocomic fashion, *The Golden Ass* transforms a rather dim, arrogant man into a beast of burden for a period of life akin to the worst existence of a slave. Finally, An *Ethiopian Story* treats love, ethnic, and other relations in a tale that reaches beyond the frontier of Greek culture to bridge distant societies, as Greco-Roman literature had already shown itself uniquely capable of doing.

Chronology of Relevant Events

Classical Literature and Its Times

DAWN OF THE CLASSICAL WORLD:
FROM THE BRONZE AGE TO THE DARK AGE

While it is difficult to pinpoint the beginnings of Greek or Roman civilization, many historians regard the Bronze Age, an era when humans used bronze tools and weapons, as the approximate starting date for both. During this period, Mycenaean-Minoan culture dominated the region that would become Greece. Legend has it that the Mycenaean people were united under a single king, Agamemnon, although there is no historical evidence for his existence. This same king, it is said, served as the model for Agamemnon in Homer's Iliad, an epic poem about Mycenae's destruction of the city of Ilium (also known as Troy). By 1100 BCE, Mycenaean civilization had collapsed, which led to three centuries of economic, political, and artistic decline among the Greek-speakers. Early in this period, around 1050 BCE, some of the Greek-speaking mainlanders began to migrate to the Aegean Islands and the coast of Asia Minor, occupying an area later known as Ionia. This expansion would lead to a gradual resurgence of Greek culture, with the help of the new Iron Age, which ushered in sturdier tools and weapons. Artistically, Greece entered the first of five eras based on changing pottery styles: the proto-Geometric Period (1050–875 BCE). Turning to Roman culture, its origins are more nebulous than Greek beginnings. A Bronze Age society developed in west-central Italy in the Apennine region, and archaeological evidence attests to one or more villages on the hills of Rome from 1000 BCE. Also Rome is known to have arisen on the fringes of the nearby Etruscan civilization, with which the Romans would later have to contend for independence and influence.

Historical Events		Related Literary Works in *WLAIT 7*
c. 3000–1400 BCE	Bronze Age: Minoan civilization flourishes on island of Crete	
c. 1600–1100 BCE	Mycenaean Period: Ancient Greek city of Mycenae flourishes as the most powerful civilization on the Peloponnesian peninsula; Greeks of this period are sometimes called "Achaeans"	

c. 1500 BCE	Shaft graves, cut into rock to a depth of several meters, are built in Mycenae
c. 1500–1200 BCE	Bronze Age Apennine culture exists in western central Italy; Apennine economy progresses from semi-nomadic pastoralism, to stock-raising, to settled agriculture
c. 1400 BCE	Mycenaeans come into contact with Minoan culture, take over palace settlements on Crete
c. 1300 BCE	Earliest Celtic culture emerges on Upper Danube River
1100s BCE	Destruction of Mycenaean palaces in Greece, perhaps as a result of Dorian invasions, the Dorians being a Greek-speaking group from the north
1184 BCE	Traditional date given by ancient scholars for destruction of Troy VIIa (Ilium), often considered the model for Homer's Troy
c. 1150–750 BCE	Dark Age: The Mycenaean world collapses, leading to a period of decline for Greek civilization; poverty is widespread and writing is lost
1050 BCE	Greeks renew contact with Cyprus
1050–950 BCE	Greeks migrate to islands of the eastern Aegean Sea and west coast of Asia Minor, an area later known as Ionia
c. 1000 BCE	Settlements are built on Roman hills
950 BCE	Most of the weapons and tools in Greece are made of iron
c. 900–600 BCE	Iron culture in western central Italy

ANCIENT GREECE:
FROM THE GEOMETRIC TO THE ARCHAIC PERIOD

In the eighth century BCE, Greece experienced an important cultural and political resurgence often called the Greek Renaissance. Historians attribute this resurgence to various causes: colonial expeditions throughout the Aegean Sea, contact with Near Eastern civilizations, adaptation of the Phoenician alphabet, and the invention of writing, which spread all over the Greek world and led to the transcription of Homer's and Hesiod's epic poems. Meanwhile, styles of Greek pottery passed through three more eras—the Geometric (875–750 BCE), Orientalizing (720–620 BCE), and Archaic (750–480 BCE) periods. In politics, the polis—a city-state with its own law code, army, and system of government—came to dominate the Greek heartland. Altogether there were several hundred poleis in Greece and its colonies. Though the systems of government varied, they generally included an assembly, a council and magistrates, and, aside from obeying the laws, their citizens had to perform military service. During the Archaic Period, control of the polis was commonly seized by a tyrant, an aristocrat who ruled with the aid of his cronies. While some tyrants—such as Peisistratos in Athens—provided a stabile regime that promoted growth, others were oppressive. Sixth-century BCE Athens saw the introduction of reforms (by Cleisthenes) that weakened the aristocracy and made government more representative. In the fifth century BCE, the Greek states clashed with an outside enemy—the Persian Empire. Two separate Persian expeditions were launched against Greece, and both ultimately met with defeat.

c. 900–725 BCE	Geometric Period: Named for the prevalence of geometric motifs on painted pottery, this era witnesses rise of the polis—or city-state—in Greece, as well as closer contact between Greek world and Near Eastern countries of Phoenicia and Syria

Historical Events		Related Literary Works in *WLAIT 8*
c. 800 BCE	Earliest evidence of writing in Greece; beginning of a resurgence of cultural activity (called the Greek Renaissance)	
c. 750–650 BCE	Greek alphabet is invented, spreads throughout Greek world; Homer and Hesiod compose Western world's first-known epic poems; Greek colonies are established in southern Italy and Sicily	*Iliad* by Homer; *Odyssey* by Homer; *Theogony* by Hesiod
c. 750–479 BCE	Archaic Period spans the era of Greek tyrannies; elimination of the Persian threat by Greeks brings greater stability and formality to the Greek world	
c. 744–612 BCE	Height of Assyrian Empire in the East	
c. 735–715 BCE	First Messenian War between Messenia and Sparta; Sparta wins	
c. 730 BCE	Colonization movement begins in Black Sea area	
c. 725–630 BCE	"Orientalizing" Period in Greek art: Near Eastern and Eastern motifs replace geometric designs	
c. 700 BCE	Introduction of hoplite warfare—the name refers to the equipment of the hoplites (infantrymen), including a breastplate, helmet, shield, and spear	
c. 700–600 BCE	Period in which Lycurgus is said to have established military and political institutions in Sparta; dawn of Greek lyric poetry— individual poets first distinguish themselves	Poems by Sappho
c. 680–620 BCE	Pheidon at Argos and Cypselus at Corinth become first to rule Greek states as tyrannies	
c. 669 BCE	Argives defeat Spartans at Hysiai	
c. 660 BCE	Second Messenian War ends with Spartans crushing revolt	
c. 657–570 BCE	Most Greek states ruled by tyrants	
c. 650 BCE	Formation of the Peloponnesian League, a network of alliances of Greek states under Sparta's leadership; Greeks found colonies on Iberian peninsula	
621–620 BCE	Dracon introduces new laws in Athens, becomes the first to put Athenian laws in writing; death is the penalty for most offenses, large or small	
595–586 BCE	First sacred war for control of Delphi	
594–593 BCE	Solon introduces economic and social reforms in Athens, repeals all of Dracon's laws except for those dealing with murder	
587 BCE	King Nebuchadnezzar of Babylon captures Jerusalem; Jewish Diaspora begins	
585 BCE	Greek philosopher and mathematician Thales of Miletus predicts eclipse of sun	
560–510 BCE	Tyranny of Peisistratos and his sons at Athens, which results in a lengthy period of stability for Athens and an increase in military power	
c. 550 BCE	Cyrus founds Persian Empire, which emerges as a threat to Greece	
546–545 BCE	Persians conquer Ionian Greeks	
543 BCE	First tragedy is performed at the City Dionysia in Athens	
c. 530 BCE	Greek philosopher Pythagoras settles in southern Italy, promotes reincarnation of souls and vegetarianism	
c. 525 BCE	Persians invade Egypt, annex neighboring African territories, including Ethiopia	

Historical Events		Related Literary Works in *WLAIT 8*
522–486 BCE	Reign of Darius I, king of Persia	
520–490 BCE	Reign of Cleomenes of Sparta	
c. 514 BCE	Darius of Persia conquers Thrace	
508 BCE	Cleisthenes introduces constitutional reforms in Athens, weakening the power of the aristocratic kin groups	
501–500 BCE	Institution of board of ten generals, or strategoi, at Athens as military commanders	
499–493 BCE	Ionian cities revolt against Persia	
490 BCE	First Persian expedition into Greece; Greeks defeat Persians at Marathon	
487 BCE	Athenian magistrates are henceforth chosen by lot; state provision of comedies at City Dionysia begins	
486 BCE	Death of Darius of Persia, accession of Xerxes	
482 BCE	Construction of Athenian fleet	
480–479 BCE	Xerxes launches Persian invasion of Greece, sacks city of Athens; Greeks defeat Persians at both Salamis and Plataea	
478–477 BCE	Formation of the Delian League; Athens leads alliance of Greek states against Persia	
c. 454 BCE	Treasury of Delian League is moved from the island of Delos to Athens, signifying development of the league into an Athenian Empire	

THE CLASSICAL PERIOD
FROM THE ATHENIAN GOLDEN AGE TO THE DEATH OF ALEXANDER THE GREAT

In the wake of the second Persian retreat, many Greek states formed a confederacy under the leadership of Athens to protect themselves from further attacks. Headed by the statesman and general Pericles, Athens reigned as the dominant political, social, and artistic power, incurring the resentment of other city-states, especially Sparta and Corinth. The internal friction escalated, culminating in the Peloponnesian Wars. While the First Peloponnesian War concluded with a pact that called for 30 years of peace, only 15 years later relations between Athens and Sparta deteriorated so severely that the Second Peloponnesian War broke out. Ultimately Athens lost much of its power and empire in the struggle, surrendering to Sparta in 404 BCE. During the next century, the northern kingdom of Macedon emerged as a powerful force. Shrewdly exploiting the rivalries among the Greek city-states, King Philip II of Macedon gained control over mainland Greece. His son, Alexander the Great, further extended the borders of the Macedonian Empire into Persia, Egypt, and India before his sudden death. Meanwhile, artists and writers reached Greek cultural heights in what has since become known as the Classical Period, which stretched from the Greek defeat of the Persians (480–479 BCE) to Alexander's demise (323 BCE).

c. 488 BCE	Magistrate is given duty of providing comedy performances each year at City Dinoysia, annual festival in Athens to honor Dionysus, god of wine, theater, and impersonation	
479–431 BCE	Athenian Golden Age: Athens becomes increasingly populous and prosperous, emerging as dominant Greek city-state; genre of tragedy undergoes major developments	*Oresteia* by Aeschylus; *The Theban Plays* by Sophocles; *Medea* by Euripides

Historical Events		Related Literary Works in *WLAIT 8*
c. 467 BCE	The Athenian statesman and soldier Cimon defeats Persians at Eurymedon	
464 BCE	Sparta suffers an earthquake; brief Messenian revolt for independence from Sparta	
462–461 BCE	The Athenian statesman Ephialtes introduces democratic reforms, limiting power of the Areopagus, the aristocratic governing council	
460s–429 BCE	The statesman and general Pericles dominates politics in Athens; among other reforms, Pericles introduces payment for Athenian jurors	
460–446 BCE	First Peloponnesian War: Athens fights Corinth and Sparta; Thirty Years' Peace declared at war's end	
459–456 BCE	Athenian expedition into Egypt to aid in rebellion against Persians; a Persian force expels Athenians	
451 BCE	Athenian citizenship law forbids marriages between citizens and foreigners and does not recognize children of such relationships	
447–429 BCE	Pericles initiates extensive building program in Athens; construction of the Parthenon, a temple dedicated to Athena	
446–425 BCE	Tenuous peace between Sparta and Athens	
c. 440–430 BCE	Socrates raises provocative questions about nature and morality; other Greek philosophers gain notoriety, such as Plato, Democritus, Hippocrates, and Protagoras	
430–425 BCE	Herodotus becomes first Western writer to investigate past events (Persian Wars) and try to explain them rationally	*The Histories* by Herodotus
430–400 BCE	Sparta beats Athens in Second Peloponnesian War (431–404 BCE); Thucydides writes an account of the conflict	*The Peloponnesian War* by Thucydides
429 BCE	Pericles dies	
425 BCE	Initial performance of Aristophanes' Acharnians, the earliest Greek comedy to survive complete	
423	Tension between poetry and philosophy in Athens—comic poet Aristophanes ridicules Socrates, depicts philosophy as dangerous force	*Clouds* by Aristophanes
421 BCE	Peace of Nicias between Athens and Sparta achieves temporary truce in Peloponnesian War	
415–413 BCE	Athens embarks on ill-fated military expedition against Sicily	
413 BCE	Hostilities between Athens and Sparta resume	
412–411 BCE	Sparta enters into treaties with Persia	*Lysistrata* by Aristophanes
411 BCE	Coup of 400 at Athens	
405 BCE	Battle of Aegospotami: Spartans destroy Athenian fleet in a final naval defeat	
405–367 BCE	Dionysius I reigns as tyrant in Syracuse	
404 BCE	Athens, much of its power and empire lost, surrenders to Sparta after a siege	
404–403 BCE	Spartan-supported oligarchy, known as the Thirty Tyrants, rules Athens	
403 BCE	Restoration of democracy at Athens	
401–399 BCE	Cyrus the Younger and the Ten Thousand (Greek mercenary soldiers) lead an ill-fated expedition against the Persian king Artaxerxes II	*The Persian Expedition* by Xenophon

Historical Events		Related Literary Works in *WLAIT 8*
late 300s–mid-200s BCE	New Comedy flourishes; Menander is recognized as its premiere playwright	
399 BCE	Trial and execution of Socrates, who commits suicide by drinking hemlock	*Apology* by Plato
395–386 BCE	Corinthian War: Persia, allied with Athens and other Greek states, fights Sparta and wins control over Greek Anatolia via the King's Peace	
387 BCE	Plato founds the Academy, develops philosophy of Platonism, theorizing that substantive reality is merely a reflection of a higher truth	*Republic* by Plato
387/386 BCE	Peace of Antalcidas ends Greek-Persian hostilities in Asia Minor and nearby islands	
386 BCE	Spartan hegemony in Greece	
382–379 BCE	Sparta seizes Thebes, then loses it in the popular uprising of 379 BCE	
378–377 BCE	Athens founds a second league of city-states, the Second Athenian Confederacy	
371 BCE	Battle of Leuctra: Thebes defeats Sparta, crushing its hopes for lasting power	
370 BCE	Assassination of Jason, tyrant of Pherae in Thessaly	
362 BCE	Battle of Mantinea: Thebes defeats Sparta but the Theban army weakens in the process	
359 BCE	Philip II becomes king of Macedon	
357–355 BCE	Athenian naval alliance dissolves because of internal conflicts	
356 BCE	Sacred War erupts between Macedonians and Phocians	
350 BCE	Oratory flourishes; Aristotle publishes Rhetoric, on theory, audience's state of mind, and style and metaphor in art of spoken argument	
348 BCE	Philip II captures Olynthos	
347–322 BCE	Political instability and flux within the Greek world challenges the survival of the polis, or city-state	*Politics* by Aristotle
346 BCE	Peace of Philocrates between Macedon and Athens	
338 BCE	Philip II of Macedon defeats Thebans and Athenians at Chaironeia, comes to dominate mainland Greek states	
337 BCE	Foundation of League of Corinth, which declares war on Persians	
336 BCE	Philip II is murdered; accession of Philip's son Alexander the Great	
335 BCE	Aristotle founds the Lyceum	
334–332 BCE	Alexander the Great crosses into Asia, defeats Persian king Darius III, occupies Phoenicia, Palestine, and Egypt	
331 BCE	Alexander defeats Persians again; city of Alexandria is founded in Egypt; Persia and Egypt pay tribute to Macedon	
330 BCE	Darius III is murdered; Alexander the Great claims right to rule Persian Empire; the Greek orator Demosthenes delivers his foremost speech, defends himself as a champion of Athenian independence	*On the Crown* by Demosthenes
323 BCE	Alexander the Great dies suddenly in Babylon	

THE HELLENISTIC PERIOD
FROM THE DEATH OF ALEXANDER TO THE
ROMAN CONQUEST

In the wake of Alexander the Great's unexpected demise, his heirs and generals tried separately to seize as much of his far-flung empire as possible. Ultimately three stable kingdoms emerged: the realms of Macedon, Egypt, and Syria, ruled respectively by the Antigonid, Ptolemy, and Seleucid dynasties. The Atigonids ruled Macedon for more than a century (c. 277–168 BCE), while the other two dynasties endured far longer. The Ptolemies, themselves of Macedonian Greek descent, ruled Egypt until its conquest by Rome (323–30 BCE). The Seleucids, also a Macedonian Greek dynasty, gained control of Syria in stages (beginning in 301 BCE), then lost it when Syria became a province of Rome in 64 BCE. The result of all this domination was a cultural blending, in which the ways of the Greeks, who called themselves "Hellenes" (hence the terms "Hellenized" and "Hellenistic") were adopted alongside local customs. Greek culture was disseminated throughout the realm, so the period featured states that were subject to the three dynasties and characterized by the adoption of Greek ways. The empire lasted 300 years (early fourth to early first century BCE), from shortly after Alexander's death to the domination of Greece and the Hellenized East by the Romans. From their small part of the Italian peninsula, the fierce Romans rose to challenge and ultimately subdue the Greek world. Macedon, Syria, and finally Egypt surrendered, yet their Greek ways of life retained preeminence. Even in defeat, the Greeks held cultural sway, their customs greatly affecting Roman religious, intellectual, social, and artistic thought. Politically the Roman Empire entirely supplanted the Hellenistic; culturally the Roman realm gave pre-eminence to a blend of Greek and Roman ways.

c. 323–281 BCE	Alexander's heirs divide his empire
323–30 BCE	Greek culture—poetry, drama, philosophy—spreads throughout Macedonian, Egyptian, and Syrian empires; Egypt is ruled by the Ptolemies, descended from one of Alexander's generals
322 BCE	Demosthenes commits suicide
c. 320–301 BCE	Macedonian general Antigonus I tries to found a kingdom in Greece, Macedon, and the Near East but is killed in battle at Ipsus in Anatolia
c. 310 BCE	Zeno founds Stoicism, a philosophy teaching that all happens according to divine reason and urging people to accept and live in harmony with nature, or divine reason
c. 307 BCE	Greek philosopher Epicurus founds school in Athens, which teaches that there is no providential god and promotes philosophical pleasure as life's main goal
c. 306–304 BCE	Alexander's successors declare themselves kings
303 BCE	Seleucus I cedes the eastern territory of his kingdom to Indian ruler Chandragupta
301 BCE	Seleucus I gains control of north Syria
300 BCE	King Ptolemy I (r. 323–283 BCE) establishes the Museum at Alexandria, which becomes the cultural center of the Hellenistic world

Historical Events	Related Literary Works in *WLAIT 8*
285–246 BCE	Rule of Ptolemy II, who develops the Library at Alexandria; probably founded by Ptolemy I, it becomes the leading center of ancient texts, is said to include official copies of works by Aeschylus, Sophocles, and Euripides, along with Aristotle's library	
284–281 BCE	Achaean League is revived in southern Greece	
281 BCE	Seleucus gains control of Asia Minor; Achaean League of Greek cities is formed to resist Macedon, revives a league of the prior century	
c. 280 BCE	First contact between Greek and Roman civilization	
279 BCE	Gauls invade Macedon and Greece; Pyrrhus of Epirus wins costly victory over Romans at Battle of Asculum	
274–217 BCE	Four Syrian wars fought between Ptolemies and Seleucids	
263–241 BCE	Eumenes I establishes Attalid kingdom in Anatolia	
247 BCE–224 CE	Arsacids control Parthia	
239–130 BCE	Independent Greek kingdom established in Bactria (modern Afghanistan)	
238–227 BCE	Attalus I of the Attalid dynasty defeats Gauls and confines them to Galatia	
229 BCE	Piracy of Illyrian tribes, who live in an area that borders Macedonia, leads to Roman intervention in the east	
227 BCE	Reform of Spartan state by Cleomenes III	
214–205 BCE	Philip V of Macedon fights First Macedonian War against Rome, which leads to Roman involvement in Macedon, Greece, Egypt, and the Near East	
200 BCE	Antiochus II establishes Seleucid rule over south Syria, Phoenicia, and Judaea	
200–197 BCE	Second Macedonian War	
171–167 BCE	Third Macedonian War; Roman legions defeat Macedon, which leads to break-up and reorganization of the kingdom into four federal republics	
168–167 BCE	Maccabees lead revolt in Judaea against the Seleucid ruler Antiochus IV Epiphanes	
168 BCE	Romans defeat Perseus of Macedon at Pydna on northeast coast of Greece; end of Macedonian monarchy	
149 BCE	Third war between Rome and Carthage	
146 BCE	Rome crushes Macedonian revolt; Greek cities of Carthage and Corinth are destroyed; Macedon becomes Roman province	
142 BCE	Jews expel Seleucids; rise of Hasmonean kingdom of Jewish rulers in Judaea (they will endure until 63 BCE)	
88 BCE	Sack of Delos by soldiers of Mithridates of Pontus; 20,000 inhabitants are killed	
86 BCE	Sack of Athens by the Roman general Sulla	
64 BCE	Syria becomes a Roman province	
51–30 BCE	Reign of Cleopatra VII of Egypt, the last pharaoh and the last Macedonian ruler of the Hellenistic period	
40 BCE	Parthians capture Jerusalem	

Historical Events	Related Literary Works in *WLAIT 8*
37 BCE — Romans recapture Judaea and support Herod the Great as king; Hasmonean dynasty ends, Herod begins his 33-year reign (37–34 BCE)	
31 BCE — Octavian defeats Mark Antony and Cleopatra at Actium	
30 BCE — Double suicides of Antony and Cleopatra; Egypt becomes a Roman possession	

ANCIENT ROME
FROM THE FOUNDING OF THE CITY TO THE END OF REPUBLICAN ROME

Although archaeological evidence testifies to permanent settlements on the hills of Rome from about 1000 BCE, Rome has traditionally dated its origins at 753 BCE, when the legendary Romulus is said to have founded the city. Ancient sources recount the lives of Romulus and successive, possibly legendary kings over the next two centuries. According to these sources, in 509 BCE the people expelled their seventh king, Tarquinius Superbus, and established the Roman Republic, a government of the aristocratic populace. This early republic appears to have been led by two elected officials (called consuls) and a Senate of wealthy citizens who held office for life. In external affairs, Rome overwhelmed the Latin tribes in the region and defeated the native Etruscans, in whose shadow the Romans had long dwelt. Even the temporary capture of Rome in 390 BCE by Celtic tribes from Gaul could not halt the city's growth. During the fourth and third centuries BCE, Rome undertook a series of military and colonial expeditions that led to its occupation of all Italy south of the Po Valley as well as most of Spain and parts of Africa. Between 200 and 167 BCE the Romans brought much of the inhabited world under their control, including the once-mighty kingdoms of Macedon and Syria. Meanwhile, Roman society flourished, constructing roads and aqueducts and settling down to enjoy the fruits of successful military conquest. In art and literature, the Romans borrowed from and built on the Greek civilization they had subdued. In politics, individual statesmen gained distinction, among them, Pompey, Cicero, and, most remarkably, Julius Caesar, whose military prowess, intellect, and personal charisma contributed to his meteoric rise in Roman society. After winning a civil war, Caesar assumed supreme control of all Rome's political affairs. The Senate finally proclaimed him dictator for life, a status that would lead not only to his own assassination but also to the demise of the republican government and the rise of imperial rule in Rome.

c. 1000 BCE — One or more settlements exist on the hills of Rome, each formed by a few thatched huts	
c. 753 BCE — Legendary founding of the city of Rome by Romulus, who descends from Aeneas, a survivor of the Trojan War	
753–509 BCE — Seven kings (some of whom may be legendary) rule Rome, beginning with Romulus and ending with Tarquinius Superbus	
c. 700–400 BCE — Etruscan culture influences life in central Italian peninsula; Etruscan alphabet leads to spread of writing	
c. 600 BCE — Emergence of Latin states in central Italy	
509 BCE — Superbus expelled and monarchy falls; the Roman Republic is established	

Historical Events		Related Literary Works in *WLAIT 8*
c. 496 BCE	Rome defeats Latin League at Battle of Lake Regillus	
c. 450 BCE	Publication of the Twelve Tables, first codification of Roman law	
c. 445 BCE	Lex Canuleia permits marriages between plebeians (mass of Roman citizens) and patricians (aristocrats)	
396 BCE	Romans destroy Etruscan town of Veii after ten-year siege	
c. 390 BCE	Invasion of Celtic tribes from Gaul and sack of Rome	
367 BCE	Lex Licinia Sextia makes plebeians eligible for the office of consul, a right formerly enjoyed only by patricians	
c. 343–341 BCE	First Samnite War: Romans fight Samnites in central Apennine region of Italian peninsula	
341–338 BCE	Latin War, dissolution of Latin League	
c. 327–321 and 316–304 BCE	Second Samnite War	
c. 312 BCE	Work begins on Appian Way, Rome's main road to south Italy; Aqua Appia, the first Roman aqueduct, is constructed	
298–290 BCE	Third Samnite War	
287 BCE	Lex Hortensia affirms the resolutions of plebeian assemblies as law	
280–275 BCE	Greek general Pyrrhus invades Italy and defeats Romans but at a tremendous cost in Greek lives (experiences "Pyrrhic victories—wins that are offset by great loss of life)	
272 BCE	After capture of coastal city of Tarentum, Rome acquires control over southern Italy	
264–241 BCE	First Punic War between Rome and Carthage; Rome remedies weakness in cavalry and light-armed troops by hiring mercenaries; first gladiatorial games in Rome	
241 BCE	Sicily becomes first Roman province	
240 BCE	Livius Andronicus translates works by Homer into Latin	
218–201 BCE	Second Punic War between Rome and Carthage; Rome's use of mercenary soldiers grows	*The Braggart Soldier* by Plautus
218 BCE	Carthaginian general Hannibal crosses the Alps Mountains into Italy	
217–216 BCE	Hannibal defeats Romans at Lake Trasimene and village of Cannae; Romans suffer enormous losses	
215–205 BCE	First Macedonian War between Rome and Philip V of Macedon, an ally of Hannibal	
204 BCE	Roman general Scipio invades Africa; later he becomes known as Scipio Africanus in tribute to his success	
202 BCE	Scipio defeats Hannibal at Zama in North Africa	
200–196 BCE	Second Macedonian War ends with Battle of Cynoscephalae; Philip retains his kingdom	
192–188 BCE	Syrian War between Rome and Antiochus III of Syria ends with Syrian defeat	
191 BCE	Rome completes conquest of Cisalpine (Nearer) Gaul	
168 BCE	Battle of Pydna: Perseus, the king of Macedon is captured and his kingdom is divided	
160 BCE	Death of Aemilius Paullus, a Roman general given to extravagant ways, in contrast to conservative ways of the statesman Cato the Censor	*The Brothers* by Terence

Historical Events	Related Literary Works in *WLAIT 8*
155–133 BCE — Celtiberian War: Romans control most of Iberian peninsula (Spain and Portugal)	
146 BCE — Rome destroys Carthage (146 BCE), wins Third Punic War; later in year Rome sacks Greek city of Corinth, and crushes Macedonian revolt, Greece and Macedonia become provinces ruled by Rome	
144 BCE — Construction begins on the Aqua Marcia, Rome's first high-level aqueduct, to bring water to Capitoline Hill	
135–132 BCE — First Slave Wars in Sicily, led by Eunus and Cleon	
133 BCE — The tribune Tiberius Gracchus proposes land distribution to help poor, gets law passed by irregular means, leading to a riot that claims his life	
21 BCE — The tribune Gaius Gracchus, attempting to enfranchise Italians, is murdered	
112–106 BCE — War against Jugurtha of Numidia in North Africa	
104–103 BCE — Second Slave Wars in Sicily, led by Athenion and Tryphon	
104–100 BCE — Roman leader Gaius Marius serves as consul for five consecutive terms	
91–89 BCE — Social War between Roman Republic and other Italian cities; citizenship is extended to all Italian lands south of the Po River	
89–63 BCE — Series of wars between Rome and King Mithridates of Pontus, the region of Asia Minor south of the Black Sea	
88–82 BCE — Civil war between Roman generals Gaius Marius and Lucius Cornelius Sulla	
88 BCE — Sulla becomes consul, marches on Rome	
86 BCE — Death of Marius	
82–81 BCE — Dictatorship of Sulla, proscriptions against his enemies—they are listed as outlaws whose property is forfeit and who can be killed with impunity	
79 BCE — Sulla resigns dictatorship, dies the following year	
73–71 BCE — Spartacus leads slave revolt in southern Italy	
70 BCE — Consulships of Pompey and Crassus; Cicero delivers Verrine Orations against governor Gaius Verres, who has plundered province of Sicily for self-gain	
67 BCE — Pompey eliminates pirates from Mediterranean area	
66–62 BCE — Pompey conquers lands in the East, creates new provinces, returns to Rome in triumph	
63 BCE — Cicero serves as consul, denounces Catiline conspiracy against Rome; Pompey begins settlement of East	*Speeches* by Cicero
60 BCE — Formation of "First Triumvirate," misnomer for a coalition of Caesar, Pompey, and Crassus, a group that has no official power to rule	
c. 60–55 BCE — Lucretius promotes ideas of Greek philosopher Epicurus in Rome	*On the Nature of The Universe* by Lucretius
c. 50s BCE — "New Poets" create fresh style of lyric verse in Rome	*Carmina* by Catullus
59 BCE — Caesar serves as consul	
58–57 BCE — Exiled from Rome, Cicero flees to Greece but, with Pompey's support, is recalled	
58–52 BCE — Expansion of the Roman Empire; Caesar campaigns in Gaul and Britain, writes his own versions (commentaries) of his military victories	*Commentaries on the Gallic War* by Caesar; *The Republic* by Cicero

	Historical Events	Related Literary Works in *WLAIT 8*
55–54 BCE	Caesar's invasions of Britain	
53 BCE	Romans, ambushed by Parthians, suffer a serious defeat; Crassus and his eldest son are killed	
49 BCE	Caesar incites civil war, crosses the Rubicon, stream that serves as the boundary between his domain and the empire's Italian heartland	
48 BCE	Caesar defeats Pompey at Greek city of Pharsalus; Pompey flees to Egypt, is murdered upon his arrival	
48–47 BCE	Caesar invades and captures Alexandria, Egypt, has liaison with Cleopatra VII of Egypt, who gives birth to a son she names Caesarion ("little Caesar" in Greek)	
44 BCE	Roman Senate proclaims Caesar dictator of Rome for life	

THE RISE AND DECLINE OF IMPERIAL ROME

Julius Caesar's political ascendancy stirred grave concern on the part of certain Romans. To thwart the transformation of their republic into a dynasty-oriented monarchy, a band of conspirators assassinated Caesar on March 15, 44 BCE. Caesar's heir and grandnephew Octavian later seized the consulship, then pursued and defeated Brutus and Cassius, ringleaders of the assassination. For the next decade, Rome was ruled by the Second Triumvirate (Octavian, Mark Antony, and Marcus Lepidus), whose members divided the empire among themselves. Antony's involvement with Cleopatra VII led to the triumvirate's dissolution, the defeat of Antony and Cleopatra at Actium in 31 BCE, and their suicides within the following year. Octavian assumed solitary control over the Roman state. Taking the name Augustus ("revered one") in 27 BCE, he restored the traditional offices of state and then ruled Rome until his death in 14 CE. During his tenure, Augustus oversaw Rome's final transition from Republic to Empire. His reign, which was peaceful and prosperous, boded well for the future of the Julio-Claudian dynasty he established. In the end, however, few of his heirs ruled so successfully. The turbulent dynasty ended with the suicide of Nero in 68 CE. A series of short-lived emperors followed before stability was restored under Vespasian, founder of the Flavian rulers. This second Roman dynasty ended with the assassination of the repressive emperor Domitian. There followed a generally peaceful, prosperous era under five successors known as the "Good Emperors." Then came a new set of civil wars, the rule of the Severan dynasty, and a chaotic era under the rule of soldier-emperors. Restoring order in 284, Emperor Diocletian set up separate governments for the eastern and the western halves of Rome's empire. Meanwhile, a new faith, Christianity, had begun taking hold in the imperial world. In 324 Constantine I became the first Christian ruler of the Roman Empire.

	Historical Events	Related Literary Works in *WLAIT 8*
44 BCE	Assassination of Julius Caesar on the Ides of March during a Senate meeting	
44–43 BCE	Civil war in Rome; Octavian (Augustus) seizes consulship; Octavian, Mark Antony, and Marcus Lepidus form Second Triumvirate; Cicero is killed in the proscriptions	
42 BCE	Battle of Philippi ends with the suicides of Brutus and Cassius	
41 BCE	Antony forms an alliance with Cleopatra VII of Egypt	
41–40 BCE	Octavian oversees confiscation of lands from Italian farmers to reward veteran soldiers; siege of city of Perusia by Octavian	*Eclogues* by Virgil
40 BCE	Second Triumvirate divides Roman provinces; Antony's wife Fulvia dies; Antony marries Octavian's sister, Octavia	

Historical Events		Related Literary Works in *WLAIT 8*
40 and 36 BCE	Cleopatra gives birth to three of Antony's children: in 40 BCE, after he returns to Rome, where he marries Octavia, Cleopatra bears him twins (Alexander Helios and Cleopatra Selene); in 36 BCE, she bears Antony a third child (Ptolemy Philadelphus)	
37 BCE	Second Triumvirate renewed for another five years	
36 BCE	Lepidus is forced to retire from the Second Triumvirate	
32 BCE	Antony divorces Octavia	
31–30 BCE	Octavian defeats Antony and Cleopatra in naval battle at Actium, then triumphs over them at Alexandria; suicides of Antony and Cleopatra	
27 BCE–68 CE	Reign of first Roman dynasty, the Julio-Claudians, though existence of the Roman Empire is never openly proclaimed	
27 BCE–14 CE	Octavian takes the name Augustus ("revered one") and assumes complete control of Rome, oversees its transition from Roman Republic to Roman Empire; era of stability and peace known as the Pax Romana ensues	*From the Founding of the City* by Livy; *Roman Elegy* by Tibullus and Propertius
23 BCE	Augustus grows ill, recovers, assumes powers of a tribune; Marcellus, nephew of Augustus and likely heir, dies	*Odes* by Horace
20 BCE	Successful diplomatic negotiations with Parthia	
19 BCE	Virgil dies before finishing a Roman epic designed to be as lofty as Homer's Greek epics	*Aeneid* by Virgil
19–18 BCE	Augustus implements the Julian laws to encourage marriage and childbirth, and punish adultery as a public crime	
13–9 BCE	Expansion of Roman Empire up to the Danube Rive	
11 BCE	Tiberius (son of Augustus's wife Livia) is ordered to divorce first wife and marry Augustus's daughter Julia	
c. 5–6 BCE	Birth of Jesus of Nazareth in Judaea	
4 BCE	Death of Herod the Great	
2 BCE	Augustus banishes his daughter Julia from Rome on charges of adultery	*The Art of Love* by Ovid
8 CE	Augustus banishes Ovid from Rome for reasons that are never fully explained	*Metamorphoses* by Ovid
9	Three Roman legions are lost in Germany; Rhine-Danube riverway is ultimately established as northern frontier of Roman Empire	
14–37	Augustus dies, is deified; Tiberius reigns, continues most of Augustus's policies; conflicts erupt within imperial family; Tiberius's reign ends in period of terror	
26	Tiberius leaves Rome and governs the empire from isle of Capri until his death	
c. 30	Preacher and healer Jesus of Nazareth is active in Judaea, suffers death by crucifixion	
31	Trial and execution of Sejanus, commander of praetorian or household troops of Roman emperors and former friend of Tiberius	
37–41	Reign of Gaius Caesar, popularly known as Caligula; after serious illness, Caligula behaves cruelly and irrationally, is assassinated by his own palace guards	
c. 40s–60s	Paul of Tarsus, a follower of Jesus, travels through Roman Empire as missionary, preaching gospel of Christianity; Paul dies c. 62	
41–54	Reign of Emperor Claudius restores political stability; Seneca is recalled from exile to tutor Claudius's stepson, Nero	*Phaedra* by Seneca

Historical Events		Related Literary Works in *WLAIT 8*
43	Invasion of Britain by Rome	
44	Judaea becomes a Roman province, is ruled by a procurator, an employee of the Roman emperor	
54–68	Reign of Nero, whose court becomes notorious for its vice, corruption, and cruelty	*Satyricon* by Petronius; *Moral Letters to Lucilius* by Seneca
65	Conspirators against Nero are found and put to death; Seneca is ordered to commit suicide	
64	Great Fire of Rome	
66–67	First Jewish revolt against Roman rule; Vespasian, a general of the rising Flavian family, is sent to regain control	*The Jewish War* by Josephus
69–79	Reign of Emperor Vespasian restores political and economic stability to Roman state, creates a new dynasty (the Flavians)	
70	Vespasian's son Titus takes charge of siege in Judaea, destroys Jerusalem and temple	
74	Fall of Masada, a Judaean fort, ends first Jewish revolt	
79–81	Brief reign of Emperor Titus	
79	Eruption of Mt. Vesuvius destroys Pompeii; Pliny the Elder, admiral of Roman fleet and author of Natural History, dies in the disaster	
80	Completion and inauguration of the Colosseum, Rome's great amphitheater, in which spectators witnessed fights involving beasts and men	
81–96	Reign of Domitian, which grows increasingly repressive and harsh; Domitian is assassinated by members of his own household, soon after is satirized in verse	*Satires* by Juvenal
96–180	Rule of five "Good Emperors": Nerva, Trajan, Hadrian, Antoninus Pius, and Marcus Aurelius; Rome experiences peace and prosperity	
96–98	Reign of Roman emperor Nerva	
98–117	Reign of Roman emperor Trajan; rebirth of Roman literature after an era of censorship and tyranny	*Annals of Imperial Rome* by Tacitus
106	Arabia becomes a Roman province	
113	Building of Trajan's column, commemorating his military campaigns	
117–c. 122	Hadrian's early reign; his secretary Suetonius has access to imperial records; construction of Hadrian's Wall as boundary of Roman territory in Britain (c. 122)	*The Twelve Caesars* by Suetonius
117–138	Hadrian enjoys lengthy reign, distinguishes self as an intellectual and a patron of arts, favors Greek culture	*Parallel Lives* by Plutarch
135	Suppression of Jewish revolt under Bar Kokhba in Palestine	
138–161	Reign of Roman emperor Antoninus Pius	
161–180	Reign of Marcus Aurelius, last of Rome's five "Good Emperors"; Greek culture continues to predominate in artistic life of Rome; Galen serves as court physician	*The Golden Ass* by Apuleius
167	Rome suffers outbreak of the plague	
168–175	War with Germany	
180–192	Reign of Roman emperor Commodus, who later shows signs of derangement and is finally strangled	

Historical Events		Related Literary Works in *WLAIT 8*
193–211	Reign of Roman emperor Septimus Severus, who founds new dynasty	
244–255	Greek philosopher Plotinus settles in Rome, begins to write, develops Neoplatonism (dominant philosophy of pagan antiquity), shows how individual soul can reach God	
211–217	Reign of Roman emperor Caracalla	
212	All free inhabitants of Roman Empire gain citizenship, which allows them to be taxed	
218–222	Reign of Roman emperor Elagabulus	
222–235	Reign of Roman emperor Aurelius Severus Alexander	
226–641	Reign of Sasanid dynasty in Persia	
235–284	Period of instability; succession of short-lived military rulers; economic and cultural decline	
267	Herulian Goths sack Athens	
284–305	Period known as the Late Roman Empire begins with the reign of Diocletian	
293	Diocletian renews control of the Roman state through system known as tetrarchy— separate governments are set up for the empire's eastern and western halves	
300s	Eastern Germanic peoples challenge Roman rule; conquered areas of Persia and Ethiopia are relatively quiet	*An Ethiopian Story* by Heliodorus
303	"Great persecution" of Christians in East and West	
305	Abdication of Diocletian	
306–337	Reign of Constantine I	
312	Battle of Milvian Bridge, in which Constantine, who claims to have seen the sign of the cross emblazoned on the sun, defeats Maxentius for control of Rome	
312–324	Constantine controls the western empire; Licinius controls the eastern empire	
313	Edict of Milan legitimates Christianity	
324	Emperor Constantine converts to Christianity, rules as sole emperor	
330	Constantine moves capital of Roman Empire to Byzantium (present-day Istanbul in modern Turkey); city is renamed New Rome but called Constantinople by the people; Greeks enter artistic and historical period called the Byzantine Age (ends in 1453)	
354	Birth of St. Augustine of Hippo	
361–363	Reign of Roman emperor Julian the Apostate	
379–395	Theodosius the Great reigns; is last to control whole empire; leaves eastern part to his son Arcadius, western part to his son Honorius	
386	Augustine of Hippo converts to Christianity after studying Neoplatonism	*Confessions* by St. Augustine
393	Abolition of the Olympic games	
395	Christianity becomes state religion; Roman Empire divides into eastern and western empires, each with its own administration and line of emperors	

FALL OF THE EMPIRE AND THE CLASSICAL LEGACY

Now governed as two kingdoms, eastern and western, the Roman Empire proved increasingly vulnerable to foreign invaders during the fifth century CE. In 476 CE the Germanic general Odoacer deposed Romulus Augustulus, the last Roman emperor of the West. The eastern half of the Roman Empire, centered in Byzantium (renamed Constantinople, then Istanbul) would endure for nearly a thousand more years. Meanwhile, the West suffered a millennium of repeated strife and upheaval. During the sixth century, the eastern emperor Justinian reclaimed some of the lost territories in the West, including Italy, northwest Africa, coastal Spain, and the Mediterranean. All the while, Byzantium, the heart of the surviving Roman Empire, remained Greek in culture, except for a few decades (1204–1261) during which the city was captured by the French and the Venetians. Ultimately the Eastern Roman Empire fell to the Turks (1453). But the legacy of the classical world endured, thanks to an already longstanding cultural pursuit. For more than a century, Italians had been rediscovering classical manuscripts, including ancient works from Rome (which had been preserved by Benedictine monks) and Greece (which had been preserved by Byzantine scholars). Together these works became the object of study and imitation by Renaissance humanists.

401	Alaric and the Visigoths invade Italy	
406	Germanic tribes invade Gaul	
407–408	Formation of new Gallic Empire	
410	Sack of Rome by Visigoths; Rome formally renounces Britain	
418	Roman treaty with Visigoths	
439	The Vandals, a Germanic people, conquer Carthage and Africa	
451–452	Romans and Visigoths defeat Attila the Hun; Pope Leo I persuades Attila not to enter Rome	
455	Rome is sacked by Vandals for two weeks	
476	Last Roman emperor in the West, Romulus Augustulus (r. 475–476) is deposed; Germanic general Odoacer becomes king of Italy, accepts eastern Roman emperor as his overlord	
493	Accession of Theodoric, the Ostrogothic king, to Italian throne	
c. 500s	Preservation of classical Latin texts by Benedictine monks	
524	Boethius, a high official under Theodoric and the classical world's last Latin-speaking scholar to master Greek, is imprisoned	*The Consolation of Philosophy* by Boethius
527–565	Justinian reigns as eastern Roman emperor; recovers former Roman territories in Africa (533/534), Spain (551), and Italian peninsula (561/562); arranges and systematizes Roman law	
527–1453	Eastern Roman Empire (Byzantium) preserves Greek literature, abridging and commenting on classics; develops new Greek writings in history and theology	
529	Justinian orders closure of the Academy at Athens	
533	Publication of *Justinian's Digest*, the result of effort to excerpt and codify works of classical jurists	
609	Pantheon, temple at Rome formerly consecrated to the pagan gods, is converted to a church	
846	Arabs sack Rome	

Historical Events	Related Literary Works in *WLAIT 8*
1084 Normans sack Rome	
1204–1261 Rome falls to the French and Venetians, who capture it in the name of Christianity, during the Fourth Crusade	
c. 1325–1330s Italian poet Petrarch begins recovery of classical texts, focuses first on Virgil, Livy, and Cicero; restores Livy's *History of Rome*; finds forgotten speech by Cicero— *Pro Archia* (*In Defense of Archias* [a Greek poet])	
1349 Earthquake in Rome	
1354 Petrarch receives manuscript of Homer's writing from Nicholas Sygeros, a Byzantine envoy to the papal court	
1360 In Florence, Byzantine scholar Pilato is hired to teach Greek, an unknown language in early 1300s Italy	
1453 Fall of Constantinople (Byzantium) to the Turks; end of Roman Empire in the East	
c. 1500 Renaissance humanism spreads northward through Europe, reigniting interest in classical studies	

Contents by Title

Contents by Title

Contents by Author

Contents by Author

Aeneid

by
Virgil

THE LITERARY WORK

An epic poem set in Asia Minor, Greece and Italy in the years following the Trojan War (c. 1200 BCE); first published in Latin after 19 BCE.

SYNOPSIS

Aeneas leads a band of Trojan refugees to the future home in Italy promised to them by the gods.

Publius Vergilius Maro, better known in English as Virgil (or Vergil), was born in the Italian village of Andes near the city of Mantua on October 15, 70 BCE. He was educated at home and then in Rome for a public career that he would never pursue. His level of education suggests that his family was fairly wealthy. During the Civil War (49-45 BCE), Virgil went to the city of Naples, where he would spend most of his adult life. In the early 40s or late 30s BCE, Virgil published his first poetic collection, the *Eclogues* (also in *Classical Literature and Its Times*). At this point, Maecenas, a close associate of the Roman emperor, Caesar Augustus, took an interest in Virgil, becoming his patron for the rest of his career. Virgil probably published his next poem, the *Georgics*, on farming and humankind's place in the natural world, in 29 BCE. Thereafter, he devoted himself to writing the *Aeneid*, a pursuit that would continue for the rest of his life. Though Virgil wrote all his poems in the traditional epic meter—dactylic hexameter—the *Aeneid* gained distinction as both his lengthiest work and a national epic. In 19 BCE Virgil left for Greece to finish composing the *Aeneid* and to continue his study of philosophy, which appears to have been a lifelong passion. In Athens he encountered Augustus, the Roman emperor for whom the poem was being written. Persuaded by Augustus, Virgil prepared to return to Italy with him. On a hot day in Greece, stricken with an illness, the 51-year-old Virgil set out for Italy. He died in Brundisium (modern Brindisi) on September 20, 19 BCE. A story circulated that his last request was that the unfinished

Aeneid be burned, but the truth of this report cannot be checked; according to tradition, Augustus himself prevented the poem from being burned. In any event, Virgil's literary executors, his fellow poets and friends Plotius Tucca and Lucius Varius Rufus, seem to have readied the poem for publication and wider release in 17 BCE. Already before his death, a great many people—most notably Augustus himself—had heard Virgil give readings of parts of the poem, most likely books 2, 4, and 6. Like the rest of Virgil's *Aeneid*, these books reflect on fundamental changes in Rome during Virgil's lifetime, even as they establish in writing Rome's founding myth.

Events in History at the Time of the Epic

Layers of time in the *Aeneid*. Both directly and indirectly, the *Aeneid* involves different time periods. The action takes place around the fall of

Troy, thought by the Romans of Virgil's day to have occurred in 1184 BCE. As often recounted, the Trojan War was touched off by a contest among three goddesses—Juno, Minerva, and Venus, who asked Paris, a Trojan prince, to judge which of them was most beautiful. Paris chose Venus, the goddess of love, who had bribed him (as the others tried to do). Delivering on the bribe, Venus caused the most beautiful woman in the world, Helen, to fall in love with Paris. The two lovers stole away from her home in Sparta to Troy. Helen was already married to Menelaus of Sparta at the time. Enraged, Menelaus called on his fellow Greeks to marshal their armies and together they formed a fleet that sailed forth to wage a ten-year war against Troy. The ensuing war claimed the lives of great warriors, including the Trojan prince Hector and the Greek champion Achilles. Ultimately the Greeks won the war, gaining the advantage by trickery. They constructed a wooden horse, loaded it with a band of their warriors, and made a show of boarding their ships and quitting Troy for good. Slyly, the departing Greeks hid behind a nearby island and waited. The Trojans, believing the horse to be an offering to the war goddess Minerva, hauled it into their city and retired. That night, under the cloak of darkness, the band of warriors inside the horse slipped out and brazenly opened the city gates for their fellow Greeks, who returned to do battle. The reunited army slaughtered the Trojans, who were both surprised and exhausted from celebrating what they had mistakenly thought was the war's end. A few escaped the final slaughter, among them, Aeneas. With a band of fellow Trojans, he sailed through the Mediterranean region until he reached Italy. Legend has it that Aeneas finally settled here, in Italy, going on to become the ancestor of Romulus, whom further legend identifies as the founder of Rome. Romulus is said to have built the city named after him in 753 BCE, peopling it with runaway slaves and other outlaws. They warred against a neighboring people (the Sabines) whose women they stole for wives (known as the "Rape of the Sabines"), after which the two peoples settled down together under the rule of Romulus for 40 years. These beginnings hark back, the belief was, to Aeneas's landing.

Again according to legend, the queen god, Juno, was opposed to Aeneas's arrival in Italy for several reasons, one being her affection for the recently founded North African city of Carthage. Juno worried about Carthage because she knew that Aeneas's descendants, the Romans, would

Virgil. © Massimo Listri/Corbis.

destroy it. Historically the Romans finally did destroy Carthage in 146 BCE, after the third Punic War (named after the Carthaginians, who are called "Poeni" in Latin). Carthage had put up a mighty fight in the three Punic Wars (264-241 BCE, 218-201 BCE, 149-146 BCE). Most famously, in the second of the three wars, its general Hannibal led an army across the mountainous Alps to invade Italy. In *Aeneid* 4, Virgil draws on myth to explain the origins of the enmity between Rome and Carthage, referring to the curse of Dido, a lover from Carthage whom Aeneas has forsaken. While the poem itself takes place much earlier than the Punic Wars, they provide key background for the story of Aeneas and Dido contained in Virgil's poem.

Through prophecies and the like, Virgil's poem invokes a third time period: his present day. He refers to numerous events in Roman history after Aeneas's arrival in Italy. Virgil lived through an especially turbulent time in Roman history; he was born not long after the Italian or Social Wars (*socii* is the Latin term for "allies") during which the Romans fought against their Italian neighbors and allies who revolted against Roman attempts to control them. The second half of the *Aeneid*, which centers on the war between the survivors of Troy and the Italians, two groups that finally reconcile and fuse into a single culture, recalls the civil conflict of these Social Wars.

As an adult, Virgil had experienced the civil war between Julius Caesar and Pompey, which ended with Caesar's becoming the undisputed ruler of Rome. Soon after, however, Caesar was assassinated, and Rome once again entered a period of turmoil. Finally in 31 BCE, Caesar Augustus, grandnephew and adopted son of Julius Caesar, became the sole power in Rome. Its first emperor after Rome's existence as a Republic for almost 500 years, his reign ushered in a new era of peace. By his death in 19 BCE, Virgil had experienced about a decade of peace under Augustus, the longest calm Rome had known in almost a century. Dubbed "father of the fatherland" in 2 BCE, Augustus was regarded as Rome's second founder, after Romulus, the city's original founder.

The Epic in Focus

Plot summary. The *Aeneid* comprises 12 large sections, referred to as "books." In book 1, we meet the Trojan leader Aeneas, son of Prince Anchises and the goddess Venus. Having escaped the final slaughter in Troy, Aeneas and his seafaring band encounter a storm stirred up by the queen of the gods, Juno, to prevent them from reaching Italy. Worried about Aeneas, Venus confronts Jupiter, king of the gods, who reassures her by revealing the future glory of Aeneas's descendants, the Romans. Venus nonetheless comes to Aeneas's aid. He and his Trojan companions land near the newfound city of Carthage on the northern coast of Africa. In disguise, Venus advises Aeneas to seek help from Carthage's queen, Dido. With the help of Venus's son, Cupid, who also appears in disguise, Dido falls in love with Aeneas. The book ends on a lovestruck Dido asking Aeneas to speak of his travels.

In books 2 and 3, Aeneas flashes back to his recent past, describing the fall of Troy and the travels that brought him to Carthage. Particularly notable in book 2 are the narratives of the Trojan horse and Aeneas's loss of his wife, Creusa, during his escape from Troy. The last he sees of her, she has returned as a spirit to tell him to go on without her, to pursue his destiny (and another wife). Although Aeneas rescues his father, Anchises, from Troy, the old man dies early in the subsequent voyage.

In book 4, the action returns to Dido and Aeneas in the present. The two goddesses Juno and Venus, the first of whom tries to interfere with Aeneas, the second of whom favors him, come to terms. They agree to establish a bond between Dido and Aeneas while they are on a hunting expedition. The goddesses send a storm that forces Dido and Aeneas into a cave, where they consummate their union. Time passes as Aeneas helps build Carthage. When Jupiter sends Mercury, the

---

LISTENING TO POETRY IN ROME

In ancient Rome, works of literature were not published or read as in the modern era. Rather, all literature was recited aloud, even if one was reading alone. The *Aeneid* was a poem that audiences heard recited either by Virgil (who is said to have been a good reader) or a reader he chose before his death in 19 BCE. We know that the emperor Augustus asked Virgil to show some of what he had written, and there is a well-known story that Virgil recited parts of the poem to Augustus and his sister Octavia at some point after 23 BCE. When Virgil read the part in the *Aeneid* (book 6) about the death of her son Marcellus, who had been a youth of great promise, Octavia supposedly fainted.

Part of a Roman's education was learning how to recite with the proper inflections and tones, and in the proper meter. Almost immediately after its publication, Virgil's *Aeneid* became the primary school text for Roman children, who no doubt focused on reading Virgil's epic aloud. First the teacher would read them the text so they could memorize it. Then they would recite it back, and finally they would write it in Latin. Ancient graffiti has been found that quotes lines from the *Aeneid*. No doubt this graffiti is the handiwork of educated students, but their social status is open to question, since even the slaves of Rome were schooled in this epic (along with other Latin texts).

---

messenger god, to remind Aeneas of his destiny to establish a new home in Italy, he leaves Carthage. A distraught Dido curses Aeneas, then commits suicide. With her dying breath, she swears enmity between his descendants (the Romans) and hers (the Carthaginians).

In book 5, Aeneas returns to Sicily, where his father had perished a year earlier. He commemorates the old man's death with funeral games, including a ship race, foot race, archery contest, and boxing match. During the games, at the bidding of Juno, another messenger god, Iris, appears disguised as a Trojan woman and convinces the other women in Aeneas's band to set its ships ablaze so they will have to stop their endless wandering. Some ships are burned before rain douses out the flames. Aeneas and his group sail off, leaving behind those who want to stay.

In book 6, Aeneas finally reaches Italy, but obstacles lie ahead. He encounters the prophetess Sibyl of Cumae, who warns that the worst is yet to come: Aeneas will face another war like the one at Troy. Can he visit the underworld to see his father, Anchises? Aeneas asks. Granting him a rare privilege, the Sibyl leads him through the underworld, where he encounters many figures, including Dido, who refuses to speak with him. Aeneas spies his father, who explains that the soul is immortal, then bids him to gaze at a collection of souls lined up to become Romans of future distinction. The son returns to earth's surface.

In book 7, Aeneas encounters Latinus, king of a group of inhabitants known as the Latins, and agrees to marry his daughter. Latinus received a prophecy telling him to make the pact, but his daughter, Lavinia, was already engaged to Turnus, leader of the Rutulian tribe. Ignoring the engagement and heeding the prophecy, Latinus makes the pact. Turnus promptly declares war on Aeneas, gathering many Italians to fight on his side. Still trying to undo Aeneas, Juno calls upon the fury Allecto, a punishing spirit to help stir up the war. The text presents a catalog of Italian forces arrayed against Aeneas and the Trojans.

Book 8 begins with the river-god Tiber appearing to Aeneas, telling him to seek help from some Greek colonists of Arcadia who have settled in Italy. Aeneas acts accordingly, meeting Evander, king of the Arcadians, who lives with his people on the future site of Rome. Evander introduces his son, Pallas, and gives Aeneas a tour of the land that will become Rome. Meanwhile, Venus obtains some divine armor for Aeneas made by Vulcan (god of the forge and metalwork). Virgil describes the armor in detail, especially the shield with images from Rome's future (from Aeneas's viewpoint, or Rome's past from Virgil's).

With Aeneas away at the future site of Rome, the Trojans are besieged by Turnus. They fare poorly against him in book 9. In a bold nighttime attempt, two Trojan friends, Nisus and Euryalus, slip out to get help but are distracted by the prospect of killing sleeping members of the enemy

Italian tribes. The two meet with some success until they are discovered and then killed.

Book 10 opens on the gods, who convene for the first time in the poem. Jupiter tells them to cease their meddling. Back among the mortals, Aeneas at last returns to his men and a battle ensues. Both sides score victories, killing each other's allies. Turnus fells Pallas (Aeneas's ally); Aeneas kills Mezentius and his son Lausus (Turnus's allies). Now Aeneas becomes a dominant fighting force.

In the assembly that begins book 11, the Italian tribes falter in their resolve; only Turnus still wishes to fight. Aeneas holds a funeral for Pallas, offering many gifts to the dead warrior, including human sacrifices. The warrior woman Camilla aids the Italian enemy by leading a cavalry action, but she is soon cut down in battle.

In the final book, the two sides call a truce so that Aeneas and Turnus can resolve matters in single combat against each other. Spurred on by Juno, Juturna (Turnus's sister and a minor deity in her own right) breaks up the truce and more fighting follows. Aeneas and Turnus confront each other in battle, one on one. But just then, the gods reach an agreement. Juno gives in to Jupiter, appeased by his promise that the Italians and Trojans will merge, becoming a people who speak Latin and honor her as no others do. Finally, with Aeneas gaining the upper hand in battle, Turnus begs for mercy. Aeneas is ready to spare him, until he spies the baldric (sword belt worn across the chest) Turnus stole off Pallas's dead body. The poem ends with Aeneas killing Turnus:

> He sank his blade in fury in Turnus' chest.
> Then all the body slackened in death's chill,
> And with a groan for that indignity
> His spirit fled into the gloom below.
> (Virgil, *Aeneid*, book 12, lines 950-952)

Virgil and Augustus. The first Emperor of Rome, Caesar Augustus (63 BCE–14 CE), looms large in the *Aeneid*, as does the propaganda of his new settlement—an arrangement (introduced in 27 BCE and later modified) by which he agreed to command the standing armies in the three mightiest Roman provinces (Spain, Gaul, and Syria). To do so, he removed the top Senate officials (proconsuls) in charge of these provinces and put in their place his own subordinates. Augustus is present in the *Aeneid* both implicitly as a descendant of the Trojan leader Aeneas, son of the goddess Venus, and explicitly in several prophecies, all of which highlight key themes of Augustan propaganda.

Virgil's choice to include Augustus in a poem focusing on much earlier history draws attention to developments in Roman government when he was writing. Augustus's name, given him in 27 BCE, means "reverend" or "deserving to be revered." After a long series of civil wars, Augustus—who was called "Octavian" before receiving the new name—brought peace to Rome. It was probably clear to many that the old republican government was gone forever, but Augustus tried anyways to maintain the appearance of old forms. For the rest of his life, he would claim to have restored the Republic, all the while amassing new powers for himself. That he took the title *princeps,* or "first among equals" rather than emperor indicates the way he wished to be seen in the new Roman government. In truth, he was the first Roman emperor, though it would be centuries before they were designated as such. Augustus's power was unprecedented, consisting of the formal powers of almost all the traditional public offices in the Republic, never before granted to one man at the same time.

The issue of Augustus's appearance in the *Aeneid* is further complicated by Virgil's personal relationship with the emperor, about which we know far less than we would like. We do know that Virgil enjoyed the patronage of Gaius Maecenas, a wealthy and well-connected patron to whom many famous works were dedicated, including Virgil's *Georgics.* Maecenas was a key advisor to Augustus, and Maecenas's support of several poets (Virgil, Horace, Propertius) reflects some link between them and the emperor. Judging from numerous refusals in the works of various poets of the day, it seems as though Maecenas was looking for someone to compose an epic for Augustus; to Virgil fell this task.

While Augustus and the new era of Roman history he ushered in lurk just below the surface throughout the entire epic, they rise to the fore on three occasions. Through prophecies, Virgil is able to refer directly to contemporary events, and it is in these passages that the importance of Virgil's historical context is most clear. This focus on the present is part of what makes Virgil's version of Roman history unique: "In all three prophecies [Virgil] links the rule of Augustus with the end of external war and internal discord; he describes the arrival of universal peace under Roman rule, and he heralds the outset of a new golden age" (Zetzel in Martindale, p. 200). All three themes in the major prophecies of the *Aeneid* reflect central themes of Augustus's own propaganda.

War, peace, and Caesar. The first major prophecy comes near the beginning of the poem, and is part of our introduction to key divine figures in the story. Venus, worried about the Trojan refugees, who have just suffered a sea storm sent by Juno, goes to Jupiter to question if he has changed the promises he once made her about the future of the Trojans. Jupiter's response centers on the spread of Roman power and refers to "Caesar," which likely refers to both Julius Caesar and his adopted son Augustus:

> For these [Romans] I set no limits, world
>   or time,
> But make the gift of empire without end.
> Juno, indeed, whose bitterness now fills
> With fear and torment sea and earth and sky,
> Will mend her ways, and favor them as I do,
> . . . .
>   . . . From that comely line
> The Trojan Caesar comes, to circumscribe
> Empire with Ocean, fame with heaven's stars.
> Julius his name, from Iulus [the son of
>   Aeneas] handed down:
> All tranquil shall you take him heavenward
> In time, laden with plunder of the East,
> And he with you shall be invoked in prayer.
>   (*Aeneid*, 1.278-282, 286-294)

Here Virgil lays out the genealogical connections between Aeneas, the main character of the poem and the Julian clan, which traced its lineage back to Iulus, the son of Aeneas and forward to Emperor Augustus, one of its latest members.

The ambiguous nature of "Trojan Caesar" points to the connection between the named Julius and his adopted son, Augustus. Much of Augustus's early success came from his ability to capitalize on his connection with Julius Caesar, whom the Senate deified in 42 BCE. In this first prophecy from the *Aeneid*, Virgil connects dominion on earth with a place among the gods, suggesting that Augustus will eventually be deified, too (as he would be after his death in 14 CE).

This prophecy also fits with Augustus's propaganda. As Augustus says in his *Res Gestae*, record of things accomplished (c. 2 BCE):

> It was the will of our ancestors that the gateway of Janus Quirinus [the temple of the god of gates and doorways] should be shut when victories had secured peace by land and sea throughout the whole empire of the Roman people; from the foundation of the city down to my birth, tradition records that it was shut only twice, but while I was the leading citizen the senate resolved that it should be shut on three occasions.

> (Augustus, *Res Gestae*, 13)

The doors of this temple, which stood in the Roman Forum, were closed only in peacetimes, hence rarely. While the date of the third of these closings is unknown, Virgil would have known of those in 29 BCE (after the Civil War) and 25 BCE (after a war against the Cantabrians in Spain). Under Augustus, the closing of these doors signified the military dominion of the Romans abroad and suggested an empire without end. The consequence was peace at home.

Like many other archaic religious practices, the closing of the religious doors had fallen into disuse, but Augustus revived the custom to serve his own ends. He essentially developed a new language of symbolism by resurrecting older Roman practices, brought to the fore in Virgil's poem. His Aeneas is devoted to the gods, and his descendant Augustus cultivated a similar reputation. Additionally, Augustus surrounded himself with imagery and symbols of an earlier Rome, making his new settlement seem to be a return to better days, rather than a total revolution (as it was).

A new Golden Age. When Aeneas visits the underworld, he gains insight from his father, Anchises. In what serves as a centerpiece of the poem, Anchises explains the immortality of the soul and the doctrine of metempsychosis, a type of reincarnation. As he points out the souls waiting to return to the world of the living, he provides a catalog of future Roman figures, famous and notorious. The climax of this list is the soul who will become Augustus:

> Turn your two eyes
> This way and see this people, your own
> Romans.
> Here is Caesar, and all the line of Iulus,
> All who shall one day pass under the dome
> Of the great sky: this is the man, this one,
> Of whom so often you have heard the
> promise,
> Caesar Augustus, son of the deified,
> Who shall bring once again an Age of Gold
> To Latium, to the land where Saturn reigned
> In early times. He will extend his power
> Beyond the Garamants and Indians,
> Over far territories north and south
> . . . .
> The truth is, even Alcidës [another name for
> Hercules]
> Never traversed so much of earth. . . .
> (*Aeneid*, 8.788-807)

Virgil again combines two key bits of Augustan propaganda, peace at home in Italy and military

power abroad, with the notion that everything Aeneas does will lead to the rule of Augustus. To stress these ideals, Virgil compares Augustus to Hercules, thought to have been mortal (or at least only semidivine) and to have become a god through his cultural contribution and military achievements. By linking Hercules to Augustus, Virgil suggests that Augustus, too, deserves to become a god.

The issue of lineage is also central, for Augustus faced many difficulties in obtaining an heir. Shortly after the above passage, Anchises explains with great distress that Marcellus will die too young. This Marcellus was Augustus's nephew and likely heir until 23 BCE, when he died while still a young man. Almost 30 years later, following the unexpected deaths of his two young grandsons, Augustus reluctantly adopted his stepson Tiberius as his heir. Tiberius succeeded Augustus in 14 CE.

The general tone is, despite the loss of an heir, optimistic, invoking a central image of the Augustan regime: the return of the Golden Age. Early Italian myth held that the current heavenly ruler, Jupiter (the Greek Zeus), had ousted a deity called Saturn (the equivalent of the Greek god Cronus). Saturn fled to Italy, where he reigned over a Golden Age of peace and abundance, which would some day return. Augustus tapped into this complex of ideas, and officially declared that the Golden Age had in fact returned at the celebration of the "secular games" of 17 BCE (a *saeculum* was traditionally a cycle of 110 years). Long before this, however, he and his supporters had used images of peace and prosperity to announce the advent of a new Golden Age, as Virgil does in this passage from the *Aeneid*.

Actium and a unified Italy. The third major prophecy is not a divine utterance like the other two, but a work of art. In book 8, Venus brings her son the armor that Vulcan has wrought for him, and Virgil provides an elaborate description of the shield's decorations:

> Vivid in the center were the bronze-beaked
> Ships and the fight at sea off Actium.
> Here you could see . . .
> Augustus Caesar leading into battle
> Italians, with both senators and people,
> Household gods and great gods: there he
> stood
> High on the stern, and from his blessed brow
> Twin flames gushed upward, while his crest
> revealed
> His father's star . . .

Virgil writes the *Aeneid* alongside Clio, the Muse of History (left), and Melpomene, the Muse of Tragedy (right).
© Roger Wood/Corbis

Then came Antonius [Mark Antony] with
    barbaric wealth
And a diversity of arms, victorious
From races of the Dawnlands and Red Sea,
Leading the power of the East, of Egypt
. . . .
And in his wake the Egyptian consort
    [Cleopatra] came
So shamefully . . .
            . . . The queen
Amidst the battle called her flotilla on . . .
Mars [god of war], engraved in steel, raged in
    the fight . . .
Overlooking it all, Actian Apollo [god of
    prophecy and healing]
Began to pull his bow . . .
      (*Aeneid*, 8.675-681, 685-688, 696-700,
                     704-705)

Central here is the naval victory of Augustus over the forces of Mark Antony and Cleopatra near Actium in northwestern Greece in 31 BCE. The battle itself was transformed into a symbol, the foundation of the new regime. Virgil celebrates it accordingly, making the battle mythological by focusing on the actions of the gods, especially Apollo, god of prophecy, whom he took as his special patron god and Augustus regarded as a patron of the new regime.

Virgil portrays the battle as one between Italy and a foreign power instead of a civil war between Romans, as it was. The poem depicts Antony, as a non-Roman, a barbarian from the East, who associates with the foreign Cleopatra. As it appears on Aeneas's shield, Actium is a victory of all Rome over barbarians. The propaganda here is clear. Virgil's poem is thus in keeping with the Augustan presentation of events.

Augustus emphasized not only the unity of Italy, but also the collaboration of all classes. Thus, on the shield are senators and people of Rome. In his record of deeds, Augustus himself boasts of the unified support of Italy in his war against Antony and Cleopatra, the enemies the poem clearly has in mind, though they are conspicuously unnamed.

> The whole of Italy of its own free will swore allegiance to me and demanded me as the leader in the war in which I was victorious at Actium. . . . More than seven hundred senators served under my standards at that time . . .
> (Augustus, *Res Gestae,* 25.2-3)

While Virgil never saw the complete record above, he was certainly in touch with the language that Augustus and his circle used in constructing an identity for the regime.

As the description of the shield comes to a close, Virgil makes the significance of the whole *Aeneid* clear: the deeds of Aeneas are directly connected to those of Augustus. At the close of book 8, the speaker declares:

> All these images on Vulcan's shield,
> His mother's gift, were wonders to Aeneas.
> Knowing nothing of the events themselves,
> He felt joy in their pictures, taking up
> Upon his shoulder all the destined acts
> And fame of his descendants.
> (*Aeneid,* 8.729-731)

These descendants include all the Romans especially Augustus, whose deeds comprise the center of the shield.

Sources and literary context. The most obvious models for the *Aeneid* are the two epics of Homer, the **Iliad** and **Odyssey** (eighth century BCE; both also in *Classical Literature and Its Times*). From the very first line, Homer's influence pervades the *Aeneid*: its famous beginning, "I sing of warfare and a man at war" (literally, "I sing of arms and a man") announces a combination of the two Homeric epics, with the "arms" suggesting the *Iliad* and the "man" suggesting the *Odyssey*. Other examples of Homeric influence would be Aeneas's trip to the underworld in *Aeneid* 6, which recalls that of Odysseus in *Odyssey* 11, and the description of Aeneas's shield in *Aeneid* 8, which resembles that of Achilles's shield in *Iliad* 18.

A third Greek model is the *Argonautica* of Apollonius of Rhodes (mid-third century BCE),

especially its portrayal of the relationship between Jason and Medea, which underlies Virgil's account of the Dido episode. Apollonius's psychological portrayal of Medea greatly influenced Virgil's depiction of Dido's thoughts during her affair with Aeneas, and the characterization of the hero Jason lies behind some of Virgil's treatment of Aeneas.

On the Roman side, there are numerous sources and models, the influence of Lucretius's **On the Nature of The Universe** (c. 55 BCE; also in *Classical Literature and Its Times*) being especially pervasive. According to some ancient sources, Virgil was a lifelong student of philosophy, and Lucretius's poem was one of the boldest attempts to write philosophy in Latin, certainly in Latin verse; Virgil often echoes the language of Lucretius and the philosophical thought of Epicurus, whom Lucretius favored, too. Another key Roman model is Catullus, especially poem 64, which again influenced Virgil's treatment of the relationship between Dido and Aeneas. In general, Catullus and his contemporaries greatly influenced Virgil in terms of stylistic developments in Latin, moving away from earlier, less elegant forms (see Catullus's **Carmina,** also in *Classical Literature and Its Times*).

Like most poets of his day, Virgil was steeped in both Greek and Latin literature, and the *Aeneid* abounds in echoes of and allusions to authors of all types and genres. Besides drawing on the works of Homer himself, for instance, Virgil makes use of the wide scholarship on the Homeric poems that existed by that point. Like some predecessors of the Greek poetry in Alexandria, Egypt, in the third century BCE, Virgil was very much a scholar-poet.

Reception. The *Aeneid* is one of the few works to become an "instant classic," gaining prominence as the key school text for Roman children shortly after Virgil's death. Even during his lifetime, Virgil was lauded for his accomplishments, as shown by this poem by Propertius (another poet in Maecenas's circle):

> [Virgil] now calls up the arms of Trojan Aeneas
>   And the walls he built on the Lavinian
>   shore.
> Make way, you Roman writers, and you
>   Greek, make way!
> A greater than the *Iliad* is born
>   (Propertius, 2.34.62-66)

According to Propertius, Virgil's new poem was easily worthy of comparison with Homer's time-honored epics.

As his poem was connected with Augustus, so was Virgil's fame. According to Tacitus (c. 55-117 CE), "the people, when they heard [Virgil's] verses in the theater, all rose and cheered the poet, who happened to be present, as if he were Augustus himself" (Tacitus in Zanker p. 194). The popularity of the poem is reflected as well in its effect on Augustan sculpture: "[Virgil's] depiction of Aeneas as heroic founder-figure almost certainly contributed to the prominence of Aeneas in major Augustan monuments such as the Ara Pacis (planned between 13 and 9 BCE) and the Forum of Augustus (dedicated in 2 BCE). In both settings Aeneas...is... presented as a...national icon" (Tarrant in Martindale, p. 57).

In Roman poetry of the next several generations, Virgil was an inescapable influence. The *Aeneid* looms large in Ovid's **Metamorphoses** (c. 8 CE), toward the end, when Ovid playfully fills in some gaps left by Virgil (also in *Classical Literature and Its Times*). Moreover, the influence extends beyond the learned poetry of Virgil's successors. Graffiti citing or parodying the poems of Virgil abound. In the ruins of Pompeii are 63 Virgilian graffiti, 46 from the *Aeneid*; of these, 17 are from the first line of the poem ("I sing of warfare and a man at war" [*Aeneid*, 1.1]) and 15 from the first line of the second book ("The room fell silent, and all eyes were on him" [*Aeneid*, 2.1]). Such graffiti appear even in places as unlikely as a gladiatorial barracks and a brothel. Clearly students were not the only ones scribbling lines from Virgil on walls throughout the city.

Virgil remained a key author throughout antiquity and the middle ages. From **The Confessions** (1.13) of St. Augustine (also in *Classical Literature and Its Times*), we know that he wept in response to the death of Dido in *Aeneid* 4. A remarkable testament to Virgil's enduring influence (and the difficulties some readers have had with the way the *Aeneid* ends) is the composition of a thirteenth book of the *Aeneid* by the Italian poet Maffeo Vegio (c. 1407-1458; known also by his Latin name, Mapheus Vegius).

Perhaps most famously, Virgil influenced Dante's *Divine Comedy* (1306-21). His appearance as guide for much of this epic suggests that Dante, too, read the *Aeneid* in school and practiced his Latin by modeling Virgil. At their first meeting in the epic, Dante acknowledges his debt:

> Art thou then that Virgil, and that fountain which pours abroad so rich a stream of speech?
> ....
> Thou art my master and my author; thou alone art he from whom I took the good style that hath done me honour
> (Dante, *Inferno,* 1.82-87, p. 13)

—Kristopher Fletcher

For More Information

Augustus. *Res Gestae Divi Augusti: The Achievements of the Divine Augustus*. Oxford: Oxford University Press, 1967.

Dante Alighieri. *Inferno*. In *The Divine Comedy*. Trans. Carlyle-Okey-Wicksteed. New York: Vintage, 1950.

Gransden, K. W. *Virgil, the Aeneid*. Landmarks of World Literature. Cambridge: Cambridge University Press, 1990.

Horsfall, Nicholas, ed. *A Companion to the Study of Virgil*. Mnemosyne Supplement 151. Leiden: E. J. Brill, 1995.

Martindale, Charles, ed. *The Cambridge Companion to Virgil*. Cambridge: Cambridge University Press, 1997.

Propertius. *The Poems*. Trans. Guy Lee. Oxford: The Clarendon Press, 1999.

Quinn, Stephanie, ed. *Why Virgil? A Collection of Interpretations*. Wauconda, Ill.: Bolchazy-Carducci, 2000.

Virgil. *The Aeneid*. Trans. Robert Fitzgerald. New York: Vintage, 1983.

Zanker, Paul. *The Power of Images in the Age of Augustus*. Jerome Lectures 16. Trans. A. Shapiro. Ann Arbor: University of Michigan Press, 1988.

Annals of Imperial Rome

by
Tacitus

THE LITERARY WORK

A historical narrative set in the Roman Empire from 14 CE to 68 CE; written in Latin c. 105-120 CE

SYNOPSIS

Tacitus tells the story of the first dynasty of Roman emperors, the Julio-Claudians, from the death of Augustus (14 CE) to the death of Nero (68 CE).

Publius Cornelius Tacitus has been referred to as the greatest of the Roman historians, followed by Livy and Sallust. His life story is a sketchy one. Tacitus was probably born about 55 CE in northern Italy or across the Alps to the northwest in the province of Gaul (modern France), more exactly in Narbonese Gaul (Provence). Scholars suspect that he was related to a financial officer of the same name and so originally came from the equestrian order in Roman society. Equestrians tended to be those wealthy citizens who chose to pursue careers in big business rather than politics and so occupied second place in the Roman hierarchy, below the members of the Senate and their families. This situation changed after Rome became an empire, however: equestrians were recruited as government officials and assigned financial, military, or judicial responsibilities in the provinces. Such equestrians could rise through the ranks of the imperial administration to become senators, which apparently happened to Tacitus's family. He became a senator of Rome.

Our knowledge of Tacitus's life is mostly gleaned from his works, especially from the *Dialogue on Orators* (written c. 101/102 CE) and the *Agricola* (written c. 98 CE). Tacitus tells us that he came to Rome in his teenage years. As was the custom, he apprenticed himself to adult men of society to train for a future career. Tacitus trained for the law, following some prominent lawyers of the day to learn their work. We also learn that he married the daughter of Agricola (a Roman general and the governor of Britain) in

77 CE and that he had personal connections with the emperor's son, Titus, who would become emperor himself two years later. Under Titus, Tacitus served as a financial official (*quaestor*) and under Titus's successor, Domitian, as a judicial official (*praetor*) and religious commissioner (*quindecimvir sacris faciundis*). From 89-93 CE, Tacitus served as a military commander in the provinces. He subsequently returned to Rome, where he witnessed (and may have aided and abetted) Domitian's growing savagery toward the Roman upper classes. The experience appears to have scarred Tacitus, leaving him with a sense of shame and guilt that is apparent in his writings, including the *Agricola* and the *Annals of Imperial Rome*. But, despite the shame, Tacitus was both a political survivor and a social climber (he has also been described as snobbish and as someone with little respect for the political opposition). In his view, traditional valor was gone and moderation in politics was the key. Tacitus had an

opportunity to put his belief into practice; he served as one of two consuls in 97 CE, filling a post that was the most important in the old Roman Republic and still carried prestige under the emperors. Tacitus would later (in 112) serve as governor of the province of Asia, an office of the highest distinction. Most scholars place his death about 117, the same year as the emperor Trajan's, though some have suggested that he lived to see Trajan's successor, Hadrian, and incorporated some of that experience in his *Annals* as well. What we know about the first century of Roman emperors comes largely from Tacitus; his facts and interpretations of them have influenced our understanding of this period for the past 2,000 years.

Events in History at the Time of the Narrative

From Republic to empire. The Roman Republic, a system of aristocratic government grounded in the authority and the powers of the Roman Senate, existed and flourished for almost 500 years (509-27 BCE). It was under the direction of this Republican government that the Roman people forged an empire in the Mediterranean basin. But the empire brought undreamed of wealth and power into the hands of the senators, which resulted in corrupt policies and reckless decisions. In the last century of the Republic, particular senators competed with one another for dominance in the Republic; they used bribery, rigged elections, and even pitted gangs and armed forces against their rivals. By 44 BCE, one of these ambitious senators, Julius Caesar, had made his way to the top of the heap. Fearing that he would transform the Republic into a monarchy, a number of fellow senators assassinated Caesar to prevent the possibility. Supporters of Caesar at this point stepped into action. His political lieutenant (Mark Antony) and the heir to his private estate (Octavian) each saw his assassination as their opportunity to rise to the top. For the next 13 years, they waged a war of political propaganda against each other, dividing the Roman world into two camps. Finally, this war of words exploded into open conflict on land and sea, developing into a civil war. Octavian emerged the victor, the most successful warlord and senator of Rome by 30 BCE. Thanks to political maneuvering and military victory, he gained complete control of the Roman world. But Octavian strove not to end up like his great-uncle Caesar. He saw the merits of keeping elements of the Republican system intact (continuing to have a Senate, to hold elections for political officials, to delegate responsibilities to them rather than to overburden himself with the tasks of governing); he recognized that the Republic was a way of life, a treasured tradition, not just a political apparatus. Within three years, Octavian had "trimmed the fat" off the old Republic—that is, he had eliminated any "unnecessary" institutions and offices—and manipulated what remained. He dressed and conducted himself like an average senator, but he had far more wealth than any one of them. Although he consulted senators frequently on all of the important issues, they knew that his was the final decision. He commanded Roman armies on campaign like other generals, but only he had the allegiance of all Roman forces everywhere in the Empire. He held official posts like other magistrates, but he often held multiple offices at once; he combined in his position of *princeps* or "first citizen," duties that used to be handled separately by separate senators. Technically the Senate was in charge, and it formally recognized Octavian's extraordinary powers. It even conferred a new name on him—Augustus, the revered one. The Republic seemed still to exist in certain particulars, but there was little doubt that Augustus was making all the decisions.

Augustus's immediate successors, the Julio-Claudian emperors who are the focus of Tacitus's *Annals,* would struggle to follow his example and maintain this strange hybrid of military dictatorship and free government. But they would not always be up to the challenge of such a careful balancing act, primarily because their personalities or preparation were not suited to the task. Some would feel uncomfortable working with a subservient Senate, while others wished to discard the Senate altogether and rule as monarchs. Some would understand how to lead Rome's military, while others lacked the experience to do so. In the end, the new system of government would only be as good as its emperor.

The Narrative in Focus

Contents overview. It was during the reigns of the emperors Nerva (96-98 CE) and Trajan (98-117 CE) that Tacitus, already known for his skill at oratory and the law, composed his great works of history, the *Annals,* which covers much of the initial half of the first century (14-68 CE) and the *Histories,* which treats most of the latter half (69-96 CE). Together they would become humanity's primary source for Roman history in this period. What we know of events at the time of the narrative comes most directly from Tacitus. His *Annals* tells the story of the Julio-Claudian Dynasty, the first dynasty of Roman emperors, which was founded by Caesar Augustus, grandnephew and adopted son of Julius Caesar. Tacitus's history, however, does not begin with Augustus's rise after defeating Antony and Cleopatra in 31 BCE. Rather, it starts with Augustus's death in 14 CE and the rise to power of his stepson and successor, Tiberius. Tacitus explains: "Others have memorialized the good times and the bad times of the Roman People and the age of Augustus, but the affairs of Tiberius, Caius, Claudius, and Nero were falsely recorded when they were still alive, because of fear, and after they died, because of still fresh hatred. Thus, my conception is to relate . . . the reigns of Tiberius and the rest, without anger or partisanship (*sine ira et studio*)" (Tacitus, *Annals of Imperial Rome,* book 1, chapter 1; all quotations from the *Annals* are translated by M. Lovano).

Tacitus's original account would have traced the events of 54 years, through the reigns of Tiberius, Caligula, Claudius, and Nero, ending with Nero's suicide in 68 CE. Unfortunately, the surviving text of the *Annals* is missing the entire section on Caligula, the first half of Claudius's reign, and the fall of Nero (most of book 5 and all of books 7 through 10 and books 17 and 18). We cannot even be certain that Tacitus lived long enough to complete all 18 books. From the text that does exist, we can, however, see that Tacitus focuses on political affairs at Rome, particularly the personal relationships of influential individuals at the imperial court. Occasionally he glances at the rest of the empire, especially at developments in the provinces that affected or were affected by the court in Rome.

Contents summary—book 1. Tacitus begins his history in 14 CE with a brief account of the collapse of the Roman Republic and the subsequent dawn of the *principate* (a term the Romans preferred to *empire*) under Augustus. The historian speaks of the rising tide of flattery and the fictions that people came to believe about the emperors, even Augustus, whose reign is greeted with a long list of criticisms by Tacitus. These criticisms are especially interesting because Nerva and Trajan, the rulers in power as Tacitus was writing, modeled themselves on Augustus, and Tacitus knew it. Still, Tacitus boldly questions the rule of one man and notes how Augustus, with his unprecedented degree of authority, used gifts

of food to the people, bonuses to the army, and the promise of everlasting peace to justify and cloak his assumption of total political power under the facade of a continuing Republic; the weary survivors of almost 100 years of civil war eagerly accepted his rule to avoid more conflict.

Augustus proceeded to set up a dynasty of one-man rule, first designating one son-in-law as successor, then another, and finally his grandsons. As Tacitus notes, "Nothing opposed him. . . . The most spirited men had fallen in the battle lines" or had otherwise been eliminated (*Annals,* 1.3). Augustus's plans went awry, however, when he lost all these heirs to untimely deaths; circumstances forced him to promote his dour stepson Tiberius as successor. Augustus did so, but on the condition that Tiberius adopt as his next-in-line his brother's son, Germanicus, not his own son, Drusus. So, although less than happy about the choice, on his deathbed, Augustus could feel secure that he was leaving Rome a dynasty of rulers for at least the next two generations.

Tacitus begins his account of these successors on a condemning note. Tiberius's character contained the seeds of immense cruelty and arrogance, and he did not rule alone: behind the throne was a force to be reckoned with, his mother, Livia. She was an arch-intriguer—duplicitous, cunning, and suspicious. Tacitus, like other Romans, suspected that she had actually paved the way for her son's rise to power as the designated emperor by having the more favored candidates—Augustus's two sons-in-law and his grandsons—eliminated one by one.

The historian's judgment of Tiberius's reign can be seen from the very first sentence devoted to it: "The first crime of the new principate was the death of Agrippa Postumus," Augustus's last surviving grandson, who was then living in exile (*Annals,* 1.6). Tacitus goes on to fill out the portrait of Tiberius, painting him as sneaky, hesitant, in need of a bodyguard to feel secure, and dishonest with the Senate. When it offered Tiberius the same powers Augustus had earned by "saving" the government of Rome from years of internal friction and war, Tiberius pretended not to want these powers but accepted them anyway, says the *Annals* (*Annals,* 1.7-11). He created the illusion that the Republican form of government still existed, but in fact controlled elections to high office, something Augustus had never dared to do openly. As these initial moves suggested, Tiberius would prove to be "cunning, suspicious, unjust, and ruthless" (*Grant,* p. 105).

Tiberius was greeted at the outset of his reign by a military mutiny: the Roman garrisons protecting the Danube frontier along the province of Pannonia (modern Hungary) had been serving longer than their proper terms, had not been appropriately paid, and had not received other benefits promised by Augustus. Now under Tiberius, they made their demands known, turning violently against their commanding officers; a similar mutiny took place among the forces guarding the province of Lower Germany (modern Holland and Belgium). Tiberius sent his son, Drusus, to settle the first mutiny, and his nephew/stepson, Germanicus, to quell the disturbance in Lower Germany; the former took a hard-line approach with the mutineers, browbeating them into eliminating their own ringleaders while the latter shamed the mutineers into surrendering. Germanicus ordered his wife, Agrippina, and their little son Gaius (whom the troops nicknamed Caligula because he wore little military boots) to leave camp, creating the shameful impression that life among the Germanic "barbarians" was safer than among the Roman soldiers.

The resolution of the mutiny on the northern frontier of the Roman Empire, where Tiberius had sent Germanicus, was followed by fresh campaigns under the young general into hostile German territory on the other side of the Rhine and Danube rivers. According to Tacitus, Tiberius was displeased with the popularity that Germanicus had begun garnering with the troops and did not want the young general to be too successful at penetrating the German wilderness either.

Meanwhile, back at Rome, Tiberius had revived and revised the law against treason, using it to punish and grab the wealth of senators who refused to agree with him. Under the old treason law, explains Tacitus, "Deeds were denounced, words had impunity" (*Annals*, 1.72). Now anything one said or even thought might make the person guilty of treason on penalty of death, since treason was a capital offense. There began a number of treason trials based on trumped-up charges, framing innocent men. Rome would suffer such trials for the next 50 years.

Book 2. After briefly reviewing some of Tiberius's minor projects, the second book relates the end of Germanicus's wars in Germany and his transfer to the Eastern frontier to deal with fresh troubles between Rome and the Parthian Empire. Since the days of Augustus, the Romans had tried to maintain at least the semblance of peace with the

Parthians, the Iranian rulers of much of the Middle East, who for years were bent on conquering Rome's eastern provinces (modern-day Greece, Turkey, Syria, Lebanon, Israel, and Egypt). Tiberius, interested in having his own son, Drusus, negotiate with the Germans to secure the northern frontier, ordered the recall of Germanicus for the more complicated service against the Parthians. But Germanicus stalled by pressing deeper into Germany in his campaign against Arminius, Rome's archenemy among the German chieftains, who had earlier arranged for the massacre of three Roman legions. Germanicus avenged the massacre, securing the assassination of Arminius by his own followers and the destruction of many of Rome's other German enemies as well before turning the command over to Drusus and heading east.

Once there, he found that not only did he have to confront Parthian aggression and rebellious buffer states in the region that were supposed to be allies of Rome, but he also had to confront the jealous, insubordinate Roman commander in charge, Piso. Piso was encouraged by his wife, Plancina, to murder Germanicus in order to retain personal power in the east. When Germanicus, after many altercations with Piso, fell ill at Antioch in 19 CE, recovered fully, and then suddenly relapsed and died, many believed Piso had a hand in the matter. The Roman people's sorrow at Germanicus's passing was deep and heartfelt.

Book 3. The third book relates a wide range of information. First comes Germanicus's funeral and Rome in the throes of mourning. Piso, accused and tried for murder, committed suicide, while his wife, similarly accused and tried, was rescued through the good graces of Empress Livia, who thereby attracted even more ill will from the Roman populace. Next Tacitus provides details of several trials for immoral behavior and extortion in the provinces. Other details concern guerilla warfare in the North African deserts and the hills of Thrace, rebellion in Gaul against high taxes and debts, and an account of the death of Vipsania, Tiberius's first wife.

With Drusus rising in reputation and authority and the empire more or less stable, Tacitus takes a few moments to reflect on the cyclical nature of history and to observe, "That [Tiberius's] age was so corrupt and tainted with servility," that even the leading citizens had to hide their distinction by subservience," and Tiberius himself characterized Rome's Senators as "men ready to be slaves" (*Annals*, 3.65). Those who tried too quickly to rise above the slavish crowd fared poorly: "hastiness . . . has ruined many good men, who[,] despising the slow but secure way, rush to their end too quickly" (*Annals,* 3.66). In such an environment, gradual progress, implies Tacitus, was the key.

Book 4. While Tacitus begins the fourth book with a happy reference to the "ninth year of stability for the state and prosperity at home" (*Annals,* 4.1), this statement is only apparently positive. The promising beginning sets the reader up for a tragic irony—the rise of Sejanus, Tiberius's lieutenant in governing the Empire. Sejanus wielded authority over the Praetorian Guard (the 9,000 troops who protected the emperor and the Italian peninsula) and influenced the paranoid, mistrustful Tiberius. Sejanus maneuvered other members of the imperial family out of power and even eliminated them. According to Tacitus, Sejanus seduced Drusus's wife, poisoned Drusus to death, and encouraged a distraught Tiberius to isolate himself from his duties and from reality by retiring from Rome, eventually to the isle of Capri, which became his haven of debauchery and decadence. Heaven's anger ("*ira deum,*" *Annals,* 4.1), says Tacitus, brought Sejanus to wreak catastrophe upon Rome! Amid disturbances in Germany and North Africa, debates over temples being dedicated to Tiberius in Spain and the East, and natural disasters in Italy, Sejanus acquired unlimited power, which allowed him to orchestrate the exile or trial and condemnation of possible foes.

Book 6. "Now there was sheer, oppressive despotism," remarks Tacitus near the start of his fifth book (*Annals,* 5.3). A two-year gap in the surviving text follows. When the narrative resumes, Sejanus's reign of terror has been stopped by Tiberius and the lieutenant's co-conspirators find themselves on the receiving end of harsh punishments. Tacitus reports that Tiberius, still governing from outside Rome, unleashed a savage series of treason trials, and many tried to avoid the axe of execution by pointing the finger at others: "The fear of violence had severed the binding ties of human relations, and just as much as cruelty grew, so much did compassion shrink" (*Annals,* 6.19). Amid all this turmoil, the emperor, ever suspicious and fearful of threats to his power, failed to rescue his family members from exile: he allowed Agrippina and her sons (except Gaius) to die of starvation or suicide in confinement. And for the next six years, the judicial executions did not stop: "At Rome, continuous was the slaughter" (*Annals,* 6.29).

When Tiberius fell ill at his villa in Campania in 37 CE, his new lieutenant, Macro, conspired with Caligula, the emperor's grandnephew, to smother the emperor in his own bed. Caligula wanted power for himself, and Macro wanted to be the power behind the throne. Tacitus sums up Tiberius like this:

> His character had its separate phases of development. While he was a private citizen or serving in command under Augustus, his life and reputation were outstanding; while Germanicus and Drusus were around, he was crafty and hid behind fake virtues; while his mother lived, he was still a mixture of good and evil. As long as he either respected or feared Sejanus, he was hated for his savagery but concealed his lusts. In the end, when shame and fear were gone, and he could do as he pleased, he plunged himself into crime and disgrace.
>
> (*Annals,* 6.51)

Book 11. There is at this point in the manuscript a gap of the ten years that comprise the entire reign of Caligula and the first half of Claudius's reign. Tacitus had already commented on Claudius several times in previous books, especially in book 3 where he remarked: "The more I think back about recent or past events, the more ludicrous all the affairs of mortals appear to be. For in reputation, expectation, and esteem, anyone else seemed more destined for the throne than that future emperor [Claudius] whom fortune kept waiting in the wings" (*Annals,* 3.18). Now, in book 11, Tacitus reveals to us a bumbling, drunken Emperor Claudius in the midst of scheming women (his wife Messalina and his niece Agrippina the Younger) and intriguing freedmen (Callistus, Narcisssus, and Pallas).

Again, there are brief descriptions of diplomatic and military problems in Armenia and Germania, and even a proud account of Claudius's decision to enroll leading citizens of Gaul in the Roman Senate. But mostly, the focus of the narrative is on Messalina's abuse of power and her attempt to seize her husband's throne for her lover, a young senator named Silius. Claudius, the wronged husband, was the last one to know, because his freedmen tried to cover up the affair and then turned on Messalina, eliminating the traitorous wife. When Claudius was told she had died, he grieved not, reports Tacitus. "Nor did he inquire" about the method of her death. "He simply called for his wine-cup and celebrated the party as usual" (*Annals,* 11.38).

Book 12. Competition now commenced among the elite women to become Claudius's fourth wife; each of them had her own "agent" making her case before the emperor. In the end, the most persuasive argument was made by his financial minister Pallas on behalf of Claudius's own niece, Agrippina the Younger; the Senate in 49 CE granted them a dispensation from Roman marriage law, which otherwise forbade such an incestuous union.

According to Tacitus, Agrippina proceeded to control the empire with a "masculine tyranny" (*Annals,* 12.7). Austere and arrogant, she was also greedy for wealth. Agrippina ruthlessly dominated the scene, maneuvering against Claudius's children, Octavia and Britannicus, so that her own son from a previous marriage, Nero, would rise to become emperor instead.

New troubles erupted between Rome and first the Parthians, then the Armenians, and finally the Jews in Palestine. In the midst of these problems and Claudius's conquest of Britain with a Roman force of perhaps 40,000 (43 CE), Nero married his stepsister Octavia, and was adopted officially by Claudius. Supporters of Britannicus in the Senate, bureaucracy, and Guard were killed by the agents of Agrippina. Finally, according to Tacitus, Agrippina eliminated Claudius himself, poisoning him at dinner and then delaying the announcement of his death until her earmarked successor, Nero, could emerge from the palace and be transported safely to the camp of the protective Praetorians. Claudius received a grand funeral like that of Augustus and was similarly deified, but his official will was never read. Agrippina had achieved her goal.

Books 13-16. In the concluding books, Tacitus chronicles the sheer horror that was the reign of Nero. He starts book 13 with: "The first death of the new principate was that of Marcus Junius Silanus, governor of Asia" (*Annals,* 13.1). Purely private reasons motivated this execution, and similar jealousies, fears, hatreds, and resentments caused the deaths of many other men and women over the next decade.

Agrippina's and Nero's advisors, Burrus and Seneca, managed to steer the emperor in his actions for the first few years, but the young Nero refused to focus on the war with Parthia (as Tacitus saw it, a true test of his leadership), instead whiling away the time with his freedmen friends and his mistress, the actress Acte. In this early part of the reign, Nero's mother wanted to rule in place of Nero. Gradually, however, Agrippina

felt her influence over her son waning, and ultimately she turned against Nero and sided with her stepson, Britannicus, as the legitimate ruler; Britannicus soon died from a poisoned drink prepared by Nero's henchmen. Agrippina now turned to support Nero's wife Octavia against the adulterous emperor and apparently also began to foment plots against his power. The result was the prosecution of her closest confidants on various charges.

Nero had broken free of his mother's or anyone else's control. "Disguised in the outfit of a slave, he roamed the streets, brothels, and motels, with a gang who stole goods from shops and assaulted people on the way" (*Annals,* 13.25). By 59 CE, Nero had decided to eliminate his own mother, who was still attempting to check his power from behind the scenes. The most famous episode in this whole affair was a boating accident in the bay of Naples. Nero invited his mother to dine with him at his seaside villa and then offered her a ride home by boat along the coast; he had ordered one of his cronies to sabotage the boat so that it would collapse and sink with Agrippina on board. The scheme worked just right, except that Agrippina managed to swim ashore safely. When Nero responded to her survival by sending guards to assassinate her, his mother simply directed their blades toward her womb and accepted death. The whole business was covered up with the believable story that Agrippina had plotted to eliminate Nero and seize power herself.

The reign of Nero amounted, says Tacitus, to the plummeting of Roman society into an immoral abyss. "It was hard to maintain decency in honest walks of life, much less chastity or modesty or any bit of morality in that contest of vices" (*Annals,* 14.15). Nero proceeded through judicial trials, exiles, and executions to steal the wealth and possessions of the elite and to remove all obstacles to his exercising a free hand in public affairs. Burrus died; Seneca fell from grace and retired. Falling in love with Poppaea, the wife of one of his commanders, Nero forced the couple to divorce so that he could marry her; of course, he divorced Octavia, Claudius's daughter, to make this work and so appeared even less the legitimate heir of Claudius. Octavia suffered further, from charges that she had committed adultery. Exiled, she was abandoned; no one came to her rescue. Around the same time, the captured Armenian king Tiridates was brought to Rome, and sizing up the situation, he observed, "Great empires are not preserved by idle cowardice; they are made by the contest of men and arms" (*Annals,* 15.1). In Tacitus's mind, the Senate revealed its cowardice and weakness when it abandoned the innocent Octavia. Rome was no longer a great empire under a ruler like Nero.

Nero's most despicable moment came in 64 CE when a fire broke out near the Circus Maximus in Rome and then devastated 10 of the 14 wards of the city. According to some, Nero celebrated the disaster and perhaps even started it in order to gobble up a huge section of downtown real estate and convert it into his *Domus Aurea,* his huge private pleasure palace (Nero's efforts to organize fire brigades during the outbreak, however, and the relief that he afterward extended to victims suggest otherwise). Attempting to suppress the rumor that he was behind the catastrophe, Nero rounded up and executed Christians as scapegoats, but the strategy did not have the intended effect. Blaming the Christians only excited pity from the people and did not stop the rumors. Although Tacitus himself was not particularly kind to the early Christians, whom he viewed as "haters of mankind," his text neither blames them for nor excuses them from responsibility for the Great Fire (*Annals,* 15.44).

The next year some senators took action. Led by Seneca and C. Calpurnius Piso, they formed a plot against Nero for the sake of their own survival. But the plot was discovered, and, one-by-one, conspirators confessed to save their own skins and pointed the finger at other victims: "Free men, Roman knights and senators, untouched by any tortures, were betraying each one his nearest and dearest" (*Annals,* 15.57). Piso and Seneca were forced to commit suicide. Tacitus apologizes for the tedious list of trials and deaths, including those of the poet Lucan and the satirist Petronius, again asserting that the cause of all of this was heaven's anger with Rome (*Annals,* 16.16). "After the slaughter of so many distinguished men, Nero in the end desired to extinguish virtue herself through the murder of Thrasea Paetus and Barea Soranus," two exemplary men who were leading opposition Senators (*Annals,* 16.21). They were charged simply with espousing Republican values, were tried by other senators, not by Nero himself, and despite vigorous speeches in their own defense, were both convicted and sentenced to suicide.

Unfortunately, the surviving text of Tacitus's account breaks off just as Thrasea Paetus is dying; we do not see his last moments nor those of the other leading men and women whom Nero condemned to death. The remaining two years of his reign must be pieced together using other sources, primarily the biography by Suetonius and the much later history in Greek by Dio Cassius.

The Roman army. Much of the *Annals* is caught up with the military, which was reformed under imperial rule. After Augustus's victory over Antony and Cleopatra at Actium in 31 BCE, all surviving Roman troops from both sides of the civil war swore an oath of personal allegiance to Augustus. In 23 BCE, the Senate declared his authority to command and govern greater than that of all other military commanders. This position of *imperator* (commander-in-chief of all Roman armies) was passed down to his successors by approval of the Senate.

After making some only moderately successful attempts at expanding the empire, Augustus decided to deploy Roman forces (about 28 legions plus auxiliary troops and naval contingents) along its perimeter as a permanent, standing defensive barrier. It would defend the empire especially against the Parthians to the east and the German tribes to the north. Service in the military was voluntary: a male citizen of Rome volunteered for a 20-year period of service, plus 5 years as a reserve soldier. During that time, he had to be totally committed to the emperor and the empire, which meant he was not permitted to legally marry or have children. In return for such devoted service, the Roman legionary or sailor received an annual salary, occasional bonuses on holidays or upon the accession of a new emperor (Claudius started this latter tradition), awards (often in the form of precious metal) for distinguished conduct, and a sizable retirement pension in land or money. Scholars, however, estimate that only about 10 percent of the enlisted lived to retirement.

Not only Roman citizens became soldiers and sailors. The empire also relied on auxiliary forces made up of inhabitants of the provinces, the territories outside Italy that were subject to Rome. Provincial soldiers served five to ten years longer than citizens and earned one-third less pay. On retirement, they received Roman citizenship for themselves and their relatives, gaining legal and political rights and privileges unavailable to other provincials. By Tacitus's day, there were at least as many auxiliaries defending the empire as Roman citizen soldiers.

Tacitus's account indicates that Roman forces in the provinces were both the basis of the Emperor's power and, when not properly treated, the source of much trouble. Tiberius faced mutinies along the Rhine and Danube Rivers almost as soon as he came to the throne; the soldiers had been abused by their officers and had not received pay or been discharged on time. If Augustus's new military arrangements were going to work, the emperor in power could not neglect the frontier armies. Even Claudius, who had no military background, realized that he had to maintain discipline and order among the troops, and needed to keep them occupied with new frontiers, like the conquest of Britain. He himself appeared in Britain for part of its capture. But his successor, Nero, neglected Rome's armies during much of his reign, failing to ever visit them and threatening some of the units and their commanders with elimination. Consequently his last days as emperor were greeted by multiple mutinies along the frontiers and Rome was once again plunged into civil war. The soldiers, it seems, had rediscovered the "secret of empire," as Tacitus calls it—that the armies make the emperors wherever they please (Tacitus, *Histories*, 1.4).

No doubt with this in mind, the emperors built up their military backing at home in Italy. Augustus guaranteed the security of Italy by expanding the old camp guard of campaigning generals, called praetorians after the general's headquarters (*praetorium*). His new Praetorian Guard consisted of 9,000 men selected from among Roman citizen soldiers; they were divided into nine units, three stationed near Rome, the rest at key sites throughout Italy. Praetorians only had to serve 16 years, unlike the 20 years typical of rank-and-file infantry, and were paid about one-and-a-half times as much as the ordinary foot soldier. Their commanders (or prefects) exercised much authority in Italy, especially in Rome.

Tiberius put Sejanus in control of the guard. Under his direction, all of its units were concentrated in a massive fortress on the outskirts of Rome, where he could use them to terrorize Rome's senators and populace. We can clearly see how central the Praetorians were to control of the empire when we consider Sejanus's virtual takeover of the government for a while and his reign of terror against rivals in the imperial family. Without such backing, the history of Rome under the early emperors would have been much different, perhaps less bloody. Especially after Tiberius, the Julio-Claudian emperors relied ever more heavily on this military force and its leader, not only to gain and maintain power but to function, or at least appear to function, as

commander-in-chief, for none of these emperors had true military experience. Later emperors, after the Julio-Claudians, generally had stronger military credentials and enough power to closely control the Praetorian Guards.

Augustus revamped the military system, and it was modified by his successors in ways that in hindsight had several desirable effects. First, emperors promoted loyalty among the troops by being their central paymaster and on occasion commander-in chief in the field. Second, the revamped system centralized and streamlined the chain of command and opportunities for promotion, making the military a more efficient institution. Third, the new army provided a permanent defense of Rome's 6,000 mile long frontier, thereby encouraging peace within the empire. Fourth, the army helped Romanize the provincial peoples. And last, it constituted a skilled workforce that could be and often was diverted to vast engineering projects like roads, aqueducts, baths, temples, fortifications, even whole towns. As a result, the new Roman military was an essential support of the *Pax Romana*, the "Roman Peace."

Sources and literary context. Roman authors had experimented with various forms of history writing before Tacitus turned to composing his own. Later, in the sixteenth century, scholars gave his work the name *Annals*; they recognized how Tacitus followed the same sort of strict chronological sequencing of events typical of earlier historians in the Roman Republic and how he similarly focused on political and military details. But Tacitus went beyond simply chronicling events. Like the Republican historian Sallust, whose rapid, staccato style of writing he consciously imitated, Tacitus blended the traditions of biography, ethnology, psychology, rhetoric, theatricality, and philosophy into a seamless whole. He saw the recording of history as an art form, but certainly not as fiction. He seems to have regarded himself as superior to preceding historians, such as Livy, who, in Tacitus's view, had been first and foremost a teller of tales (see Livy's **From the Founding of the City**, also in *Classical Literature and Its Times*). Yet modern views vary on the degree of accuracy that Tacitus attained in his history: some have characterized him as irresponsible and careless; others as resentful, too sensitive, and/or brooding. Most scholars concur that Tacitus was generally careful, reliable, and factually sound in his account, even using a speech confirmed by a real archaeological source from Gaul.

The similarities in detail and arrangement between Tacitus's account and those of the biographer Suetonius and the historian Cassius Dio suggest that they all relied on one common source for large chunks of material (see Suetonius's **The Twelve Caesars**, also in *Classical Literature and Its Times*). We must also consider that Tacitus would have been influenced by his reading in Greek and Roman literature; scholars have noted the parallels between his portrait of Sejanus and Sallust's portrait of Catiline and between some of Tacitus's battle scenes and those recorded by Julius Caesar in his **Commentaries on the Gallic Wars** (also in *Classical Literature and Its Times*).

There are several sources that Tacitus himself identifies. He consulted the *diurna acta senatus*, the daily records of Senate meetings, and the memoirs of Agrippina the Younger ("who recorded for posterity her life and the events that befell her own family" [*Annals*, 4.53]). Also he refers to four prominent historians: the Elder Pliny, Cluvius Rufus, Fabius Rusticus, and Aufidius Bassus. Pliny the Elder had composed not only an exceptional *Natural History*, but also a 20-book study of Rome's wars against the Germans; Cluvius Rufus devoted his historical work to the period 37-69 CE, with special focus on Nero. The politician Fabius Rusticus composed a history quite hostile to Nero. Tacitus probably also used Aufidius Bassus's works on Roman history and German history; Tacitus points to Aufidius's eloquence with admiration in the *Dialogue on Orators*. Probably he also had access to the memoirs of general Gnaeus Domitius Corbulo for his campaigns in the East.

Though he availed himself of all these more learned sources, Tacitus was also seduced by sensational, suggestive rumors and allegations, which he interfused with his accurate facts. He is also suspected to have relied heavily on partisan, anti Julio-Claudian political pamphlets for some of his material.

Like a portrait painter, Tacitus depicted individuals briefly but vividly, giving us studies in character and personality, and he made frequent use of the aside, as though to demonstrate his ability to see beyond the apparent facts to a deeper reality. He believed that historians possess the gift to penetrate appearances and discern fundamental truths, as he attempts to do, for example, in his portrait of Tiberius.

Tacitus was something of a prophet of history and politics, becoming didactic in his messages in the process. Though claiming to be impartial, he set out to show his readers how Roman society had declined from the virtues of the Old Republic (with which he was almost obsessed) to the vices of the emperors, and to show the Romans of the "happiest age" (his own) how to avoid another such slide into an immoral abyss: "I consider it the prime duty of history to make sure that virtuous deeds are not kept silent and that wicked words and deeds fear posterity and infamy" (*Annals*, 3.65). The *Annals* can be regarded as a series of chronological episodes that fulfills this purpose. The historian and his work become agents for potential change. Vice takes center stage in the history. Tacitus apologized for this strategy in his work, yet he insisted that it was useful and necessary: "few men discern through their own wisdom the good from the bad, the useful from the harmful—most men learn such from the experience of others" (*Annals*, 4.33). For Tacitus, the practice of history could never be anything less than a supreme study in morality. He was no doubt influenced in his approach by the dominance of satire in early Roman society; with its biting edge of social and moral criticism, satire was the most popular literary form of his day.

Events in History at the Time the Narrative Was Written

A world of difference—ruling justly. Scholars place Tacitus's *Annals* as his last work, dating its composition to sometime between 105 and 117 CE. Curiously it deals with the earliest period of interest to Tacitus in all of his writings. The composition of the *Annals* fell entirely within the reign of the Emperor Trajan (98-117 CE), considered by Tacitus's generation to be the "*optimus princeps*," the "best of emperors." In his *Histories*, Tacitus himself referred to the time of Trajan and his predecessor, Nerva, as the "*beatissimum saeculum*," the "happiest age" yet in the Mediterranean (Tacitus, *Histories*, 1.1). Not fully known to Tacitus, Nerva had inaugurated a pattern of smooth successions from one adoptive "good" emperor to another that would last for nearly a century; Tacitus's writings suggest that he knew Nerva and Trajan had ushered in a remarkable period of peace and prosperity for the empire, something to be grateful for after the convulsive politics under the preceding Julio-Claudian and Flavian dynasties.

Certainly Tacitus felt free enough under Trajan to critically appraise the latter's predecessors on the throne and indeed to drag their memories through the muck in his search for the truth about their reigns. The era during which he wrote the *Annals*, or more precisely the emperor under whom he wrote the *Annals*, allowed Tacitus the freedom to express repressed feelings, to vent his political and moral frustrations and anger especially with the terror he had suffered under Domitian's rule. Tacitus places in the mouth of a historian of the previous century, Cremutius Cordus (who wrote during the time of Tiberius about the collapse of the Roman Republic), words that probably reflected Tacitus's own sentiments: "But what above all was customary and unrestricted [during the Republic] was writing about those whom death had removed from hatred or favoritism" (*Annals,* 4.35). Under Tiberius, such freedom of expression did not exist (Cremutius Cordus was driven to suicide for something he said). Nor did it exist under any Julio-Claudian or Flavian emperor, and Tacitus knew it. But it existed under Trajan, whom Tacitus happily linked to the earlier Republican freedom of speech.

Before becoming emperor, Trajan, a native of Italica in Spain, had enjoyed a distinguished military career under the Flavians. He served in Asia Minor, Syria, and on the borders of Germany. As emperor, he ruled with the support of all the armies of Rome and received full powers as Princeps from the Senate. Through his wife Plotina, he won over the faction of philosophers and other Roman intellectuals who had objected strenuously to one-man rule under the Flavian dynasty. Indeed, we should mention how contemporary authors took special note of the model Roman woman, like Plotina, or his sister Marciana, or his niece Matidia, with whom Trajan surrounded himself (compare Tacitus's portraits of the Julio-Claudian women).

Trajan reestablished a standard of excellence for the position of emperor: people remembered him as honest and flexible, generous and merciful, dutiful and brave, equitable and respectful of the law. He guided the leaders of the empire by example. His policies appear to have been liberal and well-ordered; his relations with all influential groups in Roman society, careful and practical. Trajan appointed qualified legal, financial, and military experts to key posts in the government and always made decisions in consultation with these experts and other representatives of the Senate. Making it more representative, the emperor introduced into the Senate additional aristocrats from the provinces, especially from Asia Minor, Spain, North Africa, and Gaul. He insisted, however, that all senators own a substantial amount of their property in Italy so they would have a vested interest in the heart of the empire.

Trajan dispatched traveling commissioners, *correctores,* throughout the empire to promote agricultural growth and provide solutions for local economic problems. He provided for army veterans by establishing for them new colonies that grew into cities along the Rhine River, in the ancient European country of Dacia (modern Romania), and in North Africa. He was well known for his public works projects, especially the new port at Ostia, Rome's harbor, as well as new aqueducts, baths, and markets.

Trajan demanded and received from the armed forces greater discipline, order, and hard work; his foreign policy was one of strong frontiers and expansion. In foreign affairs, he waged major campaigns against the Dacians (in 101-102 CE and 105-106 CE) in central Europe and against the Parthians (in 113-117 CE) in the Middle East. As a consequence of these wars, Trajan added sizeable territory to the Empire, famously extending its reach to the Persian Gulf, original heartland of Western civilization. Certainly these events dominated the imagination of those who lived during Trajan's reign, not least because of the monuments he erected to honor his victories—for example, the famous Column of Trajan, which commemorates his military campaigns and still stands in Rome today. Trajan's campaigns likely inspired Tacitus to devote considerable attention in his *Annals* to previous Roman wars against the Parthians and others beyond the Danube River instead of just to politics and intrigues at Rome.

Trajan's expansionism beyond Rome's natural frontiers over-extended the military resources of the empire, however, and not long after his death (from a stroke in the summer of 117), his successor, Hadrian, pulled Roman forces out of Mesopotamia (modern-day Iraq) and established client-kingdoms in that region while holding on to the new Dacian provinces and strengthening border defenses generally. Trajan's passing was greeted with a huge public funeral in Rome and honors from the Senate, including his transformation into a god, or deification.

Even a cursory reading of Tacitus's *Annals* will demonstrate how much previous emperors like Tiberius and Nero, whom the historian loathed, were polar opposites of Trajan. Trajan's approach to politics and warfare, his personality and character traits, and his choice of advisors reminded

THE POLITICAL WIFE

Our evidence about women of the imperial family comes entirely from biased male authors who provide us with anecdotes illustrating the activities and character of these women. Tacitus is no exception. It has long been recognized among scholars that his portraits of imperial women, though complex, are largely rooted in his moralistic approach to human nature and Roman society. Tacitus's history provides some reliable indication of the activities of powerful women in the first two centuries CE. But, with a few notable exceptions, his portrayals suggest that he resented the rising power and influence of elite women in Roman politics. To him, this development signified a decline in Roman society from the days of Republican propriety.

In the Roman Empire, as in the days of the Republic, both elite and lower-class women were married off at young ages in matches arranged by their fathers. Especially among the elite, a woman was always supposed to be under some male's supervision. Tacitus vividly illustrates what men believed could happen if even married women were left unsupervised, when he describes the sexual escapades of Claudius's wife, Messalina. His eleventh book characterizes her as greedy, jealous, and lustful, and describes her adulterous love affair with Gaius Silius as well as her notorious drinking parties in the palace. On the other hand, her daughter, Octavia, is portrayed as chaste and modest, a perfect wife cast aside by Nero and framed for adultery. Messalina and Octavia are opposite stereotypes of the Roman wife.

Traditional Roman men, Tacitus among them, favored women in the roles of dutiful daughter, then mature, nurturing wife and mother. In the *Annals*, we see Augustus's granddaughter, Agrippina the Elder, fulfilling both these roles exceptionally well: she is devoted to her natal family (especially her father, Agrippa, and grandfather, Augustus) and to her husband, Germanicus, and their children. She furthermore dedicates herself to what these famous men of her family supposedly stood for: the Roman Republic and its virtues of good government, law, equity, honesty, and bravery. While she aims to achieve the morally good, she also lets nothing stand in the way of exacting revenge from those who threaten her family, an unwomanly pursuit, as Tacitus sees it. She is a mixture of ideal female and male traits. Livia, by contrast, appears to be a perversion of the ideal: she is a compliant wife to Augustus and the power behind her son Tiberius, but never allows him to forget it. Unlike a good Roman mother, she probably causes the deaths of Augustus's grandsons and perhaps even of her own popular son Drusus, whom she regards as a threat to her first-born, Tiberius. Livia, says Tacitus, was driven by hunger for power, not motherly love. But, in light of the fact that no evidence exists beyond his innuendoes, scholars argue that his image of Livia relies on untrue and malicious rumors. Agrippina the Younger is also fiercely critiqued by Tacitus. He paints her as a woman who used sexual allurements to get what she really wanted—power and wealth. Agrippina tried to rule alongside her husband Claudius while he lived, then killed him to seize his throne for her son, Nero. When that son broke from her control, she switched her support to his step-siblings and tried to overthrow him. Certainly there was no love lost here, despite reports of her attempts to seduce Nero into obedience (*Annals*, 13.13, 14.2).

Tacitus of the great men from the Republic who had built Rome and the Empire, the men of virtue and tradition whom he so greatly admired. Trajan was a "new, old Roman" and his era perhaps reminiscent of the good old days of the Roman Republic for which Tacitus so longed.

Reception and impact. Versions of Tacitus's work have barely come down to us. The only manuscript containing *Annals* 1-6, the First Medicean (now in Florence), was probably produced in the mid-ninth century in Germany. *Annals* 11-16 survive through both the Second Medicean (also in Florence), produced perhaps in southern Italy in the eleventh century, and from later manuscripts derived from this Second Medicean.

Tacitus's writings were meant to be read privately, not to be recited publicly. They were in a style that many ancient orators would have regarded as inelegant, and students in Roman schools or monks in medieval monasteries would not have considered his unusual, atypical Latin prose worth imitating. This may explain why his works were not much appreciated in ancient times and through much of the Middle Ages.

We know that the late medieval and early Renaissance writers Giovanni Boccaccio and Poggio Bracciolini read Tacitus firsthand. His works, including the *Annals*, are known to have been highly regarded in the later Renaissance and during the revolutions of the eighteenth and nineteenth centuries. Thinkers like Italy's Francesco Guicciardini, England's Francis Bacon, France's Montesquieu and Michel de Montaigne, and America's Thomas Jefferson and John Adams saw in his history the struggle between individual conscience and corrupt society, between freedom and tyranny that so resonated in their own time. They, and their opponents, avidly pored over his anti-tyrannical analysis and borrowed slogans from Tacitus for their respective political causes. Guicciardini in his *Ricordi* (C-18) remarked that Tacitus teaches us all good and all bad of which humans are capable, while Montaigne in his *Essays* (2.10 and 3.8) called Tacitus the master of both truth and exaggeration. Rulers like Napoleon disliked Tacitus precisely because he condemned one-man rule so effectively. In the later nineteenth century, when a growing number of Europeans subscribed to the notion of infinite human progress, Tacitus's pessimism about human nature—that it stays the same and is always corruptible and basically sinister—fell out of step with a more modern, positive outlook. But the disastrous wars of the twentieth century revived his reputation among the educated as they embraced more negative views of history and man's future. Our modern concepts of tyranny, of political freedom, and of martyrdom for a great political cause derive largely from Tacitus's work. Tacitus's influence today can be seen even in the way sinister political forces and imperial government are depicted in popular culture. The recent *Star Wars* trilogy, which chronicles the fall of a virtuous Republic and the rise of a diabolical one-man rule through the manipulation and machinations of an ambitious senator and his cronies, owes its characterization and the very essence of its message to the *Annals* of Tacitus.

—Michael Lovano

For More Information

Africa, Thomas W. *Rome of the Caesars*. New York: Wiley and Sons, 1965.

Gardner, Jane. *Women in Roman Law and Society*. Bloomington: Indiana University Press, 1986.

Grant, Michael. *Roman Literature*. New York: Penguin, 1954.

Keppie, L. *The Making of the Roman Army*. London: Barnes and Noble, 1984.

Mellor, Ronald. *From Augustus to Nero: The First Dynasty of Imperial Rome*. East Lansing: Michigan State University Press, 1990.

———. *The Roman Historians*. London: Routledge, 1999.

———. *Tacitus: The Classical Heritage*. New York: Routledge, 1995.

Syme, Ronald. *Tacitus*. Oxford: Clarendon Press, 1958.

Tacitus, Cornelius. *The Histories*. Trans. Clifford H. Moore. *The Annals*. Trans. John Jackson. [Latin with English translations.] Cambridge, Mass.: Harvard University Press, 1937.

———. *The Annals of Imperial Rome*. Harmondsworth, England: Penguin, 1977.

Watson, Graham. *The Roman Soldier*. Ithaca: Cornell University Press, 1969.

Apology

by
Plato

Plato was born in Athens in 429 BCE to an influential, politically active aristocratic family and given the fine education typical for an Athenian boy of his status. His interests included wrestling (he was a champion), politics (he wanted to run for office), and writing. According to ancient tradition, Plato, in hopes of becoming the next Sophocles, began to compose dramas that showed some promise. However, after first hearing Socrates, Plato went home and set fire to these writings. Plato subsequently studied under Socrates for nearly a decade, until the teacher was tried and condemned to death in 399 BCE. These events so disillusioned Plato that he left Athens to travel, visiting parts of Egypt and present-day Italy. Plato returned to Athens at the age of 40. It was probably at this point that he founded his philosophical school, the Academy, where he would spend most of his remaining time writing and teaching (one of his students was Aristotle). Twenty years later Plato went to Syracuse, a city-state of Sicily that had invited him to become its advisor. By then, Plato had written the **Republic**, a dialogue describing the ideal ruler as a philosopher-king, a model the new Syracusean ruler could possibly emulate (also in *Classical Literature and Its Times*). In the end, however, Plato's proposals were seen as too radical and life in Sicily grew politically unstable and dangerous: the number of exiles and assassinations mounted. Taking heed, Plato returned to Athens and devoted himself to his Academy for the remainder of his 81 years. Plato's *Apology* (from the Greek *apologia*, meaning "a speech in

---

> ## THE LITERARY WORK
>
> A dialogue written in Greek and set in Athens in 399 BCE; probably written soon after 399 BCE.
>
> ## SYNOPSIS
>
> The *Apology* dramatizes the trial that condemned Socrates to death for being insufficiently religious and for corrupting Athenian youth.

---

defense, usually self-defense") is the first of 35 dialogues ascribed to him. Many of them explore the relationship between morality or virtue and politics. In his *Apology,* Plato presents Socrates as a man committed to the truth at all costs and as a defendant who is standing trial largely because of the misperceptions and wounded vanity of some preeminent Athenian citizens.

Events in History at the Time of the Dialogue

Socrates and his trial. Socrates was born to a middle-class family in 469 BCE. His mother was a midwife and his father, an artist or craftsman who earned enough to leave Socrates the small inheritance that he lived on until his death at the age of 70. Socrates had a wife, Xanthippe, and three children but never held a job or worked at

Plato. © Gianni Dagli Orti/Corbis.

a trade. He spent all his time practicing philosophy in Athens, without payment. Apparently his family received little financial or emotional support from him, coming second to his philosophic mission.

Although Socrates is sometimes spoken of as the first philosopher, he built on the work of a group of early Greek thinkers (including Thales, Parmenides, and Heraclitus). Known as the pre-Socratics, these thinkers grappled with cosmology (from *cosmos*, the Greek word for "universe"), asking questions about the nature and structure of the cosmos. This first wave of Greek philosophers shared a focus on the external, material world. Although Socrates began as a natural philosopher, he ultimately abandoned that inquiry to become a moral philosopher, a thinker interested in the human being and his or her search for truth.

Socrates was reputedly a prolific philosopher. Yet the only written records of his thought are those related by other people, most notably Plato, who was not just Socrates' student but also one of his closest friends. Xenophon (c. 430-356 BCE), another student of Socrates, wrote versions of the trial too, and of Socrates' philosophic conversations. A third account comes from the poet-playwright Aristophanes, a strident critic of Socrates. But most of Socrates' ideas come to us from Plato.

We know for certain that Socrates was tried on charges of corrupting Athens' youth, of not believing in the city's gods, and of recognizing new divinities. He was found guilty and put to death by poison, more precisely, by hemlock. There is much conjecture about exactly what happened at the trial. Plato was present; Xenophon was not. To what extent the Socrates presented by Plato is the true, historic Socrates is nonetheless open to debate.

Development of Athenian democracy. From the sixth century BCE onward, three types of regimes predominated in the Greek states: monarchies (or kingships), oligarchies (the rule of a few), and democracy (rule of the people). Athens ultimately provided the most salient example of the last.

In 594 BCE Solon, an *archon,* or high official, of Athens, instituted a series of legal reforms, including the *Seisachtheia* laws, which attempted to ease the poorer citizens' burdens by canceling certain mortgages and debts and by abolishing a creditor's power to imprison or enslave. Solon also reorganized the Athenian citizens into four property classes and widened eligibility for public office, breaking the monopoly of the noble families. However, Athens' development as a true democracy did not begin until after the fall of the Peisistratid tyranny (560-510 BCE) and the ascension of the Athenian statesman Cleisthenes, almost a century later.

Coming to power in 508 BCE, after a brief period of political struggle, Cleisthenes introduced a series of reforms that resulted in less power for the aristocratic upper class and more for common citizens. He converted the approximately 139 demes (local districts) of Attica, including the city of Athens itself, into political units, each with its own local assembly, cults, treasury, and *demarch,* or mayor. Each deme had to keep a register naming all male residents who were 18 years of age or older, which served as an official record of the citizen body. Citizens thus identified themselves by their demotics, the demes in which they were registered, and they retained those demotics even if they subsequently went to live elsewhere in Attica.

Cleisthenes also stripped the four traditional tribes, based mainly on family relations, of most of their importance and reorganized the citizenry into ten tribes, according to their demes. This, in turn, led to a reorganization of the *boule,* or council, which had been created under Solon. Instead of 400 members, the *boule* now consisted of 500 members, 50 of whom were chosen annually by lot from each of the ten tribes formed by Cleisthenes. No citizen could serve in the council more than twice during his lifetime.

Cleisthenes' democratic policies were not wholly uncontested, however: during the early decades of the fifth century BCE, there were several disputes between Athenians who favored an oligarchic regime, like the statesman and general Cimon, and Athenians who desired radical democratic reforms, like Ephialtes and Pericles. For most of the century, the more radical democrats maintained the ascendancy and democracy flourished in Athens, especially under Pericles, who dominated the political scene from the 450s to 429 BCE. Pericles' policies included negotiating a lasting peace with Sparta, revising citizenship laws to favor native Athenians, and commissioning numerous public buildings, among them, the famous Parthenon, a temple dedicated to Athena, the city's patron goddess. But during the second Peloponnesian War (431-404 BCE), there was increasing dissatisfaction with the democratic government in Athens. The discontent led to oligarchic revolutions, beginning, in 411 BCE, with a moderate oligarchy, headed first by a council of 400 (the Four Hundred), then by an assembly of 5,000 (the Five Thousand). In 410 BCE, the democracy was restored, temporarily. Athens' defeat in the war led to rule by another, more radical oligarchy in 404-403 BCE, which was supported by Sparta and known as the Thirty Tyrants. In 403 BCE, a democratic revolution attacked this oligarchy and the king of Sparta himself abolished it. At this point, democracy returned.

The Athenians' experience of Spartan tyranny may have heightened their suspicion in the matter of potentially anti-democratic activities and those who engaged in them. Indeed, the political misadventures of some of Socrates' students possibly prompted the charges against the philosopher. One former student, Alcibiades, fled into exile to escape trial for the destruction of sacred statues (the merit of the charges is unknown); seeking refuge at Sparta, he aided its citizens against Athens during the Peloponnesian War (431-404 BCE). Later Alcibiades would regain favor at Athens, then lose it once more, his actions remaining a lasting stigma to Socrates. Even more damningly, two other students, Critias and Charmides, were members of the Thirty Tyrants. Although Athenians, they had been selected by Sparta to serve in its puppet government in Athens during 404-403 BCE. None

of these instances could be brought up during Socrates' trial, owing to a general amnesty for political crimes that had been declared when Athens re-established democracy in 403 BCE. But while the amnesty made it impossible to charge Socrates with political crimes, it has been argued that he suffered guilt by association with these students. Presumably these are the students to whom Socrates refers when, in Plato's *Apology,* he says, "I have never been anyone's teacher; but if anyone, whether younger or older, desired to hear me speaking . . . I never begrudged it to him. . . . And whether any of them becomes an upright man or not, I would not justly be held responsible, since I have never promised or taught any instruction to any of them" (Plato, *Apology,* 33a-b).

Trial by jury in Classical Athens. By the mid-fifth century BCE, the judicial process in Athens had developed into a system of juries, each consisting of a certain number of citizens who tried an individual case. All citizens older than 30 could volunteer for jury service at the beginning of each year. It was from this pool that the list of about 6,000 jurors for the year was compiled. Hoping to encourage volunteers, the Athenian statesman Pericles introduced payment for jurors around 425 BCE. However, payment amounted to less than the wages an able-bodied citizen could earn in a day's work. Consequently, many of the volunteers were men too old to work.

The number of jurors varied according to the case, but a jury usually consisted of several hundred members, chosen by lot. A magistrate or group of magistrates presided over each trial, with different magistrates handling designated cases. For example, the *archon* took charge of cases dealing with family and inheritance rights; the *basileus,* of cases involving homicide; and the *strategoi* (generals), of cases concerning military and naval matters. The *thesmothetia* tended to be responsible for any public case that did not fall within the purview of another magistrate.

The popular courts (*dikasteria*) met about 200 days a year. On each meeting day, a number of courts would be appointed to try cases as they arose. Actions were classified as private or public. Private actions concerned wrongs committed against an individual and could be raised only by the offended party. Public actions, wrongs committed against or affecting a whole community, could be raised by a magistrate or any official acting on the state's behalf. A session generally lasted about eight hours, during which the jury heard speeches, first from the prosecutor, then from the defendant. After both speeches, the jury voted, placing objects like pebbles or shells into urns that designated conviction or acquittal. The votes were counted and the verdict determined according to the majority; a tie was treated as an acquittal. If the verdict resulted in conviction, the jury then determined the appropriate punishment. A defendant could not appeal the jury's verdict. But to discourage malicious or frivolous prosecutions, the accuser would be fined if less than one-fifth of the jury returned a verdict of conviction.

Socrates' trial in the *Apology* follows the established Athenian procedure. However, Plato includes only the philosopher's speeches: his self-defense, his counterproposal to the death penalty, and his final response to the verdict and sentence. The first and longest of these speeches displays the "Socratic method," a technique that employs questions to identify false or contradictory assumptions. Not once but several times, Socrates deftly persuades his dialogue partner—the prosecutor Meletus—to abandon his initial belief and proclaim another one true. The technique helps Socrates demonstrate that even on the gravest matters, people's opinions are often not based on fact or careful scrutiny. In his second and third speeches—delivered after the verdict—Socrates demonstrates another harsh reality: the unyielding nature of the Athenian judicial process. Although the exact number of jurors in his trial remains uncertain, many suppose there were about 500, of whom 280 voted for conviction and 220 for acquittal. "[I]f only thirty of the votes had fallen differently," says Socrates in Plato's *Apology*, "I would have been acquitted" (*Apology*, 36a).

The sophists. During Socrates' lifetime, the term "sophist" (expert on wisdom) was applied to an intellectual who traveled widely through the Greek world, giving scholarly lectures and offering paid instruction in a wide range of subjects. Sophists were not considered a school or a single movement, as each sophist tended to have his individual ideas and doctrines to expound.

The sophists' fields of expertise could include natural philosophy, mathematics, history, geography, and speculative anthropology. Other areas of interest were practical knowledge and rhetoric. Generally the sophists approached traditional subjects with inquisitiveness and skepticism. They were renowned for their argumentative powers. Indeed, the word "sophistry," as now used, denotes a clever, specious argument, one that appears plausible but is built on

fallacy. The Greek sophist Protagoras (c. 481-420 BCE) reportedly composed a treatise on argumentative techniques and gained notoriety for claiming that he could make the weaker argument the stronger. Still, he employed persuasion to a higher purpose, to develop good citizens. Sophists aroused strong positive and negative reactions. Some enjoyed highly successful careers and their services were much sought after. The Greek statesman Pericles enjoyed close friendships with the sophists Damon (c. 500 BCE) and Anaxagoras (c. 500-428 BCE); Pericles also invited Protagoras to Athens. However, those who held more conservative views regarded sophists as a subversive element, a force that could undermine morality and tradition, especially among the young and impressionable.

As the writings of the sophists appear to be lost, historians must draw upon the accounts of others for information, including Plato, who was one of the sophists' harshest critics. The predominantly negative impressions of the sophists are partly the result of his writings. Keen to determine the direction of philosophy, Plato deliberately distinguished himself from the sophists, whom he viewed as operating without "a coherent positive doctrine" (Gagarin, p. 4). Plato may also have blamed the suspicion with which sophists were often regarded as a contributing factor to the death sentence pronounced upon Socrates, whom conservative Athenians often associated with sophists, although he denied sharing their ideas or practices.

Sophists, in fact, seem to have been among Plato's favorite targets; the most famous make frequent appearances as characters in his dialogues. Like most of Socrates' conversational partners, they are usually on the losing side of an argument, and Plato never misses an opportunity to ridicule their flowery speeches, their tendency to focus on trivial details during a debate, and their utter irreverence for the truth. One of Plato's dialogues, called the *Protagoras,* after the sophist of the same name, is quite telling in this respect. In this dialogue, Socrates, who also appears as a character, concedes that Protagoras is superior in "speechmaking," but not in verbal exchanges of question and answer. Socrates furthermore objects to the tactic of making "a long speech in reply to every question, staving off objections and not giving answers, but spinning it out until most of the people listening forget what the question was" (Plato, *Protagoras,* 336d). He himself cannot make such a speech, admits Socrates, but this skill is entirely different from genuine discussion and argument.

POETRY VS. PHILOSOPHY

Belief in the gods played a major role in most aspects of daily life in ancient Greece. In addition to the 12 major gods of Olympia, which all Greeks worshipped, each city-state had its own set of deities with its own local mythology, which often involved the founding of the city. Citizens regularly participated in public religious rituals, and statesmen and military leaders commonly consulted the gods when there were decisions or policies to make. Poets were thought to have divine insight, partly because of the inspiration they received from the goddesses known as the Muses. Others furthermore recognized that the poets transmitted Greek mythology through their verse and respected them for the service. While Socrates' generation thought of poets as spokesmen for the gods and preservers of the religious traditions, it regarded philosophers more ambivalently: some were celebrated; others, distrusted. The *Apology* showcases the rivalry between the two groups. As a philosopher, Socrates upheld a distinction between knowledge and opinion. In his view, all of the people he engaged in dialogue had *opinions* about what was true, but they were often contradictory and illogical, not the result of careful thought. Philosophers like Socrates, Protagoras, and Antiphon also distinguished between nature and convention, and this too posed a challenge to poets and religious tradition. Is it not possible, asked the philosophers, that the existence of gods is conventional rather than natural? The gods may simply be an invention by the poets, one that prevents men from asking basic questions about the origin of man and the nature of the universe. From the perspective of philosophy, poetry does not answer the myriad questions of human existence. Meanwhile, the poets see the philosophers as challengers to piety, justice, and support of the city's laws and traditions. It is hardly surprising, given the conflict between poetry and philosophy, that a number of Socrates' accusers were poets; Meletus, who was either the son of a minor poet or a poet himself, apparently initiated the charges against Socrates. In fact, one view of the *Apology* regards it as Plato's response to the poets' charges against philosophy.

In Plato's *Apology*, Socrates denies that he is a sophist and differentiates between his teachings and theirs:

> How you, men of Athens, have been affected by my accusers, I do not know. For my part, even I nearly forgot myself because of them, so persuasively did they speak. And yet they have said, so to speak, nothing true. . . . They said you should beware that you are not deceived by me, since I am a clever speaker. They . . . will immediately be refuted by me in deed, as soon as it becomes apparent that I am not a clever speaker at all. . . . I am an orator—but not of their sort. So they, as I say, have said little or nothing true, while from me you will hear the whole truth.
>
> (*Apology*, 17a-b)

Socrates also points out that he, unlike the sophists, receives no payment for his discussions with young people. He mentions by name well-known sophists such as Gorgias, Prodicus, and Hippias, pointing out that they have earned a handsome living teaching the art of persuasive rhetoric to young men from wealthy families. Socrates, on the other hand, lives in abject poverty. (Actually Socrates' financial standing was not quite as dire as the *Apology* suggests. He had ties to elite families through his marriage and his father, as noted, had left him a small inheritance. Of course, Socrates may still have had less wealth at his immediate disposal than a well-paid sophist.)

The Dialogue in Focus

The contents. The *Apology* is Plato's portrayal of the trial and sentencing of his teacher, Socrates. In the course of the dialogue, Socrates delivers three speeches to the jury: the first is a defense of himself and his work; the second, a counter-proposal to the death penalty; and the third, a response to the jury's pronouncement of the death sentence upon him.

As the dialogue begins, Socrates, in traditional rhetorical fashion, prepares his audience, the jury, not to expect too much of his defense. First, he attempts to distinguish himself from the clever rhetoricians of his day by warning the jurors that, unlike them, he will simply speak the truth "at random in the words that [he] happen[s] upon" and not "in beautifully spoken speeches like theirs" (*Apology,* 17c). He calls the jurors "the men of Athens," entreating them to deal with him leniently, stating that although he is 70 years old, this is the first time he has ever appeared in court. As a *xenos*, a stranger, or outsider to these proceedings, he asks for the court's sympathy.

After this introduction, Socrates lays out the charges against him. He divides them into two groups, emanating from the "old" and the "new" accusers. The new accusers are the men who brought the specific, "official" charges against him for which he is on trial. But the older accusers, says Socrates, are far more dangerous; they are the ones who have been slandering him and turning public opinion against him for years. Since he views them as the larger threat, he deals with their charges first.

Socrates refers to some older poets as his original accusers, specifically Aristophanes, who parodied Socrates in his comedic satire **Clouds**, a play performed in Athens 24 years before this trial (also in *Classical Literature and Its Times*). According to Socrates, Aristophanes' play had made an informal charge against him, accusing him of the following: "Socrates does injustice, and is meddlesome, by investigating things under the earth and the heavenly things, and by making the weaker speech the stronger, and by teaching others these same things" (*Apology,* 19b). Socrates dismisses these accusations, saying simply that "none of these things is so" (*Apology,* 19d). If anyone in the jury has ever heard him conversing about these topics, they should come forward. But, says Socrates, none of them can because he has never discussed the things Aristophanes accuses him of, and the same holds true for the rest of the rumors Aristophanes has spread about him. Socrates also expresses concern at the unfair advantage that the comic poet has over him: Aristophanes has had more than 20 years to slander Socrates, while the philosopher has only a day to defend himself. Socrates then admits that a juror might well ask why he has been so slandered if he is innocent. His response is that the Athenians resent him because he possesses wisdom. In order to explain what kind of wisdom he has and why it is unique, he tells the jury how his quest for the truth began.

Socrates' friend Chaerephon paid a visit to the Oracle of Delphi and asked if there were any man alive wiser than Socrates. The Oracle replied that Socrates was the wisest. Socrates recounts his reaction to the Oracle's pronouncement for the jury:

> Whatever is the god saying, and what riddle is he posing? For I am conscious that I am not at all wise, either much or little. So what ever is he saying when he claims I am wisest? Surely he is not saying something false. . . . And for a long time I was at a loss about what ever he was saying, but then very reluctantly I turned to something like the following investigation of it.
> (*Apology,* 21b)

Socrates' inquiry consisted of questioning the three most well-respected segments of society to prove that they were wiser. He questioned politicians, poets, and craftsmen, always seeking out those reputed to be the wisest. Each time he found that while the person knew quite a lot about his particular pursuit, the individual did not possess true human wisdom.

Ironically Socrates' wisdom consists of being able to recognize and admit what he does not know, which distinguishes him from his fellow citizens: "As I went away, I reasoned . . . . 'I am wiser than this human being. For probably neither of us knows anything noble and good, but he supposes he knows something when he does not know, while I . . . do not even suppose that I do'" (*Apology,* 21d). Socrates then demonstrated to those who thought themselves wise that they really were not. This, according to Socrates, is the source of the slander against him. His line of questioning made him hateful, not only to the person questioned but also "to many of those present" at the time (*Apology,* 21d). Was the person embarrassed or insulted by Socrates' questions? If so, the person could easily fall back on the standard prejudices against philosophy.

Next Socrates turns to the charges against him by his new accusers, led by the poet Meletus. The charges are that Socrates corrupts the city's youth, and that he does not believe in the gods of the city but in other *daimonia* (or spirits). Socrates brings Meletus to the stand in order to cross-examine him, and what follows is worthy of the most popular courtroom drama. As far as the first charge goes, Socrates, using his dialectic method, succeeds in getting Meletus to agree that 1) one person alone cannot corrupt the youth—that would take an effort by many, and furthermore 2) no one would deliberately corrupt the youth in his society, since it would be foolish to turn them into dangerous villains and then be forced to live among them.

> [Socrates] But tell us further, Meletus, before Zeus, whether it is better to dwell among upright citizens or villainous ones. . . . Do not the villainous do something bad to whoever are nearest to them, while the good do something good?
> [Meletus] Quite so.
> [Socrates] Is there anyone, then, who wishes to be harmed by those he associates with, rather than to be benefited?
> [Meletus] Of course not. . . .
> [Socrates] What then, Meletus? Are you so much wiser at your age than I at mine, that you have become cognizant that the bad always do something bad to those who are closest to them . . . whereas I have come into so much ignorance that I am not even cognizant that if I ever do something wretched to any of my associates, I will risk getting back something bad from him?
>
> (*Apology*, 25c-e)

Perhaps he has corrupted the youth involuntarily, admits Socrates, but in that case, the city should simply teach and admonish him, not punish him.

Socrates does a similarly brilliant job of disposing of the second charge against him, that of not believing in the gods of the city. Considering the official charge, Socrates gets Meletus to refine it while he is on the stand. Meletus accuses Socrates of not believing in any gods at all. Yet Socrates always claimed to hear a *daimon*, the voice of a spirit that warned him against or encouraged him toward a given action (this concept of an inner source of moral authority that supersedes conventional religious, political, or cultural authorities is one of Socrates' main contributions to Western moral philosophy). Since such spirits are thought to be the children of gods, or nymphs, or some sort of divinity, Socrates is able to demonstrate that he does believe in gods after all, for "what human being would believe that there are children of gods, but not gods? It would be as strange as if someone believed in children of horses or asses [mules] but did not believe that there are horses and asses" (*Apology*, 27d-e). Getting Meletus to

change his accusation is a very clever move on Socrates' part, for it allows him to avoid discussion of the original charge—not believing in the city's gods.

Having dispensed with the official charges against him, Socrates delivers one of the most poignant parts of his speech. He tries to reconcile himself and his philosophy to the city of Athens. Socrates explains to the jury that his relentless questioning and criticizing of fellow citizens is ultimately beneficial for both individual citizens and the city as a whole:

> Best of men, you are an Athenian, from the city that is greatest and best reputed for wisdom and strength: are you not ashamed that you care for having as much money as possible, and reputation, and honor, but that you neither care for nor give thought to prudence, and truth, and how your soul will be the best possible? . . . So I, men of Athens, am now far from making a defense speech on my own behalf. . . . I do it rather on your behalf, so that you do not do something wrong . . . by voting to condemn me. For if you kill me, you will not easily discover another of my sort.
>
> (*Apology*, 29d-e, 30d-e)

In his argument, Socrates compares himself to a gadfly on the sluggish horse that is Athens. He admits that his relentless questioning of citizens is annoying but maintains that it is also necessary, portraying himself as an engaged social critic concerned for his city's well-being, in contrast to the self-absorbed, materialistic sophist-scientist described by Aristophanes. According to Socrates, Athens desperately needs him to remind its citizens of the high and noble aspects of life that are more important than individual wealth, beauty, or glory. He enlightens them about what is just and virtuous, encouraging them to develop these attributes and thereby improve their individual souls. Socrates pursues wisdom not only for its own sake but also so he can exhort citizens to virtue (which, for him, encompasses excellence, knowledge, courage, wisdom, self-control). Socrates believes that virtue can be taught to others. Thus, there is a public-spiritedness to his philosophy.

Next Socrates tries to garner sympathy from the jury as he explains his aloofness and detachment from ordinary obligations, which Aristophanes has criticized. Socrates says he has neglected many aspects of his private life to fulfill his mission to the city of Athens. He lives in poverty and his own family has been "uncared for" all these years so that he might go to citizens privately, "as a father or an older brother" and persuade them to care for virtue (*Apology*, 31b). His is a practical philosophy. It deals not with abstract subjects such as stars and gnats but with the city and its affairs, and to such an extent that Socrates neglects his personal needs.

Socrates turns to his lack of involvement in public affairs, which would have been very damning to the ancient Athenians. Citizens were expected to attend public assemblies, hold public office, make speeches, and sit on juries. Accounting for the lack, Socrates admits that it might seem strange that he is "a busybody in private," while "in public I do not dare go up before your multitude to counsel the city" (*Apology,* 31c). His divine voice, Socrates explains, warned him not to enter politics, probably because if he had he would have been killed: "For there is no human being who will preserve his life if he genuinely opposed either you or any other multitude" (*Apology*, 31e). If he had died young, he would not have fulfilled his god-given purpose of goading his fellow Athenians to virtue.

All of Socrates' skillful arguments come to naught, for the jury finds him guilty. In the sentencing phase of the trial, Meletus makes a speech requesting the death penalty, and Socrates delivers his second speech, a counterproposal. Considering his options, he rejects exile, realizing that if his fellow citizens cast him out because of his philosophizing, so will every other city in the world. But what about "being silent and keeping quiet" in exile? Socrates rejects this alternative too, uttering the famous dictum that "the unexamined life is not worth living" (*Apology*, 37e-38a). In accordance with his view that all his philosophizing has been for the good of humanity, Socrates makes a counterproposal: he should be rewarded for his service to the city by being housed and fed at Athens' expense, like the victorious Olympic athletes. (To some of the ancients, Aristotle among them, this counterproposal almost seemed calculated to infuriate the jury.) Socrates concludes with a second counterproposal, a fine of 30 *minae*, a large sum of money. Again, the options of exile and silence as alternatives to death are unacceptable. In his pursuit of truth, Socrates opts rather to make the ultimate sacrifice: that of his life.

Once the jury hands down the death sentence, Socrates addresses the jurors for a third and final time. He now refers to them as *judges*. (While it was customary to address jury members as *judges* during court proceedings, Socrates waits until this point to do so.) He says that he will call only the men who voted to acquit him *judges*, because they are the only "judges in truth" (*Apology*, 41a). He adds that he is not worried about death, because his divine voice is silent. It has not warned him of impending evil or tried to stop him from anything he was going to say during his trial. He surmises that death is either like a quiet restful sleep, which is nothing to fear, or it is a journey to Hades, the underworld. But if there is a Hades, even death will not stop him in his pursuit of true knowledge:

> Certainly the greatest thing is that I would pass my time examining and searching out among those there—just as I do to those here—who among them is wise, and who supposes that he is, but is not. How much would one give, judges, to examine him who led the great army against Troy, or Odysseus, or Sisyphus, or the thousand others whom one might mention, both men and women? To converse and to associate with them and to examine them there would be inconceivable happiness.
>
> (*Apology*, 41b-c)

Public vs. private life. Towards the end of his defense, Socrates presents the jurors with two examples of his political activities, attempting to prove his commitment to virtue "not in speeches, but what you honor, deeds" (*Apology*, 32a). The first example occurs during his tenure on the Athenian Council, the one political office he held during his lifetime. As noted, Athenian citizens were divided into administrative units called tribes, and each year men were chosen by lot to serve on an administrative council as *prytanes*, or board members, for part of the year. In 406 BCE Athens was near the end of the second Peloponnesian War, a 27-year conflict with Sparta that pitted democracy against oligarchy in a struggle for control of the Greek city-states. Socrates was serving as a *prytanes* when the ten generals who had commanded the Athenian naval fleet at the Battle of Arginusae were facing trial. Although the generals had orchestrated a brilliant victory at Arginusae (an island in the Aegean Sea), they were forced to leave behind disabled ships and the corpses of Athenian soldiers because of the post-battle confusion and the onset of a violent storm. Upon their return to Athens, the generals were brought up on charges of neglecting their duty; included was a charge of impiety because they failed to insure that the dead soldiers received a decent burial with all the appropriate rites.

The board decided to try the generals together, which Socrates argued was blatantly illegal; each commander had, by law, the right to be tried separately based on the merits of his own particular case. Socrates brought a motion challenging the decision. According to legal procedure in fifth-century BCE Athens, the trial should have been suspended until his motion was considered. But public indignation against the generals was so strong that the presiding officers brushed the motion aside and proceeded with the trial. All of the *prytanes* except Socrates succumbed to threats and other attempts to intimidate them, and the trial ended in the execution of the Athenian generals. Later, when cooler heads prevailed, the Athenians realized that they had committed an injustice. He alone, Socrates reminds his fellow citizens, had refused to be a party to the "mob mentality" that prevailed in Athens at the time:

> I alone of the prytanes opposed your doing anything against the laws then, and I voted against it. And although the orators were ready to indict me and arrest me . . . I supposed that I should run the risk with the law and the just rather than side with you because of fear of prison or death when you were counseling unjust things.
>
> (*Apology*, 32b-c)

The second instance of Socrates' involvement in the unjust proceedings of Athenian politics occurred not during the democracy, but during Athens' rule by an oligarchy in 404-403 BCE. Again, Sparta, the victor in the Peloponnesian War, installed a puppet government in Athens known as the Thirty Tyrants. Made up of Athenians with anti-democratic leanings, this government enjoyed little popular support, relying during its brief tenure on a garrison of Spartan soldiers stationed in Athens to protect it. In order to raise money to support the garrison, the Thirty Tyrants began to execute wealthy residents who were not Athenian citizens and then liquidate their assets. When the Thirty Tyrants summoned Socrates, along with several other prominent citizens, and gave them the order to "arrest Leon the Salaminian and bring him from Salamis to die," Socrates refused: "Perhaps I would have died because of this, if that government had not been quickly overthrown" (*Apology*, 32c-d).

With these two examples, Socrates demonstrates the difficulties of a public and political life. Communities—even democratic ones—do not always act justly, so there is often a conflict between true justice and the laws or will of the city.

In Plato's *Apology*, Socrates defends his choice of a private rather than a public life by pointing out that any individual prepared to speak the truth puts himself at the mercy of a possibly corrupt majority: "Now do not be vexed with me when I speak the truth. For there is no human being who will preserve his life if he genuinely opposes either you or any other multitude and prevents many unjust and unlawful things from happening in the city" (*Apology*, 31e). In several other dialogues by Plato, Socrates expresses reservations about various aspects of democracy, especially majority rule. The dialogue *Laches* features a Socrates who is asked to cast a deciding vote but protests this method: "It is by knowledge that I think one must make decisions, not by the greater number, if one intends to decide well" (Socrates in Kraut, p. 197). Finally, in the *Crito*, Socrates asks, "And in particular, concerning the just and unjust and shameful and noble and good and bad things, . . . must we follow the opinion of the many and fear it rather than that of the one—if there is such an expert—whom we must be ashamed before and fear more than all others?" (Plato, *Crito*, 47d). As one scholar explains, Socrates distrusted the rule of the many. He "thought moral experts should rule, and he urged withdrawal from everyday politics only because he realized that he and his followers were far from being experts" (Kraut, p. 194). However humble this opinion may have been, it clashed with the standard esteem for the public and political life, which many saw as a civic responsibility.

Sources and literary context. The primary source for Plato's *Apology* was an actual event, the trial of Socrates. Although it is known that Plato was an eyewitness to the trial, some argue that his *Apology* idealizes Socrates. These scholars contend that in attempting to deflect criticism leveled against his teacher, Plato transforms him into a model of civic virtue, interested in the concerns of Athens; he is depicted as an instructor who has turned away from abstract philosophy as the lone pursuit of wisdom, and employs it to assist his fellow citizens in the attainment of true knowledge, which can be used in settling disagreements over what is good and just in Athens.

Xenophon, as noted, wrote the other surviving account of the philosopher's trial, but his version was composed years later and based on hearsay. Also as noted, discrepancies exist between the two accounts: according to Xenophon,

PARALLEL DISAPPOINTMENTS: PLATO AND ATHENS

Plato, like Socrates, was deeply troubled by the behavior of Athens. It dealt brutally with city-states that proved too independent for its taste, a pattern that Plato viewed with "moral revulsion" (O'Hare, p. 2). Any city-state that joined the Delian League (an alliance for mutual protection against Persia) had to follow Athenian rules. The city-state had to adopt a constitution modeled on that of Athens, send offerings to Athenian religious festivals, receive Athenian inspectors, adopt the Athenian systems of money and weights and measurements, and require all of its own officials to swear an oath of loyalty to Athens. When Athens suffered losses during the second Peloponnesian War, city-states that tried to assert their independence were harshly punished. The mistreatment of these city-states troubled Plato, who saw a great disparity between the ideals of freedom and democracy that Athens proclaimed and its often ruthless practices. In another of his dialogues (*Gorgias*, 519a), Plato criticizes the founders of the city's empire for filling Athens with harbors, dockyards, walls, tribute money, and other such nonsense instead of with moderate and upright ways. The decline of the empire, its decades-long struggle between oligarchy and democracy, and the dissolution of Greece's political system based on the *polis* explain why so much of Plato's writing concerns basic political questions: What is the organization of the best regime? the proper relationship between philosophy and politics? between religion and politics? And how should we define virtue and justice? a question that goes to the heart of Socrates' trial and conviction as presented by Plato in the *Apology*.

Socrates wanted to provoke a guilty sentence in order to escape old age (he was 70 at the trial). He therefore did not suggest a counter- or milder penalty "and would not let his friends do so, saying that this would be an admission of guilt" (Vlastos, p. 291). But Plato's version disagrees, saying that Socrates reacted first by saying that he should be rewarded, not penalized, then by relenting and proposing a monetary fine as punishment. Despite these discrepancies, Xenophon's *Apology of Socrates* is sometimes considered corroborating evidence for Plato's account, since the two are similar in many other respects. Both authors wished to refute the charges against Socrates, to counter the unflattering portrait of him in Aristophanes' *Clouds*, and to extricate their teacher from damaging associations with the sophists.

Plato's *Apology* is classified as a philosophical dialogue, an argument presented in dramatic form between at least two characters; some contend that Plato introduced or at least popularized this literary form. Socrates functions as the central character and Plato's mouthpiece in several dialogues, which are thus called the Socratic

dialogues. Among Classical dialogues, Plato's are distinctive for their humor, irony, vivid characterization, and inclusion of such secondary texts as myths and legends. They are also notable for their authorial detachment. Plato himself rarely appears and never speaks in his dialogues, distancing himself from the issues raised and leaving the reader to decide which position to adopt. The technique is in keeping with his beliefs about learning: Plato "remains convinced throughout that anything taken on trust, second-hand, either from others or from books, can never amount to a worthwhile cognitive state; knowledge must be achieved by effort from the person concerned" (Hornblower and Spawforth, p. 539).

Reception and impact. Devastated by their teacher's death sentence, Socrates' students urged him to flee (as depicted in Plato's sequel, the *Crito*), but Socrates refused. Instead he carried out his execution by drinking hemlock. Plato's *Apology*, written within a few years of these events, became the earliest contemporary account of Socrates' trial. Few immediate reactions to Plato's *Apology* are recorded. However, Aristotle, Plato's student, analyzed Plato's

The Death of Socrates (1787), by Jacques-Louis David. © Francis G. Mayer/Corbis.

account of the trial and concluded that Socrates neglected to follow the most basic rule in using persuasive rhetoric: do not anger those whom you are trying to persuade. In Aristotle's reading, Socrates antagonized the jury, which was no way to win their vote.

Interestingly, what Aristotle saw as a defect, others have regarded as inspiration. In the eyes of many, Socrates became a martyr for truth and knowledge; he refused to pander to mass opinion and fought for the individual's right of free inquiry and free speech against the power of the state. The philosopher's trial and execution inspired other Classical writers. Xenophon, also a Socratic disciple, wrote his own *Apology of Socrates* several years after the trial; Libanius (314-393 CE), a Greek orator, composed yet another version centuries later. Isocrates (436-338 BCE), an Athenian orator and teacher, even envisioned himself as a second Socrates and composed his own apology (*Antidosis,* 353) after he lost a court case involving an exchange of property.

Scholars have long debated the respective merits of Plato's and Xenophon's versions. Indeed, the phenomenon known as the "Socratic problem" springs from historians' continuing difficulty in distinguishing the personality and philosophy of the real Socrates from the somewhat idealized representations provided by his two disciples. Still, most contemporary scholars consider Plato's account to be the most reliable source of information about Socrates' trial and Socrates himself.

Whatever its degree of accuracy, Plato's *Apology* has continued to intrigue audiences for 2,400 years. It furthermore remains the first of a series of dialogues that are unparalleled in philosophic and literary achievement and have gone far to ensuring the fame of both teacher and student through the ages:

> It is to Plato's literary genius that Socrates owes his pre-eminent position as a secular saint of Western civilization. And it is Socrates who keeps Plato on the best-seller lists. Plato is the only philosopher who turned metaphysics into drama. Without the enigmatic and engaging Socrates as the principal character of his dialogues, Plato would not be the only philosopher who continues to charm a wide audience in every generation.
>
> (Stone, p. 4)

—Despina Korovessis and Pamela S. Loy

For More Information

Brickhouse, Thomas C., and Nicholas D. Smith, eds. *The Trial and Execution of Socrates.* Oxford: Oxford University Press, 2002.

Gagarin, Michael. *Antiphon the Athenian: Oratory, Law, and Justice in the Age of the Sophists.* Austin: University of Texas Press, 2002.

Hornblower, Simon, and Antony Spawforth, eds. *The Oxford Companion to Classical Civilization.* Oxford: Oxford University Press, 1998.

Kraut, Richard. *Socrates and the State.* Princeton, N.J.: Princeton University Press, 1984.

O'Hare, R. M. *Plato.* Oxford: Oxford University Press, 1996.

Plato. *Apology.* In *Four Texts on Socrates.* Ed. Thomas G. West and Grace Sterry West. Ithaca, N.Y.: Cornell University Press, 1984.

———. *Crito.* In *Four Texts on Socrates.* Ed. Thomas G. West and Grace Sterry West. Ithaca, N.Y.: Cornell University Press, 1984.

———. *Protagoras.* Trans. C. C. W. Taylor. Oxford: Clarendon Press, 1991.

Stone, I. F. *The Trial of Socrates.* New York: Random House, 1989.

Vlastos, Gregory. *Socrates: Ironist and Moral Philosopher.* Cambridge: Cambridge University Press, 1991.

The Art of Love

by
Ovid

Born at Sulmo in the Abruzzi (central Italy) in 43 BCE, Ovid (Publius Ovidius Naso) was the son of a wealthy family. Like most young men of his class, Ovid was educated in Rome, where he studied rhetoric under Arellius Fuscus and Porcius Latro; after completing his education, he toured the Greek lands. Although his family wished him to pursue a political career, Ovid soon abandoned public life to become a poet. With the help of an influential patron, Marcus Valerius Messalla Corvinus, Ovid quickly gained prominence as a writer, becoming the leading poet in Rome by 8 CE. Most of Ovid's early work explores romantic and erotic themes. His *Amores* ("Loves," c. 25 BCE), for example, recounts the poet's seemingly autobiographical misadventures in love. Other works, composed between 15 BCE and 2 CE, include *Heroides* (*Heroines*), a series of verse letters written by mythological heroines to their beloveds; *Ars Amatoria* (*The Art of Love*), a didactic poem concerning the arts of courtship and erotic intrigue; and the *Remedia Amoris* ("Remedies of Love"), a poem instructing readers how to end a love affair. In 8 CE, Emperor Augustus, offended by Ovid's poetry and by some other transgression, exiled the poet to Tomis on the Black Sea (in modern Romania). Ovid himself identified the causes of his offense, speaking of them vaguely as an error and a *carmen* (poem). While the error was an unspecified indiscretion that remains a mystery to this day, apparently the poem was *The Art of Love*. Ovid would continue to live in exile until his death in 17 CE. Before he was banished, the poet

THE LITERARY WORK

A didactic poem written in Latin in three books on the art of courtship and erotic love, set in Rome during the late first century BCE; published around the first year BCE.

SYNOPSIS

Ovid tutors young men and women on the arts of finding, courting, and keeping a lover.

married three times and fathered a daughter, probably during his second marriage. Ovid's third wife remained steadfast throughout his exile; scholarly texts speak of her devotion and the tender feelings between them. However much offense Emperor Augustus may have taken to *The Art of Love*, it quickly became and has long remained a favorite with readers, who celebrate the poem for its vivid scenes of life in imperial Rome as well as its witty treatment of amorous intrigue.

Events in History at the Time of the Poem

Sexual morality in Augustan Rome. Most of Ovid's works were composed during the long reign of Rome's first emperor, Augustus. He ruled from 27 BCE to 14 CE, preferring the title "princeps" (first man) of Rome to emperor. Prosperous and relatively peaceful, the era, which

Illustration of Ovid.

followed on close to a century of civil wars, came to be known as the *Pax Romana* (Peace of Rome).

Besides providing a centralized government, restoring religion to prominence, administering a uniform system of law and justice throughout the expanding empire, and constructing numerous public works, Augustus attempted to reform public morality. Enriched by the wealth flowing in from various parts of the empire, Rome developed into a thriving, cosmopolitan city; however, Augustus felt that Rome's very prosperity was contributing to moral laxity among its citizens. Adultery was common; divorce, easy to obtain; and the family had lost much of its coherence. Augustus sought to restore such virtues as sobriety, chastity, self-restraint, and piety, often associated with the Roman Republic. Augustus lived austerely and dressed modestly, and besides setting an example, implemented legislation for social and moral reform. By presenting himself as a strong moral force, Augustus gave legitimacy to his increasingly authoritarian rule.

In 18 BCE Augustus introduced two important though highly unpopular laws, the *Lex Julia de maritandis ordinibus* and the *Lex Julia de adulteriis coercendis.* The first law encouraged larger families through the procreation of legitimate offspring and prohibited bachelors and widows unwilling to remarry from receiving legacies (this law was replaced in 9 CE by the milder *Lex Papia*

Poppaea). The second law, the *Lex Julia,* sought to eliminate adultery (defined here as sexual intercourse between a married woman of freeborn status and a man not her husband) among the senatorial and equestrian (business) classes by imposing harsh penalties on the offenders. If found guilty, both parties were banished to separate islands for the rest of their lives; the man forfeited half his property, the woman a third of hers, as well as half her dowry. The law also permitted fathers to kill daughters and their partners in adultery; cuckolded husbands could kill the partners under certain circumstances and had to divorce their adulterous wives. Finally, the law divided all free women into two categories: *matronae honestae,* with whom all extramarital liaisons were illegal, and women *in quas stuprum non committitur* (an expression implying that they are too lowly to suffer from contamination). Including prostitutes, this second category was established for all women with whom extramarital liaisons were acceptable. A married man who had an affair with such a woman was not blamed or regarded as an adulterer, a concession that did little to mute the negative reaction both laws elicited. Romans generally greeted the two laws with disdain, which may have fuelled the popularity of Ovid's poetry.

Adultery was to prove a continual sore point with Augustus, especially in his own family. Although strictly reared as a child, his daughter Julia allegedly had several adulterous affairs as an adult, and in 2 BCE, after her indiscretions came to light, Augustus banished her to the barren island of Pandateria. In 8 CE Julia's daughter and namesake suffered the same fate; on their deaths, both women were denied burial in the royal tomb. The year of the younger Julia's banishment, Ovid was also exiled from Rome, partly because his poetry seemed to encourage adultery by offering women advice on how to deceive their husbands.

Meretrices and prostibulae. A double standard dictated sexual behavior in imperial Rome. Middle- and upper-class women were expected to remain chaste, engaging in sexual intercourse only with their husbands. While men could be severely punished under the law for seducing innocent maidens or respectable matrons, they suffered no such penalty for conducting liaisons with prostitutes, women who provided sex for money. Romans classified prostitutes into two basic types: the *meretrix,* viewed as a courtesan or *hetaira* (companion), and the *prostibula,* seen as a common whore. The *meretrix* might enjoy an ongoing relationship with one or two men, whereas the *prostibula* catered to a larger, more varied, and generally poorer clientele. Additionally *meretrices* were registered with the state and often worked out of brothels while the unregistered *prostibulae* plied their trade at public venues. In *The Art of Love* Ovid creates a speaker who is a teacher of love. The speaker-teacher seems initially to be referring to *meretrices* when he offers advice to the poem's male readers. In book 1 he warns off "respectable ladies" from his teachings, yet states that "[s]afe love, legitimate liaisons / Will be my theme. This poem breaks no taboos" (*The Art of Love*, 1.31, 33-34). The distinction between matrons and *meretrices* blurs in book 3, however, when Ovid's speaker counsels bored wives on how to deceive their husbands and conduct discreet extramarital affairs.

In general, the Roman attitude towards prostitution was pragmatic: since the trade could not be eliminated, it was regulated. Solon, king of Athens, introduced the idea of state-controlled brothels in the sixth century CE; Romans likewise instituted state control of their brothels, known as *lupanares* (houses of she-wolves). Not until the emperor Augustus, however, were tight restrictions imposed on the behavior and privileges of prostitutes. During his tenure and after, Roman prostitutes could not veil their faces in public. *Meretrices* were forbidden from wearing shoes or putting their hair in ribbons in public, and they had to dye their hair red or yellow as a sign of their profession. The law prohibited prostitutes from owning property and from marrying men of the senatorial class, even if the women renounced their trade.

Imperial expansion. While *The Art of Love* concerns itself mainly with the details of private life, the poem occasionally refers to larger historical events, such as the growth of Rome's empire. Expansion had accelerated during the first century BCE, with the military campaigns of Augustus's granduncle and predecessor, Julius Caesar. By 50 BCE Caesar's victories had extended Rome's frontiers to the English Channel and the Rhine River in Germany.

As princeps, Augustus continued the process of expansion. However, he also wished to consolidate the existing provinces, a policy that involved extending some boundaries and abandoning others. Galatia (central Asia Minor) and Judaea were made Roman provinces in 25 BCE and 6 CE, respectively; Spain was finally subjugated to Roman authority; and to the north, the frontier was extended to the Danube. However,

Rome abandoned further plans for eastward expansion in 20 CE, after negotiating a peace with the Parthian Empire (located in what is now eastern Iran), against which Rome had waged several previous military campaigns, in 20 BCE. Under the terms of the agreement, Parthia acknowledged Rome's protectorate over Armenia.

Around 1 BCE Rome again became involved in Parthia's affairs after a pro-Roman client king was expelled from Armenia with the Parthians' assistance. Augustus dispatched his grandson and designated heir, Gaius Caesar, to settle the problem. Ovid's speaker alludes to this incident in book 1 of *The Art of Love*, confidently

---

ROMAN ENTERTAINMENTS

Despite the new austerity of Augustus's reign, the Romans frequented the many forms of available entertainment. Games involving dice were especially popular with Romans, including Augustus, who liked to gamble. But chariot racing was clearly the most exciting of the public entertainments in ancient Rome. The largest of eight racetracks around the city of Rome itself, the Circus Maximus held 250,000 spectators. The contests themselves featured four chariot-racing companies (Red, White, Blue, and Green), owned by businessmen, as are American football teams today. Other well-known venues for entertainment were the amphitheater, where gladiatorial games were held, and the theater, which staged comedies, tragedies, and mimes (short burlesque skits). In Ovid's poem, the speaker mentions all three locales as likely places to meet and pursue women. He is especially enthusiastic about the "spacious Circus," which offers "chances galore" as well as opportunity for physical closeness, since men and women were not seated in separate sections (Ovid, *The Art of Love*, book 1, lines 135-136).

---

predicting a triumphant outcome for the young Caesar (*The Art of Love*, 1.177-228). Ironically, Gaius did not return victorious to Rome but died in 4 CE of a lingering wound suffered during a minor skirmish in Armenia. Ovid's poetry engages with Rome's military-minded culture, comparing determined lovers to warriors and love itself to a hard-fought military campaign: "Love is a species of warfare. Slack troopers, go elsewhere! / It takes more than cowards to guard / These standards. Night-duty in winter, long route-marches, every / Hardship, all forms of suffering: these await / The recruit who expects a soft option" (*The Art of Love*, 2.233-237).

The Poem in Focus

The contents. Composed in elegiac couplets, *The Art of Love* consists of three books, the first two addressed to young men, the third to young women. The poem adopts a didactic yet humorous tone as it gives practical instructions on acquiring and

---

THE RAPE OF THE SABINE WOMEN

Throughout *The Art of Love*, Ovid's speaker refers to various myths and legends. The rape of the Sabine women is one of a series of tales surrounding Romulus, legendary founder of Rome and son of the war-god Mars. Suckled as infants by a she-wolf, Romulus and his twin brother, Remus, established the future city of Rome on the Palatine hill. Romulus built walls around the city and slew Remus for leaping over those walls. To people the city, Romulus offered asylum to all fugitives and then found them wives by inviting the Sabines, inhabitants of a neighboring town, to a festival. The gesture was a ruse, for the newcomers abducted the Sabine women, who were then forced to marry their rapists. Although the Sabine men returned in arms to reclaim their women, the latter—now reconciled to their new husbands—brought hostilities to an end by placing themselves between the opposing forces. With characteristic irreverence, Ovid's poem compares romantic assignations at the theater with the Sabine rape: "The Palatine woods supplied a leafy backdrop (nature's / Scenery untouched by art), / While the tiers of seats were plain turf, and the spectators shaded / Their shaggy heads with leaves" (*The Art of Love*, 1.105-108). The distress of the victims as they are carried off is almost comically rendered: "Some tore their hair, some just froze / Where they sat; some, dismayed, kept silence, others vainly / Yelled for Mamma; some wailed; some gaped . . . / . . . Ever since that day, by hallowed custom, / Our theatres have always held dangers for pretty girls" (*The Art of Love*, 1.122-124, 133-134).

---

keeping a lover. Although it seldom dwells on such philosophical issues as the nature of love itself, the poem sometimes draws on already well-known myths to illustrate points about erotic dalliance.

Book 1. The first book deals with finding and courting one's chosen lady. Describing himself as "Love's preceptor," or teacher, the poem's speaker offers to share his expertise in erotic dalliance with the young men of Rome (*Art of Love*, 1.17). After warning off respectable married ladies from his teachings, the speaker promises to help Ovid's readers find, woo, win, and keep their ladies.

To choose a potential mistress, says the speaker, men need not travel far, as Rome is full of beautiful women. The speaker goes on to name various temples, the law court, the theaters, and the races as ideal places to meet women. He devotes particular attention to the last two venues, recalling how theaters have always held dangers for pretty girls, since the rape of the Sabine women, and describing how the races increase chances for physical contact with women: "[Y]ou'll sit / Right beside your mistress, without let or hindrance, / So be sure to press against her whenever you can— / An easy task: the seating-divisions restrict her, / Regulations facilitate contact" (*The Art of Love*, 1.138-142). Men will thus have many opportunities to ingratiate themselves with women. Additionally, public shows, spectacles, and triumphs can unite prospective couples in celebration; Ovid's speaker anticipates just such an occasion should Rome's latest military campaign against Parthia succeed. In peacetime, on the other hand, banquets and seaside resorts are likely places for romance.

To attract one's female of choice, says Ovid's speaker, a man just has to be confident and persistent. All women desire love and passion, he argues, just as men do. To further one's suit, it is wise to win over the lady's maid, who can carry letters back and forth or report on her mistress's moods. The speaker-teacher raises the possibility of the male lover seducing the maid as well as her mistress, but considers the gambit too risky, unless the man also finds the maid appealing. In this case, one should seduce the mistress before the maid.

A wooing lover should write many letters to his beloved, says the speaker, and they should be full of entreaties and flattery. Moreover, a lover should persist in his attentions until he wears down his lady's resistance, taking advantage of every opportunity to be in her company. He must enhance his own attractiveness by practicing good personal hygiene and dressing becomingly.

Ovid's speaker mentions the usefulness of wine in softening the mood and providing opportunities to speak more freely to one's beloved.

Tears and pallor may likewise stir a lady's pity, while stolen kisses and embraces may excite her ardor. However, a man must not praise his beloved too freely before his male friends, lest they become rivals and pursue the lady themselves. Finally, Ovid's speaker reminds readers that all women are unique: "To capture a thousand hearts demands / A thousand devices" (*The Art of Love*, 1.756-757). In other words, the wise man adapts, changing his methods of courtship to suit each quarry.

Book 2. The second book deals with keeping a mistress, which Ovid's speaker regards as no less important than winning one: "To guard a conquest's / As tricky as making it. There was luck in the chase, / But *this* task will call for skill" (*The Art of Love*, 2.13-15). The speaker advises readers against trying charms, spells, and drugs to accomplish their goal: these methods are useless, dangerous, and potentially harmful to the beloved.

Just being handsome will not do the trick either, because looks fade. Therefore, a man should cultivate his mind and spirit as well as his body: "Then build an enduring mind, add that to your beauty; / It alone will last till the flames / Consume you" (*The Art of Love*, 2.119-121). Ovid's speaker suggests that the lover practice such virtues as tolerance, tact, and gentleness; he should also adapt his moods to fit those of his mistress. A lover should never quarrel with his mistress, not least because reconciliation might require purchasing expensive gifts. He should let her win at games, perform various mundane tasks for her, and show himself attentive to her every need. When a mistress falls ill, the lover should constantly attend her to show his solicitude for her health. However, he should not prescribe noxious medicines and restrict her diet, but leave prospective rivals to make these mistakes.

Love requires nourishment and careful attention to thrive, cautions the speaker-teacher. The lover must make himself indispensable to his mistress's comfort: "Habit's the key, spare no pains till that's achieved. / Let her always see you around, always hear you talking / Show her your face night and day" (*The Art of Love*, 2.345-348). However, the lover should also know when to absent himself for brief periods so that she misses him. Ovid's speaker cites several mythical relationships, such as that of Odysseus and Penelope, to show that absence can make the heart grow fonder (see the ***Odyssey***, also in *Classical Literature and Its Times*).

Discretion is also important. If a man has several mistresses, he must take care that none finds out about the others, unless he deliberately wishes to arouse jealousy. If a mistress suspects a lover's infidelity, he should deny his guilt and placate her with ardent lovemaking. Ovid's speaker contends that the heart requires "a sharp stimulus," such as jealousy or anxiety, to keep love alive (*The Art of Love*, 2.444).

The speaker-teacher claims that the god Apollo visited him and informed him that men must know their own strengths and weaknesses to succeed as lovers. Agreeing with Apollo, Ovid's speaker promises that, with the aid of his poem, intelligent lovers will usually triumph, but warns that not every love affair will bring complete satisfaction. A man must be prepared for disappointments; it is more prudent to tolerate a rival than to confront or expose him. A lover should not conduct himself like a jealous husband.

Reemphasizing the importance of discretion, the speaker-teacher advises against bragging of one's romantic conquests to other men. A lover should protect his mistress's reputation, even if she *has* been involved in various scandals. He should furthermore refrain from criticizing his lady's physical imperfections, instead using her "virtues to camouflage each fault" (*The Art of Love*, 2.662). A lady's age is another sensitive topic that the lover should avoid discussing. But if one's mistress is older, the lover can benefit from her wider experience. Mature women, who tend to be more enthusiastic and enduring, often make better lovers.

Ovid's speaker concludes the second book with a detailed discussion of the proper lovemaking techniques. A lover should take the time to discover what positions and caresses his mistress prefers. Ideally both partners will experience equal satisfaction in lovemaking. Declaring himself the expert at "the love-game," a master teacher, the speaker exhorts young men to ascribe their erotic triumphs to his guidance: "And when you've brought down your / Amazon, write on the trophy *Ovid was my guide*" (*The Art of Love*, 2.739, 743-744). The next book, the speaker promises, will offer similar advice to young ladies.

Book 3. In the third book of *The Art of Love*, Ovid's speaker argues that in the interests of fairness, he must share his expertise with young ladies. He even claims that Venus, goddess of love, visited him with this demand: "Two books you've written instructing / Men in the game;

high time the opposite sex / Got benefit from your counsels" (*The Art of Love*, 3.47-49).

The speaker-teacher begins by advising girls to make the most of their youth, to experience erotic love before they grow too old and undesirable to attract men. On the subject of appearances, he says ladies should work to preserve their beauty. The speaker offers detailed advice on hygiene, cosmetics, and fashion. Few women are gifted with extraordinary beauty; however, every woman can make the most of her looks with the proper hairstyle and clothing, insists the speaker-teacher. Ladies should not, he adds, let men observe their beautification rituals, lest the men find the process unattractive.

PROCRIS AND CEPHALUS

In *Metamorphoses,* Ovid creates his version of the myth of Procris and Cephalus. The newlyweds are very much in love when the goddess Dawn spies Cephalus hunting one day and falls in love with him. After trying in vain to win him over, an enraged Dawn tells Cephalus that he will one day regret ever being with Procris. This accusation plants doubt in Cephalus, who then begins to question the faithfulness of his wife. Cephalus returns to Athens in disguise and attempts to seduce his own wife. Although firmly rebuffing his many attempts at seduction, Procris finally starts to waver, at which point Cephalus throws off his disguise in anger and accuses her of being a shameful traitor. Horrified, Procris flees to the mountains to worship and follow the goddess Diana. Cephalus feels remorse at tricking his wife and, deeply missing her, begs for her forgiveness. Procris does so and returns to him, giving him two gifts that were given to her by Diana: a magical spear that always hits its mark and a hunting dog who runs with incredible speed. Eventually Procris grows suspicious of Cephalus after hearing rumors of his infidelity and follows him hunting one day, hiding in the bushes. Cephalus hears rustling leaves and, imagining that he has heard an animal, throws the magical spear into the bushes, killing his beloved Procris. It is only just before she dies that Cephalus convinces her of the falsehood of the rumors. Procris has jumped to conclusions and paid for it with her life.

Ovid's speaker suggests that ladies figure out ways to conceal physical imperfections. A short girl should be seen reclining, so as not to draw attention to her height. A girl with bad teeth ought not to smile too broadly or laugh too openly. As a rule, girls would be well advised to study how to walk, talk, and laugh gracefully but without appearing affected. Those who have the talent should practice singing, dancing, composing poetry, or playing a musical instrument. Ovid's speaker recommends that girls study some literature, so they can converse intelligently on the subject. If a girl plays competitive games, she should exercise self-control whether she wins or loses.

To attract a lover, a woman needs to make frequent appearances at public venues. Let her take heed in these public places, however. She should be on her guard against men who appear too smooth and glib in their attentions, and against those who have notorious reputations as womanizers. Did a prospective lover write her a letter? Then she must read it carefully and not yield too quickly to his entreaties. Her reply should be elegant, and, for her own protection, she should have one of her servants write the actual letter.

The speaker-teacher moves on to the way women interact with men. Besides caring for their looks, women should cultivate a pleasant demeanor. It is important not to appear ill-tempered or overly disdainful; rather, a woman should smile and be charming to the men she wishes to encourage. Let her cultivate and value each man for his individual talents and be especially generous towards poets, who can make women immortal in their verses. Women should be aware of the different advantages offered by youthful and mature lovers: the former is more passionate; the latter, more lasting.

Once involved in a romance, a woman must be coy. Her lover should believe that he has rivals who might interrupt their dalliance, for this will make their own affair more titillating. If a married woman wishes to take a lover, she should learn such wily tricks as sending letters with disappearing ink, administering sleeping potions to her husband or guardian, and bribing those appointed to watch over her movements.

Just as Ovid's speaker advised men not to speak of their mistresses to their friends, he offers similar counsel to women. Speaking of their lovers invites trouble. In counseling women, he cautions them to beware of potential rivals in the form of acquaintances and pretty maidservants. Let men believe they are desired and loved. Re-

Cephalus and Aurora (Dawn) by Nicholas Poussin (c. 1630). © National Gallery Collection/Corbis.

main calm even if one hears that one's lover might have another mistress. Ovid's speaker uses the myth of Procris and Cephalus to illustrate his point about the dangers of jumping to conclusions.

If attending a party, a woman should arrive late, in order to make a graceful entrance. Her manners, once there, ought to conform to certain standards. She should eat daintily and not stuff herself; likewise, she should not drink to excess, partly because a drunken woman is a disgusting sight, partly because revelers might take advantage of a female who has drunk herself into a stupor.

In the closing section of the third book, Ovid's speaker again discusses the techniques of lovemaking. There are various positions a woman can assume in the bedroom to show her body to best advantage. Ideally a woman should experience the same pleasure as a man in lovemaking, but if she fails to climax, she should feign ecstasy. Having imparted these final instructions, the speaker-teacher concludes with a flourish, "so now let my girl-disciples / Inscribe their trophies: *Ovid was my guide*" (*The Art of Love*, 3.811-812).

The Roman body. One striking feature of *The Art of Love* is Ovid's emphasis on the importance of physical hygiene. While his speaker

also recommends that readers cultivate their minds, he continually exhorts them to pay close attention to their appearance. He advises young men: "Keep pleasantly clean, take exercise, work up an outdoor / Tan; make quite sure that your toga fits / And doesn't show spots.../ Keep your nails pared, and dirt-free; / Don't let those long hairs sprout / In your nostrils, make sure your breath is never offensive" (*The Art of Love*, 1.513-515, 519-521). Ovid's speaker offers similar counsel to young women: "True beauty's a gift of / The gods, few can boast they possess it—and most / Of you, my dears, don't. Hard work will improve the picture: / Neglect your looks, and they'll go to pot, even though / You're a second Venus" (*The Art of Love*, 3.103-107).

The advice of Ovid's speaker, designed to help readers attract lovers, may seem frivolous initially, but his admonishments are rooted in a major concern of Roman society: the control and care of the physical body. A Roman citizen consisted of a name and a body, upon which his fellow citizens based their assessment of his character and abilities. From birth, the physical body had to be contained, its crudest functions mastered, and its movements carefully schooled. Roman nurses were advised on how to mold the shape of an infant's body, by swaddling and massage. Correct control over one's body was expected of a good citizen, when he took his place in public life.

The clothing in which the body was attired became important as well, because clothing was one feature that separated humans from animals. Although Roman art frequently depicted nude male figures, Roman citizens were supposed to keep their genitals covered in public: "The body that the citizen put on display should be clothed, scrubbed, and under control. Nature—that is, anything to do with procreation or defecation—had to be concealed" (Dupont, p. 240). Citizens were expected to bathe, keep their hair and beard trimmed, exercise, and eat properly—in short, to follow advice very like that offered by Ovid's speaker in *The Art of Love*. Dupont explains,

> If a man let himself go, abandoning this minimum of *cultus* [bodily care], he became repugnant, despicable, sordid, bestial, and savage. He became a stinking tramp and could no longer regard himself as a citizen or a man. In Roman eyes, there was no such thing as a "natural man." To repeat the old adage: it was natural for a man to be part of a culture; if he rejected that culture, he was no longer himself.
>
> (Dupont, pp. 240-241)

Sources and literary context. In *The Art of Love*, Ovid drew upon his own experiences—social and romantic—in contemporary Rome. His detailed descriptions of the temples, colonnades, piazzas, theaters, and streets brought the city alive for his readers. Although many question whether Ovid intended *The Art of Love* as serious or humorous instruction, there is little reason to question his truthfulness as a social observer or as an enthusiastic participant in the game of love. Certainly it is on the basis of such observation and/or experience that he offers such copious advice.

As a work, *The Art of Love* has been described as a practical handbook and even as a satire. However, it is most often interpreted as a parody of didactic literature. Intended to instruct and enlighten, didactic works featured a speaker who often presented himself as an authority upon the chosen subject, who commanded his audience to heed his words, and who shaped his argument in orderly fashion. Serious didactic works that Ovid would have known include Hesiod's *Works and Days* (c. eighth century BCE), Lucretius's *On the Nature of the Universe* (c. 55 BCE) and Virgil's *Georgics* (29 BCE). While the earlier poems dealt, respectively, with the virtues of honest work, Epicurean philosophy, and the homely details of a farmer's life, *The Art of Love* explored the racier topic of seduction, purporting to treat it with the utmost seriousness. The incongruous pairing of the frivolous subject with the sober tone made *The Art of Love* a particularly devastating parody. Ovid's style was as distinctive as his choice of subject: while most didactic works, like epics, were composed in hexameters, *The Art of Love* was composed in elegiac couplets, linking it more closely to Ovid's earlier *Amores*, a poem detailing the poet's affair with a woman named Corinna.

Impact. Having recently banished his daughter Julia from Rome for promiscuity, Augustus may have taken personal offense at the themes of Ovid's poem. At his command, *The Art of Love* was banned from all of Rome's libraries. It appears to have been popular with its intended audience (cultured, upper-class Romans), but Ovid soon distanced himself from the poem. While in exile, he composed *Tristia* (Sorrows), a series of poems lamenting his banishment and pleading for the mitigation of his sentence. He meanwhile attempted to disassociate himself from *The Art of Love*, which he felt had ruined him. Ovid argued that the poem had been no more than a frivolous trifle, intended to amuse. Far from encouraging adultery, he continued, the poem warned off married women from participating in the game of love, and he avoided pursuing them himself. His appeals fell upon deaf ears, however; neither Augustus nor his successor, Tiberius, permitted Ovid to return to Rome. Still Ovid remained a favorite with the empire's readers. Graffiti containing quotations from his verses was found scrawled upon walls in Pompeii during the first century CE, an unusual testimony to his popularity.

Responses to *The Art of Love* have varied through the ages. When considering the work, Heloise, a twelfth-century nun and scholar, described its author as "that master of sensuality and shame" (Heloise in Mack, p. 83). The poet Francesco Petrarch, writing during the Italian Renaissance, harshly condemned the "dirty" mind that had produced *The Art of Love*, calling the author "lascivious, lecherous, and altogether mulierous [sic]" (Petrarch in Mack, p. 83). But others embraced the poem: during the twelfth and thirteenth centuries, *The Art of Love* gave rise to allegories, morals, works on the pursuit of sexual love, and, "to Ovid's probable chagrin had he been alive," to works on spiritual love (Myerowitz, pp. 17-18).

Polarized responses to *The Art of Love* persisted into the late nineteenth and early twentieth centuries. The critic J. W. MacKail, writing in 1895, called it "perhaps the most immoral poem ever written" (MacKail in Myerowitz, p. 20). Lord Macaulay designated *The Art of Love* "Ovid's best," although he also noted that Ovid reduces love to "mere sexual appetite" (Macaulay in Myerowitz, p. 190, 2n). More recent critical commentaries have focused less upon Ovid's immorality and more upon the poem itself. A. S. Hollis called *The Art of Love* "the gayest and wittiest among Ovid's love poems" (Hollis in Myerowitz, p. 21). Finally, Sara Mack, in her 1988 study of Ovid, contends that modern readers should find the poet more accessible and entertaining than ever:

> We need not be put off . . . or irrelevantly titillated by his occasional sexual explicitness and his typical sexual suggestiveness. And Ovid should appeal enormously to the generation that has fought to make equal rights a reality. No one but Ovid would have written two thousand years ago that sexual satisfaction should be equal for both partners, that sex was no good if the woman acquiesced because it was her duty.
>
> (Mack, p. 4)

—Pamela S. Loy

For More Information

Boardman, John, Jasper Griffin, and Oswyn Murray, eds. *The Oxford History of the Roman World.* Oxford: Oxford University Press, 2001.

Casson, Lionel. *Everyday Life in Ancient Rome.* Baltimore, Md.: Johns Hopkins University Press, 1998.

Dupont, Florence. *Daily Life in Ancient Rome.* Trans. Christopher Woodall. Malden, Mass.: Blackwell, 1994.

Hardie, Philip, ed. *The Cambridge Companion to Ovid.* Cambridge: Cambridge University Press, 2002.

Hornblower, Simon, and Antony Spawforth, eds. *The Oxford Companion to Classical Civilization.* Oxford: Oxford University Press, 1998.

Jones, Peter, and Keith Sidwell, eds. *The World of Rome.* Cambridge: Cambridge University Press, 1997.

Mack, Sara. *Ovid.* New Haven, Conn.: Yale University Press, 1988.

Myerowitz, Molly. *Ovid's Games of Love.* Detroit, Mich.: Wayne State University Press, 1985.

Ovid. *The Art of Love.* In *The Erotic Poems.* Trans. Peter Green. Harmondsworth, England: Penguin Books, 1982.

———. *Metamorphoses.* Trans. A. D. Melville. Oxford: Oxford University Press, 1986.

Wyke, Maria. *The Roman Mistress.* Oxford: Oxford University Press, 2002.

The Braggart Soldier

by
Plautus

Titus Maccius Plautus, whose name means "Flat-Footed Clown," gained renown as a popular comedic playwright in Rome. Ironically, he himself was probably not Roman. According to the ancient biographical tradition, Plautus was born around 255 or 250 BCE north of Rome in the town of Sarsina in Umbria, well out of range of either the bustle of urban Roman culture or the Hellenized regions of southern Italy. We know very little about his background, save for what we find in later authors. The Latin writer Aulus Gellius (c. 130-180 CE) tells us that Plautus once lost his fortune in a trade investment gone awry, and to recover from this disaster, he simply wrote and produced more comedies. It is presumed that prior to being a playwright Plautus probably worked as a comedic actor. Some scholars believe he even acted in his own productions. Approximately 130 comedies were once attributed to Plautus (most of them, falsely), but only 21 of these plays survive, all of which are considered his. *The Braggart Soldier*, the longest of the group at 1,437 verses, is regarded as one of his masterpieces.

Plautus was one of the first professional playwrights in western history, that is, one of the first to earn his living by writing for the public. In contrast, Terence, a playwright one generation after Plautus, relied on the financial support of wealthy patrons (see Terence's **The Brothers,** also in *Classical Literature and Its Times*). Although Plautus remained unconcerned with the reactions of the Roman elite, he won widespread public approval. The fact that his name was

> ## THE LITERARY WORK
>
> A Roman adaptation of a Greek comedy (called *Alazon*) written and set in Ephesus around 287 BCE; adapted into Latin (as *Miles Gloriosus*) and first performed around 206 BCE.
>
> ## SYNOPSIS
>
> A young man from Athens relies on his clever slave to steal back the girlfriend who was kidnapped from him by an outrageously conceited soldier-for-hire.

falsely attached to works more often than any other ancient Greek or Roman writer suggests that he gained enough influence to increase the popularity of any play, whether written by him or not. Plautus likely died in or around 184 BCE. The comedy that survives him reveals a Roman culture that delighted in temporarily overturning its own social structure through irony, satire, slapstick bawdiness, and all-around mayhem.

Events in History at the Time the Play Takes Place

Mercenary soldiers and Hellenistic kings. *The Braggart Soldier* takes place squarely in the Hellenistic period, often delineated as the era between the death of Alexander the Great (323 BCE) and Rome's domination over Greece (c. 27 BCE). The period was a time of political upheaval, great transformations in art and literature, and a sort of ancient multi-cultural cosmopolitanism. Greeks, Macedonians, Egyptians, Jews, Persians, Italians, and Phoenicians mingled and conducted business across the Mediterranean, and the cultural influences they exerted on one another are apparent in art and literature. This cosmopolitanism is seen in *The Braggart Soldier* by the ease and frequency with which the characters travel to and fro by sea, as if leaving home were standard practice. The play is set in third-century BCE Ephesus, a city on the Mediterranean coast of Asia Minor (modern-day Turkey). The title character, the braggart soldier, is the type of mercenary fighter and cosmopolitan citizen characteristic of the period. At the beginning of the play, he makes references to wide travels (including campaigns in India) and to recruiting soldiers who would fight with him for King

---

READING THE HUMOR IN PLAUTUS

Like all of Plautus' plays, the storyline of *The Braggart Soldier* is humorous, but its true hilarity lies in the witty dialogue and slapstick interactions of the characters. The playwright's language is rife with exclamation, idiom, alliteration, punning, double entendre, and perfect comedic timing. Adding to this comedic dialogue is the dimension of physical hilarity in the performance (side-stage eavesdropping, a tug-of-war with human body parts, and so forth), which, unfortunately, must be envisioned in the mind of the reader, since the original stage directions do not appear in any of the surviving manuscripts. It is important to remember that *The Braggart Soldier* was not intended to be a work of literature, but a live performance that appealed to the five senses. One needs to imagine the sights and sounds of the ancient Roman theater—the bustle and catcalling of the audience, sound effects from backstage, dramatic costumes and masks, the visual set of the play, and the festive atmosphere. The set for Plautus' plays was normally constructed as a public street in front of the façade of two or three adjoining buildings. In *The Braggart Soldier*, the two buildings are the houses of Periplectolemus and Pyrgopolynices, and all the action of the play takes place on this street in plain view of the audience.

Seleucus. The soldier is a foreigner living in Ephesus, although we are not told his nationality. In fact, he is so new to town that he does not even know his next door neighbor is unmarried (a significant detail that contributes to the plot). Like other Hellenistic kings, Seleucus (d. 280 BCE), for

whom the soldier works, rose to power out of the fractured political world left behind by Alexander the Great's defeat of the Persian Empire and subsequent death. The Seleucid Empire occupied the central coastal region of Asia Minor, and its most immediate threat was the territory surrounding it, controlled by the Attalids of Pergamum. Hellenistic kingdoms (like Seleucus') widely enlisted soldiers-for-hire who were not always native to the kingdoms or otherwise invested in the stability of the side for which they fought. These mercenary armies tended to be mobile, multi-ethnic, and comprised of part-time crooks like Plautus' braggart soldier.

Courtesans in classical culture. Prostitutes and courtesans constituted a significant part of Greek and Roman culture and sexual life. Regarded as a less respectable class than freeborn marriageable women, the prostitutes themselves were further divided into classes: courtesans were highly educated, trained in music, "self-employed," and occasionally they took up residence with their male lovers. Other prostitutes were akin to poor streetwalkers or sex slaves living in the brothels of seaport towns. Still others, especially in Greece, were temple prostitutes who offered religiously sanctioned relief to the customer. Their proceeds went to funding the upkeep of temples and to financing sacrifices and religious festivals. For both Greece and Rome, while most prostitutes were originally slaves, many were freed and able to do as they pleased. The controversy over the status of prostitutes was not a moral controversy in the cases of the Greeks or Romans. Rather the class raised questions related to male dominance over women and to the legitimacy of offspring. Indeed, it was socially acceptable for men to visit prostitutes, but the prostitutes themselves presented a problem with regards to paternity. In a patriarchal culture, as both Greece and Rome were, the question of legal inheritance created great anxiety, and the offspring of a freeman and a prostitute did not have the right to inherit from the father. The prostitute was viewed as very distinct from proper marriageable women, who were entitled to bear children (preferably sons) to carry on the family name. On the other hand, a married woman was considered the legal property of her husband, and prostitutes, while suffering the stigma of their profession, often enjoyed greater autonomy than she did. In *The Braggart Soldier*, Philocomasium appears to be a well-cared-for courtesan, while Acroteleutium is clearly a local Ephesian prostitute hired for the day and trained to pull off a scam.

The Play in Focus

Cast of Characters

Pyrgopolynices: The Braggart Soldier, his name means essentially "Conqueror of Many Fortresses"; the character steals a courtesan from Athens and brings her, against her will, to Ephesus.

Philocomasium: The abducted courtesan, whose name means "Lover of a Good Time."

Pleusicles: The young Athenian man, whose courtesan and slave are abducted. He must sail to Ephesus to get them back.

Palaestrio: Slave of Pleusicles; he must concoct a plan to free himself and Philocomasium from the soldier.

Periplectolemus: Older Ephesian gentleman, friend of Pleusicles' father, who aids in the scheme to reclaim Philocomasium and Palaestrio.

Acroteleutium: A hired courtesan in Ephesus who pretends to be married to Periplectolemus and to passionately long for Pyrgopolynices. Her name roughly means "Highest End," which we could interpret as "Top Prize."

Plot summary. The play begins in Ephesus in front of the house of Pyrgopolynices, a military officer whose friend, a flatterer, lavishes praise on him as they reminisce about his extraordinary military accomplishments. Inside Pyrgopolynices' house is Philocomasium, a courtesan whom he kidnapped from Athens and brought to his hometown as his lover. Magnifying his deeds outrageously, Pyrgopolynices and his companion, Artotrogus, discuss the golden-armored legion Pyrgopolynices once blew away with one breath, the elephant in India whose forelegs he smashed, and the scores of opponents that he slew in one day: 150 Cilicians, 100 Jugotheevians, 30 Sardinians, and 60 Macedonians. A practiced flatterer, Artotrogus fuels the soldier's ego by telling him he is the most feared warrior ever, that Mars (the god of war) is no match, and that all women crave him desperately because of his courage and stellar looks. Between each morsel of flattery, Artotrogus turns to the audience and reveals the truth about the soldier—that he is a pathetic liar and a braggart, but a sure source of food for the flatterer. This initial scene, disembodied from the action of the play, alerts the audience to the bombastic character of Pyrgopolynices, the braggart soldier. The two exit the stage and head for the forum or city "square" (a rectangle, really), where they will attempt to recruit soldiers for the Seleucid army.

A clever slave named Palaestrio then enters the scene and informs the audience of the circumstances

Greek vase representing a scene of an ancient comedy. Painting on vase by Asteas. © Photo Museum. Reproduced by permission.

that have led up to the play. Palaestrio is the servant of a young man of Athens named Pleusicles. Pleusicles has been sent on official government business to Naupactas, a Greek city on the northern coast of the Gulf of Corinth. At Athens he has a courtesan lover named Philocomasium, for whom he feels passionately. In his absence, the swaggering soldier, Pyrgopolynices, courts and abducts this courtesan lover. The wronged lover's clever slave, Palaestrio, takes a ship to Naupactas to inform his master that the courtesan was abducted, but en route his ship is attacked and captured by pirates, and he is given as a slave to someone new. Coincidentally, his new master happens to be the same soldier who abducted Philocomasium, and Palaestrio finds himself enslaved in the soldier's household in Ephesus with the courtesan. The slave secretly sends a letter to Athens to alert his master of their whereabouts, and Pleusicles sets sail to Ephesus to reclaim them. He stays in the home of his father's friend, Periplectolemus, who, remarkably, lives next door to the braggart soldier. Like many ancient urban houses, the two share a wall in common. While devising a way to get back his original master's courtesan, Palaestrio digs a secret hole through a shared wall that connects the two houses. Through this hidden passage Philocomasium can slip secretly and freely to see her lover Pleusicles.

After these two initial ground-setting scenes, the action of the play begins with Periplectolemus distraught and enraged that his friend's secret intent to reclaim the courtesan and the slave has been compromised. The kidnapper, Pyrgopolynices, has a slave named Sceledrus whose sole responsibility is to keep an eye on Philocomasium. One day Sceledrus chases a monkey across the rooftops and, peering down through a lightwell, he spies Philocomasium embracing her original Athenian lover in Periplectolemus' house. The question now is, how will the foursome (the neighbor Periplectolemus, the lovers Philocomasium and Pleusicles, and the clever slave Palaestrio) handle this discovery? Palaestrio instructs Periplectolemus to have the courtesan cross back over to her captor's house, so that when the other slave, Sceledrus, reveals what he has seen, her undisturbed presence in the soldier's house will prove his testimony wrong. Palaestrio then deliberates on how he can convince the slave that the woman he saw in Periplectolemus' house was not Philocomasium. After some dramatic gesturing and visibly hard thinking (Periplectolemus narrates the slave's thought process and physical demeanor), Palaestrio presents his plan: he will tell the servant that Philocomasium's twin sister has arrived from Athens with a lover, and that the twin is the lip-locked girl whom the slave saw. As soon as Palaestrio reveals his plan, Periplectolemus deems it brilliant. Now the clever slave and the neighbor must work to pull the charade off while figuring out how to rescue the courtesan permanently.

Moments later Palaestrio encounters the monkey-chasing Sceledrus. He is in a frenzy over what to tell his master about the promiscuous girl and the strange man next door. He knows he may be beaten or crucified because his only charge managed to end up in another man's house. Palaestrio pretends not to believe that Sceledrus could have witnessed such a scandal and insists on entering the soldier's house to double-check the whereabouts of the courtesan. By this time, Philocomasium has been coached about the farce and has returned to the soldier's house. Palaestrio goes inside, finds Philocomasium, and rushes back out to accuse the slave of being dimwitted, trouble-seeking, and bleary-eyed. After bantering to and fro about the slave's delusionary eyesight, Palaestrio brings Philocomasium outside to prove her whereabouts. From this point on, the suspicious Sceledrus insists on guarding the neighbors' front doors so that he can see exactly who enters and leaves. So Philocomasium must pass through the hole in the wall; moving from house to house, she poses as two different young women.

Moments later Sceledrus has his first confrontation with Philocomasium-as-her-twin. The courtesan leaves Periplectolemus' house, and the slave calls out to her. She, pretending not to know him, ignores his biddings. He hurls insults her way, and in response, still playing her twin sister, she feigns shock and seems offended. When Sceledrus grabs her, she claims to have arrived the night before in search of her twin and threatens to have him beaten for his insolence. She escapes his grip, enters Periplectolemus' house, and rushes through the wall to her room in Pyrgopolynices' house. Sceledrus enters his master's home and finds the courtesan there again.

Periplectolemus bursts from his house to punish his neighbor's slave for assaulting the female guest who arrived last night fresh from Athens. Feigning rage, he opens his own house to Sceledrus the slave, insisting that he look inside to see the newly arrived twin. Having just spotted Philocomasium on her couch in his master's house, Sceledrus finds the twin visitor inside his neighbor's house. Dumbfounded, he finally accepts the existence of two identical young women. After begging forgiveness and winning mercy from Periplectolemus for roughing up the female guest, Sceledrus goes into hiding to avoid being sold by his master for such a grave blunder.

With their initial plan a success—to convince Sceledrus that two twin sisters exist—the play moves into its more important comedy-laden objective, namely, to trick Pyrgopolynices into giving up Philocomasium willfully. Palaestrio, ever the scheming slave, concocts a crafty plan involving the lovers (Philocomasium and Pleusicles) and the neighbor, Periplectolemus. He instructs them to find a local courtesan of exceptional beauty and wit to pretend to be Periplectolemus' wife. Via her fake maidservant and Palaestrio, the pretend wife will send Periplectolemus' ring next door to Pyrgopolynices as a testament of her desire for him. The fake maidservant will insist the wife is madly in love with the soldier and cannot live without him. In fact, the wife will claim to have divorced the neighbor, who is elderly, simply to make herself available to the soldier. Naturally, this will come as no surprise to Pyrgopolynices, who believes all women fall in love with him at sight. If Palaestrio's plan is successful, the soldier will be tempted to get rid of Philocomasium in order to make room for his neighbor's stunning, lustful wife.

When presenting the ring to the soldier, Palaestrio builds up the physical and material assets of the lustful wife to such an extent that Pyrgopolynices cannot help but be interested. Palaestrio refers to her as dazzling, cheerful, beautiful, stunning, and desperately in love with him. As is hoped, Pyrgopolynices' immediate reaction is to wonder how to get rid of the captive courtesan in his house so he can pursue his neighbor's wife. Palaestrio seizes the moment and suggests that the soldier free the girl into the possession of her mother and twin sister who just happen to be next door. (The "mother" never appears in the play, however. The dialogue just alludes to her.) Palaestrio instructs him to make a gift of all the jewels he has decorated her with, and to send her on her way as pleasantly as possible. Taken by the plan, the soldier allows the fake maidservant to approach and describe how her mistress is home writhing in pain with longing for the soldier. Pyrgopolynices is so taken with the maidservant, he becomes ever more eager to meet her mistress. Upon meeting the fake wife, he decides that Philocomasium must be dismissed from his house at once. If she refuses, he declares aloud that he will have to use force. At this precise moment, Pleusicles appears on the scene dressed as a shipmaster and claims to be ready for sailing back to Athens. He comes to lead the twin back to port, whether she has reclaimed her sister or not. It seems to Pyrgopolynices that he must seize the moment to get rid of the courtesan, so he can marry the neighbor divorcée. Pyrgopolynices frees Philocomasium despite her feigned protests. Tearfully she finally consents to leave his company. The soldier, in a moment of joyous goodwill, even gives his recently acquired slave, the same Palaestrio, to her as her personal servant. Thus, the courtesan and slave are freed in the same instant. Palaestrio, like Philocomasium, pretends to be upset at leaving the soldier. Both the courtesan and the slave cry bitterly as they depart from Pyrgopolynices' home and head to port with the "shipmaster."

With Philocomasium out of his way, the soldier answers an invitation to enter his neighbor's house and visit with the wife. This is a pre-set trap, however. Once inside, Periplectolemus barges in, finds his fake wife with the soldier, and attacks him for adultery. Periplectolemus' slaves, wielding eager knives, drag the soldier outside as ordered by their master. They confiscate his cloak, sword, and money, beat him with clubs, and threaten to castrate him for attempting to seduce the wife. Pyrgopolynices begs that they spare his life and testicles, and promises that he will never in the future hurt any of the slaves for this beating. They agree to spare him, after which he inquires after the whereabouts of Philocomasium. Told that she has set sail for Athens, he finds out that the "shipmaster" was no shipmaster, but her lover from Athens. The play concludes with Pyrgopolynices bereft of his cloak and sword, suffering a terribly wounded ego, and humiliated in the knowledge that he has been duped out of his female lover and slave.

Roman conservatism and comedies of inversion. The cornerstone of Roman morality was a sense of *pietas*, or deep reverence for the gods and duty to one's parents. Furthermore, Romans valued hierarchy, authority, obedience, and tradition. If one word were to be used, however, to characterize the strategy of Plautus in this well-ordered universe, it would be "inversion," arranging elements in a topsy-turvy way. Plautus turns the orderly Roman world on its head. His comedy, in the non-threatening environment of a state-sanctioned festival, subverted deeply held values. Instead of unquestioned obedience to the *pater familias* (head of household), Plautus portrays adolescent boys who dupe their elders and behave saucily without apology. Instead of conservative, demure matrons, Plautus showcases courtesans or prostitutes and conniving women. Instead of subservient slaves, Plautus depicts clueless slaveowners and the intelligent servants who manipulate them. In the midst of the Second Punic War (218-202 BCE), when Rome treats its war heroes with the highest respect, Plautus dares to portray his main character as a bombastic soldier whose military feats are little more than fantasy. In short, Plautus presents his characters doing precisely the things Romans are not supposed to do. He breaks the bonds of appropriate social behavior and violates the *pietas* so integral to Roman identity. His comedy is deeply irreverent toward all things esteemed by Roman culture; the sacred becomes profane and the vulgar takes charge.

The dialogue between Pyrgopolynices, the braggart soldier, and his kidnapped slave Palaestrio shows the irreverence with which Plautus treats Roman customs. Here Palaestrio begins telling the soldier about his neighbor's lustful wife (who is really a prostitute):

> **Pyrg**: What about her? Is she freeborn, or some slave freed by the rod? [In early Rome, legal ownership was sometimes indicated by touching the object in question with a stalk or rod. Slaves were freed by being touched in this

manner by a Roman official, indicating that they were no longer private property, but part of the general public.]

Pal: Really, sir! Would I dare to bring a message to you from a freed slave, when you aren't even able to give a decent reply to the freeborn ladies already chasing you?

Pyrg: Well, is she married or unmarried?

Pal: Uh, both. Married and unmarried.

Pyrg: Exactly how can the same lady be married and unmarried?

Pal: Because she's a young wife stuck with an old husband.

Pyrg: Fabulous!

Pal: Oh, she's beautiful—what a woman she is!

Pyrg: You better not be lying to me!

Pal: I swear, she's the only woman who deserves someone like you.

(Plautus, *The Braggart Soldier,* lines 961-970; trans. J. Eyl)

In this scene, Palaestrio makes a mockery of the soldier, and in the play, all the actors make a mockery of marriage. Not only does the "wife" next door pretend to attempt adultery (a crime punishable by death for women in Rome), but she is actually a prostitute pretending to be a wife pretending to attempt adultery. Driving the entire plot is a brilliant slave who controls his masters like marionettes. Plautus is expert in transferring power away from traditional authority figures and into the hands of Rome's disenfranchised servants, disreputable courtesans, and irresponsible youths. Within the context of the festival, this reversal of traditional power dynamics allowed the audience to temporarily reject their own values by inverting them in a distant and foreign (Greek) setting.

Festivals, games, and temporary madness. In *The Braggart Soldier,* as shown, a slave—Palaestrio—drives the action by coming up with a shrewd plan that achieves its aim. The slave, the lowliest member of society, regarded as a thing rather than a person, rules the day. Knowledge of the social context of the play is essential to understanding this inversion. All Roman drama is linked to festival holidays, when citizens abandoned the constraints of daily life to view parades, tightrope walkers, fire-eaters, acrobats, dancers, and theater. Several festivals (called *ludi,* or "games," in Latin) were celebrated each year, and the staging of plays was strictly limited to these holidays. The festivals, native to the Italian peninsula, date from the earliest Roman times and were originally tied to agriculture and the changing of seasons. However, the first plays were not incorporated into festivals until the *ludi Romani* (Roman Games) 240 BCE, when Livius Andronicus produced Latin translations of two Greek plays. Over the centuries the festivals took on a progressively more licentious, or immoral, tone. In view of the other festival activities, theater became associated with immoral behavior; in fact, it was so associated with disreputable behavior that Rome did not erect a permanent theater until 55 BCE.

At each festival, wealthy politicians funded the theater in an attempt to curry favor with voters by showing their interest in public entertainment and relaxation. The Saturnalia, celebrated every year in December, was perhaps the festival at which celebrants took the greatest license. The Saturnalia encouraged the temporary toppling of social structure; masters served dinner to their slaves, immorality and drunkenness were forgivable, and general mayhem was tolerated throughout the city.

Scholars have theorized on the social function of the *ludi,* suggesting that it operated as a sort of safety valve to relieve the pressure that accumulated through daily social constraints. Inverting roles or other elements of society provided a periodic catharsis, a release of emotions within the safe context of ritualized festivals. Allowing for this release, the festival ultimately re-inscribed traditional social structure and boundaries of behavior. Festivals provided an approved space for people to invert all that was deemed appropriate, good, and valuable in Roman society, and the tactic forestalled any serious breakdown in values and traditions. This same theory can be applied to modern-day celebrations such as 1) Mardi Gras, celebrated in New Orleans and 2) Brazil's annual Carnival, where "normal" people cast off regular identities and enjoy a sort of temporary madness. Plautus' comedy was an integral part of the mild madness of these festivals. They provided festival-goers with a vicarious form of release and relief. Through his comedy, Romans temporarily erased the rigid social boundary between respectable married women and prostitutes or courtesans. Through his comedy, this profoundly militaristic culture turned military leaders into fools. Through his comedy, young inexperienced men sought guidance from their social subordinates (slaves and courtesans) instead of revering the examples of their fathers.

Sources and literary context. At the beginning of *The Braggart Soldier* we are told that the play was adapted from an earlier Greek play, the *Alazon* (which means "braggart" in Greek). We do

STOCK CHARACTERS IN PLAUTINE COMEDY

Like contemporary situation comedy, Plautus' comedy relied heavily on stereotyped characters whose names and personal psychologies were less important to the plot than the comic role they filled. The following list is in no way exhaustive, but provides a general synopsis of the type of *dramatis personae* Plautus included in most of his plays:

Adulescens (Young Man): The Adulescens is in his late teens or early twenties, and is always passionately in love with a prostitute or other young woman whose social standing is far below his. Circumstances place him temporarily beyond the jurisdiction of his absent father, and thus he must be watched over by the family slave. Because of his limited life experience, he frequently makes terrible decisions, for which the slave must shoulder the blame. In *The Braggart Soldier,* Pleusicles is less troublesome than the Adulescens of other plays. Still he goes to extraordinary lengths to reunite himself with his lover, relying on his watchful family slave.

Parasitus (Parasite): Always angling for a free meal, the Parasite will stoop to any degree of flattery to gain it. He may be a traveling companion, businessman, or paid witness in a court trial. His allegiance is determined by who offers him the most financial gain or whose food satisfies his stomach best. The motives behind his compliments are painfully transparent to the audience, and he is frequently irritating to his patron. This character role is usually evident in the name of the Parasite. In *The Braggart Soldier,* the Parasite is Artotrogus, whose name means "Bread-Chewer."

Meretrix (Courtesan/Prostitute): The Courtesan is the object of the Adulescens' unrelenting desire. She is usually in some sort of immediate trouble—financial, emotional, or familial. In *The Braggart Soldier* the Courtesan has been kidnapped and taken from Athens to Ephesus against her will.

Servus (Slave): Plautine comedies have more than one slave, but there is usually a "lead" slave, who is responsible for the well-being of the Adulescens. Clever beyond belief and full of sass toward his master, the Servus concocts absurdly implausible plans to solve the problems caused by his wayward charge. In the role of the Servus in this play is Palaestrio; a double-dealing slave, he serves both Pleusicles and Pyrgopolynices and masterminds the play's action.

Senex (Old Man): Usually either the father of the Adulescens or a friend/relative of the father, the Senex operates as a symbol of authority and frequently expresses anger toward the Servus and Adulescens. More infrequently the Senex acts in concert with the Servus to bring a hair-brained plan to fruition. This less frequent option is what happens in *The Braggart Soldier;* the hero's slave and the hero scheme in concert with his father's friend, Periplectolemus.

Miles (Soldier): The Soldier is pompous and self-congratulating. He inflates his military accomplishments and exaggerates his worth. Because he is blind to the reality of his unimpressive life, he is easily duped through flattery, as the braggart soldier is in Plautus' play of the same name.

not know the author of the *Alazon*, but we do know that Plautus adapted many of his works from the Greek playwright Menander, who belonged to an era of Greek theater called New Comedy. Thus, it is possible that Menander wrote the *Alazon*, but we have no evidence to support or refute such a claim. As far as we know, none of Plautus' plays are complete originals. Segal writes, "Like Shakespeare and Molière, Plautus begs, borrows, and steals from every conceivable source, including himself" (Segal, p. 6). Because the Alazon is lost to history, it is impossible to say how much of the play Plautus copied directly and how much he transformed to suit his Roman audience. Yet we do know that Plautus tailored his plays to suit the humor of his Roman audience. Thus, none of his plays are translated verbatim from the original.

Events in History at the Time the Play Was Written

Rome meets Greece. No study of Plautus would be complete without looking at the effect of Greek culture on Rome. *The Braggart Soldier* was adapted from a Greek play not long after Romans had come into contact with Greeks through maritime trade, through the Greek slaves who served Roman families, and through Greek settlements in the southern Italian region called Magna Graecia, or, Great Greece. Earlier in the fifth century, Greek city-states had established colonies in southern Italy and Sicily. As Rome expanded, it became involved in military disputes in this region, and the Greek influence filtered north, resulting in profound cultural change for Rome. Greeks were also taken as slaves to Rome when it entered into mainland Greek political and military disputes in the third century BCE. Romans adopted and adapted various aspects of Greek culture including sophisticated marble sculpture, the complex genealogies of the human-like Greek gods (who were subsequently reassigned Latin names), the idea of leisure time, public exercise, and theater.

Early Roman culture was more austere than Greek culture, and the Hellenizing of Rome was met with a great backlash by some of Rome's most powerful politicians who feared a "softening" of Roman men. Though most Romans were eager to import Greek culture and adapt it to their liking, legal and social measures were taken to thwart the spread of it. For example, partly to curtail a perceived growing decadence and partly to shore up national wealth during the Second Punic War, Rome's Senate passed the *lex Oppia* in 215 BCE, which sought to control the physical appearance and behavior of women. This law, passed just a few years before the production of *The Braggart Soldier*, barred women from wearing gold jewelry and multi-colored clothing in public—particularly garments dyed with the expensive purple ink of the murex mollusk, imported from the southeast Mediterranean. Women were also barred from traveling in

horse-drawn carriages unless they were traveling to a temple for religious sacrifices. By legislating the behavior of wealthy women and by denouncing the physical luxury that women represented to Roman men, the *lex Oppia* reinforced a conservatism championed by Rome's most staunch traditionalists. After much heated debate, the law was repealed in 195 BCE, just 11 years after the debut of *The Braggart Soldier*.

Reception and impact. While we have no evidence for the initial reception of *The Braggart Soldier*, we do have a sense of Plautus' great popularity as an entertainer. Many scholars have contrasted Plautus with Terence, suggesting that Plautus won enormous popularity among the masses but that Terence survived off the approval of a small circle of wealthy patrons. Plautus has even been referred to as Rome's most popular playwright, but there is no ancient evidence to support this claim. While it is true that the comedy writer Terence enjoyed the patronage of wealthy Romans, this does not mean Plautus was more appealing to the masses. On the contrary, Terence's wealthy patrons may have chosen to support him *because* of his popular reputation (Parker, p. 606). What we know for certain is that Plautus wrote many plays over a lengthy career and that several playwrights attempted to borrow his name. It is furthermore known that his influence spread far and deep, from ancient Rome to distant places and times. At the turn of the seventeenth century, William Shakespeare drew heavily on Plautus' work for his comedies, and more recently Stephen Sondheim used it as the basis for his long-running 1962 Broadway musical *A Funny Thing Happened on the Way to the Forum*.

—Jennifer Eyl

For More Information

Conte, G. B. *Latin Literature: A History*. Trans. Joseph B. Solodow. Baltimore: Johns Hopkins University Press, 1994.

Livy. *Ab Urbe Condita* [A History of Rome from Its Founding]. Trans. T. J. Luce. Oxford: Oxford University Press, 1998.

McCarthy, Kathleen. *Slaves, Masters, and the Art of Authority in Plautine Comedy*. Princeton: Princeton University Press, 2000.

Packman, Z. M. "Feminine Role Designations in the Comedies of Plautus." *American Journal of Philology* 120, no. 2 (1999): 245-258.

Parker, Holt. "Plautus vs. Terence: Audience and Popularity Re-Examined." *American Journal of Philology* 117, no. 4 (1996): 585-617.

Plautus. *The Braggart Warrior* [The Braggart Soldier]. Trans. Paul Nixon. Cambridge, Mass.: Harvard University Press, 1952.

———. *Miles Gloriosus.* Ed. Mason Hammond, Arthur Mack, and Walter Moskalew. Cambridge, Mass.: Harvard University Press, 1997.

Segal, Erich. *Roman Laughter: The Comedy of Plautus.* Cambridge, Mass.: Harvard University Press, 1968.

Slater, Niall. *Plautus in Performance: The Theatre of the Mind.* Singapore: Harwood Academic Publishers, 2000.

Walbank, F. W. *The Hellenistic World.* Cambridge, Mass.: Harvard University Press, 1993.

The Brothers

by
Terence (Publius Terence Afer)

Most scholars agree that Publius Terence Afer was born a slave in Carthage about 190 BCE, between the Second and Third Punic Wars. Sold to the Roman senator Terentius Lucanus, Terence was brought to Rome, given a gentleman's education, and freed from slavery—supposedly because of his intelligence and good looks. At this point he began to translate plays from ancient Greek into Latin, capitalizing on the Roman thirst for all things classically Greek. Terence elevated himself into the upper ranks of Roman society by writing his own first play *The Girl from Andros* (166 BCE), after which he secured a patron. By the age of 25, he had published six plays, all part of the genre of Greek theater known as New Comedy. These six comedies—*The Girl from Andros, The Mother-in-Law, The Self-Tormentor, The Eunuch,* and *Phormio,* along with *Brothers*—constitute Terence's body of surviving works. Based on the Greek play *Adelphoe* by Menander, *The Brothers* is considered Terence's masterpiece. At the height of his career, Terence left Rome for Greece, never to return. His disappearance and death remain a mystery. *The Brothers* demonstrates Terence's gift for irony and his ability to add sophistication to the works he adapted from Greek to Latin. He conceived a complex style of characterization that would influence future comedic writers of the West, from England's Geoffrey Chaucer (c. 1340-1400) to France's Molière (1622-1673) and beyond. In *The Brothers,* Terence tackles such issues as the generation gap, class conflict, and the tension between traditional and modern ways in the Rome of his day. He furthermore does

THE LITERARY WORK

A Latin adaptation of a comic Greek play set in fourth-century BCE Athens; written and performed in 160 BCE.

SYNOPSIS

Two brothers are raised separately, one in the country by their strict biological father, the other in the city by their liberal uncle. The brothers fall in love with girls below their social class and contrive, with their uncle, to outwit their father, but he has the last laugh.

so in a manner that conveys his humanistic approach and belief in universal truths, such as *Homo sum: humani nil a me alienum puto* (I am human myself, so I think every human affair is my concern). At the heart of *The Brothers* is a young man's right to woo and wed the woman of his choice; the play features two attempts to exercise this right and the powerful reaction from established society.

Events in History at the Time of the Play

Second-century Rome and Carthage. After the Romans defeated Hannibal and his troops at Carthage in 201 BCE in the Second Punic War, the Roman general Publius Cornelius Scipio *Africanus* (as he became known) returned home master of the Mediterranean region. Conquering its most formidable regional enemy had in fact made Rome the undisputed leader of the known world, turning the Roman state into an international empire. Rome and Carthage had long been vying for control of the western Mediterranean region, North Africa, and southern Europe. Though a third war would be fought in 149 BCE, the victory in the second war and the 50-year reprieve that followed gave Rome time to conquer the Hellenistic (culturally Greek) kingdoms to the east and to consolidate its power in Europe. In essence, the end of the Second Punic War signaled the birth of a global Roman Empire. Conversely, the loss by Carthage reduced it to a de-

---

ROME WAGES WAR TO FORGE AN EMPIRE

264-241 BCE First Punic War
First of the three wars in which Rome fights Carthage for control of the western Mediterranean
238 BCE Roman Conquest of Sardinia
229-228 BCE First Illyrian War in the Balkans
First of two wars between Rome and Illyrii for control of a region east of the Adriatic Sea, near Macedonia
219 BCE Second Illyrian War
218-201 BCE Second Punic War
215-205 BCE First Macedonian War
First of four wars fought for control of the kingdoms of Macedonia, a region covering parts of today's Bulgaria, Greece, and Serbia
200-191 BCE Gaul invades northern Italy
Romans beat Boii, the main Gallic tribe, after which Gaul never successfully threatens Roman military might
192-189 BCE Syrian War
Rome defeats Antiochus III, king of the Seleucid Empire
171-168 BCE Third Macedonian War
149-148 BCE Final Macedonian War
149-146 BCE Third and final Punic War

---

pendent state of Rome, forced to pay it tribute and reparations. As in other conquered regions, many Carthaginians were enslaved and sold to Romans as a result of the war. From throughout the Mediterranean, millions of former opponents were taken to Italy to perform slave agricultural and domestic labor for wealthy citizens. By the end of the first century BCE, slaves comprised 40 percent of the Italian population. The luckier

ones—those considered beautiful, skilled, or talented—were sold to the nobility at high prices (a highly skilled slave could fetch 50 times the price of an unskilled slave); thereafter, they were provided with an education and the opportunity to do meaningful work. Terence was one such slave. Prized for his handsome appearance as well as his literacy and intelligence, he was sold to a Roman senator.

Rise of Hellenism. Back in 338 BCE, Macedonia's ruler conquered Greece. An area between the Balkans and the Greek peninsula, Macedonia had by this time established cultural ties to the Greeks, inviting their artists and poets to its capital city and adapting Greek customs. The culturally Greek Macedonian Empire expanded and endured for the next hundred years, then became embroiled in a series of wars against Rome. Macedonia lost, which led to the breakup of its empire and its decline into a Roman province. For Rome, the spoils of war included not just slaves and reparations but Hellenistic, or culturally Greek, artifacts and treasures. The Romans had conquered a Hellenistic domain, including Macedonia and the Mediterranean islands of Sicily, Sardinia, and Corsica, repositories of vast Greek libraries and old objects that sparked a keen public interest in earlier Greece. Slaves such as Terence, who could speak Greek and Latin, were put to work as translators and soon the works of Menander, Diphilus, Philemon, and other celebrated Greek comedians and tragedians were being produced throughout Rome.

Hellenism was embraced especially by young, educated Romans since it valued youth and promoted a break with old values. The Hellenistic regard for the *jeunesse dorée* (wealthy and fashionable youth) contrasted sharply with a more traditional and conservative Roman culture, based on patriarchy, family, and loyalty. Mainstream society was heavily influenced by Cato the Censor (234–149 BCE), who won renown for his devotion to the old Roman ideals of simplicity, honesty, and unflinching courage. A strict disciplinarian, Cato believed in austerity (as does Demea, the stern father in Terence's play) and sharply criticized excesses of wealth and personal gratification. Hellenism, in stark contrast, promoted sophistication, worldliness, and some self-indulgence. The Roman general Lucius Aemilius Paullus Macedonicus (229-160 BCE), to take one example, practiced these forms of excess in the extreme. Paullus was famous for the immense plunder he collected in Macedonia and Epirus, his love of pageantry, and the vast amounts of war spoils he kept for himself. In 164 BCE, he was elected censor—the official in charge of public morals; his election reflects Rome's shift in cultural values during this era and the increasing influence of Hellenism on Roman society. Capitalizing on the shift, Terence produced *The Brothers* in 160 BCE. One of its main characters—the liberal uncle, Micio—embraces the new Hellenistic approach that has begun penetrating Roman society. In fact, the play speaks directly to the culture clash between Cato and Paullus, whose contrasting viewpoints are articulated by the brothers Demea and Micio.

Roman society. Roman society in the second century BCE was highly stratified. At the highest level was the emperor, who alone commanded the loyalty of everyone below (all swore allegiance to him personally, not to a flag, country, government, or empire). Under him were the politicians (the senators) and the wealthy businessmen (known as equestrians); next, the ordinary citizens; then, the freedmen; and, finally, the slaves. Though the boundaries between social classes were fairly rigid, slaves could be freed by their masters or buy their freedom for the price their masters had paid for them (often a virtually impossible feat). It was possible for citizens to climb the social ladder through politics, military service, acquisition of wealth, or marriage. Bribery and flattery also went a long way toward elevating one's status—particularly currying favor with the emperor. But such social climbing did not occur easily or commonly. Rome's leaders saw class divisions as key to preserving the empire's strength, so they were not lightly crossed and even when they were, the social climber stepped into the new status with indication of their old status. Roman law limited the rights and activities of freed slaves, prohibiting them, during Terence's era, from serving in the regular Roman army or becoming a senator.

Roman families, like Roman society, were ruled from the top down. Often an entire family line lived in one household, from grandparents to grandchildren, with the eldest male (the *paterfamilias*) acting as family head. The *paterfamilias* owned the property and wielded complete authority—including the power of life and death over each family member. It was understood that every family had the right to follow its own household customs and rules. The patriarch could run the household strictly or liberally, as he saw fit. He assumed full responsibility for the actions of his family; if a family member committed an offense, he was liable and could be

held accountable. The males had total dominion over the females—typically even a woman who became a widow did not become independent; she was instead assigned a male guardian by the patriarch of the family.

Roman women of Terence's day enjoyed more physical freedom than their counterparts in ancient Greek society. In 195 BCE the women of Rome demonstrated for and won the repeal of an edict (the Oppian Law) that prohibited females from riding about the city in carriages (i.e., in public). Today's scholars observe that such "progress" amounted to a freedom that was more apparent than real. As in Greek society, the primary role of Roman women continued to be bearing children and managing the household. These were the priorities, not a romantic relationship with one's husband. Though the evidence shows some marriages were genuine love relationships, young men learned to look outside upstanding families for sexual satisfaction. The men turned mostly to slaves or to former slaves to find "women of easy virtue." Among other cues, these women could be spotted by their clothing—while a "proper woman" wore a long dress that reached to her heels, the female servant or slave wore shorter dresses and it was mandatory for professional courtesans, or high-level prostitutes, to dress in togas. By the late Republican period, when *The Brothers* takes place, men were also having affairs with some of the married upper-class matrons (who wore the long dresses). Wealthy male citizens often kept a mistress and a second family in a separate household. There is little information about the marriage patterns that developed among the lower classes.

Another facet of personal life that often involved people outside the immediate family was child-rearing. If a household had too many young people to support, the patriarch might ask childless relatives or friends to adopt the burdensome child—or, in extreme cases, might sell the child into slavery. In Terence's play, Demea, a married citizen, gives one of his two sons to his wealthy single brother Micio because he cannot afford to raise both.

Rural versus urban life. Until the end of the Second Punic War, 90 percent of Romans were rural dwellers. Most lived in shanties or huts and worked the lands of the wealthy citizens and landowning nobility. Although these wealthy landowners lived in the cities and looked down on peasants, they nevertheless idealized rural life. Overseers meanwhile ran the farms of the absentee owner however they saw fit; the average overseer became notorious for his harsh treatment of the peasants. Because working and living conditions were so difficult, the peasants tried by all means to migrate to the cities where life seemed less brutal. At the end of the Second Punic War (202 BCE), they began flocking en masse to urban centers. The rural migrants were joined by a vast influx of slaves flooding into the cities after Rome's military victories. Exerting a profound influence on urban life, the slaves brought with them a myriad of cultural influences. Most came from Hellenistic cities outside or in other parts of the empire, their presence adding to the Greek influence spreading over Rome.

INTO THIN AIR—TERENCE'S DISAPPEARANCE

Terence's disappearance at approximately age 25 (some say as late as 36) has been a source of conjecture for centuries. His critics charged that he had homosexual relationships with the Roman nobility, that they were ghostwriting his plays, and that he fled Rome in order to avoid public exposure and humiliation. The widely accepted theory is quite a different story: Terence had run out of material to translate and was returning to Greece to find more plays and more closely study Greek culture and history. Where and how he disappeared remains a mystery. Some say he died in a shipwreck returning to Rome from Greece, others that he died of grief in Arcadia or Leucadia because his newly written plays were lost at sea as he tried to return to Rome; still others believe he died on the way to Greece or went into a self-imposed exile.

Urban life had its pluses, however, particularly in the city of Rome. Politicians of the late Republican period tried to win votes by providing for the entertainment of Roman citizens. The popular entertainments were chariot races, theater plays, and wild animal "hunts" (pitting a wild animal [e.g., a lion or panther] against a man given a weapon but no protective clothing before a crowd in the public arena—the man almost never survived). The enthusiasm for spectacles only increased over time, with the staging of comedies and tragedies becoming especially popular in the 100s BCE, when Terence wrote his play.

The city population was divided into different social classes, much as it is today. While the impoverished majority occupied overflowing rooms or apartments in a house, above a shop or factory, or in an apartment building that often featured communal cooking and bathroom facilities, the elite occupied palaces and large houses that sheltered not only the owners and their children but also relatives and family slaves. Rome housed at least one million inhabitants by the second century BCE, and Rome's nobility wanted nothing to do with most of them. Aside from daily household contact and reliance on perhaps hundreds of slaves (depending on the nobleman's wealth), the aristocrats often did not mingle socially with lower-status Romans (except for sexual relations, as noted). Public venues were segregated—the privileged elite had their own private boxes and sections, entertained lavishly for one another at private parties, and attended theatrical and musical performances not open to the general public. Like most playwrights and performers, Terence catered to this demographic. His plays were "written for a small, cultivated audience" that was in his day captivated by all things Greek (Radice, p. 12). Though his plays were often performed in public venues, Terence clearly tailored his craft to the taste of the nobility.

Roman education. In ancient Rome, education was mainly for boys and usually took place at home. Fathers and/or gifted slaves taught sons reading and writing as well as Roman law, history, and customs, and gave them a physical education befitting a soldier. Reverence for the gods, respect for law and order, obedience to authority, and truthfulness were traditionally regarded as the most important lessons to learn. Girls too were taught basic reading, writing, and arithmetic skills, but their education focused mainly on the domestic sphere. They learned from their mothers to play music, spin, weave, and sew—all the things needed to run a household.

About 200 BCE, the Romans began implementing the ancient Greek system of education. They started sending their boys to school outside their home at the age of 6 or 7. The primary school concentrated on reading, writing, math, and memorization of legends, laws, and poetry, educating boys until about the age of 11. Alternatively the family might bring a Greek tutor into the home, which gave girls a rudimentary education too. Girls as young as 12 got married, and in keeping with this fundamental goal, their focus was mainly on household skills (boys were forbidden to marry before 14). From 11 to 14, upper-class boys might study with a higher-level teacher, who taught them to refine their writing and speaking skills, to analyze poetry, and to attain a command of the Greek language; thereafter, a few boys acquired an even higher education, training for careers in public speaking, law, and politics. In the play, Terence shows the importance of education to the father and uncle in rearing the young men featured in the play. Though the two older characters, Demea and Micio, have different approaches, both emphasize that the primary role of a Roman father is to properly educate his son.

Greek New Comedy, Plautus, and Terence. Rome conquered Macedonia in the decades leading up to Terence's adaptation, between the 190s BCE and the 160s BCE (the community of Cynoscephalae in 197 BCE, Pydna in 169 BCE). By extension, Rome conquered all of the Greek city-states that had been dominated by Macedonia under Alexander the Great. His conquest had encouraged the spread of Hellenistic or Greek literary works throughout the Mediterranean region. Once Hellenism took hold, Roman writers produced very little that was not inspired by or taken directly from the Greeks. This is especially true of a genre that resurfaced in Terence's day—Greek New Comedy—which had first flourished in Athens c. 323-c.263 BCE. Adapting the New Comedy of such Greek writers as Menander, Diphilus, and Philemon, Roman playwrights produced theater that turned a humorously critical eye on society. The plays ridiculed people and institutions, often using obscenity, abuse, and insult to do so. The works of Menander, who was considered the finest of the ancient New Comedy writers, dealt mainly with matters of everyday life, such as young lovers, stern fathers, and bawdy and clever slaves.

Like Plautus (254-184 BCE), the great Roman playwright before him, Terence adapted the works of Menander, including *The Brothers*. Far more than a translator, Terence refined, combined incidents from different Menander plays, and recovered passages that Plautus had omitted in his own earlier adaptations. Terence comments on Plautus's versions, for example, of the play *Joined in Death*:

> Plautus made a Latin play out of it with the same name. In the beginning of the Greek play there is a young man who abducts a girl from

The Brothers is based on a Greek play by Menander (c. 343-292 BCE), shown here. Library of Congress.

> a slave-dealer. Plautus left out this incident altogether, so the present author took it for *Brothers* and translated it word for word.
> (Terence in Radice, p. 52)

Plautus's comedies brightened the Roman stage 20 years earlier than Terence's, before Hellenism had truly taken root in Roman society. A product of more liberal times, "unfettered by the conventions of an earlier age," Terence appealed to an entirely different audience (Radice, p. 12). His adaptations tapped the pulse of his contemporary Roman climate and spoke directly to an ongoing struggle between old and new moral values. While the ancient Roman tended to be based in practicality and prized discipline, loyalty, and consistency, the new Hellenized Roman gravitated more to hedonism and romance; he or she believed in the concept of love and was more given to self-gratification and the pursuit of earthly pleasures. Terence's adaptation does not necessarily condone this shift (some read the play as a condemnation of it, in fact), but it certainly speaks to it and reveals important changes that were taking place in the attitude and behavior of his contemporaries.

In addition to updating Greek New Comedy for a 100s BCE Roman audience, Terence changed the staging to more closely resemble Roman life and furthermore infused the plays with a more subtle irony—considered by some a higher form of comedy. Whereas Plautus delighted mass audiences with faithful translations of Menander's caricatures and satires, Terence strove for more nuanced characterization that would reflect his society and appeal to the sophisticated tastes of his day.

The Play in Focus

Plot summary. A so-called "problem comedy," *The Brothers* begins with a problem outside the play—that is, the author's personal conflict with certain critics who accused him of plagiarizing. In a carefully worded prologue, full of irony and wit, Terence details his source material and vehemently denies "the spiteful accusation that eminent persons assist the author and collaborate closely with him" (Terence, *The Brothers,* p. 137). He implores the audience to "watch carefully" and "judge whether his conduct deserves praise or blame" as he sets the stage for the action to begin (*The Brothers,* p. 137).

Situated in Athens, the play opens in front of a citizen's house. The citizen, Micio, is one of two brothers who are raising two brothers. It is morning and Micio is frantic because his son Aeschinus has not come home from the previous night. He chides himself for worrying so much, as he is supposed to be very tolerant and liberal:

> Now look at me when my son hasn't returned, full of fancies and forebodings. The boy may have caught a chill or fallen down and broken a leg. . . . Why on earth should a man take it into his head and get himself something to be dearer to him than his own self? It's not as if he's my own son—he's my brother's, and my brother and I have had quite different tastes since boyhood.
>
> (*The Brothers,* p. 139)

Elaborating on how he and his brother Demea differ, Micio describes himself as an urban bachelor who enjoys leisure and spending money. Demea, in stark contrast, is a highly thrifty married man who lives in the country and works very hard. Demea had two sons but could not afford to raise both so Micio adopted the eldest and brought him up as his own. Because the fathers are so different the boys have been reared in opposite ways. A strict disciplinarian, Demea has raised Ctesipho in a highly authoritarian and austere manner, while Micio has indulged Aeschinus and raised him very liberally. Demea's motto is "fear authority"; Micio's is "if

the threat of punishment alone drives a man to do his duty, he'll be careful only so long as he thinks he may be detected" (*The Brothers,* p. 140). Echoing closely the contrasting philosophies of Roman conservatism and Greek liberalism, Demea and Micio illustrate the conflict of values occurring in Roman society at the time this play is being produced.

Nearly full adults, Aeschinus and Ctesipho are growing into their manhood, beginning love affairs, and getting into common types of trouble. As Micio paces outside his house, fretting about Aeschinus, Demea walks up. He is very angry with Micio because he has learned where Aeschinus is. It seems that Aeschinus has abducted a slave girl, severely beaten her pimp, and the entire town knows it. Demea blames Micio entirely for this act because of his permissive, "amoral" child-rearing philosophy. Micio retorts:

> It is no crime, believe me, for a young man to enjoy wine and women; neither is it to break open a door. If you and I didn't do these things it was only because we hadn't the money.
>
> (*The Brothers,* p. 141)

Though relieved that Aeschinus is all right, Micio is secretly perturbed by the news and thinks Demea has a point about Aeschinus behaving badly. But he is not about to admit it to his brother. They both leave to look for their respective sons.

In the next scene, Aeschinus enters Micio's house with the slave-girl Bacchis, followed by her pimp, Sannio. Sannio is demanding that he be paid for Bacchis. Micio's clever middle-aged manservant, a slave named Syrus, stops Sannio and urges the pimp to humor Aeschinus because he is young and impetuous. Syrus promises Sannio will be paid in due time if he leaves them alone. Sannio reluctantly agrees and leaves for a trip to the slave auction in Cyprus, where he was planning to sell Bacchis along with many others.

Next, the other younger brother, Ctesipho, enters the house, ecstatic. It seems that the girl whom Aeschinus has abducted is actually Ctesipho's girlfriend. He praises Aeschinus to Syrus: "The splendid man! He put my interests before all his own, took on himself all the hard words and gossip, my own trouble and misdeeds" (*The Brothers,* p. 148). He thanks his brother, then goes to the slave-girl.

The scene moves away from Micio's house, next door to the house of a woman named Sostrata. Her daughter, Pamphila, is nine months pregnant. From the nurse comes the news that

Pamphila is about to give birth and the suggestion that they send for a midwife and for Aeschinus, who apparently is the father. Just then a household servant, Geta, runs in, screaming, "What times! What crimes! O wicked world, O vile wretch!" (*The Brothers*, p. 151). She tells her mistress, Sostrata, that the whole town is talking about how Aeschinus ran off with the slave-girl Bacchis and beat up her pimp. Sostrata is furious and laments the situation her daughter is in. "Things couldn't be worse than they are now. In the first place she has no dowry, and then she's lost the next best thing—her reputation is ruined and she can't be married without one" (*The Brothers*, p. 153). It seems that Aeschinus promised to marry Pamphila (he gave her a ring), but now Sostrata and her servants are convinced that he has abandoned both Pamphila and his soon-to-be-born baby to run off with Bacchis. Sostrata vows to take him to court as Geta runs out to get the midwife.

Next Demea returns to Micio's house looking for Ctesipho, the son he raised. He continues to regard Aeschinus as the bad son, and Ctesipho as the wholly good and innocent one because he has been raised "properly." Alert as well as clever, Syrus intercepts Demea before he can enter the house and find Ctesipho with his love, Bacchis. The slave has never liked Demea because of his constant condescension toward him. Now Syrus delights in giving Demea the run-around. He sends him off in the wrong direction, to search for Ctesipho at the outskirts of town on what will turn out to be a wild goose chase.

Meanwhile, Micio is out looking for Aeschinus and runs into Geta. Still fuming, she tells him of her mistress's intention to take Aeschinus to court for reneging on his obligation to marry Pamphila, who is about to bear his child. Micio is shocked to hear this news—his day is just getting worse and worse—and promises to find Aeschinus and set things straight.

Micio returns home and finally discovers what is really going on with the two younger brothers, Aeschinus and Ctesipho, and the two young women: Aeschinus has abducted Bacchis not for himself but for his brother; he truly loves and intends to marry Pamphila. In fact, both brothers are in love and want to marry—Aeschinus to Pamphila and Ctesipho to Bacchis. Micio resolves to make this happen but just then Demea reappears. He is livid, having searched all over town for his son, only to find him back at Micio's house with a slave-girl. He too learns the truth of the complex situation and, again, blames Micio's

overly indulgent child-rearing philosophy for everything.

Then suddenly Demea does an about-face. He starts agreeing to all the two boys and his brother want, promising that they can marry the young women they love if Micio pays for everything. Next he turns Micio's own logic against him and reasons that if he is so indulgent and liberal he should free Syrus and his wife from slavery, marry Pamphila's mother, and put all the newly-weds under his own roof. In a strange and unforeseen twist, Demea assumes the role of *paterfamilias*, convincing everyone that he, in his conservative wisdom, is the brother to manage things. Micio is a pushover who finds it hard to say "no." If they follow his lead, they will squander their lives. But Demea will keep them on the right path, he promises as he offers the family his services. They accept and enter Micio's house for the wedding celebrations. Whether the final victory goes to Demea or Micio is debatable, as all in the end get more or less what they want.

Romance in Rome. In *The Brothers*, as in other New Comedy plays, romantic love is a key ingredient in marriage. The attention given it is remarkable in view of the minimal or nonexistent role it customarily played in real-life Greek marriages. Menander nevertheless bases dramatic relationships on genuine affection; his marital partnerships involve physical passion and emotional intimacy borne of an attraction to fine manners, intelligence, loyalty, and the like. Literature had already introduced physical and emotional intimacy in marriage as significant in Homer's Greece in his *Odyssey* (also in *Classical Literature and Its Times*). Now four centuries later it gained new importance in Menander's Greece, with the help of New Comedy. Also novels of the period concerned themselves with marriage for love (see *An Ethiopian Story*, also in *Classical Literature and Its Times*). By the end of the next century, the 200s BCE, "marriages by consent, for love, had become commoner" in Greece (Grant, p. 25).

Terence tailors his adaptation of the play to second century BCE Rome, in which attitudes about love were also changing. Marriage in Rome had long been a businesslike transaction, entered into to make life more stable, to move up in society, to conserve wealth, and to bear children, preferably sons who would care for parents in old age. Patriarchs, who generally arranged the matches, considered bloodlines and social class, not love. But with the influence of Hellenism, which stressed passion, the self, and the arts, Romans began to seek emotional intimacy in marriage, a shift represented by the women pursued in the play. The two younger brothers chose for themselves a couple of young women who meet none of the traditional requirements for men of their status.

Aeschinus, who is a respectable citizen, falls in love with Pamphila, a lower-class young woman whose family cannot provide a dowry and whose condition of pregnancy before marriage is viewed

BAD PRESS, GOOD PRESS— TERENCE AND THE SKEPTICS

~

An elite group of Roman nobles and intellectuals surrounded the adopted grandson of Scipio Africanus, the famed general and conqueror of Carthage. Because of his ties to these nobles and his previous slave status, Terence was accused of not writing his material at all. His enemies reasoned that no slave could produce such sophisticated work and suggested that his powerful friends were writing it on his behalf. Clearly aware of these vicious rumors, Terence prefaced *The Brothers* with this witty rebuttal:

The author is well aware that his writing is scrutinized by unfair critics, and that his enemies are out to deprecate the play we are about to present; he therefore intends to state the charge against himself in person, and the audience shall judge whether his conduct deserves praise or blame. . . . As to the spiteful accusation that eminent persons assist the author and collaborate closely with him: his accusers may think it a grave charge, but he takes it as a high compliment if he can win the approval of [such] men who themselves find favour with you all and with the general public.

(Terence in Radice, p. 52)

as one of disgrace. In traditional Roman society, these factors would make her an unsuitable match for Aeschinus. But he has given her his love and an engagement ring as a token of it promising they will marry no matter what his family or society says. He "in whom we put all our hopes," explains Pamphila's mother, "swore he could not live a day without [Pamphila]!" (*The Brothers*, p. 152). Not only did he profess his undying love for her daughter, but he promised to "put the baby in its grandfather's arms and beg the old man's leave to marry her!" (*The Brothers*, p. 152). As indicated by this promise, Aeschinus plans to seek approval for the marriage from his adoptive father, Micio, recognizing that traditionally he is the one with the authority and responsibility to give it. However, the young man plans to marry whether or not Micio approves, placing love above conformity to tradition.

Ctesipho has fallen in love with a young woman even further down the social scale. She is a slave who entertains men with singing and dancing, so her status is the lowest possible. But Ctesipho loves her and is ready to flee the country to marry her. When his brother asks why he did not confide in him about this love sooner, Ctesipho replies, "I was ashamed" (*The Brothers*, p. 149). Rather "stupid," counters Aeschinus, "to let a little thing like that nearly drive you out of the country. It's ridiculous. Perish the thought!" (*The Brothers*, p. 149).

The older generation is not so sold on love. Demea, Ctesipho's father, who represents stolid Roman tradition, objects. Though he finally relents, Demea is vehemently opposed to the brothers marrying below their stations, whether or not they are in love. He blames Micio for encouraging such romantic notions and feels that Micio's son, Aeschinus, has corrupted the son whom Demea has done such a proper job of raising. But Micio is not as radical an influence as Demea would have others believe. Micio's ways are more liberal than his brother's, to be sure. But Micio is a transitional figure, a father who still adheres to many traditions. When he learns of Aeschinus's predicament, Micio warns his son to be more responsible.

What kind of a country do you think you live in? You seduced a girl you never should have touched. . . . That was your first fault. But afterwards, did you give it a thought? . . . You delayed and did nothing while nine months went by. This was the greatest wrong you could do, to yourself, to that poor girl, to the child. . . . I trust you are not so thoughtless in all your personal affairs.

(*The Brothers*, p. 169)

For Micio, the problem is not that Aeschinus "seduced a girl he never should have touched," but that he did not take immediate responsibility for it (*The Brothers*, p. 169). He teaches his son that it is natural enough to fall in love, but romance must be taken seriously; romantic love is more than a dreamy ideal—it must be rooted in reality. As he gives his consent to marry, he arranges to have the brothers and their wives move into his house, where they will have stability. Demea is naturally appalled:

Here's a bride coming without a penny, and a kept woman in the house! Too much money in the home, a young man ruined by indulgence, and the old one off his head!

(*The Brothers*, p. 173)

In the end, Demea accepts the matches, drawing them into an otherwise traditional family setting, in which he will serve as patriarch. The play ends happily in a spirit of compromise, and in the process, romantic love takes root.

Sources and literary context. *The Brothers* is a "problem comedy" based on Menander's original, which the Greek playwright wrote to be performed at a ritual in honor of the wine god, Dionysus (renamed Bacchus by the Romans). In Athens, comedies became an official part of the celebration in 486 BCE and prizes were awarded for the best productions. Unfortunately Menander's originals did not survive (except for the play *Dyscolus*). Because Menander's original is lost, we do not know if Terence's ironic ending is his own invention or a restoration of the original.

Scholars have suggested possible parallels between the father figure, Demea, and Rome's conservative politician Cato. Likewise, they have pointed to possible similarities between Micio and the earlier-mentioned extravagant leader of Rome, Paullus (in whose honor the play was performed). But, while Terence's characters are certainly articulating some of these separate real-life figures, there are vast differences between them and their proposed fictional counterparts. Attributes of the characters may in fact come from Terence's own experiences as a slave, freedman, and friend of the nobility. We simply do not know. We do know that he drew from both Menander's original and incorporated the scene of the young man abducting a girl from a slave-dealer from the Greek play *Joined in Death* by Diphilus.

Reception and impact. The sixth and last of Terence's plays, *The Brothers* was very well received. It was first performed along with the gladiatorial games as part of the funeral rites in honor of the same Paullus mentioned above, who, again, had served as a general and consul. The games were held by Quintus Fabius Maximus and Publius Cornelius Scipio Africanus, who was the adopted grandson of the famous general Scipio Africanus. Both of the younger men were great friends of Terence, and gossips claimed they had a hand in writing his scripts, a rumor Terence pointedly denies in the prologue to his play. Competing playwrights furthermore accused him of plagiarizing and of altering the original Greek texts. Terence, perhaps his own best promoter, refuted all these charges, and despite them, earned high acclaim in his day.

Cicero, Horace, and Quintillian all praised Terence for developing a form of Latin in his plays that was subtle and stylish yet unaffected (Radice, p. 13). He has also been credited with laying the groundwork for the Western comedic tradition. Terence's influence has resounded through the centuries, affecting the plays written by Spain's Lope de Vega, England's William Shakespeare, and Ireland's George Bernard Shaw. Perhaps the greatest influence has been on the French playwright Molière, who further perfected Terence's humanist approach.

—Diane R. Mannone

For More Information

Flacelière, Robert. *Love in Ancient Greece.* Trans. James Cleugh. New York: Crown, 1962.

Grant, Michael. *Greeks and Romans: A Social History.* London: Weidenfeld and Nicolson, 1992.

Grimal, Pierre. *Love in Ancient Rome.* Trans. Arthur Train, Jr. New York: Crown, 1967.

Hadas, Moses, ed. *Greek Drama.* Toronto: Bantam Books, 1962.

Howard, Anne. *Penelope to Poppea: Women in Greek and Roman Society.* London: Macmillan, 1990.

Plautus and Terence. *Five Comedies.* Trans. Deena Berg and Douglass Parker. Indianapolis / Cambridge: Hackett, 1999.

Radice, Betty, ed. *The Brothers and Other Plays,* by Terence. Baltimore, Md.: Penguin, 1965.

Shelton, Jo-Ann. *As the Romans Did: A Sourcebook in Roman Social History.* New York: Oxford University Press, 1998.

Terence. *The Brothers.* In *The Complete Comedies of Terence.* Ed. Palmer Bovie, et al. New Brunswick, N.J.: Rutgers University Press, 1974.

Carmina

by
Catullus

Very little is known for certain about the life of Gaius Valerius Catullus. A late source informs us that he was born in Verona (the principal town in the Roman province of Cisalpine Gaul in northern Italy) in 87 BCE and died at the age of 30 in Rome. However, these birth and death dates are contradicted by evidence in the poems themselves. On the strength of this poetic evidence, scholars conclude that Catullus was born in 85 or 84 BCE and died in 55 or 54 BCE. The ancient biographer Suetonius claims that Catullus' father was a prominent man in Verona who often hosted Julius Caesar at banquets, probably when he was governor of Cisalpine Gaul (see Suetonius' ***The Twelve Caesars***, also in *Classical Literature and Its Times*). Catullus had a brother, whose death and burial in Asia Minor (modern Turkey) he mourned in a famous elegy (poem 101). Later, Catullus served in the Roman province of Bithynia in Asia Minor in association with the governor Gaius Memmius. Catullus' family must have been wealthy enough to have the poet educated in Rome, where Greek studies were prominent at the time, for his verse reflects a deeply rooted love of Greek literature and a topnotch literary background. When Catullus arrived in Rome, he no doubt associated himself with other young writers interested in making the Latin language and its poetry as flexible and sophisticated as the Greek. Instead of epic verse about Roman legends or heritage, Catullus and his fellow *Poetae Novi* (New Poets), as Cicero called them, wrote sometimes concise, sometimes lengthy poems

> ## THE LITERARY WORK:
> A collection of 113 poems, grouped into three sections based on various meters; written in Latin in the middle of the first century BCE.
>
> ## SYNOPSIS
> A poet addresses lovers, friends, enemies, and his family, responding to personal and larger social circumstances in poems ranging from marriage hymns to short, witty lampoons that ridicule their subjects.

about a wide span of subjects. Many of these poems were on subjects of a personal nature, and many were based on the Greek-style lyrics these poets so fervently admired. Catullus was the most famous representative of this artistic movement and of all the New Poets, only his works have survived, thanks to a single manuscript, the Codex Veronensis, once lost, which resurfaced around 1300 and upon which all existing manuscripts are based. Scholars agree that the book of his poetry—called *Carmina* (meaning "Poems" or "Songs")—was arranged by Catullus himself. They showcase his specialties; Catullus is as famous for his erotic love poetry as he is for his scathing epigrams and harshly critical verse. His corpus includes an extensive selection of meters, moods, and themes. Catullus' chief contribution is his so-called "Lesbia Cycle"; a series of poems to his married lover, "Lesbia" (the name derives from the Greek island of Lesbos, home of the poet Sappho, who is perhaps the most famous composer of love poems in antiquity and an important influence on Catullus; see Sappho's *Poems,* also in *Classical Literature and Its Times*). The poems of the Lesbia cycle vividly recreate the rise and fall of a love affair. Catullus' poetry exerted great influence on ancient writers such as Propertius, Horace, Ovid, and Martial, and on Renaissance writers such as Italy's Francesco Petrarch and England's Robert Herrick and Ben Jonson. Commonly considered the most "modern" of ancient poets, Catullus wrote verse that expresses a personal reaction to life events, whether public or private. In so doing, he contributed enormously to our understanding of the late Republican culture of Rome and to the evolution of poetry in ways still felt by new generations of writers.

Events in History at the Time of the Poems

Catullus' Rome—the remarkable individuals. Catullus' poetry is vivid, personal, daring, and unabashedly emotional. It is also a remarkable record of the turbulent era in which he lived. His poems were most likely intended for both oral recitation and publication, and he mentions many known figures of his era throughout his work. Some are lauded; others are pilloried or ridiculed. Because of his works' profuse mixture of history and art and of public figures and private relationships, many readers since his era have assumed that his poetry is autobiography. Though he undoubtedly drew on elements of his own life, it must be remembered that "the tradition in which Catullus wrote called . . . for the artful projection of an image or *persona,* literally a mask behind which the poet manipulates the tools of poetic rhetoric" (Garrison in Catullus, *The Student's Catullus,* p. ix). In keeping with this tradition, literary scholars like to separate the poetic voice, the narrator of his poems, from the biographical man. We cannot be certain that Catullus' famous love affair was "real" in the biographical sense. His poetry, however, is so powerful—and seems so sincerely personal—that many scholars believe his poetic persona to have been inspired by actual events in his life.

This view is supported by the fact that late Republican Rome is well represented in the *Carmina.* Catullus enjoyed skewering prominent citizens with his often obscene accusations. Gaius

Julius Caesar (100-44 BCE) was stung by Catullus' stylus no less than four times (in poems 29, 54, 57, and 93), despite Caesar's friendship with the poet's father. The foremost military man and politician of his day, Caesar achieved his greatest feats after Catullus' death. But already by 60 BCE, he had formed a political alliance with Pompey and Crassus (the so-called "First Triumvirate"). Thereafter, Caesar was elected consul (in 59 BCE) and began his famous campaigns in Gaul (in 58 BCE; see *Commentaries on the Gallic War,* also in *Classical Literature and Its Times*). By this time, the young Caesar was already one of the most powerful figures in the Republic, and seemingly the most ambitious. Yet Catullus felt socially and financially secure enough to criticize Caesar openly for supposedly promiscuous sexual behavior with both genders. Caesar, says the biographer Suetonius, nevertheless favored Catullus. Apparently the poet apologized for his lewdly insulting verses, then was invited to dine with Caesar.

The Roman orator Marcus Tullius Cicero (106-43 BCE) is another towering figure in Catullus' verse. In poem 49, Catullus metes out lavish praise to Rome's greatest speechmaker. Cicero, however, often disparaged the group of writers with whom Catullus associated himself. The orator called them the "new (or novel) poets" (in Latin, *novi poetae,* and in Greek, *neoteroi*), a label reflecting the group's modern approach. This was no compliment. Cicero sneered at the so-called "modernists," though he and their most famous representative, Catullus, circulated in the same social circles. In 58 BCE, Cicero was banished from Rome and his house destroyed, thanks to his political enemy Publius Clodius Pulcher, brother of the most mysterious and provocative woman in Rome in his day. Was this woman also Catullus' love interest "Lesbia"?

Indeed, Clodia Metelli (c. 95 BCE-post 45 BCE) has long been identified as the "Lesbia" of Catullus' most famous poems. Sister to Publius Clodius Pulcher, she was also the wife of Quintus Metellus Celer, consul of Rome in 60 BCE. Her brother's surname, *Pulcher,* means "beautiful" in Latin, and she was, by all accounts, a well-educated and lovely woman as well as an important political asset to her brother. Their family gained distinction as one of the most ancient and well respected in Rome. Catullus evidently met Clodia sometime before 59 BCE and at once began to poetically immortalize his passion for her. How much of the emotion behind his verse belonged to his poetic persona and how much to the real Catullus remains unanswerable. In any case, the relationship soon soured, and in place of the exuberant lyrics testifying to their undying love came insulting diatribes from Catullus, both brilliant and obscene. Clodia's husband had died suddenly in 59 BCE, and as her brother's power grew, she apparently threw off Catullus for another lover—Marcus Caelius Rufus. Caelius, as he was called, had been a protégé of Cicero's.

In 57 BCE Cicero returned from exile and used his relationship with Caelius to take revenge on the man responsible for banishing him, Clodia's brother, Clodius. A case presented itself as a perfect opportunity. Caelius was brought to court on charges of attempting to murder Clodia. Acting as his lawyer, Cicero seized the opportunity to defend Caelius and publicly humiliate the sister of his worst enemy (see *Cicero's Speeches,* also in *Classical Literature and Its Times*). In presenting his case, Cicero famously labeled Clodia "the Medea of the Palatine," the most fashionable district in Rome. In comparing Clodia to Medea, Cicero identifies her with the female paradigm of jealousy and murder in Greek mythology. Medea was infamous as an enchantress who killed her own children to exact vengeance on her husband, who abandoned her for another woman. It was a condemning metaphor.

The charges against Caelius are fashioned in Cicero's court drama as nothing more than the vindictive action of a Roman Medea who had lost her younger lover (Caelius) to another woman. Cicero painted Clodia as an indecent woman with a bottomless appetite for sex who violated Roman custom by choosing her own lovers and who watched young men bathe nude at her famous garden parties. Cicero's biting rhetoric and Catullus' poetic attack both sought to pillory her for her sexual independence. Cicero even slyly accused her of incest with her brother Clodius, describing him as her husband, then adding, "I meant to say 'her brother'—-I'm always making that mistake" (Cicero, *Pro Caelio,* 13.32; trans. Kelli Stanley). In a clever pun in poem 79, Catullus exploits this well-known slander against Clodia to identify his lover. He writes that "Lesbia" prefers "Lesbius" to Catullus ("Lesbius" is the Latin masculine adjective to the feminine *Lesbia,* and so suggests a family relation like brother and sister). He furthermore builds on this beginning, adding that "Lesbius" is "pulcher" (the Latin adjective for "beautiful"), playfully punning on the third element in Clodius' name (Publius Clodius Pulcher). So, to convert Catullan poetics to a

mathematical equation, if Lesbius = Clodius Pulcher, then Lesbia = Clodia.

Aside from people, places in Catullus' Rome—the bustling marketplace, the glittering soirees of the upper classes, the carefully rehearsed drama of the court—are also captured in his lyrics. No ancient poet so vividly records everyday activities of his era, from dining out with friends (poem 12), to bragging in the forum (central marketplace) (poem 10), to demanding repayment of a loan (poem 103). At the same time, Catullus was equally comfortable with the unusual circumstance or topic—a thoughtful and moving elegy to his recently deceased brother (poem 101), a metrically complex narrative about the mythological wedding of Peleus and Thetis (poem 64), or a haunting story of religious fanaticism (poem 63).

Roman patronage. The patronage system was one of the firmest foundations of Roman society. For the Romans, social influence amounted to political clout: there was no dividing line between the social and political spheres. A member of the political elite was powerful precisely because other citizens and at times entire cities came under his influence. How did patronage work? The politically elite individual caused these "clients," as such citizens were called, to vote for or otherwise support issues that he, their patron, favored. In return, the patron bestowed favors on his clients—he might offer them money, legal help, or possibly even a political appointment.

Cicero's life and relationships provide the best documented examples of how the patronage system worked in Rome during the late Republic. Whole towns in southern Italy, the island of Sicily, and the Roman province of Cilicia (in Asia Minor), where he served as governor, were his clients. This meant he could count on their support, quite literally: several of the Italian towns sent men to help protect the orator when he believed his life was in danger in 63 BCE, during his term as consul. In return, Cicero could provide assistance to his clients by recommending citizens to political appointments or providing legal help in a lawsuit. In essence, he represented their interests in the Senate and acted as an advocate for their interests, as they did for his. The total number and status of a politician's clients are what granted him authority in the highly competitive world of the Roman aristocracy. Catullus lived during a transitional time, when Rome was shifting from a Republican form of representative government (albeit one dominated by the Roman aristocracy) to imperial rule under the

Medieval Latin manuscript of the poems of Catullus. Public Domain.

authority of one man. The concept of patronage narrowed in scope during the imperial era, when such competition was no longer a factor because power was concentrated in a single individual—the emperor.

One kind of patronage that continued to flourish during the imperial era was that of a writer and his benefactor. It is unlikely that Catullus himself had a patron—it appears as if his social position was secure enough without one. However, any writer not wealthy or well placed socially needed a patron for material support and to attain sufficient fame. Another writer of the first century BCE, Virgil, did need a patron. The patron, Maecenas, was a key figure in Emperor Augustus' circle and the very model of an ideal literary benefactor.

Writers catered to a small population, which made literary patrons especially important. Studies suggest that books were purchased and circulated among just the elite, the only class capable of enjoying them. Poets also shared their lyrics by delivering them orally. Recitations, a popular mode of literary dissemination, were organized for the enjoyment of the same group. Since writers received no money for publication, they depended on inheritances or the monetary gifts of a patron in order to practice their art. If the status of the poet's own family did not entitle him to a reserved seat at the table, the patron would be his entryway into the highest social circles. In exchange for a chance to write and have his work read and recited among the best people in Rome, the writer would glorify his patron in prose or verse, thus adding to the patron's glory with each copy read or each nightly recital. The opportunity for literary immortality spurred many a politician to support poetry. Cicero spoke on behalf of the Greek poet Archias when Archias was defending his claim to Roman citizenship (Cicero, *Pro Archia*). In the speech, Cicero, Archias' patron, discusses the importance of literature and poets in immortalizing the heroic deeds of generals and leaders. He more specifically notes that Archias is working on an epic poem glorifying his (Cicero's) heroism in saving the Republic during his consulship in 63 BCE (*Pro Archia*, 11.26). Though Cicero almost certainly prevailed in the case, Archias seems never to have finished the poem that he had promised his patron.

Latin lyric. Before Catullus, Latin poetry had been limited to mostly long, drawn-out epics on Roman history. There was some circulation of epigrams—short poems that expressed a certain mood or attitude of the author in a mannered Greek style. Also there were theater pieces that employed a variety of meters. All poetry was based on Greek meter, except the early Saturnian verse, which was an ancient Italian form native to the Latin language. Lyric poetry was a much later literary development in Latin literature, essentially the creation of Catullus and other New Poets in the middle of the first century BCE. Though many of his poems were inspired by earlier Greek poets, Catullus' lyrics stretched the Latin language into a pliable, piquant tongue. His poetry mixed elevated diction and street language and spread the whole on a frame of meter typical of Greek lyric, elegy, and even epic. According to one literary historian, "the poet most responsible for the development of Latin lyric was Catullus, even though the poet Horace later attempted to claim this honor for himself" (Forsyth, p. 4; see Horace's *Odes*, also in *Classical Literature and Its Times*).

Catullus did more than adapt a Greek form to Roman language and literature. In addition to his experiments with his native tongue, he stamped a vividly emotional style on an elegant, learned format. One of his own literary heroes was Callimachus (c. 310-240 BCE), a Greek poet born in North Africa who flourished in Alexandria and was famed for his erudite and concise poetry. In poem 66 Catullus translates into Latin verse a famous elegy by Callimachus known as the *Lock of Berenice*. Gaining distinction himself, Catullus was termed "doctus" (learned or polished) by later poets because his poetry demonstrated an obvious awareness of the Greco-Roman literary heritage. Ultimately his melting pot of Greek sophistication and Roman immediacy, of emotion and precision, and of vulgarity and lyricism make Catullus not only a founder of the Latin lyric, but its ideal practitioner. He invented a type of verse whose appeal would endure for more than 2,000 years. "Of all the Latin poets," observes another literary historian, "Catullus is the one who seems to speak most directly to us" (Wiseman, p. 1).

The Poems in Focus

Contents and arrangement. The *Carmina* numbers 116 poems but actually consists of 113 poems (three poems—numbered 18-20—inserted into the standard collection in the sixteenth century, are now excluded, though the numbering remains unchanged). The poems are arranged in three sections, featuring various rhythmic patterns and subjects.

> **Poems 1-60** are polymetric poems. These generally brief poems are full of insult and satire. Catullus wrote them in several lyric meters (especially in the Greek meters known as the hendecasyallable and choliambic or "limping iambic" meter).

> **Poems 61-68** are seven long poems in additional meters, including elegy-style (or elegiac) couplets and epic-style (or dactylic) hexameters. Elegy, composed in alternating verses or couplets, was originally a meter associated with mourning or warfare in archaic Greece, but already by Catullus' era the meter was associated with epigrams, satire, and love poetry.

Poems 69-113 are poems written in the elegy-style couplet. They include Catullus' moving tribute to his dead brother, epigrams that attack various people, often in obscene language (the so-called "Mentula" poems), and intense declarations of love and its sorrows.

It is generally believed that Catullus himself ordered the poems as described above. In addition to the overarching metrical arrangement, there are many "cycles" of themes—the Lesbia poems, marriage and the gods, the "Juventius" poems (addressed to a young male lover), and invective verse that denounces someone or something. The individual poems are most commonly named by their number. Below are three typical poems in the *Carmina*, all taken from the polymetric section of the work.

Poem 5. Catullus wrote two poems about kissing, but poem 5 is the more well-known, as it embodies the principle of *carpe diem* ["seize the day"], which would later be made famous by Horace.

> Let's live, my Lesbia, and let's love—
> And not give a damn for the gossip
> Of sanctimonious old fools.
> Suns may fall—yet rise again;
> For us, when once the brief light has dimmed
> One eternal night must be slept.
> Give me a thousand, then a hundred kisses
> Followed by a thousand and another hundred
>   more—
> Then again a thousand, again a hundred,
> And when we've kissed so many, many
>   thousands,
> We'll mix them all up, so we won't know the
>   number
> Or so some jealous sort can't jinx us
> When he discovers just how many kisses
>   there are.
>
> (Poem 5, *The Student's Catullus*;
> trans. K. Stanley)

In this early Lesbia poem, the narrator entreats his lover to indulge her passion in a giddy flourish of countless kisses. Yet something ominous hangs over the atmosphere of extreme happiness or euphoria: death (the eternal night) is inevitable—therefore, one must love while one can. Superstition, too, threatens the lovers—if their passion is discovered, they could fall victim to the baneful "evil eye" of the gossip. Their erotic indulgence is dangerous to quantify, even by the lovers themselves, as if analyzing their passion will dissipate or sap it. In keeping with this conviction, the poem concludes on a note of secrecy and protection that balances the expansive exuberance of the first lines. "We'll mix them all

up . . . so some jealous sort can't jinx us" ends the poem, against "Let's . . . not give a damn for the gossip," which begins it.

Poem 13. The following poem offers an entertaining example of Catullus' disarming wit, along with a view of upper-class Roman nightlife.

> You'll dine well at my house, Fabullus
> In a few days, if the gods favor you.
> And if you bring a large and tasty dinner
> And don't forget a pretty girl, and wine, and
>   salt
> And plenty of loud laughter.
> I repeat, if you bring these things, you
>   charmer,
> You'll dine well;
> For your Catullus' wallet is full of spiders'
>   webs.
> But, in return, you'll earn unadulterated
>   affection
> And something even more elegant and
>   precious—
> For I will offer a perfume
> Which the love gods gave to my girl.
> And after you smell it, you will beg the gods
> To change you, Fabullus, into
> One
> Big
> Nose.
>
> (Poem 13, *The Student's Catullus*;
> trans. K. Stanley)

The poet uses the opening lines to describe the most crucial ingredients of a successful evening party and to emphasize the poverty of the male speaker: the man's wallet has been empty so long that it contains nothing but cobwebs. Yet within this short work, the speaker goes on to jokingly explain the state of his finances. He claims that Love, personified by the love gods (Venus and Cupid), has given his Lesbia a precious aromatic perfume. He himself may have in fact given "his girl" the perfume. This would account for both his exaggerated poverty as well as his taking on the identity of the "love gods" when he offers the perfume to Fabullus and then equates himself with the essence of Love in the closing lines. The humor implicit in the idea of Fabullus being transformed into a large nose—in order to smell the rarified scent so much more powerfully—probably contains some sexual innuendo as well. Fabullus is an affectionate nickname for "Fabius." The historical personage, the real Fabius, was a male friend of Catullus who served in the Roman army in Spain.

Poem 49. At first this next poem reads like a high compliment to Cicero, whom everyone would understand was meant by "Marcus Tullius," the first two parts of his name. It was known that Cicero, the great orator, did not restrain himself when it came to self-praise, and Catullus playfully outdoes the orator in the lavishness of this seeming tribute. He even opens with the rhetorical flourish of epic, calling Cicero a grandson of Romulus, one of the legendary founders of ancient Rome.

> To the most articulate grandson of Romulus
> Of those that are, of those that were,
> O Marcus Tullius,
> And of those who will be in later years—
> Catullus gives his greatest thanks.
> He, the worst poet of all. . . .
> As much the worst poet of all
> As you are the best patron . . . of all.
> (Poem 49, *The Student's Catullus*;
> trans. K. Stanley)

But the poem's excessive praise holds true only if Catullus is truly declaring himself "the worst poet of all"—and his tone is seldom so self-critical. Thus, this apparent compliment to Cicero may actually be mocking him.

The poem is a short masterpiece and its meaning is double-edged. Thanks to the flexibility of Latin word order, "the best patron . . . of all" could mean either the *best (of all) patrons*, or the *best patron of everyone*—a sense that would sarcastically refer to Cicero's famous ability to defend anyone—even those whom he had formerly prosecuted. Though the surface meaning expresses gratitude, a mixture of elements suggests irony: the elaborate formality of the poem, Catullus' overly and uncharacteristically modest stance to his own poetry, and, depending on the sense of *best patron of all,* the ambivalent ending (which could either be a compliment or a sarcastic jibe). Without knowing the circumstances under which Catullus wrote the poem, we can never be sure of its purpose.

Roman culture and the poetic insult. That Catullus was able to perhaps slyly attack Cicero or to forthrightly insult Caesar in verse demonstrates not only the comparative artistic freedom of this poet (thanks largely to his high social status), but also the prominence of the insult in Roman culture. The competitive Roman aristocracy used a variety of tools to keep politics and social prominence (which were virtually identical concepts in Rome) on a level playing field. When one person became too powerful, it was quite common to see him publicly attacked or humiliated. A *military triumph* was a rare honor

accorded to a general for military accomplishments, and it physically paraded the leader's troops, booty and captives before the Roman populace. During such a triumph, it was traditional for the Roman soldiery to insult their general with loud and rude name-calling. The insults not only enhanced the tough reputation of their commander; they also helped keep the triumph a symbol of Republican power, one that celebrated the state, not the individual. By demeaning him, the insults kept the general in his place; they firmly anchored him as not the leader but as a citizen of the Republic, dispelling the implicit physical threat of his army marching through Rome. The insults also served an important function in the Roman belief system: they helped prevent a jealous enemy from cursing their general's good luck. By minimizing his good fortune, name-callers sought to avert bad fortune from plaguing him.

Such equalizing social customs were regarded as necessary in the Republic, where power was shared. The insult was one way of emphasizing the importance of the state over the individual, and the fact that it was an accepted part of Roman life meant that Catullus' invective poetry would not have been startling to his Roman audience. In fact, the ancient Athenians, who also lived in a political state in which power was shared, used this same tool. Demosthenes' *On the Crown* is an excellent example of insult in oratory. In theater, too, Greek Old Comedy leveled abusive attacks at public figures such as Socrates or Euripides. (See **On the Crown** and, for theater, see **Clouds;** both also in *Classical Literature and Its Times.*)

Sources and literary context. Catullus was the foremost of the Roman *Novae Poetae* or "New Poets," a literary movement that aimed to transform the Latin language and its literature and to breathe new life into "a poetic tradition [that they] considered stale and stagnant" (Forsyth, p. 1). Others in Catullus' circle of poets included Valerius Cato, Gaius Helvius Cinna (Cinna the poet in Shakespeare's play *Julius Caesar*), and Gaius Licinius Calvus, apparently Catullus' best friend. A description of a day they spent together while trying to outdo each other in on-the-spot verse writing is the subject of poem 50. Another member of the literary circle may have been Parthenius, a Greek poet who encouraged the young men to write in the style of some Hellenistic (Greek) poets in the Alexandrian school, when Alexandria, Egypt, was the center of learning and education in the Mediterranean world.

The already mentioned Greek poet Callimachus, who wrote in this style, became the single greatest influence on Rome's New Poets, including Catullus.

Others influenced the New Poets too. The older Greek verses of Sappho and of Archilochus (a master of satire and invective) especially affected the polymetric poetry that Catullus wrote. For his epigrams, Catullus may also have found inspiration in the native Italian or Etruscan tradition of *Fescennini*. These were blunt, obscene songs performed mainly at weddings to ward off envious spells or prevent the "evil eye" from attacking the fortunate couple. Such a "warding off" function is called *apotropaic*, and it surfaces in the desire to minimize good fortune reflected in Catullus' poem 5.

From this blend of sources, Catullus produced a collection of poetry with the Greek learnedness of Alexandrian scholarship and the raw Roman street language used earlier in plays by Plautus (c. 250-184 BCE) (see Plautus' **The Braggart Soldier**, also in *Classical Literature and Its Times*). Catullus concocted a happy mixture of traditions, thereby becoming the leader of a revolutionary poetic movement and a singular poet of his day.

Impact. Catullus' impact on subsequent Roman poetry cannot be overestimated. He invented words to increase Latin's pliability, and he successfully adapted very complex Greek meters into the far less metrically sophisticated language of Latin. He also had tremendous impact on the poets who followed. Horace's *Satires* owe a large debt to Catullus, and Catullus is mentioned (and venerated) by the epigram writer Martial. Propertius, too, with his love poems addressed to Cynthia, was inspired by Catullus' verses, as was Ovid in his writing of love poetry (see **Roman Love Elegy**, also in *Classical Literature and Its Times*).

During the fourteenth century, copies of Catullus' poems appeared in Italy, perhaps through Petrarch. who followed such verse with his own series of love poems addressed to a woman named Laura. But it was in English poetry, beginning in the sixteenth and seventeenth centuries, through such leading poets as Edmund Spenser and William Shakespeare, that Catullus probably exerted the strongest influence. John Donne and Ben Jonson drew on Catullus' poem 5 for inspiration, as did Andrew Marvell when he penned "To His Coy Mistress." By the end of the eighteenth century (1798), Samuel Taylor Coleridge had translated this same poem into English:

> My Lesbia, let us love and live
> And to the winds, my Lesbia, give
> Each cold restraint, each boding fear
> Of age and all her saws severe.
> Your sun now posting to the main
> Will set—but 'tis to rise again—
> But we, when once our mortal light
> Is set, must sleep in endless night!
> (Coleridge in Duckett, p. 39)

Lord Byron paraphrased a different part of the same poem in the nineteenth century (1806), when addressing his own love interest, Ellen: "Nought should my kiss from thine dissever / Still would we kiss and kiss for ever; / E'en though the numbers did exceed / The yellow harvest's countless seed" (Lord Byron in Duckett, p. 40). In the United States, Eugene Field, best known for his children's poetry, published a translation of poem 5 in 1896, calling it "Catullus to Lesbia."

> Come, my Lesbia, no repining
> Let us love while yet we may!
> Suns go on forever shining,
> But when we have had our day,
> Sleep perpetual shall overtake us
> And no morrow's dawn awake us . . .
> (Fields in Duckett, p. 40)

Every generation of poet—especially those who wrote about love—seems to have rediscovered Catullus' legacy. Far from "the worst of all poets," as he so cheekily dubs himself in poem 49, after 2100 years, Catullus has proven to be one of the most enduring—and enchanting—lyric voices of all time.

—Kelli E. Stanley

For More Information

Adkins, Leslie, and Roy A. Adkins. *Handbook to Life in Ancient Rome.* Oxford: Oxford University Press, 1994.

Catullus. *Catullus: The Complete Poems.* Trans. Guy Lee. Oxford: Oxford University Press, 1990.

———. *The Student's Catullus.* Ed. Daniel H. Garrison. Norman: University of Oklahoma Press, 1995.

Cicero. *Pro Caelio.* Ed. R. G. Austin. Oxford: Clarendon Press, 1952.

Duckett, Eleanor Shipley, ed. *Catullus in English Poetry.* Smith College Classical Studies 6. Northampton, Mass., 1925.

Ferguson, John. *Catullus.* Oxford: Clarendon Press, 1988.

Fitzgerald, William. *Catullan Provocations: Lyric Poetry and the Drama of Position.* Berkeley: University of California Press, 1995.

Forsyth, Phyllis Young. *The Poems of Catullus: A Teaching Text*. Lanham, Md.: University Press of America, 1986.

Hornblower, Simon, and Antony Spawforth. *The Oxford Classical Dictionary*. 3rd ed. Oxford: Oxford University Press, 1996.

Martin, Charles. *Catullus*. New Haven, Conn.: Yale University Press, 1992.

Quinn, Kenneth, ed. *Approaches to Catullus*. Cambridge, England: W. Heffer and Sons, 1972.

Wiseman, T. P. *Catullus and His World: A Reappraisal*. Cambridge: Cambridge University Press, 1985.

Cicero's Speeches

by
Marcus Tullius Cicero

M arcus Tullius Cicero was born January 3, 106 BCE, in Arpinum, a city 70 miles southeast of Rome. As boys, Cicero and his younger brother, Quintus, were trained for legal careers. By the time Cicero tried his first legal case (*For Quinctius*) in 81 BCE, he had already embarked on a writing career, publishing *On Invention* (about finding topics for speeches) and earning a reputation as a skilled poet, though little of his poetry survives. From 79 to 77 BCE Cicero studied rhetoric and philosophy in Athens, Rhodes, and Smyrna (modern Izmir in Turkey). Returning to Rome, he began his political career in earnest, moving up the traditional *cursus honorum* ("course of political offices"). Winning many high-profile legal cases, Cicero earned a reputation as the leading advocate in Rome. He was elected as one of the two consuls for 63 BCE, with the consulship being the highest elected office in the Roman Republic. In his year as consul, Cicero uncovered a revolutionary plot led by Lucius Sergius Catilina (in English, often changed to *Catiline*) to topple the government. The discovery led to Cicero's delivering four speeches against Catilina, the first of which is covered here. For the rest of his life, Cicero considered his exposure of Catilina's conspiracy his greatest achievement and contribution to Rome. In another famous speech that provides a window into the social circles of Rome during his day, Cicero defended Marcus Caelius Rufus, a former lover of Clodia, who was the notorious sister of Clodius, a diehard enemy of Cicero. Cicero himself had a stable marriage for 30 years

> ## THE LITERARY WORK
> Two speeches set in Rome in the mid-first century BCE; delivered in Latin in 63 BCE and 56 BCE.
>
> ## SYNOPSIS
> In *Against Lucius Sergius Catilina I* Cicero exposes to the Roman Senate a conspiracy aimed at the state. His *In Defense of Marcus Caelius Rufus* reveals Cicero's view of the real reason for the case against Caelius— a spurned lover's desire for revenge.

to a woman named Terentia, but in 46 BCE he divorced her and then married an adolescent named Publilia, who, like his first wife, came from a wealthy family. Cicero seems to have been in constant debt (Roman politicians received no salaries, and lawyers could not technically charge for their services, though they were often rewarded in other ways). The ill-fated second marriage lasted only a year. Divorcing Publilia, Cicero retreated to his villa at Tusculum to devote himself to his philosophical writings.

Caesar's murder in 44 BCE drew Cicero back into public life. He struggled to uphold Rome's republican government while others strove to circumvent the constitution and work outside the system. In 44-43 BCE, Cicero delivered 14 speeches that harshly criticized Mark Antony; called the *Philippics*, they were named after some earlier speeches by the Greek orator Demosthenes against Philip of Macedon. Antony retaliated when he gained power, having Cicero executed on December 7, 43 BCE. It is reported that Antony (or his wife Fulvia) ordered Cicero's head and the hand with which he wrote the *Philippics* to be staked up for all to see on the speaker's platform in the forum at the center of Rome. Yet, despite all the official punishment, Cicero has endured as Rome's greatest orator. He considered the first speech featured here (originally called *In Catilinam I*) his greatest contribution to Rome. In the second speech (originally called *Pro Caelio*), he offers a snapshot of aristocratic life in a Rome in political turmoil.

THE *CURSUS HONORUM*

A Roman man who opted for a career in politics had to climb a ladder of governmental positions. By Cicero's time, the progression was more or less standardized. The first rung was *quaestor,* an administrative position that often involved service to the governor of a province and made one a member of the Senate. There were 40 quaestorships in Cicero's day. The next higher position was *aedile,* for which there were four openings a year. Since aediles took charge of public buildings, games, and festivals, the position helped politicians win popularity with the people. After aedile came *praetor,* a mostly judiciary position held by eight Romans at a time. The next rung up was the key position of *consul,* occupied by two men yearly. Consuls commanded the army, conducted the chief elections, presided over the Senate, and enforced Senate decisions. The office of consul usually led to a subsequent position as chief magistrate of a province. Above the consulship came the *censor,* an office in effect only every five years, when two ex-consuls were appointed to conduct a property census. Censors were also in charge of public morals and could expel senators if they wanted. Finally, the hierarchy of offices provided for the special position of *dictator,* an emergency post filled only in times of military crisis and then only for six months.

Events in History at the Time of the Speeches

The social and civil wars. Cicero lived during one of Rome's bloodiest periods, when the Republic was wracked by internal wars. During his teenage years, Rome became enmeshed in the Social Wars (91-89 BCE), fighting against its erstwhile Italian allies, who wanted more rights for themselves, including the right of Roman citizenship. Technically Rome won the Social Wars, but in the end it granted citizenship to the allies, enlarging its electorate (although the new citizens had to come to Rome to vote). Cicero, it will be remembered, came from outside Rome, a fact that would in one respect work in his favor as he rose to distinction: he always had a measure of support from other Italians, especially the wealthy business class.

In the 80s BCE, Rome moved from the Social Wars to a civil war that pitted Lucius Cornelius Sulla Felix against Gaius Marius, who was a distant relative from Cicero's hometown of Arpinum. Sulla won this conflict. At the same time, Rome was fighting a war in the East against Mithridates VI, King of Pontus (in the Black Sea region), who tried to take advantage of Rome's troubles at home to gain power. He put to death perhaps as many as 80,000 Romans—mostly businessmen—who were in Asia Minor. Sulla helped curtail Mithridates' power for the time being. Returning to Rome, Sulla seized control and, in 82 BCE, had himself appointed dictator. He made some attempts to reform Rome's political system, then shocked everyone by retiring and disappearing from the public scene in 79 BCE.

With Sulla gone, his former generals jockeyed for power. The civil war between Marius and Sulla gave rise to many of the figures that would dominate the Roman political scene for the next few decades, including Pompey (106-48 BCE), Crassus (c. 112-53 BCE), and Caesar (100-44 BCE). Cicero was making a name for himself as a lawyer at the time and launching his own political career. In 66 BCE, Cicero gave his first political speech ("On the Command of Pompey"), aligning himself with Pompey in the competition for power. For the rest of Pompey's life, Cicero championed him as often as he could, though he admitted to often being disappointed by Pompey's actions. Cicero was, despite these disappointments, convinced that Pompey would uphold the Senate and constitution of the Roman Republic, whereas popular leaders like Caesar threatened to do away with the system altogether. In terms of his own work, Cicero saw himself as a figure who should constantly strive to get all parts of the Roman state to work in harmony (with the Senate in control) for the good of all Roman citizens.

The First and Second Triumvirates. In 60 BCE, with the help of Pompey and Crassus, Caesar was elected to be consul for the next year. Largely to fight the Senate's attempts to curtail their power, the three—Caesar, Pompey, and Crassus—formed an informal alliance (known now as the "First Triumvirate") and became the effective rulers of Rome. Cicero had been asked to join this alliance, but the orator turned them down. His primary responsibility, as he himself states throughout his career, was to uphold the constitution that he saw as the heart of the Roman Republic; he feared that popular leaders like Caesar would undermine the Republic and try to assert individual rule.

When Crassus died in 53 BCE, the only major players left were Pompey and Caesar. The situation led to another bloody civil war, which began in 49 BCE and ensued for several years before Caesar emerged victorious. Early in 44 BCE, now the solitary power, Caesar had himself declared *dictator in perpetuo* (dictator for life), which demonstrated the obvious: Rome's Republican system of government no longer worked. Caesar now held more power than any one man in Rome for nearly 500 years. Shortly thereafter, on the Ides of March (March 15) in 44 BCE, a group of senators assassinated Caesar, plunging Rome into another period of political uncertainty. Cicero was not asked to take part in the assassination, but after the deed was done, the conspirators sought his approval; his response was lukewarm by his own admission, as he disapproved of the violence and was troubled by the possibility of further instability. Caesar's second-in-command, Mark Antony, emerged as the leader of the faction that backed the murdered leader. At the same time, an heir apparent appeared on the scene—Caesar's 18-year-old adopted son, Octavian (63 BCE-14 CE). Octavian quickly showed himself an able leader and soon had much of Caesar's military force on his side. He allowed the Senate to use him as a force against Antony, and in return secured the consulship in 43 BCE, which gave him a certain legitimacy. Cicero had hopes of playing Antony and Octavian off each other to minimize the threat of either one becoming too powerful, but the two were eventually reconciled and, along with one of Caesar's former lieutenants, Marcus Aemilius Lepidus, formed what became known as the Second Triumvirate. Unlike the First Triumvirate, this arrangement was a constitutional one, ratified by the Senate.

The new leaders drew up a list of people who were considered enemies, calling for their lives and property to be confiscated by the state. According to some sources, there was disagreement over whose names should appear on the list.

Cicero. © Araldo de Luca/Corbis.

Antony demanded that Cicero and his family (his son Marcus, brother Quintus, and nephew Quintus) be included; supposedly Octavian was against this but agreed for the sake of the alliance. Cicero was not alive to see the ultimate dissolution of the Second Triumvirate, which gave way to another civil war. The three leaders squabbled. Lepidus lost any influence he had because of military failures, which Octavian had to reverse. Eventually Octavian and Antony vied for supremacy off the coast of Actium in western Greece in 31 BCE; Octavian won the battle, ending the civil war and becoming master of the Roman world. In 27 BCE, he was given the title *Augustus* (means "reverend," or "deserving reverence"), a milestone that for many scholars signifies the death of the Roman Republic and the beginning of the Roman Empire. Augustus had become Rome's first emperor.

In sum, history shows that the fears of Cicero, who devoted his life to preserving the republican form of government, were well founded. Imperial rule would continue thereafter, with little more than lip service being paid to some vestiges of the Republican government. In their own ways, Caesar, Pompey, and Octavian all did what the target of Cicero's first speech, Catilina, had tried to do 36 years earlier: seize power unconstitutionally by military force. Cicero stopped Catilina, but his political efforts against the others were in vain.

ROMAN NAMES AND ANCESTRY

By Cicero's day, Rome's male citizens had at least two names, while Roman men of the nobility had three names and sometimes more. Cicero had three—Marcus Tullius Cicero, including the following parts:

- The **praenomen** (literally "before the name"). Serving as a first name, the *praenomen* was chosen from a few possible options, including Gaius, Gnaeus, Publius, and Marcus.
- The **nomen** (or name). The most important part, the *nomen* identified the clan to which a person belonged; in Cicero's case, this is Tullius.
- The **cognomen** (like a nickname). The *cognomen* made it possible to differentiate among various branches of a clan, all of which kept the same *nomen*. Thus, Cicero's branch of the Tullius clan was the Ciceros (Latin *Cicerones*), possibly because one of Cicero's ancestors had a scar or a wart shaped like a chickpea.

The naming of children was more or less predetermined, with the eldest son being named after the father. Cicero's father's name was also Marcus Tullius Cicero. Cicero's own son was in turn named Marcus Tullius Cicero. To differentiate, people would sometimes refer to a father as "the elder" and the son as "the younger." If there were more than two people with the same name, they would use other degrees ("the youngest") or a cognomen. Female children, on the other hand, legally had only one name, the feminine form of the clan name. So, Cicero's daughter was simply "Tullia." If Cicero had had more than one daughter, each would have been named Tullia, and then distinguished as "the first," "the second," and so on.

Names were further complicated if a person was adopted. Julius Caesar, for example, had a grandnephew and adopted son who was originally named Gaius Octavius Caepias. When Caesar adopted him, his name was changed to Gaius Julius Caesar Octavianus to show that he now belonged to the Caesarian branch of the Julian clan but had once been a member of the Octavian clan.

A conspiracy to thwart, a friend to rescue. When Cicero was consul in 63 BCE, a nobleman named Catilina threatened the government of Rome. Having failed to win the consulship two times already (he had lost to Cicero the previous year), Catilina seems to have abandoned the constitutional process. Apparently he planned a violent coup, appealing to people from various social classes, in part by promising debt relief. Debt was a constant problem among the Romans. It plagued not only aristocratic family members, who had to spend to maintain their positions, but also the less well-to-do, because interest rates were unregulated and hence outlandishly high. According to some, both Caesar and Crassus secretly supported Catilina's plot but distanced themselves from him when it became clear he would fail. When Cicero discovered the conspiracy and revealed it to the Senate, the main threat was over. Some of the conspirators were executed within the city, despite the uncertainty that existed about a consul's right in times of emergency to execute Roman citizens without a full trial. Catilina, who openly rebelled, was killed along with some fellow conspirators in a battle outside Rome.

Venues for rhetoric. There were three main places in which a Roman orator spoke: in the law courts, in the Assembly, and in the Senate. All of these met in or right off Rome's central *forum* (a name that derives from the Latin *for*, meaning "I speak"). A public square (or rectangle) at the center of town, the forum served as the focal point for government, business, and social affairs. For the orator, it offered different challenges depending on whether he was arguing a law case or speaking in the Assembly or Senate.

Law courts. The courts met in the forum itself and provided entertainment to those who happened by and decided to watch. Both sides agreed on a judge (usually one of the praetors) and established beforehand the actual charges. After this point, there could be no divergence from the charges laid out. The courts conducted their proceedings in the open air, and the juries were large; the norm was probably around 75 people, including senators, businessmen, and other well-to-do Romans. The prosecution spoke first, followed by the defense, after which evidence was produced. That the evidence came only after lengthy sets of speeches highlights the relative importance accorded to rhetoric (the art of public speaking) by the Roman justice system.

The speakers were not lawyers in the modern sense. No one paid for their services; instead, Roman defendants relied on personal connections for legal aid. A powerful Roman often acted as an advocate in exchange for favors (usually votes) from less powerful clients. Though Cicero preferred to speak on behalf of the defendant, he spoke on both sides and was often the final speaker. In delivering *For Caelius* (or *In Defense of Marcus Caelius Rufus*), Cicero was the third of three advocates on the side of the defense.

To modern readers, Roman court speeches seem irrelevant to the case and too concerned with issues of character. *For Caelius*, for instance, is all about Caelius' relationship with a woman named Clodia; Cicero barely mentions any of the real charges. The focus on character, however, was extremely important; it was considered worthwhile to defend a good person regardless of their guilt or innocence in the particular matter at hand. Cicero deems Caelius a good person who can help Rome, and so defends him. As a rule, the most important thing at stake in the Roman courtroom was a person's reputation; a person's actions and general behavior were the central issue.

Assemblies. For close to 500 years (510 BCE-27 BCE) Rome was a republic. In theory, its government was representative, with supreme power resting in the people, although only over time did the ruling class grow to include not just aristocrats but commoners too. By Cicero's day, male citizens (all the free adult males) could vote for magistrates and on issues of legislation. The citizens formed various assemblies In some assemblies, the men voted by tribe (by group determined on a geographic basis); in others, by property rank. In either case, the whole group got one vote. Limited in power, these assemblies did not create legislation (the Senate did); they only voted on it. Each type of assembly dealt with different kinds of legislation and had the power to elect certain officials. The assemblies usually met outdoors in the forum.

Sometimes Romans congregated more informally, providing Roman politicians with opportunities to address the general public. Because there was no way of magnifying sounds, an orator had to be very loud. Cicero tells us that, as a young man, his voice was weak and needed work.

The Senate. In the Senate the focus was on issues of policy, in the development of which oratory played a key role. In theory, the Senate was only an advisory body, and the people voted on all major issues. In fact, however, the Senate was the only consistent power in Rome, as most other offices had terms of only one year. Membership in the Senate was for life and could be taken away only under extraordinary circumstances. Sons tended to inherit the right to belong from their fathers, though the two men who served as the consuls, or chief officials, of Rome selected members of the Senate. As a body, it proposed laws and brought them before the people for a vote, produced resolutions, administered the government's finances, assigned magistrates to the provinces, handled foreign relations, and supervised state religious practices.

Like all other official government posts, the position of senator offered no salary. There were stricter requirements placed on senators than on other officials. Senators could not earn their livelihood from any business that required constant attention. It followed that a Roman had to be quite wealthy to belong to the Senate. The Senate met throughout the year, whenever a consul called a meeting, usually in the *curia*, a building in the forum. Technically these meetings were closed to the public, but they tended to be held with the doors open, so a large crowd could often be found listening outside.

The two consuls for the year had the right to speak first. Next came the *princeps senatus* or "chief of the Senate," followed by former consuls and then former praetors. Given all the rules and the size of the Senate (it grew to 600 members under Sulla), most senators probably did not speak at a given meeting, though it typically lasted from early in the day until the evening. It was considered improper to continue to meet past sunset.

The Speeches in Focus

Contents summary. Cicero, like most politicians of his day, was trained to speak in private court cases as well as in meetings of the Senate. In the course of his lifetime, he delivered all types of speeches. The following two speeches exhibit the different circumstances under which Cicero would speak and the tactics that he and others like him would use.

Against Lucius Sergius Catilina. Cicero delivered this speech to the Senate on November 8, 63 BCE. Instead of meeting in the Senate house, the body met in the Temple of Jupiter Stator ("the Stayer," the deity who stopped battle routs or retreats) on the Palatine hill in the middle of Rome. The case was heard here to guard against attack from the accused party's fellow conspirators. As consul, Cicero convened the meeting and, in this instance, was the first to speak.

Before this meeting took place, Cicero had gathered information from informers about Catilina's plans of conspiracy against the state. Cicero refers to these plans throughout his speech. Because the danger is still at hand, he cannot reveal the names of his informers, so he presents no real proof of his charges. Still he has enough information to charge Catilina under the Plautian law concerning violence. We do not know the exact nature of this law, but surviving references suggest that it involves some kind of armed violence or even an attack on the state, including inciting a public riot (which seems to be how the law was leveled against Catilina). The charges were brought against Catilina sometime after October 21 and before Cicero made his speech on November 8. In the interim, while the investigation was underway, Catilina either had to post bail or give himself over to house arrest; as Cicero mentions, Catilina chose the latter. The Senate had also passed what is known as a "final decree" (*senatus consultum ultimum*), giving Cicero as consul special power to deal with threats to the state. It was under these auspices that he would eventually order the execution of some of Catilina's followers without trial, though with the approval of the Senate. Before Cicero delivered this speech, then, people were aware that Catilina was plotting something, but he had not yet been confronted with any serious charges. This speech marks the beginning of Cicero's efforts to confront this conspiracy head-on.

Cicero begins his speech by revealing to Catilina that he knows all he has been plotting. Also Cicero reminds the Senate that everything he had said would happen did, in fact, happen (about two weeks earlier Cicero had informed the Senate of preliminary aspects of Catilina's plan, including attempted attacks in other Italian cities). Cicero adds new details about the conspiracy, informing the Senate about a recent meeting of the conspirators (at which they talked about how to divide power and whom to kill) and about a subsequent attempt on his own life.

The central debate involves what to do with Catilina. Cicero argues for letting him go as opposed to killing him immediately (as the earlier Romans would have done), since no one knows the extent of the conspiracy. If they kill Catilina, they will not know how many conspirators are left. If they let Catilina go, he will either leave and take his fellow conspirators with him or meet with the army he is amassing and make the threat clear to everyone:

> Make war on your own country; behave like a godless brigand, and revel in the fact. For then it will be abundantly clear that I have not driven you into the arms of strangers, but that you have merely responded to an invitation to join your own friends.
>
> (Cicero, *Selected Political Speeches,* p. 88)

Either way, it will be easier to deal with the problem. Thus, Cicero argues, he is actually serving Rome better by letting such a dangerous enemy go. Cicero is not worried about his own glory, but about the safety of Rome.

The day Cicero gave this speech, Catilina did flee the city to join another disgruntled Roman, named Manlius, who was amassing weapons and recruiting men for a bona fide revolt. After Catilina joined Manlius, they were both declared public enemies. The conspirators left in Rome were put to death, and Catilina and his forces were crushed in battle soon thereafter.

***For Caelius* (or *In Defense of Marcus Caelius Rufus*).** Cicero delivered this speech on April 4, 56 BCE, before the law court, defending his client against charges of "political violence," which included the assault and murder of a foreign envoy.

Before this trial, Rome had been involved with politics in Egypt. An embassy led by a man named Dio had come from Alexandria to Italy to plead a case before the Roman Senate, and a number of the foreign visitors were killed. The trial against Caelius is part of the attempt to call the killers to account. The formal charges against Caelius are 1) civil disturbance at Naples; 2) assault on Alexandrians at Puteoli; 3) damage of the property of one Palla; 4) taking gold for the attempted murder of the ambassador Dio; 5) attempted poisoning of Clodia; and 6) the murder of Dio. For these charges, Caelius faced possible exile or even death. It is perhaps surprising to modern readers that Cicero does not even mention most of these charges. Instead he argues on a more personal level, focusing on issues of character. It is important to note that since in this case he was the last speaker for the defense, it is likely that the preceding two speakers (one was Caelius himself) treated these charges in more detail.

Cicero begins his speech by commenting that an outsider would think this was a serious case, because the court is meeting on a holiday. But the threat is not really serious, Cicero says. The case in fact has much to do with the malice of Clodia, a woman formerly involved with Caelius.

Cicero combats the charges of the prosecution by defending Caelius' character, pointing out that Caelius trained with Cicero as a young man. It is true that Caelius was a friend of Catilina, but this is irrelevant, since many young men were. In any case, Caelius was not part of the conspiracy.

Caelius' only mistake, if any, was moving to a new neighborhood, where he unfortunately met Clodia:

> And that, gentlemen, hints at what I am going to demonstrate when I come to the appropriate point in my speech: namely that all this young man's trouble, or rather all the gossip about him, has been caused by his change of residence—and by this Medea of the Palatine.
> (Cicero, *Selected Political Speeches*, p. 176)

(Cicero here uses Medea as a metaphor for a troublemaker or villainess; see **Medea,** also in *Classical Literature and Its Times.*) After briefly discrediting the witnesses against Caelius, Cicero notes that he will focus on the facts.

Caelius' prosecutors have gone too far in relying on vague moral assertions, says Cicero. There is no crime in enjoying dinner parties and wearing perfume. Instead, this case should focus on particular charges, which involve gold that Caelius allegedly took from Clodia, and his subsequent attempt to poison her. Thus, "the whole of the case revolves around Clodia. She is a woman of noble birth; but she also has a notorious reputation" (*Selected Political Speeches*, p. 183).

But how shall he proceed against Clodia—in a "mild and civilized fashion" or in "the bleak old manner and style" (*Selected Political Speeches*, p. 184)? If the latter, then he will have to call up the spirit of Clodia's famous ancestor, Appius Claudius the Blind, to reprove her. He would certainly say that she is not acting according to the traditions of her family and that her rampant lust is disgraceful. But this is not, continues Cicero, the way he wants to proceed; he will be mild instead, thinking of what her brother, Clodius, would say. He would tell her that she could find many other men for her bed and that she should leave Caelius alone. And how should Cicero treat Caelius? If Cicero treats him like the father figure

CAELIUS, CLODIA, AND CATULLUS

Cicero's speech holds additional interest for students of Roman literature because of the possible identification of Clodia, the woman whom Cicero attacks, with Lesbia, the woman in some of the love poems of Catullus (c. 84-54 BCE; see Catullus' **Carmina,** also in *Classical Literature and Its Times*). Like other Roman love poets, Catullus did not use his mistress' real name. He calls her "Lesbia" in his poetry, as a tribute to the Greek poetess Sappho, who was from the island of Lesbos. While it is impossible to know if Clodia and Lesbia are one and the same (we first hear of the connection from Apuleius [in the mid-100s CE]), Cicero's portrait of Clodia and her circle of admirers casts interesting light on some of Catullus' poetry, much of it a testament to a love/hate relationship. All we know about Clodia's relationship with Caelius is what we hear from Cicero, namely that they had an affair, indulged themselves together, and then separated on unpleasant terms.

in the comedies by a favorite playwright of Rome (meaning Caecilius [d. 168 BCE]), then Caelius only has to claim that it is all gossip. If Cicero treats him like a father in the comedies of another favorite (meaning Terence [d. 159 BCE]), then Caelius need only say that Clodia made the advances. Perhaps Cicero is being overindulgent. Yet morals are not what they used to be; every young man will have his dalliances. Caelius, however, is not out of control, as his ability in oratory shows. Such skill only comes from hard work, and Caelius could not have worked so hard if he was as depraved as the prosecution asserts. Thus, it is only the spurned lover, Clodia, who is responsible for this case being brought against Caelius.

Cicero addresses the charges that Caelius borrowed money from Clodia to hire hit men to kill Dio, the ambassador from Alexandria. If Clodia knew what the money was for, says Cicero, then she was involved; if she did not know, then her relationship with Caelius was not as close as the prosecution says. Also, Lucceius, the man who hosted the ambassador, had testified as to Caelius' innocence (his testimony was read in court but is not included with this speech). Accordingly, the Clodii (Clodia's family) must have fabricated these charges.

Regarding the poison that Caelius allegedly tried to give Clodia, Cicero notes that the prosecution never really provided a motive. Caelius would have to have conspired with Clodia's slaves, who are known to be unreliable and more like bedmates than slaves. Would Caelius be this foolish? As for poison, Clodia should be careful mentioning poison, considering how suddenly her husband, Quintus Caecilius Metellus Celer, died. The whole story of Caelius trying to acquire the poison is a poorly constructed tale and is nothing but a ludicrous stage show with no proof behind it.

In summation, Cicero remarks that the law on violence is to be reserved for serious charges and that Caelius has done nothing to merit such a charge. It is clear to everyone that he is a respectable young man; he lapsed only in being briefly involved with Clodia after moving into her neighborhood. When he broke off this affair, she acted out of hatred and had this case brought against him, concludes Cicero. Caelius is such a noble young man and such a benefit to the Republic that he should be acquitted—and he was.

Rhetoric in the Roman Republic. In his defense of Caelius, Cicero must deal with Caelius' prior association with Catilina, whom Cicero himself had earlier maligned. In the later speech, to suit the case, Cicero provides a very different portrait of Catilina, one that speaks of him as impressing even Cicero as a man full of positive character traits:

> Let no blame attach to Caelius because he associated with Catilina. For that is something which he has in common with many people, including persons who are beyond reproach. Indeed, I declare that I myself was once nearly deceived by him. I took him for a patriotic citizen attached to our national leaders, and for a faithful and reliable friend. I did not believe his misdeeds until I saw them; until I had actually caught him in the act I had no suspicion they even existed. If Caelius, too, was one of his numerous friends, he would, I agree, be right to feel annoyed that he made such a mistake, just as I sometimes regret my own misconception about the man. But the fact should certainly not give my client the slightest cause to fear that the friendship might be used as the basis for an indictment in court.
>
> (*Selected Political Speeches*, pp. 173-174)

This part of Cicero's speech highlights the training of Roman orators, who learned numerous approaches to public speaking, including arguing both sides of an issue as the occasion arose. Like many of his contemporaries, Cicero was trained from an early age to engage in all the aspects of oratory because it was so integral to the life of a Roman politician. His defense of Caelius shows the importance of rhetoric, as it "is another example of Cicero's success in defending a client by cleverness, wit, and style rather than by evidence or proof" (Kennedy, p. 139).

Cicero's training allows him to draw on a wide range of skills in the speech against Catilina and the speech for Caelius. The first speech is full of invective; the second, a speech to entertain. His contemporaries regarded Cicero as a master of both types. A highly serious speech, the one against Catilina involves attacking a person to convey a threat at hand. In keeping with this purpose, Cicero stresses Catilina's vices and emphasizes (and perhaps overemphasizes) the danger to Rome.

In the second speech, a legal defense, Cicero focuses on entertaining his listeners as the final speaker in a case that took place on a holiday. He fills his speech with jokes, quotations from comic plays, and humorous caricatures of some of his personal enemies and their ancestors: "The speech for Caelius is by common consent Cicero's wittiest" (MacKendrick, p. 264). Throughout the speech, for example, Cicero makes cutting remarks about Clodia's character, as when he alludes to a possible incestuous relationship between her and her brother Clodius:

> Indeed, my refutation would be framed in considerably more forcible terms if I did not feel inhibited by the fact that the woman's husband—sorry, I mean brother, I always make that slip—is my personal enemy. Since that is the situation, however, my language will be as moderate as I can make it, and I will go no farther than my conscience and the nature of the action render unavoidable. And indeed I never imagined I should have to engage in quarrels with women, much less with a woman who has always been widely regarded as having no enemies since she so readily offers intimacy in all directions.
>
> (*Selected Political Speeches*, p. 184)

Cicero identifies wit as one of an orator's essential tools. In the following passage, he rails at the dismal qualities of a group of orators that he has heard, and in the process reveals what he considers to be the best attributes of a skilled orator:

> Of them there was not one who gave me the impression of having read more deeply than the

average man, and reading is the well-spring of perfect eloquence; no one whose studies embraced philosophy, the mother of excellence in deeds and in words; no one who had mastered thoroughly the civil law, a subject absolutely essential to equip the orator with the knowledge and practical judgement requisite for the conduct of private suits; no one who knew thoroughly Roman history, from which as occasion demanded he could summon as from the dead most unimpeachable witnesses; no one who with brief and pointed jest at his opponent's expense was able to relax the attention of the court and pass for a moment from the seriousness of the business in hand to provoke a smile or open laughter; no one who understood how to amplify his case, and, from a question restricted to a particular person and time, transfer it to universals; no one who knew how to enliven it with a brief digression; no one who could inspire in the judge a feeling of angry indignation, or move him to tears, or in short (and this is the one supreme characteristic of the orator) sway his feelings in whatever direction the situation demanded.

(Cicero, Brutus, pp. 279-281)

Reading, studying philosophy and Roman history, mastering civil law, joking at an opponent's expense, moving from the particular to the general—these skills make up the ideal rhetorician as Cicero saw it (in 46 BCE) and, to some extent, as Cicero's contemporaries would have seen it. In the two speeches covered here, Cicero places most emphasis on the ability to sway the feelings of the audience.

The importance of rhetoric in ancient Rome cannot be overstated. Persuasive speech was one of the main paths to distinction, especially for those, like Cicero, who did not hail from a distinguished aristocratic family. To a great extent, it was Cicero's speaking ability that allowed him to rise to the highest-ranking office in Rome.

Ability in rhetoric and military affairs went hand in hand. A soldier was supposed to be able to exert influence at home as well as on the campaign: "Rhetoric is the special speech of the state. It is also, in effect, the occupation of off-duty soldiers" (Habinek, p. 2). For Cicero, who had little military experience, rhetorical ability was especially key. Throughout his career, Cicero, his own best public relations agent, reminded listeners that he had saved his country without bloodshed by foiling the Catilinarian conspiracy. In terms of the accolades he received for his role in the affair, Cicero did achieve something akin to military success, as the rewards, praise, and political clout given him were usually reserved

for victorious generals. He was also the first to be called "Father of the Fatherland," a title later used by Caesar Augustus.

Sources and literary context. To produce the two speeches featured here, Cicero drew upon his rhetorical training in both Rome and Greece. Several years after the Catilinarian affair, Cicero likened his speeches against Catilina to Demosthenes' speeches against Philip of Macedon, called the "Philippics." Cicero considered the Athenian speaker Demosthenes (384-22 BCE) to be one of the orators most worth imitating, and the "Philippics" were famous for their invective. Cicero would return to them when he wrote his own "Philippics" against Mark Antony.

In his defense speech for Caelius, Cicero shows the influence that drama had on his style. Roman comedy exercised a particular influence; Cicero even discusses characters from the plays of Caecilius and Terence (see Terence's **Brothers**, also in *Classical Literature and Its Times*). To discredit the witnesses' story that his client tried to poison his former lover, Cicero treats it as if it were part of a play, which allows him to critique it for its lack of sensible plot. As suggested, such a treatment was especially appropriate because this speech was delivered during a period of holiday celebration, when such comedies were performed (MacKendrick, p. 264).

Reception. Of these two speeches, the one against Catilina has proven to have a more lasting influence, in part because Cicero himself continued to remind people of his role in suppressing what he paints as one of the most serious threats in Roman history. He refers to this threat numerous times in later speeches and in "On His Consulship," a poem he wrote in 60 BCE (only fragments of this poem survive today). His repeated references to the conspiracy and the enduring popularity of his speeches helped build an image of Cicero as the savior of Rome.

A younger contemporary of Cicero's, however, provides a slightly different account of the conspiracy. Gaius Sallustius Crispus (86-c. 35 BCE) wrote a historical monograph about Catilina and his plot that gives Cicero a less individual role than the orator gives himself. On the other hand, Sallust, as he is called, refers to Cicero's speech against Catilina in positive terms: "the consul Cicero, alarmed by Catilin[a]'s presence or, it may be, moved by indignation, rendered the state good service by delivering a brilliant oration, which he afterwards wrote down and published" (Sallust, p. 198). Sallust also tells us of Catilina's reaction to the speech, including a derogatory remark about Cicero being "a mere immigrant," a reference to his status as a "new man," not a proud descendant of a forefather who had served before him, but the first in his family to become consul (Sallust, p. 198).

Later references to Cicero often focus on his oratory in general rather than on specific speeches. According to Quintilian (c. 35 CE-before 100?), famous as a writer on and teacher of rhetoric, Cicero was considered the ideal orator; as Quintilian himself saw it, Cicero was "the name not of a man, but of eloquence itself" (Quintilian in Rawson, p. 299).

—Kristopher Fletcher

For More Information

Austin, R. G. *Cicero. Pro M. Caelio Oratio*. Oxford: Clarendon Press, 1960.

Catullus. *The Poems of Catullus*. Trans. Guy Lee. Oxford: Oxford University Press, 1991.

Cicero. *Selected Political Speeches of Cicero*. Trans. Michael Grant. London: Penguin, 1989.

Cicero. *Brutus*. Trans. G. L. Hendrickson. Loeb Classical Library. Cambridge, Mass.: Harvard University Press, 1962.

Everitt, Anthony. *Cicero: A Turbulent Life*. London: John Murray, 2001.

Habinek, Thomas. *Ancient Rhetoric and Oratory*. Oxford: Blackwell, 2005.

Kennedy, George A. *A New History of Classical Rhetoric* Princeton, N.J.: Princeton University Press, 1994.

MacKendrick, Paul. *The Speeches of Cicero: Context, Law, Rhetoric*. London: Duckworth, 1995.

May, James M., ed. *Brill's Companion to Cicero: Oratory and Rhetoric*. Leiden, The Netherlands: Brill, 2002.

Rawson, Elizabeth. *Cicero. A Portrait*. Ithaca, N.Y.: Cornell University Press, 1983.

Sallust. *The Jugurthine War/The Conspiracy of Catiline*. Trans. S. A. Hanford. New York: Penguin Books, 1963.

Warmington, E. H., ed. *Ennius and Caecilius*. In *Remains of Old Latin*. Vol. 1. Loeb Classical Library. Cambridge, Mass.: Harvard University Press, 1988.

Clouds

by
Aristophanes

Not much is known about the personal life of the poet Aristophanes, whose comic genius is undisputed. The dates of his birth (c. 446 BCE) and death (c. 386 BCE) are estimates. We do know that Aristophanes was educated at Athens, of which he was a loyal, if consistently critical, citizen. Of the 44 plays ascribed to him, 11 survive. These 11 testify to Aristophanes' talent for biting public satire. In addition to *Clouds*, which lambastes the philosopher Socrates and his followers, Aristophanes' other works are all ruthlessly critical of various aspects of Athenian society and public policy: The so-called "peace-plays" (*Acharnians*, *Peace*, and *Lysistrata*) attack Athens' seemingly endless war with Sparta. Aristophanes criticizes the corrupt and overused legal system of Athens in *Wasps*; he condemns the "new" poetry of Euripides in *Frogs*. And lest we think that Socrates was the only well-known public person to figure so prominently in Aristophanes' works, another surviving play (*Knights*) criticizes and even ridicules the Athenian ruler Cleon. In fact, so fierce was Aristophanes' criticism that Cleon brought a lawsuit against the poet, charging him with slander and treason.

The comedy of Aristophanes' day typically transgressed acceptable behavior. Still, the coarse, vulgar, and even obscene nature of Aristophanes' comedies has led to a great deal of speculation about his traits. A few have assumed that the poet-playwright himself must have been fairly crude and somewhat of a buffoon, while others have pointed out the need to distinguish

> **THE LITERARY WORK**
>
> A Greek play set in Athens in the early fifth century BCE; first performed in 423 BCE but surviving only in the revised version of 418-416 BCE.
>
> **SYNOPSIS**
>
> The somewhat bawdy political satire demonstrates the dangers that Socratic philosophy poses to Athens.

between his morals and manners and those of his characters. With so little information to go on, scholars have been unable to settle the debate about what kind of man Aristophanes was. Most, however, describe him as a man who was conservative, romantic, and even reactionary. Plato's dialogue the *Symposium* depicts Aristophanes as circulating in the highest levels of society, a portrayal that many consider fairly accurate. Though his comedies are bawdy and ribald, like the others of his age, the poet had high expectations for his comedies and what they could accomplish. In all his plays, his harsh criticism of the modern approach to values, morals, art, public policy, and ways of viewing the world demonstrates an unequivocal longing for Athens' "good old days" and a desire to uphold the religious and social conventions of tradition. Aristophanes is said to be the first literary critic, and he judged poetry based on what he thought was its primary function—to make us better human beings. His

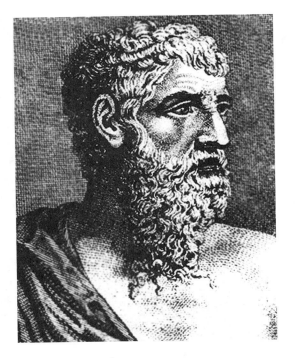

Engraving of Aristophanes.

Clouds aims to save Athens from the "danger" of developments in Greek philosophy.

Events in History at the Time the Play Takes Place

Determining who the real Socrates is. There is no doubt that the character of Socrates in Aristophanes' *Clouds* was inspired by the historical Socrates (469-399 BCE), the famous philosopher who was tried, found guilty, and sentenced to death by the city of Athens in 399 BCE, 24 years after the performance of Aristophanes' play. Since Socrates did not produce any written documents, we must glean much of what we know of him from the writings of others, especially his student Plato. Plato believed that *Clouds* was in no small measure responsible for Socrates' conviction. Although Plato's *Apology* reads like a transcript of the trial and seems to have been written fairly soon after Socrates' death, scholars disagree about how much of the dialogue records actual events and how much artistic license was taken. Another friend of Socrates, Xenophon, wrote his own *Apology,* and its account of the trial differs. In any case, Plato's *Apology* condemns the way that Aristophanes portrayed Socrates as irresponsible and characterizes him very differently than *Clouds.*

In Plato's *Apology,* Socrates begins his defense to the jury by outlining the charges against him. He divides his accusers into two groups, the "old" and the "new." The new accusers are the men who have charged him with the specific, "official" offenses for which he is on trial: not believing in the city's gods and corrupting the youth of Athens. But the old accusers, according to Socrates, are far more dangerous; they have been slandering him and turning public opinion against him for years. Socrates refers to a "certain comic poet," to whom members of the jury listened when they "were most trusting, when some of you were children and youths" (Plato, *Apology,* 18d). Socrates laments that this comic poet (Aristophanes) had more than 20 years to malign him, while Socrates had only one day to change their minds. He summarizes the charges leveled against him:

> "Socrates does injustice [commits a crime], and is meddlesome, by investigating things under the earth and the heavenly things, and by making the weaker speech the stronger, and by teaching others these same things." It is something like this. For you yourselves also used to see these things in the comedy of Aristophanes: a certain Socrates was carried around there, claiming that he was treading on air and spouting much other drivel.
>
> (*Apology,* 19c)

In response, Socrates simply states "None of these things is so" (*Apology,* 19e). He asks if any jury member has ever heard him conversing about these topics, and if so, to come forward. None can, he adds, because he never discussed the things Aristophanes has accused him of, and the same holds true for the rest of Aristophanes' rumors about him.

Based on what we know of Socrates from Plato and other sources, Aristophanes' portrayal is not entirely accurate. First, Plato's Socrates is not concerned with the physical sciences and investigations into material causes, although he admits in another dialogue by Plato (*Phaedo*) that he pursued such inquiries as a youth. Second, Plato's Socrates never taught or purported to teach anyone how to "make the weaker speech the stronger." Moreover, he, in contrast to the sophists, did not place high value on wealth. He *did* refute prominent men in public discussions, often making them look ridiculous in the process. He admits too that some of his followers learned to speak cleverly by his example. And he is indeed revolutionary in pushing for a new understanding of the virtues, which is no longer founded on the traditional myths about the Greek gods. However, Plato's Socrates also champions justice and virtue, while Aristophanes' Socrates in *Clouds* is a pompous charlatan who undermines traditional morals and values, such as piety and a son's obedience to his father.

Would Aristophanes have been aware of these differences between his portrayal of Socrates and the actual man? Perhaps he was, but took artistic license with his subject. Aristophanes might have concluded that Socrates would make a useful scapegoat and prime example of all that was wrong with the sophists and philosophers. According to the *Apology*, Aristophanes' play did great damage to Socrates' case. There are scholars, however, who counter that "the power of Aristophanic satire to influence political events is grossly overestimated" and "no firm evidence can connect the philosopher's condemnation and the comic poet's caricature" (Segal, p. 45). According to this view, Socrates merely provided great material for comic inspiration. Not only was he well known in Athens as an eccentric who went around barefoot questioning people, but, as already noted, his unusual physical characteristics (such as his odd gait) made him ideal for comic caricature.

The conservative poet and a city in flux. When Aristophanes wrote his plays, Athens was undergoing a dramatic transformation. Advances were being made in art, architecture, music, literature, science, and philosophy, and these advances posed serious challenges to established religious tradition and its associated morality and ethics. Militarily, Athens took an ever more aggressive stance, pursuing a policy of expansion and internationalism that brought a flood of merchants, traders, and soldiers to the city, all foreigners who introduced the Athenians to new beliefs, value systems, and worldviews. Tributes from a growing empire and the discovery of silver deposits outside Athens, at Laurion, further enriched the city. In keeping with these developments, the pursuit and accumulation of wealth became a central concern for an increasing number of people. These are all changes that Aristophanes perceived as threats to the old, established order in Athenian society and that he criticized in his works.

In such an atmosphere, it is easy to see why Aristophanes would have viewed Socrates and his philosophy as a serious threat to Athenian society. Socrates did not believe in accepting conventional wisdom or public opinion on any given subject. His whole method of philosophy was one based on questioning. As practiced by Socrates, philosophy consisted of verbal exchanges, wherein an important query such as "What is the nature of justice?" was discussed with conversation partners or interlocutors in a series of question-and-answer sessions. In the *Apology*, Socrates claims that of all the Athenians he has questioned, the politicians and the poets have been the most ignorant. Not only do they know nothing about justice or politics or the gods; they pretend that they do! Socrates reasoned that he was more knowledgeable than the Athenians he questioned: "I am wiser than this human being. For probably neither of us knows anything noble and good, but he supposes he knows something when he does not know, while I, just as I do not know, do not even suppose that I do" (*Apology*, 21d). For Socrates, wisdom amounted to recognizing one's ignorance. This realization marked the beginning of the quest for the truth, which required one to question and even to blatantly disregard established opinions and myths. No doubt the spirit of rebellion in this approach alarmed Aristophanes, a poet who has been characterized as "The great reactionary who opposes with all the means at his disposal all the new-fangled things, be it the democracy, the Euripidean tragedy, or the pursuits of Socrates" (Strauss, *Rebirth*, p. 103).

The sophists. Traveling scholars and intellectuals known as sophists (derived from the Greek term for "wisdom") traveled the Greek world, lecturing and teaching for a fee mathematics, history, natural philosophy, rhetoric, and more. Too diverse in their interests and approaches to be considered a unified movement, sophists elicited both positive and negative reactions from the cities they frequented. Several sophists were highly regarded, and many had successful careers. The Athenian statesman Pericles took pride in his friendships with the sophists Damon and Anaxagoras, both active during the fifth century BCE; also he invited another well-known sophist, Protagoras of Abdera (c. 481-420 BCE), to Athens.

Other Athenians considered sophists a disruptive and possibly dangerous element in society, mainly because of their argumentative skills, which could be used to undermine or at least call into question the validity of traditional religion, morality, and government. Many also feared the sophists' possible influence on the aristocratic youth of fifth-century Athens. Three of Socrates' former disciples—Alcibiades, Critias, and Charmides—became involved in anti-democratic activities, colluding with Sparta, Athens' enemy in the Peloponnesian War, and initiating a coup known as the reign of the Thirty Tyrants. When democracy was restored in Athens, Socrates himself fell under suspicion.

Those hostile to the sophists, like Plato, tended to depict them mainly as clever rhetoricians, convincing speakers who used the art of persuasion to win any argument, without any regard for right and wrong. Indeed, the modern term "sophistry" is often applied to clever, specious arguments.

Probably the public at large found it hard to distinguish between the kind of arguments the sophists were famous for and what Socrates referred to as his questioning of Athenian citizens in pursuit of the truth. At the time, there was no clear-cut distinction between the two types of discussions, so Socrates tended to be tarred with the same brush as the sophists. If Aristophanes shared the prejudices of his fellow Athenians, he might have truly believed Socrates to be a sophist and thus have focused on all that the philosopher had in common with that disreputable group: intellectual pretension, an outlook that embraced moral relativism rather than strict morality, and a skepticism that made people question basic values, like belief in the gods and obedience to the laws.

The Play in Focus

Plot summary. Aristophanes' *Clouds* uses its main character to present Socrates and his philosophy as a corrupting and dangerous influence on Athens. Strepsiades, the main character, is a simple, traditional farmer from the countryside who has married unwisely, relates poorly with his son, and is struggling with huge debts because of his family's extravagance. His wife, a "classy, luxurious, aristocratic" townswoman, has very expensive tastes (Aristophanes, *Clouds*, line 48). He blames her not only for spending so freely but also for spoiling their son, Phidippides, whose costly habits she encourages. The son dabbles in horses and gambling, indulging his taste for racing with an abandon that has thrown his father into debt. After a night of fretting, Strepsiades comes up with a plan: he decides that he and his son will attend Socrates' school, which is known as the thinkery, to learn how to make the "weaker speech the stronger" and thus convince his creditors to forgive his debts.

At the thinkery, a student of Socrates recounts the brilliant investigations conducted by his teacher that very day. Socrates figured out how

Socrates conversing with students. © Archive Photos. Reproduced by permission.

many of its own feet, or how far, a flea could leap when it jumped from person to person by making wax slippers for the flea and measuring them. Also he sought to discover whether "gnats hum through their mouth or through their behind" by examining the intestines of a gnat, after which he declared that the "gnats' anus is a trumpet!" (*Clouds*, lines 158-159). When Strepsiades wonders why a group of young men are bent over with their own anuses looking at heaven, the student replies that their anuses are learning astronomy. As if these descriptions of Socrates and his pursuits were not derogatory enough, the student makes it known that Socrates, while "gaping upwards" as he investigated "the courses and revolutions of the moon" was "crapped on" by a lizard from the roof (*Clouds*, lines 193, 171-173).

Not only does Aristophanes portray Socratic investigations as useless and ludicrous in the extreme, but also as distracting Socrates and his students to such an extent that they forget even their most basic needs. The student tells Strepsiades that Socrates was so engrossed in his studies the previous evening that he forgot to prepare or get them dinner, so they all went hungry. In much the same way, philosophy seems to have distracted Socrates and his students from Athenian politics; the student has no idea what Strepsiades is talking about when he refers to the Peloponnesian War. Philosophy, as Aristophanes depicts it, is concerned only with scientific knowledge and universal definitions and concepts. It posits a Socrates who seeks a philosophic detachment from the affairs and concerns of the city. In fact, when the play first introduces Socrates, he is physically detached from the city. He comes into view suspended in a basket in the air, attempting to emulate the free and formless clouds, which he chooses to worship instead of the traditional gods. For Aristophanes' Socrates, "Zeus does not even exist . . . the true gods are the Clouds" (West in Aristophanes, p. 29).

Aristophanes makes his attack on philosophy even more explicit in the subsequent scene. When Phidippides, the son, decides to enter the thinkery, the characters representing Just Speech (an old man) and Unjust Speech (a young man) have a contest to determine which will have the privilege of educating him. Just Speech blames Unjust Speech for the current corruption of the city's youth, who no longer have respect for their parents, the gods, or the city and its laws. Moderation and restraint are the behaviors to practice, says Just Speech. In the good old days, when Just Speech was the norm, the youth were silent, respected their elders, and became courageous and strong through gymnastics and athletics. Unjust Speech counters with arguments of its own. It warns the young man of all the pleasures he will have to give up in the name of moderation: lovers, drinking, gambling, delicacies. If he acquires Unjust Speech, he will be able to act however he wants. Next, Unjust Speech points out contradictions in the various elements of religious traditions. It ends its "pitch" with a flourish, pointing to the audience and stating that even the leading men of Athens, its orators, lawyers, and poets, no longer live by the beliefs that Just Speech espouses. Not knowing how to respond, Just Speech concedes defeat.

The next time we see Phidippides, he has returned home from the thinkery after completing his study of the unjust speech. He instructs his father in what arguments to make to his creditors in order to avoid paying his debts. Strepsiades manages to use these rhetorical tricks successfully, which makes him deliriously happy until he gets into an argument with his son. The next scene finds him running from the house and hurling names at his son, calling him a wretch and a father beater. Apparently Phidippides physically assaulted his father during an argument, and

when Strepsiades told him to stop, the son refused, claiming he could use his argumentative powers to persuade his father that parent-beating is just.

At this point, Strepsiades realizes the consequences of what he has done and the full ramifications of life in a society that throws off its laws and traditions. Distraught, he asks the god Hermes what to do and is told to burn down Socrates' thinkery. Fire is the only way to destroy it; lawsuits or other civil remedies will not do

THE PELEPONNESIAN WAR

The war between Athens and Sparta from 431 to 404 BCE was the most important and possibly the most troubling aspect of Athenian policy during Aristophanes' lifetime. During the war, Sparta besieged Athens, forcing its citizens to remain within the city's defensive walls, which the Spartans could not breach. The plague that resulted from those crowded, unhealthy conditions claimed about a quarter of the Athenian population, including the leading statesman Pericles. Aristophanes criticized the war and its political supporters in no fewer than three plays, the most famous of which is *Lysistrata* (411 BCE), a hilarious comedy wherein the women of Athens conspire to end the war by withholding sex from their husbands (also in *Classical Literature and Its Times*). In *Clouds*, the main character, Strepsiades, often refers to this war, most humorously when he asks one of Socrates' students to move Sparta farther away from Athens on the map they are studying.

because the philosophers can simply talk their way out of them. Heeding the advice, Strepsiades sets the edifice ablaze to rid society of the disease of unjust speech.

Aristophanes' true targets. While Aristophanes' play makes Socrates the butt of the satire, it in fact attacks pretentious intellectuals in general for their impact on daily life in Athens. Using Socrates as a representative appears to have been a practical choice, since most of the other intellectuals were foreign migrants to Athens and so less familiar to the Athenian public. Also Socrates was someone with physical characteristics—a snub nose, large eyes, and an odd gait—on which a comedy could capitalize. Moreover, he was known for his habit of drawing people into conversations in public.

Besides employing these character traits, Aristophanes assigned to Socrates "all the intellectual theories and activities which he wished to ridicule"; that some of them did not really apply to Socrates mattered little to him (MacDowell, p. 132).

Aristophanes' reasons for making Socrates his comic scapegoat apparently stem from a harmful legal development in the city, for which the playwright blamed the intellectuals. Many Athenians were bringing weak cases before the courts and setting out to win nonetheless. By Aristophanes' day, it had become possible for the side with the weaker evidence to prevail if the evidence was presented cleverly enough. Plato's student Aristotle described such a scene, using the example of a man accused of assault: a physically weak man charged with assault might argue that his weakness made him an unlikely culprit; charged with the same crime, a strong man could argue that he would not have committed it because others would immediately suspect him on account of his strength. Aristotle notes that both arguments *appear* probable, but the strong man's argument only *seems* to make sense because of the way it is presented: "[T]his is what making the worse argument the better is" (Aristotle in MacDowell, p. 128).

Such attempts at legal wrangling were attributed, with some justification, to the teachings of the sophists. Protagoras, perhaps the first man to identify himself as a professional sophist, became most widely associated with the claim that he could teach people "how to make the worse argument the better" (MacDowell, pp. 128-129). He was also credited with the authorship of a treatise on argumentative techniques. However, Protagoras was not universally condemned as a malign influence. He also taught the art of citizenship, arguing that, whatever sorts of things seem just and honorable to a given city are indeed that way as long as the city deems them so. Others of the age condemned Protagoras for not drawing an absolute distinction between truth and falsehood, or right and wrong. While Protagoras employed persuasion to a higher purpose, hoping to develop good citizens, his followers—who arrived in Athens during the 420s—perfected the art of persuasion for its own sake. Several used it to excuse terrible crimes, arguing, for example, that if a king wins power (the end), it justifies his having killed or banished others (the means) to attain it.

Sources and literary context. Although *Clouds* does not name real individuals, it "contains more or less clear allusions to theories and activities which we can attribute to Anaxagoras, Protagoras, Diogenes, and Antiphon," among others (MacDowell, p. 130). The poetic comedy furthermore reflects a very real competition between poetry and the fledgling field of "philosophy" (not yet known by that name when *Clouds* was written). The poets of fifth-century Athens vied with the newer intellectuals for the position of supreme dispensers of wisdom in society. Aristophanes manipulates it so that poetry, in the form of his play, emerges the victor.

Aristophanes' plays are among the earliest surviving comedies in Western civilization; we only have descriptions or fragments of earlier comedies. The particular comedic style of fifth-century Athens is referred to as "Attic Comedy" or sometimes as "Old Comedy." The Greek *komoidia*, from which "comedy" derives, refers to a song, often sung by a group of costumed men who would entertain audiences at festivals or other public events. Not much is known regarding the transformation of *komoidia* into comic plays, but apparently Old Comedy preserved the antagonistic relationships between characters (or between a character and the chorus), as well as the biting social and political critiques of the costumed men. The plays of Old Comedy seem to have revolved around issues of the day. In the fifth century BCE, comic plays were directly political in a way that tragedy was not; their jokes had a bite and were

OLD COMEDY, MIDDLE COMEDY, NEW COMEDY

Toward the end of Aristophanes' career, Old Comedy fell into a serious decline. Aristophanes' last plays, particularly *Plutus* (388 BCE), heralded the beginning of "Middle Comedy," in which the chorus was less involved with the actors (as was already in the case in tragedy) and the satire targeted political figures less often. In the fourth century BCE, the poet Menander completed the transformation of the genre into "New Comedy," wherein luck and fortune provide plenty of surprises and plot twists. Gone were the biting satire and scathing criticism of Aristophanes; Menander replaced them with more subtle observations about people and human nature in what can best be described as comedies of manners. Significantly, Menander's career covered a period in which democratic rule was replaced by an oligarchy in Athens. The more biting or critically laced comedy would reappear once the democracy was restored.

often meant to be taken very seriously. Although the comedies generally featured a fantastic plot, they were "part of a real democracy" (Boardman, et al, p. 168). They commonly ridiculed key figures in society or portrayed them as villains, and also showed irreverence for myths and other sacred beliefs. The chorus, made up of 24 members, figured prominently in Old Comedy, playing a dramatic role and at times speaking directly to the audience for the poet.

Along with its cutting edge, Old Comedy had some standard lyrical and humorous elements. It contained beautiful melodies and meters as well as base verses that referred to bodily functions, such as vomiting or evacuating one's bowels. Costuming and staging contributed to the comic effect. It is not only "the chamberpot [toilet] that is so omnipresent," in the comedies but the phallus as well, notes one scholar (Segal, p. 36). In Old Comedy all the actors, even those portraying gods, wore costumes featuring a dangling phallus, which could be manipulated by a string to indicate sexual excitement.

Performance and impact. Aristophanes' comedies and those of his peers were performed at festivals for Dionysus, god of wine and merrymaking. These festivals, each of which lasted several days, were state holidays. They were held twice a year, in spring and winter, and they included religious rites such as prayer and an animal sacrifice. In Aristophanes' age, Athens went to great effort to finance lavish performances of plays at the festivals. Men wealthy enough to finance a dramatic production were required by law to do so at least once in their lives. Athens' theater could hold around 17,000 spectators—perhaps half the citizenry. Among the festival events were various processions and musical competitions, but most important was the staging of tragic and comic plays. Normally three tragedy writers would compete in a festival, each of them producing several plays, and five comic poets would compete, each with a single play.

Unfortunately for Aristophanes, *Clouds* did not do as well as he hoped, placing third (last) in the Great Dionysia festival, a fact that the Chorus laments in the later, revised version of the play that survives. We have no explanation of why the judges relegated the play to third place, but Socrates had recently behaved bravely on Athens' behalf in the real-life Battle of Delion,

so it may have been the wrong time for a play that ridiculed him, although there were other plays that did (Dover, p. 119). Sorely disappointed, Aristophanes, who regarded *Clouds* as his finest work, began to revise the play in hopes of being given another chance to present it at a festival. This hope probably never materialized, since plays were seldom performed twice. Most scholars agree that the version that has come down to us is a partially revised second draft.

Along with the rest of Aristophanes' surviving plays, *Clouds* is still regularly performed, sometimes with modern touches. A production by the Ancient Comic Opera Company in Toronto, for example, set Aristophanes' lyrics to the music of Gilbert and Sullivan, Wagner, and Mozart. The production also characterized Phidippides in a way that included impersonations of popular screen stars (Johnny Depp, Jim Carrey, Keanu Reeves, and William Shatner), and it referred to the television game show *Jeopardy*. Such adaptations testify to the continuing popularity of the playwright and his works.

—Despina Korovessis

For More Information

Aristophanes. *Aristophanes' Clouds.* In *Four Texts on Socrates.* Trans. Thomas G. West and Grace Starry West. Ithaca, N.Y.: Cornell University Press, 1984.

Boardman, John, Jasper Griffin, and Oswyn Murray, eds. *The Oxford Illustrated History of Greece and the Hellenistic World.* Oxford: Oxford University Press, 1986.

Dover, K. J. *Aristophanic Comedy.* Berkeley: University of California Press, 1972.

Grant, Michael. *The Classical Greeks.* New York: Charles Scribner's Sons, 1989.

MacDowell, Douglas M. *Aristophanes and Athens.* Oxford: Oxford University Press, 1995.

Nichols, Mary P. *Socrates and the Political Community: An Ancient Debate.* New York: State University of New York Press, 1987.

Plato. *Apology.* In *Four Texts on Socrates.* Trans. Thomas G. West and Grace Starry West. Ithaca, N.Y.: Cornell University Press, 1984.

Segal, Erich. *The Death of Comedy.* Cambridge, Mass.: Harvard University Press, 2001.

Strauss, Leo. *The Rebirth of Classical Political Rationalism.* Chicago: University of Chicago Press, 1989.

——. *Socrates and Aristophanes.* Chicago: University of Chicago Press, 1966.

Commentaries on the Gallic War

by
Julius Caesar

For a modern audience the enduring reputation of Gaius Julius Caesar (100-44 BCE) is owed partly to his infamous portrayal in Shakespeare's *Julius Caesar* and partly to his political and military domination of the Roman world during the 50s and 40s BCE. Born on July 13, 100 BCE into a noble family, Caesar benefited from his family connections, which included an uncle, Gaius Marius, who was a general and seven times occupied the office of consul (the highest ranking government official in Rome). Like most young noblemen in Rome, Caesar served a military apprenticeship. In 79 BCE he won the Civic Crown (a military decoration of oak leaves woven into the shape of a crown) for saving the life of a Roman citizen, an indication of greater things to come. He also showed himself to be a rising star in the Roman law courts. His success as an orator led to political and social advancements, which by the late 60s BCE had placed him among the most important men in the state.

Caesar's fellow Romans understood that a considerable factor in his rise to power was his rhetorical and literary talent. According to his contemporary, the famous orator Cicero, Caesar spoke and wrote on a daily basis. In his youth he composed the poem *Praises of Hercules*, a tragedy called *Oedipus*, and a collection of sayings (apophthegms). Later works include his dispatches to the Senate, letters to Cicero and others, two speeches against the Roman statesman Cato the Younger (95-46 BCE), and

THE LITERARY WORK

Annual reports by Julius Caesar of his campaigns in Gaul and Britain between 58 and 52 BCE, published in Latin in the 50s BCE, plus a supplement for 51 and 50 BCE by Caesar's general Aulus Hirtius, published in the mid-40s BCE.

SYNOPSIS

Appointed governor of Rome's ancient provinces of Gaul and Illyricum, Julius Caesar battles the tribes of Gaul, Germany, and Britain. Despite setbacks, Caesar establishes Roman dominion over the area that is modern-day France and the low countries (Netherlands, Belgium, and Luxembourg).

the poem *The Journey*. An interest in grammar and style resulted in *On Analogy*, a lost work in which Caesar advocated the lucid, pristine style used in his two surviving historical works: *Commentaries on the Gallic War* and *Commentaries on the Civil War*. The two works arise out of a chaotic period of self-styled military rulers, growing corruption of governmental processes, gang warfare, and civil war. Intended to do more than document events, the commentaries are the product of someone who understood the importance of propaganda to increase his power and to achieve his autocratic ambitions.

Julius Caesar. Bettmann/Corbis. Reproduced by permission.

Events in History at the Time of the Commentaries

Politics in the Late Republic (146 BCE–44 BCE). In theory, the governance of the Roman state was shared jointly by the Senate and the people of Rome (*senatus populusque Romanus*). In practice, power rested in the hands of a small landowning minority who controlled the Senate. Their complex systems of patronage and factional alliances allowed them to influence public assemblies, fix elections, and control access to the magistracies (political offices). As one historian remarks, "The Senate was a club, and club members decided whether or not a man had the social profile necessary for membership, whether or not he could add to the prestige of the group" (Veyne, p. 95). A politician's self-worth, or *dignitas*, was closely associated with the glory (*gloria*) and honor (*honos*) he attained from military accomplishments and political offices. Such military and civic distinctions bestowed *auctoritas*, an authority that entailed the respectful admiration of one's contemporaries. Each successive generation could augment the *auctoritas* earned by their ancestors and increase their own *dignitas* through the position, status, and wealth of their family. Access to the highest magistracies was restricted, even to nobles. Out of every eight praetors elected each year, only two could become

consuls, and every year there were more ex-praetors competing for those top two positions. It was even harder for the lower classes and equestrians (businessmen with property worth at least 400,000 *sesterces*—Roman coins) who had neither the necessary *dignitas* nor *auctoritas*, although from time to time the nobles were willing to concede the consulship to a new man, or *novus homo*, who showed promise. Within the Republic, ancient eulogies and funerary inscriptions testify to a preoccupation among the oligarchy with magistracies and priesthoods, public building works, military successes, and, above all, contests to prove themselves "first," "best," or "greatest." The citizens of ancient Rome competed fiercely to gain access to the Senate, to ascend the *cursus honorum* ("ladder of honors"), and to become consul. In the last century or so of Republican life in Rome, "it mattered who was first and who was second" (Wiseman, p. 7).

Political offices of the Roman Republic. The leading citizens of Rome could hold a number of political positions as follows, from highest to lowest:

Dictator A six-month (or shorter) appointment held by one Roman citizen. His power superseded all other magistrates in a military (and occasionally domestic) crisis.

Censor Two censors were elected every five years from among the ex-consuls. In office for 18 months, they took the census, controlled public morals, and had the right to expel senators from the Senate.

Consul The two annually elected chief magistrates of Rome. They commanded the army, conducted the chief elections, presided over the Senate, and implemented Senate decisions.

Praetor At the time of the Gallic War, Rome elected eight praetors a year. The *praetor urbanus* (city praetor) was the supreme civil judge of Rome. The *praetor peregrinus* (alien praetor) dealt with lawsuits involving foreigners. The praetors oversaw the permanent law courts.

Aedile Each year four aediles were elected. They maintained the streets of Rome, regulated traffic and the city water supply, and were responsible for the upkeep of public buildings. They also oversaw markets and weights and measures as well as public festivals and games.

Quaestor Financial and administrative officials, the 20 quaestors at the time of the Gallic War maintained public records and oversaw the treasury. They acted as paymasters to generals on campaign and supervised the sale of war booty.

Tribune of the People (tribunus plebis) A one-year position held by 10 men, charged with defending the legal interests and property of plebeians (common people). Tribunes could veto Senate laws, and the election and actions of magistrates.

In Caesar's day, senators typically belonged to one of two groups:

Optimates These senators followed the traditional senatorial routes to authority and political success, and were often seen as a less democratic and more conservative group.

Populares These senators used the people to achieve their political aims and objectives, and were often seen as a more democratic and radical group.

The Late Republic and the rise of Caesar. During the second century BCE the traditional systems of the Roman Republic began to fracture in the face of protracted foreign wars, an influx of foreign slaves, and extraordinary opportunities for wealth and prestige to be amassed by generals and their legates (military commanders). Citizens often returned home to find their land allotments in ruin. Many had to sell them to wealthier landowners to avoid bankruptcy. The era saw the growth of enormous estates (the infamous *latifundia*), whose rise came at the expense of the smaller landowners. Unable to compete, they quit their holdings and flocked to Rome with other dispossessed citizens. The resultant urban problems led to genuine attempts at political and social reforms (in 133 and 123-122 BCE), aimed at relieving the plight of Rome's poorer classes. Yet in the struggle for personal *auctoritas*, it became clear that an ambitious politician could use the people to his advantage. The so-called *popularis* politician exploited the needs of the people to serve his own self-interested ends. None understood this more than Caesar's uncle, Gaius Marius. Marius had first gained public recognition in 134 BCE as a military tribune at Numantia in Spain. Later, as tribune of the people, he passed a measure limiting the influence of the nobility at elections. In 108 BCE Marius campaigned for the consulship of 107 BCE. His platform rested on the inability of nobles in the Senate to find either a diplomatic or military solution to the conflict in Numidia. After he was elected consul, Marius promptly enrolled in his army numbers of the urban proletariat, the *capite censi*, those without the necessary property qualification. Working closely with the army, tribunes, and the people, Marius's military successes in Numidia resulted in his election *in absentia* for the consulship of the Republic in 104 BCE. Further successes against tribes from Gaul prompted the people to re-elect Mar-

ius consul every year until 100 BCE. With the help of the tribunes of the people, he distributed cheap grain to the poor and guaranteed land to his veteran troops. The presence of Marius's army veterans in the forum, Rome's civic and commercial center, effectively silenced any opposition. For the first time the Roman army no longer owed allegiance to the state but to the general who could provide for them. The influence of Marius cannot be overestimated, either on Roman politics in the first century BCE or on the young Caesar. Later on, in 68 BCE Caesar was to win acclaim as the new champion of the *populares* when he proudly displayed images of Marius at his aunt's funeral.

THE REPUBLICAN *CURSUS HONORUM*

The *cursus honorum,* or "ladder of offices," was the means by which a Roman official, or magistrate, advanced politically. Each office bestowed a certain amount of *potestas* (political authority) or *imperium* (military authority). The highest offices, praetors and consuls, had the right to wage war, to punish citizens, and to impose the death penalty. These officials had aides called *lictors,* who carried bundles of rods, known as *fasces* (for flogging) and (when the official was a consul) also carried axes (for executions).

A law of 180 BCE, the *lex Villia Annalis,* prescribed a fixed order in which magistracies had to be held and also prescribed minimum age limits for each office. The conventional order was quaestor (28), praetor (39), consul (42), and potentially censor (which could only be held after the consulship), although a magistrate could also hold the tribunate or aedileship (the former traditionally held before, and the latter after the quaestorship). After their year of office in Rome, praetors and consuls sometimes governed outside Rome in a province, where they were known as propraetors or proconsuls. A dictatorship was a temporary six-month appointment made by the Senate only during times of war. By the time of the Gallic War, Rome had decreed that a ten-year interval was necessary between the holdings of the same office.

Caesar grew up during the bloody struggle between Sulla and Marius in the 80s BCE. At the time, Sulla earned the dubious distinction of being the first Roman citizen to march an army on the city of Rome. Later he demonstrated how easy it was to pervert the traditional Republican constitution when he had himself declared dictator for the purpose of rewriting the constitution. Sulla subsequently tried to shore up the power of the *optimates* (those who believed in the traditional authority of the Senate) and to prevent popular agitation by muzzling the tribunes of the people. But his measures were short-lived as the actions of certain nobles undermined his constitutional reforms.

Men like Lepidus or Catiline, thwarted in their attempts to gain power or to pass social legislation, raised armies against the state in 78 and 63 BCE respectively. Others such as Pompey the Great used their popular influence to gain extraordinary commands. At the age of 25, Pompey joined Sulla and campaigned in Italy, Sicily, and Africa, then refused to disband his army unless he was granted a triumph (a celebratory procession that wound its way through the streets of Rome to the temple of Jupiter Optimus Maximus on the Capitoline Hill). In 78 BCE Pompey marched against Lepidus and in 77 BCE demanded the power of proconsul to fight in Spain against the rebellious general Sertorius. In the two decades that followed, Pompey used his military successes against Rome's enemies to persuade the Senate to give him a consulship and further commands. His actions resulted eventually in the annexation of the Near East and an ingenious settlement that took account of the complex geographical and political factors of the region. Despite a magnificent third triumph, the Senate's refusal to ratify Pompey's eastern settlement led him to seek support from equally ambitious nobles.

As a young man, Julius Caesar served briefly in Asia between 80 and 78 BCE before returning to Rome to make a name for himself in the law courts. He studied rhetoric and philosophy in Rhodes, after a brief delay *en route* when he was captured by pirates. On returning to Rome, Caesar was elected to the college of pontiffs (a priesthood with duties ranging from overseeing state sacrifices to serving as an advisory body on sacred law). Thereafter, he occupied a series of political offices: military tribune in 72 BCE, quaestor in Spain in 69 BCE, aedile in 65 BCE. Meanwhile, he lent support to Pompey and earned popular favor as aedile through his lavish games. Undoubtedly Caesar's skill as an orator was a powerful factor in his election in 63 BCE to *pontifex maximus,* head of the college of pontiffs. Election to the office of praetor followed. Though an able orator, Caesar understood that true power at Rome was possible only through military success and a supportive army. To ad-

vance his ambitions, he joined forces with Pompey and Crassus in an unofficial political alliance known as "The First Triumvirate," a pact that foreshadowed the end of the Republic.

The three allies engineered a consulship for Caesar in 59 BCE, during which he oversaw the ratification of Pompey's eastern settlement and supported the financial interests of Crassus in Egypt and the East. The coalition was cemented by the marriage of Pompey to Caesar's daughter, Julia. At the end of the year the triumvirs conspired to award Caesar a five-year governorship of some Roman provinces in Europe—Illyricum and Nearer Gaul (or Cisalpine Gaul, Gaul on this side of the Alps). To this was soon added Farther Gaul (Transalpine Gaul). In Roman politics, alliances were always unstable because of external pressures and wavering ambitions, and this three-way coalition was no different. In 56 BCE Caesar's command in Gaul was extended for another five years, but the peace did not last long. In 54 Julia died and in 53 Crassus was killed in Parthia, seeking military glory. Meanwhile, the yearly reports from Gaul and Britain were adding to Caesar's growing popularity. Caesar's fearless style of generalship, marked by his famed *celeritas* (speed) was as impressive as his oratory. Exposing himself to the same risks as his troops, he won their confidence and trust. In Rome, the people celebrated. Twice Caesar had been granted unprecedented periods of public thanksgiving and prayers to the gods. All of this was enhanced by Caesar's own reports to the Senate and his *Commentaries on the Gallic War,* which kept the Roman people abreast of his latest conquests.

Power became ever more polarized in the hands of Caesar and Pompey. To make matters worse, there was open gang warfare between their supporters in the streets of Rome, which prevented elections being held for 52 BCE. Pompey was granted special authority to deal with the crisis. He tried to grant Caesar the special privilege of being eligible to stand for the consulship *in absentia* so that when he finished his Gallic command he could step directly from one office to the next without a year's interlude that would have left him open to prosecution. A small group of powerful senators, however, continued to provoke a rift. A request that Caesar's command in Gaul be extended from 51 through 49 BCE was rejected. To add insult to injury, in 51 BCE, one of the consuls, M. Marcellus, publicly flogged a senator from Novum Comum (a town in Gaul) to demonstrate that the town did not enjoy Roman citizenship. In 50 BCE, the question of a successor to Caesar became a pressing issue. When the measure to remove Pompey and Caesar from their commands was vetoed, some senators requested that Pompey protect the Republic from the ambitions of Caesar. On January 10 and 11 of 49 BCE, Caesar, his *dignitas* irreparably slighted, crossed the Rubicon, a stream separating Gaul from Italy. After several years of civil war from which Caesar emerged victorious, in 44 BCE he had himself declared *dictator in perpetuum* (dictator for life), which demonstrated the obvious: the Republican system of government no longer worked. But the Roman world was not yet ready for a monarch. After Caesar's assassination, it would take another 14 years of civil war for the emergence of an autocrat who was capable of unifying the Senate and the people of Rome.

Relationships with Gaul prior to 58 BCE. In Caesar's time the ancient region of Gaul (roughly equivalent to France, Belgium, the Netherlands, and Luxembourg) was inhabited by disparate nations, or tribal groups. Along with the tribes of Britain, Germany, and the Danube region, these nations were known collectively as the Celts. The Romans had a deep-rooted fear of Celtic tribes because of past history. At the river Allia, on July 18, probably in 390 BCE, a notorious "black" day (*dies nefastus*) in the Roman calendar, the Senones inflicted a crushing defeat on Rome's legions and then sacked the city of Rome, destroying houses, temples, and public records. In the centuries that followed, Celtic tribes continued to encroach on Italian territory and to offer aid to Rome's enemies. Rome annexed Nearer Gaul, but matters came to a head in the late second century BCE, when two German tribes, the Cimbri and the Teutones, migrated there. In 113 BCE they roundly defeated the Roman consul Cnaeus Papirius Carbo at Noricum (in Nearer Gaul). Fortunately for Rome the tribes moved westward toward Switzerland. They were joined on their march by another tribe known as the Tigurini. In 109 BCE the Romans sent out a new army under the consul M. Iunius Silanus to defend the new Roman province of Farther Gaul. Silanus was defeated. A new army and a new general, L. Cassius Longinus, advanced against the Tigurini. In 107 BCE his army was defeated and forced to march under the yoke as if they were oxen, a terrible humiliation. In 105 BCE at Arausio (modern Orange, France) the combined armies of the Cimbri and Teutones decisively routed the Roman legions of the proconsul Quintus Servilius Caepio and Cnaeus Mallius with the reported loss of 80,000 men. In 102 and

101 BCE, under the command of Marius, the Romans defeated first the Teutones and then the Cimbri. This gave some relief to the Romans, ever mindful that the Gauls had once sacked Rome.

In the years that followed Marius's victory, the inhabitants of Farther Gaul were heavily taxed and closely monitored. In 63 BCE, a Gallic tribe, the Allobroges, who had long been faithful to the Roman cause, rebelled when their appeal for debt relief fell on deaf ears. At Rome it must have seemed that the threat posed by the tribes of Gaul would never be averted. A few years later, when the Senate added Farther Gaul to Nearer Gaul as one of Caesar's territories, he redirected his attention toward the unruly tribes of Gaul.

The Commentaries in Focus

Contents summary. Seven "books," which are in fact parts of a single book, make up *Commentaries on the Gallic War*. The books are further subdivided into chapters, or subsections. Beginning with 58 BCE, each book narrates one year of campaigning. An additional book by Caesar's general, Aulus Hirtius (consul 43 BCE), relates events of 51 and 50 BCE.

The events in Caesar's commentaries unfold in chronological order, always by year and subdivided by summers and winters, resembling the method characteristic of Roman historiography. Beginnings of books are often marked off with threats to the peace of Gaul, which continue to justify Caesar's presence in the territory. Endings are signaled by a return to winter quarters (books 1, 3, 5, and 6) or the more climactic reference to public thanksgivings in Caesar's honor (2, 4, and 7).

Book One (58 BCE). "As a whole Gaul is divided into three parts..." (*Gallia est omnis divisa in partes tres...*) (Caesar, *C. Iulii Caesaris Commentarii rerum gestarum,* book 1, chapter 1; trans. A. Nice). Instead of a conventional prologue, Caesar begins with a description of Gaul and its inhabitants. His troops' first action is against the Helvetii (chapters 2-29), who have been inspired by their chieftain Orgetorix to migrate from their homeland (in modern-day Switzerland) to Gaul through Roman territory. Moving swiftly, Caesar prevents them from crossing the Rhine River. When they threaten two Gallic tribes—the Aedui and Allobroges—that are Roman allies, Caesar pursues the Helvetii to the town of Bibracte, where his troops defeat them.

In the second part of the book Caesar responds to a request from the tribes of Gaul for aid against a German chieftain named Ariovistus (chapters 30-59). Reports of incursions by two Germanic peoples (the Harudes and the Suebi) inspire Caesar to march north to prevent Ariovistus from capturing a major town of Gaul—Vesontio. Here Caesar confronts the first threat to his command when his inexperienced military tribunes and other high officials search for reasons to avoid combat. The "mutiny" spreads and Caesar is compelled to call a council of war. In a remarkable speech, he shames the remainder of the army into action. There ensues a battle in which Caesar's legions rout the army of Ariovistus. Leaving his lieutenant Titus Labienus in winter quarters among the Sequani, Caesar returns to Nearer Gaul to conduct the administrative duties of a governor.

Book Two (57 BCE). In light of a reported conspiracy by the Belgae, a group of tribes in Northeastern Gaul, Caesar raises two new legions and marches on their territory. He crosses the river Axona (now called Aisne) to aid the town of Bibrax. Routing the enemy, he presses forward into the territory of other Belgic peoples. He advances on the Bellovaci, who surrender themselves to the Romans. At the river Sabis (now Sambre) the ferocity and courage of the Nervii tribe proves a worthy match for Caesar's legions. The tide is turned by the arrival of Rome's Tenth Legion and the Romans are victorious. Caesar draws attention to the significance of the victory and takes the opportunity to display his famous *clementia* (clemency):

> So ended this battle, by which the tribe of the Nervii was almost annihilated and their name almost blotted out from the face of the earth. On hearing the news of it, their old men . . . sent envoys to Caesar and surrendered. . . . Caesar, wishing to let it be seen that he showed mercy to the unfortunate suppliants, took great care to protect them from harm, confirmed them in possession of their territories and towns, and commanded their neighbours to refrain from injuring their persons or property.
>
> (*Gallic War*, 2.28; trans. S. A. Handford)

Only the Aduatuci tribe now withstands Rome's might. Caesar agrees to spare the people but only if they lay down their weapons. Attempting to deceive Caesar, the Aduatuci appear to comply but then attack the Romans by night. Caesar's response is savage. All 53,000 Aduatuci are sold into slavery.

Meanwhile, on the Atlantic coast, Publius Crassus, the son of the triumvir, secures the submission of the maritime tribes. By the end of the year Gaul is at peace, and Caesar is rewarded

an unprecedented honor—a 15-day period of thanksgiving to the immortal gods.

Book Three (56 BCE). With the armies settled in winter quarters, Caesar's lieutenant Servius Galba attempts to open up a secure trade route across the Alps. The peace of just a few weeks earlier is shattered by an unexpected onslaught on Galba's camp. Galba shows initiative and the Romans counterattack from the gates of the camp:

> It was a complete reversal of fortune: the Gauls who had counted on capturing the camp were surrounded and cut off. Of the forces that had taken part in the attack—known to number over 30,000—more than a third were killed; the rest fled in terror and were not allowed to halt even on the mountain heights.
>
> (*Gallic War* 3.6; trans. S. A. Handford)

After repulsing the enemy, Galba retires to the Roman province, where he winters amid the Allobroges.

In 56 BCE, assuming peace, Caesar heads for Illyricum. His back is not long turned before the Veneti, a tribe of seafarers, reveal themselves to be unwilling subjects. They capture some Roman officials and demand the return of their own hostages. Caesar hastens back to the province. Doing battle, his Roman fleet proves itself superior to the enemy in oarsmanship, speed, and tactics. The Veneti Senate is executed by sword, and the remaining adult males are sold as slaves. In other arenas his lieutenants quell some unruly tribes, including rebels in the territory of Aquitania (in today's southwest France). With winter approaching, Caesar plunders territory of two Belgic peoples in the North—the Morini and the Menapii.

Book Four (55 BCE). Book Four reminds us of the ever-present German threat to peace in Gaul. The Usipetes and the Tencteri cross into Gaul under pressure from the Suebi, who are the largest and most warlike of the German nations.

> It is said that they have a hundred cantons, each of which provides annually a thousand armed men for service in foreign wars. Those who are left at home have to support the men in the army as well as themselves, and the next year take their turn of service, while the others stay at home.
>
> (*Gallic War*, 4.1; trans. S. A. Handford)

With typical *celeritas*, or speed, Caesar marches against the German tribes, defeating them in two separate engagements. In a demonstration of Roman might, Caesar crosses into Germany in order to deter further German incursions into the new Roman province and to encourage another Germanic group, the Ubii, to resist the Suebi. Just ten days later, a 400-yard Roman-built bridge spans the Rhine. After 18 days of maneuvers and raids, his point made, Caesar withdraws to Gaul.

Now late in the summer, Caesar directs his attention toward Britain. He offers reasons for campaigning outside his province: the Britons have been helping the tribes of Gaul fight the Romans and Rome will gain knowledge of Britain's land and peoples. Unnerved by the unusual spectacle of charioteers in Britain and by the British weather, the Romans survive an ambush and an attack on their camp. Despite their success, the Britons petition for peace and promise to return hostages. Fearing the approach of winter, Caesar departs for Gaul. Once there, he sends his men against the Morini and Menapii, who have renewed hostilities. In honor of his achievements, the Senate grants Caesar 20 days of public thanksgiving.

Book Five (54 BCE). Caesar orders the construction of new ships to facilitate a full-scale invasion of Britain. Setting out for Britain from Portus Itius (perhaps today's Boulogne), he leads an army of 2,000 cavalry and five legions (approximately 25,000 infantry soldiers). His movement inland is temporarily checked when news arrives that a storm has destroyed 40 ships. After ordering new ships built, Caesar continues his advance and encounters Cassivellaunus, lord of the land north of the Thames River. Though the Britons keep bothering his men on the march, Caesar eventually reaches the Thames. There he receives the surrender of the Trinobantes and other tribes and attacks the stronghold of Cassivellaunus. Cassivellaunus attempts to divert Caesar's attention by urging tribes in Kent to attack Caesar's naval camp. When this attack fails, the Britons sue for peace. Cassivellaunus promises hostages and a yearly tribute, after which Caesar returns to Gaul and settles his troops in winter quarters.

Suddenly a revolt breaks out incited by a member of the Treveri tribe, a Gallic tribe that provided Caesar with cavalry. The Roman winter camps are assaulted by the Gauls. The first blow is struck by Ambiorix, chieftain of the Eburones, a Belgic tribe. The Nervii then besiege the camp of Quintus Cicero. When his slave brings word to Caesar, Caesar advances swiftly to break the blockade of Cicero's camp. Report of the victory causes the rebellious Treveri to call off another planned attack, but they continue to incite rebellion and taunt the Romans. Eventu-

ally the Romans launch a counterattack, their cavalry pursuing and beheading the Treveri leader, Indutiomarus. The forces of the Eburones and Nervii disperse. The book ends laconically: "After this deed Caesar found Gaul somewhat quieter" (*Commentarii rerum gestarum,* 5.58; trans. A. Nice).

Commentaries on the Gallic War

BRITISH CHARIOT FIGHTING

These are the tactics of chariot warfare. First they drive in all directions hurling spears. Generally they succeed in throwing the ranks of their opponents into confusion just with the terror caused by their galloping horses and the din of their wheels. They make their way through the squadrons of their own cavalry, then jump down from their chariots and fight on foot. Meanwhile the chariot-drivers withdraw a little way from the fighting and position the chariots in such a way that if their masters are hard pressed by the enemy's numbers, they have an easy means of retreat to their own lines.

Thus when they fight they have the mobility of cavalry and the staying power of infantry; and with daily training and practice they have become so efficient that even on steep slopes they can control their horses at full gallop, check and turn them in a moment, run along the pole, stand on the yoke and get back into the chariot with incredible speed.

(*Gallic War* 4.33; trans. A. Wiseman and P. Wiseman)

Chariots had not been encountered by a Roman army in over 150 years. In this passage, Caesar, who tended to avoid "the unusual word as a sailor avoids a rock," captures their novelty by his introduction of the nouns *essedum* ("chariot") and *essedarius* ("charioteer") into the Latin language. His vivid description of the British charioteers soon gripped the Roman imagination. For not long after the conquest of Gaul, the unusual antics of the *essedarii* made them a regular feature in the Roman amphitheater.

Book Six (53 BCE). After amassing fresh troops to counter the threat of war, Caesar finds himself occupied in the North, again in Menapian territory. After Caesar's lieutenant Labienus routs the Treveri, his force and Caesar's set out once more for Germany. Over one-third of the book is then taken up with a lengthy digression on the differences between the societies of Gaul and

Germany. Finally, failing to engage the Suebi, Caesar returns to Gaul, leaving part of the Roman-built bridge standing as a warning to the Germans. In the territory of the Eburones, Caesar sets up camp, appointing Cicero to guard the baggage. The Romans launch simultaneous attacks against the restless northern peoples—the Menapii, Aduatuci, and the Treveri. In the absence of Caesar, the cavalry of a west Germanic group, the Sugambri, attack Cicero's camp. Cicero's band, foraging away from the camp, is caught off guard. Only through instances of individual valor do the Romans retain the camp. The Sugambri retire across the Rhine. Caesar's arrival soon after revives morale. He ends the year harassing the enemy, searching for Ambiorix, chief of the Eburones, a Belgic tribe, and conducting an enquiry into a conspiracy by two Gallic tribes (the Senones and Carnutes). The ringleader, Acco, is flogged to death in accordance with Roman custom, and Caesar heads back to Italy.

Book Seven (52 BCE). The first words of Caesar's climactic seventh book: *Quieta Gallia* ("Peaceful Gaul") could not have been more precisely chosen. They are ironic in view of the tumultuous events then happening in Rome (Caesar notes that he had learned of the murder of a leading Roman political figure, Clodius [*Gallic War*, 7.1]), and the events about to unfold in Gaul itself.

Book seven is the story of Vercingetorix, a young nobleman of another Celtic tribe, the Arvernians, who becomes the leader of the resistance movement in Gaul. The narrative paints Vercingetorix as a suitably intelligent and resourceful opponent to the Roman commander. After he fails to relieve the town of Avaricum (today's Bourges), it falls to Caesar, whose troops have besieged it. Caesar withdraws to settle a dynastic squabble among the Aedui people. When they join forces with Vercingetorix, he turns to the Germanic peoples for aid.

The climax of the work is the siege of Alesia. Encircling the ramparts of the enemy, the forces of Gaul are successively beaten back. Caesar arrives, resplendent in the scarlet cloak of a general (*Gallic War*, 7.88), and ends the resistance of the Gallic tribes. The leading rebel, Vercingetorix, submits nobly to Caesar. His brief speech to his own people is a moving demonstration of self-sacrifice:

> The next day Vercingetorix addressed an assembly. "I did not undertake the war," he said, "for private ends, but in the cause of national liberty. And since I must now accept my fate, I place myself at your disposal. Make amends to

> the Romans by killing me or surrender me alive as you think best."
>
> (*Gallic War*, 7.89; trans. S. A. Handford)

Vercingetorix was given over to Caesar. Six years later, after being displayed in Caesar's triumph, he was executed.

Caesar also recovers the loyalty of the Aedui and of the Arverni, stations Roman officials and troops throughout Gaul, and personally winters at Bibracte. Caesar's work ends on the positive and self-congratulatory note: "When these messages were made known at Rome a public thanksgiving of twenty days was granted" (*Gallic War*, 7.90; trans. A. Nice).

Book Eight (51-50 BCE). After an apologetic preface, Hirtius, Caesar's general, opens with a verbal reference to books one and seven of the *Gallic War*: "The whole of Gaul was defeated." (*omni Gallia devicta*) (*Gallic War*, 8.1; trans. A. Nice). As with Caesar's exaggerated claims, it is not true. In the subsequent sections Caesar and his legates reduce the remnants of Gallic resistance. The final sections shift the focus to the challenges to Caesar's authority at Rome. The final word of the incomplete manuscript "*contendit* . . ." (He strove . . .) (*Gallic War*, 8.55; trans. A. Nice) suspends the narrative indefinitely on the brink of civil war. It is perhaps an appropriate, if less than satisfying, conclusion.

The rhetoric of conquest. When Aulus Hirtius remarked in his preface to book eight that "Caesar possessed not only the greatest skill and elegance in writing, but also the surest ability to explain his own plans" (*Gallic War* 8, Preface, section 7; trans. A. Nice), he acknowledges that Caesar had exceeded the limits of his command. As Caesar's opponents knew very well, his campaigns in Gaul, Britain, and Germany were illegal. He had operated outside the limits of his provinces without senatorial authority and, by rights, should have been prosecuted. The year-by-year publication of the *Gallic War* was necessary to justify Caesar's actions to his adoring public and to promote his calculated subjugation of areas outside Roman control.

Caesar presents real or imagined threats to explain away his intervention in Gaul. For example, Caesar claims that the Helvetii threaten the Roman province and promote anti-Roman sentiment. Four times he recalls their annihilation of the Roman army of L. Cassius Longinus in 107 BCE. Also his reports always portray the enemy as the aggressor, even when his troops plunder Gallic lands or he sells a population into slavery.

Caesar compares and contrasts the civilized ways of Rome to the barbarism of those he conquers. He portrays the Gauls as deserving to be subjugated because they lack Roman qualities. They are fickle and undetermined, rash and frenzied, greedy and lazy. Caesar's men defend their nation with discipline, hard work, and traditional virtue.

Digressions on the characteristics of the Gauls and Germans are essential to Caesar's account. They justify his conquests by encouraging the reader to draw comparisons between Roman ideals of nationhood and the ways of these foreign nations. Although the Gauls have some degree of a social class structure, they fight one another and the Germans. They are less developed than the civilized Romans: they make human sacrifices; they treat the common people like slaves; they do not have democracy.

Among the Gallic peoples, Vercingetorix is the Gallic equivalent of Caesar: a capable orator, strategist, and warrior. His nobility is apparent from the beginning of book seven to the moment that he surrenders willingly to the decision of his own people and to Caesar. Generally, though, Caesar sets up a framework of Roman versus barbarian, portraying the region as a threat to the survival of Roman civilization itself.

Despite the use of the third person for his account, Caesar himself is ever present. Often he appears suddenly and dramatically: to save the Seventh Legion in Britain, to rescue Quintus Cicero, at the forefront of the battle, robed in his general's red cloak at the siege of Alesia. As appropriate, Caesar metes out pardon or punishment. He takes care to mention individual officers, centurions, and even slaves. In the account and through the account, Caesar emerges as a model of Roman virtue *par excellence*. He is the diplomat, general, warrior. As Lindsay Hall remarks:

> He ponders things, acts in accordance with pre-arranged plans or principled habit, explains his reasons for strategic or tactical decisions and his other *consilia* or policies; he . . . anticipate[s] political or military movements on the part of potential enemies, or the results of actions that have come to an end; he regularly foresees . . . eventualities, or . . . carefully excuses failure to do so.
>
> (Hall in Welch and Powell, p. 21)

Caesar's narrative is a masterpiece of rhetorical or persuasive composition. He encourages his Roman audience to believe in his actions and in himself. It is perhaps no wonder that just two years later his Roman troops were ready to follow him to the bitterest of encounters—civil war.

Sources and literary context. The full title on surviving manuscripts of Caesar's single, continuing set of accounts on the Gallic and Civil Wars is *C. Iulii Caesaris Commentarii rerum gestarum* (The Commentaries of C. Julius Caesar on His Achievements). The *commentarius* was a genre that had its origins in the Greek *hypomemnata* (or 'memoranda'), such as public legal records and accounting expenses, or private notes for speeches and personal diaries. At Rome the form developed in the writings of the priestly colleges or of the leading magistrates, in senatorial dispatches and reports, and in the diaries of army generals and provincial governors. In general, *commentarii* were not for publication, but were intended as raw material for the historian.

It was customary for Romans to celebrate the *res gestae* ("things done") of their ancestors in speeches of praise at funerals and in funerary inscriptions. It was also common to praise one's own achievements when dedicating a monument or writing memoirs. As time passed, generals and politicians recognized that by publishing their *commentarii* or *res gestae* they could justify their actions and promote themselves in Rome. They now intended for their works to be publicly disseminated. The memoirs of P. Rutilius Rufus, the autobiography of M. Aemilius Scaurus, or Cicero's account of his consulship are worthy predecessors to Caesar's commentaries. But the most obvious inspiration is the dictator Sulla's lost *Commentarii rerum gestarum*, on his life and achievements.

Caesar's narrative, written in the third person, lays claim to a more impersonal and objective approach. The annual structure, geographic and ethnographic digressions on the Gauls and Germans, rousing speeches by the Celts and Romans, records of his own and his generals' achievements, the results of his campaigns—all these suggest the writing of history rather than autobiography. In ancient Rome, history was above all a rhetorical and literary genre. The ideal form focused on the doubtful and varying fortunes of an outstanding individual and would contain contrasting emotions of surprise and suspense, joy and distress, hope and fear. Ancient and modern readers would be hard pressed to find a purer example of historical writing that is tailored to the views and desires of its central figure than Caesar's *Gallic War*. In addition to the influences of genres, one can detect the impact of Caesar's teachers, the orator Apollonius Molon of Rhodes, and the grammarian Antonius Gnipho. The former advocated an austere style of oratory. The latter

ASTERIX THE GAUL

In the modern world, Caesar's accomplishments have rarely gripped the popular imagination. Although there have been a plethora of excellent TV and film adaptations of Shakespeare's *Julius Caesar*, there have been few that deal with the historical Caesar. Occasionally Caesar has been the subject of the historical novel, most notably in the recent works of Colleen McCullough, Allen Massie, or Steven Saylor but none have achieved anything similar to the phenomenal success of the comic book series created by René Goscinny and Albert Uderzo. Situated in 50 BCE, each book begins as follows:

The year is 50 B.C. Gaul is entirely occupied by the Romans. Well, not entirely . . . One small village of the indomitable Gauls still holds out against the invaders. And life is not easy for the Roman legionaries who garrison the fortified camps of Totorum, Aquarium, Laudanum and Compendium . . .

(Uderzo, p. iii)

Their unlikely hero is a very small Gallic man named Asterix, who is accompanied by his faithful companion, an oversized man named Obelix, and his pet hound, Dogmatix. Asterix's small village fends off the Roman invaders with a little help from a magic potion prepared by a Druid named Getafix.

Ingenious storylines paint a caricatured portrait of overbearing and stuffy Romans and of boorish and guileless Gauls. Cleverly the authors exaggerate themes of Roman and barbarian found in Caesar's *Commentaries*, although in their version the barbarians always have the last word. Since 1959 Goscinny and Uderzo's 32 books have been translated into over 100 languages (including ancient Greek and Latin), used as educational materials, and adapted for animation and motion picture (*Asterix and Obelix vs. Caesar* [1999]; *Asterix and Obelix: Mission Cleopatra* [2002], starring Christian Clavier as Asterix and Gérard Depardieu as Obelix).

had a special interest in word forms. Caesar's style in the *Commentaries* is smooth and concise. He avoids coining new words and standardizes the use of vocabulary and grammatical structures.

Publication and reception. The standard position is that Caesar's *Commentaries on the Gallic War* were a synthesis of his earlier campaign reports, and that he wrote and published them after the successful completion of business in Gaul in 52-51 BCE. A slightly different stance suggests that Caesar wrote the *Commentaries* in stages but published them all at the same time. A third view argues that the books were produced and published at stages during the campaign, probably yearly. Publishing a section of *Commentaries on the Gallic War* annually at the end of a military campaign season would have enabled Caesar to promote himself to the Roman public and to enhance his immediate political ambitions.

During his own lifetime and the century that followed, Caesar's *Commentaries* received high praise for their uncomplicated style. Cicero, the foremost rhetorician of the era, wrote in 46 BCE: "They [the *Commentaries*] are greatly to be approved. For they are unadorned, direct and graceful, stripped of every oratorical ornament as though divested of clothing" (Cicero, *Brutus*, chapter 292).

The *Commentaries on the Gallic War* had a widespread impact on later ancient biographers and historians. The subject matter provided raw material for Livy's *From the Founding of the City*, for Plutarch's *Parallel Lives*, and for Suetonius' *The Lives of the Twelve Caesars* (all also in *Classical Literature and Its Times*). More generally, Caesar's descriptions of the Celtic tribes helped shape later Roman views of the "barbarian," including those of historians, such as Tacitus, Ammianus Marcellinus, and Orosius.

The *Commentaries on the Gallic War* influenced writers and thinkers in Britain, France, and Germany. The English scholar Francis Bacon (1561-1626) thought that the *Commentaries* revealed Caesar to be the most complete and unique figure to emerge from antiquity. In eighteenth-century France, the value of the *Commentaries* as a military handbook was not lost on Napoleon Bonaparte, who wanted the work to be part of the education of every general and wrote his own *Summary of the Wars of Caesar* (*Précis des Guerres de César*, 1836). The German historian Theodor Mommsen, winner of the Nobel Prize for Literature in 1902, regarded Caesar as the only creative genius produced by Rome and the last produced by the ancient world.

Nonetheless, there are traces of a tradition hostile to the content of Caesar's *Commentaries*. Asinius Pollio, who had fought with Caesar, thought they had been composed carelessly and with too little regard to the truth. Pollio believed that Caesar gave a false account, either purposely or because of a faulty memory (Suetonius, *Caesar* 56.4). It was impossible for Caesar to have fully falsified his account since it would have been competing with his own reports to the Senate, with his correspondence and the letters of his officers to Rome, and with other literary compositions by the men under his command. However, Caesar had an agenda he wished to promote. As one historian suggests, he was "presenting himself in contemporary terms to his fellow Romans as the greatest and most worthy of them, striving beyond all else to outdo his most significant rival, Pompey the Great" (Welch and Powell, p. ix).

As a historical document, the *Commentaries on the Gallic War* remain enormously valuable as the memoir of a Roman commander in provinces of the empire. The extent to which Caesar may have exceeded the truth of history should be considered in relation not just to the historical events or circumstances that shaped the work. Rather the *Commentaries on the Gallic War* should be regarded as a key to understanding the sophisticated linguistic, rhetorical, and historical processes of one of ancient Rome's most dynamic politicians and foremost thinkers.

—Alex Nice

For More Information

Bradley, P. *Ancient Rome: Using Evidence.* Cambridge: Cambridge University Press, 1992.

Caesar, Julius. *The Battle for Gaul* [Commentaries on the Gallic War]. Trans. A. Wiseman and P. Wiseman. Boston: David R. Godine, 1980.

———. *C. Iulii Caesaris Commentarii rerum gestarum* [Caius Julius Caesar, Commentaries on His Achievements]. Ed. O. Seel. Leipzig: Teubner, 1968.

———. *The Conquest of Gaul* [Commentaries on the Gallic War]. Trans. S. A. Handford. Harmondsworth, U.K.: Penguin, 1951.

Cicero, Marcus Tullius. *Brutus.* Trans. G. L. Hendrickson. Cambridge, Mass.: Harvard University Press, 1962.

Meier, Christian. *Caesar.* Trans. D. McLintock. London: HarperCollins, 1995.

Mommsen, Theodor. *A History of Rome.* London: Routledge, 1996.

Parenti, M. *The Assassination of Julius Caesar: A People's History of Ancient Rome.* New York: New Press, 2003.

Suetonius. *Lives of the Twelve Caesars.* Trans. R. Graves. Harmondsworth, U.K.: Penguin, 1957.

Uderzo, Albert. *Asterix and the Secret Weapon.* Trans. Anthea Bell and Derek Hockridge. London: Orion, 2002.

Veyne, Paul, ed. *From Pagan Rome to Byzantium.* In *A History of Private Life.* Vol. 1. Trans. A. Goldhammer. Cambridge, Mass.: Harvard University Press, 1987.

Welch, Kathryn, and Anton Powell, eds. *Julius Caesar as Artful Reporter.* Swansea: Duckworth and the Classical Press of Wales, 1998.

Wiseman, T. P., ed. *Roman Political Life 90 BC-AD 69.* Exeter: Exeter University Press, 1985.

Confessions

by
St. Augustine

Augustine (November 13, 354 to August 28, 430) was born in the town of Thagaste, in the Roman province of Numidia Proconsularis, in North Africa, to a well-to-do pagan father and a Christian mother. Intellectually precocious, the boy, whose full name was Aurelius Augustinus, responded well to the initial stages of his education. He seems to have been devoted and happy, both as a student and as the son of loving parents. After advanced studies in Carthage, he began a career as a teacher of rhetoric, first in Thagaste, next in Carthage, then in Rome, and finally in Milan, a large and important city in the later Roman Empire. A great success as a teacher, he sought the company of like-minded intellectuals who were interested in the great philosophical questions: What is the good? What is the nature of God? How can we account for the presence of evil? Such concerns had preoccupied thinkers since before the days of Socrates. Now Augustine wrestled with them, embracing and rejecting a series of philosophical positions that claimed to offer answers. As a young man, he rejected his mother's Christian religion, finding it intellectually unsatisfactory. He afterward aligned himself with various schools of thought before going on to experience first an intellectual, then a spiritual conversion to the Christian faith, in which at last he found the answers he sought. Augustine's restless search for a system of belief that would satisfy both his intellect and his heart brought him into contact with Ambrose, the celebrated Christian bishop of Milan. Attracted to Ambrose's preaching,

THE LITERARY WORK

A spiritual autobiography, written in Latin and set in North Africa (Thagaste, Carthage and Hippo) and Italy (Rome and Milan) from 354 to about 387 CE; published in the first decade of the fifth century CE.

SYNOPSIS

Augustine describes the circumstances of his birth, education, and professional career as a teacher of rhetoric, while at the same time meditating on his intellectual and philosophical formation from the perspective of a committed Christian.

Augustine was persuaded to receive baptism in 387. He subsequently returned to North Africa and established a Christian community dedicated to prayer, study, and Christian intellectual conversation. His rapidly spreading fame as a writer and thinker of the first order made it inevitable that he would take an official position in the Church, which he did by accepting ordination as priest in 391, and as bishop of the North African community of Hippo in 395. He would later become an amazingly prolific writer; letters, theological treatises, biblical commentaries, polemics, and other such works seemed to fly from his pen. The *Confessions*, his spiritual autobiography, occupies a special place among his writings. It describes how a man, suffused with happiness and

Saint Augustine, bishop of Hippo. Library of Congress. Reproduced by permission.

the certainty that he has finally found the peace he sought for so long, came with difficulty to achieve his present state. At the beginning of the *Confessions*, addressing God, he states, "you have made us for yourself, and our heart is restless until it rests in you" (Augustine, *Confessions*, book 1, chapter 1).

Events in History at the Time of the Autobiography

The later Roman Empire. When Augustine was born, Rome had been the undisputed master of the Mediterranean and much of northern Europe for several centuries, and there was no hint that its supremacy in the West would falter. In another 120 years, around 476 CE, Rome would fall. But at this juncture, in Augustine's lifetime, Rome *was* Western civilization. To be a functioning member of this civilization required participation in Rome's educational, civic, and social programs. The rise of Christianity did little to change this, even though the Christian leaders were to a large extent hostile to the existing social order, in light of its pagan origins and scope. Christian youth were educated with the same texts (Virgil's *Aeneid*, Cicero's *Speeches*, etc.) as everyone else, and major Christian figures of the day—such as Ambrose (340-397)—generally

mastered a secular profession (like law or rhetoric) before devoting themselves full-time to the Christian cause. To be sure, Christian bishops tried to convert pagans, but this evangelical impulse lacked the political urgency that it had possessed in earlier centuries when Christians were a persecuted minority, and Roman paganism was at a very basic level identified with the Roman state. Augustine grew up in a world where the emperors (with the exception of "Julian the Apostate" [r. 361-363]) were Christian and the decision of whether or not to embrace the new religion was primarily a personal or familial one. No one was being thrown to the lions. On the contrary, Christians and pagans lived and worked together in relative harmony. Augustine's own family was a case in point—his mother was a devout Christian, his father a pagan, and Augustine himself a dabbler in various systems of belief until he accepted the religion his mother had taught him in boyhood. Though their belief systems differed, the three appear to have been equally Roman to the core.

This situation would change considerably in Augustine's lifetime, not during the period covered in the *Confessions* but certainly during the early years of its circulation. The 390s saw an increasing level of hostility among Christians towards paganism, with Christian monks, bishops, and emperors attacking pagans and their temples verbally and physically. Various edicts stripped pagan temples of their financial subsidies and prohibited certain modes of pagan sacrifice. In 392 the Christian bishop of Alexandria successfully encouraged his followers to destroy the Serapaeum, one of the main temples devoted to the Egyptian god Serapis, who was worshipped in many parts of the Greco-Roman world. This same decade saw Rome's military fortunes declining at an ever more rapid pace. Whether the escalating Christian attacks on paganism had anything to do with Roman military weakness is uncertain, but we do know that after 410, the battle lines of Christian against pagan grew sharper than they had been since the late 200s.

In 410 the Visigothic king Alaric took Rome, the capital city of the Western Empire. Though the Visigoths soon left, the shock felt throughout the Roman world was massive; no foreign army had occupied Rome for 800 years. The sense of unique permanence that Romans accepted as their birthright vanished. Seeing newly emboldened foreign armies start to move more freely across Roman lands in northern and central Europe, pagans began to suggest that

Rome's fortunes had fallen because the old gods were no longer worshipped. Without divine protection, Rome would be at the mercy of its enemies, and the blame could be laid squarely at the feet of the Christians. Augustine's last great work, *The City of God*, was composed as a refutation of this claim; it was begun in 413, and was substantially completed in 426, just before the Vandal army crossed over into Africa after running amok in Spain. This army besieged Hippo in 430, as Augustine lay dying within its walls.

The Church in the fourth century. Christianity was well and widely established in the Roman Empire by the fourth century, with dioceses (or bishop-centered districts) in every province and a strong presence in all major cities. For the most part, the bishops were able and energetic men, dedicated to the security and spiritual welfare of their flocks, and to the ultimate conversion of the world as they knew it. The end of large-scale persecution enabled them to pursue these goals without much hindrance, but the Church found new antagonists, this time from within.

Heretics were by definition those who preached a version of Christianity different from the one the Church had now been teaching for several hundred years. The Church was embroiled throughout the fourth century in combating heresies and their adherents. In the long run, these disputes would be fruitful: they would make the Church refine and focus its doctrines to create an orthodoxy of Christian doctrine. For example, most Christian denominations now hold that while a priest or minister should ideally be as free from sin as possible, his ability to perform the duties of his sacred office by no means depends on his personal moral character. If a priest gives a blessing, it is God who confers the blessing, and that blessing is full and valid even when the priest is a sinner. If a bishop ordains a priest or another bishop, that ordination is valid irrespective of the moral state of the one performing the rite. Not all Christians believed this in the early Church, which led to a controversy born of the anti-Christian persecutions under the emperor Diocletian in the first decade of the fourth century. Faced with a choice between recanting their faith or suffering a grisly execution, many Christians (priests and bishops among them) chose to save their lives. After the persecutions ceased, some of these apostates attempted to resume their positions in the Church. One set of Christians—members of the Novatian heresy—held that such *traditores* ("traitors")

should not be readmitted to the Church, that they deserved to be permanently excommunicated for their failure to hold fast in the face of persecution. In a similar vein, another set of Christians—members of the Donatist heresy—

RISE OF CHRISTIANITY IN THE ROMAN EMPIRE

60-62 CE St. Paul preaches in Rome to win converts to the Christian faith

64 Nero blames the Christians for fire in Rome

95 Emperor Domitian persecutes Christians

203 Emperor Septimius Severus issues an edict against Christianity and Judaism

250-251 Emperor Decius orders the first empire-wide persecution of Christians, leading to the deaths of several dozen martyrs

251-253 Persecution under Emperor Gaius Trebonianus Gallus

257-260 Persecution of Christians under Emperor Valerian

260 A period of toleration begins

284 Diocletian ascends the Roman imperial throne

298-302 Christians in the Roman army refuse to worship Roman imperial cult (which deifies emperors upon their deaths), are considered untrustworthy and are forced to resign

300 The population of the Roman Empire is 60 million (about 15 million Christians)

303-304 Diocletian orders a general persecution of Christians; his minions destroy places of worship, imprison clerics who refuse to make pagan sacrifices, and execute both clerics and laypeople

306-312 Persecutions continue under Emperor Maximian

313 The Edict of Milan (by Emperor Constantine the Great and his co-emperor Licinius) proclaims religious freedom in the Roman Empire and declares toleration for Christianity

337 Constantine is baptized and dies shortly thereafter

354 Augustine is born

361-363 Emperor Julian attempts to restore paganism

391-392 Emperor Theodosius I proclaims Christianity the official faith of the Roman Empire

395 St. Augustine becomes bishop of Hippo

---

held that sacred rites performed by *traditores* were invalid, even if the recipient of the sacrament was a good and holy man. Augustine took strong issue with both heresies; for him, man was by nature a sinner, in constant need of God's grace and the sacramental comfort of the

Church. To believe that *any* Christian, however holy, was sufficiently sinless to perform a sacred office on his own merit was to deny the necessity of grace, and to give humankind a moral stature it did not possess. In fact, some of the harshest words Augustine ever wrote were directed against another heresy (Pelagianism), which held that people could perform good works on their own and essentially "earn" their way to heaven. The story of Augustine's conversion in the *Confessions* is essentially a story of how God's grace made that conversion happen. Augustine asserts that he did not do it himself; he deserves no credit for finding faith. In fact, according to his writings, his whole experience of Christianity, as it unfolded throughout his conversion and career as a bishop, was one of realizing his own sinfulness and the absolute necessity of God's grace to do anything of value.

Other heresies focused on the nature of God himself, and the relationship between God and Jesus. Orthodox Christianity now holds that God is three persons (Father, Son, and Holy Spirit) in one God—both three and one, at the same time. The second person of the Trinity, the Son, is co-eternal with the Father and the Holy Spirit but at a specific point in human time took on human flesh and became incarnate as Jesus Christ. Jesus was both God and man; he had two natures, one human and one divine. Some early Christians, unwilling to accept apparent contradictions such as these, attempted to define God and Christ differently, and some of the fiercest battles within the early Church were over these issues. At the root of many heresies concerning God and Christ was a body of beliefs collectively known as Gnosticism.

Derived from the Greek word *gnosis*, or "knowledge," Gnosticism was in origin pagan. The movement gave rise to a number of different sects, each claiming possession of a secret body of knowledge detailing the true nature of a supreme God and the purpose of mankind. This knowledge was supposedly revealed by God to the founder of the sect and made available to the sect's adherents after a probationary period of study and (usually) self-disciplined, ascetical practice. By the second century, Gnosticism in various forms had appeared in all major centers of Christianity, causing grave concerns among Church leaders, primarily because Gnosticism at its heart was dualistic. That is, the movement taught that there was a supreme God who was distant from the material world and another deity who created the material world and was connected to evil. Gnosticism held that not one but two divine principles (or divinities) existed in the cosmos, with the evil divinity being responsible for the material world. The existence of the material world was essentially a catastrophic accident, in which spirit (good) was mingled with matter (evil) and human beings were the most significant locus of this malign commingling. Man can see the good and strive after it, but his body continually seeks to drag him away from the good, towards the wickedness that lies in bodily gratification.

Religion during this period was widely individual, with followers adopting elements of various belief systems to create their own unique blend. Some Gnostics adopted a number of Christian beliefs, and certain early Christian groups showed definite Gnostic tendencies. Obviously Gnostic Christians were disinclined to accept the doctrine of the Trinity, since Gnosticism's idea of God was, on one hand, singular (God was the undifferentiated source of good) and, on the other hand, dual (there were two divine principles, one good and one evil). Gnostics explained the existence of evil by laying it wholly at the feet of an evil god, which left the one that they worshipped free of all responsibility for evil. Followers were furthermore disinclined to accept the doctrine of the Incarnation—the idea that God purposely took on material form was anathema to them. Augustine had been a Gnostic for a number of years before leaving the movement and converting to Christianity, but his *Confessions* do not reflect these Gnostic beliefs. On the contrary, the work makes a case for orthodox Christian teachings: that the material world is as much the product of divine creation as the spiritual world and that whatever evil is to be found in the cosmos cannot rationally be ascribed to God, because God is by definition wholly good. Disobedience, whether by man or the fallen angels, is the sole source of evil.

The intellectual life—rhetoric. The word "rhetoric" now sometimes has a negative connotation; terms like "empty rhetoric" convey the idea that rhetoric is all form and no content, a way to express opinions (even erroneous or wicked opinions) in an attractive manner so as to lead the unwary astray. Christian leaders of the fourth century were certainly aware of the dangers of misguided or ill-intentioned rhetoric, but at the same time they saw rhetoric's extraordinary potential as a tool for conversion. All educated Romans were schooled from an early age in rhetorical modes; they studied the great rhetoricians of the past, such as Cicero and Demosthenes, and they practiced—through formal classroom exercises—techniques in verbal persuasion. If a position was true and worthwhile, then it deserved to be expressed as artfully as possible, and furthermore (especially in public life, such as law or politics) the worth of an opinion was to a significant degree measured by the rhetorical skill of the man expressing it. If the Church was to grow, its leaders had to show that its teachings were not just spiritually compelling, but rhetorically defensible—in spite of the fact that the gospels were widely regarded by pagans as simplistic and rhetorically crude. Since this was the very perception that for many years prevented Augustine from accepting Christianity, he knew all too well that the task of conversion was in many ways a rhetorical one. Potential converts had to be shown that the gospels were charged with meaning of a special sort, one that rhetorical analysis could discover and rhetorical skill could express. Consequently Augustine and other prominent Christians of his day wrote a great deal of scriptural commentary about how intellectually substantial the scriptures were. This approach can be found throughout Christian writings of the fourth century. The last three books of the *Confessions*, for example, embody a meditation on the first chapter of the Book of Genesis, a mere 31 verses that at first glance do not seem terribly complicated (or in need of clarification). Beyond such close readings of sacred verse, Christian scholars also employed the language of scripture to discuss complex philosophical and theological topics, showing that biblical ideas and vocabulary had useful roles to play in weighty intellectual matters.

The intellectual life—philosophy. The intellectual tradition of the ancient world was primarily a philosophical one in two ways. First, the basic topics of philosophy (the nature of good, man's duty towards the gods, the nature of true happiness, and so on) were the primary subjects addressed by the various philosophical schools. And second, philosophy was thought to underlie all other fields of knowledge. What we call the natural sciences, such as chemistry and biology, the ancients called natural philosophy. This helps explain why Aristotle was as much at home writing about the properties of stones and the structure of birds' eyes as about the nature of the soul. The ancients took a holistic approach to the life of the mind, and this approach influenced the development of the Church in fundamental

ways. Perhaps most fundamentally, it affected how early Christians understood and made use of scripture. They noted that the Bible is not a single book, but rather an anthology of books, differing in subject, genre, and purpose. Just as philosophical inquiry encompassed all fields of human activity and being, so in a sense did the Bible. In other words, the early Christian writers had ready at hand a collection of texts, and it had as wide a range of applicability as the Greco-Roman philosophical tradition. Further, the reading public was predisposed to consider Christian thought as an interconnected whole, just like other ancient systems of belief. Whereas now someone might accept Christian ethics but

---

IN THE TRADITION OF PLATO

After breaking with a Gnostic cult (the Manicheans), Augustine joined a group of intellectuals who were devoted to the philosophy of Plato, as modified by an Egyptian Greek named Plotinus (250-70). Building on Plato's ideas, Plotinus taught that all existence came from a single, ultimate reality, known as the One. "The animating force of the universe was the soul of God; and the material world was the outer limit of divine emanation" in which humans were "ensnared in ignorance" from which they should awaken so they could embark "upon a spiritual journey of the soul back to the eternal being of the One" (Chidester, p. 128). Though others had built on Plato's ideas before him, Plotinus did so much to revitalize them that his work gave rise to Neoplatonism, the philosophy that would dominate the Roman Empire from his day to the early sixth century.

---

reject the doctrine of the Trinity, a Roman would be unlikely to do this; all aspects of Christianity are interrelated, much as Aristotle's biological theories depend ultimately on his metaphysics. It follows that the ancient intellectual tradition made the step toward Christian universalism a natural one. Just as Stoic philosophy, for instance, determined how a Roman Stoic would act and think both publicly and privately, so did Christian ideology determine how a Christian man of Rome saw himself in relation to all aspects of life. His Christianity, professed as a full-scale philosophical worldview, went far beyond simple acts of private devotion; it caused him to regard the world around him in specifically Christian terms, and act accordingly, both ethically and politically. If the ancient philosophical tradition had not been so wide-ranging in scope, Christianity would have had a much more difficult time taking hold. In the pagan tradition, it was not uncommon for writers to derive full-scale worldviews from a single body of texts; such was the method with the followers of Plato as they studied his dialogues. Augustine made use of scripture in a similar way, and the intellectual world he inhabited was predisposed to take such claims seriously.

The Autobiography in Focus

Contents overview. The *Confessions* is made up of 13 books (what we call chapters, the ancient world called books), and most modern scholars believe that these books should be gathered into three main divisions within the text. Books 1-9 cover the years of Augustine's life before his conversion to Christianity (his mother taught him the fundamentals of the Christian faith, but he did not then embrace them and so saw his pre-conversion life as non-Christian). Book 10 describes his current state and books 11-13 employ his newly found Christian vision to explore the full implications of the first chapter of Genesis. The title gives a good idea of what the work contains.

While the *Confessions* is now generally called an "autobiography," this word did not exist in the ancient world, and it is not very useful as a description of what the *Confessions* is. The Latin noun *confessio* can pertain to a number of things, all of which apply to Augustine's book. It can refer to "confession" in the modern sense—a confession of sin or wrongdoing; it can refer to a statement expressing belief in or praise of God; and it can refer to a formal declaration of belief, with the confessor giving witness to an individual or assembly as to his religious convictions. The *Confessions* is all these things and more, but it is not an autobiography in any strict sense, because nothing is included that does not bear on these three applications. Most autobiographers give accounts of their childhood and upbringing; Augustine does this too, but not because he regards these details as significant in themselves. Rather, what the reader learns about Augustine's youth is essential to a proper understanding of the young man who would reject his mother's faith, only to embrace it again after an intellectual and spiritual journey of many years.

Plot summary. Book 1 describes Augustine's early childhood, but in an idiosyncratic manner that sets the tone for the work as a whole. He begins with a series of addresses to God, expressing in a heartfelt manner his intense devotion and gratitude that God should love such a lowly and wretched creature as man. He refers to his own infancy, but only to discuss how evil resides in humankind from the very beginning. Infants are greedy, selfish, violent creatures; their conduct is reprehensible, and as such, fully human. He notes, "it is not the infant's will that is harmless, but the weakness of infant limbs. I myself have seen and have had experience with a jealous little one; it was not yet able to speak, but it was pale and bitter in face as it looked at another child nursing at the same breast" (*Confessions*, 1.7). He speaks of his own behavior as a baby but admits that he does not remember acting this way; the actions he describes are those of newborns in general, all steeped in sin from birth. This sin manifested itself in different ways as Augustine grew older. At one point, near death from a stomach ailment, he entreated his mother to let him undergo the sacrament of baptism. She, of course, was more than willing, but he speedily recovered and soon forgot his fear of death and the religious fervor it inspired. His baptism was put off, because (he thought) he had no more need of God. His education occasioned further opportunities for sin; he gloried in academic success, he read erotic verse and filled his head with the "wine of error" proffered by "drunken teachers" (*Confessions*, 1.16). It was at this time that he developed a taste for theatrical spectacles, which in the Roman Empire of the mid-fourth century often featured violent gladiatorial contests and nude dancing. Book 2 briefly recounts the particular vices of his sixteenth year—lust and theft. Having discovered sex, he indulged in it with abandon. He fell in with low companions. Together they perpetrated the crime that for him would come to represent the full depravity of sin. Out in the streets late at night, they stole the fruit of a pear tree—not because they needed the pears (they had plenty of better pears at home) and not because they were hungry (they ended up throwing most of the pears to swine), but because it was wrong. They had no appetite for pears, but for sin itself.

Ready for more advanced studies, Augustine moved in 370 to the larger city of Carthage. In the famous opening sentence of book 3, he writes, "I came to Carthage, where a cauldron of shameful loves seethed and sounded about me on every side" (*Confessions*, 3.1). The immoral habits of his earlier youth became more pronounced, but in some ways more refined. The pleasures of the flesh remained dear to him, but he found a mistress and remained faithful to her. She soon gave birth to his beloved son, Adeodatus. He continued to visit the theater, but now, rather than indulging in vulgar entertainments, he attended plays (he found himself moved by the actors' dramatic skills in conveying emotion). Growing more and more enamored of Cicero's writings, he found that he desired greatly to come to terms with the classic philosophical questions. When he reexamined the Christian scriptures he remembered from his childhood, they paled before Cicero's fiery rhetorical brilliance. Augustine abandoned them and became a special type of Gnostic—he joined the Manichean sect. Throughout book 4 and into book 5, he describes what it was like to belong to this sect, but his words are always those of a Christian who grew to despise a faith he had professed for nine years. As he explains it, the Manicheans preyed upon his youth, his arrogance, and his desire for certainty in an uncertain world. Their words were glib and polished (he liked this); they were contemptuous of the vulgar paganism of the common people (so was he); and they made sense of a world in which sorrow and mischance were to be found at every turn. A dear childhood friend of Augustine's died. Augustine's students ran off without paying their tuition. His professional career was not going as well as expected. For a time, the sect's doctrine of a dual godhead helped him endure these reversals, mostly because the belief was that the "good" god is wholly concerned with spirit. The material world is the province of the evil god, and our time here on earth (i.e., imprisoned within a material body) is to be regretted and renounced; there is no happiness to be found here, not until we return to the spirit world that is our proper home.

Several factors were responsible for Augustine's gradual rejection of the Manichean sect. One was his long-awaited meeting with Faustus, a highly regarded sage and master of Manichean teaching. This meeting proved to be something of a disappointment. He found Faustus to be an intellectual lightweight, deficient in learning and, though smooth and polished in his speech, unable to answer Augustine's questions about the faith. His allegiance shaken, Augustine moved from Rome to Milan, where he met Ambrose, the bishop of that city. Ambrose was as well-known in Christian circles as Faustus was among the Manichean, and Augustine began to attend Ambrose's lectures and sermons. At that point he was not seeking instruction in the Christian religion but simply wanted to hear the words of a man famous for his rhetorical skill. Augustine was intrigued by his own reaction to Ambrose's words:

> I listened carefully to him as he preached to the people, not with the intention I should have had, but to try out his eloquence, as it were, and to see whether it came up to its reputation, or whether it flowed forth with greater or less power than was asserted of it. I hung eagerly on his words, but I remained uninterested in his subject matter or contemptuous of it. With the sweetness of his discourse I was delighted, which, although more learned, was less lively and entertaining than was that of [the bishop] Faustus. This applies to his style of speaking, for with regard to their subjects there was no comparison.
>
> (*Confessions*, 5.13)

In other words, Ambrose was no empty showman; he did not conceal insubstantial ideas with flashy rhetoric.

Augustine was becoming more and more aware of what distinguished form from content, and how a pleasing form can conceal error of the worst kind. His philosophical training also led him to question some of the basic tenets of Manicheism; ultimately, it made no more sense to him than did classical Roman paganism. Logically, if God is infinite in all attributes, there can be only one God. To propose with the Manicheans that there are two gods, or with pagan Romans that there are many, is to maintain a contradiction. The universe is only big enough for one god—there is either one or none. His friend Alypius had a role to play as well. A fellow native of Thagaste and a former student of Augustine's, Alypius was also a Manichean for many years; under the influence of Ambrose, Alypius finally became a Christian. Three years after abandoning Manicheism, and after a period of intense soul-searching punctuated by intervals of skepticism and Platonism (detailed in books 6, 7, and most of 8), Augustine was intellectually ready to become a Christian, but he found himself unable to take the plunge. He was still addicted to the pleasures of the opposite sex and knew that if he were to accept Christianity, the conversion must be total and permanent. Even when provided with a convenient opportunity to renounce fornication he found himself unable to take advantage of it. His mother wished him to marry (he never would), and family pressure compelled him to send his mistress back to Africa. A solitary bed was unendurable to

Augustine, so he took on another mistress. One day, in an agony of mind, he threw himself on the ground beneath a tree and wept. In the distance he heard the voices of children chanting repeatedly, "Take up and read. Take up and read" (*Confessions*, 8.12). He knew of no child's game that involved the recitation of these words, and a certainty stole over his mind that the words were a command from God, that he should take up a book of scripture and read the first lines he came across. This he did, and the lines were these: "Not in reveling and drunkenness, not in debauchery and licentiousness, not in quarreling and jealousy. But put on the Lord Jesus Christ, and make no provision for the flesh, to gratify its desires" (Paul in Romans 13:13-14). Augustine evidently took this passage as a condemnation of his lifestyle as well as the reason he had failed to fully and formally accept Christianity. Rather than feeling guilt and shame, however, he felt a sense of peace entirely new to him. He was now completely converted and rushed to tell his mother the news.

Book 9 is an account of joy tempered by grief. Wishing to occupy himself full-time in the practice of his religion, he had no desire to continue his career as a teacher of rhetoric. A sudden lung ailment that rendered him unable to speak made this decision easy; after a short leave of absence to recuperate, he went in 386 on a retreat with friends to Cassiciacum (near Milan) to prepare for baptism. Returning the following year, he resigned his position as professor of rhetoric to the citizens of Milan, and was baptized, along with Alypius and Adeodatus. While awaiting their return to Africa, his mother fell ill and died. This was a grave blow to him, to be sure, but she had died in the fullness of joy and he knew it. A lifetime of prayers had been answered, and her work was in a sense complete; her husband had passed away some years before, and her son was now ready to make his mark on the faith that had sustained her for so long.

If none of his prior religious or philosophical beliefs had given him the answers he sought, Christianity now did, and in book 10 he sets these answers out. In it, we read of the nature of the soul and mind, of the relation between the mind and bodily sensation, and of the attributes and capacities of memory, mathematics, music, God, happiness, and love. These same subjects had occupied the attention of philosophers since Socrates, and now they all became plain to Augustine in the light of Christian faith and the revelation that makes sense of faith.

For example, the nature of happiness had long been a subject of philosophical speculation. The subject was considered problematic because each person seeks happiness differently and experiences happiness (or unhappiness) in different ways. How, then, can happiness be a single quality, a common goal for mankind? For Augustine, true happiness consisted of only one pursuit; anything else was an illusion. Addressing God, he writes, "This is the happy life, to rejoice over you, to you, and because of you: this is it, and there is no other. Those who think that there is another such life pursue another joy and it is not true joy" (*Confessions*, 10.22). Intellectually, Augustine had known of such answers for years, but it was only after his spiritual conversion that these answers satisfied him.

Augustine was not simply a believer, but a believer of experience, knowledge, and wisdom who had seen and lived everything else the world had to offer and rejected it. To his way of thinking, faith resided in his mind, faith that had been planted there by words—the words of scripture containing divinely revealed truths. It is therefore fitting that the final three books of the *Confessions* concern the beginning of the "word" itself, both in the sense that they discuss the beginning of the Bible (the first chapter of Genesis) and in that they examine the word of God coming into the universe. The six days of creation described in Genesis 1 are accomplished through words: God speaks the universe into existence (e.g., "Let there be light"). Words are the beginning of Augustine's faith, and now that he has found it, he must return to those initial words to complete his confession of faith.

Manicheism. In his restless search for a belief system, Augustine lighted on a movement known as Manicheism, a variety of the Gnostic tradition. Mani, the founder of the sect that bears his name, was born in 216 near Cteisphon (in modern Iraq), capital of the Parthian Empire. At the time, a number of different religions were practiced there, including various forms of polytheism, Christianity of various sorts, and Zoroastrianism. Zoroaster (c. 628-551 BCE) taught that the world was created by a Wise Lord who is opposed by an Evil Spirit that forever tempts people to commit evil. It is a person's duty to always seek the good and the true—forces symbolized by light and by fire. Mani incorporated much of Zoroastrianism in his teachings, but made the creator of the world the evil god. Originally spirit (the realm of the good god) and matter (under the control of the evil god) were entirely separate, but through a massive cosmic accident the two regions became mixed, and the two gods wrestled for control of the universe. In Mani's view, good will win out in the end, but it is the duty of humans to fight on its side. As corporeal humans, we are victims of the cosmic accident, and whatever wickedness we feel, experience, or commit is a result of the evil god's efforts on behalf of the material world. The devout Manichean therefore shunned the world and its pleasures. All bodily delights were the work of evil, with one of the greatest evils being to bear children, since this imprisoned yet another soul within a base material body.

Beyond these basic outlines, Manichean theology was extraordinarily complex, with thousands of details to keep track of. This was doubtless one of the reasons why Augustine was attracted to it, since it made considerable demands on the intellect. Not everyone could become a full-fledged Manichean, and among those who did, there must have been a feeling of superiority to the common folk who could not master the cult's intricacies. In any case, the cult spread rapidly eastward and westward, and although the Roman emperor Diocletian persecuted adherents to the sect in 296, it survived in the West for centuries. Augustine, however, grew disenchanted. The intricacies came to seem to him complex simply for the sake of being complex. Furthermore, the Manichean insistence on the divine origin (from the evil god) of evil was at odds with Augustine's experience of human nature. In his view, humanity is the source of evil, and it is a shirking of moral responsibility to place our sins at the feet of a god.

Sources and literary context. The ancient world knew the genre of biography. Lives of famous poets, philosophers, politicians, and generals were widely read, and these works were considered to be profitable reading insofar as the subjects were worthy of imitation. Some writers even wrote about themselves in a way that approached autobiography (see Caesar's **Commentaries on the Gallic War,** also in *Classical Literature and Its Times*). Some historians sought to get into the minds of their subjects, proposing unstated motives and psychological compulsions. Thucydides (c. 455-400 BCE) employed these methods in his analysis of the major participants in the Peloponnesian War, as did the Roman historian Tacitus (c. 55-117 CE) in his descriptions of early Roman emperors. The *Confessions,* however, stands alone; no one had ever before written about himself (or

anyone else) with the same degree of autobiographical detail and unflinchingly honest psychological insight. We know more about Augustine than we do about anyone else in history before the fall of the Roman Empire.

We will never know why Augustine decided to write the work, but many think the reason lies in one of the definitions of the word *confessio.*

THE PEAR THEFT AND DIVINE GRACE

Many readers of Augustine are puzzled by his preoccupation with this incident from his childhood. After all, taking fruit from a neighbor's tree is about as harmless an offense as one can imagine; there seems to be more mischief-maker than devil at work here. The key is Augustine's concept of the utter depravity of the human will. His belief was that we are all born in sin, fully tainted by Original Sin, inherited from Adam and Eve. Their primordial sin in the Garden of Eden permanently ruptured the relation between man and God and rendered man's volition, or free will, corrupt and evil. Without God's grace, we are capable *only* of evil; we cannot gain merit in God's eyes because any good that we do is a gift from him. This innate tendency towards evil is manifest in humans from birth, as Augustine takes pains to observe in his discussion of infants in book 1 of the *Confessions.* Furthermore, since we know that the evil things we do are evil (evil is by definition an act of the will) and that they do nothing but harm us and those around us, it follows that we commit evil not for the sake of a perceived good, but for the sake of the evil itself. This is sometimes difficult to realize, because most sins at least seem to carry with them a perceived good. For example, an adulterer knows that what he is doing is wrong but seeks the pleasure of the act. And what if he loves his mistress? This does not make his sin excusable, for in this case too the love is nothing more than an illusory "good," blinding the sinner to the essential wickedness of his act and making it more difficult for him to recognize his sin. What made the pear theft unique in Augustine's experience was that there was no distracting "good" involved. He and his companions sought nothing but the pure encounter with evil, since they did not even want the pears.

The confession of sin was and is a sacrament in the Church, based on a highly individualistic concept of personal responsibility. For pagan Greeks and Romans, one could be guilty (and subject to divine punishment) in many ways, not all of them within the control of the guilty party. A good example is the tragic hero Oedipus, the subject of the famous play by Sophocles (see **The Theban Plays,** also in *Classical Literature and Its Times*). Oedipus killed his father and married his mother. These are grave sins for which he is punished, and the fact that he did not know what he was doing when he committed them proves to be irrelevant. Another example is the story of the house of Atreus (King Agamemnon, Queen Clytemnestra, Prince Orestes, and so on—see the **Oresteia,** also in *Classical Literature and Its Times*). In this story, we have a vast catalogue of cannibalism, fratricide, matricide, and other gruesome crimes, all because the very bloodline of the family has been cursed. Its members are guilty by virtue of being born into it.

Christianity made the radical proposal that humans—and only humans—are responsible for the state of their souls. It did not matter what one's family members did. God is perfectly just, and holds people accountable only for what they deliberately do in spite of knowing that it is wrong. The catch was that each Christian had to confess his sins publicly, before the body of the faithful. Each sin needed to be honestly and fully confessed. As a detailed confession of his sins, Augustine was only doing with his pen what all other Christians had to do verbally.

Reception and impact. By the time of his death, Augustine was as well-known a figure as the Church possessed, because of his writings. Widely recognized for their brilliance, they were copied and transmitted throughout Christendom. The *Confessions* was among his most popular works from the outset. Christian writers have never ceased quoting from it, mostly because of its confessional honesty. Clearly Augustine knew himself (and his failings) in a way that all Christians are called to emulate. Two of the most frequently quoted passages are "You have made us for yourself, and our heart is restless until it rests in you" and "I came to Carthage, where a cauldron of shameful loves seethed and sounded about me on every side" (*Confessions*, 1.1, 3.1). The first reflects on the quest for truth; the second describes the snares of the world.

The impact of the *Confessions* can be compared to that of the King James Bible on English literature: an impact so pervasive that its influence on most later works can almost be taken for granted. The *Confessions* had a profound impact on Christian moral theology that can be traced through the introduction of monasticism. In the early Middle Ages, monasteries were often islands of learning and piety in a turbulent world. The study of Augustine flourished in these monasteries. A monk spends much of his time in solitary prayer and spiritual self-analysis, and the *Confessions* has always been valued as a guide to this sort of activity. Medieval monks wrote thousands of manuals on the practice of penance and on how to recognize and avoid sin within themselves. These manuals, along with the *Confessions* (ever-present in spirit and through direct quotations), formed the foundation of how moral norms were transmitted to Christians at large from the pulpits of parish churches. Again and again, priests would admonish their parishioners to repent, confess their sins, and return to the faithful practice of Christianity. Augustine showed in detail how this could be done. The *Confessions* was also valued by worshippers directly, without priestly guidance. By the late Middle Ages, popular piety had become grounded in the home as well as in church. Christians avidly sought books on moral instruction that they could read themselves, and with the Protestant Reformation, this tendency became even more pronounced. Augustine became a valued authority for Catholics and Protestants alike. A rise in literacy brought on by the advent of the printing press resulted in the *Confessions* finding a place on bookshelves in homes across Europe, with families using it to show how through perseverance and faith an individual can be brought to God.

The *Confessions* was influential outside the realm of religion as well. Jean-Jacques Rousseau (1712-1778) titled his autobiography *Confessions* quite deliberately, not because it was a Christian confession of faith (it was not) but because he sought to lay open his life as fully and honestly as Augustine had his. Thus, Augustine can be considered in some way the forefather of the modern "confessional" mode of writing, where the author keeps nothing hidden and reveals his or her innermost thoughts, desires, and feelings to the reader. A great deal of contemporary autobiographical writing is composed in this manner; readers now want to read about the inner person, the "real" figure behind the public mask. Hollywood tell-all books continue to sell well, especially if the author has recently reformed after a dissolute life. Their authors are a long way from St. Augustine, but they are following in his footsteps.

—Matthew Brosamer

For More Information

Augustine, Saint, Bishop of Hippo. *The Confessions of St. Augustine.* Trans. John K. Ryan. Garden City, N.Y.: Doubleday, 1960.

Battenhouse, Roy W., ed. *A Companion to the Study of St. Augustine.* New York: Oxford University Press, 1955.

Brown, Peter Robert Lamont. *Augustine of Hippo.* Berkeley: University of California Press, 1967.

Cameron, Averil. *The Later Roman Empire, AD 284-430.* London: Fontana, 1993.

—————. *The Mediterranean World in Late Antiquity.* London: Routledge, 1993.

Chidester, David. *Christianity: A Global History.* San Francisco, Calif.: HarperSanFrancisco, 2000.

Encyclopedia of the Early Church. Ed. Angelo Di Berardino. Trans. Adrian Walford. New York: Oxford University Press, 1992.

Fitzgerald, Allan D., ed. *Augustine Through the Ages.* Grand Rapids, Mich.: William B. Eerdmans, 1999.

The Holy Bible: Revised Standard Version. Catholic ed. San Francisco, Calif.: Ignatius Press, 1994.

The Consolation of Philosophy

by
Boethius

Born c. 480 CE into a distinguished Roman aristocratic family, Anicius Manlius Severinus Boethius achieved success in politics, along with his other accomplishments; he was made consul in 510, and in 523 became Master of the King's Offices, the highest post in the administration of Theodoric, the Ostrogothic king who since 493 had governed the western half of the Roman Empire. Now better known for his philosophical and theological writings, Boethius translated a number of the works of Aristotle into Latin, wrote commentaries on Cicero, and authored original treatises on music, logic, and theology. Among his theological works, the *De Fide Catholica* (On the Catholic Faith) was valued throughout the succeeding Middle Ages as a masterful explication of Christian teachings on (especially) redemption. He also wrote other tractates on the Trinity and against the heretics Nestorius and Eutyches, whose teachings about the relationship between the divine and human natures in Christ had been condemned by the Church. But Boethius is best known for *The Consolation of Philosophy*, a work he wrote in prison in 524 after his sudden arrest on charges of conspiracy and treason. Though he knew he would soon meet his death (he was executed in 525 or 526, never having regained his freedom), his final work teaches that the truly philosophical man must be indifferent to shifting fortunes. To the limited human intellect, it seems paradoxical that God presides over a universe in which the good suffer and the wicked prosper. In the face of a necessarily transcendent and beneficent divine

---

THE LITERARY WORK

A prose-poetry work (*prosimetrum*) set in Rome; written in Latin in 524 CE and published c. 536 CE.

SYNOPSIS

A high official under Theodoric, ruler of the Western Roman Empire, experiences a sudden reversal of fortune and languishes in prison under a death sentence. The prisoner wallows in self-pity until Lady Philosophy arrives, bringing instruction, comfort, and the key to control over one's inner equilibrium no matter what happens.

---

providence, however, the only rational response to this apparent paradox is a humble (even worshipful) acceptance of the divine will.

Events in History at the Time of the Prose-Poem

The later Roman Empire and the Germanic invasions. Originally a local power, centered around the city of the same name, Rome grew into master of the ancient Mediterranean world in the last few centuries BCE. Through conquest and assimilation, it amassed an empire that ultimately included most of Europe, North Africa, and the Near East. The Romans had long looked eastward to Greece for cultural inspiration, when in the second century BCE, they began finding themselves master of more and more territory where Greek was the language of the people. Greece itself numbered among the conquests of Rome, as did much of the land formerly conquered by the Greek-speaking Alexander the Great. In fact, virtually the entire eastern Mediterranean was Greek, and had been for some time. While this was in many ways to the advantage of Rome (Greeks were highly valued as teachers, civil servants, doctors, and the like), it created a situation that was never resolved: the eastern Roman Empire became less Romanized than the western provinces (of today's Spain, France, and England), retaining the Greek language and culture. This situation sowed the seeds of a political controversy that would eventually cost Boethius his life.

Since Rome's empire was too large to be governed directly by one man, the emperors delegated local and regional power to administrators and provincial governors. The strategy went awry in the third century, however, when Roman power was besieged on a number of fronts; foreign invasions, rebellions by ambitious generals, and a series of weak emperors all took their toll. This crisis prompted the emperor Diocletian to establish in 293 a "tetrarchy," a system whereby one emperor ruled the West from Rome, one ruled the East from Constantinople, and both (bearing the title *Augustus*) would have a second-in-command, called a *Caesar*. Since each emperor would be responsible for only half the empire, he could respond more quickly and decisively to military threats. Further, he could effectively be in two places at once, with his *Caesar* handling one crisis while he handled another. This new system of government was taken a step further in 395; upon the death of Emperor Theodosius, the empire was formally divided into two. Instead of one empire having two emperors, there were simply two separate Roman Empires—one in the East and one in the West. Within the next several decades, disaster struck the West. A series of invasions by Germanic peoples quickly shattered Roman power in the Western Empire; Spain, Gaul, Roman North Africa, and ultimately Italy itself all fell to the invaders. In 476, the Germanic general Odoacer (or Odovacer) deposed and exiled Romulus Augustulus, the last emperor in the West, and proclaimed himself king of Italy.

Until fairly recently, the invasions that destroyed Roman power in the West were called the "barbarian" invasions because the "barbarians" (i.e., the Visigoths, the Ostrogoths, the Vandals, the Huns, and so on) were from outside the boundaries of the Roman Empire; in the eyes of some, this made them uncivilized and hence barbaric. The term "barbarian" is falling into increasing disuse because it is now realized that the invaders were in many ways quite similar to the Romans themselves. (The preferred term now is "Germanic," from the language group to which the invading groups all belonged.) Also, contact with such peoples was far from new to the Romans. Their empire had long since ceased to have an army made up entirely of Roman citizens; for centuries, it had made use of "barbarian" troops who fought not out of patriotism, but for money, or even in the hope that they might eventually be offered citizenship. These troops hailed from outside peoples who had long maintained commercial and cultural relations with Rome; some of the noble families among these outside peoples even sent their sons to Rome to be educated.

The "Fall of the Roman Empire" is often spoken of as if it were a great watershed in history; yet for many Romans very little changed with the transfer of power to the new Germanic kings. Rome had been weak for generations, a mere shadow of its former greatness. Its new ruler was a king rather than an emperor, to be sure, but Odoacer knew Rome and its people very well—he and his people (the Scirae) had in fact served with distinction in the Roman army for several years. To the old senatorial class in Rome, the change in rule meant more. These men came from illustrious families, and to serve a foreign king went against everything they cherished as Roman citizens. But the shock soon wore off, and prominent Romans continued to serve in the Roman government under Odoacer and his successors just as they had served the emperors.

Italy's new Germanic kings appeared to be a suspicious and volatile lot, however, for a number of reasons. First, they were well aware of how they were seen by the old Roman aristocracy—as uncultured foreign interlopers—and they never fully trusted their Roman subjects. Second, they had the ambitions of their own highly competitive countrymen to contend with; Odoacer himself was murdered in 493 by Theoderic, the Ostrogoth king who employed Boethius and had him executed. Third, the Eastern Roman Empire was alive and well, and the Germanic kings knew that the emperors in the East would like nothing better than to re-take the West. In 565 the Emperor Justinian did just that, conquering (though only briefly) all of Italy, most of North Africa, and parts of Illyria and Spain. Thus, Theoderic's suspicions about a possible collusion between Boethius and the Eastern Roman Emperor Justin I (518-527) were not outlandish, especially since he himself had originally come to power at the expense of Odoacer, with the blessing of the Eastern Roman Emperor, Zeno; like his successors, Zeno liked nothing better than to sow dissension among the various Germanic factions. Finally, there was the question of religion. As noted, the Germanic peoples were generally Arian Christians, whereas the Romans (in both the East and the West) were orthodox Christians. This was important because by this time the Roman world had become almost entirely Christian, and the unity of the state largely depended on religious consensus. Now that Christianity was by far the majority religion, what used to be small-scale internal disputes over theology developed into matters of state.

The Christianity of the Romans held that the three persons of the Trinity—God the Father, Jesus Christ the Son, and the Holy Spirit—were each God: three persons, but only one divine being. Thus, God could in no way be considered the creator of Jesus, since they were co-eternal, and they were both equally God. Arians, on the other hand, believed that the Son was created by the Father, and that therefore Christ (as a creature) could not be God. Named after a priest from the city of Alexandria, Arius (c. 250-c. 336), Arianism gained many adherents (and provoked much controversy) until it was formally condemned by the Church at the Council of Nicea (325). While it soon died out within the Roman Empire, it gained many converts among the Germanic peoples. Christians outside the empire were far more apt to embrace heterodox dogmas, which explains why Arianism ran unchecked throughout the various Germanic nations in the fifth and sixth centuries. Gradually the Germanic peoples abandoned Arianism, but during Boethius' lifetime the divide was more or less absolute: Germanic peoples were Arians, and Romans were not (rather they were orthodox Christians). Within the confines of Rome, Theoderic knew that his Arianism was regarded as heretical and dangerous by orthodox Christians like Boethius and the Emperor Justin, which must have added to Theoderic's suspicions about Boethius' loyalty to him.

Historians remain in disagreement about whether, or to what extent, Boethius was guilty of the conspiracy attributed to him by Theoderic. Like most ancient rulers, Theoderic had many enemies, and he was well aware of this. Boethius was Master of Offices for Theoderic's court at the capital city of Ravenna; this was a position of power second only to the king himself. Thus, Boethius was in a position that made it uniquely possible to do Theoderic harm, and even if Theoderic had indefinite suspicions, perhaps he thought it better to be safe than sorry.

The ancient philosophical tradition. The ancient Greeks are commonly held to have "invented" philosophy, and, if the discussion is limited to the Greco-Roman world of classical antiquity, this is not far from the truth. The Greeks spent leisure time wrestling with questions about the nature of reality, the good life, and the like, developing a culture of rational inquiry. Socrates, for one, preferred to discuss the nature of beauty in general rather than the beauty of a specific work of art. The ancient Greek world also greatly valued (and enjoyed) argument. The mark of a cultivated and intelligent man was his ability to employ finely-honed rhetorical and logical skills in conversational speculation about ethics, politics, the nature of man, the nature of god (or the gods), and so forth. This highly intellectualized culture gave rise to many different "schools" of philosophy based on the teachings of their supposed (or actual) founders. Major schools of philosophy included

- **The Cynics,** inspired by Diogenes (c. 400-c. 325 BCE), who held that to be happy one must disdain material wealth and property, and feel no shame about one's body or its functions
- **The Epicureans,** founded by Epicurus (341-270 BCE), who held that there is no providential god, that the universe is an accident, and that the goal of life should be philosophical pleasure, which is promoted by limiting bodily desires
- **The Stoics,** founded by Zeno of Citium (335-263 BCE), who held that the good man maintains philosophical self-possession in all circumstances, however dire or painful, and that the only duties of man are to avoid vice and practice virtue, which is based on knowledge
- **The Peripatetics,** who followed the teachings of Aristotle (384-322 BCE), and valued scientific inquiry, the rational classification of fields of knowledge, and the usefulness of observation and empirical inquiry
- **The Platonists,** who followed Plato (c. 429-347 BCE) and through Plato, Socrates (469-399 BCE), who taught that the material world is a shadowy and insubstantial reflection of the true, immutable, and eternal world of ideas.

Other schools of thought existed as well and within each school substantial variations in teaching over the years. In short, there was a great variety of philosophical beliefs in antiquity. Also philosophy was of general interest at the time; people cared deeply about the "big questions" and saw the life of the mind as a noble calling.

In inheriting the Greek cultural patrimony, Rome faced questions that had preoccupied Greek philosophers for centuries. Most educated Romans identified with one school or another. For example, Lucretius (94-55 BCE, the author of the didactic poem *De Rerum Natura* [*On the Nature of The Universe*, also in *Classical Literature and Its Times*]) was an Epicurean; Cicero (106-43 BCE) and Seneca (c. 1-65 CE) were both Stoics; and Boethius was influenced by Stoicism, as indicated by his calm acceptance of the loss of power, position, wealth, and even his life. With the long, steady rise of Christianity in the ancient world, the influence of the ancient philosophical tradition did not dwindle. Many of the early Christians were adults when they converted and those with formal educations had in earlier years been steeped in the teachings of one or more ancient schools of thought. Not surprisingly, many doctrines of the pagan philosophers were absorbed into the work of the Christian theologians. A devout Christian could retain his earlier philosophical beliefs, as long as they did not contradict the teachings of his new faith.

By the early sixth century, the gulf between the West and the Eastern Roman Empire had widened indeed. In the West, knowledge of Greek had been quickly dying out among the Romans; Boethius was one of the few who could still read the language. Though a Christian, he valued the thought and writings of Aristotle and endeavored to translate Aristotle's complete works into Latin for the benefit of his fellow citizens. Much as a patriotic American now might revere the writings of George Washington and Thomas Jefferson while repudiating their slave ownership, Boethius saw the irreplaceable good in pagan philosophy while repudiating its paganism. Christianity could provide salvation, but Boethius would not abandon the texts that gave him (and Rome) civilization.

Christian Neoplatonism. Of all the ancient philosophical schools, that of Plato was perhaps the most influential on early Christianity. This is not surprising, given the sometimes startling similarities between Plato's teachings and the Christian faith. In a polytheistic culture, Plato reasoned

his way to the notion of a single, eternal god, an achievement remarkable enough to prompt some ancient commentators to speculate that he borrowed the idea from the Jews. Neoplatonism originated with the teachings of Plotinus (c. 205–270 CE), who adapted the teachings of Plato to provide the basis for a life of the mind centered on religious devotion. Plotinus and his successors were mystics, seeking through mental exercise a degree of union with the "One," the source of all being. Like the Christian God, the One is beyond human comprehension. All that we know and experience falls far short of the One, and our bodily sensations act as especially dense barriers to true philosophical contemplation. This holds true for the entire material world; the One is the source of being, but the most perfect being is immaterial, and the sensible world (including our bodies) prevents us from coming closer to the One. In fact, all creation is hierarchical, extending from the One down through increasingly imperfect categories of form, spirit, and matter. (This notion draws on Plato's original notion of ideas, his teaching that a flower, for example, may be beautiful but does not embody the perfect "idea" of beauty, which exists beyond time and space, and which—unlike a flower's beauty—can never change.)

It is easy to see why Christians were attracted to Neoplatonism; with a few changes, the One can be seen as the Christian God, the source of all creation, who is beyond human understanding. Neoplatonism also can be accommodated to the hierarchy of creation in the Christian system; it explains the hierarchy of the angels, the relation of the soul to the body, the superiority of man over animals, and so forth. The rigidly moral dimension of Neoplatonism was also attractive to Christians. For the Neoplatonist, the moral life was a way to rid one of distractions and prepare the way for eventual union with the One; this aligns well with the Christian notion of sin as a barrier on the path to eventual union with God in heaven.

This is not to say that the fit was perfect, however. Most Neoplatonists were quite hostile to Christianity, largely because of the dogma of the Incarnation (the idea that God became a human being in the person of Jesus Christ); it was inconceivable to them that God (which they saw as the One) could (a) be three (Father, Son, and Holy Spirit), and (b) live on earth as a man, in a corruptible body. Further, while the Neoplatonic idea of creation (which they called *emanation*, in the sense that all things emanate from the One) is more or less consonant with the Christian idea of creation, Neoplatonists taught that all things (including individual human souls) would eventually return to the One and be absorbed by that singular perfection. Intrinsic to Christian teaching is that humans retain their individuality in the afterlife, and live forever in blissful contemplation of the divine. There were other difficulties as well, but for many Christians they were readily overcome. Neoplatonism provided a solid philosophical and intellectual foundation for Christian belief, something that Christianity (based, as it was, on the revelation contained in Scripture) lacked.

In Book 3 of *The Consolation of Philosophy* Boethius is taught by Lady Philosophy that God is not only the supreme and perfect good, but also simultaneously the source and fulfillment of man's happiness. True happiness cannot be found in things of this earth, nor can it be found *on* earth; true and complete happiness can be achieved only by a full encounter with the divine (the highest good) after all other, lesser goods are stripped away, including our material bodies. This is a recognizably Neoplatonic idea, one that few Christians would argue with, though it is expressed not in religious but in philosophical terms. Many readers of *The Consolation of Philosophy* are surprised to discover that its author was a Christian: there is no explicit Christian doctrine in the work, no mention of Jesus or even of an identifiably Christian God. Seeing it as a Christian Neoplatonic work removes this problem—Boethius seemingly intended his work to be useful to both pagans and Christians who find themselves confronted by adversity, and made use of a philosophical tradition that by then had come to be acceptable to both.

The Prose-Poem in Focus

Contents summary. *The Consolation of Philosophy* is divided into five books, each containing a series of passages in alternating prose and poetry. The prose passages are generally straightforward narrative, made up mostly of the instructional dialogue between the character Boethius (who must be distinguished from the author, Boethius) and Lady Philosophy. The verse passages provide a commentary of sorts on the prose passages they accompany.

The work opens with a poem: a woeful lament in which Boethius bemoans his fallen fortunes. His enemies have prevailed, all his wealth and worldly honors have disappeared, and he

Boethius and Philosophy Personified, a fifteenth-century painting. © Leonard de Selva/Corbis. Reproduced by permission.

languishes in prison. While before he wrote happy songs, now he composes poetry of sorrow and despair. Engulfed in misery, and attended only by the muses of the poetry he writes, he is suddenly confronted with an awe-inspiring sight: a serious and noble lady, who at one moment is of normal height and at the next towers to the heavens. She is Lady Philosophy; just as the muses personify the poetic arts that Boethius practices, so she personifies the philosophic mindset, which he has recently lost due to his present condition. He has allowed his grief to overwhelm him, which has robbed him of his philosophical abilities. His grief, she tells him, stems not from his unfortunate circumstances but from his failure to react to them wisely. He used to possess such wisdom; to regain it he must be cured of the mental illness that imprisons his thoughts just as securely as prison walls confine his body. Lady Philosophy chases away the muses, and his lessons begin.

Book 2 details Boethius' philosophical difficulties with the notion of a benevolent and providential God. Essentially, his problem stems from a dissatisfaction with the workings of "Fortune," or chance. Like the muses, whom Lady Philosophy calls "harlots" because they distract Boethius from the pursuit of wisdom by giving him pleasure of

Lady Philosophy with Boethius (left); Fortune, the goddess of luck or chance, with her wheel.
© Wallace Collection, London, UK/Bridgeman Art Library.

another sort, Fortune was traditionally viewed as a harlot. Some even viewed Fortune as worse than a harlot, as a whore who distributed favors indiscriminately, regardless of the moral stature of the recipient. A wicked man may have good fortune, while a just man, like Boethius, may face ruin and undeserved execution. The power of Fortune seems absolute to Boethius, and he cannot reconcile this with any rational concept of God. If God is perfectly good and all-powerful, then why does he allow those who follow his will to suffer? Why does he allow evil to triumph over good? Lady Philosophy is amazed that Boethius has allowed himself to fall so deeply into error. Why, she asks, does he regard the gifts of Fortune as his? She quotes Fortune herself:

> Why, good man, do you indict me day after day with your complaints? . . . When nature brought you forth from your mother's womb, I adopted you; you were naked then, and bereft of everything. I nurtured you with my resources, and—this is what now makes you so angry with me—I bent over backwards to spoil you, and to give you a pampered upbringing. . . . It now suits me to withdraw my gifts. You owe me a debt of gratitude for having enjoyed possessions not your own; you have no right to complain as if you have lost what was indisputably yours. . . . Wealth and position and all such things are at my discretion.
>
> (Boethius, *The Consolation of Philosophy*, p. 21)

Lady Philosophy then proceeds through the remainder of Book 2 and halfway through Book 3 to review the gifts of Fortune, and to investigate whether any of them can lead to true happiness. Wealth, honor, power, health, physical pleasure—none can bring the perfect happiness that can be found in God. At the midpoint of *The Consolation*, we learn that it is only through and with God that this happiness may be found. Even the most fortunate of men eventually dies; his power and honors disappear, and his wealth stays in this world while he passes to the next. The gifts of Fortune are indeed good (as long as we do not let them blind us to their limitations), but they are by definition temporary and imperfect. And it is this limited quality of their goodness that points beyond the material:

> The universe does not take its rise from things which were curtailed or incomplete; rather, it issues from things which are intact and fully developed, and it disintegrates into this parlous and sterile world of ours. Now if . . . there is what we may call imperfect happiness in a good that is brittle [fragile, temporary] there can be no doubt of the existence of some unalloyed and perfect happiness.
>
> (*Consolation*, p. 57)

God is perfection in all things, including not only goodness and happiness, but also power; the universe must necessarily be ordained according to his will. Book 3 closes with a restatement of Boethius' original paradox: how can this sort of

divine providence govern a world in which evil exists? Lady Philosophy's answer is both puzzling and unsatisfactory to Boethius. If evil exists in a world subordinate to the providence of an all-powerful and benevolent God, she argues, then there is only one way to avoid concluding that God commits evil. This is to realize that "evil is a nothing, for there is nothing that he cannot do, but he cannot commit evil" (*Consolation*, p. 68).

Book 4 is a sustained explanation of the above point. Boethius cannot bring himself to accept it; the suffering of the good and the prosperity of the wicked seem so very real to him, and he is unable to conclude that they are both illusions. Lady Philosophy admits that the problem is a difficult one, but she maintains that this is because humans rarely see the world without emotion. By banishing the muses at the beginning of the treatise, she was attempting to rid Boethius of this blinding emotion. Poets celebrate the joys and triumphs of this earth; they mourn disasters such as the deaths of loved ones and defeat in battle. To a philosopher, though, all aspects of worldly existence, good and bad, must be accepted with equanimity. This process of philosophical resignation is in itself a good that is ultimately greater than any material possession or worldly achievement, since it leads directly to God. Thus, the good *are* rewarded, without fail. Similarly, the wicked are always punished, since their apparent prosperity prevents them from attaining the good that just men invariably possess through their wisdom and virtue. If evil is not a thing, but rather a nothing or a privation, then the wicked do not truly gain anything through their vice, but are instead diminished; they are not only less good, but less real as well. Evil, in other words, is an absence rather than the presence of something. To explain by comparison, cold is not a thing; rather cold is the absence of heat. In much the same way, the dark is not a thing—one does not place darkness into a room but rather prevents light from entering the room. Like cold, darkness is a privation. So is evil. Boethius accepts the logic of this argument but remains unhappy with it; the sufferings of good people are too real to be explained away by simple argument. Sympathetic to his state of mind, Lady Philosophy suggests that he not expect to be able to understand this subject fully. Divine Providence (the eternal will of God that orders the affairs of creation) is beyond human understanding. We see its effects in the world (this is what we call Fate), but our inability to know what God knows prevents us from seeing that all things, even apparent evils, are ordained by God and necessarily are directed toward an ultimate good.

In the fifth and final book Lady Philosophy discusses the last remaining problem—the reconciliation of divine foreknowledge with human free will. How can God reward the good and punish the wicked if, by virtue of his perfect knowledge, he knows what they are going to do before they do it? For Boethius, God's foreknowledge of human actions makes nonsense of any system of reward and punishment. Lady Philosophy's solution is again to make a distinction between human and divine knowledge. It is a mistake, she says, to regard God's knowledge as "foreknowledge." God exists outside of time, and all things

---

FROM *THE CONSOLATION OF PHILOSOPHY*

"Father of earth and sky, You steer the world
By reason everlasting. You bid time
Progress from all eternity. Yourself
Unshifting, You impel all things to move.
No cause outside Yourself made you give shape
To fluid matter, for in You was set
The form of the ungrudging highest good.
From heavenly patterns You derive all things.
Yourself most beautiful, You likewise bear
In mind a world of beauty, and You shape
Our world in like appearance. You command
Its perfect parts, to form a perfect world."

(*Consolation of Philosophy*, p. 56)

---

are present to him. Our futures seem uncertain and our actions seem free to us because they *are* so, to us. We exist in time, and our actions are freely chosen because to us the future has not happened yet. God's knowledge includes all events in time, and also the freely chosen dimension of events:

> [A] future happening which is necessary when viewed by divine knowledge seems to be wholly free and unqualified when considered in its own nature. In fact, there are two kinds of necessity. One is simple; for example, it is necessary that all men are mortal. The other is conditional; for example, a man must be walking if you are aware that he is walking.
>
> (*Consolation*, p. 113)

This notion of conditional necessity allows for both free will and divine omniscience. Accord-

ing to this notion, if I know something, then that thing must be true; it cannot be otherwise. If I know a man is walking, then he must be walking. It would be nonsense, however, to claim that my knowledge somehow causes him to walk. A man can take a walk of his own free will. God's knowledge works the same way.

Free will vs. divine foreknowledge. Boethius concerned himself with the philosophically well-ordered life as a system of ethics. To give an account of this philosophically well-ordered life, he needed to address the issue of human freedom. The subject required explanation because human freedom, on the face of it, seemed incompatible with God's absolute knowledge, and with his nature as the cause of all things. It has never been easy for philosophers, theologians, or scientists to make sense of the idea of free will. For the materialist (one who does not believe in the supernatural), human activity is just a more complicated version of balls ricocheting off each other on a pool table. Things move because they are moved by something else, and nothing can move itself. How then is free will possible, given that we can only do what we are caused to do, and nothing else? Adding God and spirit to the mix makes for a more complicated scenario, but it does not solve the problem. The Christian doctrines of sin, virtue, punishment, and salvation depend for their sense on the concept of free will. God, the religion teaches, gave Moses the Ten Commandments; implicit in this is the idea that people are free to obey or violate these commandments. Why tell people not to steal if whether they steal is not up to them? Likewise, Jesus taught that if a person is struck, he or she must turn the other cheek. Clearly, this person has a choice: turn the other cheek or strike back. If people had no free will in the matter, it would make no sense for Jesus to say do the former instead of the latter.

This all seems self-evident, until we consider the element of divine foreknowledge. Among the traditional attributes ascribed to God is omniscience; the belief is that God knows everything—all that has happened, and *will* happen. For God, there is no past, present, and future; he exists in the eternal now. Since God knows everything, God also knows things that have not happened yet. To God, these things are not in the future, they simply are. Now we return to being struck on the cheek. A man stands there, his face stinging with pain. Despite his anger, he recalls Christ's injunction to turn the other cheek. He considers his options—should he do the right thing, or should he hit back? But to God, he has already done one or the other. The man does not know yet what he is going to do, but God does. And when that man finally acts, he will do precisely what God knew he was going to do all along. In fact, he can do nothing else, since God's knowledge cannot be faulty.

There are several obvious problems here. First, it seems that the man has no free will at all. He has the illusion of deciding, but in reality he is simply running through a mental process that has a foregone conclusion. There is only one thing that he can do, and he is going to do it. Hence, he has no free will. Second, what does this mean as far as Scripture is concerned? The Bible is full of exhortations and prohibitions, but all for naught; people seemingly have no choice in whether they follow God's commandments or not. Third, what does this do to Christian teachings about salvation and damnation? The belief is that God punishes the wicked with hellfire but rewards the just with eternal life. But if it is not up to people whether they act justly or wickedly, then how can it make sense for God to reward and punish? Even a person's postmortem destination is believed to be known to God. The person will either be saved or not, and God already knows which will happen. What is the point, then, of telling someone who is bound for heaven to act virtuously? Why warn the hell-bound to avoid evil if it will not do them any good?

Boethius was neither the first nor the last to be troubled by this seemingly insoluble paradox, but his solution was enormously influential. Scholars of his day were familiar with the concept of conditional necessity— the idea that if you know something, then it must exist. By applying this concept to divine knowledge and removing the element of causality, Boethius preserved both God's omniscience and human freedom. He resolved the paradox in a satisfying way, one that later generations of writers (especially poets) would find especially congenial. First, his resolution neatly encapsulated the mindset of the times. Christian culture was established and stable, but within a still-vital classical tradition that was highly intellectualized, philosophical-minded, and pagan. By framing his discourse around the figure of Lady Philosophy, Boethius accommodated both traditions; *Philosophia* could be both a pagan goddess and the personification of Christian divine wisdom. *The Consolation* was not a specialized philosophical treatise; it was meant for a wide readership, and its poetic qualities gave it an immense popular appeal. Few thinking people have remained untroubled by

the problem of free will, but Boethius' solution, while it did not satisfy everyone, gave the West a conceptual vocabulary that would last a thousand years.

Sources and literary context. *The Consolation of Philosophy* is an example of Menippean Satire, an ancient literary genre of complex and uncertain origins, whose most identifiable quality is that its exemplars are *prosimetra*. A prosimetrum is a literary work containing both prose and poetry; such works were often satirical, treating philosophical topics in a light vein, usually accompanied by an at least superficially non-serious narrative. A good example of this genre is the **Satyricon** of Petronius (also in *Classical Literature and Its Times*), a work detailing the amorous and picaresque escapades of a pair of ne'er-do-wells in early imperial Rome. Obscene even by modern standards, the *Satyricon* nevertheless addresses in a lighthearted, whimsical fashion a number of topics of perennial philosophical interest, and in the Renaissance came to be regarded as a work of considerable value, despite its licentious content. By the time of Boethius, however, the prosimetrum had lost its essentially flippant character, and was used primarily to treat philosophical (or learned) subjects in a somewhat popular mode, with the prose supplying the serious doctrine and the poetry providing the reader with artistic delight. This is precisely how the prose and verse sections of *The Consolation* interact. Menippean Satire was no longer identifiably satirical (at least in the modern sense of "satire"), but the formal links of *The Consolation* to the older tradition gave it a quality that made it appealing to philosophers and lovers of literature alike.

The sources of *The Consolation* are many and varied. The influence of Neoplatonism is noted above. There are, furthermore, parallels between the works of Boethius and Plato. In Plato's *Crito* and *Phaedo*, the condemned Socrates spends his last hours in the company of his friends, discussing philosophy. The parallels between Socrates and Boethius in this respect are not likely coincidental. In the ancient world, the standards for what constituted a noble or praiseworthy death were fairly exacting. The critical factor was that of control; ideally, one would exercise the maximum degree of control over the circumstances of one's death. Suicide was praiseworthy, because it showed the subject embracing death, instead of the reverse. Philosophical self-possession and control over one's emotions (and body, to the extent possible) were always to be maintained. The example of Seneca was famous in this regard. Stoic

LADY PHILOSOPHY AND ANCIENT METAPHOR

The ancients were wont to create gods by simply naming them after abstract terms, or something associated with them. Thus, the Greek god Zeus is easily recognized as a variation on the Greek word *theos*, which simply means "god." The goddess Athena is quite naturally named after the city of Athens (though legend has it the other way around), and the Greek god of sexual love (Cupid) was known to the Romans simply as Amor—that is, "love." Especially in the case of minor deities, their names were often identical with that quality over which they had governance. Thus, for the letter "F," we find Flora, the goddess of flowers and vegetation; Fornax (i.e., furnace or oven), the goddess of bread-making ovens; Fides (i.e., faith), the goddess of good faith; Fons (spring), the god of springs with drinkable water; Fama (fame), the goddess of fame or reputation; and of course Fortuna, the goddess of fortune, or luck. Though the extent to which these gods and goddesses were ever actually worshipped is a matter of debate, by the beginning of the Common Era most educated Romans considered them to be personified abstractions rather than literal deities. As a Christian, Boethius did not believe such creatures actually existed, but as an educated Roman he would not have believed in them even if he were a pagan. Latin literature for centuries had built narratives around such personified abstractions, and the intent was that they be read allegorically. Reading a poem in which Cupid is described as shooting an arrow into a young man, a reader would immediately understand that what was being illustrated was the sudden crush of romantic love. Neither author nor reader was under any illusion about the actual existence of Cupid. When Boethius wrote about himself in prison, the voice of Philosophy came not from a Lady but from within his own head, and his readers understood this.

philosopher, playwright, and courtier of the tyrant emperor Nero, Seneca finally incurred the fatal suspicion of his master, and was invited to commit suicide rather than being executed (see Seneca's **Moral Letters** and **Phaedra,** both also in *Classical Literature and Its Times*). Gathering his friends about him, he commended to them as his legacy his pattern of life and death, and proceeded to show them how a true philosopher met his end. He made deep incisions in his arms, and sat in a bath of warm water while his life ebbed away, all the while discussing eternal truths with his friends. A third model was Jesus. By Boethius' lifetime, the period of Roman persecution of Christians had long ended, but the example of the martyrs as heroes of the faith was ever-present. Of course, the view of death as a public performance and a measuring-stick of ideological fortitude was not just a Christian concept. The entire ancient world was in many ways a cult of martyrs, with each martyr dying in the best possible manner for the sake of the belief system to which he or she ascribed. As

he sat in his prison facing certain death, Boethius was in good company; he had the examples of many—both Christian and pagan—to guide him.

Reception and impact. Little is known about the reception or readership of *The Consolation* in the centuries immediately following its composition, but by the end of the first millennium CE it was part of the literary canon. *The Consolation* survives in over 400 manuscripts—a very impressive figure for an ancient author—and was regularly quoted by theologians and poets throughout the medieval and early modern periods. It was translated into Old English by King Alfred the Great (c. 897), into Middle English by Geoffrey Chaucer (c. 1380), and into Modern English by Queen Elizabeth I (mid-1590s); there are also medieval translations into French, German, and Greek. Its popularity actually increased over time; both Catholics and Protestants found it inspiring, and the Renaissance vogue for Neoplatonism ensured its continuing popularity in learned circles. With the advent of printing, *The Consolation* was reprinted

70 times before the year 1500. Translated into English again and again through the succeeding centuries, it retains its vigor and relevance to the present day, and is easily the best-known work from the sixth century. John Kennedy Toole's *A Confederacy of Dunces* (1980), a Pulitzer Prize-winning comic novel, centers on *The Consolation* both thematically and literally—the protagonist is robbed of his copy by a woman of ill-repute, and spends the rest of the novel seeking its return.

—Matthew Brosamer

For More Information

Boethius, Anicius Manlius Severinus. *The Consolation of Philosophy*. Trans. P. G. Walsh. Oxford: Oxford University Press, 1999.

Cameron, Averil. *The Mediterranean World in Late Antiquity: AD 395-600*. London: Routledge, 1993.

Chadwick, Henry. *Boethius: The Consolations of Music, Logic, Theology, and Philosophy*. Oxford: Oxford University Press, 1981.

Fox, Robin Lane. *Pagans and Christians*. New York: Knopf, 1986.

Lerer, Seth. *Boethius and Dialogue: Literary Methodology in The Consolation of Philosophy*. Princeton: Princeton University Press, 1985.

Moorhead, John. *Theoderic in Italy*. Oxford: Oxford University Press, 1992.

O'Daly, Gerard. *The Poetry of Boethius*. Chapel Hill: University of North Carolina Press: 1991.

Relihan, Joel C. *Ancient Menippean Satire*. Baltimore: Johns Hopkins University Press, 1993.

Tacitus, Publius Cornelius. *The Annals of Imperial Rome*. Trans. Michael Grant. New York: Penguin, 1977.

Eclogues

by
Virgil (Publius Vergilius Maro)

According to classical sources, Publius Vergilius Maro (70-19 BCE) was born in Andes near Mantua (modern Mantova) in Cisalpine Gaul to a modest family, where he grew up on a farm. He received his early education in the nearby towns of Cremona and Mediolanum (modern Milan), later traveling to Rome to study philosophy and rhetoric (and possibly mathematics and medicine). Ancient tradition relates that Virgil studied the philosophy of Epicureanism near Naples with an inspiring teacher named Siro. Recently published papyri scrolls found in the buried city of Herculaneum in the Bay of Naples confirm that he was closely associated with the most famous Epicurean philosopher at the time, Philodemus, who dedicated one of his works to Virgil. It is generally assumed that the budding poet returned from the Epicurean "garden" to his father's farm where he continued his studies, but this intellectual idyll was interrupted by the military confiscations of farmers' property in his region. Virgil composed his *Eclogues* in this troubled time, and their success assured him of the protection of Octavian. From then on, the poet's life moved between Rome and an estate at Nola (near Naples) given to him by Octavian. It was at this estate that he composed the four books of the *Georgics* (29 BCE), a poem on farming and other rural pursuits (*georgika* is Greek for "things of the earth"), composed in the didactic tradition of Alexandrian verse. Virgil's next project was the *Aeneid* (also in *Classical Literature and Its Times*), an epic poem on the Trojan hero Aeneas, modeled on the Homeric epics

---

THE LITERARY WORK

Ten pastoral poems set in an imaginary landscape after the battle of Philippi (42 BCE); first circulated in Latin between 42 and 38 BCE, though some argue for a later publication or revision c. 35 BCE.

SYNOPSIS

The reader is invited to bear witness to life in "Arcadia," a place created by poetry, an idealized rural scene where people live in harmony with nature.

---

and widely recognized as one of the most important and greatest works of Roman literature. Virgil died in Brundisium in 19 BCE and was buried in Naples. His life and work have been cleverly condensed into verse featuring a list of places and landscapes (lines cited in this and all excerpts that follow have been translated by D. Dutsch):

Mantua me genuit, Calabri rapuere, tenet nunc
Parthenope: cecini pascua, rura, duces.

Mantua gave birth to me; Calabria then
    snatched me away.
Now [Naples, the city where the Siren]
    Parthenope [is buried] holds me.
I sang of pastures, farmlands, and leaders
    [of armies].
          (Donatus, *Tiberius Claudius, vita,*
                   paragraph 123)

Eclogues

The title of Virgil's *Eclogues* is derived from the Greek *ekloge*, meaning "choice" or "selection," although the collection has also been well-known since antiquity as the *Bucolics* (Greek *boukolikos*), the origin of our word "bucolic," or pastoral. To understand Virgil's journey from his pastoral poems, or *Eclogues,* through didactic poetry to the epic *Aeneid*, we must begin with the dramatic events following the assassination of Julius Caesar in 44 BCE.

Events in History at the Time of the Poems

Up front—(un)civil war. The political murder of Julius Caesar in 44 BCE ignited a civil war between

---

VIRGILIAN GOSSIP

While we know little about Virgil's private life, two affectionate allusions in the poems of Horace afford us glimpses of it. The first speaks to Virgil's friendly disposition, as Horace gratefully remembers how "Virgil, the kindest of men" introduced him to the literary patron Maecenas (Horace, *Satires*, book 1, poem 6, line 54). The second is a brief allusion to an episode during the trip to Brundisium in 37 BCE (made famous by Horace's fifth satire). It shows both poets unable to play ball with their companions because of poor health: Horace is indisposed because of an eye problem, while the author of the *Eclogues* apparently suffers from indigestion (Horace, *Satires,* 1.5.49). Chronic health problems are a recurring theme of Aelius Donatus's *Life of Virgil* (fourth century CE), which also abounds in tidbits unconfirmed by more reliable sources. For example, Donatus offers a description of Virgil's physical appearance, claiming that he was dark and tall, and had a "rustic appearance" (whatever this might mean). Donatus also speaks of Virgil's paralyzing timidity: the poet apparently visited Rome rarely and when recognized on the street used to run and seek refuge in the nearest house. This shyness allegedly prevented Virgil from becoming a lawyer; as the *Life* would have it, the poet's one and only attempt to deliver a speech in court ended in disaster, since the brilliant writer was an appallingly dull speaker. Shyness seems also to have been why the inhabitants of Naples, where Virgil lived as an adult, nicknamed him "Parthenias," or "Mr. Virgin." Finally, Donatus offers that "when it came to pleasure, he [i.e., Virgil] preferred boys," a statement possibly made up on the sole basis of the poetic declarations of love for men or boys in the *Eclogues* (Donatus, *Tiberius Claudius, vita,* paragraph 25).

Caesar's assassins, led by Marcus Brutus and Cassius Longinus, and those who declared themselves Caesar's heirs and avengers. Three powerful figures emerged from the latter faction: Caesar's former allies, Mark Antony (83-31 BCE) and Marcus Lepidus (d. 12 BCE), and Octavian, the dictator's 19-year-old grandnephew, who was posthumously adopted by Caesar in his will as his son and legal heir (63 BCE-14 CE). Octavian was Virgil's future protector, who would later assume the name of Caesar Augustus. The three joined their forces in an official alliance, the second triumvirate (43 BCE) and were formally appointed by the Assembly as "Officials to Reestablish the Order in the Republic." They set about this task by publishing the *List* of politically undesirable individuals to be hunted down and executed. This brutal procedure, known under the innocuous name of "proscription," was an effective way not only of eliminating political and personal enemies, but also of obtaining funds, since those who were listed had their property confiscated for the benefit of the Roman treasury. The Caesarians desperately needed these funds to pursue the forces of the anti-Caesarians who had fled to Greece. First, however, they had to face the infamous pirate Sextus Pompeius (also on the *List*), whose forces, strengthened by the arrival of some of the proscribed, prevented the armies of the triumvirs from crossing the Adriatic Sea. Only after a great battle outside the straits of Messana was Sextus's grip weakened enough to allow the triumvirs' armies to cross and confront their adversaries. Two decisive battles then took place at Philippi in Macedonia (42 BCE), where first Cassius and then Brutus committed suicide. The victors proceeded to divide the Roman world among themselves: Antony obtained the East, reputed for its wealth; Africa fell to Lepidus; and the western provinces of the Empire and Italy to young Octavian, who was also in charge of confiscating the land from Italian farmers to be distributed to the veterans. The confiscations made Octavian the most hated man in Italy and, as the relationships among the triumvirs quickly soured, the partisans of Antony did their best to take advantage of this extreme unpopularity. Antony's wife Fulvia and his brother Lucius attempted to seize power in Rome, encouraging those affected by the confiscations to ignore Octavian's orders; Octavian struck back immediately, chasing the Antonians and their army away from Rome. They then took refuge in the town of Perusia, which surrendered to Octavian only after several months of siege (in 40 BCE); according to ancient sources, mass executions of

Illustration of Virgil. © The Gamma Liaison Network. Reproduced by permission.

sometimes the shorter period beginning with the assumption of his new name in 27 BCE) is known as "the Augustan era." The literary output of the poets active in this short period whose works have survived—Virgil, Horace, Propertius, Tibullus and Ovid—would be a source of inspiration for readers and writers for the next 2,000 years. A part of this era of impressive literary creativity coincided—paradoxically—with war, famine, confiscations, and displacements that affected all of the older poets, Virgil, Horace, Propertius, and Tibullus. (Ovid would have his share of bad luck later, when he was banished by Augustus for an unspecified "crime" to Tomis in 8 CE.)

Backdrop—famine and confiscations. The triumvirs' proscriptions (43 BCE) directly affected 300 families of senatorial rank and 2,000 of equestrian, or business-class, rank. Prizes were awarded to those who helped capture the victims; freedom was granted to slaves willing to denounce their masters. Soon bands of lawless prize-hunters roamed Italy. No one—proscribed or not—was entirely safe. At the same time, the country was torn by famine as the ships of Sextus Pompeius frequently kept vital supplies of Egyptian grain from reaching Rome. The confiscations that began after the battles at Philippi (42 BCE) weakened an already ailing economy through the forced change in ownership of thousands of estates. The injustice of these confiscations, which touched thousands of innocent inhabitants of Italian cities, provoked an outrage.

The Caesarians had promised land to the soldiers recruited before the confrontation with Cassius and Brutus. Eighteen cities had then been marked out as prizes for the soldiers' valor, Cremona near Mantua, the town where Virgil went to school, among them. Now, after the war, the veterans who had fought at Philippi demanded their prize. The cities and their inhabitants protested in vain, suggesting that the burden be shared by all; Octavian carried out the plan. More than a hundred years later, Appian of Alexandria in his *Roman History* offered a dramatic reconstruction of the popular feelings at the time when the dispossessed marched to Rome:

> They came to Rome in crowds, young and old, women with children, to the forum and to the temples; they lamented, saying that they had committed no crime for which they—Italians— should be driven from their fields and their houses, like people conquered in war. The people of Rome felt their pain and wept with them, especially because they knew that the war had been waged and the prizes of victory given

Antony's partisans followed. In the summer of 40 BCE Antony came back to Italy from the East, bringing an army with him; open confrontation seemed inevitable when, in the fall of 40 BCE, the friends of the two triumvirs managed to orchestrate an agreement between Octavian and Antony at Brundisium. The poet and politician Gaius Asinius Pollio (Virgil's friend and protector) represented Antony, while Gaius Maecenas (the same Maecenas whose name became synonymous with the patronage of art and whom Virgil was soon to meet) represented Octavian. The alliance they negotiated was to be strengthened by the marriage of Antony (his enterprising wife Fulvia was now dead) to Octavia, the sister of Octavian. But the prospect of peaceful alliance did not live up to its promise. The relationship between Octavian and Antony continued to deteriorate, finally ending, nine years later, in Octavian's triumph in the battle of Actium (31 BCE) and Antony's death. Thus ended the civil wars and the Roman Republic: though the tradition of the Roman Senate and Republican political offices remained, Octavian (later as Augustus) became de facto the sole ruler of Rome.

A period of relative peace and prosperity followed. The time between the proscriptions of 43 BCE and the death of Augustus in 14 CE (or not on behalf of the Republic but against the people themselves, to change the form of government, . . . so that democracy should never again lift its head.

(Appian, *Roman History*, 5.2.12)

The confiscations most severely affected the owners of middle-sized estates (the tiniest farms were eventually exempted and the wealthy and influential citizens holding the largest ones often managed to keep their property). These midsize estate owners received no compensation and were often condemned to misery. Violent protests and armed conflicts between the dispossessed and the veterans ensued. Years were to pass before the turmoil finally subsided. The frustration, injustice, violence, and famine of the years of the civil war provide the emotional background for Virgil's *Eclogues*. This nightmarish anti-Arcadia is more than a shadow passing over the pastoral scenes—it is the very *raison-d'être* behind the compassionate landscape of Virgil's pastorals.

Closeup on local history—paradise confiscated. Mantua (modern Mantova) was a town in the province of Cisalpine Gaul that covered the Po Valley and extended to the Alps. Virgil's town lay on the river Mincius (modern Mincio) in a particularly lush part of this fertile region, now in northern Italy. The town was and still is quite literally encircled by small lakes full of fish that attract swarms of waterfowl. This corner of paradise has always drawn settlers, the oldest traces of whom date to the second millennium BCE. In the middle of the first millennium BCE, an Etruscan village was built on the site of previous settlements; the Romans conquered it a few hundred years later, in the second century BCE. This opulent, quiet town provided an ironically idyllic background for the drama of Octavian's dispossessions.

Since antiquity, scholars have speculated about the degree to which the *Eclogues* reflect the details of Virgil's personal experience and his relationships with the prominent Mantuans who oversaw the redistribution of lands between 43 and 40 BCE. Was his father's Mantuan farm confiscated? Did Virgil at any time appeal to the governor of Cisalpine Gaul or to Octavian himself for its restoration? Did he succeed? The honest answer is: we do not know. We can, however, identify three historical figures of Virgil's patrons and friends and pinpoint the time each of them spent in Cisalpine Gaul as well as his position in Mantua. The rest is a matter of conjecture.

Pollio, the man whom Virgil flatters in Eclogue 3 and to whom he dedicates his fourth eclogue, is Caius Asinius Pollio. Governor of Cisalpine Gaul in 43 BCE and a supporter of Mark Antony, Pollio would later help negotiate the agreement between Antony and Octavian at Brundisium. Pollio was also a poet, tragedian, and historian of the Roman civil wars, and he founded the first public library in Rome in the atrium of the Temple of Liberty. The cowherds Damoetas and Menalcas in Eclogue 3 (one of the earliest composed) suddenly sing of Pollio. Damoetas boasts that Pollio appreciates his pastoral Muse, "albeit she is rustic," to which Menalcas responds praising the "novel verses" that Pollio composes himself. These verses were probably tragedies, of which we have nothing except for the opinion of Tacitus, who dismisses them as "old-fashioned and dry" (Tacitus, *Dialogus*, 21.7). For Virgil's shepherds, however, Pollio was nothing less than an inspiration: "Whoever loves you, Pollio, may he come / Where you too are happy to come! [to the place visited by Muses] / May honey flow for him, harsh bramble bear fragrant spice" (Virgil, *Eclogues*, poem 3, lines 88-89). This blessing for those who want to enter the realm of the Muses together with Pollio is addressed to a circle of literati surrounding the governor in Mantua; Virgil was in all likelihood one of them.

Gaius Cornelius Gallus would also have been a part of this Mantuan circle. Like Pollio, Gallus was both a poet and a politician. He was destined for a brief but brilliant career: Octavian was to appoint him the first Roman governor of Egypt (after Antony's death), but later would formally renounce his friendship, which led to his prosecution by the Roman Senate and eventually his decision to commit suicide in Egypt. At the time Virgil was composing his *Eclogues*, Gallus was already an established poet who later would be considered the founder of the new literary genre of Latin Love Elegy (of his four books of *The Loves*, or *Amores*, we have today only one line). His poetry was greatly admired by Virgil, who later paid a passionate homage to Gallus in his tenth and final eclogue: "[Muses of Pieria] you shall make my song great for Gallus; / For Gallus, my love grows every hour as fast as green alder shoots upwards in early spring" (*Eclogues*, 10.72-73).

Publius Alfenus Varus was another prominent figure in Mantuan politics, succeeding Pollio as the governor of Cisalpine Gaul in 42 BCE. His name appears in Eclogues 9 and 6. Number 9 quotes a "yet unfinished" song that Menalcas (one of the cowherds of Eclogue 3) sang for Varus: "Varus! Your name, if only Mantua survives, / —

Alas! Mantua, too close to wretched Cremona!—singing swans will carry up to the stars" (*Eclogues*, 9.27-29). Varus was a well-educated man (author of legal treatises) and a clever politician who later rose to the consulship (39 BCE). When he was governor, Mantua might have indeed been threatened by confiscations. The 18 municipalities originally marked for the veterans proved insufficient and eventually as many as 40 towns might have become involved. The most common practice was to extend the territory of dispossessions to include towns in the vicinity of those whose lands had already been redistributed. This practice is probably behind the bitter complaint about Mantua's closeness to the town of Cremona in the poetic lines above.

Mantua was apparently known for the swans that visited the surrounding lakes: Virgil treats the reader of the *Georgics* (2.198-199) to a nostalgic glimpse of the field that Mantua lost (possibly in the confiscations) with his description of snow-white birds against the green tide. The birds, the lakes, and the grass are still near Mantua for all to see. As for the singing swans of Eclogue 9, they obviously allude to a poet's appeal to the governor Varus for the town to be spared. One cannot infer that this is a formal plea concerning Virgil's personal estate. Nor can one link the skirmish that almost ended with the death of two shepherds, described in Eclogue 9, to an event in Virgil's own life. Displacement or violent death would, however, have been the fate of many a citizen of Mantua and Cremona, and traces of their collective experience are interwoven in the vibrant tapestry of Virgil's pastorals.

The Poems in Focus

Contents summary. Virgil's *Eclogues* is an elaborately arranged book of pastoral poems. First composed by Theocritus of Sicily, such poems usually feature shepherds who compete in songs praising the beauty of the landscape along with the charms of a beloved boy or girl. Most eclogues are miniature scenes that introduce diverse pastoral figures and their songs. Eclogue 4, sung by Virgil and his Sicilian (Theocritean) Muses, is an exception.

The *Eclogues* fall into two sequences of five poems each, 1-5 and 6-10; the longest poems, 3 and 8, occupy symmetrical positions within this arrangement. Poems 2 and 7, which are quite faithful to the type of poetry they model (Greek verse by Theocritus), follow the more daring poems, 1 and 6, which likewise occupy parallel po-

sitions in the collection. The fifth eclogue contains subtle allusions to the first, thus enclosing the first half. The sixth eclogue, with its reference to previous pastoral writing ("My Muse was first to deign to amuse herself with Syracusan poetry"), marks a new beginning. These are only the most conspicuous patterns of Virgil's design; there are others as well—"Virgil," it has been noted, "is a poet of labyrinthine intricacy" (Clausen, p. xxii). Here is an overview of the labyrinth in relation to his *Eclogues*:

Eclogue 1   Tityrus, an older man who, thanks to a "divine" youth, will keep his land, discusses his destiny with Meliboeus, whose land has been confiscated.

Eclogue 2   Virgil tells his reader how Corydon wooed Alexis, a handsome boy who rejected Corydon's rustic attentions.

Eclogue 3   Two shepherds, Menalcas and Damoteas, compete in alternating verses (which include praises for Pollio); old Palaemon declares both worthy of the first prize.

Eclogue 4   Invoking the pastoral Muses, Virgil sings a prophetic song announcing that Pollio has begun his year as one of the consuls of Rome. A new age of peace will begin, symbolized by a newborn child.

Eclogue 5   Two shepherds, Menalcas and Mopsus, meet to sing together; they propose several themes we know from the previous eclogues before settling on a theme of their choice—the death of Daphnis, an idealized shepherd who was deified after his passing.

Eclogue 6   Virgil, addressing Varus, tells how two boys have captured Silenus, an ever-intoxicated old sage (in keeping with an old motif of the wise man who needs to be forced to share his immense knowledge). In exchange for his freedom, Silenus sings a song about the origin of the world, ending in a eulogy for Cornelius Gallus, the poet and politician in Virgil's circle who later kills himself.

Eclogue 7   Meliboeus recounts how Daphnis summoned him to witness the contest between Thyrsis and Corydon. (The latter wins.)

Eclogue 8 Two songs of unhappy love are cited and dedicated to an unidentified patron. Damon's song is a lament over an unhappy lover who committed suicide; Alphesiboeus's song recounts the magical gestures and incantations that a woman uses to bring back her beloved Daphnis.

Eclogue 9 Lycidas and Moeris (figures from Theocritus's *Idylls*) meet as Moeris drives his flock to its new owner; they try to remember the songs of Menalcas.

Eclogue 10 Virgil (invoking the nymph Arethusa as his muse or spirit of artistic inspiration) tells how Cornelius Gallus, represented as an unlucky lover, was received in Arcadia as a new living form of Daphnis. In the final strophe, or stanza, Virgil takes his leave from pastoral poetry.

This general "map" of the *Eclogues* can hardly do justice to the complexity of the poems. Close-ups of two poems will better serve this purpose.

Eclogue 1. Two shepherds discuss their destinies—Meliboeus's land, the verse implies, is being confiscated; Tityrus's is not. Meliboeus, who speaks first, contrasts the leisure enjoyed by Tityrus with his own fate:

Tityre tu patulae recumbans sub tegmine fagi
silvestrem tenui Musam meditaris avena.
Nos patriae finis et dulcia linquimus arva,
nos patriam fugimus. Tu Tityre lentus in umbra
formosam resonare doces Amaryllida silvas.

Tityrus, reclining under the cover of a
  spreading beech,
you rehearse woodland music on your slender
  reed. We are
leaving our native land and its gentle fields.
  We are
fleeing our own country. You, Tityrus, at ease
  in the
shade, teach the woods to echo the name of
  pretty Amaryllis.
                                    (*Eclogues*, 1.1-5)

The intricate beauty and music of the Latin lines is impossible to render in an English translation; note the reiterations of *tu* and *nos* ("you" and "we") and the echo resounding in the Latin reference to the forests that repeats the name of Tityrus's beloved: *Amaryllida silvas*. In Latin, Virgil's reference to the echoing sounds echoes itself.

Tityrus explains that his happiness is god-given and takes a solemn oath to worship always that god who permitted his cows to graze and his music to be: Tityrus's poetry comes as a natural consequence of the wellbeing of his flock: "He allowed my cows to wander, as you can see, and me / To play anything I wish on my rustic reed" (*Eclogues*, 1.9-10). Meliboeus answers; first he sings of the herd of goats that he must hastily drive to their new master in town. One of the goats has just given birth (and can hardly walk); her twin kids, "the hope of the flock," had to be abandoned. But he does not wish to dwell on this outrage against nature's creative act. With curiosity rather than with envy (*Eclogues*, 1.11), he gently asks Tityrus for the name of the "god" who answered "his plea" (probably to spare his land from being confiscated). To this, Tityrus gives an evasive yet pointed answer—the city of Rome, he says, is greater than any other city. In Rome, he, an old man and apparently a slave, found "freedom" and is infinitely grateful to the one who granted it to him. The solemn tone of this confession is deflected when Tityrus playfully adds that he would have visited Rome earlier but was too much in love with Galatea to care. Only recently, since his feelings for his current beloved (Amaryllis) allowed for some leisure, he undertook the journey to Rome that gave him his freedom.

The praises Meliboeus sings for Tityrus's fate offer the readers an opportunity to glimpse this extraordinary setting where Greek shepherds/poets deify Roman political figures. It is a place where people share emotions with elements of landscape: pines and orchard trees call upon the now-absent Tityrus along with Amaryllis. Meliboeus knows this scenery in intimate detail and imagines Tityrus's future in Arcadia with photographic precision: his song zooms in on the rocks surrounding the pasture, the marshy plants, the shade, the sound of the bees, the species of birds that visit the nearby crags and trees. Such precision contrasts with the crude outline of the outside world. Meliboeus envisages his own future in stock-epithets: it will take him to "thirsty Africa," "swift-flowing Amu-darya," or "Britain cut off from the rest of the world" (*Eclogues*, 1.63-66). But this all will happen tomorrow. Tonight Meliboeus is welcome to stay with Tityrus; the menu will feature: "ripe fruits, soft chestnuts, and a generous quantity of cottage cheese" (*Eclogues*, 1.81-83).

Eclogue 4. This often-misunderstood eclogue is the brightest in the collection; for all its erudite references, it is most of all a true explosion of joy with playful, almost childlike, qualities. The poem opens with an invocation to the Muses of pastoral poetry, who are asked to sing with the poet a *slightly* grander song than usual, one worthy of a consul (this is the reader's first clue to the identity of the poem's addressee). The next seven lines speak in a roundabout fashion (which lends itself easily to mystical interpretations) of the new era about to begin, alluding to the birth of a child who will bring back the Golden Age.

> Now the last age of the song of Cumaean
> Sibyl [a prophetess] has come,
> and the great sequence of centuries begins
> anew: the Virgin [Justice] returns,
> old Saturn's realm returns; a new offspring is
> sent down from heaven.
>
> *(Eclogues, 4.1-4)*

Though apparently sent from heaven, the child described in Eclogue 4 will be human: he will need the help of Diana-Lucina (here the goddess of childbirth) to come into the world and will be born after several months (of his mother's pregnancy). The birth year will be that of Pollio's consulship—40 BCE. (Since this was the year Octavia and Antony married, some scholars suggest that the mysterious "boy" could well be the child eagerly expected from that union, but Virgil himself never says so.) The child will lead the life of gods and "by ancestral virtues will rule a world at peace" (*Eclogues*, 4.17). The next strophe flashes forward to offer a graceful pastoral image of the divine child living in an earthly paradise replete with flowers, milk, and spices:

> Earth herself will cradle you, spreading gentle
> flowers.
> Goats themselves will bring home their
> udders full of milk
> and the cattle will not fear mighty lions.
> Destroyed will be
> the snake and the faithless herb of poison will
> be destroyed.
> Assyrian spice will grow everywhere.
>
> *(Eclogues, 4.23-25)*

As soon as the child learns to read, he will study the praises of heroes and the deeds of his father—apparently his ancestry is human after all. As he grows, the earthly paradise will acquire new miraculous features: grapes will grow on thorny bushes and oak trees will ooze honey. But even this paradise will not yet be complete: traces of ancient treachery will still remain and the Age of Heroes with its wars will be repeated. Only when the child turns into a man will the true Golden Age arrive. As recounted by the ancient Greek writer Hesiod in *Theogony*, not only wars, but also all other kinds of labor, including agriculture, will then cease. Virgil caps this description of nature undisturbed by any craft with a humorous image:

> Not any more will the wool learn to deceive
> with different colors,
> but in the pastures the ram himself will dye
> his fleece
> to the gentle blush of purple or to saffron
> yellow.
> Golden-red dye on its own accord will clothe
> the feeding lambs.
>
> *(Eclogues, 4.42-45)*

FOUR (OR FIVE) AGES OF HUMANKIND

In Roman myth, the god Saturn (in Greek, Cronus) is father of Jupiter (Zeus), king of the gods. Saturn's name is associated with the good old days, an earlier, happier age occupied by a Golden Race. The idea comes from the Myth of the Ages or Generations, most famously presented by the Greek writer Hesiod in **Theogony** (c. 700 BCE; also *in Classical Literature and Its Times*). According to this version, Cronus ruled over the earliest generation, that of Gold; people lived long and happy lives and the earth brought forth fruits of its own accord. The Silver Age followed; the people of that generation were children for the first hundred years of their lives and then died after a short and violent adulthood. The next two generations, that of Bronze and that of Heroes, can be conflated into one, as there are few differences between them and the notion of heroes is grafted upon an otherwise coherent scheme that associates the generations with metals of decreasing value. The heroes of the Bronze Age saw violence and war (the great epic wars, such as the siege of Troy). Hesiod's own time was the Age of Iron, a time of cruelty and injustice in which people must labor to sustain themselves. There were still worse times, taught Hesiod, to come.

After discussing the purple sheep with golden stripes, Virgil turns his attention to a grander scale; he imagines the Fates both ordering their spindles to spin such golden times and urging the child "offspring of gods, offshoot of Jupiter" to grow faster (*Eclogues*, 4.49).

Needless to say, the Golden Age will also be the perfect time to write. Virgil playfully promises to surpass all the legendary poets of nature—Orpheus, Linus, and even Pan, the god

ARCADIA—FANTASY OR REALITY?

Arcadia is in fact a central region of Peloponnese, the peninsula that forms the southern part of Greece. The inhabitants of this region, which is divided by mountains into isolated valleys, regard themselves as the descendants of the Pelasgians, the mythical pre-Greek population. One of the local legends has it that the tribe's hero, Pelasgus, grew out of the uncultivated Arcadian soil. Among divinities, Pan, the goat-god, patron of goatherds, shepherds, and their music, was worshipped on every mountain in Arcadia. His name, meaning "everything" in Greek, prompted ancient interpreters to view Pan as the embodiment of the universe. This name also offers an apt description of the god's immense sexual appetite; Pan is one of mythology's most relentless rapists. His victims are often the nymphs, gentle female spirits who personified their different habitats: springs and streams were personified by nymphs known as *Naiads,* trees by nymphs known as *Dryads,* meadows and flowers by the *Limoniads,* and grottos and hills by yet other varieties of these semi-divine female spirits. With its peculiar legends and history of isolation, Arcadia functioned in the Greek imagination as a metaphor for the wilderness and rusticity.

Pastoral poetry was born of an urbane nostalgia for a simpler world of shepherds who sing of Pan and the nymphs. It was for a cultivated audience of weary inhabitants of the large Hellenistic cities that Virgil's predecessor, the poet Theocritus, fantasized such a world into existence. Theocritus chose to locate it in his native Sicily, also reputed for rustic simplicity, but his narrative poems mentioned specific sites located elsewhere as well (including some in Arcadia). Virgil's "Arcadia" is more a product of the poet's fantasy, serving as an imaginary background for his Latin poetry. The name itself occurs rarely in the poetry and is always combined with features of Italian, not Greek, topography and with facts of Roman life under Octavian (war and dispossessions). It is perhaps best to compare Virgil's attitude towards Arcadia with his attitude towards Sicily. Consider the famous invocation, "Sicilian Muses, let us sing a slightly grander song," at the beginning of Eclogue 4. By mentioning Sicily (Theocritus's setting) Virgil indicates that he expects the originality of his poem to be measured against the literary conventions established by Theocritus. More precisely, Sicily is a place of departure for Virgil; he will take his Muses and readers beyond the limits of the genre. In a similar fashion, the actual Arcadia needs to be understood as a place we must leave behind if we are to reach the literary *Arcadia* that Virgil's poetry establishes for readers.

of Arcadia himself. He ends his poem addressing the mysterious newborn boy:

> Begin, my little boy to smile, recognizing your
>   mother.
> Ten months [of pregnancy] has brought her a
>   long hardship.
> Begin my little boy! Who has not smiled at
>   his parent has never
> feasted with a god or slept with a goddess.
>   (*Eclogues*, 4.60-63)

Augustan poets and the concept of Arcadia—nostalgia for the Golden Age. Exquisitely beautiful, endlessly surprising in its playful transformations, the background of the *Eclogues* is more than an empty theatrical décor. It is a living landscape whose presence is not to be taken for granted. There is only one way to summon it——through singing or, if we wish to lift the veil on Virgil's pastoral disguise, through poetry. In the very first lines of the first eclogue, Meliboeus sums up the difference between Tityrus's fate and his own as that between *singing* and *leaving*: "you rehearse your songs" and "we [whose lands have been confiscated] must leave" (*Eclogues*, 1.1-4). "Singing" in this equation stands for "remaining in Arcadia," so it comes as no surprise that exile will condemn Meliboeus to silence, for there is no pastoral song without Arcadia. Nor is there an Arcadia without its songs: Lycidas in Eclogue 9 fears that, had the singers (Menalcas and Moeris) died, his comforting world would simply have ceased to exist: "Who would sing the nymphs into being," he wonders; "Who would sprinkle the ground / With flowering herbs? Who would clothe the springs in fresh shade?" (*Eclogues*, 9.19-20).

The landscape of the eclogues is clearly one of joy and beauty (*locus amoenus*) sung into existence by poetry. But the motives for its creation are not purely aesthetic; Arcadia is an emotional necessity. Lycidas in Eclogue 9 says so when he refers to the songs as *solacia*—a source of relief from sorrow. In Eclogue 5 Menalcas goes so far as to describe pastoral poetry as fulfilling an urgent physical need:

> O divine poet, to us your song is as welcome
> as sleep in the grass is to those who are
>   weary, as
> quenching of thirst with fresh water from a
>   leaping brook
> is in the midst of the summer.
>
> (*Eclogues*, 5.45-47)

Against weariness (excess) and thirst (lack), poetry offers soothing scenery attuned to human emotions. The programmatic first lines of the first eclogue suggest that the experience of knowing and being known to the surreal literary countryside is the essence of the pastoral song. Tityrus, stretched out in the shade, teaches the forests the name of his beloved; when she, in her turn, misses him, the pines and springs call upon Tityrus—they presumably *know* his name. Harmony between the landscape and the figures within it permeates the *Eclogues*. Nymphs and naiads (river nymphs) spice wildflowers with cinnamon to help Corydon woo his "cruel Alexis" (*Eclogues*, 2.45-50). Nymphs and fierce lions mourn Daphnis—rivers and hazel bushes bear witness to the mourning. The presence of beautiful Alexis, whom so many desire, assures the fertility of chestnuts and juniper trees. Rocks of the cold Lycaeon stream feel for Gallus when, abandoned by his beloved, he mourns. Virgil suggests that this imaginary place of connectedness and compassion is "Arcadia," alluding to an ancient Greek land that, according to myth, grew its first inhabitant, Pelasgus, out of its own soil (*Eclogues*, 10.31-33). Through poetry the composer and the listener are briefly transferred into a place beyond historical time, where people are one with nature.

Eclogue 4 promises a similarly blissful experience, but situates it in computable time—the future. Here Virgil evokes a more familiar myth, that of the Four (or Five) Ages of humankind. The conceit of the poem, that the cycle of time is complete, that the present Iron Age is over, and that the world should begin anew with the Golden Age, allows Virgil to represent the gradual fading of the present forms of evil: vipers and poison; open warfare, and toil. The expected age of plenty is strongly reminiscent of the idealized countryside evoked in the other eclogues.

While this is never stated directly by Virgil, it is legitimate to assume that the desire to create a safe haven, be it a poetic Arcadia or a dream of the Golden Age, would have been inflamed by the grim circumstances of the civil war and the reality of the confiscations in Virgil's native Mantua. Virgil's friend, Horace, in his Epode 16 (written at the same time as some of the eclogues), openly expresses an intense weariness with Rome's constant wars:

"A second generation is now worn out by civil wars; Rome herself is ruined by her own strength" (Horace, Epode 16.1-2). The poet speaks in the name of the entire "generation of cursed blood"; he expects the sacrilege of the fraternal war to ruin Rome and does not wish to see the relics of Romulus desecrated. Horace's solution (like Virgil's) is an escape to a Utopia, but this time the sanctuary is painfully beyond reach; it lies in the Islands of the Blest, which Jupiter reserved for the survivors of the Golden Age to occupy in this Age of Iron. On the islands, as in the countryside of Virgil's Eclogue 4, goats offer their udders of their own accord and no vipers hide in the grass. And, like Virgil, Horace believes that his writing directs the worthy towards this unattainable refuge:

> . . . *saecula quorum*
> *piis secunda vate me datur fuga.*
>
> . . . the Ages [of Bronze and Iron] from which
> a propitious escape is granted to those who
>   are pious with
> me as their poet.
>
> (Horace, Epode 16.66)

The same feelings—weariness with the complexities of the present and nostalgia for an imaginary Golden Age—are discernible in the work of the elegiac poets of the Augustan period, only they locate the longed-for sanctuary in different places. Tibullus contrasts an idyllic description of the Golden Age, free of toil and warfare, with the perils of contemporary life. In another poem he suggests that the idyllic peace is neither in the future nor in some remote group of islands; it *was* the reality in Rome's pre-urban past, at the time before the city was founded by Romulus; now Rome's chance to become Arcadia is lost forever. His younger contemporary Propertius uses the Golden Age ironically, with reference to love affairs, implying that it may still be alive in those ephemeral happy moments lovers spend together. Later, however, he reverts to Tibullus's wistful vision of past (and lost) happiness.

The *Eclogues* thus can be read as Virgil's answer to the same question that Horace was to pose (and answer) in his Epode 16: "Is there any refuge from the trauma of civil war?" Of all the responses mentioned, Virgil's is not only the most extensive but also the most compelling, perhaps because the genre he used to write his poetry is particularly amenable to escapism.

Sources and literary context. The *Eclogues* was the first book of pastoral poems in Rome, but the genre was a Greek invention. It was developed in the 270s BCE by Theocritus, a poet who left his native Sicily for Alexandria. There he composed his *Idylls* ("Pictures"), some of which offered the urban(e) audience a literary refuge of affected rusticity. Theocritus's well-organized "pictures" were *poêmes à clef* (that is, poems featuring barely disguised real people). His poems dramatized debates between Alexandrian literati, transforming them into contests between Sicilian goatherds. Thus, from the very beginning, pastoral poetry was both a place of refuge and a metaphor representing the literary vocation. Theocritus may have invented pastoral poetry, its tone, its distinctive form called "amoebean dialogue" (a version of the traditional singing contest, wherein one speaker responds to the other's utterance with the same number of lines, preferably on the same topic), even the names of some of Virgil's shepherds and cowherds. But he did not create Arcadia; Arcadia is the intimate landscape of Virgil's mind. The Greek poet's descriptions of the landscapes of Sicily or the Island of Cos (the birthplace of his patron, Ptolemy) read like a versified guidebook for learned tourists. To sense the difference, compare the following excerpt from Theocritus's first idyll with its imitation in Virgil's Eclogue 10:

> Where were you, when Daphnis was in pain,
>   where were you Nymphs?
> Was it the pretty valley of Peneius or Pindus
>   [the names of a river and a mountain
>   range in Thessaly]?
> Certainly it was not the big stream of the
>   [Sicilian] river Anapus,

> Nor the pike of Aethna, not the holy water of
>   Acis [another Sicilian river].
>   (Theocritus, 1.66-69)

> What groves, what glens have kept you
>   maiden Naiads
> When Gallus was pining away from unworthy
>   love?
> For neither the ridges of Parnassus [mount
>   near Delphi] nor those of Pindus
> Held you back, nor yet the Aonian
>   [Thessalian spring of] Aganippe.
>   (*Eclogues*, 10.9-12)

Differences in precision and focus are immediately apparent: for Theocritus's general "Where?" Virgil substitutes nouns suggestive of various places in the woodland (glens and groves) that make the presence of his naiads (river nymphs instead of Theocritus's general nymphs) more tangible. The suffering lover is Gallus, a real person, rather than a pastoral stereotype as in Theocritus. Virgil substitutes for the references to Sicilian rivers in Theocritus's verse, the name of the spring Aganippe, probably taken from Gallus's poetry, thus adding another personal touch to his description. Most important, unlike the predictable nymphs of Theocritus, who must be in Sicily because they are not in Thessaly (they seem to visit only well-advertised places), Virgil's nymphs spend their time in unnamed woodlands. They could be everywhere. The geography of the *Eclogues*, though tangible, is ultimately elusive: readers can glimpse it, briefly touch its textures, smell its flowers, hear its sounds, but they can never explore it, or point to it on a map. Virgil's Arcadia at once is and is not the stylized Sicilian scenery in Theocritus's idylls; Virgil's is and is not the countryside of Mantua tormented by Octavian's confiscations. Unlike the knowable landscapes of the *Idylls*, Arcadia remains a mystery.

Reception. Virgil's *Eclogues* was an immediate success. Even before its publication the book gained Octavian's approval and ensured his protection for its author. Soon not only the literary circles, but also larger audiences recognized Virgil's talent. In his *Dialogue*, the historian Tacitus reports the following event: one day Virgil happened to be present in the theater when his poems were recited (most likely the *Eclogues* or excerpts from the *Georgics*). When the audience realized he was there, they gave him a standing ovation, "just as though he were Augustus himself" (Tacitus, 13.5). Even before the *Aeneid*, Virgil had already become a classic, an author to study in the schools (thanks to the grammarian Caecilius Epirota). After Virgil died, his reputation as a sage and the conviction that he knew everything (including the future) led to the practice of using his poetry for fortune-telling. Virgil's fourth eclogue was, along with the *Aeneid*, the best-known Latin poem in early Christianity. This eclogue, with its invocation to the Virgin and to the coming of the holy child, lent itself easily to Christian interpretations. Very few Romans of late antiquity would have believed that Virgil meant the Virgin "Justice" rather than the Virgin "Mary" or that he was writing about the expected child of Antony and Octavia (who would turn out to be a daughter) rather than Christ. Instead, the author of the *Eclogues* was pronounced a "natural Christian," having allegedly prophesized the birth of Jesus Christ, foreseeing Christianity without having been exposed to its teaching. This "odor of sanctity" did not prevent others from perceiving Virgil as a magician of sorts. The English spelling *Virgil* instead of the expected *Vergil* (the poet's Latin name was Vergilius) dates to that time and in fact reflects the linking of his name to the word *virga* ("branch" and "magic wand") or *virgo* ("virgin").

—Dorota Dutsch

For More Information

Alpers, Paul. *The Singer of the Eclogues: A Study of Virgilian Pastoral.* Berkeley: University of California Press, 1979.

Appian of Alexandria. *Roman History.* Trans. Horace White. Cambridge, Mass.: Harvard University Press, 1964.

Clausen, Wendell. *A Commentary on Virgil, Eclogues.* Oxford: Clarendon, 1994.

Conte, Gian Biagio. *Latin Literature.* Trans. J. B. Slodow. Baltimore, Md.: Johns Hopkins University Press, 1994.

Donatus, Tiberius Claudius. *Interpretationes Vergilianae* [Interpretations of Virgil]. Stuttgart, Germany: Teubner, 1969.

———. *Life of Virgil.* Trans. David Scott Wilson-Okamura. http://virgil.org/vitae/

Horace. *Odes and Epodes.* Trans. Niall Rudd. Cambridge, Mass.: Harvard University Press, 2004.

———. *Satires, Epistles, and Ars Poetica* [Art of Poetry]. Trans. H. Rushton Fairclough. Cambridge, Mass.: Harvard University Press, 1991.

Leach-Winsor, Eleanor. *Vergil's* Eclogues. *Landscapes of Experience.* Ithaca, N.Y.: Cornell University Press, 1974.

Levi, Peter. *Virgil: His Life and Times.* New York: St. Martin's Press, 1999.

Pelling, Christopher. "The Triumviral Period." In *The Cambridge Ancient History: The Augustan Empire.* Vol. 10. Cambridge, Mass.: Cambridge University Press, 1996.

Tacitus. *Dialogus de Oratoribus* [A Dialog on Oratory]. Trans. W. Peterson. Cambridge, Mass.: Harvard University Press, 1992.

Theocritus. *The Greek Bucolic Poets.* Trans. J. M. Edmonds. Cambridge, Mass.: Harvard University Press, 1977.

Virgil. *Eclogues, Georgics, Aeneid.* Vols. 1-6. Trans. H. Rushton Fairclough. Cambridge, Mass.: Harvard University Press, 1999.

An Ethiopian Story

by
Heliodorus

Heliodorus, the author of *An Ethiopian Story*, claims to be a Phoenician from the Syrian city of Emesa and to belong to the priestly clan of the sun god. He lived during the Roman Empire (probably in the late fourth century CE) and wrote his novel in ancient Greek in an archaic style more characteristic of the writings of Thucydides or Plato (fifth century BCE) than the contemporary "common" (*koine*) form of Greek. Little else is known about him, aside from an unverified account in Nicephorus' *Church History* (early ninth century CE) that Heliodorus later became a Christian bishop in Tricca, Thrace, and was given the choice either of destroying his "pagan" novel or relinquishing his position as bishop of a district. Heliodorus then surrendered his bishop's headdress. Probably this story is a fabrication designed to make the writing of a "pagan" author legitimate for Christian readers, much as Dante makes the pagan author Virgil worthy of the readers of his *The Divine Comedy*. Racine, the famous seventeenth-century French dramatist, had a son who tells an amusing anecdote about his father in relation to this novel. In his youth, an official at the monastery school he attended caught the young Racine devouring a copy of *An Ethiopian Story*, immediately confiscated the pagan novel, and burned it. The same thing happened again and Racine was severely reprimanded. Not long after, he cockily approached the official and surrendered a third copy to the furnace—for by then, we are told, the stubborn young student had memorized it! An adventure-packed novel, *An Ethiopian Story* unravels like a detective tale

THE LITERARY WORK

A novel set in Ethiopia in the third or second century BCE; written in Greek in the mid-fourth century CE.

SYNOPSIS

A young Greek priestess learns that she is the long-lost daughter of the rulers of Ethiopia and embarks with her fiancé on an adventure-filled quest from Greece, to Egypt, to the royal court of Ethiopia, where she reclaims her birthright.

and contains not only a sentimental love interest but also a nuanced portrayal of ethnic relations in the ancient world.

Events in History at the Time the Novel Takes Place

Ancient conceptions of the Eastern world. *An Ethiopian Story* takes us on an adventurous journey from what the ancient Greeks and Romans perceived as the "civilized" West to the "barbarous" unfamiliar East. Both the Greeks and the Romans (who conquered Greece in the third century BCE) showed dislike mixed with fear of foreigners. In fact, the degree of dislike was inversely proportional to the distance of a particular people from Greece (or Rome). A neighbor, such as the Persians, whom the Greeks or Romans were more likely to have knowledge of and engage in conflict with, were more feared than, for example, the Ethiopians or the Chinese. It is not that the Greeks necessarily thought of themselves as the wisest. In fact, Philostratus, a Greek writing in the early third century CE, describes the hierarchy of world wisdom as moving from the Greeks, up to the Egyptians, then up to the Ethiopians, and at the top to the Indians. There was a general tendency in Greek and Roman society to honor other peoples with a longer history of civilization. Yet at the same time, a sense of superiority, or ethnocentrism, prevails in much of Greek thought and writing. In the ancient novels, Greekness is a prerequisite for what is stylish and admirable: "good" characters of every ethnicity are always able to speak Greek; those who cannot are "bad" and inferior morally, intellectually, and physically.

The Greeks had a history with the East, or more exactly with the Persians, harking back to the mid-sixth century BCE. It was during the reign of the Persian King Cyrus that the Greeks first came into contact with the Persians. Cyrus began expanding the Persian Empire over the known Eastern world, eventually taking it all the way to the borders of India. Beginning his enterprise close to home, he set the Persians against the Lydians, who occupied an ancient country, Lydia, spread over much of the western part of Asia Minor (present-day Turkey). On the coast were many Greek colonies (Miletus, Ephesus, Smyrna) across a district known as Ionia. By paying yearly tributes to the Lydian kings, these Greek colonies that occupied the Ionian coast for the most part lived in peaceful co-existence with the Lydians. The situation would change dramatically when the Persians conquered Lydia. The Persians ravaged the Greek cities of the Ionian coast, sparing only Miletus. At the beginning of the fifth century BCE, the Ionian Greeks revolted against the Persians, who were now under the leadership of Darius.

Darius soon demanded the submission of all of Greece, and when the Greeks refused, he waged war. During the course of these hostilities, the Acropolis of Athens was devastated and Greek works of art were irrevocably lost. But the Greeks successfully resisted conquest, convincing the Persians and Xerxes, who had taken over after Darius, that victory was neither possible nor profitable. The Greeks had fended off the Easterners, bringing the Persian Wars to an end, but an uneasy relationship between the Greeks of Ionia and the Persians ensued. The Persians established satrapies, provinces ruled by governors who answered directly to the king himself. So while Persia had been kept out of mainland Greece, part of Greek territory was always under Persia's thumb, a disquieting reality.

There was also in Greek mythology a pretext for Persian-Greek enmity in the stories associated with Medea, the legendary barbarian princess from Colchis on the Black Sea, whose liaison with the Greek hero Jason had been treated by the poet Hesiod in the eighth century BCE. Medea's son Medeus (or Medus) helps found a new people, the Medes, the ancestors of the Persians, who attract the ill will of the Greeks. The hatred they harbor for Medea is transferred to her son's people. In Greek art, especially Greek vase paintings, Persians are characteristically denoted by their unfamiliar dress: pointy hats, elaborate fabric, and trousers. In the eyes of the Greeks, the Persians were a decadent people, whose love of luxury testified to their moral corruption. Book 7 of Herodotus' *Histories* (also in *Classical Literature and Its Times*) depicts the Persian king Xerxes as a megalomaniac, a leader obsessed with gaining ever more power. The distinction between themselves and the Persians is evident in the Greek names for styles of rhetoric or oratory. The Greeks called the plain, elegant style of rhetoric "Attic," from Attica, the name of the region in which Athens sat; they called the ornate, bombastic style of rhetoric "Asiatic." There were political differences, too. At the end of the sixth century, Athens had rid itself of tyrants and instituted a more representative government. Many other Greek city-states, such as Corinth, went through a monarchic period before they, too, established proto-democratic regimes. Ever after, the word "tyrant" stuck in the Greeks' throats, and they came to view with disgust and disdain kings and kingdoms. They considered their elective system superior. In actuality, though, Greek democracy more closely resembled the democracy in the United States at the end of the eighteenth century, in that Greek society also ran a partially slave-based economy, and only free males were allowed to vote.

Egyptians and Indians. The Greeks knew more about the Egyptians than about the Persians and maintained an active fascination with Egyptian culture. Herodotus in book 2 of his *Histories* asserts that the Greeks derived their gods from the Egyptian gods. This does not necessarily mean that the Greeks literally invented their gods based upon the Egyptian gods, in a one-to-one type correspondence.

What it does mean is that Herodotus is laying a claim to prestige for the Greek pantheon based upon an association with an older, more established tradition.

The four areas of Egyptian culture most impressive to the Greeks were its art, architecture, religion, and socio-political system. The influence of Egyptian style on Greek art is evident in many ways, for instance, in the *kouros* ("young man") and *kore* ("young woman") statues of the Archaic Period, which bear great similarities to well-known Egyptian pieces. There is good evidence for healthy trade between various Greek city-states and Egypt, an activity that declined following the conquest of Egypt by the Persians under Cambyses in 525 BCE. Thereafter, the Persians established a satrapy in Egypt. But Egypt did not submit to subjugation easily; the cultural memory of 2,000 years of independence was difficult to dispel. In the mid-fifth century BCE, there was a revolt in Egypt against the Persians, and Egyptian rebels appealed to the Athenians for aid, mindful of the fact that Athens operated the finest navy of the day. The Athenians sent a fleet to Egypt, a force that was at first quite successful in vanquishing the Persians, helping to free Egypt from Persian rule for five years. The Persians, realizing that their best defensive strategy was to exploit an internal rivalry for power in Greece—the contest between Athens and Sparta—did their best to aggravate this hostility. They sent envoys to the Spartans, encouraging them to attack Athens while its fleet was in Egypt. In the end, the Spartans decided not to raise tensions to such an extent, and Persia had to move against the Athenians itself. It took almost two years, but Persia eventually routed the Athenians and reclaimed Egypt, which periodically revolted against the Persians until 331 BCE, when Alexander the Great annexed Egypt to the Macedonian Empire. The Egyptians, who are described as having detested Persian rule, regarded the Macedonians as liberators, and Alexander founded the first of the many cities to be named after him, Alexandria, at the mouth of the Nile River. When Alexander died and the Macedonian Empire was divided into quarters (Asia, Egypt, Thrace, and Macedonia and Greece), the Macedonian leader Ptolemy gained control of Egypt. Ptolemy's dynasty endured until his final descendant, Cleopatra VII, committed suicide in 30 BCE. Hers became the last of all the Macedonian dynasties to fall to Rome.

Once Egypt became a Roman province, it seems to have lost some prestige in Roman circles. It had been a long time since Egypt had governed itself as an independent country, and to the minds of many Romans, it shared an unhappy fate with Greece. The decline of Greece could be seen in the transformation of Athens; once an empire unto itself, the city became little more than what today might be called a college town, a place wealthy Romans sent their sons for education. Once a great power, Egypt had withered from its former glory. The land, long admired for its age-old wisdom, became associated with arcane lore and magic. In *An Ethiopian Story,* all older Egyptian women are proficient in potions and spells, and an Egyptian priest (Kalasiris) speaks at length (book 3, chapter 16) about lower (magic) and higher (divination) kinds of Egyptian wisdom.

Finally, the Greeks knew comparatively little about the Ethiopians, aside from their skin color—in Greek *aithiops* means "burnt-face." They believed them to dwell at the eastern edge of the known world. As such, the Ethiopians existed on the border between reality and fantasy, which allowed the Greeks to lend the Ethiopians certain attributes in the earliest literature. In Homer's the **Iliad** and the **Odyssey** (eighth century BCE), the Ethiopians are one of the few peoples who enjoy the privilege of the gods' personal company (both works also in *Classical Literature and Its Times*). That the gods allow physical contact with the Ethiopians denotes a great honor, for most often in mythology any direct contact between god and mortal results in that mortal's demise. For example, Semele, a princess of Thebes in Greece, has a son with the god Zeus and convinces him to appear to her in the same form as to his heavenly wife; he appears as a thunderbolt, and Semele is blasted into oblivion.

While *An Ethiopian Story* mentions other exotic people too, such as the Troglodytes, the Blemmyes, the Seres, and the Indians, the Greeks had little factual evidence about them beyond travelers' tales. The Troglodytes ("cave dwellers") and the nomadic Blemmyes, who supposedly had no heads but eyes and mouths in their chests, lived to the south of Egypt. The Seres refer to the silk-producing Chinese, whom the Greek travel writer Pausanias (second century CE) confuses with the Ethiopians and the Scythians. Though Aristotle (fifth century BCE) knew of the silk worm (*ser* in Greek), the famed Silk Road overland trade route linking the East to the West was not established until the second century BCE. The Romans nevertheless had direct contact with the

Chinese when Chinese envoys visited the Roman emperor Augustus. Regarding the Indians, the Greek geographer Strabo (first century BCE) admits that any accurate information about India is shrouded in the obscurity of third-hand reports. This does not stop him from passing on fantastic accounts of Indian tribes, animals, and cultural practices—including an erroneous summary of the caste system. Also in India were the Gymnosophists, or Naked Sages, groups of philosophers who saw food and clothing as counterproductive to pure thinking. Strabo locates the Gymnosophists, who were as famous for their wisdom as for their habit of meditating in the nude, in India. But Heliodorus places them in Ethiopia for narrative convenience.

Kingdom of Meroe. In *An Ethiopian Story,* Meroe, the capital of Ethiopia, is a land of fantasy, a place of extremes. Not only is it home to the renowned Gymnosophists, but its king is also a model of sophistication, learning, and military prowess who commands the respect and tribute (it seems) of all the Eastern world. The land's customs include human sacrifice.

In real life, ancient Meroe appears to have been settled in the early sixth century BCE by Cushites, who were from Nubia (present-day Sudan). They conquered their way northward, up to middle Egypt (Thebes), where their progress was arrested, first by the Assyrians and then by the Egyptians, who forced them to retreat and move their capital south to Meroe, near the sixth cataract of the Nile. Irrigation from the river helped the settlement at Meroe thrive. Meroe Island, a triangular landform south of the fifth cataract on the east bank of the Nile, was the cultural and social center of the kingdom. The isle was bordered on the north by the Atbara River, on the west by the Nile, and on the south by the Blue Nile River. Following Egyptian custom, the inhabitants of Meroe erected pyramids (still standing today) and commemorative stone slabs as monuments to their rulers' accomplishments. The Cushites of Meroe adopted many aspects of Egyptian culture, then developed independent offshoots of these traditions over time. For instance, Meroe's pharaohs answered to a priestly council, and they included a line of female rulers, known as the *Kentake* or, in Greek, as the *Candaces*. The Ethiopians also adapted their own writing system (which has yet to be deciphered) based upon the popular script of the Egyptians.

Meroe gained wealth through trade by exploiting its convenient position between sub-Saharan Africa and the Middle East, Europe, and North Africa. It reached its zenith of power in the third and second centuries BCE, at which point its territory extended from the third cataract of the Nile southward almost to modern Khartoum. The kingdom of Meroe was successful enough to attract the attentions of ancient superpowers. After the Persians' invasion of Egypt in 525 BCE, Ethiopia was soon added as a vassal state of Persia. Then when the Persian Empire fell to Alexander the Great and the Macedonians in 330 BCE, Ethiopia began sending tribute to this new imperial power. During the reign of Augustus at the beginning of the Roman Empire, Ethiopia once again switched, now paying tribute to its new Roman rulers. At the same time, in a quest to extend its boundaries, Meroe made forays north into Egyptian territory, causing so much trouble that the Roman army razed the formerly Ethiopian town of Napata in ancient Egypt but did not venture further south, deeming the territory unfit for colonization. In the second century CE, the Blemmyes, a nomadic people living in the regions of Ethiopia and Egypt, made many incursions against Roman territories in Egypt. To suppress them, the Roman emperor Diocletian at the end of the third century CE in effect hired the Nobatae, a tribe of uncertain origin that had settled in the northern territory of Meroe, as mercenaries to contain the Blemmyes.

Priests, prophets, and sacrifice. Greek religion is founded around the principle of exchange: *do ut des,* Latin for "I give so that you give." Humans traded offerings to the gods in return for boons—good crops, purification, success, wealth, health, love, or knowledge. Priests were intermediaries who performed the sacrifices and interpreted messages from the gods. In this way, the priests filled a prophetic function, which helps explain why most prophets in Greek literature are also priests. Gods were believed to communicate with mortals through patterns in nature: the movement and character of birds, the entrails of those sacrificed, or the positions of the heavenly bodies (astrology). Priests could interpret these signs and, through sacrifice, could coax the gods to reveal more. The items to be sacrificed included food, animals (chickens, goats, cows, pigs), and perhaps even humans. Human sacrifice occurs in Greek mythology—King Agamemnon's sacrifice of his daughter Iphigenia to obtain good weather to sail to Troy, for example. Andromeda, a legendary princess of Ethiopia, is herself a human sacrifice to appease the anger of the gods. Archeological evidence, which is not without its critics, suggests that human sacrifice might have played a part in Greek culture during the second millennium BCE and perhaps into the early first millennium. There does not appear to be archeological evidence for human sacrifice in Ethiopia, though it would not be surprising to find human sacrifices in the royal tombs, given that the Ethiopians adopted the art of pyramids and the pharaonic system from Egypt, where human sacrifices have been discovered.

An alternate way of consulting the gods was through oracles. In his *Histories,* Herodotus describes how King Croesus of the Lydians tested the accuracy of all the oracles in the ancient world and found the one at Delphi, which is consulted in *An Ethiopian Story,* to be the most reliable. At Delphi, the Pythia, or priestess, served in the temple of Apollo, the god of prophecy. Visitors would bring offerings to Apollo and await their turn to approach the priestess with their questions. People typically consulted her about business, health, wealth, and love. The Pythia would then enter into a frenetic trance. Some ancient writers supposed the Pythia would enhance this trance by breathing vapors from a chasm in the rock or by chewing on laurel leaves. Though attempts to replicate the latter method have been unsuccessful, recent findings support the vaporous gas (ethylene) hypothesis. Inspired by the god, the prophetess would speak in unintelligible words, which the priests of Apollo would then render into hexameter verse. In Greek literature, oracles are always correct, almost always misinterpreted at first, and properly understood only upon their (often tragic) fulfillment. Herodotus (book 1) records a famous consultation in which King Croesus is told that if he attacks Persia, a great kingdom will fall. Croesus arrogantly assumes that he will triumph, and only after he has lost his own kingdom of Lydia to the Persians does he understand the oracle's intended meaning.

The Novel in Focus

Plot summary. *An Ethiopian Story* concerns a young woman's quest to reclaim her birthright, which takes her from Greece through Egypt to distant Ethiopia. On the way, she and her fearless fiancé do battle against brigands, suffer slavery, fend off amorous foreigners, and brave torture before landing, literally, on the sacrificial chopping block in Ethiopia.

After years of childlessness King Hydaspes and Queen Persinna of Ethiopia finally conceive, but when the baby is born with white skin, Persinna abandons it, fearing a charge of adultery. A philosopher, one of the Gymnosophists, rescues the newborn and fosters the child at Delphi in Greece with a priest named Charikles, who names his foundling daughter Charikleia. When she grows to maturity, unbeknownst to Charikles, who intends to marry her to his son, Charikleia falls in love with Theagenes, a young man from Thrace, who is visiting Delphi. In shrouded language, the oracle of Delphi predicts adventures, hardship, and eventual success for this pair. Their romantic predicament is solved by the appearance of Kalasiris, an Egyptian priest, who is on a secret mission for Queen Persinna to find and retrieve her long-lost daughter and only child. The three of them abscond from Delphi, set out for Ethiopia, and encounter an amazing array of mishaps—shipwreck, lewd pirates, an equally lecherous Persian queen, battles, a witch, torture, and slavery. At one point, Theagenes is rescued from Persian captivity by a renegade son of Kalasiris and taken to Memphis in Egypt. When Kalasiris and Charikleia arrive, there unfolds a dramatic scene of reunions, of Charikleia with Theagenes and of Kalasiris with his two sons. Egypt, however, is under Persian control, and the satrap's wife, Arsake, lusts after Theagenes, vowing to stop at nothing until she seduces him. When he is summonsed to appear before the queen, Theagenes refuses to bow to her, which outrages the court, but she lets the offense pass, excusing the blunder. "You must forgive him. . . . He is every inch a Greek and is afflicted with the scorn that all Greeks feel for us" (Heliodorus, *An Ethiopian Story*, 7.19). Theagenes and Charikleia pose as brother and sister, so there seems to be no obstacle to her designs on him, though, of course, there is. Complications ensue, including an attempt on Charikleia's life.

Fortunately, during a war between the Ethiopians and the Persians, the couple is captured by the Ethiopian King Hydaspes. The story now centers only on the two lovers, as their companion the priest has died mid-adventure. At first, their capture seems far from a happy turn-of-events. The king orders that his captives be delivered to Meroe for sacrifice and that his queen prepare a celebration in honor of his military victory. During the festivities, Charikleia and Theagenes impress everyone by testing positive for virginity on the gridiron, a magical device that measures sexual purity. Charikleia also takes the opportunity to reveal her identity to her father King Hydaspes. After much drama, including the abolition of human sacrifice in the kingdom at the behest of the Gymnosophists, both she and

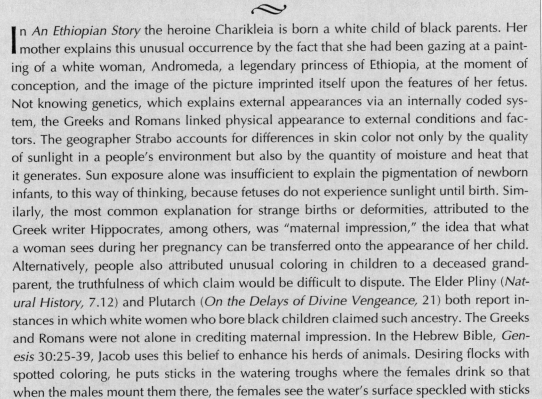

UNDERSTANDING SKIN COLOR—THE WAY THE ANCIENTS WOULD

In *An Ethiopian Story* the heroine Charikleia is born a white child of black parents. Her mother explains this unusual occurrence by the fact that she had been gazing at a painting of a white woman, Andromeda, a legendary princess of Ethiopia, at the moment of conception, and the image of the picture imprinted itself upon the features of her fetus. Not knowing genetics, which explains external appearances via an internally coded system, the Greeks and Romans linked physical appearance to external conditions and factors. The geographer Strabo accounts for differences in skin color not only by the quality of sunlight in a people's environment but also by the quantity of moisture and heat that it generates. Sun exposure alone was insufficient to explain the pigmentation of newborn infants, to this way of thinking, because fetuses do not experience sunlight until birth. Similarly, the most common explanation for strange births or deformities, attributed to the Greek writer Hippocrates, among others, was "maternal impression," the idea that what a woman sees during her pregnancy can be transferred onto the appearance of her child. Alternatively, people also attributed unusual coloring in children to a deceased grandparent, the truthfulness of which claim would be difficult to dispute. The Elder Pliny (*Natural History,* 7.12) and Plutarch (*On the Delays of Divine Vengeance,* 21) both report instances in which white women who bore black children claimed such ancestry. The Greeks and Romans were not alone in crediting maternal impression. In the Hebrew Bible, *Genesis* 30:25-39, Jacob uses this belief to enhance his herds of animals. Desiring flocks with spotted coloring, he puts sticks in the watering troughs where the females drink so that when the males mount them there, the females see the water's surface speckled with sticks and their progeny become similarly marked.

Theagenes are welcomed into the royal family and parade off to celebrate their wedding.

Cultural identity in the ancient world. Whereas today many people identify their ethnicity with a combined term (African American, French Canadian, and so on), until recently ethnic identity seemed to be simpler in the ancient world. Greeks were Greeks, Persians were Persians, and the two never mixed. Scholars of late have realized that identity in the ancient world could have been just as complicated as it can be today. How does a child born of parents from different countries yet living in a third country describe his or her cultural identity? Or, to put it in ancient terms, what label could be put on a man born in Syria, educated in the Greek language and culture, and yet living in the Roman (Latin speaking) Empire? Such a man is Heliodorus, author of *An Ethiopian Story.* The more people are inclined to migrate, the more difficult it becomes to use country of origin to determine a person's

culture. This issue is played out in the novel, where cultural identities seem to be exchanged as easily as clothing, and a person's appearance does not necessarily correspond with her or his cultural identity. The heroine's appearance, both physical and cultural, belies her multilayered heritage: by the novel's end Charikleia realizes that she has not one, not two, not three, but four parents—King Hydaspes, a painting, the priest Kalasiris, and her foster father Charikles. She owes to each a part of her identity. Kalasiris' appearance is likewise misleading, for he hides an Egyptian identity beneath Greek garb. The story questions the relationship between appearance and identity on many levels—in fact, the novel itself is a Greek tale about Ethiopians written by a Syrian.

Language is a significant marker in the novel. It does not necessarily designate culture so much as it indicates *paideia,* a Greek term meaning sophistication, education, and cultivation all rolled into one. *An Ethiopian Story* is the only ancient novel that attempts to represent the multilingual milieu of the ancient world. Not all characters speak Greek, and some speak only broken Greek. This situation leads to problems in communication and understanding. It is worth noting, however, which characters are able to speak which languages. All of the sympathetic characters speak Greek—Charikleia, Theagenes, Kalasiris, Hydaspes, Persinna. A certain Egyptian brigand who at first appears hostile does not speak Greek, but after he befriends the hero, he learns Greek. Greek-speaking characters are adept at learning other tongues. Speaking Greek is in fact an indicator of *paideia*. All the characters who speak Greek exhibit a fine sense of truth, justice, responsibility, and morality; they all are *pepaideumenoi*, "well-educated and civilized." *Paideia* is not an innate quality; it is an acquired one, and it becomes apparent in the way that a character behaves. As suggested by the languages and other habits learned and exhibited by the novel's characters, identity pivots on behavior and not birth. Characters can adopt any cultural identity they want and even entertain two simultaneously, if they are willing to alter their behavior, as Charikleia and Theagenes do at the end of the novel, when they prepare to be initiated into the more mystic aspects of the Ethiopian wedding ceremony. *Paideia* cannot be lost by the adoption of other cultures, and it is this spirit of cultural interpenetration with which the novel closes.

Sources in literary context. The ancient novel was the last major genre to emerge from Greek literature. Stylistically it is a grab bag of genres, incorporating aspects of all other literary forms. Epic is an obvious influence on the novel, in that the quest of the model epic hero (i.e., Odysseus) becomes the heroine Charikleia's quest. Also influential are historical writing (for its narrative descriptions of peoples, places, and events) and lyric poetry (with its themes of love and desire). Philosophy has a place in the novel, for characters muse on the nature of human beings and the world. Tragic elements are infused into the storyline as well—the saga of Kalasiris, for instance. The priest not only loses his wife, but a divine premonition that his sons will battle each other drives him to self-exile in order to forestall this family conflict. This action proves to be futile, and he is reunited with his sons in Memphis just as they are about to kill each other. Perhaps the most direct influence on the novel comes from comedy—not the political plays of Aristo-

phanes but the situational comedies of Menander, which feature long-lost children abandoned with recognition tokens (in Heliodorus' novel, Charikleia has a breastband that is embroidered with her mother's story in Ethiopian hieroglyphics). Other elements featured in these comedies are young lovers overcoming the obstacles to their relationship, mistaken identities, all sorts of suffering, and, finally, reunion of families and marriage. Because they encompass all these influences, *An Ethiopian Story* and the other ancient novels touch on most aspects of human experience, from the amusing to the erotic, suspenseful, and always the dramatic. In another ancient novel, *Daphnis and Chloe* by Longus, a shepherdess and goatherd fall in love but are so unsophisticated that they do not know what is happening to them and spend the rest of the novel finding out. In the end it turns out that they are the long-lost children of wealthy citizens, so they can marry and continue their idyllic existence.

The question of sources is problematic because the dating of *An Ethiopian Story* is uncertain. As the novel does not refer to any events of its day, there are no internal clues. Heliodorus claims to be a descendant of the clan of the sun god, which has led some scholars to speculate that he wrote during the height of sun worship in the third century CE, but most think this unlikely. The most tantalizing bit of evidence for dating the novel comes from the remarkable similarity between the siege of Syene that the Ethiopian king Hydaspes leads against the Persians in book 9 of *An Ethiopian Story* and the historical third siege of Nisibis in 350 CE when King Sapor II of Persia attempted to wrest the city from Roman hands. Sapor used an unprecedented technique of diverting a river to undermine the city walls, and *An Ethiopian Story* features this same exact strategy. The two earliest historical sources that describe this siege are a sermon by St. Ephraim, an eyewitness, and two letters by the emperor Julian, written in the 350s CE. The versions of Ephraim and Julian do not completely match, and there is confusion over who used whom as a source. Did Heliodorus copy Julian? Was it the other way around? Or did they both use Ephraim to compose independent versions? The current thinking is that Heliodorus and Julian wrote separate accounts and that Heliodorus may have consulted Julian's version. *An Ethiopian Story* may have influenced a set of biographies of Roman emperors known as the *Historia Augusta*, written about 400 CE. If this is the case, then the composition of *An Ethiopian Story* can be placed in the second half of the fourth century.

Events in History at the Time the Novel Was Written

East-West relations in the fourth century CE. Historically the Ethiopian kingdom of Meroe continued to exist until the mid-fourth century CE, about the time in which Heliodorus sets his novel. The historical records mention Meroe earlier, under the first Roman emperors, Augustus and Nero. Under Augustus, a Roman official in Egypt (a man named Petronius) sent a punitive force into Meroe, capturing and burning cities and leaving behind a Roman garrison. When the native inhabitants attacked this garrison, the official himself led a force to defend it until the queen of Meroe sued for peace. Apparently later the emperor Nero sent soldiers to explore the hinterlands, and they reached the renowned city of Meroe, reporting that the area had more greenery than they had seen in a while and that they had spotted the tracks of rhinoceroses and elephants there. But several hundred years later, in the fourth century CE, no mention is made of any expeditions or punitive campaigns in the area. In the fourth century CE, the Roman Empire was preoccupied with expanding its rule into new areas and subjugating the inhabitants of these areas. Lands that had already been conquered and turned into colonial territories, the way Ethiopia had a few centuries earlier, seldom appeared in the records unless their inhabitants revolted. To be sure, such revolts were occurring in the fourth century, but

not, according to the records, in any troublesome way in Ethiopia. More problematic in the fourth century were the eastern Germanic peoples (like the Goths), who challenged Roman sovereignty.

Reception and impact. The English word "novel" comes from the French for "new." The ancient novel was the last literary form to emerge from antiquity, and given the respect that the Greeks and Romans showed for tradition, its newness was hardly a benefit. The ancient Greek novel was born so late (our earliest examples date to the first century CE) that it was not included among the major literary genres. Only a handful of references to ancient novels survive. One is a quip to the novelist Chariton: "You think that the Greeks will remember your words when you die, but what does someone who is a nobody in life become when he is dead?" (Pseudo-Philostratus, Epistle 66). Another is the emperor Julian's letter to his high priests, urging them to avoid reading novels because they are written in the form of history and, since they are *not* historical documents, can fool the unsuspecting reader. Clearly the ancient novel was not a well-respected form of literature.

An Ethiopian Story is the last-known ancient novel. At the end of the fourth century, this literary form was discontinued in Greek and Roman society. However, the novels were read through the Byzantine period, and the genre enjoyed a revival in twelfth-century Byzantium, with four new novels that imitated and outdid the ancient ones (in length, in the number of shipwrecks and attempted rapes, and so forth). The ancient novels continued to attract attention, so much so that in the sixteenth century the Spanish writer Alonso

López de Pinciano named the three major epic "poets" of antiquity as Homer, Virgil, and Heliodoros, using the word "poet" loosely as a term for creative writer. Perhaps this third "epic poet" was on Cervantes's mind when he wrote the book that many describe as the world's first modern novel—*Don Quixote* (1605, 1615)—which borrows imagery and style from *An Ethiopian Story*.

—Kathryn Chew

For More Information

Bowersock, G. W. *Fiction as History: Nero to Julian*. Berkeley: University of California Press, 1991.

Hägg, Tomas. *The Novel in Antiquity*. Berkeley: University of California Press, 1983.

Heliodorus. *An Ethiopian Story*. In *Collected Ancient Greek Novels*. Ed. B. P. Reardon. Berkeley: University of California Press, 1989.

Hughes, Dennis D. *Human Sacrifice in Ancient Greece*. London: Routledge, 1991.

Hunter, Richard, ed. *Studies in Heliodorus*. Cambridge: Cambridge University Press, 1998.

Lightfoot, C. S. "Facts and Fiction—The Third Siege of Nisibis (AD 350)." *Historia* 37 (1988): 105-25.

Schmeling, Gareth, ed. *The Novel in the Ancient World*. Leiden: Brill, 1996.

Sealey, Raphael. *A History of the Greek City States 700-338 B.C.* Berkeley: University of California Press, 1976.

Tatum, James, ed. *The Search for the Ancient Novel*. Baltimore: Johns Hopkins University Press, 1994.

From the Founding of the City

by
Livy

The first great Roman historian without a political background, Titus Livius (Livy) is famous for his monumental 142-book history of Rome, *From the Founding of the City* (the *Ab Urbe Condita*). Only books 1-10 and 21-45 have survived intact. The contents of almost all of the remaining books (except for 136 and 137) are known from a summary, or *Epitome*, of the entire work by an unknown author, from papyrus fragments discovered in 1906 at Oxyrhynchus in Egypt, and from the work of Julius Obsequens, a fourth-century writer, who excerpted brief sections of Livy's text. According to St. Jerome, Livy was born in 59 BCE at Padua, Italy. As a member of the provincial elite, he would have had the usual schooling in rhetoric and philosophy. In his youth he wrote philosophical essays and later wrote a rhetorical treatise for his son; none of these works has survived. Livy moved to Rome in the 30s BCE, when he began work on his history of Rome, *Ab Urbe Condita*. This project occupied him until his death in 17 CE. In writing the history, Livy adopted a traditional, annalistic (year-by-year) framework. There is a pro-Republican, strongly moralistic outlook to his history, though it is clearly shaped by the tumultuous civil wars of the 40s and 30s BCE and the rise to power of the first emperor of Rome—Augustus. The inherent dangers of absolute power and the erosion of Rome's traditional Republican way of life during this troublesome period are of particular concern to Livy. His analysis of Rome's expansion through military conquest

THE LITERARY WORK

A historical narrative of the history of Rome from c. 753 BCE to c. 9 BCE; written in Latin and published during the reign of the Emperor Augustus (31 BCE to 14 CE) and the early years of his successor Tiberius (14 to 37 CE).

SYNOPSIS

Likening history to a monument on which are displayed good examples to follow and bad to avoid, the author traces the rise and expansion of Rome from the twin founders, Romulus and Remus, to the Emperor Augustus.

and of the development of its political, religious, and social institutions is therefore imbued with valuable lessons for Livy's own time.

Events in History at the Time of the Narrative

Early Rome and the regal period. Around the tenth century BCE onwards, the Iron Age peoples of Italy began to settle on easily defensible hilltops. The site of the future Rome was ideal. Some 12 miles inland from the Mediterranean Sea, a series of hills rose next to the River Tiber. The hills provided refuge from floods and hostile influences, while the valleys irrigated by the Tiber and by fresh spring water provided excellent farmland and pasture. Evidence for early settlements at the

Illustration of Livy. The Library of Congress.

future site of Rome has been confirmed by archaeological excavations that have revealed Iron Age huts and burials dating to the ninth century BCE on the Palatine and Esquiline hills. This early settlement at Rome was a pastoral community, similar to other settlements in the region. These settlements seem to have been ruled by a "king" or chief, who was probably the most powerful man of a small aristocratic class. Most people were probably peasant farmers dependent on the aristocrats for protection from hostile tribes.

Rome nonetheless benefited from its position close to the Tiber River. Its central position for river and land routes meant that its people could exploit the opportunities offered by trade and could forge links with neighboring communities.

Rome's growth attracted the attention of the Etruscans to the north, who spoke a different language and had different social and religious practices. They appear to have exerted control of Rome in the sixth century BCE. During the next century and a half, Rome grew into a major city, constructing the great foundation of the Temple of Jupiter on the Capitoline Hill, large aristocratic houses from stone, and a defensive wall. During this period the Romans also developed an army of well-drilled infantry soldiers, who fought shoulder-to-shoulder. In the Roman historical sources, the Etruscan dominance of the city is captured in the reigns of the legendary Etruscan

kings, Tarquinius Priscus and Tarquinius Superbus, who receive credit for major temple and building work.

While the greater sophistication of the Etruscans had a considerable influence on Rome, trade and contact with the Greek colonies in the south of Italy and with the Phoenicians in the eastern Mediterranean left their marks too, particularly on the literature and archaeology of early Rome. The evidence suggests a vibrant, cross-cultural dissemination of knowledge and ideas.

The Republic. Livy tells us that the kings were expelled from Rome in 510-509 BCE. The date is a convenient Roman fiction that coincides with the democratic reforms of Cleisthenes at Athens during the same period. Probably the aristocratic classes, dissatisfied with the monarchy as their form of government, exerted their wealth and influence to institute an oligarchy ("rule of the few"). The basis of power now lay in the hands of two annually elected magistrates known as consuls, supported by the Senate (which derives its name from the Latin word *senex* or "old man"), effectively a body of elders. The patrician, or aristocratic, class—a wealthy, landowning elite—controlled access to the consulship, to other magistracies (offices of state), and to priesthoods.

The change in government coincided with threats to Rome from neighboring tribes. This led to extensive wars of Roman conquest throughout Italy, including campaigns against the Etruscans. The wars exposed serious problems at home, especially a growing dearth of manpower for the army and mounting debt among the lower (plebeian) classes. Not only were the plebeians compelled to fight wars that did not benefit their position in society, but they were also oppressed by the patricians, who at times compelled them to become enslaved when they could not repay their debts.

These factors and the exclusion of the plebeians from government led to their agitation for reform. Over time, the patricians relinquished their rights to control the laws, magistracies, and priesthoods. Key turning points were the codification of Roman law by way of the Twelve Tables (451-450 BCE), the opening up of the consulship (367 BCE) to plebeian candidates, and the election of plebeians to the priestly colleges (300 BCE). The ceding of powers from the patricians to the plebeians (commoners) coincided with Rome's reliance on the common people to man its armies during a time of expansion. It also marked the formulation of a more rigid constitution, one in which both the rich and the poor had parts to play.

The later Republic. Rome's wars of conquest brought Rome into conflict with Carthage, as both powers were eager to acquire Sicily and its natural resources. Emerging the victor, Rome acquired Sicily in 241 BCE. In 202 BCE, Rome defeated Carthage again, gaining parts of Spain, and in 146 BCE Rome razed Carthage altogether. At the same time, Rome turned its attention to the Greek east, fighting four wars with Macedon, finally overcoming the Greek state in 146 BCE. This resulted in an influx of Hellenistic art, culture, and religion. The effects of Roman expansion throughout the Mediterranean were beyond estimation. The nobility acquired wealth at a pace they never had before. Huge numbers of slaves flooded into Rome and the Italian countryside. Exacerbated by the wars of conquest, the divide between rich and poor became ever more apparent, and this inevitably led to more serious political and social upheavals.

Livy's narrative survives only in summaries for the later Roman Republic, but our evidence is well supplemented by other authors: Sallust, Cicero, Appian, and Plutarch. They paint a bleak picture of Rome from the mid-second century BCE onwards. These writers emphasize Rome's declining morality and the abandonment of traditional political and religious practices. They paint a picture of a class of nobility that is given to luxury, greed, and an overriding desire for personal acclaim at any cost. Indeed a survey of the last years of the Republic shows continual internal strife and civil war from 133 BCE.

In 133 BCE, the tribune Tiberius Sempronius Gracchus tried to institute a rather modest land reform that would help the poor and nobles alike. In the ensuing disturbances, he was killed along with many of his supporters, whose bodies were thrown into the River Tiber. The nobility resisted such reforms because of worries that they gave ambitious individuals too much influence amongst the people. Ultimately their obstruction led in the first century BCE to the rise of the "military dynast": men who would not hesitate to use the army to augment their personal reputation and glory. Gaius Marius, an army general, ignored the restrictions that prevented Roman magistrates from acquiring successive political offices or holding the same office within a ten-year period; he himself occupied the consulship seven times (five times in succession). Lucius Cornelius Sulla, another general, fought against his fellow citizens and was declared dic-

tator for the unprecedented reason of rewriting the constitution. Sulla occupied the dictatorship (normally a six-month appointment) for the equally unprecedented period of three years. Pompey the Great held military commands and political offices before he was legally permitted to do so. Finally, after gaining unparalleled acclaim from his Gallic campaigns, Julius Caesar showed a thirst for ultimate power. On January 15, 49 BCE, he led his forces across the Rubicon (a tiny stream separating Gaul from Italy) to embroil Rome in another bloody civil war and, eventually, to be elected dictator for life.

THE ETRUSCANS AND THE ROMANS

Rome's early tribal organization was based on Etruscan distinctions. Etruscan kingly regalia, special clothes, and a ceremonial chair survived as symbols of Roman magistrates. The progress of Roman drama is also attributed to the Etruscans. In particular, they influenced Rome's religious institutions. Members of the Etruscan nobility were adept in interpreting the signs sent by the gods (thanks to a system they developed from a mixture of Mesopotamian, Greek, and native beliefs). The Roman Senate regularly turned to the Etruscan divinatory experts—the *haruspices*—to assist them in the interpretation of particularly dreadful portents.

In recounting Rome's earlier and later history, Livy evokes the sense of a glorious past that has, by stages, been forgotten. He draws the reader back to Rome's origins in hopes that traditional values can be recovered, while outlining a history that traces the rise and fall of the Republic.

The Narrative in Focus

Contents overview. Livy's original intention was to write the whole of Rome's history from its foundation to his own day. Sometimes called his *Annales* (Annals) because of its year-by-year format, the work mentions the arrival in Italy of Aeneas, a survivor of the Trojan War, and then traces the rise and expansion of Rome from its twin founders, Romulus and Remus, to the death of Drusus in 9 BCE. Livy probably published the first five books before 26 BCE and the remainder in groups of ten books roughly every three years, until his death in 17 CE. Of the 142 books, only 1-10 and 21-45 have survived intact. However, the fortunate survival of summaries for books 11-20 and 46-142 means we can reconstruct at least the outlines of his entire account.

In the preface to the first book, Livy emphasizes that his task is to put on record the deeds (*res gestae*) of the Roman people, the greatest nation in the world, tracing its development from slender beginnings to the present, which labors under its own enormity. He goes on to warn that the fabulous and supernatural elements in Rome's early history might not be to the taste of all his readers. These readers will hasten to his later books, which record the story of Rome's rise and fall. It is a pessimistic record of waning discipline, sliding morals, and an outright collapse into the evils of his day. Livy, on the contrary, hopes that his stories of early Rome will provide at least some relief from the troubled times of his own day. The preface ends with a memorable metaphor in which Livy stresses the didactic purpose of his work, likening it to a monumental building that displays the Roman people's achievements—both the good examples to follow and bad ones to avoid.

In barest outline, Livy's history is structured as follows:

Book	Events
1	Preface; Aeneas and the seven Kings of Rome (pre-753 BCE-510 BCE)
2-5	The formation of the Roman Republic, including the Laws of the Twelve Tables, to the Sack of Rome by the Gauls (509 BCE-390 BCE)
6-15	A second preface, claiming to introduce a clearer and more certain historical account; the conquest of Italy (265 BCE)
16-20	The First Punic War to the first Roman census (264 BCE to 219 BCE)
21-30	The war against Hannibal (The Second Punic War) (218-201 BCE)
31-40	A third preface lamenting the magnitude of Livy's task; the wars with Philip V of Macedon and Antiochus of Syria (201 BCE-179 BCE)
41-45	The Third Macedonian War against Perseus, son of Philip V (171 BCE-167 BCE)
46-70	Spanish Campaigns, the Third Punic War, and the war with Perseus of Macedon down to the outbreak of the Social War (178 BCE-91 BCE)
71-80	The Social War to the death of Marius (91 BCE-86 BCE)
81-90	The ascendancy of Sulla to his death (86 BCE-78 BCE)
91-108	The war with Sertorius to the end of Caesar's Gallic campaigns (78 BCE-51 BCE)
109-116	From the causes and beginning of the Civil War to the assassination of Julius Caesar (51 BCE-44 BCE)
117-133	The deification of Julius Caesar and the rise of Octavian, the First Triumvirate, Actium, and the deaths of Antony and Cleopatra (44 BCE-30 BCE)
134-142	The rule of Augustus to the death of Drusus and the disaster of Quintilius Varus (29 BCE-9 BCE)

Books 1-5. There is emphasis in the preface and throughout the narrative on the theme of foundation and re-foundation. Livy's first book, which lays the groundwork for the remainder of the history, is a testament to those notions: Rome is founded through "august augury," or divine omens, when the legendary twin brothers Romulus and Remus compete to see favorable signs from the birds. After the killing of his brother Remus, Romulus establishes Rome's early community and laws; the priest-king Numa founds Rome anew on religious grounds. The succeeding kings, Tullus Hostilius, Ancus Marcius, Tarquinius Priscus, and Servius Tullius, make their own military, religious, and legal contributions. In telling the tale, Livy ensures that the reader comprehends the dangers of kingship. Its flaws are laid bare in the person of Tarquinius Superbus, whose overbearing qualities end with the expulsion of the Etruscan. Maintaining the metaphor of his work as a building, Livy's first book maps out the city of Rome and its monuments: the Palatine and Aventine hills of Rome, where Romulus and Remus competed to control the founding of the city; the swampy site of Rome's future forum; the Capitoline Hill, the temple of Janus, where Servius Tullius (a king of 578-535 BCE) was murdered; the Circus; Rome's great sewer, the Cloaca Maxima, and more. Livy's reader is enticed into a world familiar but simultaneously set in a distant and mythical past.

Consistently Livy plays down Greek and Etruscan elements in his early stories to emphasize the grandeur of Rome. At the start of book 2 he indicates the importance of law: "From this point onwards I shall narrate the achievements of the Roman people now free, in peace and war, their annual magistracies, and the authority of statutes more powerful than men" (Livy, *From the Founding of the City*, book 2, chapter 1, section 1; trans. A. Nice). The emphasis on law is significant. Having shaken off the tyranny of the Etruscan kings, the Roman people can look to success at home and abroad through their annually elected magistrates and laws from which no man, not even a king, will be exempt. This second beginning, resting on Republican ideals, marks a change of tone in Livy's narrative.

It is in books 2-4 that we begin to see the first evidence of Livy's annalistic scheme. Invariably a new year opens with the naming of the two consuls and yearly events begin to be divided on the basis of internal-external-internal affairs. The rigid structure does not prevent Livy from including dramatic material. For example, Mucius Scaevola's heroic attempt to kill the Etruscan king Lars Porsenna results in the would-be killer's capture. When threatened with being burnt alive, Mucius Scaevola thrusts his right hand into a fire on an altar and is set free by the Etruscans, who admire his bravery (*From the Founding*, 2.12.12-13). Also in book 2, Horatius defends the Milvian Bridge, then swims heroically to safety across the River Tiber; and the heroine Cloelia escapes her Etruscan captors and similarly swims the river. Worthy examples such as these testify to Roman courage and endurance. The narrative passes through a series of internal struggles between the patricians, or wealthy landowners, and plebeians, or commoners, as well as war with various Italian tribes to the north and south of Rome: the Etruscans, Volscians, and Aequians. Constant warfare gives the plebeians leverage. In 494 BCE they go on strike, forcing the patrician leadership to elect officials—the tribunes of the people—to protect plebeian interests. Later in book 3, a commission of ten men establishes the earliest Roman code of law, the Twelve Tables. This moment is a pivotal one in the first five books. But Roman troubles continue. Book 4 relates the ongoing struggles against Rome's southern neighbors and the growing threat posed by the Etruscan hilltop town of Veii (situated on the River Tiber, 9 miles northwest of Rome), which reach a climax in book 5.

Book 5 is divided between the Roman capture of Veii, and the Gallic invasion of Italy. The book abounds in the miraculous and supernatural: the portentous rise in the water level of the Alban Lake; the seizure of Veii after the Romans capture an Etruscan diviner and steal the entrails of a sacrificial victim from the very altar on which the Etruscan king was sacrificing; the sacred geese that saved the Capitol; and the words of a centurion (a unit commander in the Roman army), who orders his troops to stand fast in the Roman forum, an omen confirming that the Romans should not move their capital from Rome to Veii. Cementing the book is the patriot Marcus Camillus, who after his glorious capture of Veii, falls from grace, but later returns in glorious triumph to defeat the Gauls. After the Romans recapture their city, he is acclaimed as "another Romulus and parent of the homeland, a second founder of the city" (*From the Founding*, 5.49; trans. A. Nice). Rome rises once more from the ashes of the Gallic destruction, its disorganized street plan—which was obvious in Livy's own time—a testament to the people's haste to reconstruct their city.

Books 6-10. At the start of book 6, a second preface emphasizes the new foundation: "From its second founding, as though reborn from its roots more fortunate and more fertile, the deeds of the city in domestic and military affairs may be set out more clearly and more certainly" (*From the Founding*, 6.1.3; trans. A. Nice). From this moment, despite considerable variation in the treatment of individual years, the building blocks of the annalistic form are more evident: notices of elections, the elections of magistrates, the announcement of and remedies for prodigies (unexplained and, therefore, ominous natural events), more religious material, famines, plagues, and floods, administrative business, troop dispositions, and other military information.

Two main themes dominate books 6 to 10—the renewal of the struggle in Italy and continuing domestic problems. In the first case, Rome is compelled to subdue once more the southern tribes. Much of these books is taken up with Rome's war with the Samnite nation. For Livy, the freedom of the Roman people continues to be a double-edged sword. Rome's success in war is threatened by internal dissension (the so-called "Struggle of the Orders") between the plebeians and their patrician overlords, who remain reluctant to cede power. The patricians are compelled to make more concessions in order to keep the peace. Eventually book 10 reaches a convenient stopping point. By 300 BCE, the patricians have allowed the plebeians to become candidates for both the consulship and the major priesthoods (the pontificate and augurate); Rome, victorious over the Samnites in 293 BCE, now effectively controls most of Italy. Nonetheless, at the end of book 10 any optimism is undermined when a plague devastates Rome and the countryside. The Sibylline Books (a collection of oracles) advise the Senate to bring the cult of the Greek god of healing, Aesculapius, from Epidaurus to Rome.

Engraving of Hannibal crossing the Alps during the Second Punic War, 218 BCE. Archive Photos. Reproduced by permission.

Books 11-45. The next decade begins on a more optimistic tone, with the arrival of Aesculapius and a cure for Rome's woes. It requires, however, another five books to subjugate the Etruscans. Rome's control of the Italian peninsula brings Rome into conflict with the great seafaring nation of Carthage for control of Sicily. Five books on the First Punic War (264-241 BCE) record Rome's surprising victory over the Carthaginians at sea and lay the seeds for the centerpiece of the *Ab Urbe Condita*: the war with Hannibal, or the Second Punic War. In ten books (books 21-30), Livy traces a wide range of developments: Rome's dubious claims to Saguntum (a city in Spain); the origins of Hannibal's hatred for Rome and his famous march across the Alps; the role of the general Flaminius in Rome's catastrophic defeat at Lake Trasimene; a second and equally devastating rout at the village of Cannae; the reversal of Roman bad fortune through the delaying tactics of the Roman general Fabius Maximus; and the role of Scipio Africanus in the Roman defeat of Hannibal on Carthaginian soil at Zama. Essential to the narrative is the harmonious union of all sectors of Roman society and their religious piety, especially that of Scipio Africanus, who is acclaimed as a second founder of the city. Overwhelming despair in book 22 changes to hope and finally triumph by book 30. At this point, the tone of Livy's narrative is wholly optimistic.

At the start of book 31, however, Livy is distressed and wearied:

> Although it is not at all right that someone who has dared to promise that he would record the whole of Roman history should become tired in the individual portions of such a great work, nevertheless, when it occurs to me that 63 years—for there have been that many between the beginning of the First Punic War and the end of the Second—have filled as many volumes for me as were required for the 488 years from the foundation of the city to the consulship of Appius Claudius, who began the first war with the Carthaginians, already I foresee in my heart that . . . I am being carried, whatever progress I make, into yet vaster depths and, as it were, into an abyss.
>
> (*From the Founding*, 31.1.2-5; trans. A. Nice)

Rhetorically Livy's despair at the magnitude of his task suggests that this is also the moment from which he traces Rome's descent towards the troubles of his own generation. Now Rome's history is not clearer and more assured as at the beginning of book 6, but rather more obscure and more doubtful.

Rome's wars against Philip V of Macedon and Antiochus of Syria strain Livy's annalistic or year-by-year method as he strives to associate internal affairs with events happening overseas. In book 31 (201-200 BCE) Rome declares war on Macedon but simultaneously must deal with an uprising among the Insubrians (a tribe in the very north of Italy). Domestic affairs at the end of the year concern the general Lucius Furius and his disputed claims to a triumph over the Gauls. In books 32 and 33, campaigns against the Macedonians continue under the great Roman general Quinctius Flamininus. He defeats the Greeks at Cynoscephelae in 197 BCE and, after terms have been settled, argues for the freedom (autonomy) of Greece from Roman rule. At the same time Rome campaigns continually against the Boii, Insubrians, and Ligurians (tribes in north Italy), and in Spain. After the withdrawal of Flamininus from Greece in book 34, conflict arises when King Antiochus of Aetolia (a country in central Greece) adopts a new policy towards Rome and aggressively interferes in Greece, threatening Rome's claims to dominion. Ultimately the Romans are triumphant under the consul Marcus Acilius (book 36). Nonetheless, the books that follow see continuing problems with Macedon and a renewal of Macedonian power under Philip in 185 BCE (book 39). There follows, in a piecemeal fashion, campaigns in Greece, northern Italy, and Spain right through to book 40. Amid these foreign affairs, Livy traces the fates of the Carthaginian general Hannibal (who is forced to leave Carthage in disgrace) and Scipio Africanus, who is prosecuted and then dies. In domestic affairs, the period witnesses senatorial attempts at religious control: the suppression of the cult of Dionysus in 186 BCE (book 39) and the discovery in 181 BCE (book 40) of the alleged Pythagorean books of Numa (containing subversive religious and philosophical material). Also woven into the narrative is the rise of the Roman statesman Cato the Elder, from his commands in Spain (195 BCE, book 34) to his election as censor (184 BCE, book 39).

Books 41 to 45 are the last of Livy's surviving books and are plagued by gaps in the narrative. Their subject matter is dominated by the rise of Perseus, son of Philip V of Macedon. The Third Macedonian War is declared in 171 BCE (book 42). Perseus's defeat is finally wrought by L. Aemilius Paullus at the Battle of Pydna in 168 BCE (book 44). Book 45 outlines the surrender of Perseus and the Senate's terms for Macedonia and Illyria (northern Greece). An inquiry into Greek affairs leads to further conditions being imposed on the Greek nations. Like Scipio Africanus, Paullus comes under attack for his conduct in office but overcomes the charges to celebrate a triumph, which is marred by the death of one of his two remaining sons a few days before and of the other son just three days later. His speech is a testament to Roman character and tradition. In his sadness he finds a consolation for the disaster to his family in the happiness and good fortune of the Republic (*From the Founding*, 45.42.1).

***The periochae* (summaries).** After book 45 the reader is dependent on the summaries to reconstruct the remaining books of Livy's history. There are hints that the pessimistic tone of the first preface returns in these remaining books. The second century BCE is marked by ever more expansive wars abroad: the subjugation of Spain; a further campaign against Macedon (149-146 BCE, books 49-52); and a third and final bitter war against Carthage (149-146 BCE, books 49-51). Brief notices of wars in other arenas suggest that Livy's purpose in these books is to give an overwhelming picture of a Rome fighting on several fronts, weighed down by responsibilities to allies and a compulsive desire for imperialistic expansion.

At home Livy appears to have been interested in challenges to the traditional authority of the Senate in politics and religion. To bring water to the Capitoline, the praetor Quintus Marcius builds an aqueduct in defiance of a prophecy of the Sibylline Books. Tiberius Gracchus, a tribune of the people, passes an agrarian law; and his brother, Gaius Gracchus, also a tribune, passes a more sweeping series of legislative reforms. Both are killed in the violence that follows their attempts to alleviate the problems of Rome's poorer classes.

These themes are a good prelude to the circumstances surrounding the military and political successes of Gaius Marius, who is victorious over the Numidian prince, Jugurtha, and the migrating Gallic tribes, the Cimbri and Teutones. His consulships in the late 100s BCE are marked by his deceptive dealings with the controversial tribunes Saturninus and Glaucia and by the increasing use of force to pass legislation. In contrast to the tumultuous later years of the second century BCE, Livy requires only one book to narrate the years 99-91 BCE (*Epitome* 70). Nine books later, after the devastating Social War, a conflict waged by Rome against its Latin allies (its *socii*), Marius returns to march on Rome and to declare himself (with another general, Cinna) master of the city. Marius is everything good and bad about Rome, as Livy remarks,

> As a man, if his faults are examined along with his virtues, it is not easy to say, whether he was better in war or more dangerous in peace. So true is it that armed he saved the state, but as a private citizen first overturned it with every manner of deception, and then in a hostile manner with weapons.
>
> (Livy, *Epitome* 80; trans. A. Nice)

Increasingly the books that follow are concerned with the growth of military power, first of Sulla (dictator from 82 to 79 BCE), then of Gnaeus Pompeius (Pompey), and finally of Julius Caesar. Livy traces the progress of the state towards the civil wars of the 40s BCE. Caesar's assassination is seen as a direct result of his intentions at monarchy (*Epitome* 116). Not long afterwards, as his adopted son and grandnephew, Octavian, is parading his troops on the Campus Martius, six vultures appear and then another six, a sign that indicates he is to found the city anew under the same omens as the city's founder, Romulus.

The tone of optimism does not continue, however, as Livy describes the strained relations among Marc Antony, Lepidus, and Octavian, and the events that result in a new civil war. Even the defeat of Antony and Cleopatra at Actium does not seem to have captured Livy's imagination in the same way as it did the Augustan poets. In his books on Augustus's rule, Livy seems to have been more interested in the wars waged by Roman generals and Augustus's relatives than in the achievements of Augustus himself, who brought peace to the Roman Empire. The remnants of Livy's history end, perhaps appropriately, on an inconclusive yet pessimistic note: "Disaster to Quinctilius Varus"—a reference to the slaughter of three legions under the command of this Roman general in Germany's Teutoburg Forest.

Religion and divination in Livy. According to the Greek historian Polybius, the Romans were the most religious of nations. Religion played a vital role in the political and military affairs of the Roman people; it was also an ever-present facet of their daily private lives. Other Roman historians, in particular Sallust and Caesar, had paid little attention to the supernatural. Like the Greek historian Thucydides, they strove to give their accounts a "scientific" and objective appearance. Livy's narrative, on the other hand, is more like

Herodotus's **Histories** (also in *Classical Literature and Its Times*); the work is imbued with religious material relevant to Livy's historical account.

Just a few years before Livy began his history, the orator and statesman Cicero divided Roman religion into three categories—the *sacra*, *auspicia*, and prophecies drawn from signs and omens (*On the Nature of the Gods*, 3.5). The first division, the *sacra* (sacred things), was the domain of the college of pontiffs (one of several bodies of state priests). Livy's history describes the pontiffs as maintaining the ancestral customs of the Roman state and preventing its contamination by foreign ritual. The *auspicia*, the second category, was the responsibility of the Roman augurs, who oversaw the rules pertaining to various supernatural signs, particularly those shown by birds (auguries and auspices). The importance of augury and the taking of the auspices is a constant theme in Livy's work. The consul Appius Claudius states that nothing is done in war and peace, whether at home or abroad, without first taking the auspices (*From the Founding*, 6.36.6). If a general goes to war under unfavorable auspices, disaster invariably follows. Cicero's last religious category was for prophecies obtained from prodigies and portents, which were interpreted by the Board of Ten (later Fifteen) men in charge of the Sibylline Books or by the Etruscan soothsayers (the *haruspices*). In Livy's narrative Roman political and military success depends on maintaining the *pax deorum* (the "peace of the gods") and avoiding divine displeasure. Pious regard for the signs sent from heaven and pious performance of rituals, prayers, and vows are essential to Roman expansion and victory in battle. Improper regard for the gods and impiety lead to political or military failure, sometimes death for the individual. This is most evident in the lists of prodigies (natural phenomena for which there was no apparent rational explanation) that appear in the narrative. These lists are usually inserted into the narrative at the beginning of the year, before the consuls set out with their armies for war. Invariably the lists are followed by a description of the remedies (expiation ceremonies) recommended by Rome's priests to avert the gods' anger. For example:

> On the Alban Mount a statue of Jupiter had been struck by lightning, also a tree near the temple; at Ostia, a fountain had been struck, at Capua the wall and the temple of Fortune, and the wall and a gate at Sinuessa. In addition to this, it was reported by some that the Alban Lake had flowed red, like blood, and in Rome,

inside the shrine of the temple of Fors Fortuna, a figure fixed to the wreath round the head of a statue fell without apparent cause into the statue's hand. It was common knowledge that at Privernum an ox talked and a vulture, while the forum was full of people, flew down on to a shop, and that at Sinuessa a child of ambiguous sex was born, half male half female—an *androgynous* child, to use, as often, the popular term. . . . At Sinuessa it also rained milk and a male baby was born with an elephant's head. These prodigies were expiated with sacrifices of full-grown victims, and a decree was issued for prayer.

> (Livy, *The War with Hannibal*, 27.11.2-6)

Livy takes a liberal approach to this type of material: "He is prepared to expand it, shorten it, change the order of events within it, alter its position within the year, and even occasionally place it in the wrong year altogether" (Levene, p. 242). He thereby makes the prodigy lists and expiation ceremonies more relevant to events in his narrative and shows how human fortune and divine favor are intertwined.

The official divination systems of the Roman Republic did not allow for individual "prophets," and in keeping with this convention, Livy omits or plays down evidence for prophecy. Only occasionally does he admit evidence that points to the existence of diviners and a religious life outside the practices of the Roman state. He therefore creates the impression of a state religion that was universally observed when other evidence suggests that Roman religion included multiple approaches and beliefs.

For Livy, religion is an unavoidable feature of Roman civic life, one that it is his duty to record, more than a question of his own belief or skepticism:

> I am not unaware that, from the same negligence that makes the populace believe that the gods do not send portents, prodigies are no longer announced in public or included in the annals. But, for my part, when I am writing about ancient events by some agreement or other my mind becomes antiquated itself, and a certain religious awe prevents me from regarding such events (which those wisest of men thought should be taken up in public) unworthy of inclusion in my annals.
>
> (*From the Founding*, 43.13.1-2; trans. A. Nice)

Livy appreciated how interconnected human and divine affairs were in Rome. This helps to explain why, at various junctures in his account, supernatural explanations co-exist with rational ones. A religious current permeates the main narrative and promotes Livy's historical objectives. When the historian records the rise of the Roman Republic, proper religious behavior and ritual observance are essential for the state to prosper. In Livy's own day, when political power was located in the hands of one man, the Emperor Augustus, the need for correct balance between political power and religious piety constituted an obvious model for the new regime to imitate.

Sources and literary context. Livy's choice to write annals meant that he subscribed to a form with a long tradition at Rome, that of the yearly record of events. The form, which neatly corresponded to the yearly election of magistrates as laid down by the Republican constitution, also affected Livy's style, his tone and manner of expression, and his interpretation of history.

The origins of the annalistic tradition lie in the records of Rome's *pontifex maximus* (chief priest and head of the College of Pontiffs), the *Annales Maximi*. This was primarily a religious chronicle that documented prodigies and the associated rites of expiation, eclipses of the sun and moon, corn shortages, and the like. Evidence from other sources suggest that the records probably also included mythical and miraculous stories relevant to the foundation legends of early Rome. Similar chronicles, known as *fasti*, which named magistrates and brief notices of political and religious material, were posted in temples. In the second century BCE the Romans began to consolidate lists of magistrates and other information from these records, and to compose Rome's earliest continuous historical accounts. It may be at this point that the annals began to be divided neatly into affairs at home and abroad, in war and peace, on land and sea, and in winter and summer.

The earliest literary work in Latin to use the title *Annales* was the epic poem of Quintus Ennius, arranged as a year-by-year account based on the consuls for each year. Ennius included traditional stories that are found in the work of later Latin annalists and, like Livy, wrote from the foundation of the city to his own day (753-169 BCE). The writing of actual annals seems to have begun with Lucius Calpurnius Piso Frugi (consul in 133 BCE). Piso's work demonstrates the essential building blocks of the later annalistic scheme: reports of elections, entry of magistrates, allotment of provinces to the consuls, the levying of troops, the announcement and expiation of prodigies, the reception of embassies, administrative business, departure for provinces, shortages of food, building and dedicating temples, establishing colonies, granting or imposing Roman citizenship, troop dispositions, and other information.

The last two centuries BCE represented a period of experimentation for Roman historians. A few, such as Cato the Elder, attempted to distance themselves from the arid style of the annals. Others, such as Sallust, wrote historical monographs on a single event in Roman history. By the time of Livy, the Roman annalistic form appears to have developed into a mix of a restrained, ceremonious record and a more extended narrative of wars and political events. Livy's choice to use this form hearkened back to Rome's earliest historical records but his technique elevated it beyond its traditionally rigid approach. After book 1, Livy shows considerable flexibility in his adaptation of the form. The typical internal-external-internal format and the different categories of routine material are lengthened, shortened, displaced, or otherwise varied.

For a long time, many scholars thought of Livy as being at the mercy of his sources, but in fact he skillfully chooses and uses them to underscore his view of history. Among the Romans who influenced his work are Aelius Tubero, Licinius Macer, Valerius Antias, Coelius Antipater, and Julius Caesar. Livy also drew on the works of the Greek historians Polybius and Posidonius. Livy's working method suggests that he sought out the best available sources, adapting them to emphasize Rome's Romanness and to offer a didactic, ethical history that would provide good examples to follow and bad ones to avoid.

Events in History at the Time the Narrative Was Written

The First Triumvirate and the 50s BCE. If Jerome is right in placing Livy's birth in 59 BCE, then it coincided with Julius Caesar's term as consul. The recent formation (c. 61-60 BCE) of the unofficial political coalition known as the First Triumvirate, consisting of Caesar, Pompey, and Crassus, had placed the three men in an unparalleled position to promote their own political ambitions. During the next decade they did so with a ruthless enthusiasm that ignored the democratic processes of Republican government and ultimately caused the Civil War in 49 BCE.

Although the three men were nominally united in a political alliance, their ambitions were self-serving. In 58 BCE Caesar left for Gaul to seek the military glory that had so far eluded him.

There he produced a remarkable record of his own successes, his *Commentaries on the Gallic War* (also in *Classical Literature and Its Times*), a self-promoting work written partly to outdistance his closest rival, Pompey. Pompey meanwhile remained at Rome, governing Spain through subordinates. At the same time, Crassus, the richest man in Rome, continued to campaign for the affections of the people and for his own personal self-enrichment.

The three triumvirs wanted to use the services of Clodius, a tribune of the people. In 58 BCE, he seemed to act in their favor by exiling the orator Cicero, whose critical voice was a thorn in the side of the triumvirs. Clodius's tribunate soon degenerated into something more sinister. He employed gangs to achieve his political purposes, forcing Pompey to marshal his own gang under another tribune, Milo. The 50s BCE were marked by clashes between the gang leaders as the various individuals jostled for power. Things came to a head after 54 BCE, with the death of Caesar's daughter, Julia, whose marriage to Pompey had helped cement their alliance. The next year Crassus's death allowed members of the upper classes to drive a wedge between Caesar and Pompey. Pompey was pushed towards the *optimates* (aristocrats who used the Senate to gain their political objectives). Meanwhile, street violence became more open, climaxing in 52 BCE with the murder of Clodius. The disturbances prevented elections from taking place, and the Senate chose Pompey to be sole consul, an unprecedented position. After various attempts to make Caesar a consul or to get both him and Pompey to surrender their separate provinces (Spain and Gaul), the Senate finally called on Pompey to save the Republic. On January 10, 49 BCE, in an open declaration of war, Caesar marched his army from his sanctioned territory (the province of Gaul), across the Rubicon (the stream separating Gaul from Italy) and plunged the Roman world into a bitter civil war.

The war continued in various arenas until 45 BCE, dividing fathers from sons and brothers from brothers. The decisive battle was fought at Pharsalus in Greece in 48 BCE. Pompey fled to Egypt but was killed as he stepped off his boat. At Rome Caesar had to set about the process of rebuilding. He showed mercy towards his enemies, but more was required to bring peace and stable government. Caesar was elected dictator for a year, then dictator for ten years, and finally, in 44 BCE, dictator for life. The overthrow of the Republican constitution was now complete. As dictator, Caesar had greater military authority than any other official and was immune from the veto of the tribunes, the people's representatives. He could therefore pass legislation without seeking the mandate of the Senate or the people.

Caesar was careful during this period to continue the normal processes of Republican elections and offices. But he used his tenure to pass legislation to make the Senate more representative of the Roman Empire, to create jobs through an extensive building program, and to establish law and order by placing colonies of veteran troops and the poor in locations scattered throughout Rome's territories. Caesar's preeminent position and his tendency to favor his own men and to exclude former opponents (whom he had pardoned) heightened opposition to his rule. When Mark Antony appeared to offer him a crown during a religious festival, the offer aroused deep-rooted Roman fears of kingship and the despotism it implied. On the Ides of March, 44 BCE, Caesar was killed by a group of senators who claimed to have liberated the Republic and to have rid themselves of a tyrannical master. Undoubtedly Livy's narrative drew parallels between Caesar's murder and transformation into a god, and the death of King Romulus over 700 years earlier.

A new struggle for power. The conspirators' joy was short-lived. Popular anger drove them into hiding, and Mark Antony took the initiative. He claimed leadership of Caesar's supporters and replaced him as their patron. Opposition came from an unexpected source: Caesar's grandnephew, Octavian, who had become his adopted son. Octavian staked his claim to Caesar's inheritance and quickly showed his leadership. He appealed to Caesar's army veterans and won the public approval of Cicero, who thought Octavian might be a new savior for the Republic.

In the months that followed, Antony was declared an enemy of the state by the Senate but escaped with the assistance of Octavian and Lepidus, the new *pontifex maximus*. These three men now formed a new triumvirate. This was not an informal coalition, as in the case of the First Triumvirate, but one formalized by law. The Second Triumvirate took up arms against the self-proclaimed "liberators" of the Republic, Brutus and Cassius. To fund their cause, the triumvirs had their henchmen assassinate would-be opponents and confiscate their estates. Cicero was one such victim.

After Brutus and Cassius were defeated at Philippi in 42 BCE, the triumvirs carved up the Empire among themselves. Antony received Gaul and the East; Lepidus, Africa; and Octavian,

Spain, Italy, and the islands. Gradually Lepidus's position weakened. He was marginalized within the coalition, and power again polarized around two individuals—Octavian and Antony.

From the 30s onwards, Octavian used his position as the adopted son of a god (the appearance of a comet at Caesar's funeral games had convinced the populace to make Caesar a god after his death). Octavian now began to attack Antony, who had begun a love affair with the Egyptian monarch, Cleopatra. Antony made a grave mistake by declaring Cleopatra and their children his heirs. Octavian showed an adept understanding of propaganda. He discredited Antony's position, painting him as an effeminate, degenerate Roman who was trying to subvert the liberties of the Roman people and subjugate Italy and the West to the rule of an oriental queen. Things came to a head after the triumvirate agreement lapsed at the end of 33 BCE. Octavian advanced on Antony's troops in Greece and the two armies confronted one another at Actium on September 13, 31 BCE.

Little fighting occurred as Antony's forces quickly turned tail:

> Actium was a shabby affair; the worthy climax to the ignoble propaganda against Cleopatra, to the sworn and sacred union of all Italy. But the young Caesar [Octavian] required the glory of a victory that would surpass the greatest in all history, Roman or Greek.
>
> (Syme, p. 297)

In contrast Octavian's propaganda machine made Actium part of the birth legend of the new empire, the climax of the struggle between East and West. Well might Livy have hoped that the early parts of his work would provide relief from the evils of his own day: a world marked by mob rule in the streets of Rome, proscriptions, and Roman army fighting Roman army. There could be no guarantee that the new autocracy of Octavian (renamed Augustus in 27 BCE) would be different from that of Julius Caesar or that the Roman world would not again be plunged into bitter civil war. The pessimism of the time is captured by Horace, in a poem written between 42 and 38 BCE:

> Already a second generation is being ground to pieces by civil war, and Rome through her own strength is tottering. The city that neither the neighbouring Marsians had power to ruin nor the Etruscan host . . . nor Hannibal . . . this selfsame city we ourselves shall ruin, we an impious generation of stock accursed.
>
> (Horace in Liebeschuetz, p. 55)

CLASSICAL LITERATURE AND ITS TIMES

161

It is no wonder that Livy's work warns of the dangers of kingship and calls for a return to older, more traditional values: virtue, honor, and traditional pursuits of glory. Nor is it a surprise that his values include a strong emphasis on the reverence of Rome's gods to ensure continued prosperity.

PHILOSOPHY AND RELIGION IN THE FIRST CENTURY BCE

In Livy's day there were three major schools of philosophy: the Stoics, who believed that the gods existed and showed their concern for mankind through signs; the Epicureans, who thought that the gods did not care for humans; and the New Academy, whose followers suspended judgment, played "devil's advocate" and allowed questioners the freedom to make up their own minds. The leading exponent of the New Academy was the Roman orator, Marcus Tullius Cicero. After the death of his daughter Tullia in 45 BCE, Cicero turned to philosophy for consolation. Before his own execution, in 43 BCE, he wrote three major works on Roman religion: *On the Nature of the Gods*; *On Divination*; and *On Fate*.

Central to Cicero's discussion is whether the gods send messages to humankind that can be interpreted. In a manner typical of the Academy, he steers a careful course between Stoic and Epicurean worldviews, between belief and disbelief in divination, between determinism (fate) and free will. If there is a message, it is one that Cicero had already offered in *The Republic* (also in *Classical Literature and Its Times*): that religion and certain types of divination are essential to the state in order to control the masses.

Like Cicero, Livy emphasizes the need for the correct and proper observance of prodigies and other phenomena, yet he sometimes criticizes the masses for their superstitious belief in the supernatural. If Livy has a philosophical position in his religious outlook, it is most like that of the New Academy.

The new age of Augustus. Since early in his career, Octavian recognized the value of religion to support his claims to power. At the funeral games for his adoptive father, Julius Caesar, in 42 BCE, a comet had appeared in the sky. Octavian not only interpreted this as the soul of Caesar ascending to heaven (thus making him, Octavian, the son of a god) but also as a positive sign from the gods, an indication that he was destined for great things. From this time too, Octavian emphasized his divine links to two gods—Mars (father of Romulus, the founder of Rome) and Venus (mother of Aeneas, the legendary founder of the Roman race and ancestor of the house of Julius Caesar).

Throughout the 30s BCE Octavian had repeatedly contrasted his preference for traditional Roman ways with Antony's attraction to Eastern ways, including support of Egyptian gods and goddesses such as Isis. After Actium, Octavian emphasized his piety towards the Roman gods and undertook public works on their behalf: "As consul for the sixth time [28 BC] on the orders of the Senate I restored eighty-two temples of the gods in the city, neglecting none that needed to be restored at that time" (Augustus, *Res Gestae*, 20.4; trans. A. Nice). The physical reconstruction of Roman temples was accompanied by a literal restoration of priesthoods and ceremonies that had fallen into disuse. In 27 BCE Octavian was renamed *Augustus* (meaning "most hallowed one") to emphasize the holy and revered character of the new master of the Roman world. A temple of Apollo was built on the Palatine Hill with a ramp linking it to the house of Augustus. Augustus himself adopted the position of *pontifex maximus* when the position was vacated in 12 BCE. From this point, the emperor was also a member of the College of Augurs and of the Board of Fifteen in charge of the Sibylline Books. In short, Augustus controlled all the mechanisms of Rome's religion. Meanwhile, he recognized the importance of other forms of "worship," consulting astrologers and minting on coinage his sign of the zodiac, Capricorn. Closely connected with Augustus's religious legislation was a series of less successful laws designed to prevent adultery and reward members of the nobility who married and had children. These laws aimed also to reduce excessive expenditure and to reinforce the traditional hierarchic positions of senators, equestrians, and plebeians. Through a series of "settlements" (in 27, 23, and 19 BCE), Augustus gradually maneuvered himself into position as head of the Roman state without abolishing any of the Roman Republic's regular institutions. He had the power of a consul and the sacrosanct position of the tribunes of the people. His position was emphasized in the adoption of the titles "princeps" (leading citizen) and "primus inter pares" (first amongst equals). A careful politician, Augustus made sure not to alienate the elite classes and to share power. Elections for the traditional political offices (consuls, praetors, quaestors, and so on) continued. The Senate likewise kept meeting and making decisions essential to running the Roman state. In 17 BCE Rome celebrated the arrival of Augustus's new Golden Age by holding Secular Games, games to celebrate the end of one *saeculum* (normally understood as a period of 100 years) and the start of another. Not since 149 BCE, says Livy, had the last games been held.

The reign of Augustus, then, is marked by an apparent reconstruction of Rome's religious monuments and customs as well as its moral foundations, and by the apparent restoration of Republican political institutions: an intermingling of things divine and human. It was a carefully calculated and successful strategy: Augustus ruled, mostly peacefully, as Rome's first emperor from 27 BCE to 14 CE.

But Livy's work, also one of religious "reconstruction," avoids the overwhelming optimism that marks the literature and monuments of the new reign. He continues to remind his audience of the dangers of despotism and the necessity of adhering to traditional Roman custom, including proper devotion to the gods.

Reception and impact. Livy's reputation was well established before his work was completely finished. Pliny the Younger (*Letters,* 2.3) records that a man from Cadiz in Spain, very impressed with the name and fame of Livy, went so far as to come from this distant outpost of the Roman Empire simply to see the historian. His curiosity satisfied, the man turned round and went home again. Praise for Livy's work was not wholly positive, however. His contemporary Asinius Pollio noted that the writer's eloquence revealed his provincial origins, that it was too full of his Padua origins. But others praised Livy's work. In the century following his death, Livy received high compliments from the rhetorician Quintilian, who compared Livy's eloquence and scope to that of Herodotus, the "Father of History." Livy's work was recommended reading for the youth of Rome. In 79 CE the Younger Pliny, aged 17, was even more engrossed in Livy's work than in the eruption of Vesuvius.

Perhaps Livy's most profound and infamous impact was on the sixteenth-century political theorist Niccolò Machiavelli. Some influence may be detected in *The Prince,* in which Machiavelli hoped to secure the favor of Florence's ruling Medici family. This work argued that the skills of an individual leader determined the success of a state, advising that a ruler needed *virtù*—the ability to take bold amoral decisions—and urging the justice of war where it was necessary.

More significant is the political writer Machiavelli's *Discourses on Livy.* Machiavelli found in Livy's depiction of Rome's Republic the exemplary virtues he wished were present in his contemporary Florence. In Machiavelli's day Florence suffered deaths, exiles, and partisan rule because of disunity. Machiavelli urged the proper application of morality to political life in order to avoid this chaos and to achieve the same kind of success and glory attained by ancient Rome.

Inspired by a theory that legendary stories such as the birth of Romulus and Remus came from ancient Roman ballads, Lord Macaulay (Thomas Babington; 1800-1859) took these stories from Livy and transformed them into poems. The *Lays of Ancient Rome* was instantly popular (by mid-1875 more than 100,000 copies had been sold); untinged by Livy's pessimism, they captured the spirit of a British nation at the height of its own empire.

In the later nineteenth and early twentieth century, when history was conceived of as science, European scholars subjected Livy's work to close analysis in order to identify his sources. The approach reduced Livy to the status of a mere transcriber, overly reliant on his sources and lacking in originality.

The freer spirit of recent times has led to a useful analysis of Livy's historical methods and content. Recent contributions discuss, for example, his ideas of virtue, his treatment of religion, the work as Augustan propaganda, the influence of rhetoric, and his purpose in writing history, in ways that bring out the work's richness and explain why his work was acclaimed in his own lifetime. As one scholar has observed on *From the Founding of the City:*

> [Livy's] greatness as a historian . . . lies rather in his own imaginative reconstruction of the past and his representation, or rather evocation, of it to the reader . . . Livy's main engagement is not so much with the records of the Roman past as with the mind of his reader.
>
> (Solodow, p. 259)

—Alex Nice

For More Information

Augustus. *Res Gestae Divi Augusti: The Achievements of the Divine Augustus.* Ed. P. A. Brunt, and J. M. Moore. London: Oxford University Press, 1967.

Davies, J. P. *Rome's Religious History: Livy, Tacitus and Ammianus Marcellinus.* Cambridge: Cambridge University Press, 2005.

Levene, D. S. *Religion in Livy.* Leiden: Brill, 1993.

Liebeschuetz, J. H. W. G. *Continuity and Change in Roman Religion*. Oxford: The Clarendon Press, 1979.

Livy. *Ab Urbe Condita* [*From the Founding of the City*]. Ed. P. G. Walsh, R. S. Conway, J. F. Walters, R. K. Johnson, and A. H. McDonald. Oxford: Oxford University Press, 1963-1974.

———. *The Early History of Rome*. Trans. Aubrey de Sélincourt. Harmondsworth: Penguin, 2002.

———. *History of Rome*. Trans. B. O. Foster. 14 vols. Loeb Classical Library. Cambridge, Mass.: Harvard University Press, 1982-1998.

———. *The War with Hannibal*. Trans. Aubrey de Sélincourt. Ed. B. Radice. Harmondsworth: Penguin, 1965.

Luce, T. J. *Livy: The Composition of His History*. Princeton: Princeton University Press, 1977.

Solodow, J. B. "Livy and the Story of Horatius." *TAPA* 109 (1979): 251-268.

Syme, Ronald. *The Roman Revolution*. Oxford: The Clarendon Press, 1939.

Walsh, P. G. *Livy*. Cambridge: Cambridge University Press, 1961.

The Golden Ass

by
Apuleius of Madaura

Apuleius was born in the 120s CE to prosperous parents in Madaura, a city in Roman North Africa. He wrote in Latin, delivered speeches in both Greek and Latin, and probably also spoke Punic, the language of that area during the pre-Roman empire of Carthage. His birth and multilingual abilities raise some still hotly debated questions—What was his ethnicity? Was he of Italian or African descent? Did he identify with his local African origins or strive to become thoroughly Roman? Apuleius traveled widely, studying in Carthage, Athens, and Rome. Back in North Africa, he married Pudentilla, the wealthy, widowed mother of a school friend, who was considerably older than Apuleius. Suspecting his motives, her former in-laws charged him with seducing Pudentilla through magic. Apuleius, a legal advocate, was equipped to defend himself. He was also a skilled public speaker, a student of natural science, and a reputable philosopher in the tradition of Plato. In his spiritual life, Apuleius became an initiate of several mystery religions (Greco-Roman cults that promised a blissful afterlife) and a priest of the imperial cult (devoted to the health and the security of Roman emperors and their families). Most importantly, Apuleius wrote—mainly nonfiction. His works include philosophical treatises, the court speech in which he defended himself from Pudentilla's in-laws (the *Apologia*), extracts from his public orations (the *Florida*), and a fictional work. Although *Metamorphoses* is the title on the work's earliest surviving manuscripts, according to the fifth-century bishop Augustine, Apuleius himself called it *Asinus Au-*

> ## THE LITERARY WORK
>
> A novel set in Italy, the Roman provinces, and Greece in the latter half of the second century CE; first published in Latin (as *Metamorphoses*) in the second century CE.
>
> ## SYNOPSIS
>
> Lucius, a lusty young Greek under Roman rule, is accidentally transformed into a donkey when his experimentation with magic goes awry. In animal form, he passes from owner to owner, undergoing some strange and dangerous experiences before being rescued by an Egyptian goddess.

reus, or *The Golden Ass* (using *golden* to refer to excellence of character). Apuleius' adult life coincided with the growing social and economic prominence of the provinces and elite provincial families in the Roman Empire, and *The Golden Ass* reflects this fact. A novel of sometimes comical adventure, it focuses on life in Greece under Roman rule.

Events in History at the Time of the Novel

Roman law and provincial society. *The Golden Ass* was written in Latin by an African about a Greek. Africa is not discussed in the novel, but

Fourteenth-century coin depicting the second-century novelist Apuleius, along with his name. AP/Wide World Photos. Reproduced by permission.

Apuleius' African provincial background likely influenced the way he depicts his main character's Greek provincial background. By the time of Apuleius, Rome had gained control over a territory of more than 100 major and minor provinces, including much of northern Africa and all of Greece. Both had been under Roman rule for more than three centuries. Greece was divided into two administrative regions: the northern province of Macedonia, where the adventures of the Greek main character begin, and the southern province of Achaea, where they end.

Rome ruled each of its provinces through a governor, whose main duties were to keep the province "peaceful," that is, out of foreign hands and free from dissidents, insurgents, and criminals. In the words of one ancient authority, a governor "should search out persons guilty of sacrilege, brigands, kidnappers and thieves and punish them according to their offences" (Ulpian in Freeman, p. 503). The empire selected certain cities as assize towns, that is, towns where legal cases were heard. Mostly the cases involved small-scale crimes. A provincial governor would rely on local magistrates to bring the accused before him. They would cooperate with the Roman authorities to enforce the imperial laws. With cooperation, recognized the magistrates (and others in the local elite, including army veterans), came privileges—control of the local government, the food supply, various properties, and more.

Society in the provinces was comprised of two basic classes: the *honestiores* ("more honorable people") and the *humiliores* ("humbler people"). Slaves were another case altogether. Not part of the *humiliores*, they were thought of as property rather than people. The *honestiores* class, made up of the local elite, received preferential treatment. In criminal cases, their hearings were the first to be conducted, and if convicted, their sentencing involved fines or, at worst, exile, not bodily punishment or death. In contrast, though nominally free and sometimes of citizen status, the criminals who were *humiliores* suffered penalties such as torture and crucifixion. Often the accused from this class were even condemned without a proper hearing. A governor could judge only so many cases, and, again, the rich came first. Only in fiction, says one historian, such as "*The Golden Ass* . . . would a poisoned woman get instant access to justice" (Goodman, p. 193).

The "justice" meted out to slaves was especially harsh. It is impossible to arrive at an accurate number of slaves in the whole of the Roman Empire at any period. It has been conjectured that, during the reign of Augustus (31 BCE–14 CE), in the century before Apuleius, the empire had 10 million slaves in a population of roughly 50 million. In Italy itself, one in every three persons was probably a slave (Madden). These figures, while speculative, are likely not to have varied significantly by Apuleius' time. Romans enslaved war captives, abandoned children, and the kidnapped and then put them to work in various capacities. There were slave road builders, construction workers, factory laborers, cooks, house cleaners, secretaries, miners, barbers, seamstresses, and farmhands. In some cases, the captives looked like their captors and were just as educated, but, in society's eyes, slavery robbed them of any social or moral status, regardless of their talents and skills. Slaves were commonly subjected to floggings and sexual assaults. For a capital crime (adultery, treason, or murder) they would be crucified or burned alive. One Roman custom called for all the slaves in a household to be murdered if one of them had killed their master.

The adoption of imperial ways. The spread of Roman culture and the Latin language was mostly an urban phenomenon. As in other provinces, Roman ways became dominant in the cities of mainland Greece. Their inhabitants continued to speak Greek, but otherwise adopted Roman customs. In Greece and Asia Minor, the elite learned to speak Latin as well as Greek (in Roman North Africa, the elite learned to speak both Greek and Latin as well as their native Punic). The provinces also adopted the practice of holding Roman gladiatorial games, including those between unevenly matched opponents. Typically a helmeted, shielded swordsman fought an opponent equipped with a net and trident. The games made a public spectacle of pain and injury or death. After Rome conquered the Greek city of Corinth in 146 BCE, it became the first to hold gladiatorial games. This distinction fit with the city's reputation for immorality and cruelty and made it an ideal setting for Book 10 of *The Golden Ass*, which puts the hero at risk of becoming the spectacle in an arena event.

Along with acceptance of Roman customs came acknowledgement of and reverence for the Roman emperor, as indicated by the spread of the imperial cult. Discouraging inhabitants from worshipping a living emperor, officials advised them to instead worship Roma (the divine spirit of Rome) and to pray for the continued good health of the living emperor. It became common after 44 BCE (the murder of Julius Caesar) to conceive of the deceased emperor as joining the ranks of the gods, and the inhabitants in Asia Minor went so far as to worship the living emperor as a god. A comic episode of *The Golden Ass* provides a striking illustration of how revered and feared the emperor was in the provinces. After the double misfortune of being transformed into an ass and then abducted by bandits, the protagonist tries to summon bystanders in an open-air market to rescue him by invoking the name of the emperor:

> So when . . . we were passing through a largeish town with a busy market and a crowd all round us, I tried to call on the august name of Caesar in my native Greek. I did indeed produce a clear and convincing 'O', but the name 'Caesar' itself I couldn't manage. My discordant bray was not appreciated by the robbers, who laid into my wretched hide from all sides . . .
> (Apuleius, *The Golden Ass*, 3.29, p. 54)

The fact that Lucius, the protagonist, tries to rally Greek locals to his side this way is a powerful testimony to the widespread acceptance of Rome's emperor as "an ever-present protector" (Millar, p. 66). In 77 CE, out of gratitude to the Roman emperor Vespasian, who had donated desperately needed aid after a terrible earthquake, Corinth went so far as to rename itself "the colony of Julius

Flavius Augustus Corinthiensis," honoring Vespasian by invoking his family name, Flavius, and his position as emperor, indicated by the name Augustus (means "venerable"). During reconstruction, Corinth reorganized its city center so that its major buildings could be dedicated to worship of the imperial cult, in the manner of many other cities.

COPS AND ROBBERS IN ANCIENT ROME

Bandits were a pervasive phenomenon throughout the Roman Empire, as suggested by their presence in Apuleius' novel. The bandits in *The Golden Ass*, however, are more imaginative than real. Simplistic stereotypes of the bandit as noble or ignoble appear in the ancient novels. In fact, even the depictions of bandits by ancient historians appear to be drawn more from imagination than from life. Who, then, were the historical bandits? The real counterparts to Apuleius' robber gang were the *latrones*, a special Roman legal term. The crime of robbery committed with violence was *rapina*, the charge leveled against a *latro*. Simply committing an act of *rapina*, however, was not enough to make one a *latro*. Such a label was not conferred upon muggers. Rather the *latrones* were known for planning, wielding weapons, gathering into large bands, chasing plunder, and committing violent crime on a far grander scale than other outlaws. The Roman state attempted unsuccessfully to curtail the *latrones*, disarming civilians, building roads in rural areas to make them less convenient haunts for the outlaws, and the like, but to little avail. Conditions of extreme vulnerability (to bandits, no less than natural disasters) were the norm. No traveler anywhere in the Empire could have felt entirely safe from the threat of the *latrones*.

Religion, mystery cults, and Isis. The ancients generally sought favor in all their enterprises from their gods, who, it was assumed, intervened in human life. It was furthermore believed that the gods cared dearly about how much they were worshipped, and that a particular god was best contacted in shrines and temples devoted to him or her. People sought direction from the gods, who instructed their followers and reacted badly only when their instructions were ignored. It was standard in the Greco-Roman world for a city to recognize a single patron deity among the many that they honored. Individuals also might pay more attention to one god than the others, as Lucius does to Isis in *The Golden Ass*.

Greco-Roman religious cults that worshipped a deity through secret rites and rituals were known as mystery religions. The name comes from the Greek *mysterion*, or "secret thing," a reference to the fact that these cults concentrated on explaining the mystery of life and death. The ultimate object was union with the divine and immortal life; thus, the cults concerned themselves with questions of personal redemption, salvation, and the afterlife. Their focus on the individual, both in this life and the hereafter, made mystery religions different from Greco-Roman paganism, which emphasized stability and prosperity for the community, and offered little hope for a happy afterlife. The possibilities of divine attention to the problems of the individual in this life and of eternal bliss in the hereafter were a strong draw.

A few mystery cults gained considerable followings in the empire, among them the cult of the Egyptian goddess, Isis, and her divine husband Osiris (also known as Serapis). Other popular cults were those of Orpheus, Bacchus (Greek Dionysus), and the Persian Mithra. Already ancient by Roman times, these cults spread from Asia Minor, Greece, and Egypt. Soldiers, merchants, slaves, and immigrants transported their beliefs to every corner of the empire. They shared a few common attributes—a set of secret practices, claims to mysterious knowledge about the universe and the gods, and a complex, sometimes very costly initiation process for followers. The time, trouble, and expenses were considered worth the privilege of entering into the cult's higher levels, which gave followers access to divine secrets and greater intimacy with the divine. Since there was freedom of worship in the Roman Empire, the religious cults were allowed to flourish as long as they did not have anything to do with political insurrection. Sometimes an emperor even encouraged the spread of a cult.

In real life, Isis attracted numerous followers. By the second century CE, the cult had grown into one of the most popular religions in the Roman world. Isis was conceived of as queen of nature, of the immortals, and of the dead, as universal mother, and as single manifestation of all gods and goddesses. While Isis-worship existed throughout the empire, she had important temples dedicated to her worship in Rome and in Cenchreae, near Corinth, both of which are mentioned in *The Golden Ass*.

Magic versus religion. Imperial life included less visible figures whose practices were wrapped in secrecy as well. These were the magicians and witches, who cast spells, concocted potions, and performed rituals. At first, magical rites were almost indistinguishable from religious ones. Actually magical and religious rites were not even separated until the fifth and fourth centuries BCE, when Greek philosophers (Plato and Heraclitus) argued for isolating certain practices from the main body of religious activity. Whatever distinctions were made thereafter were the concerns of a philosophical elite. To what extent these concerns affected the thinking and practices of the Roman populace is debatable. In Apuleius' day, this marginally religious and potentially illegal (depending on the goal or purpose of the magic) category of rituals and its practitioners formed part of *mageia*, a Greek word from the Persian for "priest."

To the ancients, the universe was a field of divine forces. Some of these forces were known and could be harnessed by an established religious authority; others could only be approached by another kind of specialist, one with the knowledge to confront and manipulate them. What is called "magic" today was the manipulation of divine powers to attain a private goal. There were some common features between magicians and the followers of mystery cults. Magicians often used the language of the mystery rites in their spells, and their rites too involved secrecy, complex processes of initiation, and the goal of direct contact with the divine. But in other respects magic diverged.

The empire established a couple of laws against magic. The first was part of the Twelve Tables, a body of Roman laws written on bronze tablets in the mid-fifth century BCE. These laws guarded against magically removing or cursing someone's crops, in keeping with concerns of the predominantly agricultural society at the time. Magic itself was not targeted; the use of magic to commit theft (of the crops) was. In 81 BCE Rome passed the second act—the Cornelian Law Concerning Stabbers and Poisoners. Poisoning was a catchall category for violence committed by means difficult or impossible to verify, including magic. In Apuleius' own trial, the accusation that he seduced Pudentilla by means of magic was likely treated under the poisoning category of the Cornelian Law. Although physical violence was probably not involved, the accusers thought he had compelled Pudentilla to make a decision detrimental to themselves that she would not otherwise have made.

Whereas mystery cults maintained a public presence and remained highly conscious of the need for governmental approval, magicians operated quite differently. The mystery cults were ever mindful of the harsh measures imperial officials (the magistrates) might take against a group considered hostile to Rome's security. In the first century BCE, Rome had several times suppressed the Isis cult, perhaps most famously when Emperor Augustus was preparing for war against Cleopatra of Egypt (who considered herself the incarnation of Isis). Magic, on the other hand, was a solitary endeavor. Mindful of competition and of the air of authority that secrecy lent to their art, magicians worked individually and kept their knowledge private. Part of this knowledge was the alleged ability to transform people into animals, long considered a feature of magic. Although technically a goddess, Circe in the *Odyssey* (eighth century BCE) turned mortals into swine. Herodotus' *Histories* (fifth century BCE) records that *magi*, or Persian priests, could turn themselves into wolves. In Virgil's *Eclogues* (first century BCE), a male magician transforms himself into a wolf (all three works also in *Classical Literature and Its Times*). Subsequent works suggest that these beliefs persisted far beyond Apuleius' day, as shown by the writings of Augustine, a Christian bishop of the fifth century who described how some of the women of Italy mixed drugs with the food that they gave travelers in order to turn them into pack animals for the performance of chores. Already in Apuleius' era, intellectuals had begun to doubt that such a tale could actually be true, but they stopped short of ruling out the possibility altogether.

The Novel in Focus

Plot summary. Lucius is a wealthy, lustful, adventuresome youth from the famously decadent Greek city of Corinth. Fascinated by the occult, he is more than pleased to embark on a business trip to Hypata in Thessaly, a region of northern Greece notorious for witches and strange happenings. On the way, Lucius hears grotesque tales of witchcraft and, the day after his arrival, is even warned that Pamphile, the wife of his host, Milo, is a dangerous witch. Far from upsetting him, the information excites his curiosity. But his attention drifts to Photis, a young female slave to Pamphile. Lucius enters into a passionate sexual affair with the slave.

Returning late one night, a rather drunk Lucius stabs what he takes to be three would-be intruders trying to batter down the door of his host's house. He is arrested early the next morning and

put on trial for murder before the town magistrates. A strangeness settles over the trial. While Lucius does his best to speak in his own defense, the crowd keeps laughing. Then, just as he is to be handed over for torture, the trial is revealed as a giant hoax. It turns out that the murdered intruders are not humans after all, but three inflated goatskin bags that Pamphile had earlier turned into human form. The spectators erupt into general hilarity at Lucius' expense. The town's representatives plead with Lucius not to be angry, because everything he has just undergone has been done for an important local god. Each year the God of Laughter is honored with an improvised festival, which this year took the form of a vast practical joke on Lucius, using the slain goatskin bags as the prop. Because he has served the God of Laughter in this way, the townspeople assure Lucius, he will remain forever under Laughter's divine protection.

Although a little shaken by events, Lucius decides to spy on Pamphile as she magically changes into an owl. Anxious to imitate her, he sends Photis to grab the ointment used in the transformation, but she grabs the wrong box and Lucius is transformed into an ass instead. Worse still, while Photis is off searching for the antidote (roses), bandits suddenly burst upon the scene and rustle all the livestock, Lucius included. In the bandits' company, Lucius the ass hears the tale of Cupid and Psyche, a lengthy digression from the main storyline. An old woman who cooks for the robbers tells it to comfort a young bride named Charite, whom the gang has abducted.

Psyche, explains the old woman, is the youngest and most beautiful of three princesses; she is so breathtaking that others worship her as an earthly manifestation of Venus, the goddess of love. Venus suffers as a result, as worshippers neglect the rites and temples of the genuine goddess. Infuriated, she dispatches her son Cupid to punish Psyche. Meanwhile, despite her extraordinary loveliness, no suitors have sought Psyche's hand in marriage. Her concerned father consults Apollo (God of Oracles), who directs the father to leave his daughter on a mountaintop, where she will be claimed as wife by a snakelike monster that plagues humanity.

Abandoned on the peak, Psyche passes out, and a gentle wind transports her to a beautiful house, where she spends the day with invisible servants who cater to her every wish. That night her new husband enters her room in the dark, consummates the marriage, and then departs unseen. This pattern continues night after night, and, though she never sees him, Psyche grows to love her mysterious spouse. She conceives a child. Though elated, Psyche grieves at not being able to comfort her sisters, who mourn for her. Her husband relents, allowing them to visit, but warns her not to heed them if they urge her to investigate his identity. Despite his warnings, they convince her. She approaches him with a lamp as he sleeps only to discover that her husband is the beautiful, winged youth Cupid. Just then a drop of hot oil spills from her lamp and wakens him, whereupon Psyche is banished and punished by Venus, who tortures the girl, then assigns her a series of impossible tasks. During one of these tasks, Psyche falls into a coma and Cupid rushes to the rescue. After reviving her, the still-loving husband makes his way to Jupiter, King of the Gods, to beg his indulgence. A forgiving Jupiter rules the two shall be officially married and Psyche, turned into a goddess as befits Venus' daughter-in-law. Cupid and the now immortal Psyche have a child, a daughter named Pleasure. At this point, the robbers return, and the story stops abruptly.

Lucius the ass and the young bride Charite are rescued by her husband, who infiltrates the gang in disguise. The reunited couple's happiness is short-lived, however. When a jealous former suitor murders the husband, Charite avenges his death and commits suicide. Lucius the ass passes into new ownership and is put to work in a mill, tediously turning the mill wheel. As he plods along at the tiresome task, he observes the miserable slaves and animals at work in the mill: "As to the human contingent—what a crew!— their whole bodies picked out with livid weals [welts], their whip-scarred backs shaded rather than covered by their tattered rags, some with only a scanty loin-cloth by way of covering" (*The Golden Ass*, 9.12, p. 153). A sequence of misadventures lead to Lucius the ass falling into the possession of two slaves owned by a wealthy master in Lucius' hometown of Corinth. Since his new owners, the two slaves, are a pastry cook and a chef, Lucius now has access to delicious human food. When discovered eating various choice delicacies, his owners are amused. They summon the rest of the household to join in their laughter at the ass with gourmet tastes.

The master of the house brings Lucius to the dining room to entertain his guests with his humanlike behavior. The satisfaction of Lucius' humanlike appetites is taken still further when a wealthy lady of Corinth arranges to have secret sexual encounters with him. The master, after spying on this spectacle for his own pleasure, decides to reproduce it in the arena for the entertainment of the city at large. Since he has been awarded the highest magistracy in the city, he needs to stage an impressive event to mark the occasion, and this show promises to be a crowd-pleaser. A woman, already sentenced to die in the arena by attack by a wild animal, is chosen to become the bride of the ass. Lucius learns that while he publicly rapes her, wild beasts will be released to execute her death sentence, probably killing him in the process. He manages to escape.

The final section opens as Lucius awakens by the seaside. Sensing divine power in the night air, he prays to the mother goddess, addressing her by all the holy names that come to mind. Pleading for her mercy, he falls asleep again. He awakens later to a magnificent apparition of the goddess Isis, who explains how to find the roses that will cure him and promises him her protection forever after, provided he lives chastely and obediently in her service. Following her instructions, Lucius is restored to human form and begins the rites of initiation. In Isis' service, he journeys to Rome and, although overwhelmed by the cost of living in the imperial city, is able to cover his expenses by establishing a legal practice, the success of which he credits to Isis. The novel ends with the image of a transformed youth—his days as an ass over, Lucius has become the bald priest of Isis and a prosperous lawyer.

A world of slaves. After his transformation into an ass, Lucius' first encounter with a human being other than Photis is with his own slave, who promptly beats him. It is a telling moment. The slave, of course, fails to recognize his master and sees only an ass trying to eat roses off the statue of a deity. Even so, the incident marks Lucius' new place in the scheme of things. In antiquity, slaves were often associated with beasts of burden. Lucius himself makes the connection, noting that, in the form of an ass, he has been made the "fellow slave and yoke-mate" of the horse he once owned as a human (*The Golden Ass*, 7.3, p. 113). In truth, the beast of burden ranks even lower: until he regains his human form, Lucius becomes the slave of slaves as well as of the free.

The fictional adventure offers insight into the actual conditions of slaves and the lower economic classes under Roman rule. Tediously turning the mill wheel, Lucius the ass surveys his new surroundings, considering the human slaves first. Their heads are shaven; their foreheads, branded; and their feet, manacled. If they wear anything more than a loincloth, their clothing amounts to nothing but the barest and most tattered of rags.

Their backs are scarred with welts from whippings, and the bodies of all the slaves are coated head to toe in an eerie whitish powder, a mixture of dirt and the flour ground at the mill. Next Lucius considers the animals. Constant beatings have nearly stripped the flesh from their ribs. They are underfed, the skin hangs on their bones, and their hooves have flattened and widened from the constant circular march of turning the mill wheel. The harshness of life depicted by the novel is arresting, though it seems not to trouble its main character much.

Recounting these events long after they are over, Lucius the narrator fixes on the wide variety of people and places he met as an ass rather than the suffering. He recalls but does not condemn slavery or oppression. Apuleius himself, like all men and women of property in the Greco-Roman world, owned slaves. His wealthy wife owned so many that she gave her grown children 400 slaves as an advance on their inheritance. There is no evidence from the author's life that he considered slavery morally wrong. His novel contains no criticism of the institution, only concern for individual slaves and, perhaps, for how their treatment reflects on the humaneness of their owners.

Apuleius' perspective is shaped in part by ancient philosophical debates on slavery. The Stoics argued that someone who was enslaved could be "free" in the sense that he led the life worthy of a free man. Likewise, a free man could be a slave if he lived in a manner ascribed to slaves, who were thought of as deceitful and unable to act virtuously or to master their appetites. Slaves were also considered curious to a fault; their curiosity showed a mental slavishness insofar as they allowed themselves to be led by whatever trivia happened to absorb them. For much of the novel, Lucius demonstrates curiosity, lustfulness, and disregard for piety or reason, recalling ancient stereotypes of someone enslaved by his appetites and whims.

Sources and literary context. Although now called a novel, *The Golden Ass* is described by Apuleius as a "Milesian tale" (*The Golden Ass*, 1.1, p. 7). The name comes from Miletus, home city of the first author of such stories, the Greek writer Aristides of Miletus. This type of tale was an often erotic, low-level kind of literature, utterly at odds with the subtlety and depth of Apuleius' writing. In labeling his novel a Milesian tale, Apuleius is most likely making a sly joke.

The first ten of *The Golden Ass*'s eleven "books" (chapter-sized sections) are based on a Greek novel, which was later abridged in Greek and

entitled *Lucius, or the Ass*. The abridgement survives, but not the original. Much debate has arisen over the relationship between the three texts—the lost original, the abridgement, and Apuleius' adaptation. Apuleius' version is considerably more literary than the surviving Greek abridgement. Perhaps the best indicator of the difference between *The Golden Ass* and the abridgement, *Lucius, or the Ass*, is a glance at the latter's ending.

As in Apuleius' version, the abridgement has Lucius the ass enter into a sexual relationship with a woman shortly before he is changed back into human form. In Apuleius, we hear no more about this woman, but in the abridgement, there is further communication. Lucius imagines that she will be overjoyed to see him in his resplendent human shape after having loved him so passionately in spite of his animal form. All seems to go well as they meet, have dinner, and get reacquainted. Lucius walks to the bedroom, strips off his clothing, and waits for her on the bed. When she arrives, she is not pleased with what she sees. After a barrage of insults, she clarifies the situation for the bewildered Lucius:

> I wasn't in love with *you*. I was in love with the donkey you were. I slept with *it* those times, not you. I thought you might have saved at least one thing and still have that nice big emblem of your donkeyhood trailing between your legs. You've gone and turned yourself from a lovely, precious beast into an ape, that's what you've done.
> (Lucian, p. 93)

The abridgement closes humorously, with these sentiments. It ends with the same comic irreverence that has guided the narrative throughout, not with the concern for a new life of chastity and restraint that ends Apuleius' telling.

Reception. Ancient reactions to *The Golden Ass* are few, with those that are known ranging from the cautious to the hostile. Some of the novel's earliest readers are known to have objected to the erotic and fantastic tenor of *The Golden Ass*. Apparently Emperor Septimius Severus (193-211 CE) accused a rival of frittering away his time reading *The Golden Ass*. In a similar vein, the fourth-century scholar, Macrobius, expressed shock that Apuleius, a reputable philosopher, would indulge in literary endeavors of this sort.

> [These stories] beguile the listener in the same way as comedies, of the sort that Menander and his imitators produced for performance, or, again, as the plots told about the imaginary vicissitudes of lovers, in which kind of work Petronius so

indulged himself, and in which Apuleius also sometimes dallied—to our astonishment.
(Macrobius in Tatum, pp. 100-101)

A century later the novel impressed the bishop Augustine (354-430), who in considering whether to give the benefit of the doubt to popular reports of magical transformation, treated *The Golden Ass* as Apuleius' own autobiographical claim to have undergone a metamorphosis. A skeptical Augustine refers to Apuleius when he doubts the truth of tales about female innkeepers who transform travelers into pack animals that perform chores:

> This is what Apuleius, in the work bearing the title *The Golden Ass*, describes as his experience, that after taking a magic potion he became an ass, while retaining his human mind. But this may be either fact or fiction. Stories of this kind are either untrue or at least so extraordinary that we are justified in withholding credence.
> (Augustine, *The City of God*, 18.18, p. 782)

The Golden Ass then fell from view for close to a millennium. In the 1300s, Giovanni Boccaccio rediscovered it and responded to the story with such enthusiasm that he translated it into vernacular Italian and fused three of its episodes into his own masterpiece, the *Decameron*. The popularity of *The Golden Ass* was secure thereafter, as was its incorporated tale of Cupid and Psyche, which went on to have a healthy existence of its own. Translated into English by William Adlington (1566), *The Golden Ass* was available to Shakespeare, and probably influenced his *A Midsummer's Night Dream*. More definitely, it inspired John Keats's "Ode to Psyche" (1819) and a myriad of visual artists. European painters and sculptors from Raphael, to Orazio Gentileschi, Anthony van Dyck, Antonio Canova, Jacques-Louis David, Edward Burne-Jones, and Auguste Rodin have all turned their hands to depicting Cupid and Psyche.

—Seán Easton

For More Information

Apuleius. *The Golden Ass, or, Metamorphoses*. Trans. E. J. Kenney. New York: Penguin, 1998.

Augustine. *The City of God*. Trans. Henry Bettenson. New York: Penguin, 1984.

Feeney, Denis. *Literature and Religion at Rome: Cultures, Contexts, and Beliefs*. Cambridge: Cambridge University Press, 1998.

Freeman, Charles. *Egypt, Greece and Rome*. Oxford: Oxford University Press, 2004.

Goodman, Martin. *The Roman World: 44 BC-AD 180*. London: Routledge, 1997.

Graf, Fritz. *Magic in the Ancient World*. Trans. Franklin Philip. Cambridge, Mass.: Harvard University Press, 1997.

Grünewald, Thomas. *Bandits in the Roman Empire: Myth and Reality*. Trans. John Drinkwater. London: Routledge, 2004.

Lucian. *Selected Satires of Lucian*. Ed. and trans. Lionel Casson. New York: W. W. Norton, 1968.

Madden, John. "Slavery in the Roman Empire: Numbers and Origins." *Classics Ireland* 3 (1996): 109-128. http://www.ucd.ie/classics/96/Madden 96.html.

Millar, Fergus. "The World of the *Golden Ass*." *The Journal of Roman Studies* 71 (1981): 64-75.

Shelton, Jo-Ann. *As the Romans Did: A Sourcebook in Roman Social History*. New York: Oxford University Press, 1998.

Tatum, James. *Apuleius and The Golden Ass*. Ithaca, N.Y.: Cornell University Press, 1979.

The Histories

by
Herodotus

As the first writer to investigate past events and attempt to explain them rationally, Herodotus (c. 485-c. 425 BCE) is often called "the Father of History." Little is known for certain about his life, but according to tradition he was born in the year 484 BCE in Halicarnassus, a Greek city on the southern coast of Asia Minor (now Bodrum, Turkey). It is thought that his mother was Carian (the Carians were a non-Greek people from the interior of Asia Minor), which may have contributed to his lively curiosity about other cultures. This interest shows itself repeatedly in the *Histories*, which includes detailed descriptions of a wide range of non-Greek peoples. Many of these often lengthy digressions seem based on personal experience. In light of them, modern scholars have concluded that Herodotus traveled widely while assembling the material that ultimately became the *Histories*, which is his only surviving written work. Tradition also has Herodotus, late in life, joining the new Athenian colony of Thurii on the island of Sicily. It is thought that he died there sometime after 430 BCE, the approximate date of the latest events alluded to in the *Histories*. Scholars believe that before leaving for Thurii, Herodotus probably lived in Athens. He certainly celebrates the city in the *Histories,* portraying it as Greece's savior against the mighty Persian Empire.

Events in History at the Time of the Narrative

Archaic Greece. Between the eighth century BCE and Herodotus' lifetime in the fifth century BCE,

THE LITERARY WORK

A historical narrative in nine books written in Greek and published c. 430-425 BCE.

SYNOPSIS

Herodotus recounts the Persian Wars (490 and 480-79 BCE), in which the small, disunited Greek city-states under Athenian leadership twice repelled invading Persian armies.

ancient Greece entered an age of vigorous expansion. This growth occurred in a number of realms, embracing political change, energetic trade and settlement in new areas of the Mediterranean coastline, and cultural and intellectual innovation. Herodotus covers developments in all these areas, often providing information in the form of vivid anecdotes. While other evidence—in particular, archaeological discoveries—have helped throw light on this crucial period, Herodotus remains by far the most valuable single source. In many cases, the *Histories* provides our only detailed account of important events.

From a political standpoint, the most important development in Archaic Greece was the rise of the independent Greek city-state, the *polis*. (In fact the Greek word *polis* [plural *poleis*] gives us English words like "political" and "politics.") Throughout Greece, groups of scattered villages coalesced into unitary states centered around a

Herodotus. The Granger Collection.

powerful urban hub, a process that the Greeks called *synoikismos* or "collective living." Sparta grew into a military power, emerging as the leading polis before the Persian wars; other important poleis included Corinth, Argos, Megara, Thebes, Sicyon, and Athens.

In the early Archaic period, the poleis were dominated by coalitions of powerful aristocratic families. By the seventh century BCE, in many poleis, these often unpopular ruling coalitions were being overthrown and replaced by popular leaders called *tyrannoi* or tyrants. (In this original sense, the Greek word lacked the negative connotation it has in English today.) When the tyrants attempted to found dynasties, however, their heirs frequently proved less popular than the original founder, and so most tyrannies did not last beyond a few generations. The major exception was the century-long dynasty (c. 665-565 BCE) founded by Orthagoras, tyrant of Sicyon. Herodotus twice recounts stories about this dynasty's most famous ruler, Cleisthenes (ruled c. 600-570 BCE). Herodotus also discusses the reigns of a number of other tyrants and their dynasties, most notably Cypselus, tyrant of Corinth (ruled c. 657-625 BCE) and his son Periander, and Peisistratus, tyrant of Athens (ruled c. 561-527 BCE), and his sons Hippias and Hipparchus.

Closely related to the rise of the polis were the growth of trade and the foundation of new settlements aimed at securing commercial benefits for the founding polis or *metropolis* ("mother city"). Indeed, just as modern historians often call the late Archaic period the "age of tyrants," they frequently refer to the entire period as the "age of colonization." From dry and rugged mainland Greece, where good farming land was always scarce, the seafaring Greeks sent out colonizing expeditions in all directions accessible from the Aegean Sea: west, to Sicily and southern Italy; south, to the Mediterranean coast of Africa; northeast, as far as the southern coast of the Black Sea; and east, to the western and southern coasts of Asia Minor.

Halicarnassus, Herodotus' birthplace, was among the earliest of such settlements in Asia Minor, originally founded around the beginning of the ninth century BCE. An even earlier Greek presence was established in the important city of Miletus a few days' voyage to the north. Originally a Carian town said to have been taken over by settlers from Athens around the eleventh-century BCE, Miletus by the eighth century had itself begun founding colonies and soon became the region's major metropolis. The Greek cities of the central coast of Asia Minor are collectively known as Ionia, after the linguistic group to which the original Athenian settlers of Miletus had belonged. (Aside from Ionic, other Greek dialects represented on the coast of Asia Minor included Doric, which was spoken in Herodotus' home city of Halicarnassus, and Aeolic.) Led by powerful Miletus, which plays a central role in the *Histories*, the Greek cities of Ionia, prosperous and proud, comprised a little realm of their own within the larger Greek world.

Ionia lay closer than the rest of Greece to the older civilizations of the Fertile Crescent, whose traditions included ancient mathematical and astronomical wisdom like that of the Babylonians. Ionia's exposure to such foreign ways of thinking, it has been suggested, helped spark the intellectual revolution that began in Miletus in the early sixth century BCE and rapidly transformed the Greek world. In fact, it was in Miletus that the first systematic attempts were made to explain the natural world in rational, rather than religious, terms. This innovation in thought eventually came to be known as philosophy (Greek *philosophia*, "love of wisdom") and its practitioner was the *philosophos* or philosopher. Herodotus does not employ these terms, however, since they did not come into wide use until after his death.

THE AGES OF EARLY GREECE

Throughout the *Histories*, Herodotus frequently refers to famous events and people from Greece's past. Modern historians divide early Greek history into the following periods:

The Bronze Age (c. 3000-c.1000 BCE) The Bronze Age is further divided into Early, Middle, and Late. During the Middle Bronze Age (c. 2000-c. 1500 BCE) the non-Greek Minoan civilization arose on the island of Crete. Named for its legendary King Minos, whom Herodotus mentions several times, Minoan civilization may have been wiped out by the massive volcanic explosion on the nearby island of Thera (Santorini) in c. 1620 BCE. In its wake, Late Bronze Age settlers on the mainland founded the first Greek civilization, called Mycenaean after its political center at Mycenae. Mycenaean civilization declined starting around 1200 BCE, probably as a result of internal warfare.

The Dark Age (c. 1100-c. 800 BCE) Population decrease and cultural backwardness characterized the next several hundred years. Trade stagnated in the Greek world, and writing was lost. However, oral culture carried on, and it was during this period that the ***Iliad*** and the ***Odyssey***, the epic poems ascribed to Homer, first took shape as oral narratives (also in *Classical Literature and Its Times*). Considered the foundation of later Greek culture and the beginning of Western literature, these poems celebrate the heroic deeds of legendary Mycenaean warrior-kings such as Agamemnon (king of Mycenae), Achilles, and Odysseus. The epics concern the Trojan War, a fabled conflict between the Greeks and the Trojans that Herodotus mentions. At the beginning of the *Histories*, he notes that, according to the Persians, the Greek siege of Troy marked the start of trouble between the Greeks and Asians (Troy lay on the northern coast of Asia Minor).

The Archaic Period (c. 800-c. 480 BCE) In the *Histories*, events from this age of renewal and expansion comprise the background to the Persian Wars, as Herodotus sets the stage for Persia's invasions of Greece. Modern historians generally see the second of these invasions, in 480 BCE, as marking the end of Greece's Archaic Period.

The Classical Period (c. 480-323 BCE) Greek culture has now reached what most observers regard as its high point, especially in the literary, intellectual, and artistic achievements of Athens, the democratic city-state that rose to leadership of the Greek world in the decades after the Persian Wars. Herodotus, historians believe, lived and worked in Athens during at least part of this time, where tradition has him meeting the great Athenian tragic playwright Sophocles. Herodotus' sympathetic portrait of Athens in the *Histories* suggests affection and respect for the city and its democratic institutions.

The first philosopher, Thales of Miletus (c. 636-c. 546 BCE), taught that water is the fundamental material for all existence. Other Ionians (including Thales' students Anaximander and Anaximenes) took up such speculative theorizing, proposing and defending their own ideas about nature and existence. Herodotus mentions the celebrated Thales several times in connection with events concerning Miletus. In a more general way, Herodotus' rationalistic outlook can be seen as reflecting his upbringing in Ionia's innovative intellectual climate, which remained vibrant into his own day.

The rise of Persia. Even as the Ionians inaugurated the Western tradition of rational inquiry, developments were taking place that soon brought Ionia and then the rest of Greece under the dark clouds of invasion, occupation, and war. First, around the middle of the sixth century, the Greek cities of Ionia were taken over by nearby Lydia's King Croesus (ruled c. 560-546 BCE), whose capital, Sardis, lay in the interior of Asia Minor, inland from Ionia. Only a few years later, in 546 BCE, Croesus' relatively benign rule ended when Lydia itself was conquered by a new power

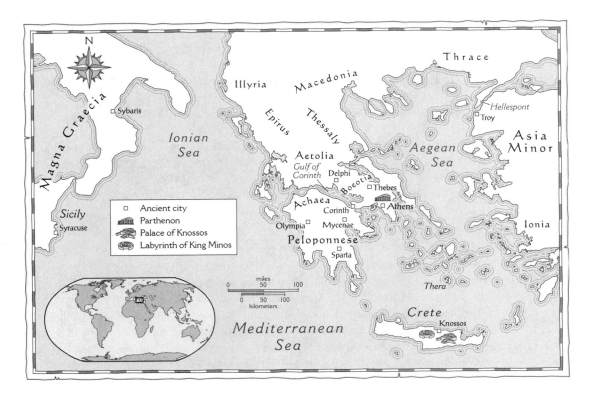

Map of Archaic Greece. © 2006 Thomson Gale

from much farther to the east, the rising empire of Persia, led by Cyrus the Great (c. 590-530 BCE). In Book 1 of the *Histories*, Herodotus devotes much space to portraits of Croesus and Cyrus, regaling his audience with dramatic tales that clearly reflect folk legends.

Cyrus had founded his empire by overthrowing the Medes, who had been the Persians' overlords when Cyrus ascended to the Persian throne in 559 BCE. From their base in Fars or Persis (now southern Iran), as Herodotus relates, the Persians under Cyrus then expanded their domains to the east and west. Cyrus' dynasty is called Achaemenid, after one of his royal ancestors. By Cyrus' death in 530 BCE, when his son Cambyses (r. 530-522 BCE) assumed the throne, the territories under Achaemenid rule stretched from India to Ionia, where the Greek cities had all been subdued.

The Ionian revolt. By 500 BCE, after nearly half a century of Persian rule, the Ionian Greeks had begun to chafe under foreign occupation. As Herodotus relates, the first indications of organized revolt came from Miletus. There the tyrant Histiaeus and his lieutenant Aristagoras, both earlier installed by the Persians, became embroiled in controversy with their Persian overlords. In 499 BCE many (though not all) of the

Ionian cities joined Miletus in rising against the Persians. Aristagoras meanwhile traveled to mainland Greece, where he tried to win support for the revolt. Sparta, the most powerful of all Greek cities and the acknowledged leader, refused, but Athens agreed, reluctantly, to aid the rebels.

Athens accordingly dispatched a fleet of 20 warships to the Ionian coast. "These ships," Herodotus observes, "were the beginning of evil for Greeks and barbarians" (Herodotus, *The Histories*, Book 5, chapter 97). After initial Greek military successes, the Persians took the offensive, and in 494 BCE they crushed the combined Ionian and Athenian fleet at the Battle of Lade. Later that year the Persians besieged and captured Miletus, plundering the city, killing many, and removing the rest of the population to be resettled deep within Persian territory. Back in Athens, Herodotus reports, people were so saddened by the Milesians' fate that when a tragic playwright presented a play about the city's capture "the audience in the theatre burst into tears" and the playwright "was fined a thousand drachmas [approximately $100,000] for reminding them of their own evils" (*Histories*, 6.21).

The Persian Wars. The Persian king who suppressed the Ionian revolt, Darius I (r. 522-486

Xerxes at the battle of Salamis. Archive Photos, Inc. Reproduced by permission.

BCE), was not satisfied with merely reestablishing his rule over Ionia. Angered by Athens' support for the rebels, he was determined to exact revenge on the mainland Greeks as well, and especially on Athens itself. In 490 BCE invading Persians crossed the Aegean Sea to the large island of Euboea, which lay just north of the territory around Athens known as Attica. The Persian force occupied the city of Eretria, and then made the short crossing from Euboea to Attica. Landing at Marathon, they were met by a far smaller Athenian force. It consisted of *hoplites* (armored footsoldiers with heavy shields and long spears who fought in a tight group or *phalanx*), aided by a group of soldiers from the nearby town of Plataea. Under the command of the Athenian general Miltiades, the Greeks boldly attacked, routing the surprised Persians in a day's hard fighting. Herodotus estimates Persian losses at some 6,400 dead, while the Greeks, he says, lost only 192 (*Histories*, 6.117). The Persians retreated back across the Aegean, and Athens celebrated its stunning victory.

Enraged, Darius again vowed revenge, but he died in 486 BCE, before he could make good on the vow. It fell to his son and heir Xerxes (r. 486-465 BCE) to do so, and immediately upon ascending the throne Xerxes began preparing a much larger invasion force. Darius had aimed merely to punish the Greeks, whereas Xerxes set out to occupy mainland Greece itself. But the Athenians, too, were readying themselves. At the urging of their statesman Themistocles, whose wisdom Herodotus praises, Athens took advantage of rich silver deposits at nearby Laurium to fund the construction of a fleet of 200 *triremes,* or warships.

Athens had a longstanding dispute with Aegina, a large island off the coast of Attica. Ancient animosities similarly entangled relations among Sparta, Corinth, Argos, Thebes, and the other cities. Yet the Greeks resolved to put aside their differences and make common cause against the Persian threat. Sparta, which had not sent soldiers to Marathon (but praised the Athenian victory afterward), agreed to assume leadership of the military alliance.

Rather than crossing the Aegean as the earlier invasion force had done, Xerxes' much larger expedition traveled in an arc along the northern Aegean coast, setting out early in 480 BCE. Also, in contrast to Darius who had remained in Persia, Xerxes accompanied his great army and navy, forces he had gathered from throughout his vast empire. The main question for the Greeks, as they conferred at Corinth in the spring of 480 BCE, was where to make their initial stand as the Persian armada drew closer. They decided on

CROESUS, CYRUS, AND THE GODS

⁓

Perhaps the best-known passages in the *Histories* are those recounting the fate of the wealthy and potent Croesus, king of Lydia, and the even mightier king who shattered his power, Cyrus the Great of Persia. Modern commentators have seen the story of Croesus as illustrating one of Herodotus' central messages, which is that the gods inevitably punish those who become too proud and ambitious. The Greeks called this combination of pride and ambition *hubris*, and it is a central theme in much Greek literature—especially the tragic drama that arose in Athens in the years after the Persian Wars, when Herodotus was composing the *Histories*. Croesus is thus portrayed as hubristic.

Herodotus also portrays the Persian king Xerxes as hubristic and describes how his hubris provokes the gods' wrath, leading to the failure of the second Persian expedition. In the following passage, Herodotus shows Xerxes ignoring a couple of "omens," which the Greeks would have considered to be messages indicating the will of the gods:

> After the whole army had reached the European shore and the forward march had begun, a great portent occurred—a mare gave birth to a hare. Xerxes paid no attention to this omen, though the significance of it was easy enough to understand. Clearly it meant that he was to lead an army against Greece with the greatest pomp and circumstance, and then to come running for his life back to the place he started from. There had previously been another portent in Sardis, when a mule dropped a foal with a double set of sexual organs, male and female—the former uppermost. Xerxes, however, ignored both omens and continued his march at the head of the army.
>
> (*Histories*, 7.58)

While Herodotus adopted a generally rationalistic approach to the past—explaining historical events in human terms rather than religious ones—he also followed tradition in keeping a place for the gods when it came to broader dimensions of those events.

Thermopylae in northern Greece, a narrow mountain pass through which the Persian army would have to march, and where Persian numerical superiority would count for less in a face-to-face battle.

There, having dismissed most of the other Greek forces, the Spartan king Leonidas and 300 elite warriors called *spartiatai* stopped the Persian advance for three days, until a local native showed the Persians a hidden trail which they used to get around the Spartans and attack from the rear. Leonidas and his celebrated 300 Spartiates fought to the death, passing immediately into glory as national heroes and giving the other Greeks time to fall back and prepare further defenses. The Greek naval fleet fought a similar holding action at Artemision, withdrawing after three days of heavy fighting.

The Persian army marched on, occupying Attica, which the Athenians had abandoned. Led by Themistocles, Athens had pinned its hopes on its navy, the backbone of the Greek fleet. Tricking the Persian naval commander with a false message, Themistocles lured the Persians into the narrow strait of Salamis, near Megara. There, in 480 BCE, the Persian fleet was defeated with heavy losses. Xerxes and the remnants of his once proud expedition retreated in confusion. A Persian army that remained in Greece was also defeated at Plataea in 479 BCE. Seemingly against all odds, Greece had again been saved.

The Narrative in Focus

Contents summary. In the broadest terms, the *Histories* can be divided in two roughly equal halves, one describing the rise of the Persian Empire and the other narrating its two invasions of mainland Greece. In the first half, Herodotus describes the various peoples conquered by the

Persians in the decades leading up to the invasions. Here he freely incorporates colorful folktales and legends (for example, those about Croesus and Cyrus). In the second part, this mythic element takes a back seat to more straightforward historical narrative, as Herodotus leaves the distant past and arrives in the firmer territory of living memory.

As Herodotus recounts the Persian wars, he invokes a highly discursive style that defies condensation. Herodotus typically expands on a subject as it arises in the course of his narrative, filling in the background before resuming the larger narrative where he left off. Thus, for example, his account of Aristagoras' journey to Athens to enlist aid for the Ionian revolt enfolds a lengthy digression about recent Athenian history and the democratic reforms that followed the expulsion from Athens of Pisistratus' sons Hippias and Hipparchus. Having brought his audience up to date, he then continues with Aristagoras' arrival and the Athenian decision to send a fleet to Ionia. This technique can be confusing to the modern reader, but it characterizes Herodotus' basic approach throughout the *Histories*. Even his digressions often have digressions.

Neither the title the *Histories* nor the division of the work into nine books originated with Herodotus. Yet, put in place by later scholars and interpreters (who named each book after one of the nine muses of Greek lore), the book divisions follow the inherent structure of the work and so prove useful in outlining its contents.

Herodotus begins by tracing the various causes put forward in his own time for the conflict between Greece and Persia. He then takes up the story of Croesus, king of Lydia, the first foreigner "so far as we know" to conquer and rule over Greeks (*Histories*, 1.6). In his attempts to defend himself against Persia by allying himself with mainland Greeks, Croesus provides an occasion for digressions on the early history of Sparta and Athens. Cyrus' conquest of Lydia prompts Herodotus to discuss Persian expansion, including accounts of the earlier Assyrian, Babylonian, and Median empires whose lands have fallen under Persian rule. Book 1 concludes with Cyrus' death while campaigning against the Massagetai near the Caspian Sea.

Soon after coming to power, Cyrus' son and heir Cambyses attacks Egypt. Herodotus takes the opportunity to give a long disquisition on Egyptian history and customs, including religious practices and the building of the famous pyramids. In one well-known passage, he

considers the Nile River, which mystified Greeks because, unlike other rivers they knew, it flowed north instead of south, and also because it flooded during the dry summer months:

> About why the Nile behaves precisely as it does I could get no information from the priests or anyone else. What I particularly wished to know was why the water begins to rise at the summer solstice, continues to do so for a hundred days, and then falls again at the end of that period, so that it remains low throughout the winter. . . . Nobody in Egypt could give me any explanation of this, in spite of my constant attempts to find out what was the peculiar property which made the Nile behave in the opposite way to other rivers. . . .
>
> (*Histories*, 2.19)

HERODOTUS AND EGYPT

Herodotus devotes much attention to describing Persian expansion, offering expository digressions on the appearance, culture, history, religion, and folkways of many of the peoples conquered by Persia in the decades before the Persian invasions of Greece. The longest such digression amounts to an extended essay on Egypt, which takes up all of Book 2 in modern editions of the *Histories*. As Herodotus makes clear, Egypt fascinated the Greeks because of its wealth, the strange behavior of its fabled Nile River (which floods during the summer, when other rivers tend to dry up), and above all the great antiquity of Egyptian civilization. Herodotus' treatment of Egypt displays several of his strongest interests, including cultural curiosities, exotic locales, and both natural and manmade marvels.

Book 3 resumes the historical narrative with Cambyses' invasion and occupation of Egypt, his failed attempt to conquer Ethiopia (as the Greeks called the lands south of Egypt), and his subsequent decline into madness and death. Herodotus gives particular attention to the Ionian island of Samos, where the tyrant Polycrates, an ally of Cambyses, survives a rebellion in which the Samian rebels are aided by an expedition from Sparta. Herodotus also describes Samos' impressive man-made marvels, including a long tunnel, a huge pier, and a large religious temple. After a struggle over succession, the Persian nobles choose Darius, an Achaemenid relative of Cambyses, to be king. Suppressing numerous revolts, Darius reorganizes the empire.

Book 4 opens with Darius' failed attempt to conquer the Scythians, which Herodotus fills out with detailed accounts of the Scythians and neighboring peoples ("Scythia" comprises the area north of the Black Sea, today's southern Ukraine). The second half of Book 4 offers a complementary report on Persian operations at the other end of the empire, in Libya, as the Greeks called the lands along the North African coast west of Egypt. Herodotus treats his audience to a detailed account of the various Libyan peoples (later called Berbers), contrasting the hot, dry conditions in their region with the cold, wet conditions of life for the Scythians.

Book 5 concludes the extended description of the Persian Empire and its conquests that occupies the first half of Herodotus' work. The book opens with the conquests of Darius' general Megabazus in Thrace and Macedonia, the regions just north of mainland Greece. Herodotus then describes conditions in Ionia, which leads to his account of the Ionian revolt and the stories of Histiaeus and Aristagoras, the Milesian rulers who initiated it. The failure of the revolt and the destruction of Miletus are recounted early in Book 6, and the rest of this book is taken up with Darius' preparations for the punitive invasion of Greece, the subsequent Greek victory at Marathon, and the return of the failed Persian expedition.

Book 7 begins with Darius' plans for another invasion, which are interrupted by his death and then renewed by his son and heir Xerxes. "At this point," Herodotus interrupts himself to declare,

> I find myself compelled to express an opinion which I know most people will object to; nevertheless, as I believe it to be true, I will not suppress it. If the Athenians, through fear of the approaching danger, had abandoned their country, or if they had stayed there and submitted to Xerxes, there would have been no attempt to resist the Persians by sea; and, in the absence of a Greek fleet, it is easy to see what would have been the course of events on land. . . . In view of this, therefore, one is surely right in saying that Greece was saved by the Athenians. It was the Athenians . . . who, having chosen that Greece should live and preserve her freedom, roused to battle the other Greek states which had not yet submitted. It was the Athenians who—after the gods—drove back the Persian king.
> (*Histories*, 7.139)

Herodotus then resumes the narrative with the second expedition's long voyage along the

northern shore of the Aegean, its progress into mainland Greece, and the battle of Thermopylae.

Book 8 covers the operations that followed, including the important naval battles. First came Artemisium (where the Greeks staged a tactical withdrawal after three days of heavy fighting) and then Salamis (where the Persians suffered a decisive defeat at sea).

Book 9 relates both sides' preparations for the decisive land battle at Plataea and goes on to describe the battle itself. In recounting the Greek victory there, Herodotus highlights the Athenians' distinguished contribution. The work concludes with the Persians' disorganized retreat, as another Greek naval victory at Mycale, near Miletus, touches off a second Ionian revolt against Persian rule.

The origins of history. As modern scholars have observed, the opening sentence of the *Histories* serves its author as the equivalent of a title page:

> Herodotus of Halicarnassus, here displays his inquiry, so that human achievements may not become forgotten in time, and great and marvelous deeds—some displayed by Greeks, some by barbarians—may not be without their glory; and especially to show why the two peoples fought with each other.
> (*Histories*, 1.proem)

The word translated here as "researches" is the Greek *historia*, meaning "inquiry," which has passed into English as "history." The word translated as "other peoples" is the Greek *barbaroi*, literally "barbarians," which for an ancient Greek merely meant "non-Greek." While the context makes it clear that Herodotus is referring primarily to the Persians, the term also embraces the many subject peoples whom the Persians would compel to fight on their side (in Book 7, Herodotus gives a long list of the various nations represented in Xerxes' army).

With these words, the study of history began. The words themselves reflect the two related impulses that have motivated historians ever since: first, to commemorate the past; and, second, to explain it rationally. In turn, these two impulses—clearly seen, for example, in Herodotus' carefully reasoned arguments crediting Athens with having saved Greece—reflect two separate traditions in Greek civilization that first came together in the work of Herodotus. The first was the epic poetry of Homer, an old legacy that reached back to Greek civilization's very origins and celebrated the deeds of its legendary heroes. The second was the much newer tradition of philosophy, which arose in Ionia in the sixth century and attempted to explain the world through rational inquiry.

Taken together, these two vibrant, influential traditions—epic poetry and rational philosophy—may be considered the two "parents" of history. Both played vital roles in shaping Herodotus' thought and writing, and both are clearly reflected throughout the pages of the *Histories*, which celebrates specific individuals and deeds but also ties them together as a way of explaining a single phenomenon, the Persian Wars. In epic poetry, however, all the action is sparked by the activities of the gods. This outlook reflects the religious explanations of both natural and human phenomena that were common to all cultures before the rise of the first secular, rationalistic philosophy in Ionia during the sixth century BCE. Where philosophy applied reason to nature, Herodotus applied it to human events (such as war) that had previously been the province of epic.

Herodotus thus brought two seminal elements in Greek civilization to bear on the most significant event of his age. In doing so he created a new discipline, the study of history, that would ultimately take its place as a vital cultural tradition in its own right. One might say that Herodotus responded to history by inventing it. The historical attitude that he inaugurated has since become so fundamental to our outlook on the past that it is difficult to appreciate just how radical Herodotus' innovation was in its day. Herodotus undoubtedly possessed one of the most startlingly original minds in history—a statement, of course, that would not be possible without the very idea of history itself.

Sources and literary context. Recent scholars stress that the *Histories* differs in important ways from what later centuries would see as "history." They point out, for example, that the *Histories* contains long stretches of geographic and ethnographic description with little or no material that later scholars would consider "historical" in nature. Nor does Herodotus seem to have relied on official documentary sources in the same way that a modern historian would have. Though it has been suggested that he used some official Persian documents (in his lists of peoples subject to the Persians, for example), Herodotus seems to have relied primarily on oral sources or interviews with people for the information he presents.

For the main topic of his "inquiry," the Persian Wars themselves, this oral information would have come from participants on both sides who were still alive when Herodotus was writing, about 50 years after the events took place. For other parts of his account, Herodotus sought out record keepers (such as religious authorities or prominent families) who for various reasons concerned themselves with preserving local traditions and developments. Gathering such information required extensive travel, and it is as a curious sojourner that Herodotus most often seems to present himself. Apart from Greece, he explicitly mentions gathering evidence in places from southern Italy to as far away as Babylon, and from Libya and Egypt to the Black Sea region, including Scythia (southern Ukraine).

Herodotus also mentions another Ionian author, the celebrated travel writer Hecataeus of Miletus, whose dates are uncertain but who wrote around 500 BCE. Hecataeus' most famous work, the *Periodos Ges* or "Journey Around the World," described his circumnavigation of the Mediterranean Sea, offering accounts of peoples and sights encountered along the way. Herodotus names Hecataeus several times, more than any other writer, and clearly emulated Hecataeus in his extensive descriptions of faraway places.

Other literary genres were taking shape as Herodotus planned and executed his work, and they likely influenced him. Local chroniclers, such as Herodotus' younger contemporary Hellanicus of Lesbos, were writing at around the same time, though their works appear to have been shorter and to have lacked the thematic unity, analytic quality, and large-scale perspective of Herodotus' work. One should also keep in mind Herodotus' general debt to the *Iliad* and the *Odyssey*, epic works whose two plots celebrate the deeds of the past and deal with war as well as exotic travel.

During this period, medical writers such as Hippocrates had begun applying the rationalistic attitude of the philosophers to areas outside philosophy. Herodotus displays wide knowledge of the new medical knowledge that resulted. Indeed, both philosophers and physicians used *historia* to describe their own inquiries; Herodotus echoes their term in characterizing his endeavor. One measure of the *Histories'* impact is that his use of the term fixed it forever as the name of the discipline he invented.

Rationalistic analysis also featured prominently in the emerging art of rhetoric or persuasive speaking, which assumed a new prominence in public life with the evolution of Athenian democracy. Indeed, persuasive speaking was already central to Greek literature. In the *Iliad*, for example, major characters deliver closely reasoned speeches

Illustration of Herodotus reading to the Greeks. Archive Photos, Inc. Reproduced by permission.

calculated to win listeners over to their points of view. Herodotus puts numerous speeches in the mouths of his characters, and a number of them suggest the influence of contemporary rhetorical practices. One of the best known of such passages features a discussion among Persian nobles just before Darius accedes to the throne; they present rhetorically polished arguments for and against three forms of government: monarchy, oligarchy, and democracy.

Tragic drama is also associated with Herodotus' work. Athenian tragic playwrights generally drew on Greek myth for their subject matter, eschewing real-life events, but Greece's conflict with Persia proved an exception. The battle of Salamis, for example, helped inspire a well-known tragic play, *The Persians*, produced in 472 BCE by the leading Athenian tragedian Aeschylus. Such productions suggest that as a subject for literature, the Persian Wars rapidly acquired an appropriate gravity and solemnity, and this perception may well have influenced Herodotus' choice of subject matter and his style. *The Persians* may also have inspired Herodotus' remarkably impartial depiction of the enemy. His portrait of Xerxes, for example, clearly suggests the downfall of a "tragic" hero—a sympathetic treatment of the Persian king that had also been central to Aeschylus' play.

Events in History at the Time the Narrative Was Written

The rise of the Athenian Empire. In the aftermath of the Persian defeat, Athens took the lead in pressing the Greek cause against the Persian threat in Ionia. Meanwhile, Sparta once again refused to become involved (according to the final pages of the *Histories*, the Spartans even suggested that the Greeks leave Ionia altogether). Other communities, however, joined Athens. Modern historians call the resulting anti-Persian alliance the Delian League, because its treasury was located on the island of Delos.

Over the 470s and 460s BCE, Athens' domination of the League grew more authoritarian. The Delian League became an Athenian Empire, based on Athenian naval supremacy. The treasury was transferred from Delos to Athens, and Athens began suppressing dissent, refusing to let any of its "allies" withdraw from the "alliance," even though Persia no longer posed a credible threat. By the middle of the century, Athens, whose sway had so far been limited to Ionia and the islands, was expanding Athenian power on the Greek mainland as well. The ambitious city soon encountered resistance, however; Athens' aggressive push brought it into direct conflict first with Corinth, then with Sparta. Still the greatest power on the mainland, Sparta had observed the growth of the Athenian Empire with misgivings that soon turned into hostility.

War between Athens and Corinth broke out in 460 BCE, and Sparta clashed militarily with Athens two years later. Modern historians call this conflict the First Peloponnesian War (460-446 BCE). A tenuous peace ensued, with further hostilities breaking out in 431 BCE. This second stage, the Peloponnesian War proper, lasted nearly three decades and resulted in Sparta's defeat of Athens (see Thucydides' **The Peloponnesian War**, also in *Classical Literature and Its Times*). By its outbreak, Athens' aggression had made the city highly unpopular in much of the Greek world, which accounts for Herodotus' prediction in Book 7 that "most people will object to" his portrait of Athens as the savior of Greece. The period of Athenian aggression that preceded the Peloponnesian War also saw unprecedented cultural vitality in Athens, as the city experienced a veritable explosion of literary, artistic, and intellectual innovation. Much of this took place under the political leadership of Pericles (c. 495-429 BCE), whose mother was a member of the influential Alcmaeonid family, which dominated

SPARTA AND ATHENS

~

Although Herodotus gives information about many Greek city-states in the *Histories*, he reserves his fullest attention for Sparta and Athens, which emerged as bitter rivals in the decades after the Persian Wars. As Herodotus makes clear, the rivalry had strong ideological overtones. Sparta was unusual in being ruled by two kings who were advised by a small council of elders called the *gerousia*. But Sparta's defining characteristic was its iron rule over the Helots—the inhabitants of the neighboring community of Messenia, which had been conquered and enslaved by Sparta in the eighth century BCE. Many of Sparta's actions during and after the Persian Wars (its hesitancy to get involved in the Ionian revolt, for example) have been attributed to the fear of a revolt by the Helots, a permanent underclass who performed all of Sparta's agricultural and other manual labor. A rigid, authoritarian system arose out of the need to control the Helots. Herodotus attributes this system to the reforms of the legendary Spartan lawgiver Lycurgus.

Athens, by contrast, developed along more democratic lines, in particular after the reforms of the Athenian statesman Cleisthenes, who lived in the late sixth century and (as Herodotus reports) was the grandson and namesake of Cleisthenes, tyrant of Sicyon. The Athenian Cleisthenes was also a member of the influential Alcmaeonid family. His democratic reforms would be expanded upon by his successor Ephialtes, and then by Ephialtes' protégé, Cleisthenes' Alcmaeonid relative Pericles. Herodotus perhaps reflects the bias of his Alcmaeonid sources when he endorses democracy as helping promote the Athenians' remarkable military performance: "so long as they were held down by authority," he writes, "they deliberately shirked their duty in the field [of battle], as slaves shirk working for their masters; but when freedom was won, then every man amongst them was interested in his own cause" (*Histories*, p. 369). Modern historians might qualify such enthusiasm by observing that participation in Athens's democracy was limited to its adult male citizens, and that its prosperity, like Sparta's and Greece's generally, relied in large part on the labor of slaves.

Athenian politics from the 460s. Herodotus mentions Pericles by name in his discussion of the Alcmaeonids, and modern scholars believe that the historian relied heavily on Alcmaeonid sources for material pertaining to Athens. If, as they further believe, Herodotus lived in Athens during its golden "Periclean" age, he is likely to have enjoyed the support of Pericles himself, and may even have left Athens in part because of Pericles' death in 429.

Publication and impact. Many modern historians have concluded that Herodotus composed the *Histories* specifically for an Athenian audience. The word "audience" is more appropriate in this regard than "readership," since it is also thought that the work was first "published" not in written form but by being publicly read aloud, in the first instance probably by Herodotus himself. It is important to recall that Greece in the fifth century BCE was still undergoing the transition from an oral culture to a written one, and that a public "readership" still lay at least several decades in the future.

Herodotus' invention of history was rapidly taken up by the younger Thucydides (c. 455-400 BCE), and then by other historians. These subsequent historians followed Herodotus' example in many respects, perhaps most notably in incorporating full-blown speeches by historical figures into their works, as Herodotus does on many occasions. The accuracy of speeches in ancient historical works has been a subject of debate. Certainly many of them were to some extent made up, as Herodotus' must also have been.

Ancient historians reacted against what seemed invented, questioning Herodotus' accuracy and truthfulness. The Greek author Plutarch (c. 50-c. 120 CE) went so far as to call Herodotus "Father of Lies" rather than "Father of History." Many of Herodotus' statements and conclusions may be justifiably rejected. According to modern scholars, for example, his estimates of Persian numbers in both invasion forces must have been highly exaggerated. However, recent research—especially in the field of archaeology—has demonstrated that in other cases Herodotus was remarkably accurate.

In contrast with their ancient counterparts, most modern historians have found little reason to question Herodotus' honesty; they instead tend to praise his candor and diligence. Nevertheless, historians have preferred to follow the model of Thucydides, who disparaged the storytelling in Herodotus' work and presented himself as more interested in fact than entertainment. Indeed, Thucydides' "scientific" approach dominated the writing of history until very recently, when historians once again began to acknowledge the validity of the historian's role as storyteller. This development has substantially enhanced Herodotus' reputation among modern historians.

—Colin Wells

For More Information

Boardman, John, et al. *Greece and the Hellenistic World*. Oxford: Oxford University Press, 1986.

Burn, A. R. *Persia and the Greeks*. 2nd ed. London: Duckworth, 1984.

Fornara, Charles. *Herodotus: An Interpretative Essay*. Oxford: Oxford University Press, 1971.

Gould, John. *Herodotus*. New York: St. Martin's, 1989.

Herodotus. *The Histories*. Trans. Aubrey de Sélincourt. Rev. J. Marincola. London: Penguin, 2003.

Lang, Mabel. *Herodotean Narrative and Discourse*. Cambridge, Mass.: Harvard University Press, 1984.

Murray, Oswyn. *Early Greece*. Glasgow: Fontana Press, 1980.

Thomas, Rosalind. *Herodotus in Context: Ethnography, Science and the Art of Persuasion*. Cambridge: Cambridge University Press, 2000.

Iliad

by
Homer

Little is known about the poet to whom the *Iliad* and the *Odyssey* are ascribed. Present scholarship believes that the two epics developed into their present form over many centuries, originating as songs. Although there has been debate over whether more than one person wrote down the two epics, most scholars also believe each poem to have had one final author who added passages that connected episodes and otherwise refined the overall story that each epic tells. The personal background of the *Iliad*'s author, who may have been called Homer, remains uncertain. The best evidence places his birth around the eighth century BCE and his home ground in the city of Smyrna or Chios by the Aegean Sea. According to ancient tradition, Homer was blind, though this attribute, like other details of his life, remains debatable. It can be said with greater certainty that legends of a Trojan war that took place in Mycenaean times, some five centuries before Homer's own day, circulated in his era and may have been frequently told in his birthplace. His epics probably preserve *memories* of events during the Mycenaean war more than the events themselves. Also they likely include elements that have been grafted onto the epics from post-Mycenaean times. Homer's *Iliad* is in any case based upon legends that developed about the war, while the sequel, the *Odyssey*, relates subsequent events. Famous for its graphic depictions of battle, the *Iliad* contains vivid scenes of human suffering while capturing the heroic values and traditions of a bygone age.

THE LITERARY WORK

A Greek epic poem, set in the ancient city of Troy (Ilios) around 1200 BCE; composed around 750-700 BCE.

SYNOPSIS

A quarrel between King Agamemnon and the warrior Achilles disrupts the tenth year of the Trojan War, resulting in devastating losses for both the Greek and Trojan armies.

Events in History at the Time of the Epic

The legend of the Trojan War. Although Homer's epic covers only a brief but pivotal span of weeks during the last year of the war, he presupposes the reader's knowledge of the various myths making up the saga. Throughout the *Iliad*, there are glancing references to those other myths.

The seeds for the Trojan War were first sown at the marriage of Peleus, king of Phthia, and Thetis, a goddess of the sea. All the gods were invited to the celebration, except Eris, the goddess of Discord. Angered, Eris intruded on the guests and flung a golden apple inscribed "for the fairest" among them. The goddesses Hera, Athena, and Aphrodite all laid claim to the apple, but none of the other gods could decide whom the winner should be. Zeus, the king of the gods, appointed a young shepherd, Paris, a son of the Trojan king Priam, to decide among the three. Vying for his favor, each of the goddesses promised Paris a reward if he picked her. Hera, Zeus' wife and the goddess of marriage, promised wealth and lands; Athena, goddess of war and wisdom, promised fame and military glory; Aphrodite, goddess of love and beauty, promised Paris the most beautiful woman in the world as his bride. Paris chose Aphrodite, incurring the lasting enmity of Hera and Athena.

Paris soon traveled to Sparta, where he became a guest of King Menelaus and Queen Helen, the beautiful woman that Aphrodite had promised to him. Aided by the goddess, Paris ran off with Helen to Troy.

Accounts vary as to whether Helen was complicit in her flight from Sparta. In any case, when Menelaus discovered Paris' treachery, he called upon his elder brother, King Agamemnon of Mycenae, for aid in recovering his wife and punishing his enemy. Agamemnon, in turn, summoned the many princes and chieftains who had wooed Helen before her marriage to accompany them. After Homer's day (beginning in the sixth century BCE), versions of the epic tale claim that prior to her marriage, Helen's many suitors took an oath to fight on her husband's side if anyone ever tried to abduct her. No doubt there were mixed motivations for joining the fight, including the winning of booty and fame. A huge expedition of Greek warriors, including the princes or chiefs and their ships full of followers, was launched to reclaim Helen and to wreak vengeance against the Trojans; its members included Odysseus, the king of Ithaca; Achilles, the son of Peleus and Thetis; and Diomedes, a ruler in the northern Peloponnesus (the peninsula that forms the southern part of mainland Greece).

Despite the might of the Greek army, the city of Troy (in northwest Asia Minor, a few miles or kilometers from the Aegean Sea) held out against the invading forces for ten years. Its strong walls and the prowess of its military leaders, especially Priam's eldest son, Hector, enabled it to endure for a decade. Many warriors perished over the course of the war, including Hector, Achilles, and even Paris. Ultimately, the Greek army conquered Troy by trickery, building a huge wooden horse, which they left outside the city walls, and then sailing their ships out of sight. Believing their enemies had departed and left the horse behind as a gift, the Trojans dragged it inside the city. At night, the Greek warriors hidden within the horse's hollow interior swarmed out and opened the city gates to the rest of their army. It proceeded

The Trojan Horse. Archive Photos. Reproduced by permission.

to sack and burn Troy, and slaughter the city's inhabitants, only a handful of whom escaped. Menelaus reclaimed Helen as his wife, while other Greeks took the surviving Trojan women as prizes, and the expedition finally sailed homeward.

Gods and heroes. While some religious practices varied from region to region, the Greek world appeared to worship the same group of major deities, or pantheon. Situated on Mount Olympus, a high mountain in central Greece, the pantheon consisted of a dozen gods, headed by Zeus, father of gods and men. The remaining eleven deities were all siblings, spouses, or offspring of Zeus: Hera (goddess of marriage), Poseidon (god of the sea), Demeter (goddess of the harvest), Hestia (goddess of the hearth), Aphrodite (goddess of love and beauty), Athena (goddess of wisdom and war), Ares (god of war), Phoebus Apollo (god of healing and prophecy), Artemis (goddess of the hunt), Hermes (god of trade, commerce, and thieves), and Hephaestus (god of the forge). Later, Dionysus (god of wine) joined the Olympians. Zeus' brother Hades, who ruled the underworld as god of the dead, figured among the mix of important deities too. There were also lesser deities, who inhabited forests, mountains, and bodies of water.

Although the Olympian gods could take other forms, they were usually envisioned as resembling humans in deeds as well as looks. Neither wholly good nor evil, they could be brave, cowardly, wise, foolish, merciful, cruel, loyal, or fickle, as the whim took them. At times, they quarreled among themselves like the members of any large, contentious family. Unlike humans, however, the gods were immortal, possessing eternal life and youth. Conscious of their own powers, they tended to treat human lives and struggles lightly, as a source of divine entertainment.

Nonetheless, mortals who won the gods' favor could achieve wealth, power, and status with their help. It was apparently furthermore thought, in Homer's day and earlier, that once a special class of mortals had existed, the *heroes*, men who were themselves born of or favored by the gods, such as Achilles, Aeneas, and Sarpedon, and therefore enjoyed certain privileges. In the *Iliad*, Homer distinguishes between these heroes, descended from or favored by the gods and so regarded as semi-divine, and the common men who follow them into battle. The heroes' continual displays of great physical strength and feats of valor set them apart from ordinary soldiers, whose roles are merely to fight and die. Significantly, though, even the heroes cannot avoid their destinies: Achilles, for example, is fated to die at Troy; Aeneas, to escape the fallen city and lead the surviving Trojans to another land.

To win the gods' favor, humans prayed to their deity of choice, then offered a sacrifice (usually an animal that they slaughtered and roasted on the god's altar), libation (drink), or gift in exchange for the god's aid. In reaction to the offering, the god either granted or denied the supplicant's prayer. Apollo answers the prayers of a priest whose daughter has been taken prisoner by the Greeks; Agamemnon refuses to give her up for a ransom, so, in response to the priest's prayer, Apollo visits a plague on the Greeks until they return her and sacrifice 100 oxen to him. Later in the epic, through prayers and votive offerings, the Trojan women beseech Athena to spare their city, but she ignores them because she favors the Greeks and resents Paris for not deeming her the fairest goddess.

Despite a tendency to treat mortal life lightly, the gods could become deeply involved in human troubles. In the *Iliad,* several of them take sides in the Trojan War. A few gods have offspring in the war and side with the army for which their children fight. From brief love affairs with humans, Aphrodite, Zeus, and Ares have mortal offspring whose army they favor. Other gods have a hand in the fray to avenge an insult—thus, Hera and Athena ally themselves with the Greeks because the Trojan prince Paris gave the golden apple not to them but to Aphrodite. Finally, a few mortals win divine aid simply because of their virtues. Apollo aids the Trojan warrior Hector on account of his valor, while Athena rewards the martial prowess of Diomedes and the cunning of Odysseus. In the end, an equal number of deities support either side:

Greeks	Trojans
Hera	Aphrodite
Athena	Apollo
Poseidon	Ares
Hermes	Artemis
Hephaestus	Zeus*

*He favors the Trojans only briefly, and then it is because of an internal squabble among the Greeks, to help Achilles avenge an affront to his honor.

Greek warfare à la Homer. Homer's writing conveys certain details about the way wars were fought, or perhaps more exactly, the way they were ideally fought. Communities at war tended to rely on friends and kinfolk to either volunteer manpower or comply with requests to join an invasion in return for a share of the expected war booty. An assortment of bands assembled, each congregating behind a head warrior. Some but not all conflicts also included a supreme commander. To mount an invasion, spearmen with shields would move together as a tight front line while archers shot their arrows over and around them. But mostly the fighting seems to have consisted of informal bouts of one-on-one combat. The focus of Homer's battle description is on such combat between the leading heroes. High-status warriors would recognize each other by the chariot, a horse-drawn lightly wooded vehicle driven to the front by the warrior's charioteer. The warrior would dismount, fight, then climb back up to stow his booty, doctor a wound, or ride elsewhere. The hit-and-run tactic was common; warriors saw no shame in fleeing before finishing off a wounded foe unless he was clearly weaker. Another common tactic was the surprise attack. Archers would leap from behind to shoot a victim unawares, warriors would stab a retreating foe in the back, and anyone recovering the corpse of a dead friend from the battlefield could easily be killed in the process.

The following scenario plays out repeatedly in Homer's work, with slight variations to suit the individuals: the warriors leave their chariots to fight on foot, exchange ritual boasts and insults in an attempt to intimidate their opponent, and then engage each other in combat. Most heroes favor spears as their weapons—lighter ones for throwing, heavier ones for thrusting—but also use the broadsword for fighting in close quarters. The bow and arrow are usually reserved for the common soldiery or for a very few heroes. Significantly, Paris, one of the least skilled Trojan warriors, uses the bow and arrow.

The Troy of history. Interest in the city of Troy persisted for centuries. Despite the lack of written sources before Homer, his audience tended to believe that Troy was a real place on the western coast of Asia Minor (modern Turkey). Ancient Greek historians such as Thucydides (c. 460-400 BCE) believed at least partly in Homer's story; Thucydides even composed a plausible account of how war might have broken out between Mycenae and Troy. Also ancient travelers claimed to have journeyed to Troy and seen the tombs of Hector and Achilles and other such sights. According to an account of the first century CE, Alexander the Great even laid a wreath on Achilles' tomb, "calling him a lucky man, in that he had Homer to proclaim his deeds and preserve his memory" (Arrian in Wood, p. 30).

The first scholarly attempts to pinpoint Troy's exact location occurred in the eighteenth century. In the mid-1800s Hissarlik, a mound on the northwest coast of Turkey, was identified with the lost city of Troy. The German archaeologist Heinrich Schliemann, who had long been fascinated with the legends of ancient Greece, received most of the credit for this discovery.

Schliemann's excavations, and later those of Carl Blegen, uncovered evidence of numerous civilizations having existed upon the site. The most likely models for Homer's Troy were the civilizations designated as Troy VI (c. 1700-1270 BCE) and Troy VIIa (early 1100s BCE). Both showed signs of having been destroyed by violence, whether natural or man-made, in the form of fallen masonry and traces of fire (at least one of these instances was probably an earthquake). Blegen asserted that the presence of a bronze arrowhead of Greek design was enough to make Troy VIIa the leading contender:

> We believe that Troy VIIa has yielded actual evidence showing that the town was subject to siege, capture, and destruction by hostile forces at some time in the general period assigned by Greek tradition to the Trojan War, and that it may be safely identified as the Troy of Priam and of Homer.
>
> (Blegen in Wood, p. 114)

While historians still question the degree of truth of Homer's story, along with the findings of Schliemann and Blegen, many agree that there is sufficient evidence to suggest hostilities between Troy and Mycenae, which contributed to the decline of both civilizations.

The Mycenaean age. Heinrich Schliemann also uncovered the Mycenaean civilization, which dominated the classical world from 1600 to shortly after 1200 BCE. The Greek-speaking Mycenaean peoples came from western Asia perhaps, settling in southern mainland Greece around 1900 BCE. Mycenaean fortifications were established at Tiryns (south of the hilltop fortress of Mycenae), Pylos (on the southwest coast of the Peloponnese), Thebes (in central Greece), Iolkos in Thessaly, and the Acropolis at Athens. Also Mycenaeans gained control over several Aegean islands, including Crete.

While many details of Mycenaean society had disappeared by the time the Homeric epics were composed, it appears that the Mycenaeans were city dwellers, governed by kings with the help of well-organized bureaucracies and a militaristic ruling class. Agamemnon in the *Iliad* may faintly recall Mycenaean rulers. Evidence of Mycenaean literacy has been found in the form of the script known as "Linear B," used mainly to keep inventories and for other bureaucratic purposes. Archaeologists also uncovered pottery, weapons, and elaborate tombs, further evidence of the civilization's wealth and craftsmanship. Unlike the Greeks in Homer's poetry, the ancient Mycenaeans buried rather than cremated their dead (likewise, in the eighth century BCE, when the *Iliad* was written, Greek society normally buried its dead). Besides their military abilities, Mycenaeans apparently flourished as traders in the Mediterranean region, exchanging goods with Egypt, Syria, Sicily, and southern Italy. Archaeological evidence—the discovery of Mycenaean weapons at the site designated as Troy—suggests that Mycenae and Troy were trading partners as well.

In 1939 an American named Carl Blegen discovered the "palace of Nestor," named after the wise old Greek counselor from Pylos in the *Iliad*. Blegen's discovery revealed the actual existence of a rich center of the Mycenaean world in the southwest corner of the Peloponnesus. Far from the great palaces of eastern and central Greece, the ruins suggest that in fact there existed widespread pockets of splendor in the Mycenaean world. From such sites comes evidence of this world's downfall. The Mycenaean Empire collapsed around 1200 BCE, after several of its great palaces were burned; it is not known whether foreign invasions or internal disputes were the cause. Then came the period from 1150 to 750 BCE—the so-called Dark Age—which was marked by the loss of written communication, an increase of poverty, and the decline of the arts. While Homer's *Iliad* is, in many respects, a product of its times and has perhaps even integrated material from a later era, it may also be read as an idealized recollection of the last years of Mycenae's might, before its civilization was destroyed and the Dark Age ensued. In fact, the epic may draw on all three periods—the Mycenaean era (1600-1200 BCE), the Dark Age (1150 to 750 BCE), and Homer's own eighth century BCE.

The Epic in Focus

Plot summary. The epic begins with an invocation to the muse, describing the rage of Achilles "that cost the Greeks / Incalculable pain, pitched countless souls / Of heroes into Hades' dark, / And left their bodies to rot as feasts / for dogs and birds as Zeus' will was done" (Homer, *Iliad*, book 1, lines 2-6). The Trojan War is entering its tenth year, and the Greeks (alternately referred to as Achaeans, Argives, and Danaans), unable to take Troy itself, have instead been sacking and plundering the surrounding cities.

During their last campaign, the Greeks took the surviving women as spoils of war; one woman, Chryseis, the daughter of a priest of Apollo, became the prize of King Agamemnon, leader of the Greek expedition to Troy. Although Chryseis' father tries to ransom his daughter, Agamemnon rejects his terms. The priest calls upon Apollo to punish the Greeks until they release his daughter; Apollo strikes the army with a deadly plague. After ten days, the foremost Greeks meet to discuss the crisis. At Achilles' urging, Agamemnon resentfully consents to return Chryseis, but only if Achilles yields to him another captive woman, Briseis. A violent quarrel erupts, and Achilles ultimately agrees to Agamemnon's terms, but he is furious and feels that his honor has been compromised.

Swearing an oath that he will no longer fight for the Greeks until Agamemnon makes recompense, Achilles retires to his own encampment and calls upon his mother, the goddess Thetis, to help avenge the slight against him. At her son's behest, Thetis appeals to Zeus, king of the gods, to make the Trojans victorious until the Greeks, especially Agamemnon, acknowledge

Achilles' superiority on the battlefield. Zeus grants her request, despite noting that his actions will cause further dissension on Mount Olympus, where even the gods have taken sides in the struggle.

Zeus sends a deceptive dream to Agamemnon that urges the king to muster the troops and attack Troy, promising that he will take the city at last. Heartened, Agamemnon assembles all the soldiers and tests their morale by suggesting that they abandon the war and sail for home. To his chagrin, the common soldiers rush to board the ships. With the help of the goddess Athena, Odysseus, king of Ithaca, manages to restore order and discipline, reminding the men of a prophecy that the Greeks will win the war in the tenth year. The soldiers agree to continue the fight, and heralds are dispatched to summon all the Greeks to battle. Achilles and his troops, the Myrmidons, are conspicuous by their absence.

Meanwhile, the Trojans, led by Priam's eldest son, Hector, have also mustered for battle. When the two armies meet on the field, Hector and Paris propose that the issue of war be settled by single combat between Paris and Menelaus. The Greeks agree, and both sides swear to abide by the outcome of the match. While not the mightiest of the Greek warriors, Menelaus easily defeats the cowardly Paris, but Aphrodite rescues the Trojan prince from certain death and carries him safely back to his chamber in the royal palace. The goddess also reunites Paris with Helen, who has long since become disillusioned with her lover and now regrets her flight from Sparta.

Back on the battlefield, Hera and Athena manipulate the Trojans into breaking the truce. Fighting erupts on the plain in front of Troy, with significant losses on both sides. One Greek warrior, Diomedes, performs amazing feats of valor with the help of Athena, even wounding two of the gods—Aphrodite and Ares—who are trying to aid the Trojans. The Greeks succeed in pushing the Trojan forces back toward the city. Reentering his father's palace, Hector urges his mother, Hecuba, to offer gifts and prayers to Athena to take pity on the Trojans. She obeys, but Athena, who favors the Greeks, ignores her supplications. Hector reunites briefly with his beloved wife, Andromache, and their infant son, Astyanax; the couple confesses their fears about Troy's fate should Hector fall in battle, but he remains determined to defend his city. After retrieving Paris, who is still dallying with Helen, Hector returns to the war, where he has an inconclusive combat against the Greek champion

LEADING CHARACTERS

Greeks

Achilles Son of Peleus, King of Phthia, and the sea goddess Thetis; leader of the Myrmidons; the mightiest Greek warrior

Briseis A woman from Lyrnessus, given as a war prize to Achilles but later seized by Agamemnon

Agamemnon King of Mycenae and commander-in-chief of the Greek forces in Troy

Chryseis Daughter of Chryses, a priest of Apollo, given as a war prize to Agamemnon who must return her to appease Apollo's wrath

Ajax Son of Telamon, leader of the band from Salamis; the mightiest in battle after Achilles

Diomedes Leader of the bands from Argos and Tiryns; a skilled warrior favored by Athena

Menelaus King of Sparta and Agamemnon's brother; the husband of Helen; a prominent warrior

Nestor Elderly king of Pylos, who serves as a wise counselor to the Greeks and participates, ineffectually, in the fight

Odysseus King of Ithaca, skilled fighter, orator, and problem-solver, favored by the goddess Athena

Patroclus A warrior in the Myrmidon contingent; Achilles' closest friend and companion

Trojans

Aeneas Son of Anchises and the goddess Aphrodite; renowned Trojan warrior who ultimately survives the war and escapes Troy

Hector Eldest son of Troy's King Priam and Queen Hecuba; military leader of the Trojan forces; Troy's foremost defender

Andromache Beloved wife of Hector and mother of their infant son, Astyanax

Paris (also called Alexandros) Hector's younger brother and Helen's lover; skilled archer but less esteemed than Hector

Helen Daughter of Zeus and Leda of Sparta, accounted the most beautiful woman in the world, married to Menelaus of Sparta until seduced and carried off by Paris, considered the cause of the Trojan War

Priam Wealthy, aged king of Troy

Hecuba Priam's wife and queen of Troy

Sarpedon Son of Laodamia and the god Zeus, co-leader with his cousin Glaucus of the Lycians, who are Trojan allies

Ajax, son of Telamon. The two warriors exchange gifts at the end, and both armies agree to a brief truce to cremate their dead. The Greeks also spend the day building a wall and ditch to protect their shore-beached ships.

On Mount Olympus, Zeus forbids the other gods to intervene in the war on either side. When the battle resumes, he fulfills his promise to Thetis on behalf of her slighted son, Achilles, by favoring the Trojans over the Greeks. The tide of battle turns and the Greeks are forced back towards their ships, with the Trojans in pursuit. At a council of war, a demoralized Agamemnon admits to his fellow chieftains that he was wrong to offend Achilles and offers immediate restitution, including the return of Briseis, whom the king has not touched. Odysseus, Ajax, and Phoenix are dispatched to convey this message to Achilles, who remains hostile toward Agamemnon and refuses to return to the war, despite harrowing accounts of the Greeks' misfortunes.

Although the appeal to Achilles failed, the Greeks are encouraged when Odysseus and Diomedes capture a Trojan spy who reveals military secrets about a Trojan ally, the king of Thrace. The two Greeks enter the Thracian encampment by night, kill several men, and steal the king's horses.

Heartened, the Greeks meet the Trojans in battle the following day, but again Zeus favors the Trojans. Despite many deeds of valor, several important Greek commanders are wounded, including Agamemnon, Diomedes, and Odysseus. At this juncture, Achilles begins to take an interest in the fighting again, dispatching Patroclus to inquire about the Greek casualties. Nestor, an elderly Greek king, informs Patroclus of their wounded commanders, laments Achilles' hardheartedness and pride, and proposes that Patroclus assume Achilles' armor and lead the Myrmidons into battle. Meanwhile, the Trojans, under Hector's command, have breached the wall built by the Greeks to protect the ships.

Fighting to defend their ships, the Greeks are given a brief respite when Hera distracts Zeus with a love charm borrowed from Aphrodite. While Zeus sleeps, Poseidon, god of the sea, aids the Greeks. The wounded commanders return to battle to boost the troops' morale, Ajax stuns Hector with a stone, and the Trojans are driven into retreat. On awakening, Zeus rebukes Hera for her duplicity, forces Poseidon to abandon the Greeks, and revives Hector, who helps his troops regain their lost ground. Reaching the ships at last, the Trojan army starts setting fire to the Greek vessels.

Patroclus persuades Achilles to lend him his armor so he can frighten the Trojans into believing he is the mighty Achilles as he leads the Myrmidons into battle. Achilles reluctantly agrees but commands his friend to return once he has driven the Trojans away from the ships. Armed like Achilles, Patroclus performs many deeds of valor, slaying several prominent Trojans and driving the army back toward the walls of Troy. With the help of Apollo, Hector slays Patroclus and claims Achilles' armor for himself. The Greeks fight fiercely to defend Patroclus' body, ultimately bearing it back to their encampment.

Grief-stricken over Patroclus' death, Achilles renounces his anger against Agamemnon and vows to return to the war so he can avenge his fallen comrade. Thetis has Hephaestus, the god of the forge, fashion splendid new armor for her son. Achilles formally makes peace with Agamemnon, accepts the king's gifts, including Briseis' return, and prepares for the upcoming battle.

Zeus grants the gods permission to engage in battle again if they choose; several descend to earth and openly oppose each other, including Hera, Athena, Apollo, Ares, and Aphrodite. The newly armed Achilles charges into battle and slaughters many Trojans on the bank of the river Xanthus, which becomes choked with corpses. The river god sends the waters rising up against Achilles in protest, but Hephaestus checks the water with fire. A disguised Apollo tricks Achilles into pursuing him long enough for the Trojan army to escape back into the city. On discovering the ruse, Achilles returns to the walls of Troy and finds Hector waiting alone for him outside the gates. They engage in single combat, which Achilles, aided by Athena, wins. The dying Hector pleads with Achilles to allow his body to be ransomed by his parents but Achilles refuses. Once dead, Hector is stripped of his armor and the other Greeks gather around to inflict more wounds on his corpse. In full view of the Trojans, Achilles ties Hector's feet to his chariot and drags the body back in the dust to the Greek encampment. Priam, Hecuba, and Andromache lament Hector's death.

Back among the Greeks, Achilles makes preparations for Patroclus' funeral: his remains are cremated and Achilles kills 12 Trojan prisoners of war, who are also laid on the pyre as a sacrifice. Funeral games are held the following day, with Achilles offering prizes in such events as chariot racing, wrestling, and javelin throwing.

Achilles' grief for Patroclus remains overwhelming, and he continues to drag Hector's corpse—miraculously preserved from decomposition by the gods—behind his chariot. After nine days, Thetis, acting on Zeus' commands, persuades her son to allow Hector's body to be ransomed. Zeus also sends a heavenly messenger to Priam, bidding him go to Achilles' tent that night with the ransom. Despite Hecuba's fears, Priam loads a wagon with a rich ransom and sets out for the Greek camp. Guided by Hermes, Priam reaches his destination safely, kneels before Achilles, kisses his hand, and pleads for the return of his dead son. Achilles receives him kindly

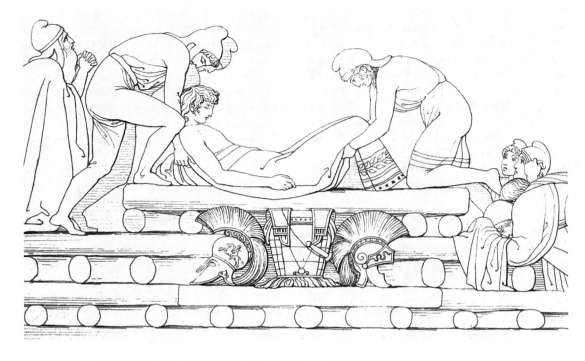

The Funeral of Hector. Archive Photos. Reproduced by permission.

and they weep together for their respective dead. Accepting the ransom, Achilles orders Hector's body bathed and dressed for transport. The two men then eat together and a bed is provided for Priam. Achilles also agrees to a truce of 11 days for Hector's funeral.

Before daybreak, Priam conducts Hector's body back to Troy, again guided by Hermes. The Trojans mourn their champion's loss, with Hecuba, Andromache, and Helen leading the laments. The epic concludes with a brief account of Hector's cremation, and interment: "That was the funeral of Hector, breaker of horses" (*Iliad*, 24.860).

A warrior's honor. In the *Iliad*, Homer's warriors take to the battlefield for various reasons. The Trojan army fights for the defense of their homeland from hostile invaders. Other warriors may fight to avenge insults or slain comrades, as Achilles does for Patroclus. However, the Homeric warrior was also deeply concerned with his honor and reputation. Fighting valiantly, slaying many enemies, and acquiring a hefty share of the spoils were all ways to increase his status in the eyes of his society.

The pursuit of glory and honor led Homer's heroes to behave in ways that modern readers might consider savage, even barbaric. In several instances, the victor not only kills his opponent

but strips him of his armor and weapons, even at risk to personal safety. Warriors considered the acquisition of such trophies necessary to demonstrate their martial prowess. It was, in fact, common practice to plunder the enemy dead, even to the extent of going onto the battlefield at night to strip the corpses. Several warriors even boast about what they have taken; Idomenus, the Cretan commander, offers to lend his comrade Meriones a weapon, saying "spears I take off Trojans, / I kill in close combat. I have plenty, / Shields too, and helmets, and breastplates" (*Iliad*, 13.275-277). Not to be outdone, Meriones counters, "The hut by my tarred ships is also filled / With Trojan spoils, but it's not close by. / I know what it means to fight up front / And win my share of glory in war. There might be one or two Greeks around / Who haven't noticed, but not you" (*Iliad*, 13.279-284).

Even in death, honor remains a primary concern for Homeric warriors, who hope—often in vain—for proper funeral rites, cremation, and burial. Wartime savagery can prevent or delay such rites. The victors not only strip but also often mutilate the vanquished, mocking the latter in his last moments. The Greeks fight fiercely to prevent Patroclus' corpse from suffering indignities like the ones they themselves inflict on Hector's corpse. Gathering round, the Greeks stab

SPOILS OF WAR

In the world of the *Iliad*, a warrior won honor not only by defeating his opponent or outstripping his comrades in feats of arms but by receiving a sizable quantity of the prizes taken by the army. These spoils were distributed among the ranking warriors, each receiving a share commensurate with his position and achievements. Money, jewels, valuable weapons and artifacts, livestock, and even women all qualified as spoils of war.

The initial quarrel between Achilles and Agamemnon erupts because Agamemnon, forced to yield up his female captive to her father, lays claim to a woman whom Achilles won in a previous campaign. Each man feels that his honor has been insulted and his status diminished by having to give up a prize. Achilles literally sulks in his tent, refusing to fight until his worth as a warrior is publicly recognized with greater gifts and the return of his prize. Significantly, the victors never take the feelings of the women themselves into consideration. As spoils of war, they were expected to accept their fate, whether it involved slavery or concubinage. Hector sadly predicts such a future for his beloved wife, Andromache, once Troy falls to the Greeks:

> Deep in my heart I know too well
> There will come a day when holy Ilion will perish . . .
> All that pain is nothing to what I will feel
> For you, when some bronze-armored Greek
> Leads you away in tears, on your first day of slavery.
> And you will work some other woman's loom
> In Argos or carry water from a Spartan spring,
> All against your will, under great duress.
> And someone, seeing you crying, will say,
> "That is the wife of Hector, the best of all
> The Trojans when they fought around Ilion."
> (*Iliad*, 6.470-471,477-485)

the Trojan prince's body, jesting that "Hector's a lot softer to the touch now / Than he was when he was burning our ships" (*Iliad*, 22.413-414).

Achilles makes sure his friend Patroclus receives the funeral he requests, followed by the posthumous honors due him. Proper disposal of the dead was believed to ease the soul's passage from one world to the next. Instructed by the spirit of his dead friend, Achilles performs the rites exactly as the ghost asks, to the point of using an urn large enough to hold not only Patroclus' ashes but his own when he too must die. After Patroclus' cremation, his comrades honor the fallen soldier's memory with feasting and contests of skill. Similar rituals mark Hector's passing after Achilles relents and permits Priam to ransom his son's body. The king of Troy ne-

gotiates a lengthy truce while Troy buries its greatest defender, explaining to Achilles, "We would mourn him for nine days in our halls, / And bury him on the tenth, and feast the people. / On the eleventh day we would heap a barrow over him, / And on the twelfth day fight, if fight we must" (*Iliad*, 24.714-717).

Greek attitudes to war. The attitude toward war in the *Iliad* seems deeply ambivalent. The Greek warrior fights for everlasting fame; Achilles, destined for either a long but obscure life or a brief but glorious one, chooses the latter almost without hesitation. However, death remains the common lot of mortals, as Achilles himself points out: "It doesn't matter if you stay in camp or fight— / In the end, everybody comes out the same. / Coward and hero get the same reward: / You die whether you slack off or work" (*Iliad*, 9.324-327). The Trojans, fighting a defensive war, have even greater cause to be weary of the ongoing strife and to long for peace. At one point, Sarpedon of Lycia, a Trojan ally, remarks to his comrade Glaucus, "Ah, my friend, if you and I / Could get out of this war alive and then / Be immortal and ageless all of our days, / I would never again fight among the foremost / Or send you into battle where men win glory, / But, as it is, death is everywhere" (*Iliad*, 12.333-338).

The ambivalence toward war expressed in Homer's poems reflected that of many Greeks. War, in fact, was a recurring phenomenon, figuring largely in Greece's history. Over the years, the Greek world had participated in such major conflicts as the Persian Wars, the Peloponnesian War and its sequels, the rise of Macedonia, and the conquests of Alexander the Great, as well as numerous local wars. War shaped Greek institutions, society, and economy; the Greek philosopher Heraclitus observed, "War is the father of all things" (Heraclitus in Hornblower and Spawforth, p. 774). However, the negative aspects of war were continually emphasized in Greek literature, not only in Homer's epics but also in the tragic plays of the Greek dramatists. Moreover, the Greek historian Herodotus summed up the human cost of war in the following statement: "No one is so foolish as to prefer war to peace; in peace, children bury their fathers, while in war, fathers bury their children" (Herodotus in Hornblower and Spawforth, p. 774).

Sources and literary context. No single source appears to have inspired the *Iliad*. When composing his poem, Homer most likely drew upon the various legends concerning the Trojan War. The *Iliad* is concerned only with one slice of this war, that is, one episode in the string of these legends. Allusions to incidents not depicted in the *Iliad*—such as Helen's flight to Troy or Achilles' revelation that he is destined for an early death—suggest that the poet expected his audience to be familiar with these legends.

The *Iliad* and its sequel, the *Odyssey*, are "epics," a term generally applied to narrative poems that illustrate the past deeds of gods, heroes, and men, frequently engaged in a grand and often perilous quest. The simplicity, directness, and frequent repetitiveness of Homer's language—formulaic phrases such as "He fell / With a thud, and his armor clanged on his body" occur repeatedly throughout the *Iliad* (*Iliad*, 5.49-50)—seem to indicate that his works were initially meant to be recited before an audience rather than read. The formulaic language suggests that the works were conceived in the tradition of orally composed poetry (whether or not they were originally written).

Taken together, the *Iliad* and the *Odyssey* form part of what would later become the Epic Cycle that purports to tell the entire legend of the Trojan War. Besides Homer's two epics, there were six shorter works, written by different authors, which fit in around the *Iliad* and *Odyssey* to relate a complete sequence of events from the marriage of Thetis and Peleus to the death of Odysseus many years after the fall of Troy. Chronologically, the Epic Cycle consists of *Cypria*, *Iliad*, *Aithiopis*, *Little Iliad*, *Sack of Troy*, *Returns*, *Odyssey*, and *Telegony*. Only the *Iliad* and the *Odyssey* survive in their entirety; the others exist only as summaries, attributed to an obscure writer called "Proclus" (c. second century CE). While the *Iliad* concerns one brief phase of the ten-year war, other works in the cycle focus on different aspects. *The Cypria*, for example, treats the causes and early events of the Trojan War; the *Little Iliad*, the death of Paris among many other events; *The Sack of Troy*, the wooden horse and the final capture of Troy. In general the six other poems in the cycle are regarded as more recent efforts than Homer's epics, which were famous even in antiquity for their scope, length, and complex themes.

Events in History at the Time the Epic Was Composed

The Greek Renaissance. Around 800 BCE the Greek world experienced a resurgence of cultural and social activity that some scholars have described as a renaissance. The Euboean cities of Chalcis and Eretria became the dominant settlements in Greece; they were largely responsible for establishing overseas trade—especially with the East—and colonial expansion. Euboeans also founded a trading post at Al Mina on the mouth of the Orontes (in north Syria), which became a mixed community of Greeks and Phoenicians, a Near Eastern people inhabiting the coast of the Levant.

Contact between Greeks and Phoenicians led to several important developments, the most significant being the Greeks' adoption of the consonantal Phoenician alphabet. Writing was rediscovered, becoming widespread throughout the Greek world between 750 and 650 BCE. Written records noted the first Olympic games, held in 776 BCE; from 683 BCE onward, Athenians inscribed lists of their magistrates on stone tablets. Even more significantly, poems and legends acquired a definite form. While songs of gods and heroes had long been part of Greece's oral tradition and thus handed down to successive generations by word of mouth, they achieved a more lasting status through writing. Set down around 750 BCE, the *Iliad* and the *Odyssey* may have been among the earliest works of literature to be thus preserved.

Impact. As one of the oldest surviving examples of Greek literature, Homer's *Iliad* enjoyed lasting fame and popularity for over a thousand years. Homer himself was often hailed as an incomparable poet. Later classical writers—such as those whose works made up the Epic Cycle—drew upon Homer's version of events to complete the saga of the Trojan War. That these works were lost while the *Iliad* and the *Odyssey* survived intact is perhaps a further testament to Homer's supremacy among Greek poets.

Homer's treatment of the Trojan War influenced not only writers but warriors as well. According to historians, the Persian king Xerxes and the Macedonian conqueror Alexander the Great both made pilgrimages to the site where Troy supposedly had stood. In addition, the Romans—who conquered Greece around 146 BCE—also fell under Homer's spell. Several prominent Romans, including Julius Caesar, claimed descent from Trojan heroes, and the Roman poet Virgil composed his own Homeric epic, the *Aeneid* (c. 30-19 BCE), detailing the founding of Rome by the Trojan hero Aeneas, one of the few to escape from the fallen city.

Even after the fall of the Roman Empire in the fifth century CE, Homer's epic continued to fascinate readers and historians. Medieval and Renaissance authors integrated elements of the Trojan legend into their own works. Benoît de Sainte-Maure, an Anglo-Norman trouvère (narrative poet) at the court of Henry II of England, composed *Roman de Troie* (c. 1160; *Story of Troy*), an influential vernacular poetic version. William Caxton subsequently translated Benoît's work into English prose as *Recuyell of the Historyes of Troye* (c. 1475). Caxton's version later influenced Shakespeare's play *Troilus and Cressida* (c. 1603),

about the doomed romance between a Trojan prince and a Trojan priest's daughter, who proves faithless to her lover when given to the Greek warrior Diomedes as a war prize.

Despite the success of some of these later versions, the appeal of the original *Iliad* has endured. Numerous translations appeared in sixteenth-century England, including that of George Chapman in 1611. Noted for its vigor and energy, Chapman's Homer was later praised in a sonnet written by the Romantic poet John Keats (1795-1821). During the eighteenth century, the English poet Alexander Pope composed another translation in heroic couplets, which won high praise. The translations into English continued, with one at the turn of the twenty-first century sizing up the poem's achievement: "The violence of the *Iliad* can be overpowering . . . yet . . . Homer makes that violence coexist with humanity and compassion, as close together as the city of war and the city of peace emblazoned in Achilles' shield (Fagles in Homer, *The Iliad / Homer*, p. xiv).

—Pamela S. Loy

For More Information

Bloom, Harold, ed. *Homer's The Iliad*. New York: Chelsea House, 1987.

Cantarella, Eva. *Pandora's Daughters*. Baltimore: Johns Hopkins University Press, 1987.

Edwards, Mark. *Homer, Poet of the Iliad*. Baltimore: Johns Hopkins University Press, 1987.

Homer. *Iliad*. Trans. Stanley Lombardo. Indianapolis: Hackett, 1997.

———. *The Iliad of Homer*. Trans. Richmond Lattimore. Chicago: University of Chicago Press, 1961.

———. *The Iliad / Homer*. Trans. Robert Fagles. New York: Penguin, 1998.

Hornblower, Simon, and Antony Spawforth, eds. *The Oxford Companion to Classical Civilization*. Oxford: Oxford University Press, 1998.

Powell, Barry B. *Homer*. Oxford: Blackwell, 2004.

Van Wees, Hans. *Greek Warfare*. London: Gerald Duckworth, 2004.

———. *Status Warriors*. Amsterdam: J. C. Gieben, 1992.

Vivante, Paolo. *The Iliad*. Boston: Twayne, 1991.

Wood, Michael. *In Search of the Trojan War*. New York: Facts on File, 1985.

The Jewish War

by

Josephus (Flavius Josephus)

Josephus's life is known to history primarily from his own account. In his autobiography, called the *Life* (*Vita*), he tells us that he was born in Jerusalem in 36-37 CE, the first year of Gaius Caligula's reign. On his mother's side, he traces his ancestry back to the Maccabees and their descendents, the Hasmonean kings (175 BCE-63 BCE). Also the child of a notable father, he was born into a family of Jewish high priests, who officiated in the Temple in Jerusalem. He claims to have gained such educational mastery that when he was 14 years old, chief priests and other leaders in Jerusalem would consult with him. In 66 CE, Josephus became a leader of the Jewish revolt against Rome. Appointed a general, he went to the Galilee region, where he briefly led the effort against the Roman army before surrendering in 67 CE. Imprisoned by the Romans, he prophesied to the Roman general Vespasian that Vespasian would soon become emperor. When that indeed happened in 69, Josephus was released and traveled with the Roman army and its new commander, Titus (Vespasian's son), back to Jerusalem, where he seems to have served as an advisor to the Romans as they besieged the city, attempting to quell the Jewish revolt. The Romans captured Jerusalem and destroyed the Temple there in 70 CE, after which Josephus traveled back to Rome with his imperial patrons and received enough economic support to write his histories. He appears to have died around 100 CE, leaving behind a number of key literary works. *The Jewish War* was his first such work. Written in the 70s, the work was originally composed in Aramaic (or possibly Hebrew) for the

> ## THE LITERARY WORK
>
> A history set in Palestine from 66-70 CE; published first in Aramaic and then in Greek translation in 75-79 CE.
>
> ## SYNOPSIS
>
> Josephus, a former general in the Jewish revolt against Rome that led to the destruction of the Second Temple in Jerusalem, recounts the war. Now a Roman court historian, he explains the reasons for the revolt and provides a detailed narrative of the fighting.

Jews who lived in the east, under Persian rule. Shortly thereafter, he translated the account into Greek. His subsequent writings were most likely composed in Greek. In the 80s and 90s Josephus wrote the more ambitious *Jewish Antiquities,* which recounts the history of the "Jewish" people from Adam to 66 CE. Also in the 90s he composed his brief autobiography, the *Life,* and *Against Apion* (*Contra Apionem*), a two-book refutation of an anti-Jewish tract. Josephus claims to have written *The Jewish War* in response to the wide circulation of incorrect histories. He was particularly irked by the Roman historians who disparaged the Jews without taking into account the several years during which they had managed to hold the Roman forces at bay. Despite his claims to establish the historical record, Josephus's motives, as we shall see, were far more complex than he admits.

Fiftheenth-century illustration of Josephus. The Library of Congress. Reproduced by permission.

Events in History at the Time of the Narrative

The beginning of the Second Temple period. When does the story of the "Great Revolt" of the Jews against Rome properly begin? Josephus begins *The Jewish War* with the rise of the Hasmonean kingdom in the 160s BCE. But some background is necessary to put into context the establishment of the Hasmonean dynasty. The First Temple in Jerusalem, constructed (according to the biblical account) around 1000 BCE by Solomon, was destroyed by the Babylonians in 587/6 BCE. Following their standard practice, they deported the Israelite elite to Babylonia, in the east. Shortly thereafter, the Babylonians themselves fell to the Persians, who allowed the descendents of these Israelite exiles to return to Jerusalem and to rebuild their temple. In fact, few Jews appear to have taken advantage of this opportunity. This small group of returnees, with Persian backing, established the foundations for the second temple by 515 BCE. By 400 BCE the Second Temple appears to have been relatively well-established.

Even by the time it was rebuilt, the importance of the Temple in Jerusalem had already been well entrenched in Jewish sacred writings. The biblical books of Deuteronomy and the historical books of Samuel and Kings that follow it, written while the First Temple still stood, established the temple's centrality in Jewish thinking. It was at the Temple, and only at the Temple, that the regular sacrifices that maintained Israel's relationship with God were to be offered. The Temple had more mundane functions too. It was also a governmental and economic institution that housed the high priests and prophets who were to take a role (with the king) in the administration of the land, and to which pilgrims were to regularly flock with tithes and other offerings. By laying the foundations of the Second Temple, the returnees saw themselves as reestablishing Israel's relationship with its god, and perhaps also starting down the path to self-rule.

Whether or not they saw themselves as establishing a new independent polity, that is not what the Persians had in mind. The small Jewish community around Jerusalem was under the political rule of the Persian governor, or satrap. While the Persian authorities more or less allowed the Jews to manage their own religious institutions and affairs, the Persians kept firm control on the administrative, political, and judicial institutions of the satrapy. Over the next century, Jews in Judah or *Yehud* (the name of the Persian province) would increasingly adopt as their own the Aramaic language, a Semitic tongue similar to Hebrew that served as the *lingua franca* of the Persian Empire. They also would integrate Persian ideas into their literature. In Jewish history, the time from 515 BCE-70 CE is known as the Second Temple period.

Hellenism. The Persian Empire collapsed suddenly when Alexander the Great, the Macedonian king whose military conquests from North Africa to the Asian steppes would result in the unprecedented spread of Greek culture, stormed through the Near East in 332 BCE. Alexander died in 323, and his empire was divided among ten of his generals. Judah found itself on a slip of land between two of them, Seleucus (in the north, around the area of modern-day Syria) and Ptolemey (in modern-day Egypt). For the next century, the Seleucids and Ptolemies fought bitterly over this small strip of land. Ruled by the Ptolemies during this period, Judah, now renamed Judaea, shifted hands in 200 BCE, when the Seleucid leader Antiochus solidified his control of the area.

The period of time from Alexander's conquest of the Near East to the rise of Roman political power beginning in the first century BCE is conventionally known as the Hellenistic period (which overlaps with the Second Temple period). The term comes from Hellenes, another name for Greeks. In part, *Hellenistic* refers to the self-styled Greek heritage of Alexander and his fellow conquerors, who were actually Macedonian conquerors of Greece (in 338 BCE). More significantly, however, the term refers to the changing cultural world that Alexander brought to the Near East. Alexander and his successors might best be seen as "philo-Hellenes," Macedonians who laid claim to the heritage of Greece by enthusiastic appropriation of things that they saw or styled as "Greek." They used the Greek language in their official dealings and documents, and promoted Greek cultural productions. They often encouraged the establishment of a peculiarly Greek institution, the *polis*, a city-state that had its own constitution and administrative structures. At the center of the *polis* stood the *gymnasium*, an institution that gave upper-class boys the educational and military training that was necessary for citizenship in the *polis*. The *polis* was a central institution for the spread of a distinctly Hellenistic culture throughout the Near East. And spread it did.

Hellenism was rarely imposed—it spread widely because people throughout the Near East found it attractive. A conquered city of the Near East typically clamored for recognition of its community as a *polis*. Greek spread widely, often supplanting Aramaic as the primary language in the community. Not only did older Greek cultural products gain circulation (e.g., philosophy and drama), but new Hellenistic ones were created. A distinctly Hellenistic artistic style, dramatic forms, and philosophical schools sprang up in different regions. Judaea was no exception. The Jewish literary productions from this period demonstrate significant interest in and comfort with Hellenistic culture. The book of Ecclesiastes, a part of the Hebrew Bible written around 200 BCE, is clearly familiar with Hellenistic norms and philosophical notions. So is the book of Ecclesiasticus, or Ben Sira, a work of around the same time consisting of wisdom maxims by a Jewish scribe and now part of Catholic sacred writings. Similarly, the Jewish apocalyptic works from this time, such as 1 Enoch and Jubilees, which purport to reveal (cryptically, of course) the secrets of heaven, demonstrate familiarity with Hellenistic apocalyptic ideas. Although the use of Greek was largely confined to the cities (it never fully spread to the more rural areas of

Galilee, north of Judaea), Jews had no principled opposition to its use too.

Outside Judaea, there is further evidence of Jewish writing in Greek. Jewish communities throughout the Near East wrote histories, philosophies, poetry, and dramas in Greek, all in Hellenistic form. They read their Bible in its Greek translation—the Septuagint—produced in Egypt around 200 BCE. Despite their unwillingness to participate in many of the religious events that pervaded the life of the *polis* (they thus were excluded from the *gymnasium* and full citizenship), Greek Jews, like their brethren in Judaea, saw little conflict between their participation in Hellenistic life and culture and their adherence to the "law of Moses." Josephus writes of the many strong Jewish communities scattered throughout the Near East, and the city of Alexandria, in Egypt, appears to have had a particularly lively and cosmopolitan Jewish life. If the Jews by and large embraced Hellenistic culture, there was less ready acceptance in the other direction. The Greeks, and others, were more guarded in their reaction to the Jews. Most Hellenistic cities accepted and respected the Jews as a people with a venerable past. At the same time, they resented the fact that the Jews kept themselves apart. Jewish practices—the Jewish observance of the Sabbath and of their own holidays rather than the city's festal calendar, their circumcision, their avoidance of pork and meats that had been sacrificed to the protecting gods of the *polis*, and their tendency to marry only other Jews—all irritated many of the non-Jews. Meanwhile, the Egyptians, who were themselves looked down upon by their Hellenistic overlords, had a particular dislike for the Jews, perhaps due to what they saw as their favored treatment by the Greeks. All the cultural differences resulted in tensions that, if often repressed, could and did periodically erupt.

The Maccabees and rise of the Hasmonean kingdom. Around 165 BCE, something happened. The precise nature of that "something" remains shrouded in mystery. Two later writers, the court historian of the Hasmoneans who authored 1 Maccabees (about 100 BCE) and Nicholas of Cyrene, author of the longer, livelier 2 Maccabees, each gave their own version of events. It appears that a group of Jews wanted to transform Jerusalem into a *polis*. This somehow resulted in a civil war. As understood by the author of 2 Maccabees, the war was really about Hellenism, which was locked in mortal combat with Judaism. Most scholars today, though, see a more complex situation, in which different factions of the Jewish elite were battling over more mundane issues of money and power for themselves. In any event, the reigning Seleucid king, Antiochus IV Epiphanes, took unkindly to this civil war and initiated a short-lived religious persecution of the Jews in Judaea—an unparalleled act in antiquity that continues to puzzle modern historians. According to the scriptural books 1 and 2 Maccabees, this persecution included desecration of the Temple, prohibitions on observing the Sabbath and holy days, and compelling the Jews to eat the meat of animals that had been sacrificed to idols.

Whether their rebellion was a reaction to or a cause of the religious persecutions, the Maccabee brothers led a revolt against Antiochus IV. Helped by a weakening of Seleucid power, the result of Antiochus's misjudgments and of shifting allegiances in his realm, the Maccabees won. Eventually the Maccabee brothers installed themselves as Hellenistic kings (which suggests their revolt was not against "Hellenism"). Also they installed themselves as high priests in the Jewish faith, establishing both the Hasmonean dynasty and an independent Jewish state, or one at least as independent as any small vassal state could be.

The Hasmoneans managed both to expand their landholdings and to play the political "game" of promoting their own people's interests successfully enough to stay in power. Eventually, though, they were defeated by their own dynastic struggles. In 63 BCE one of two brothers contending for the kingship allied himself with the Roman general Pompey and invited him into Jerusalem for support. Pompey happily obliged. Roman intervention never came without attached strings, and the last years of Hasmonean rule were spent as puppets of Rome. Officially, the Hasmonean dynasty would end only in 37 BCE. But Jewish independence in Judaea actually ended 26 years earlier, with Pompey's arrival in Jerusalem in 63 BCE.

Roman rule. When Roman legions entered Jerusalem, Rome was in the process of its transformation from a republic to an empire. Rome's own internal struggles were decisively resolved at the battle of Actium in 31 BCE, at which Octavian crushed the forces of his rival, Mark Antony. Now the unchallenged ruler of Rome, Octavian took the name Augustus and began to consolidate his power. To this end, he made one, in his eyes assuredly insignificant, decision at this time. He confirmed a supporter of his, a minor Jewish (some say half-Jewish) noble, as a subordinate king of Judaea. The supporter's name was Herod.

Herod the Great had overthrown the last of the Hasmonean kings by force in 37 BCE. Beginning with Herod's reign, the records become largely dependent upon Josephus himself for the historical account. Josephus appears to have used earlier no-longer-available sources, particularly the work of Nicolas of Damascus, whose history of Herod was probably largely financed by Herod himself and naturally biased in his favor. As portrayed in these earlier sources (unlike those of the more hostile and less historically reliable Gospels of the Christian Bible, written long after Herod's death and confusing the rule of Herod the Great with one of his sons), Herod was an active and relatively good ruler of Judaea. After eliminating his foes, he launched a campaign against the "bandits" (which surely included rebels) in the countryside. In 20/19 BCE he initiated the renovation of the Temple, a massive building project that gave work to thousands and would not yet be finished 90 years later, when the Temple was destroyed. Herod established several cities during his reign. Although not observant of the religious "law of Moses" himself, he tried to give no offense to the Jewish population of his kingdom. His paranoia and ferociousness toward his own family were legendary even in antiquity, but this hardly affected most Jews of Judaea.

After Herod died in 4 BCE, things very quickly began going downhill. Herod's kingdom was divided among his children. Herod Antipas managed to hold on to his share, in Galilee, from 4 BCE to 39 CE. The other brothers did not do as well. Archelaus ruled Judaea only from 4 BCE to 6 CE, when Rome assumed direct control. After appointing a series of governors, Rome reappointed a king in Judaea, Agrippa I (ruled 41-44 CE). In 44 CE, Rome finally turned Judaea into a province, and ruled it directly by appointing a procurator as the head official. In Josephus's account, the procurators—there was a rapid turnover of them—could not have been worse. From 60 CE on, Roman rule appears to have been almost incompetent. Of the procurator Albinus (62-64 CE), Josephus writes that "there was no form of villainy which he omitted to practice" (Josephus, *The Jewish War*, book 2, paragraph 272). But compared to the next procurator, Florus, Albinus appeared "by comparison a paragon of virtue" (*War*, 2.277). Josephus accuses Florus of legalizing brigandage (as long

JOSEPHUS, *THE JEWISH WAR*

587/6 BCE	Destruction of First Temple in Jerusalem
515 BCE	Establishment of Second Temple in Jerusalem; formation of Persian province of Yehud/Judah
332 BCE	Alexander conquers the Near East (dies 323 BCE)
323-200 BCE	Struggle between Ptolemies and Seleucids over Palestine, the region that contained Judaea (which had been renamed from Judah)
200 BCE	Antiochus III (Seleucid) gains control of Judaea
165-162 BCE	Maccabean revolt; beginning of the Hasmonean dynasty
63 BCE	Pompey enters Jerusalem
37 BCE	End of Hasmonean dynasty; beginning of Herod the Great's reign
31 BCE	Octavian defeats Marc Antony; takes title of Augustus
4 BCE	Death of Herod the Great and the division of Palestine among his sons
	4 BCE – 33/4 CE: Philip
	4 BCE – 39 CE: Herod Antipas
	4 BCE – 6 CE: Archelaus

6-41 CE	Roman prefects assume control of Judaea
36-37	Josephus born
37-41	Reign of Gaius Caligula
41-44	Reign of Agrippa I in Palestine
44-66	Roman procurators over Palestine
50-92/3 (?)	Reign of Agrippa II in Palestine
54-68	Reign of Nero
66	Outbreak of Jewish Revolt; Josephus in Galilee
67	Josephus captured by Romans
68	Beginning of siege of Jerusalem
69	Vespasian returns to Rome; his son Titus takes charge of the siege
70	Destruction of the Second Temple
69-79	Reign of Vespasian
74	Fall of Masada
79-81	Reign of Titus
81-96	Reign of Domitian

as he received his share) and setting the conditions that led to an uprising against the Jews of Caesarea. In 66 CE, the Jews revolted.

The Narrative in Focus

Contents summary. *The Jewish War* relates in seven "books" (in today's language, sections) the history of the Jewish revolt against Rome. The first two books cover the period from the Maccabees to the early stages of the revolt. Josephus's de-

scription of the revolt itself begins toward the end of book 2. The remaining five books focus on the events of the war from 66 CE to 73 CE; Josephus is practically our only source for these events and certainly our most important. Despite a few short digressions, his narrative is remarkably focused and detailed as it traces the course of the war.

For Josephus, as he makes clear in book 2, Roman insensitivity and incompetence were the immediate causes of the Jewish revolt. One of the first acts of the rebels upon their seizure of

Jerusalem was burning the archives where the records of debts were stored, suggesting economic motives underlying the revolt; the looting of the land by the procurators (and probably their Jewish supporters) had led to tremendous economic hardships and disparities. But the procurators were not only thieves. They also seemed to almost deliberately provoke the Jews. They tried to erect a statue of the Roman emperor in the vicinity of the Jerusalem Temple, and later looked the other way when Gentiles rioted against Jews in Caesarea, which was the capital of Palestine at the time. As the war got underway, Romans began allowing or participating in the slaughter of Jews in major population centers throughout the Near East. This only further inflamed the rebels.

If Roman incompetencies lit the tinderbox, though, they did not create it. Josephus suggests that since the time of Herod's death more than 60 years earlier, several competing Jewish nationalist factions had arisen. These factions, loosely tied to religious ideologies, promoted Jewish independence from Rome. In 4 BCE, as Herod lay dying, two "experts in the ancestral laws" encouraged the populace to remove the golden eagle from the Temple, claiming that Jewish law prohibited all images in the Temple (the golden eagle was the standard symbol of ancient Rome). The removal was seen as a seditious act of rebellion against Rome, and the culprits were harshly punished. Another group, adherents of the so-called "Fourth Philosophy," preached that the Jews should have no king but God. Such stirrings were connected to prophetic movements that suggested the end of time was near—Jesus, although only very briefly mentioned by Josephus (see below), might be seen in this eschatological or end-of-the-world context.

Josephus condemns the rebel leaders, whom he portrays as bandits with no redeeming motivations. At several points he suggests that things could have ended differently had only cooler voices prevailed over the murderous din of the Jewish zealots. When the war was about to begin, King Agrippa II (50 CE-c. 92/93 CE) gave a lengthy speech to the Jews, advising them not to rebel against Rome. The extreme Jewish rebels responded by throwing stones at him and driving him away.

Josephus, sent to Galilee by leaders of the revolt to spearhead the rebellion there, first tried to resolve it peacefully. His efforts at a peaceful resolution were soon sabotaged by a certain John of Gischala. Driven to war, Josephus tells us how cleverly and valiantly he defended the Galilean cities in his charge. Rome had nevertheless pacified Galilee by October of 67, taking Josephus captive in the process.

John of Gischala, however, managed to escape to Jerusalem, where he assumed leadership of the faction most supportive of the war. The zealots soon entered the city and, with the help of neighboring troops (the Idumaeans) they had invited into Jerusalem, killed the leading opponents of the war, including the Jewish high priest. With Jerusalem wracked by sectarian conflict (an explanation, incidentally, often used by Greek historians to account for the downfall of a *polis*), the Roman commander Vespasian marched on Judaea in 68. Before reaching Jerusalem, however, he was distracted by affairs in Rome. Book 4 ends with Vespasian leaving for Rome, where he will soon become emperor. He sends Titus to finish the war.

Without the Romans breathing down the rebels' neck, the sectarian conflict in Jerusalem only got worse. The fighting became so bad that stray projectiles between the warring parties would fall inside the Temple precincts, killing innocent worshippers. This strife, in turn, led to a famine. It was into this situation that Titus, with his three legions, marched.

The approach of the Roman army united the three major Jewish rebel factions. Despite their continued infighting, they managed to mount a stiff defense against Rome. After describing a string of Jewish successes against the Roman army in book 5, Josephus offers a detailed report of Jerusalem and its fortifications. By May 25, 70, the tide had begun to turn. The Roman army started slowly to capture and destroy Jerusalem's fortifications. At this point, Josephus exhorted the Jews of Jerusalem to surrender, using arguments very much like Agrippa's arguments of four years earlier. Although some Jews tried to desert the city in response to this exhortation, the rebels attempted to seal Jerusalem, causing even greater hardship within its confines. Of the lower classes alone, 600,000 people perished as a result of the hardship that the siege brought upon Jerusalem, which was exacerbated by the rebels.

Book 6 opens with the final chapter of the battle for Jerusalem. The Romans regrouped, constructed earthworks, and attacked in July of 70, soon trapping the rebels in the Temple. Although Titus wanted to leave the Temple intact, unplanned things often happen in the fog of war. The Temple was looted and burned on August 30, 70.

The destruction of the Temple had been preordained. Josephus says that anyone who had paid attention to the portents over the previous years would have known that God had already decided to destroy His house. In 62, for example, "at the feast which is called Pentecost [Shavuot], the priests on entering the inner court of the temple by night, as their custom was in the discharge of their ministrations, reported that they were conscious, first of a commotion and a din, and after that of a voice as of a host—'We are departing hence'" (*War*, 6.299-300). God was planning to punish His people for their sins. By the end of September, 30, 70, the entire city lay in ruins. Josephus reports 97,000 prisoners and 1.1 million casualties of the war.

Book 7 describes the mop-up operations and ties up other loose ends as well. The rebel leaders were captured by the Romans and, along with the spoils of war, were taken to Rome for a triumph or celebratory procession for Vespasian and Titus. But the war was not quite over. Roman generals continued the campaign against pockets of rebel resistance holed up in old Herodian forts, mainly in the Judaean desert. The last of these fortresses to remain standing was Masada, occupied by the Sicarii, a fierce rebel group named for their penchant of carrying concealed knives and stealthily stabbing their opponents.

The location of Masada was excellent. Its fortifications were strong; its stores, fully stocked. Thus, it took some time for the Romans to breech the walls. The surviving rebels, facing certain death at the hands of the Romans, made a suicide pact, slaughtering each other and themselves. Only two women and five children, hiding in the aqueduct, survived (to tell the tale to Josephus). Even the Romans were impressed: "Here encountering the mass of slain, instead of exulting as over enemies, they admired the nobility of their resolve and the contempt of death displayed by so many in carrying it, unwavering, into execution" (*War*, 7.406).

The war ended thus in 73. There were repercussions of the revolt throughout the Roman Empire. The Jewish Temple of Onias, located in Egypt, was razed, and there were continuing disturbances in Cyrene (modern-day Libya). Josephus concludes with a brief epilogue in which he asserts the truthfulness of his narrative.

Josephus's mixed motives. In *The Jewish War*, Josephus tries to walk a fine line. On the one hand, he attempts to portray the Jews as a brave and courageous people who never had a chance against Rome. He thus attributes to them the

virtues of courage and valor, which would bring them respect in Roman eyes. Even with their siege preparations around Jerusalem complete, for example, the Romans were dejected by "the discovery that the Jews possessed a fortitude of soul that could surmount faction, famine, war and such a host of calamities. They fancied the impetuosity of these men to be irresistible and their cheerfulness to be invincible" (*War*, 6.13-14). On the other hand, he also attempts to portray the Jews as fundamentally peace-loving and law-abiding citizens of the Roman Empire, and Josephus does not let an opportunity pass to emphasize that the majority of Jews did not support the revolt. After Josephus's own appeal to the Jews of Jerusalem to surrender, for example, he tells us that many would have deserted the city had not the rebels "kept a sharper look-out for the egress of these refugees than for the ingress of Romans" (*War*, 5.423). By blaming the Jewish revolt on the incompetence of some prior Roman rulers (not, of course, Vespasian and Titus) and on a small group of selfish Jewish fanatics, he tries to free the Judaean Jews of blame for the revolt. At the same time he makes these pro-Jewish arguments to Roman and Greek readers, he tells Jewish readers that Vespasian and Titus had no choice but to destroy the Temple. Despite their best attempts to avoid this calamity, the stubborn resistance of the Jewish fanatics and the fog of war forced the Roman leaders into it. In view of these circumstances, the Jews should not be angry with Vespasian, Titus, and the subsequent emperors. The diplomacy in all these explanations is self-evident. Just as Josephus presented himself as earlier trying to effect a peaceful resolution to the war before the outbreak of hostilities, he here again portrays himself working to promote cooperation between the Roman rulers and their Jewish subjects. Clearly he has deeper motives for this presentation than he reveals.

Even the better historical writings on the Jewish War, Josephus claims, "either from flattery of the Romans, or from hatred of the Jews, misrepresented the facts, their writings exhibiting alternatively invective and encomium, but nowhere historical accuracy" (*War*, 1.2). One might suppose that he therefore wrote his own account to set the record straight. Modern historians, however, have long debated Josephus's true motives for writing *The Jewish War*. Clearly "setting the record straight" was not his only or even his primary concern. All ancient histories were written, ultimately, for practical reasons;

Masada. © Nathan Benn/Corbis.

they were meant to tell stories that would be useful to their readers. So what was Josephus trying to achieve? Did he want to clear himself of wrongdoing in the eyes of fellow Jews? Did he want to encourage peaceful coexistence under Roman rule?

Josephus's complex agenda muddies our ability to sort fact from fiction in his narratives. At times, he seems driven by personal motives. For example, he describes his surrender to the Romans at Jotapata in some detail. According to his account, he and the other rebel leaders hid in a cave and entered into a suicide pact, in which they would kill each other instead of falling into Roman hands. When only Josephus and one other leader were left, he says, "anxious neither to be condemned by the lot [killed first] nor, should he be left to the last, to stain his hand with the blood of a fellow countryman, he persuaded this man also, under a pledge, to remain alive" (*War*, 3.391). This explanation of his behavior, which was denounced by some other ancient Jewish historians, makes it difficult to evaluate his recounting of a similar incident at the end of *The Jewish War*: the siege of Masada and the suicide of its rebels, which had such strong parallels to his own experience at Jotapata. Was he patterning the story of Masada on his own experience? The historical problem is further com-

plicated by the archaeological remains found at Masada, which do not fully support Josephus's account.

Sources and literary context. Josephus used a wide variety of sources for his narrative. Like most ancient historians, he rarely acknowledged them. A Greek version of 1 Maccabees, along with another unknown source, appears to stand behind his description of the Hasmonean period. The history of Nicolas of Damascus clearly informed his account of Herod's era. Scholars agree that Josephus relied on official Roman records to document his narrative of the war, but there is debate over how much he used them. Throughout his other works Josephus cites many Greek historians, and although they go unmentioned in *The Jewish War*, he might well have drawn on them for this work too.

Josephus wrote as a Greek historian. We possess fragments of several earlier Jewish histories written in Greek, but none comes as close as Josephus to resembling contemporary Greek historical writings. Indeed, it might be said that Josephus did for Jewish historiography in Greek what Philo did for Jewish philosophical writings; both seem fully at home in their chosen genre.

This, however, does not translate into the conclusion that Josephus sparked Jewish historiography. Quite the contrary—like Philo, he was widely ignored by the Jews themselves. The enormous corpus of rabbinic literature produced between 70 and 640 CE pays absolutely no attention to him or to his style of historiography, and no Jewish community preserved his corpus long enough to leave even fragments in their collection of works. Early Christians preserved his writing for reasons, as we shall see below, little related to their historical value or usefulness.

Events in History at the Time the Narrative Was Written

Postwar politics. Josephus wrote *The Jewish War* while under imperial patronage in Rome in the late 70s. The ample, almost fulsome praise the work heaps on Vespasian and especially Titus is certainly linked to the lavish benefits that these two Roman leaders heaped on Josephus. Titus gave him a grant of land to replace the one that he lost in Jerusalem, and when he arrived in Rome, Vespasian gave Josephus lodging, Roman citizenship, a pension, and another tract of land in Judaea. When Titus died, Josephus remained loyal to his successor, another Flavian emperor named Domitian (ruled 81-96).

Josephus's true motives in writing his history remain tantalizingly obscure. Clearly Josephus is more than a Flavian flatterer; the destruction of Jerusalem still seems to weigh on him, and he shows not a little pride at being a Jew. Such almost militant pride appears surprising. The Romans followed their military victory over the Jews with a campaign of humiliation. In the triumph, last of all the spoils was a copy of "the law of the Jews," meaning a Torah scroll, on display perhaps to mock the Jewish God as well as the people. The defeat of the Jews and their humiliation were commemorated publicly with an engraving on the Arch of Titus and on Roman coins. Shortly following the revolt, a special tax was imposed on Jews throughout the Roman Empire. It is possible, as some scholars have recently argued, that Jewish life in Judaea and Galilee simply collapsed as Jews increasingly lost confidence in their own tradition. Despite these humiliations, Josephus stands tall as a protector of the reputation of the Jews.

Some scholars have argued that behind Josephus's narratives is a subtle political argument. He is almost our only, and certainly our best, source on the religious sects of Judaism in the Second Temple period. *The Jewish War* contains a detailed description of the sect known as the Essenes, with decreasing attention to the Pharisees and least of

all to the Sadducees. Josephus may have admired the Essenes, but in an abstract way. His true sympathies appear to have lain with the Pharisees. He claims that they were the most accurate interpreters of Scripture, were politically well-respected, and on the whole were opposed to the war. There is some scholarly debate about whether his sympathy for the Pharisees increased in his later writings, but some indication of his allegiance can already be found in *The Jewish War*.

It has been argued that Josephus's support for the Pharisees really is veiled support for the authority of the successors of the Pharisees, the Rabbis. Josephus never mentions the Rabbis. In their own literature, though, the Rabbis identify the destruction of the Temple and the establishment of a rabbinic academy by Yohanan ben Zakkai at Yavneh (a city near modern-day Tel Aviv) as a crucially important event in the development of the rabbinic movement. With the Temple in ruins, the nobility shattered, and the priesthood adrift, who would serve as the political and religious leaders of the people? In the post-destruction years, the Rabbis, or groups relating to them, appear to have been making claims on these roles.

We know almost nothing about Judaean politics after the war. Were the Rabbis really competing at this time for authority, and if so, who were their competitors? In the aftermath of the war, the sectarian groups mentioned by Josephus vanish. Might they have folded into a rabbinic coalition?

Postscript—continued unrest. Jewish life in Judaea remained unsettled. Whatever happened, it did not succeed in healing the wounds of the war. In 132 revolt broke out again, this time from the Judaean desert. Shimon bar Kosiba would become known to his supporters as Bar Kochva, "son of the star," apparently due to a belief that he was the messiah. He was also an excellent military leader. Marshaling widespread Jewish support throughout Judaea, across the Jordan into Arabia, and perhaps even in Galilee, bar Kosiba mounted a serious challenge to Rome. He probably never managed to retake Jerusalem, but he kept a significant number of Roman forces tied down in Judaea for three years as they attempted to flush the insurgents out of their elaborate cave bunkers in the Judaean desert. The Bar Kochva letters, a number of administrative documents signed by bar Kosiba during the uprising, were recovered from these caves.

This time the Roman response was brutal. Roman forces decimated Judaea, drove the Jews into Galilee, and initiated (short-lived) religious persecutions. Jerusalem was plowed under and rededicated to Jupiter as the city of Aelia Capitolina. Over 200 years later the Jews would get one more aborted chance to restore the Temple, during the short rule of the emperor Julian. For all intents and purposes, though, the practical hope for the restoration of the Temple died with bar Kosiba.

Very slowly, there began the development of a new form of Jewish worship centered not on the Temple but on the study of the Torah and adherence to its commandments. Rabbinic Judaism began its development and rise at this time, offering alternatives to the sacrificial worship of God that had previously been confined to the Temple, although it would be many centuries before the Jews would accept the vision of the Rabbis.

Publication and impact. The survival of Josephus's writings is a historical accident. Some Jews clearly read Josephus, as demonstrated by Josephus's defensive reaction to the attacks of other Jewish historians. But no Jewish community took him seriously enough to copy and preserve him. Nor did the Romans find his work compelling enough to adopt it into some kind of canon that would survive to posterity.

It was, rather, the Christians who preserved Josephus, and they did so on account of a forged half-sentence in his work. Josephus mentions Jesus and John the Baptist very briefly, in *Antiquities*. Attached to his description of Jesus, though, is the statement, "he was the Christ [Messiah]," which almost all modern scholars think is a later emendation, probably added by a Christian scribe. Whether Josephus really wrote this or not, early Christian communities saw in this line a witness to Christ, and the passage has become known as the *Testimonium Flavianum*. Josephus's account of the war, especially his descriptions of God's abandonment of the Jews and the destruction of the Temple, also fit well with early Christian theological assertions that God had abandoned the Jews and now favored the Christians. Early Christian communities thus preserved all of Josephus's writings, which, in turn, might have reinforced the Jewish avoidance of him.

Josephus represents a path not taken by the Jews of late antiquity. Jews would not begin to write "historically," modeling their work after that of the Greek historians (Herodotus and Thucydides) until the Middle Ages. The Rabbis are completely uninterested in history *as such*, and their historical narratives are short, incidental, and almost always serve a moral purpose. From early on, though, Christians such as Euse-

bius adapted modes of Greek historiography, constructing accounts of their own story historically. Whether and in what way Jews prior to the Middle Ages might have "thought historically" is an interesting and still unresolved question, but they clearly rejected the type of writing demonstrated by Josephus.

Jews oddly rehabilitated the image of Josephus in the Middle Ages. *Josippon* was an anonymous Hebrew tract from the tenth century that told a history of the Second Temple period. It was largely based on a Latin translation of Josephus's works and mentions Josephus as "Josephus ben Gorion." This book achieved relatively wide circulation; it was known by the Jewish scholar Rashi in the eleventh century, and an edited version was published in 1510. To the extent that Josephus was known to the Jews, it was through *Josippon*, which at times was thought to have been written by Josephus himself.

At the end of *The Jewish War* Josephus writes: "Here we close the history, which we promised to relate with perfect accuracy for the information of those who wish to learn how this war was waged by the Romans against the Jews. Of its style my readers must be left to judge; but, as concerning truth, I would not hesitate boldly to assert that, throughout the entire narrative, this has been my single aim" (*War*, 7.454-455). That Josephus no doubt had other aims too has already been established, but the work remains invaluable nonetheless. Along with the ways the early Christians and medieval Jews made use of his writings, they have contributed immeasurably to modern scholarship. For all of his complex motives, his defensiveness, and his biases, Josephus is our only even semi-reliable source for the Jewish War. His occasional digressions on Jewish religious life in Roman Palestine, his comments on Jewish communities outside Judaea, and his observations about Roman history are all irreplaceably enlightening. Without them, our knowledge of the last centuries of the Second Temple period would be infinitely impoverished.

—Michael L. Satlow

For More Information

Attridge, H. W. "Josephus and His Works." In *Jewish Writings of the Second Temple Period*. Ed. Michael E. Stone. Philadelphia: Van Gorcum and Fortress, 1984.

Baumgarten, Albert I. *The Flourishing of Jewish Sects in the Maccabean Era: An Interpretation*. Leiden, The Netherlands: Brill, 1997.

Bilde, Per. *Flavius Josephus between Jerusalem and Rome: His Life, His Works and Their Importance.* Sheffield, England: JSOT Press, 1988.

Cohen, Shaye J. D. *Josephus in Galilee and Rome: His Vita and Development as a Historian.* Leiden, The Netherlands: Brill, 1979.

Feldman, Louis H. *Josephus's Interpretation of the Bible.* Berkeley: University of California Press, 1998.

Josephus. *The Jewish War.* Vols. 1-3. Trans. H. St. J. Thackeray. Loeb Classical Library. Cambridge, Mass.: Harvard University Press, 1997.

Martin, Goodman. *The Ruling Class of Judaea: The Origins of the Jewish Revolt against Rome, A.D. 66-70.* London: Cambridge University Press, 1987.

Rajak, Tessa. *Josephus: The Historian and His Society.* London: Duckworth, 2002.

Schürer, Emil. *The History of the Jewish People in the Age of Jesus Christ.* Edinburgh: Clark, 1973-1987.

Schwartz, Seth. *Josephus and Judean Politics.* Leiden, The Netherlands: Brill, 1990.

Lysistrata

by
Aristophanes

ittle is known about the comic poet Aristophanes (c. 450-388 BCE). He had a father named Philippus and a son named Araros who became a playwright in his own right, but few other details have been gleaned about his background. Despite the dearth of personal information, much has been ascertained about the period in which Aristophanes lived. Fifth-century BCE Greece was dominated by the First and Second Peloponnesian Wars (461-446 BCE and 431-404 BCE), and it is during the second of these wars that Aristophanes wrote or set many of his plays, including *Lysistrata*. Although Aristophanes is believed to have written about 40 plays altogether, only 11 survive in their entirety. Aristophanes' career as a dramatist began in 427 BCE with the performance of *The Banqueters* (no longer in existence). From then on, Aristophanes, usually in partnership with a producer named Callistratus, competed regularly at two comedy festivals, the Lenaea and the City Dionysia, earning top honors several times in his career. He won first prize at the Lenaea with his comedy *Acharnians* in 425 BCE and repeated that feat the following year with the *Knights*. His play portraying Socrates as a corrupt teacher of rhetoric—*Clouds* (423 BCE; also in *Classical Literature and Its Times*)—won third (lowest) prize at the City Dionysia. How well *Lysistrata* fared when it was first performed in 411 BCE remains unknown, but its lively portrayal of the battle between the sexes, interspersed with serious commentary on the nature of war and the need for national unity, has made *Lysistrata* one of Aristophanes' most enduringly

THE LITERARY WORK

A comic play, set in Athens, during the Second Peloponnesian War; written and first performed in Greek in 411 BCE.

SYNOPSIS

Weary of the war between Athens and Sparta, the wives of both cities resolve not to sleep with their husbands until the fighting stops, while the old women of Athens blockade the Treasury.

popular plays. Through all the laughter, the comedy sends a message to Athens at a particularly tense time in its history.

Events in History at the Time of the Play

Disunity among the Greek states. According to the Greek historian Herodotus, *hellenikon*, or "Greekness," consisted of "shared blood, shared language, shared religion, and shared customs" (Herodotus in Boardman, p. 127). But while one might suppose that these common qualities would unite the Greek city-states, factors such as envy, suspicion, and mistrust of each other's motives kept them divided into separate entities. During the Classical Period (fifth and fourth centuries BCE), when Aristophanes wrote his plays, they were unwilling to forego their independence for a system that would allow each of them only

Aristophanes.© Bettmann/Corbis. Reproduced by permission.

one vote. In retrospect, "the history of the classical Greek city-states" can be seen as "a history of failure to achieve unity: Sparta would not, and Athens could not, impose it indefinitely by force" as other powers would later do (Boardman, Griffin, and Murray, p. 128).

Sparta and Athens emerged as the two leading city-states, developing into diehard rivals. Each of the powers spearheaded a separate military alliance with other Greek states. First came the Peloponnesian League, a Spartan-led alliance formed shortly before 500 BCE; then Athens became head of another alliance, the Delian League, formed in 478 BCE. Over the next 50 years Athens gained steadily in power and prestige, building an empire that extended over the Aegean Sea. Under the statesman Pericles (c. 495-429 BCE), the city-state of Athens grew into the dominant political, intellectual, and artistic force in the Greek world.

Athens's rise did not proceed without effect on Sparta. There were major differences between the two powers, and they became diehard rivals. First, Athens was a democracy, while Sparta had a mixed but a more authoritarian government (two kings, a ruling council of elders, elected overseers, an assembly). Second, the Athenian economy was multifaceted, including farmers (in the larger region of Attica), traders, manufacturers, artists, and political officials. Sparta depended almost totally on agriculture, using *helots* (serfs) to do much of the farming, leaving the male citizens free to engage in warfare. The lives of the men and women alike were austere, *spartan*. Far from coveting luxury, they learned to survive on the minimum. At age 7, Spartan males left home to undergo a toughening process, succumbing to military discipline, honing their personal endurance, their cunning, and the like. Military service began at 20 with soldiers living together until 30, though it was permissible to take a wife (and father future Spartan soldiers) in their 20s. Wars repeatedly drew the men away from home, more than in the other city-states, for Sparta was the only one with a standing army. Women in Sparta had more power than in other city-states too; they married later (at age 18) than women in Athens (age 14) while men in both places married at roughly the same age (30). Also Spartan women could inherit property. This may have something to do with the fact that Sparta seems forever to have been plagued by a lack of men, who remained eligible for military service for four long decades (age 20 to 60). No doubt, a plan such as the one concocted in the play, to bring the war to an abrupt end so the men come and stay home, would have appealed to the actual Spartan women. All the training and service seems to have paid off in terms of military prowess. Sparta had the best-trained, most experienced land force of all the city-states, gaining high repute for its military prowess. But at the same time, Sparta's simpler, ruder society elicited prejudice from the other city-states. Athenians generally regarded the Spartans as a rough lot, whose citizens ate little, dressed scantily, let their hair grow long, and rarely washed.

Since Athens, like almost every other city-state, had no standing army, it raised troops as circumstances dictated. In the fifth century BCE, Athens switched from privately raised volunteer forces to a more dependable method. The populace elected generals and other commanders, and they hand picked soldiers from the different *demes* (local communities). Once selected, the would-be soldiers were obligated to serve or else they lost their citizenship rights. In a crisis, male *metics*, people who resided in Athens but were not citizens, were enlisted to serve as well. Athens's military gave rise to a powerful navy in the fifth century BCE, based on its light, fast warships. Called *triremes*, they were powered with the help of three rows of oars, and each had a captain in charge of its operations. The generals selected the captain, usually a well-to-do Athenian, who took responsibility for hiring the crew and maintaining the vessel; one of these commanders, Pisander, was active politically—*Lysistrata* refers to him by name and with disdain.

The rivalry between Athens and Sparta becomes a major theme in *Lysistrata* as their forces hover in the background fighting the Second Peloponnesian War. The conflict lasted for 27 years. Two decades into the fight, trying to effect a peace between the warring parties, Aristophanes wrote *Lysistrata*, whose title character rebukes Sparta and Athens for letting their differences outweigh their similarities: "You two sprinkle altars from the same cup like kinsmen, at Olympia [where the supreme god Zeus has his main sanctuary] . . . yet when enemies are available [to fight] with their barbarian armies, it's Greek men and Greek cities you're determined to destroy" (Aristophanes, *Lysistrata*, p. 421).

The Second Peloponnesian War. In 411 BCE, when *Lysistrata* was first performed, the Spartans and Athenians had been fighting the Second Peloponnesian War for over 20 years, with only a brief peace between 421 and 413 BCE. The two powers were fairly evenly matched, for both had allies, and while Sparta boasted the larger, more powerful army, Athens held the mastery at sea. After a decade of fighting, the first stage of the war had ended in a stalemate, and the Peace of Nikias was negotiated in 421 BCE. It was an uneasy peace, though, with violence breaking out here and there. In 415 BCE, Athens conducted an expedition to conquer the isle of Sicily, whose chief city, Syracuse, was Sparta's ally. Sent by the Athenian democracy, the expedition suffered crippling losses. Its defeat led to a full-blown resumption of hostilities between Athens and Sparta in 413 BCE, with the Athenians beginning a downward spiral into defeat. In 412 BCE, encouraged by the loss of its rival at Syracuse, the Peloponnesian League tried to win control of Athenian territory (the eastern Aegean Sea and the Hellespont). Cities defected from the Athenian Empire, and the Peloponnesian League gained new allies, among them, Klazomenai, Teos, Miletos, Lebedos, Mytilene, Iasos, Knidos, and Rhodes. On top of these setbacks, the Persian governor Tissaphernes, anxious to arrest the growth of Athens, which had already proven itself a formidable enemy to Persia, financially aided the Peloponnesians' cause.

Athens at this point, despite the mounting odds, met the challenge and staved off further setbacks by adjusting its procedures. The Athenians established a board of ten elderly statesmen (*probouloi*), who, in a crisis, could bypass the Assembly to implement emergency measures. (*Lysistrata* portrays these statesmen as comically ineffectual when one of them opposes the female rebels in the play.) Constructing and launching more warships, Athens further strengthened its navy and stationed about 15,000 men at the island of Samos in the Aegean Sea. The naval forces scored some victories. In June 412 BCE, an Athenian fleet made 21 Peloponnesian ships take refuge at Corinth. Athens also regained some lost territories (including Mytilene and Klazomenai) and triumphed in a land battle outside Miletos. But by the end of 412 BCE, Athens's finances were stretched thin and the Spartans had won control of a part of Attica, from where they could raid the Athenian countryside.

Alcibiades, an Athenian statesman and military leader whom the democracy had exiled, offered to lend a hand. He promised to meet secretly with Tissaphernes and convince him to support Athens against Sparta. In exchange, he wanted Athens to recall him from exile and replace its "rascally" democratic government with an oligarchy. The request was not altogether unreasonable in light of the fact that many blamed the democracy for the crippling naval defeat Athens had suffered at Syracuse. Actually the military men at Samos had already begun scheming to limit the scope of the democracy before Alcibiades stepped into the picture, and their conspiracy would continue after he failed to win support from the Persian governor. Scholars have pinpointed when *Lysistrata* takes place in this string of events. The conspirators sent one of their warship captains, the above-mentioned Pisander, from Samos to Athens to win approval from the Assembly for Alcibiades to approach the Persian governor for support. Scholars have ascertained that *Lysistrata* takes place after Pisander arrived at Athens but before he presented his proposals to the Assembly. He remained in Athens for several months, and he did address the Assembly, appealing to its common sense:

> In view of the facts that the Peloponnesians have no fewer ships than the Athenians for confronting them at sea, that more cities are allied with them, and that the [Persian] king and Tissaphernes are giving them money, whereas the Athenians have none left, is there any hope of survival unless someone can prevail upon the king to switch his support to Athens? (Ostwald, p. 353)

Pisander got the Assembly to approve the plan. He left Athens in April, at the head of a team of 11 sent to negotiate with Alcibiades and Tissaphernes. As noted, their attempt to win Persian support failed. But the military men at Samos still put the second half of the plan into effect—replacing the democracy at Athens with an oligarchy (which would be short lived). Pisander himself returned to Athens to install the oligarchy. The line in *Lysistrata* refers to Pisander with revulsion, suggesting that he (and others like him) acted out of concern not for Athens but for selfish material gain (*Lysistrata*, p. 331). In real life, the Assembly at Athens had agreed to his proposals in hopes of winning the advantage in the war. Most Athenians were still bent on fighting Sparta at this juncture. As for Alcibiades, though he had failed to win Persian support, he was rewarded for his efforts by the Athenians at Samos. One of their fleets appointed him a general, and he proceeded to serve Athens with distinction for several years, directing operations in the Hellespont and winning an important victory at Cyzicus in 410 BCE. The war ended only in 404 BCE, when a worn-out Athens finally surrendered to Sparta. So indeed it was daring of Aristophanes to write a play that sought to bring about peace seven years earlier.

In *Lysistrata*, the sexes take pro-war and anti-war positions, with the appeal for peace placed in a woman's mouth, perhaps because it was an unpopular stance to take at the time. Believing victory within their grasp, men approach the Acropolis, the city fortress, which served as a religious site and a repository for the state treasury, seeking funds to buy timber for more warship oars. But they are interrupted en route by the females on strike, who conduct themselves in ways that never really happened but who make a sound historical point nonetheless. Women, no less than men, are bearing the brunt of this war, their beds empty and the prospect of widowhood or perpetual spinsterhood looming large. Husbands leave home to fight while wives give "birth to sons and [send] them off" to war (*Lysistrata*, p. 351). In this way too, the play is a bold expression, for it dares to convey a womanly point of view.

Status of women in fifth-century Athens. The audacity and determination of Lysistrata and her female companions contrast sharply with the behavior to which history constrained Athenian women in Aristophanes' day. Lysistrata, a woman, is strong, independent-minded, self-disciplined, and steadfast, and though it takes some coaxing, she convinces the other women to follow her lead.

Meanwhile, the men appear weak and capitulate quickly. These are hardly the images that one receives from the ancient sources. While scholars debate the exact nature of women's status within the classical world, it is generally agreed that women, whatever their rank, were second-class citizens at best.

Within Greek law, women were considered perpetual minors: their male relatives protected and guided them, influencing every decision, a necessity, thought society, for the female was an undisciplined creature in need of monitoring. Left to her own devices, she would not make sensible decisions. Her behavior would be immoderate. In their mid-teens, young girls of good family were married to husbands chosen for them by their guardians, usually for political and economic reasons. Lack of affection or even acquaintanceship between a future bride (again, in Athens aged about 14) and groom (aged about 30) was no obstacle. Indeed, since the primary goal of marriage was the birth of legitimate offspring, a young bride was desirable, for she would have the greatest span of childbearing years.

Women's status did not noticeably improve with marriage or even motherhood. Husbands guarded their wives' sexuality closely to ensure the legitimacy of their heirs. A couple's children legally belonged to the father, remaining with him if the couple divorced or the wife died. Women had no political rights, and marriage did not change the situation. They could not vote, attend or address assemblies, or hold political office. A male guardian had to act as their agent in all legal and economic transactions. Also society circumscribed where a woman went. Her primary duty was to maintain her husband's household and raise his children. They could leave home to visit family and friends, attend weddings and other religious ceremonies, and, if they were lower class, to sell goods at local markets or to work as midwives, wet-nurses, craftswomen, or farmhands. But women were barred from attending banquets if men unrelated to them would be present. In a funeral oration delivered by Pericles, the women most highly praised were those who maintained utmost discretion: "If I must say anything on the subject of female excellence to those of you who will now be in widowhood, it will be all comprised in this brief exhortation . . . greatest will be [her glory] who is least talked of among the men whether for good or bad" (Pericles in Spatz, p. 93). Women had to behave modestly if they were to preserve the honor of their households, a rule that *Lysistrata*'s women brashly break.

The play depicts a world in which the rigid codes dictating what women can or cannot do have been shockingly and fantastically overturned. Besides refusing to submit sexually to their husbands, women seize and occupy the Acropolis, the highest defensible spot of Athens. A line by Lysistrata, ringleader of the women, perhaps best illustrates the sexual role reversal. In a conscious revision of a remark from the *Iliad*, she proclaims, "War shall be the business of womenfolk!" (*Lysistrata*, p. 341). The line echoes what was by then Homer's already well-known poem, twisting a remark that the Trojan prince Hector makes to his loving wife: "War is the work of men, / Of all the Trojan men, and mine especially" (Homer, *Iliad*, 6.517-518).

In real-life Athens, women had easy access to the Acropolis, since the one public role sanctioned for them was caretaker and priestess of religious cults. The city's most prominent goddess, Athena, like the other gods of the Greek pantheon, had different dimensions ascribed to her. She was conceived of as protector of cities, goddess of wisdom, goddess of arts and crafts, and goddess of victory in battle. In her incarnation as the guardian of Athens, or Athena "Polias" (protector of the city), the goddess gave rise to a cult (meaning the worship of a god with rites and ceremonies). Believers made offerings to her—sacrifices, libations, and dedications—and prayed for something in return—*do ut des* "I give (to you) so that you will give (to me)" (Howatson and Chilvers, p. 151). A priestess served as an intermediary between a god and worshippers, with the priestess of Athena Polias winning renown as the most important in Athens. Her priestess could be married and have children, though Athena herself was conceived of as a virgin goddess. At the time of *Lysistrata*, a woman named Lysimache served as priestess; she held the post for 64 years, and apparently she opposed the Peloponnesian War. Another real-life woman of the era, Myrrhine, served in the temple of Athena "Nike" (goddess of victory), a separate structure on the Acropolis. Coincidentally or not, Myrrhine is also the name of one of the characters in *Lysistrata*, a female rebel who performs a key and very comical part.

Old Comedy. Aristophanes' plays represent the only existing examples of "Old Comedy," a genre that flourished during the fifth century BCE. Comparable in several respects to modern musical comedy, Old Comedy featured a loosely constructed, often fantastic plot, an irreverent tone, coarse or even obscene language, and elements ranging from broad farce to keen social satire. The play included a chorus, consisting of 24 members who delivered their lines in unison and figured heavily in song and dance numbers. The actors (all men) performed in grotesque masks and costumes that exaggerated certain body parts, like the belly. Especially significant for *Lysistrata* is the traditional comic phallus, worn by all male performers. At the same time, Old Comedy had an incisive edge to it, targeting contemporary issues, social, political, and moral. Many of Aristophanes' comedies, including *Lysistrata*, concern the Peloponnesian War.

ATHENA AND THE ACROPOLIS

According to myth, Athena, goddess of war and wisdom, and Poseidon, god of the sea, competed to be protector of a prominent Greek city. It was decreed that the citizens should choose the victor, based on the gift he or she created for the city. Poseidon created a well (some versions say he created the horse), but Athena created the olive tree, of which no part—fruit, wood, or oil—would be wasted. The citizens decreed her gift to be more valuable, chose Athena as their patron, and named their city Athens in her honor. During the Classical Period (c. 450-330 BCE), three temples were built upon the city's highest point, the Acropolis, each dedicated to an aspect of Athena: the Parthenon (Athena Parthenos, the virgin), the Erichtheioin (Athena Polias, the protector), and the Temple of Nike (Athena-Apteros Nike, the goddess of victories). The Propylaea, a monumental gateway to the sacred area, was constructed in the same time period. Although the Acropolis might have formerly boasted a military fortress or residence, it had become mainly a religious site by Aristophanes' lifetime. The city's treasury, however, was placed under the protection of Athena and located in or beside her various temples.

The structure as well as the style of Old Comedy was distinctive. There were six basic parts:

Prologue, the opening of the play, in which the leading character would conceive of some ingenious plan
Parodos, the entrance of the Chorus
Agon, a dramatized debate between the leading character and the opposition, with the latter being defeated
Parabasis, the coming forward of the Chorus to address the audience directly and express the playwright's view on any subject

Episodes, the incidents during which the leading character's plot was put into practice, and finally

Exodus, the conclusion, in which the characters celebrated at a revel or a marriage

Choral songs and dialogues were often interspersed between episodes. *Lysistrata* adheres closely to this scheme, with the heroine proposing a "sex strike" in the prologue, debating her actions with an Athenian magistrate and soundly winning the argument in the *agon*, and witnessing the effects of her plan in the various episodes. Since the Chorus does not address the audience directly, the play lacks a *parabasis*. The standard Chorus in Old Comedy included 24 members; unusually *Lysistrata* has a split chorus of 12 men and 12 women. Instead, there are frequent heated exchanges, in song and dialogue, between

---

MIDDLE AND NEW COMEDY

Following the end of the Second Peloponnesian War, Old Comedy gave way to Middle Comedy (c. 400-388 BCE), which was replaced in turn by New Comedy (c. 388-200s BCE). Neither of these later genres exhibited the same bawdiness and frankness of Old Comedy. Middle Comedy, in particular, was composed in a postwar environment in which freedom of speech had been suppressed; its social criticisms were milder and more general, lacking the bite of Old Comedy. Aristophanes' last surviving play *Plutus* (Wealth, c. 388 BCE) is considered a Middle Comedy. New Comedy, which became widely imitated by the Romans, retreated still further from satirizing social and political issues; rather, it focused more upon domestic problems and conflicts, such as love, marriage, and children. Playwrights of New Comedy include Menander, Philemon, Diphilus, and Apollodorus, although the only New Comedy to survive in its entirety is Menander's *Dyskolos* (The Bad-Tempered Man).

---

the men's Chorus and the women's Chorus regarding the women's bold and brazen behavior.

Like tragedies, comedies were performed at the City Dionysia festival each spring; later, around 440 BCE, comedies were also included in the Lenaea festival, which occurred early to mid-February. Five comedies would be staged at each festival—some historians argue that the number was reduced to three during the Peloponnesian War. A panel of judges winnowed out the top three contenders. As noted, it is not known how well *Lysistrata* fared when it was first performed—probably at the Lenaea—in 411 BCE.

The Play in Focus

Plot summary. The play begins during the later years of the Second Peloponnesian War. Lysistrata, an Athenian woman, summons the women of Athens, Sparta, Thebes, and other cities that have joined the war to her home for a meeting. She proposes a plan to end the ongoing hostilities: the wives will cease to have marital relations with their husbands until the fighting stops and peace is declared. Initially, the women reject Lysistrata's plan. They are unwilling to give up sex. However, Lysistrata finds an ally in Lampito, a woman from Sparta. She says the Spartan women can convince their men to keep the peace but fears the Athenians will keep fighting in any case because their treasury provides a bottomless fund for war. "Don't worry," Lysistrata assures her (*Lysistrata*, p. 291). While the younger women conduct their sex strike, the older women will prevent access to the treasury, an easy task since it is kept at the Acropolis, a female-tended religious site. Satisfied, Lampito and the others seal the pact. Over a ritual cup of wine, they swear to tantalize their husbands but not sleep with them unless forced. After taking the oath, Lampito returns to Sparta to help implement the plan.

On learning of the women's actions, a Chorus of Old Men—former war veterans who live on state pay—arms itself with logs, torches, and coals, and marches upon the Acropolis. The men intend to smoke out the elderly women at the Acropolis but are foiled by a Chorus of Old Women that arrives bearing jugs of water. Comically the two factions exchange heated insults, until the old women use their water jugs to douse the old men as well as their torches. The men retreat, drenched and humiliated.

A magistrate, accompanied by slaves and Scythian policemen, arrives to break open the barred gates of the Acropolis. Now in command, Lysistrata emerges to speak to the magistrate, who tries to have her seized and bound. Lysistrata's fierce female allies, however, frighten the policemen into running away. When the magistrate interrogates Lysistrata about her reasons for seizing the Acropolis, she argues that with women in control of the treasury, the war will have to end for lack of funds. She also explains that the women of Greece have had to suffer the results of men's incompetence too long. Henceforth, Lysistrata declares, women will be in charge of domestic and foreign policy, sending embassies to all the cities until a peace is negotiated. Offended, the magistrate upbraids the women for their effrontery. "Well, what did you expect?" asks Lysistrata, ". . . did you think women lack gall?" "Oh yes," replies the Magistrate, "they've got plenty of that, provided there's a wine bar nearby" (*Lysistrata*, p. 329). The women insult him in turn, first dressing him up like a woman, then bedecking him with garlands and ribbons like a corpse. Fuming, he withdraws to consult other magistrates on the women's presumption.

The Chorus of Old Men and the Chorus of Old Women continue to argue and brawl before the gates of the Acropolis. Meanwhile, Lysistrata reveals to her co-conspirators that there has been some weakening in the ranks: several women have abandoned the cause, running home to make love with their husbands. Lysistrata stops some would-be deserters, who make feeble excuses for almost breaking their oaths; to prevent further defections, she produces a scroll that supposedly contains a prophecy or an oracle favorable to the women's efforts. Convinced by the oracle, the women reluctantly return to their posts.

Cinesias, a warrior husband, arrives at the Acropolis to appeal to his wife, Myrrhine, even bringing along their infant son to convince her to come home. Instead, Myrrhine demonstrates the effectiveness of Lysistrata's scheme by teasing her husband into a painful state of sexual arousal, then retreating into the temple without satisfying his need. As Cinesias laments his plight, the men's chorus commiserates with him on the wickedness of women.

A messenger from Sparta arrives at the Acropolis, revealing that Lampito and the Spartan women have meanwhile succeeded in conducting the strike at their end. The Spartan men are now willing to negotiate for peace, and a conference is arranged. On hearing the news, the women begin to make peaceful overtures towards the men, which calms them down.

Delegates of the men from Athens and Sparta, all in a desperate state of sexual arousal, convene before the Acropolis. Lysistrata enters accompanied by the goddess Reconciliation, who appears as a naked maiden. Acknowledged as "the only one who can reconcile us," Lysistrata serves as the mediator at the conference (*Lysistrata*, p. 417). She rebukes both sides for warring against each other, arguing that they share a common heritage and many traditions. She reminds them that they were allies in times past and very sensibly suggests that their energies are better directed at fighting off foreign invaders than battling each other.

Distracted by Reconciliation's naked charms, the delegates initially agree with everything Lysistrata says. But once the negotiations begin, each side demands terms that are unfavorable to the other. Reconciliation, who personifies the resolution of their differences, now helps out. In a comic scene, her body serves to illustrate strategic elements of the peace ("reconciliation") negotiations. Lysistrata, who uses Reconciliation this way, manages to avoid another outbreak of hostilities and secure an agreement on the terms. Lysistrata then summons both

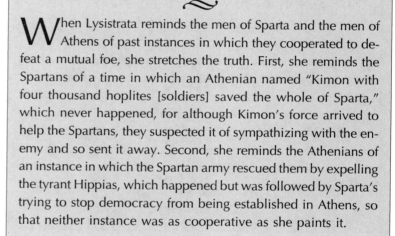

LYSISTRATA PLAYS FAST AND LOOSE WITH HISTORY

When Lysistrata reminds the men of Sparta and the men of Athens of past instances in which they cooperated to defeat a mutual foe, she stretches the truth. First, she reminds the Spartans of a time in which an Athenian named "Kimon with four thousand hoplites [soldiers] saved the whole of Sparta," which never happened, for although Kimon's force arrived to help the Spartans, they suspected it of sympathizing with the enemy and so sent it away. Second, she reminds the Athenians of an instance in which the Spartan army rescued them by expelling the tyrant Hippias, which happened but was followed by Sparta's trying to stop democracy from being established in Athens, so that neither instance was as cooperative as she paints it.

delegations to a banquet, where the women ply the men with food and liquor and a peace agreement is finally signed. The men celebrate with songs, dances, and hymns to the gods before departing with their wives for their homes and beds.

Women at war. While the men of Athens fight to defend their city's power and prestige, the women in *Lysistrata* fight no less fiercely to protect their households and families. To achieve that end, however, Lysistrata and her companions must adopt masculine traits and deploy masculine tactics, such as seizure and occupation of the Acropolis, where the treasury is kept. Even the sex strike takes on the appearance of a military campaign when the women swear an oath in wine that parodies oaths sworn by warriors:

> No man of any kind, lover or husband . . .
> shall approach me [to have sex] . . . at home

in celibacy shall I pass my life . . . wearing a saffron dress and all dolled up . . . so that my husband will get as hot as a volcano for me . . . but never willingly shall I surrender to my husband. . . . If I live up to these vows, may I drink from this cup. . . . But if I break them, may the cup be full of water.

(*Lysistrata*, pp. 300-301)

Although they adopt masculine tactics to a degree, the women use weapons and arguments of the domestic realm that they traditionally inhabit. Armed with jugs of water, the women handily defeat the men attempting to smoke them out of the Acropolis. Lysistrata uses the yarn in her weaving basket to explain to the angry magistrate how women intend to resolve international hostilities:

A MODERN-DAY VIEW OF *LYSISTRATA'S* ENDURING APPEAL

The younger wives' sex strike and their husbands' subsequent capitulation, the older women's occupation of the Athenian treasury and their physical victory over a band of decrepit and angry old men, and certainly the charisma of its eponymous heroine have all combined to make *Lysistrata* a favorite. . . . On top of that, it satisfies, as no other Aristophanic play does, an audience's desire for cohesiveness and clarity: its sustained plot has a beginning, a middle, and an end.

(Taaffe in Bloom, p. 105)

"We hold [the yarn] this way, and carefully wind out the strands on our spindles, now this way, now that way. That's how we'll wind up this war, if we're allowed: unsnarling it by sending embassies, now this way, now that way" (*Lysistrata*, p. 347). And Myrrhine delays marital relations with her sexually aroused husband—and converts him to the cause of peace—by fetching pillows, blankets, and scents under the pretext of making their union more comfortably domestic. Moreover, even as the women gain the upper hand, Aristophanes portrays them as possessing faults traditionally ascribed to their sex: they are fond of gossip as well as drink and sex, which makes the strike no easy tactic for them to employ. In keeping with the ancient stereotype, they are immoderate creatures, just as prone to having illicit love affairs as men.

Lysistrata herself is perhaps Aristophanes' most striking creation. While there had been

many heroines of classical tragedies, including Electra, Antigone, and even Medea, Lysistrata is the first comic heroine known to Western literature. As befits her position as leader, she is notably superior to her companions in determination, discipline, and intelligence. Her husband never appears onstage, but clearly she is a respectable Athenian wife. She is also a master organizer and strategist and an eloquent debater. As she explains to the delegates, her store of knowledge is attributable partly to her native intelligence, partly to an education shaped by men: "It's true I'm a woman, but still I've got a mind. I'm pretty intelligent in my own right, and because I've listened many a time to the conversations of my father and other elders, I'm pretty well-educated too" (*Lysistrata*, p. 419).

Sources and literary context. While Aristophanes' storyline and the actions of his characters are his own inventions, the playwright drew upon the Peloponnesian War and related politics for inspiration. The play's hero, Lysistrata, may have had a historical counterpart in Lysimache, the already-mentioned priestess of Athena Polias. Her name and Lysistrata's have strikingly similar meanings: *Lysimache* translates as "dissolving battles"; *Lysistrata*, as "dissolving armies."

As shown, in some ways *Lysistrata* echoes ancient stereotypes about the roles of women. Clearly Aristophanes did not write it so society would change its concept of the place women ought to hold in society. They conduct the sex strike to galvanize men to alter the way they are handling public matters, nothing more. And the boldness the women show, by holding the sex strike and barring the men from the Acropolis, is clearly fantasy, not a portrayal of anything that happened. The very characterization of strong women against weak men must have seemed outrageous to early audiences. The women's plan was not even plausible. Such a strike would have had little impact in real life, since so many men were away on military duty and would have been unaffected. Meanwhile, those still in Athens could have turned to prostitutes or other alternatives, options the play ignores. Its aim is not, however, to mirror reality, or even to convey a female point of view, although this is achieved. Rather, the comedy intends to elicit laughter and prod Athens into ending a war. The goal is peace. To this end, the play advocates ridding Athens of self-interested men (much as one would clean the dirt and burrs from fleece) and expanding Athens's loyal mass by making *metics* and foreigners who want to live in the city citizens. Beyond Athens, the play makes a bid for unity within the Greek world. This bid appears to be unique to Aristophanes during the fifth century BCE. In the words of one scholar, the call for unity seems to be "a particularly Aristophanic touch, since it is found scarcely at all in the fragments of other comic poets and does not appear prominently until the fourth century" (Henderson in Bloom, p. 97).

Lysistrata, like Aristophanes' other existing plays, belongs to the genre of Old Comedy. Of course, Aristophanes was not the only Old Comedy playwright in the fifth and fourth centuries BCE. Others include Crates, Cratinus, and Eupolis, but their works survive only in fragments, so it is difficult to compare Aristophanes' efforts with those of his contemporaries. In pondering the question, however, it is worth remembering that Aristophanes won three first-place victories in the competition at the Lenaea festival.

Impact. As indicated, no record survives of the audience's response to the first performance of *Lysistrata* or of its placement among competing plays. Although in his own day, several of his plays won prizes, they dropped in popularity in ancient Greece. As New Comedy replaced Old Comedy around the third century BCE, Aristophanes' works fell into disfavor. Menander, whose plays anticipated the Comedy of Manners (about the manners and social lives of high society) was more admired by later Greek and Roman audiences. During the second century CE, the Roman critic Plutarch compared the two playwrights, expressing a preference for Menander: "Coarseness in words, vulgarity and ribaldry are present in Aristophanes, but not at all in Menander; obviously, for the uneducated, ordinary person is captivated by what the former says, but the educated man will be displeased" (Plutarch in Spatz, p. 147).

Despite this unfavorable view, scholars found Aristophanes' plays worthy of study. His comedies were copied, examined, and interpreted from the third century BCE onward at the Library of Alexandria. Grammarians of imperial Rome pored over Aristophanes' work in their efforts to imitate pure Attic Greek, and Byzantine scholars of the ninth century CE transcribed manuscripts on which modern editions of Aristophanes' plays are based. Aristophanes won admirers in later eras too, among them the English dramatist Ben Jonson (1572-1637), who modeled his play *Every Man in his Humor* on Aristophanes' comedies.

To Plutarch, Aristophanes' mixtures of tragedy and comedy and of vulgarity and eloquence seemed flawed. The same mixtures have pleased modern audiences. Often considered the most accessible of Aristophanes' comedies, *Lysistrata* proved highly popular among twentieth-century audiences, for whom it was repeatedly staged. Still more recently, on March 3, 2003, harking back to the play, the so-called Lysistrata Project—an effort to interject more humanity into global affairs—conducted a worldwide protest against the Iraqi war of their day, with actors around the world performing more than 1,000 public readings of Aristophanes' play. Reaching back across hundreds of centuries, they likened their crisis to the one in fifth-century BCE Greece, fixing on the element Aristophanes himself counted as most important—the call for peace.

—Pamela S. Loy

For More Information

Aristophanes. *Lysistrata*. In *Aristophanes*. Vol. 3. Trans. Jeffrey Henderson. Cambridge, Mass.: Harvard University Press, 1998.

Bloom, Harold, ed. *Aristophanes*. Broomall, N.Y.: Chelsea House, 2002.

Boardman, John, Jasper Griffin, and Oswyn Murray, eds. *The Oxford History of the Classical World*. Oxford: Oxford University Press, 1986.

Bowie, A. M. *Aristophanes*. Cambridge: Cambridge University Press, 1993.

Garland, Robert. *Daily Life of the Ancient Greeks*. Westport, Conn.: Greenwood Press, 1998.

Homer. *Iliad*. Trans. Stanley Lombardo. Indianapolis, Ind.: Hackett, 1997.

Howatson, M. C., and Ian Chilvers. *Oxford Concise Companion to Classical Literature*. Oxford: Oxford University Press, 1993.

MacDowell, Douglas M. *Aristophanes and Athens*. Oxford: Oxford University Press, 1995.

Ostwald, Martin. *From Popular Sovereignty to the Sovereignty of Law*. Berkeley: University of California Press, 1986.

Pomeroy, Sarah B. *Goddesses, Whores, Wives, and Slaves* New York: Schocken, 1995.

Spatz, Lois. *Aristophanes*. Boston: Twayne, 1978.

Medea

by
Euripides

Euripides was born near Athens, Greece, around 480 BCE. Little is known about his early life, although his works show an in-depth education that suggests his family must have been financially comfortable. Also an inscription (recorded by Theophrastus) commemorates the young Euripides' service as a cupbearer to the guild of dancers who performed at the altar of Apollo, a post that suggests the family was not lacking in prominence. In 455 BCE Euripides entered Athens' dramatic competitions and placed third. He first earned the prize for tragedy in 441 BCE, winning only five times in his career (the last occasion, posthumously, for *The Bacchae*), as opposed to Sophocles' 18 and Aeschylus' 13 victories. In 408 Euripides left Athens to visit the court of King Archelaus in Macedon, where he died a year and a half later. A prolific dramatist, Euripides is credited with 92 plays, though fewer than 20 survive in complete form. *Medea* is often considered one of his masterpieces. About an already legendary figure, the play focuses on a non-Greek female, in part to explore the status and power of women, an issue that would fascinate Euripides throughout his career.

Events in History at the Time the Play Takes Place

Medea and Jason—the legend. Like other dramatists of the time, Euripides based his plays on classical myths and legends. His audience

---

THE LITERARY WORK

A tragic play set in Corinth, Greece, during an unspecified mythological time; first performed in Athens in 431 BCE.

SYNOPSIS

A wronged wife exacts a terrible revenge on her husband, who has taken a younger bride.

---

would have been familiar with the characters of Medea and Jason, who figured primarily in the story of the Golden Fleece. They would have also encountered Medea from other tales in which she made appearances, but all these stories were episodic. There was no single life story of Medea at the time. In the Golden Fleece legend, Jason, son of the king of Iolcus, a city in Greece, is sent away in secret as a child when his uncle, Pelias, usurps the throne from Jason's father.

When Jason returns as a young man to claim his birthright, Pelias first insists that his nephew free Iolcus from a curse. A generation before, a prince named Phrixus—related to the royal family of Iolcus—fled from his homeland to avoid being sacrificed, riding on the back of a divine ram with a golden fleece. Taking refuge in Colchis, a foreign land in Asia at the eastern end of the Black Sea, Phrixus sacrificed the ram to the supreme god Zeus in thanks. Phrixus then deeded the Golden Fleece to King Aeetes of Colchis, who hung the prize from a tree in a

Euripides. © Araldo de Luca/Corbis

grove consecrated to the war god Ares. A great serpent guarded the treasure day and night. Later, when Phrixus died, he was denied a proper Greek burial; a prophecy from the oracle at Delphi (the god Apollo, who answered human questions there) proclaimed that Phrixus' ghost would not rest, nor would the land of Iolcus prosper, until the Golden Fleece was retrieved from Colchis.

Agreeing to undertake this quest, Jason assembles a crew and sails for Colchis aboard a great ship named the *Argo*. After a perilous voyage that claims several lives, Jason and the surviving Argonauts reach their destination, where they are welcomed by King Aeetes. Angered by Jason's request for the Golden Fleece, the king assigns the young man a series of dangerous tasks to perform in exchange for the prize. But Princess Medea, Aeetes' daughter and granddaughter to Helios (god of the sun), has fallen in love with Jason. A powerful sorceress, she secretly helps him to accomplish all of her father's tasks and ultimately to secure the Golden Fleece as well by lulling the guardian serpent asleep. Jason and Medea then flee Colchis, Medea slaying her own brother Apsyrtus and casting his limbs before her father to delay the Colchians' pursuit of the *Argo*. During their homeward voyage, Jason and Medea marry.

On returning to Iolcus, Jason learns that Pelias brought about the deaths of Jason's parents. Jason asks Medea for help in avenging the murders. Under the pretense of restoring Pelias' youth, the sorceress tricks Pelias' own daughters into cutting up their sleeping father's body and casting the pieces into a cauldron. Too late, Pelias' daughters realize that they have been deceived.

Banished from Iolcus, Jason travels with Medea to the Greek city of Corinth, where they live for many years and have children. The ambitious Jason eventually decides to cast off Medea and make a politically advantageous marriage to a princess of Corinth, who is sometimes called Glauce, sometimes Creusa (she is nameless in Euripides' play). This princess is the daughter of King Creon. Enraged at Jason's abandonment, Medea sends a poisoned robe and crown to the bride who is consumed by unquenchable flames when she wears them. A fugitive once more, she flees Corinth in a chariot drawn by dragons. Accounts vary as to the fates of Jason and Medea's children. In one version, King Creon kills all but one of them in retaliation for his daughter's death, while the lone surviving child flees with Medea. In another version, Medea kills Creon as well as his daughter, and his relatives murder her children in retaliation. In yet another version, Hera, Zeus' wife, promises immortality to Medea's children if she will lay them on the sacrificial altar of the goddess' temple. Medea's murder of her own sons to wound Jason for his unfaithfulness seems to be Euripides' unique addition. In any case, he was first to fix this plot development into literary form. Medea herself escapes to Athens, where King Aegeus gives her sanctuary.

Thereafter, Medea appears in several other legends. She is credited with curing the Greek hero Hercules of madness and romantically linked with King Aegeus of Athens, father of Theseus, another Greek hero. Driven out of Athens after trying to poison Theseus, Medea is said to have married an Asian king and eventually achieved immortality. Jason is far less fortunate. Shunned by the gods for breaking faith with Medea, he wanders as a lonely outcast from city to city then perishes ignominiously. The prow from the *Argo*, beached on the Isthmus of Corinth, falls and crushes his skull while he is resting in the ship's shadow. In Euripides' play, Medea taunts him with her foreknowledge of his inglorious demise.

The status of women in fifth-century Athens. Although *Medea* is ostensibly set in the mythic past, Euripides portrays the characters as if they lived within his own time. Athenians of the fifth century BCE could thus identify with his characters' concerns, such as Medea's diatribe against the oppression of women: "Surely, of all creatures that have life and will, we women / Are the most wretched" (Euripides, *Medea*, lines 228-229).

Most of the information that survives on the position of women in Classical antiquity comes from male writers. Moreover, scholars disagree as to how much freedom women were truly permitted and whether their degree of freedom meant women were despised or honored. While literature and the visual arts suggest that women of good family enjoyed a prominent role in society, legal and historical data suggest that women were regarded as perpetual minors, to be protected and guided by their male relations.

Some general understandings have nevertheless been gleaned with respect to women in Classical Greece, especially those of the middle and upper classes: they were not permitted to attend, speak at, or vote in political assemblies; they could not hold office; they were considered unfit to make sensible judgments; and they required a husband, father, or guardian to be their agent in economic transactions. Also, while women might be allowed to leave the house to visit friends and relations or attend weddings and religious festivals, they were barred from attending banquets or even the theater. Women of the poorest classes actually enjoyed more freedom: they could travel to the market to sell produce or livestock. Among the higher classes, slaves probably did the shopping.

Women also had little say about whom they married. Until reaching their mid-teens, girls lived under the guardianship of their male relatives, at which point, a marriage would be arranged for them. The girls' guardians and prospective husbands saw to all the arrangements, such as the size of a bride's dowry and the groom's gifts to her father. Political and economic concerns were paramount, and marriages took place whether or not the bridal couple liked or even knew each other. Overall, the bride tended to be considerably younger than the groom, so that he could make the most of her childbearing years. Just after puberty a young woman would enter into a relationship with a man probably 10 to 15 years older (between 28 and 35) than she.

The bearing of legitimate children, especially sons, was recognized as the primary purpose of marriage because it affected inheritance of property and one's standing in the community (having sons brought honor and promised continuity of the family line). Given these concerns, women's sexuality was closely guarded, to ensure, above all, that her children were indeed her husband's. Women were supposedly wild. They had strong sexual desires and could easily fall victim to powerful emotions unless they were contained; their instincts needed to be suppressed by men or else they would create emotional havoc in society. Children were considered the legal property of their father and would remain with his family in the event of their parents' marriage ending through death or divorce.

Theoretically, either spouse could seek divorce, though the process was more involved for a wife. The husband could, without providing a reason, send his wife out of his house and back to her father's. By contrast, the wife needed the intercession of her father or some other male citizen to bring the case before the archon (chief magistrate) if she wanted permission to divorce. During the Classical period there were only three known cases of Athenian women initiating divorce proceedings (Pomeroy, p. 64).

Sexual freedom and Athenian men. While wives were expected to remain chaste and completely faithful to their husbands, men—whether married or single—endured no such restriction. Although bigamy, or marriage to two women, was prohibited, Athenian men could, according to the Greek orator Demosthenes, have three women: a wife, for the procreation of legitimate children; a concubine, for regular sexual relations; and a hetaera (companion) who attended drinking parties with aristocratic men and sometimes established an ongoing relationship with them. A man's relationships with his wife and his concubine held certain similarities. Fidelity from both women was expected and any children resulting from the man's liaison with the concubine were granted certain rights of legal succession, though not the same as those granted to the legitimate offspring of the wife. It was also not uncommon for the concubine to be received in the conjugal home.

By contrast, the hetaera was paid to provide not only sex but also social companionship. She was often more educated than either a wife or a concubine; she also had the freedom to accompany a man to public places where his two other women were not permitted to go. A man's relationship with his hetaera could therefore be socially and intellectually as well as sexually gratifying. While the hetaera enjoyed more

WOMEN AND REVENGE IN ANCIENT GREECE

In ancient Athens women had no political rights and required men to act for them in most economic and legal matters. Included were matters involving revenge, which in ancient Athens was expected to be exacted "through the laws rather than violently" (McHardy, p. 102). Women could not speak in court; to attain lawful justice, they had to depend on their private ability to influence men. In truth, the figure of the avenging woman appears repeatedly in Greek tragedy, whether she is inciting her male kin to violent retribution or influencing her sons against their fathers. Euripides takes the issue a step further by having a woman exact her own revenge and by making that woman a non-Greek. Modern scholars note that Athenians were anxious to stamp out the possibility of revenge attacks because they threatened civic order. The scholars also point to accounts that circulated about the vengefulness and deceit of foreign women; in one such tale, an Egyptian woman, Nitocris, avenges her late brother by constructing a death chamber and inviting a host of Egyptian nobles, whom she blames for her brother's death, to a dinner in the chamber. The existence of such stories suggests "that the Greeks believed powerful, foreign women were not only liable to desire revenge, but were also capable of achieving it by using these methods [of persuasion and treachery]" (McHardy, p. 104). Euripides' play features a Chorus that sympathizes with Medea's desire for revenge against the husband who has deserted her—"To punish Jason will be just. / I do not wonder that you take such wrongs to heart" (*Medea*, lines 262-263). Interestingly, Medea herself comes from Colchis, not Athens. To Euripides' audience, her hideous revenge on Jason—killing his bride, father-in-law, and children—would likely have been considered all too typical of a foreign woman.

freedom than other females, she still enjoyed far less than he. In general, the relative freedom—sexual and otherwise—enjoyed by men is another injustice upon which Medea comments bitterly in the play: "If a man grows tired / Of the company at home, he can go out and find / A cure for tediousness. We wives are forced to look / To one man only" (*Medea*, lines 245-248).

The Play in Focus

Plot summary. The play opens in Corinth, where Jason, Medea, and their two sons have been living for several years. Medea's Nurse enters, lamenting that Jason ever came to Medea's homeland of Colchis. She frets that her Medea has fallen in love with him and committed so many crimes on his behalf. The Nurse reveals that Jason has abandoned her mistress to marry the daughter of King Creon of Corinth. Medea, devastated and enraged, has taken to her bed, but the Nurse fears that she is hatching some terrible plan of revenge against her faithless husband.

Just then, the ancient Tutor of Medea's sons arrives with more bad news for Medea: fearing trouble, Creon plans to banish Medea and her children from Corinth. The Nurse and Tutor discuss Jason's selfishness and Medea's heartbreak; Medea herself is heard offstage, alternately bemoaning and cursing her fate.

> Do I not suffer? Am I not wronged? Should I
>   not weep?
> Children your mother is hated and you are
>   cursed:
> Death take you, with your father, and perish
>   his whole house!
>
>   (*Medea*, lines 112-114)

Sensing her mistress's dangerous mood, the Nurse warns Medea's sons to keep their distance from their mother.

A Chorus composed of Corinthian women arrives to inquire after Medea's troubles. As Medea continues to cry offstage for justice and vengeance, the Chorus expresses sympathy and advises caution, remarking that women have been deserted by their husbands before. At the

Chorus' request, the Nurse enters the house to persuade Medea to speak with her friends.

Medea appears, grief-stricken but otherwise composed. She reveals her misfortunes to the Chorus, relating them to the woes women have endured throughout the ages, such as faithless husbands, the difficulty of gaining a divorce, and the pains of childbirth. Medea maintains that her situation as a foreign exile exacerbates her problems and swears to avenge herself upon Jason. The Leader of the Chorus agrees that Medea has a legitimate grievance against her husband, then observes that Creon is approaching.

Confirming the Tutor's report, Creon arrives to order Medea and her sons into immediate banishment. He has heard of her threats and curses against his house and, fearing her sorcerous powers, wishes her gone for the safety of his family and his country. Medea denies that she has great powers, proclaims her innocence of any malicious intent, and pleads to remain in Corinth. Creon is unconvinced by her protestations but agrees to give Medea one day to settle her affairs before her departure. Once Creon exits, Medea tells the Chorus that she means to use that day to carry out her revenge against Creon, Jason, and Jason's new bride. She decides that poison will be her weapon of choice but wonders where she can find safe asylum after committing her crimes. The Chorus delivers a triumphant ode on how standards are changing. Someday the glory of women, it predicts, will become the focus of song and story. Medea's determination makes her such a woman.

Jason, resplendent in his royal finery, now enters and informs Medea that her banishment is her own fault. He offers her money to support herself and their sons in exile, but Medea furiously rejects his offer. She upbraids him for his abandonment of her, accusing him of selfishness and ingratitude and recalling the many times she used her powers and wiles for his benefit. Jason argues that it was the goddess of love, Aphrodite—working through Medea's infatuation—who saved him on his legendary voyage for the Golden Fleece. He furthermore contends that Medea has benefited from throwing in her lot with him, going so far as to insist that he married the princess of Corinth to improve the fortunes of his and Medea's sons. Now they are connected by marriage to the royal family. Jason considers his actions wholly unselfish and even rebukes Medea for her jealousy and possessiveness. When Medea derides him as a hypocrite and again refuses his financial assistance, Jason

departs in anger. The watching Chorus recites an ode on the dangers of unrestrained love and the sorrows of exile.

A solution to one of Medea's problems arrives in the form of Aegeus, King of Athens, who is passing through Corinth on a journey. Medea reveals her woes to Aegeus and begs for asylum in Athens, offering to use her skills to help him and his childless queen have sons. Unaware of Medea's vengeful schemes, Aegeus swears to grant her sanctuary in his land, as long as she

Medea

MEDEA THE BARBARIAN

Medea's status as a foreign exile is a recurring theme in Euripides' play. From the beginning, she is set apart from the other characters, a non-Greek woman in an alien land, who is at times considered a barbarian. Her loneliness and isolation make her a sympathetic figure, more sympathetic in many respects than Jason; nevertheless, her vengeful actions, especially the murder of her own children, only widen the gap between her and her Greek neighbors, who in real life often blamed "barbaric" behavior on a person's foreignness.

The very concept of the barbarian stemmed from a reaction to the rise of Persia, which caused the Greek city-states to identify with one another against a common threat. The concept harks back to the word *barbaros,* meaning "not speaking Greek." Largely became of the tragedy writers, a number of virtues came to be seen as distinctly Greek—intelligence, courage, order and restraint, and justice. Certain vices, on the other hand, were associated with the barbarian—stupidity, lawlessness, cowardice, and Medea's flaw, unrestrained passion. Not only the tragedies but also other works of art in ancient Athens championed a familiar set of attributes: order over disorder, self-discipline over irrational behavior, democracy over tyranny, and the Greek over the barbarian, to whom Euripides' Medea is linked.

---

gets herself to Athens without his help. Once Aegeus has left, Medea gleefully unfolds the whole of her plan to the Chorus. She will feign acceptance of Jason's new marriage, ask for their sons' sentence of banishment to be revoked, and then send the boys with poisoned gifts for the princess of Corinth that will cause her death and that of anyone who touches her. Medea also means to kill her own children to prevent them from falling into enemies' hands and to hurt their father, Jason. While still sympathetic to Medea, the Chorus pleads with her not to carry out such a cruel plan. Medea remains adamant and commands the Nurse to summon Jason to the house but reveal nothing of her secrets. The Chorus recites an ode in praise of Athens and wonders how this glorious city will receive a woman who has murdered her own children. Again it exhorts Medea to refrain from this most horrible of crimes.

When Jason arrives, Medea feigns remorse, begging his forgiveness and offering to resign their sons to his care if they are allowed to remain in Corinth. Pleased by her change of heart, Jason promises to intercede for the boys. Medea sends her sons and their Tutor back to the royal palace with Jason, bearing gifts of a gossamer robe and a gold diadem for the princess. The Chorus expresses pity for Medea's children, unwitting accomplices to murder, and even for Medea herself, because her great crimes result from Jason's betrayal.

Returning from the palace with the boys, the Tutor excitedly tells Medea that her sons will not be banished, after all. Medea is now torn between her love for her children and her hatred of Jason, but the latter ultimately prevails. Firmly resolved to kill her sons, Medea embraces them one last time, then sends them into the house. The Chorus discourses on the blessings and curses of having children, especially when the children perish young without fulfilling their promise.

A Messenger from the palace arrives in haste to tell of the terrible deaths of the king and princess. No sooner had the princess donned the robe and diadem than their poisons began to consume her flesh, the diadem bursting into flame. Embracing his dead daughter, Creon was likewise consumed. A vengeful Medea rejoices to hear this news, then enters the house to kill her sons. The Chorus prays for someone to stop this final murder and tries in vain to beat down the doors while Medea's sons cry for help on the other side.

Hoping to protect his sons from the Corinthians' rage, Jason rushes to their rescue but arrives too late. The Chorus reveals that Medea has slain the boys. In a frenzy of grief and anger, Jason orders the doors broken down and vows to kill Medea. Just then, Medea herself appears on the roof in a chariot drawn by dragons, her sons' bodies at her side. (The chariot belongs to her grand-

father, Helios, the Sun, and she sits elevated in it, as if to stress her victory and superiority.) The estranged husband and wife again exchange bitter curses and accusations, each blaming the other for the tragedy. Jason asks for the boys' bodies to bury but Medea refuses him, saying she will bury them where no one can violate their tomb. She announces that she is fleeing to Athens and mocks Jason with her knowledge of his future death, when his skull will be crushed by the hull of the *Argo*, the ship on which he first sailed to Colchis. (Such a death would have been far from ideal—young heroes hoped to die nobly to earn a public burial with all due honors.) The play ends as a broken, embittered Jason calls upon the gods to witness his wife's horrible crimes, while Medea flies away triumphantly in her chariot.

Motherhood. While Euripides follows the established legend of Jason and Medea closely, he invents or introduces into the fixed form of a play at least one striking innovation—namely, Medea's murder of her own children. In the original myth Medea either lost most of her children to vengeance by the Corinthians or gave them up to Hera (queen of gods), who promised to make them immortal. In Euripides' play, however, Medea's killing of her sons becomes the one crime no one can justify. On hearing Medea's plans, the Chorus pleads with her to refrain from this last act of vengeance:

> Contemplate the blow struck at a child.
> Weigh the blood you take upon you.
> Medea, by your knees,
> By every pledge or appeal we beseech you,
> Do not slaughter your children!
> (*Medea*, lines 851-855)

Medea herself has a difficult time resolving to go through with the deed: "Why should I hurt *them*, to make / Their father suffer, when I shall suffer twice as much / Myself? I won't do it. I won't think of it again" (*Medea*, lines 1047-1049). She wavers, but then rallies: "What is the matter with me? Are my enemies / To laugh at me? Am I to let them off scot-free? / I must steel myself to it (*Medea*, lines 1050-1052). Her final decision to carry out the murders sets Medea forever apart from her adopted country, marking her as an outsider in every sense of the word.

The nuclear family—husband, wife, and children—formed the heart of Classical Greek society. The begetting of legitimate offspring was, in fact, the main purpose of marriage; the birth of the first child consolidated the wife's position in her husband's household and family. Sons were more highly prized than daughters, who at birth could be exposed to the elements and left for rescue or death if their fathers were unwilling to raise girls.

Although children were the legal property of their fathers, mothers were responsible for their children's day-to-day rearing. Young children stayed with their mothers in "women's quarters," the most remote and protected part of the house. A close bond often formed between mothers and sons, partly because the birth of sons enhanced a woman's prestige within her husband's family, partly because women had to part with their daughters much sooner. Once a girl reached her early teens, she was groomed for marriage, then given to another household to ensure its continuance. Custom was not conducive to emotional warmth for daughters: "At birth [women] were viewed as temporary and costly members of the household, for they were destined to leave it to become mothers in a rival *oikos* (household), carrying away with them a portion of the household wealth in dowry" (Demand, p. 3).

By contrast, sons remained their mothers' concerns until they reached the age of 18 in Classical Athens. Moreover, sons were responsible for the care and well-being of their aging parents.

> As women grew older, sons became ever more important to them. Adult sons of widows acted as their mother's kyrios (guardian) and managed their dowries, which they [the sons] would eventually inherit. A son thus provided his mother with a public voice for the protection of her property and rights. The law also required him to support his mother, which was crucial in a society in which there was no public system of old-age pensions. A view to the future undoubtedly figured in the family-planning strategies of both parents and contributed to a woman's joy at the birth of sons.
>
> (Brand in Demand, p. 29)

Thus, by killing her sons, Medea destroys her own future as well as Jason's, a thought that haunts her as she contemplates their murder: "Oh, yes, I once built many hopes / On you; imagined, pitifully, that you would care / For my old age, and would yourselves wrap my dead body / For burial. How people would envy me my sons!" (*Medea*, lines 1031-1034).

Sources and literary context. Euripides' primary source for his tragedy was the extensive body of myths relating to Medea and Jason. Several written versions would have been available to the dramatist, including those in Hesiod's *Theogony* and Pindar's *Pythian* 4. Euripides chose

to concentrate not upon the legend of the Golden Fleece, but rather on the domestic tragedy that takes place many years later, when Jason abandons Medea for the princess of Corinth. While retaining the basic elements of the story, Euripides, as noted, became the first to make Medea's murder of her children part of a fixed version of the legend, an addition that has since become integrated with the original tale.

Euripides dramatized other Greek figures, including

Alcestis (438 BCE)
Medea (431 BCE)
Children of Heracles (c. 430 BCE)
Hippolytus (428 BCE)
Electra (c. 420 BCE)
Heracles (c. 416 BCE)
Trojan Women (415 BCE)
Iphigenia among the Taurians (c. 414 BCE)
Orestes (408 BCE)
The Bacchae (after 406 BCE)
Iphigenia in Aulis (after 406 BCE)

He, like other major dramatists in Classical Greece, drew on the mythology of his age. Euripides is most often considered in relation to the tragic playwrights Aeschylus (c. 525-456 BCE) and Sophocles (496-406 BCE), who also used myth as the foundation for much of their work. Euripides, however, employed a plainer style, one closer to everyday speech. Moreover, while Aeschylus chose to focus on dramatic events and Sophocles on situational irony, Euripides concentrated on the suffering individual in a way that was uniquely his own. His protagonists tend to be flawed and human, struggling with passions that frequently overpower them, which leads to a tragic outcome. Euripides' emphasis on character and realism has led some to contend that his plays anticipate the modern psychological drama.

Events in History at the Time the Play Was Written

The Golden Age of Athens. Euripides' life (c. 485-406 BCE) spanned what historians have sometimes called the Golden Age of Athens, the era when the city's power and prominence were at their height. Although sacked and burned by invading Persians in 480 BCE, Athens literally arose from the ashes in the years following the Persians' defeat at Salamis in 480 BCE. In 477 BCE Athens formed the Delian League, an alliance of Ionian cities on the west coast of Asia Minor, the strait of Hellespont, and the Propontis Sea, to repel further Persian threats. The member states began to meet on the centrally located island of Delos—hence the league's name. Athens refortified its defenses and ultimately transformed the league into an empire that extended over the Aegean area. At its height in the 430s, the empire included 150 subject states. Corinth, the city-state that is featured in *Medea,* was not one of them. Rather this city-state and Athens were bitter enemies.

COMPETING AT THE DIONYSIA

From at least the end of the sixth century BCE onwards, tragedies were performed during the Athenian spring festival of Dionysus Eleuthereus, the City Dionysia. The festival was a celebration of Dionysus, god of fertility. Poets competed with one another in the festivals for prizes, producing lyric poems, tragedies, and comedies for the occasion. Besides the dramatic competitions, the festival included such activities as processions, sacrifices in the theatre, libations, and parades of war orphans. The archon—state official—in charge of the festival chose three poets to compete, each of whom produced three tragedies about connected subjects, followed by a satyr-play— a semi-comic play with a Chorus made up of satyrs, mostly human though partly bestial creatures of the woods. Originally, the tragedian would perform in his own play, but later he employed actors to play all the characters. A panel of ten judges assessed the merits of each play, and the results were set down permanently in the public record. Once the victor had been announced, he was crowned with ivy in the theater.

Athens maintained a preeminent role in the empire. Between 479 and 431 BCE, the year *Medea* was first performed, Athens was a leading power in the Greek world politically, intellectually, and artistically. The Athenian statesman Pericles dominated the political scene from about 461 to 429 BCE, presiding over one of history's most democratic governments. While women, slaves, and foreigners were excluded from Athenian democracy, male citizens were granted equal opportunity to participate in their city's political process, whether that involved speaking at public assemblies or serving as a magistrate or juror.

While Pericles supported foreign policies that would enlarge the Athenian empire and domestic policies that clarified Athenian citizenship, his accomplishments were not only political. He also promoted festivals and financed the construction of public buildings and religious monuments during the 440s and 430s BCE. Athens grew in wealth and beauty under Pericles' administration, arousing the admiration and envy of its neighbors. In *Medea* Euripides includes a choral ode on the glories of Athens, acknowledging the city's exalted place in the Greek world: "The people of Athens, sons of Erechtheus, have enjoyed their prosperity / Since ancient times. Children of blessed gods, / They grew from holy soil unscorched by invasion, / Among the glories of knowledge their souls are pastured" (Euripides, *Medea*, lines 825-829). Ironically, tensions between Athens and the cities of the Peloponnesian League, led by Sparta and Corinth, erupted into war in 431 BCE, the same year that *Medea* was performed. The conflict, known as the Peloponnesian War, was to last nearly 30 years and cost Athens most of its wealth and prestige.

Reception and impact. During his lifetime Euripides' work tended to be underappreciated. When performed at the Dionysia in the spring of 431, *Medea* placed only third out of three tragedies, arguably because of its handling of unorthodox themes (infanticide, female vengeance). Euripides himself served as the butt of jokes: the comic dramatist Aristophanes (c. 455-385 BCE) poked fun at him in *The Frogs*, presenting Euripides as a ranting bore whose plays about bad women had corrupted the morals of Athenian wives. However, Euripides was not without his admirers. Discussing the merits of tragedy in his *Poetics*, the Greek philosopher Aristotle described Euripides as "the most tragic of the poets" and praised his handling of the infanticide in *Medea* as an effective way to arouse pity and fear in the audience (Aristotle, pp. 58-59).

Euripides, of course, influenced later classical writers, including Apollonius of Rhodes (c. 295-215 BCE), whose own epic *Argonautica* features Jason and the winning of the Golden Fleece. Other works that featured Medea were written by Ovid (43 BCE-17 CE) and Seneca (c. 4 BCE-65 CE). Ovid's *Medea,* his only tragic play, has been lost to posterity. But his *Heroides* ("Heroines"), a work of imagined letters from mythological women to their lovers or husbands, includes a letter from Medea to Jason that survives:

Ovid's *Medea*

Ah me! . . . Why did I too greatly delight in those golden locks of yours, in your comely ways and in the false graces of your tongue? . . . At your bidding I have withdrawn from your palace. . . . When, all suddenly, there came to my ears the chant of . . . a wedding-strain. . . . I was filled with fear. . . . Perhaps . . . when you wish to make boast to your stupid mate . . . you will fashion strange slanders against my face and against my ways. Let her make merry. . . . While sword and fire are at my hand, and the juice of poison, no foe of Medea shall go unpunished! . . . By the two children who are our mutual pledge—restore me to the bed for which I madly left so much behind; be faithful to your promises, and come to my aid as I came to yours!

(Medea in Ovid, pp. 143, 155, 157)

Seneca's Medea is portrayed as the vengeful sorceress, in contrast to Euripdes' image of the wronged wife. Even her final exit is more savage in this later play: before fleeing in her flying chariot, Seneca's Medea tosses down the slain bodies of their children to Jason, leaving him to rail at her as the play ends. Seneca's version was better known than Euripides' version among playwrights of the English Renaissance. But Euripides' portrayal became and remained preeminent thereafter.

Modern critics have long recognized the power of Euripides' *Medea*. In an introduction to his translation of the play, Gilbert Murray wrote, "For concentrated dramatic quality and sheer intensity of passion few plays ever written can vie with the *Medea*" (Murray in Bloom, p. 71). Much attention has been focused on the title character, who has been viewed by turns as a champion of oppressed women, an eternal outsider, a masculinized avenger, and a being at once more and less than human. Examining Medea in the light of the expectations of Euripides' original audience, Edith Hall contends that the "vengeful, competitive, sexually honest Medea," who goes

unpunished for her crimes, "was any Athenian husband's worst nightmare recognized" (Hall in Bloom, p. 86).

—Pamela S. Loy

For More Information

Aristotle. *Poetics*. Trans. James Hutton. New York: W. W. Norton, 1982.
Bloom, Harold. *Euripides*. Philadelphia: Chelsea House, 2003.
Cantarella, Eva. *Pandora's Daughters*. Baltimore: Johns Hopkins University Press, 1987.
Demand, Nancy. *Birth, Death, and Motherhood in Ancient Greece*. Baltimore: Johns Hopkins University Press, 1994.
Euripides. *Medea*. In *Medea and Other Plays*. Trans. Philip Vellacott. London: Penguin, 1963.
Garland, Robert. *Daily Life of the Ancient Greeks*. Westport, Conn.: Greenwood Press, 1998.
Hall, Edith. *Inventing the Barbarian: Greek Self-Definition through Tragedy*. Oxford: Clarendon Press, 1989.
Hall, Edith, Fiona Macintosh, and Oliver Taplin, eds. *Medea in Performance 1500-2000*. Oxford: Legenda, 2000.
Hornblower, Simon, and Antony Spawforth, eds. *The Oxford Companion to Classical Civilization*. Oxford: Oxford University Press, 1998.
McHardy, Fiona. "Women's Influence on Revenge in Ancient Greece." In *Women's Influence on Classical Civilization*. Ed. Fiona McHardy and Eireann Marshall. London: Routledge, 2004.
Ovid. *Ovid 1: Heroides. Amores*. The Loeb Classical Library. Ed. Jeffrey Henderson. Trans. Grant Showerman. Cambridge, Mass.: Harvard University Press, 1977.
Pomeroy, Sarah B. *Goddesses, Whores, Wives, and Slaves*. New York: Schocken, 1995.
Rabinowitz, Nancy Sorkin. *Anxiety Veiled: Euripides and the Traffic in Women*. Ithaca: Cornell University Press, 1993.

Metamorphoses

by
Ovid

Publius Ovidius Naso, known in English as Ovid, was born at Sulmo in the Abruzzi (central Italy) in 43 BCE. The son of a wealthy family, Ovid was educated in Rome, where he distinguished himself in rhetorical studies. He finished his education by embarking on a tour of the Greek lands, an expedition not uncommon for members of the aristocracy. Originally destined for a political career, Ovid held several minor judicial posts but soon abandoned public life for poetry. Patronage helped Ovid quickly gain prominence as a writer. His earliest work, *Amores* (Loves, or Poems about Love), may have circulated around 25 BCE, when he was still a young man. Later works included *Heroides* (Heroines), a series of fictional letters in verse purporting to be from mythological heroines to their beloveds; *Ars Amatoria* (The Art of Love), a didactic poem about the arts of courtship and erotic intrigue; and the *Remedia Amoris* (Remedies of Love), a poem that instructs readers on how to extricate themselves from a love affair. While the exact chronology of these works is not known, it is generally believed that they were composed between c. 15 BCE to 2 CE. From about the first year CE onward, Ovid was working on *Metamorphoses* (Transformations), an epic poem that narrates myths about supernatural change, and the *Fasti* (Calendar), a poem dealing with Roman festivals and religious cults (written in the rhythm known as elegiac meter). However, in 8 CE, Emperor Augustus exiled Ovid to Tomis, a remote city on the Black Sea, ostensibly because of the immoral behavior condoned in *Ars Amatoria*. There were

---

THE LITERARY WORK

An epic poem set in classical Greece and Rome, from the creation of our world to the first century CE; written in Latin c. 8 CE.

SYNOPSIS

The poet meditates upon the nature of transformation, as depicted in classical mythology and enacted within history.

---

probably political reasons for Ovid's exile as well, but they were never revealed and remain a mystery to this day. Despite pleas to Augustus and, later, to his successor Tiberius to repeal the banishment, Ovid was never permitted to return to Rome. He continued to write poems expressing his sadness at being so far from family, friends, and his beloved Rome during his exile. Ovid died at Tomis in 17 CE. Though he attempted to burn his manuscript of *Metamorphoses*, he relented and permitted friends who had kept copies of the epic poem to publish it. Often considered Ovid's masterpiece, *Metamorphoses* is a virtuoso retelling of classical myths that explores the interlocking natures of the human and the divine.

Events in History at the Time of the Epic

Augustan Rome. Despite the tumultuous events leading up to his accession, the long reign of

Augustus, "princeps" (first man) of Rome (27 BCE-14 CE) proved to be prosperous and relatively peaceful. Mindful of the Roman wariness of rule by a single person—the Romans had expelled their king in 509 BCE—Augustus claimed to have restored the Republic. In reality, however, he ruled as a monarch. He centralized the administration and implemented a uniform system of law and justice within an empire that stretched from the eastern Mediterranean to much of western Europe and extended as far north as the Rhine and Danube rivers in Germany and as far south as Egypt.

Augustus also beautified and developed Rome itself, building libraries, theaters, and roads to link his empire. He claimed to have found Rome built in brick and to have left it built in marble. His domestic policy included religious reforms. Augustus restored the Roman gods to prominence by renovating or rebuilding dilapidated temples and reviving traditional rites and ceremonies that had lapsed over the years. New temples were erected in Rome, dedicated to Augustus' predecessor Julius Caesar, who had been deified, and to various other gods—Mars, Venus, and Apollo. Augustus' own home on the Palantine, the chief hill of the seven hills of Rome, included a temple and an altar of Vesta, goddess of the hearth. The group of buildings that included his home became known as *palatia,* from which the English word "palace" would be derived.

Along with reviving religious forms and observances, Augustus also wished to improve the Roman character—at least, its public aspects. Virtues such as sobriety, high moral seriousness, and self-restraint were lauded. Augustus himself tried to set an example by embracing an austere personal lifestyle; the simplicity of his dress and the modesty of his household were intended to provide a dramatic contrast with the splendor of the public buildings he commissioned for Rome. Measures were passed to restrict private extravagance and check acts of license at public shows. Additionally, Augustus passed laws imposing severe penalties for adultery, punishing not only the culprits but others who aided and abetted in the affair as well; meanwhile, marriage and the procreation of legitimate offspring were encouraged by offering rewards to the prolific while penalizing the childless and the celibate.

Although composed during the peaceful, prosperous years of Augustus' rule, *Metamorphoses* contains little of the sobriety or moral seriousness expected from that era's poetry. Instead, Ovid's epic delves exuberantly into the amorous exploits of gods and mortals, many of which are amoral and some of which are even taboo.

The Hellenic influence. The Roman conquest of Greece began early in the second century BCE and Greece was absorbed into the Roman Empire in the first century BCE. Although Rome had dominated Greece, the wealth and beauty of its civilization seduced many Romans. Over the two centuries, Greek (Hellenic) culture spread throughout the Roman world, prompting the poet Horace to remark, "Graecia capta ferum uictorem cepit (Captured Greece captured her savage conqueror)" (Horace in Jones and Sidwell, p. 22).

Hellenization, the adoption of Greek ways, was especially noticeable in the development of Rome's spiritual, intellectual, and artistic life. The Greek pantheon, or group of gods, merged with that of Roman deities. Architects were commissioned to build monuments, temples, and other edifices in the Greek style. Aristocrats assumed Greek clothing and collected Greek art. And Roman writers studied the Greek language, rhetoric, and philosophy, and even adapted the works of Greek authors.

The Romans' attitude toward Greek literature was ambivalent. While many admired the richness of Greece's cultural legacy, some believed that absorbing it would prove detrimental to Rome's own intellectual and moral development. The conservative Roman statesman Cato the Elder (234-149 BCE) wrote to his son:

> I will show you the results of my own experience at Athens: that it is a good idea to dip into their literature but not to learn it thoroughly. I shall convince you that [the Greeks] are a most iniquitous and intractable people, and you may take my word as the word of a prophet: if that people shall ever bestow its literature upon us, it will corrupt everything.
> (Cato the Elder in Jones and Sidwell, p. 24)

Other Romans were less critical, preferring to regard Greek intellectual achievements as subjects to be imitated, absorbed, and eventually matched or even outdone. Moreover, it became a tradition for young Roman men who had completed their education in Rome to travel to Athens for further study, as Ovid himself did. Once exposed to the fruits of their own civilization and those of Greece, aspiring Roman poets frequently incorporated aspects of the latter into their own works for their own purposes. Their behavior seems to have fit into a larger pattern in the diverse empire of Rome. Apparently the Roman conquerors "acknowledged and used the strengths of the people they had subdued. The Greeks, powerful and unconquerable as a cultural force, were accepted for what they were and made to work for Rome" (Jones and Sidwell, p. 274).

For example, Virgil, often considered the foremost Roman poet, took characters from Greek myth—the Trojan warrior Aeneas and his family—and transformed them into heroes who gave rise to the Roman people and exemplified Roman virtues, such as courage, fortitude, practicality, morality and—above all—a sense of duty. While less didactic than Virgil's *Aeneid*, Ovid's *Metamorphoses* may be said to accomplish a similar purpose. After exploring the patterns of supernatural change in more than 200 Greek and Roman myths, Ovid concludes his virtuoso performance with extravagant praise for his city and its current ruler, Augustus Caesar, who in time may achieve his own metamorphosis—from being mortal into being divine.

Apotheosis and deification. The Romans took the personalities and myths of the Greek gods and grafted them onto their own native gods. Roman society, for example, identified the supreme Greek god, Zeus, with their own all-powerful sky god, Jupiter, attaching to him the personality and myths that surrounded Zeus. Given the immortality and active sex lives of their gods, most Romans believed that the divine could always have offspring, which meant the Roman pantheon was ever capable of changing and expanding.

It was further believed that mortal heroes and kings could join the Roman pantheon by undergoing an apotheosis, an elevation to divine status. This practice originated in Classical Greece, where men of extraordinary abilities and achievements might be worshiped as gods after their deaths. Altars to these heroes were established, and sacrifices made before their tombs. The most famous example of a mortal hero becoming elevated to godhood was Heracles (known as Hercules to the Romans). Although Heracles was the result of a liaison between Zeus, the father of the gods, and a mortal woman, he was granted divine status after his death. His mortal remains, poisoned by Hydra's venom, were burned upon a funeral pyre, but his spirit was carried off to the heavens and given the form of a god. In light of such examples, the Greeks found it plausible that human heroes of their time might be similarly transformed if their deeds and nature were deemed praiseworthy by the gods.

Roman civilization appears to have absorbed this belief into its own culture around the late

Roman marble relief of the mythological figures Hermes, Orpheus, and Eurydice. © Alinari/Art Resource, NY. Reproduced by permission.

second century BCE. The idea gained momentum during Julius Caesar's illustrious career as a military leader and statesman. From 46 BCE on, the still-living Caesar was granted divine honors and often identified with Quirinus, the divine form adopted by Romulus, the legendary founder of Rome. Statues of Caesar were placed in temples and prominent sites like the Capitol, a peak on one of the hills of Rome. Additionally, the Roman Senate decreed in 44 BCE that Caesar should have a house like a temple, a priest (*flamen*), and a statue in all the temples that honored Rome in the east. Caesar's assassination that same year did nothing to diminish his growing legend, especially after a bright comet coincidentally appeared in the sky around the time of his cremation. In 42 BCE Caesar was officially named as a god of the Roman state, and the month of Quintilis was renamed Julius (July) in his honor.

Similar honors were bestowed many years later, upon Caesar's adopted son and successor Augustus. In 8 BCE the month of August was named for him, and after his death in 14 CE, he too was deified. In succeeding ages, it became almost standard practice to confer posthumous divinity upon any emperor who had not committed heinous crimes against the state during his lifetime (significantly, none of the three emperors

WHAT'S IN A NAME?

Although the Romans worshipped some native deities, like Fortuna (goddess of fortune) and Janus (two-faced god of gates, doorways, and beginnings), most of their pantheon consisted of a mixed variety of gods. Roman society took the personalities and myths of the Greek gods and grafted them onto its own set of native gods, giving, for example, attributes of the Greek Zeus to their native Jupiter. The following gods are featured prominently in *Metamorphoses*:

Roman Names (Greek Names)

Jupiter, Jove (Zeus)	King of gods; god of the sky, weather
Juno (Hera)	Queen of gods; goddess of childbirth, marriage
Neptune (Poseidon)	God of the sea
Ceres (Demeter)	Goddess of agriculture (grain crops)
Pluto (Hades)	God of the underworld
Vesta (Hestia)	Goddess of the hearth
Minerva (Athena)	Goddess of wisdom and of arts and crafts
Apollo (Apollo)	God of music, prophecy, archery, and medicine
Diana (Artemis)	Goddess of the hunt
Mercury (Hermes)	God of thieves and profit; messenger of the gods
Venus (Aphrodite)	Goddess of love and sex
Mars (Ares)	God of war
Vulcan (Hephaestus)	God of the forge and metalwork
Bacchus (Dionysus)	God of wine

Tiberius, Caligula, and Nero was deified). Emperor Vespasian (r. 69-79 CE) is rumored to have quipped upon his deathbed, "My goodness, I think I am turning into a god!" (Vespasian in Boardman, Griffin, and Murray, p. 133). In *Metamorphoses*, Ovid's inclusion of several stories involving apotheoses, such as those of Hercules, Aeneas, and even Julius Caesar, suggests that even elevation to godhood represents just another transformation and further blurs the boundaries between divine and human nature.

The Epic in Focus

Overview. Composed in dactylic hexameters, the traditional meter of epic poetry, Ovid's *Metamorphoses* retells more than 200 Greek and Roman legends. Ovid links them together through a common theme of transformation and change. Most of the changes occur as a result of characters having incurred the disfavor of the gods or, more alarmingly, having attracted their amorous attentions. The passions of both gods and mortals are vividly rendered, especially those connected with the lure of the forbidden. Many episodes, for example, deal with illicit or unlawful loves, such as Tereus' for his sister-in-law, Philomela (book 6), Byblis' for her twin brother, Caunus (book 9), and Myrrha's for her father, Cinyras (book 10). Other episodes depict the folly of mortals who set themselves up as rivals to the gods; their punishments of these offenders reveal the gods' own capacity for jealousy and cruelty—in short, their human side. The line between mortal and divine blurs continually and, in some instances, disappears completely—as when a mortal is deemed worthy of godhood, undergoing the most glorious of all metamorphoses.

Book 1. The epic begins as Ovid proclaims in the opening of the first book:

> Of bodies, changed to other forms I tell;
> You Gods, who have yourselves wrought
> every change, Inspire my enterprise and
> lead my lay
> In one continuous song from nature's first
> Remote beginnings to our modern times.
> (Ovid, *Metamorphoses*, book 1, lines 1-5)

THE STRUCTURE OF *METAMORPHOSES*

Ovid's epic is divided into 15 books, each narrating a series of myths. Often the myths are embedded in other tales, and there are frequent changes in narrators as well. But the overall structure of *Metamorphoses* reads as follows:

Book 1 The Creation; The Ages of Mankind; The Flood [Lycaon]; Deucalion and Pyrrha; Apollo and Daphne; Io [Syrinx]; Phaethon

Book 2 Phaethon (cont.); Callisto; The Raven and the Crow [Apollo and Coronis]; Ocyrhoe; Mercury and Battus; The Envy of Aglauros; Jupiter and Europa

Book 3 Cadmus; Diana and Actaeon; Semele and the Birth of Bacchus; Tiresias; Narcissus and Echo; Pentheus and Bacchus [Acoetes]

Book 4 The Daughters of Minyas; Pyramus and Thisbe; The Sun in Love; Salmacis and Hermaphroditus; The Daughters of Minyas Transformed; Athamas and Ino; The Transformation of Cadmus; Perseus and Andromeda

Book 5 Perseus' Fight in the Palace of Cepheus; Minerva Meets the Muses on Helicon [Contest with Pierides]; The Rape of Proserpine [Cyane]; Arethusa; Triptolemus

Book 6 Arachne; Niobe; The Lycian Peasants; Marsysas; Pelops; Tereus, Procne, and Philomela; Boreas and Orithyia

Book 7 Medea and Jason; Medea and Aeson; Medea and Pelias: Her Flight; Theseus; Minos, Aeacus, the Plague at Aegina, and the Myrmidons; Cephalus and Procris

Book 8 Scylla and Minos, The Minotaur, Daedalus and Icarus; Perdix; Meleager and the Calydonian Boar [Atalanta]; Althaea and Meleager; Achelous and the Nymphs; Philemon and Baucis; Erysichthon and his Daughter

Book 9 Achelous and Hercules; Hercules, Nessus, and Deianira; The Death and Apotheosis of Hercules; The Birth of Hercules; Dryope; Iolaus and the Sons of Callirhoe; Byblis; Iphis and Ianthe

Book 10 Orpheus and Eurydice; Cyparissus; Ganymede; Hyacinth; Pygmalion; Myrrha; Venus and Adonis; Atalanta

Book 11 The Death of Orpheus; Midas; First Foundation and Destruction of Troy; Peleus and Thetis; Daedalion; The Cattle of Peleus; Ceyx and Alcyone; Aesacus

Book 12 The Expedition against Troy; Achilles and Cycnus; Caenis; The Battle of the Lapiths and Centaurs; Nestor and Hercules; The Death of Achilles

Book 13 Ajax and Ulysses and the Arms of Achilles; The Fall of Troy; Hecuba, Polyxena, and Polydorus; Memnon; The Pilgrimage of Aeneas; Acis and Galatea; Scylla and Glaucus

Book 14 Scylla and Glaucus (*cont.*); The Pilgrimage of Aeneas (*cont.*); The Island of Circe; Picus and Canens; The Triumph and Apotheosis of Aeneas; Pomona and Vertumnus; Legends of Early Rome; The Apotheosis of Romulus

Book 15 Numa and the Foundation of Crotona; The Doctrines of Pythagoras; The Death of Numa; Hippolytus; Cipus; Aesculapius; The Apotheosis of Julius Caesar; Epilogue

Ovid subsequently describes how the universe, which first existed in a state of chaos, was itself shaped by a god into its more ordered form. The "great Creator" established separate domains for the heavens, air, earth, and waters, shaped the world into a sphere, and populated it with plants, animals, and, finally, men (*Metamorphoses*, 1.76).

Ovid next tells of the Four Ages of Mankind: 1) the Golden Age, when all men were innocent, faithful, and good, needed neither laws

Apollo and Daphne (1470-1480), by Antonio Pollaiulo. © National Gallery Collection; by kind permission of the Trustees of the National Gallery, London/Corbis.

nor punishments, and lived in an eternal spring; 2) the Silver Age, dating from Saturn's overthrow by Jupiter, when the year became divided into four seasons, and men took shelter in caves and rough dwellings and planted the first harvests; 3) the Bronze Age, when men first became war-like and aggressive; and 4) finally the Iron Age, when "all evil straight broke out, / And honour fled and truth and loyalty, / Replaced by fraud, deceit, and treachery / And violence and wicked greed for gain" (*Metamorphoses*, 1.129-132). During the Bronze Age, King Lycaon of Arcadia tried to test the divinity of a disguised Jupiter (king of the gods) by offering him a feast of human flesh. Disgusted, Jupiter turned Lycaon into a wolf, then vowed to exterminate humanity with a great flood and afterward bring forth a new race of human beings.

Only the virtuous spouses, Deucalion and Pyrrha, survived the flood. Heeding the advice of an oracle, the couple creates new life by casting stones behind them, which are transformed into the present race of men and women, "children of the earth" (*Metamorphoses*, 1.411). The earth itself also brings forth new forms of life, including species never before seen, like the Great Python later slain by Apollo.

Ovid's narrative departs from the account of creation to relate the myth of Apollo and Daphne. After Apollo, the god of archery, rebukes Venus' son Cupid for presuming to wield a bow, Cupid retaliates by shooting the older god with an arrow that makes him fall in love with Daphne, a chaste nymph who serves the virgin goddess Diana. Wounded by an arrow that engenders hate, Daphne flees when Apollo pursues her. As he gains on her, Daphne implores her father, the river god Peneus, to save her by transforming her into something else. Daphne is quickly changed into a laurel tree, which the still-smitten Apollo claims as his particular symbol. Book 1 concludes with briefer accounts of Io, whom Jupiter loves and transforms into a white heifer in a vain effort to protect her from Juno's jealousy, and Phaethon, son of the Sun God, who is killed after he rashly attempts to drive his father's heavenly chariot and team of horses across the sky.

Book 6. Subsequent books of the *Metamorphoses* deal not only with the transformations Ovid has mentioned but the dangers of excessive pride and the destructive aspects of love and passion. In the sixth book, several mortals come to grief because they set themselves up as rivals to the gods.

In the first myth, Arachne, a Lydian girl with a talent for weaving, boasts that she can hold her own in a weaving contest with Minerva, goddess of arts and crafts. Disguised as an old woman, Minerva cautions Arachne to be content with her mortal skill and not presume to compete with the goddess. Refusing to heed this advice, Arachne repeats her boast, at which point the old woman reveals herself as Minerva and takes up the girl's challenge. Minerva weaves a scene of her victory

over Neptune for the guardianship of Athens, flanked with miniature representations of mortals who strove against the gods and were punished for their presumption. Meanwhile, Arachne weaves a portrait of mortals deceived by the gods in false guises. Incensed equally by Arachne's skill and her insult to the gods, Minerva tears up the girl's tapestry and strikes her with a shuttle, the device used for weaving. So humiliated is Arachne that she hangs herself, whereupon Minerva turns the girl into a spider, the idea being that her weaving skill will not be wholly lost.

A crueler fate befalls Niobe, queen of Phrygia (an ancient country in Asia Minor). Incessantly proud of her station and her family, Niobe boasts that she is more deserving of worship than the goddess Latona (mother of Apollo and Diana) because she has borne 14 children while Latona has borne only two. To avenge the insult to their mother, Apollo and Diana strike down all of Niobe's children with their deadly arrows. Niobe's husband, Amphion, kills himself in grief over their lost children. Wholly bereft, the weeping Niobe is transformed into stone and set on a mountaintop, from which her tears still flow.

Book 6 also relates the myth of the Lycian peasants who were changed into frogs when they rudely refused Latona a drink of water from the lake. Other myths include the tale of Marsyas— a satyr whose very skin was forfeited to Apollo after the creature rashly challenged the god to a musical contest—and the tales of Tereus, Procne, and Philomela. The last is a horrifying account of a savage king of Thrace (named Tereus) who conceives a violent, unlawful passion for his wife's (named Procne) unmarried sister (named Philomela). Charged with conveying Philomela from Athens to visit Procne in Thrace, Tereus instead spirits the girl off to a cabin in the woods and rapes her. When Philomela threatens to expose his villainy, Tereus cuts out her tongue, imprisons her under guard in the cabin, and tells Procne that Philomela died on the journey to Thrace. Unable to speak, Philomela manages to weave a tapestry that reveals Tereus' crimes and to send it to Procne, who is outraged. During the festival of Bacchus, Procne steals off to the woods to free her sister. Reunited, the two plot revenge against Tereus, killing his and Procne's son Itys, and serving the boy's flesh to his father at a banquet. On learning that he has eaten his own child, a raging Tereus pursues Procne and Philomela with his sword. All three are transformed into birds: a swallow (Procne), a nightingale (Philomel), and a hoopoe (Tereus).

Book 6 concludes with an account of how Boreas, the North Wind, carried off the beautiful princess Orithyia, by whom he had twin sons, both of whom later sailed with another Greek hero, Jason, to obtain the Golden Fleece.

Book 15. In the last volume of *Metamorphoses*, Ovid's epic comes full circle in its discussion of change and transformation. Book 15 begins with

---

THE MYSTERIOUS PYTHAGORAS

The last book of *Metamorphoses* features an unusual episode involving the Greek philosopher Pythagoras, whose views on transformation seem to reflect Ovid's, at least partially. Born in Samos around the middle of the sixth century BCE, Pythagoras settled in Crotona (in southern Italy) in c. 530 BCE, where he appears to have founded a sect that bore his name and to have played a significant role in the political life of Magna Graecia (the Greek settlements of southern Italy). A somewhat mysterious figure, Pythagoras is associated with two parallel traditions, one religious, the other scientific. In *Metamorphoses* Pythagoras delivers a lengthy speech, which expounds upon his theory of the transmigration of souls and exhorts listeners to embrace vegetarianism lest they inadvertently kill and consume the souls of departed relations, now residing in animal forms. Pythagorean religious cults did indeed impose dietary restrictions upon members, along with periods of initiation, secret doctrines and passwords, and special burial rites. Even within his own lifetime, Pythagoras seems to have taken on an almost legendary status. He is also credited with many advances in mathematics and science, and though he did not discover it, his name is attached to one of geometry's most famous theorems, the "Pythagorean theorem," which provides a formula for the relationship between the three sides of a right-angled triangle. In the works of classical authors, Pythagoras became "the pattern of the 'divine man': at once a sage, a seer, a teacher, and a benefactor of the human race" (Hornblower and Spawforth, p. 583).

---

an account of Numa from a town near Rome, who wanted to learn more of nature's mysteries and traveled widely as a younger man to broaden his mind. His wanderings lead him to Crotona, a Greek city in southern Italy. A local elder tells Numa how the gods led Mycelsus of Argos to quit his homeland and to found Crotona, named after a king who once hosted Hercules.

The elder goes on to talk of the Greek philosopher Pythagoras, who also settled in Crotona. A lengthy discourse, supposedly from Pythagoras' own lips, follows. Pythagoras' speech, based on his doctrine of reincarnation, argues in favor of vegetarianism and against eating animal flesh, primarily because animal slaughter may mean dispossessing a human soul that has been reincarnated in an animal body. The changing nature of the seasons, the human body, and other phenomena are continually discussed as well. At several points, the philosopher's words echo those of Ovid at the beginning of *Metamorphoses*:

> Nothing retains its form; new shapes from old
> Nature, the great inventor, ceaselessly
> Contrives. In all creation, be assured,
> There is no death—no death, but only change
> And innovation: what we men call birth
> Is but a different new beginning; death
> Is but to cease to be the same. Perhaps
> This may have moved to that and that to this,
> Yet still the sum of things remains the same.
> (*Metamorphoses*, 15.249-257)

Pythagoras concludes his discourse by naming various civilizations that came to power, flourished for a time, and then inevitably declined, leaving only their legends behind. The present age belongs to Rome, but it is implied that Rome too is part of this endless cycle of change.

Resuming Numa's story, Ovid recounts how Numa returned to his homeland and assumed the Roman throne, ruling for many years. After Numa's death, his grieving widow, Egeria, is inconsolable. Hippolytus, the resurrected son of Theseus, attempts to comfort her by telling her of his own tragedy. He was falsely accused of rape by his stepmother and trampled to death by his own chariot horses. But Egeria remains disconsolate and is ultimately transformed by the gods into a clear spring.

Two briefer myths follow. First is that of Cipus, who rejects the opportunity to become king of Rome because he hates tyranny, and, second, that of Aesculapius, god of healing, who—in the form of a giant snake—journeyed from his shrine at Epidaurus to Rome, where he saved the people from plague and became a deity.

Having arrived at his own times, Ovid relates how the murdered Julius Caesar, who claimed descent from the Trojan hero Aeneas, became a god with the aid of Venus (Aeneas' mother), who bore Caesar's soul up "to join the stars of heaven" (*Metamorphoses*, 15.847). Julius Caesar's soul is depicted as shining down upon the achievements of his adopted son Augustus, Rome's newest ruler. Ovid offers extravagant praise to Augustus, wishing him a long reign and hoping that when Augustus leaves this world, he achieves the same apotheosis as his adoptive father. *Metamorphoses* concludes with an epilogue in which the poet acknowledges his inevitable demise but expresses the hope that his works will confer immortality upon him: "If truth at all / Is established by poetic prophecy, / My fame shall live to all eternity" (*Metamorphoses,* 15.877-879).

Illicit passions. While many of the metamorphoses in Ovid's epic are depicted as the consequences of human pride and folly, a greater number are the result of erotic passion. Indeed, it is not inaccurate to consider *Metamorphoses*—on some level, at least—as a love poem, although that love is often unrequited (Daphne and Apollo, Narcissus and Echo), tragically curtailed (Pyramus and Thisbe, Orpheus and Eurydice), or forbidden (Tereus and Philomela, Byblis and Caunus, Myrrha and Cinyras). The involvement of the gods further complicates matters of the heart, showing that the immortals, no less than mortals, are prone to illicit yearnings and desires.

Given the emphasis that Augustus placed on forming and remaining in a marriage relationship, the popularity of *Metamorphoses* in Ovid's lifetime and beyond might seem surprising. However, the morally conservative Romans of the republican period developed more open attitudes toward sex after exposure to Greek culture. It is true that these attitudes did not affect Roman marriages, which continued to be contracted on the basis of political alliance or financial gain. The primary purpose of marriage was the birth of legitimate offspring, preferably male. Roman husbands who expressed affection for their wives or pleasure in their company, as the Roman general Pompey did, were mocked for excessive devotion to their official mate. Meanwhile, Roman wives were expected to remain modest, discreet, and chaste; a wife caught committing adultery could be divorced or even killed outright by her husband.

By contrast, Roman men enjoyed far more sexual liberty. A husband could commit adultery with a woman of a lower class, even under his own roof, without fear of repercussions. Also male family members could seek out slaves or prostitutes for sexual gratification without consequences. Finally, Roman culture produced numerous forms of erotica and pornography as a further stimulus to sexual activity. The poets Catullus and Ovid both composed works dealing

with the themes of love and sex, the former relating in verse his passionate affair with the married Lesbia, the latter producing *Ars Amatoria* (The Art of Love), a poem that reads like a manual on courtship and seduction. Additionally, some Roman homes boasted artworks and mosaics that depicted sexually explicit scenes; many bowls, lamps, and vases were similarly decorated. Thus, while Romans may have publicly moralized against sexually immoral behavior, they appeared to accept, or even embrace it, in private life. This double standard may explain the popularity of Ovid's works, including *Metamorphoses*.

Sources and literary context. Ovid drew upon a wealth of available sources—Greek, Roman, and even Etruscan—to furnish the material for *Metamorphoses*. Chief among them were Callimachus of Cyrene's *Aetia* (Causes), Hesiod's *Theogony* (Story of the Gods), Homer's *Iliad* and *Odyssey*, and Virgil's *Aeneid*. In addition, Ovid would have had access to other writings dealing with metamorphic myths, such as Boios' *Ornithogonia* (Generation of Birds, dates unknown) and Nicander of Colophon's *Heteroeumena* (Transformations, c. second century BCE). While both of these last works are now lost, they have survived as summaries and paraphrases in the writings of later authors.

Metamorphoses is most often categorized as an epic because of its scope, length, and meter. Its form, however, closely mimics that of Callimachus' *Aetia*, which connects discrete episodes through a single unifying thread. The tone of *Metamorphoses* sets it apart from the more solemn efforts of Horace and Virgil, often held up as the preeminent Roman poets. Virgil's *Aeneid*, in particular, was considered the standard for Roman epics. But while the *Aeneid* tends to be uniformly serious, didactic, and moral, *Metamorphoses* is often humorous, irreverent, and even amoral, especially when dealing with the illicit love affairs of the gods.

Impact. Around the time of his exile to Tomis in 8 CE, Ovid expressed dissatisfaction with *Metamorphoses* and burned his manuscript of it. The poet's friends, however, retained their own copies, and, eventually, Ovid sent instructions to Rome for the work's publication.

Popular during and immediately after Ovid's lifetime, *Metamorphoses* also found an audience among readers in the Middle Ages and the Renaissance, when classical themes proved especially popular. Authors as diverse as Geoffrey Chaucer, Marie de France, Christine de Pizan, and Dante Alighieri used Ovid's epic as a basis for their own works. Some medieval writings, such as the *Ovide moralisé* (c. 1300; Ovid Moralized), sanitized the amoral aspects of Ovid's poetry by transforming them into Christian allegory: for example, the goddess Diana, who had three forms, became a symbol of the Holy Trinity, while a haloed Cupid represented the Infant Christ.

Arthur Golding's first English translation of *Metamorphoses*, published in 1567, preserved the raciness and irreverence of the original. Some scholars speculate that Golding's translation was the version read by the Elizabethan playwright William Shakespeare, but it is equally likely that Shakespeare read Ovid's poems in the original Latin. Certainly *Metamorphoses'* influence can be seen in Shakespeare's *A Midsummer Night's Dream* (in the "Pyramus and Thisbe" play-within-a-play), in his poem "Venus and Adonis," and in a treatment of this same Adonis legend in Edmund Spenser's poem *The Faerie Queen*.

Throughout history, the question of Ovid's status and that of *Metamorphoses*, as opposed to that of Virgil and the *Aeneid*, has often been debated. Many have argued that Ovid has the advantage in wit, invention, and the ability to delight. In 1799 Gilbert Wakefield, a noted scholar and publisher of classical texts, called Ovid "the first Poet of all Antiquity" (Wakefield in Ovid, p. xiii). A century later, James Henry, who dedicated much of his life to explaining the meaning of Virgil's *Aeneid*, wrote that Ovid was "a more natural, more genial, more cordial, more imaginative, more playful poet . . . than [Virgil] or any other Latin poet" (Henry in Ovid, p. xiii).

—Pamela S. Loy

For More Information

Aldrete, Gregory S. *Daily Life in the Roman City.* Westport, Conn.: Greenwood, 2004.

Boardman, John, Jasper Griffin, and Oswyn Murray, eds. *The Oxford History of the Roman World.* Oxford: Oxford University Press, 2001.

Casson, Lionel. *Everyday Life in Ancient Rome.* Baltimore: Johns Hopkins University Press, 1998.

Hardie, Philip, ed. *The Cambridge Companion to Ovid.* Cambridge: Cambridge University Press, 2002.

Holzberg, Niklas. *Ovid: The Poet and his Work.* Trans. G. M. Goshgarian. Ithaca: Cornell University Press, 2002.

Hornblower, Simon, and Antony Spawforth, eds. *The Oxford Companion to Classical Civilization.* Oxford: Oxford University Press, 1998.

Jones, Peter, and Keith Sidwell, eds. *The World of Rome.* Cambridge: Cambridge University Press, 1997.

Ovid. *Metamorphoses.* Trans. A. D. Melville. Oxford: Oxford University Press, 1998.

Moral Letters
to Lucilius

by
Seneca (Lucius Annaeus Seneca)

Lucius Annaeus Seneca was born in Cordova, Spain, around 3 BCE, to a father who was an imperial administrator and a well-known student of rhetoric, or the art of persuasion. Since he and his father had the same three names, the two men are often referred to as Seneca the Elder and Seneca the Younger; however, the son's fame far outstripped that of the father. In his old age, Seneca the Elder collected model debates and speeches of advice for his sons, including arguments about problems in criminal or civil law cases. Educated in Rome for the law, Seneca the Younger became a prominent figure in the fledgling Roman Empire. Early on, he was attracted to Stoicism, an influential philosophical movement of his day, and went on to become one of its most eloquent advocates and practitioners. Some lingering criticism of Seneca has centered on the disparity between the tenets of Stoicism that he advocated, which often stressed rejection of material possessions, and his own vast wealth. Banished to Corsica (41-49 CE) for political reasons, Seneca enhanced his literary reputation by writing tragedies and philosophical essays during his exile. The empress Agrippina had him recalled to Rome in 49 CE to tutor her son, the young, future emperor Nero (reigned 54-68 CE). Thereafter, along with a leading official named Burrus, Seneca administered Rome. Tiring of the intrigues of public life and recognizing his own vulnerability after Burrus' death, Seneca went into seclusion in 62 CE until he was forced to commit suicide by a decree that Emperor Nero handed down in 65. He left be-

THE LITERARY WORK

A series of short essays in the form of letters; written in Latin between 63-65 CE.

SYNOPSIS

Seneca uses the personal letter to discuss everyday life in the early Roman Empire and to delineate his Stoic philosophy.

hind an impressive body of writings. Only his essays, letters, and tragedies have survived, though Seneca produced speeches and dialogues in his lifetime as well (see *Phaedra*, also in *Classical Literature and Its Times*). It was in the final phase of his life, while in retirement, that Seneca composed the *Moral Letters*. In them, he comments on various subjects—for example, the elements of Stoicism—focusing on choices about how to live and die.

Events in History at the Time of the Letters

Political intrigue and upheaval. Five emperors reigned during Seneca's lifetime, an age of upheaval and intrigue in which his own fortunes rose and fell.

31 BCE-14 CE Reign of Emperor Augustus; Seneca born in Cordova, Spain around 3 BCE, and moves to Rome as a young child

THE MORALLY FLAWED RULER

Aseries of civil wars following Julius Caesar's assassination left Rome morally depleted. Feeling his responsibilities as emperor keenly, Augustus embarked upon a campaign of moral improvement. For example, he passed laws regarding marriage and male-female relations. Augustus reigned for four decades (27 BCE-14 CE) and was followed by a series of successors who grappled with many of their own grave character flaws. His stepson, the emperor Tiberius (14-37 CE), was suspicious of everyone, while Tiberius' grandnephew Gaius (Caligula) is remembered for sadism during his reign (37-41 CE). After Caligula's assassination by members of his own Praetorian Guard (household troops), Claudius, Caligula's uncle and Augustus' grandson, became emperor (41-54 CE). A wise and clever man, Claudius unfortunately fell prey to the schemes of Messalina, his third wife, whom he had executed, and Agrippina, his fourth wife, who murdered him. Both women plotted endlessly and had people murdered with abandon. Before she served him poisoned mushrooms, Agrippina had Claudius adopt her 12-year-old son Domitius (Nero) and had Claudius recall Seneca from exile to tutor the boy. Nero became emperor (54-68 CE) upon Claudius' demise, ruling with a brutal hand, killing even his mother and stepbrother. Incensed by his excesses and bolstered by rebellion in the western provinces, the Senate finally declared Nero a public enemy (68 CE), whereupon he took his own life. Civil war followed, marking the end of the Julio-Claudian dynasty. Rome entered into a chaotic period, the Year of the Four Emperors (68-69 CE) before the advent of a new family of rulers (the Flavian dynasty).

14-37 CE Reign of Emperor Tiberius; Seneca begins his political career as a public official (a quaestor, recordkeeper and financial controller of the military or civil treasury)

37-41 CE Reign of Caligula; Seneca becomes well known as an orator, a lawyer, and a writer; he rises to position of senator

41-54 CE Reign of Claudius; Seneca is recalled to tutor Nero after being exiled to Corsica for eight years (41-49 CE)

54-68 CE Reign of Nero; Seneca tries to curb Nero's excesses; semi-retires, writes *Moral Letters,* receives order to take his own life

(Adapted from Motto, *Seneca: Moral Epistles,* p. 18)

The era was fraught with political strife, due perhaps partly to the fact that Rome never had adopted a clear rule for succession to the throne. The political instability had a direct effect on Seneca because, as a member of the Roman upper class, he chose a life of public service to the empire, rising to the position of senator under Caligula and administering the empire during the early rule of Nero. Of the five emperors who ruled during Seneca's lifetime, all but Augustus appear to have been inept. Our ancient sources for the period write from a senatorial perspective highly critical of the early emperors. From their pages, each of Augustus' four successors emerges as noteworthy mostly for the murders that took place during his reign, particularly among members of the upper classes. None of the ruling class was safe from plots surrounding its members. In fact, Seneca himself was condemned to death twice, once reportedly by Caligula, a sentence that was commuted when Caligula learned Seneca was sickly and wouldn't live long anyway, and later by Claudius, who chose to send Seneca into exile rather than execute him. Thanks to these reprieves, though he suffered from asthma and other physical ailments, Seneca lived to be almost 70 years old before Nero forced him to commit suicide. His two narrow escapes with his life at least partly explain Seneca's preoccupation with death and suicide in his *Moral Letters,* which he began to write when he was well into his sixties. Because of his sickly constitution and the political instability surrounding him, death was frequently on his mind.

Seneca's political position was always precarious. In his writings, there is evidence that he realized how fragile it was, indeed how fragile the position of any prominent public servant in the early empire was. Nevertheless, believing public service to be his duty, he embarked on a political career. Beginning as a lawyer, Seneca was soon recognized as a polished public speaker, a rhetorician. He grew skilled at persuading listeners to support his position or view. No doubt this skill helped him become a senator and then serve as one until he was exiled to Corsica (41-49 CE) on trumped-up charges. He tutored the young Nero as requested, gaining some influence over the future emperor. After Nero's ascension in 54 CE Seneca and Burrus, leader of the Praetorian Guard, managed to control Nero's excesses until 59 CE. Rome therefore experienced a time of stability, known as the Quinquennium Neronis (54-59 CE). However, restraining Nero's depraved and immoral character proved increasingly difficult.

In 62 CE Burrus died, from poisoning perhaps by Nero, and the risk to Seneca's own life increased. Seneca requested Nero's permission to retire from public life, but the emperor refused, whereupon Seneca went into semi-retirement. As Tacitus tells us, "He dismissed his entourage, and rarely visited Rome. Ill health or philosophical studies kept him at home, he said" (Tacitus, p. 329). He left Rome for a life of study, writing, and seclusion. This lasted until 65 CE, when Nero uncovered a conspiracy to murder him and to put Gaius Calpurnius Piso, a popular and wealthy orator, on the throne. The plot gave Nero the excuse he needed to wipe out suspected enemies. Seneca, his two brothers, and his nephew (the poet Lucan) accordingly lost their lives (Africa, p. 99). Accusing the Christians of participating in the conspiracy, Nero persecuted them too.

In his *Annals of Imperial Rome* (also in *Classical Literature and Its Times*), the ancient historian Tacitus movingly recites Seneca's last moments after Nero sends word demanding Seneca's suicide. Seneca requests but is denied the chance to leave a will, so he says the following to his assembled friends:

> Being forbidden to show gratitude for your services, I leave you my one remaining possession, and my best: the pattern of my life. If you remember it, your devoted friendship will be rewarded by a name for virtuous accomplishments. . . . Surely nobody was unaware that Nero was cruel! . . . After murdering his mother and brother, it only remained for him to kill his teacher and tutor.
>
> (Tacitus, pp. 363-364)

Teacher and philosopher to the end, Seneca offered his friends this one final piece of advice before committing suicide, a way of dying he discussed often in the *Letters*. He cut his arms, but the lifeblood seeped out too slowly, so he "severed the veins in his ankles and behind his knees" as well (Tacitus, p. 364). Then he drank poison, but without result since his limbs were already cold and numbed to the substance. Slaves then lowered him into a bath of warm water, and he sprinkled some on them, calling the gesture an offering to the god Jupiter (Zeus). Finally they carried Seneca into a bath of hot vapors, where the Stoic philosopher suffocated to death.

ROMAN SUICIDE AND SENECA'S SUICIDE

Directing someone to commit suicide instead of executing the person was a common occurrence in Rome. The emperor or Senate could order an accused man to take his own life. The practice may stem back to a belief that a noble should not be executed by others (Motto, *Seneca*, p. 39). While at one time Roman generals threw themselves on their swords to commit suicide, the more common form was by slashing the wrists. Tacitus' account suggests that Seneca modeled his suicide on that of Socrates and Cato the Younger, two men he admired greatly. In fact, when Seneca did not bleed to death, he drank hemlock, as Socrates had, to hasten the process.

From religion to philosophy. During Seneca's lifetime, Roman state religion was still a dominant force in public life. This religion revolved around a pantheon of native and imported gods, and the empire did not require by law that the people believe exclusively in it; on the contrary, a variety of religious beliefs could be practiced simultaneously. Romans mostly practiced their various observances through rituals conducted to soothe and satisfy the gods. In large part, religious belief was a matter of observing the practices of one cult or another by performing rites and ceremonies rather than by adopting fierce beliefs or moral ways of action. When they wanted to deal with moral behavior and ethical issues, thoughtful Romans opted to join various philosophical schools. Preeminent among these were Epicureanism and Stoicism.

In general, the Roman view of philosophy was quite different from later European and

American definitions, which saw it as some kind of abstract system of belief. Like the Greeks before them, the Romans viewed philosophy as a system to live by, a set of values to base their lives on and to aid them in practical decisions that they had to make on a daily basis. Seneca also saw philosophy, particularly Stoic philosophy, as a set of principles to base his actions on. The Stoic philosophy permeates his *Moral Letters*; no matter what his subject, he incorporates Stoic thought, making it the driving force of his life.

Stoicism. Seneca received a solid education directed by his father. Tutored by leading practitioners and teachers, he studied philosophy as well as rhetoric, or the art of speaking or writing to persuade. His father, a rhetorician, favored rhetoric for Seneca's preparation and advancement in his career, but clearly the young man had a preference for philosophy. In any event, he attributed his skill in speech and behavior to the study of these two subjects. His ability in rhetoric won him fame and wealth as a lawyer at an early age, while his philosophical views gained him recognition as a writer. Although Seneca studied all the major schools of philosophy in his day, he became a leading spokesman for Stoicism. The movement traces its roots back to Zeno of Citium (335-263 BCE), who developed his own system of philosophy, establishing a school in Athens that still existed during Seneca's lifetime. Except for a brief Greek work ("Hymn to Zeus"), the philosophy's only surviving complete writings are by three ancient Romans: Seneca (4 BCE-65 CE), Epictetus (c. 55-135 CE), and Marcus Aurelius (121-180 CE). Refining his Stoic beliefs throughout his literary career, Seneca reached the peak of expression about them in his last work, the *Moral Letters*. Although clearly devoted to Stoicism, he often refers to a competing philosopher, Epicurus, and another leading school of philosophy of his era—Epicureanism.

Deriving its name from the *stoa* (porch) in the *agora* (marketplace) at Athens where its members gathered, Stoicism was a philosophy embraced not only by Romans but also by many of the earlier Greeks. The Stoics taught that adherence to the wisdom achieved by the use of reason was the ultimate good. Although they developed a complex cosmology, their view on ethics has been most influential in Western history and philosophy. In fact, our word *stoic*—used for someone who is indifferent to the passions or unaffected by the changes in fortune in life—comes from the name given to the practitioners of this school.

Stoics believed that wisdom was the chief virtue and vice alone was evil. How did they define wisdom and vice? Wisdom was living according to nature, or the divine cosmic plan; everyone had a role to play and one progressed by learning what that role was. Reason guided a person's search for this role while helping the person subdue his or her passions. On the other hand, vice was equated with foolhardiness, which led to a dissolute life where the passions predominated. Everything but wisdom and vice was neutral or indifferent. In other words, poverty, pain, and death were not evils just as wealth, health, and life were not virtues. They were neutral, with some neutrals being preferred to others. Stoicism taught that the wise person is unaffected by poverty or riches because he or she recognizes that they do not matter. A wise man seeks to be as good as he can given the circumstances of his life, and to bear all, no matter what fortune has in store for him, even if it calls on him to sacrifice his life, as in Seneca's case. Concerned about more than the individual, the Stoics taught that progress also involved showing regard for people with whom one shares close ties and, beyond that, for all humankind. The Stoics further believed that only a wise one, a perfectly rational person entirely free from passion, was wholly in tune with the divine cosmic plan and that few if any such people had ever existed (except for perhaps Socrates).

Originally adherents believed there were no gradations to the formula: one could only be wise or foolish. And since it is exceedingly difficult to be wise, there were a few sages, at best, and mostly foolish people, given that almost all humans fall short of perfection. However, Seneca and others believed there was a third group, those not yet wise, or virtuous, but making moral progress. Seneca never considered himself a sage. He said he was far from one, but he would have considered himself and his friend Lucilius members of this third group, because while not perfect, they were continually striving to be virtuous by shunning false judgment about what is good (for example, wealth) yet following "good" feelings such as kindness and friendship. In fact, this striving to be better is one of the main moral teachings of the *Letters*: Seneca is constantly pointing out the path to virtue to his friend and, also, to himself.

Though they lived in a world dominated by belief in many gods, Stoics saw a divine presence everywhere, ordering all things. Seneca called this belief "the God within us" (Seneca, Letter 41,

Ad Lucilium Epistulae Morales, pp. 273-279; all excerpts that follow are from this bilingual edition). This God within us, he teaches, is manifested in the behavior of the truly good person, one who remains calm in the face of adversity. When we encounter such a person and such conduct, we feel the person is divinely inspired, that God must be touching him or her. The reason for the calm, Seneca tells us, is that in this good person is "reason brought to perfection in the soul" (Letter 41, p. 277). A human being achieves "the highest good . . . if he has fulfilled the good for which nature designed him at birth . . . to live in accordance with his own nature. But this is turned into a hard task by the general madness of mankind; we push one another into vice" (Letter 41, pp. 277-279). In spite of what the mass of humanity believes, the good person listens to this internal God because nature, fortune, or God—whatever one calls this force—controls events. Human beings have no choice but to abide by the dictates of this controlling force. But the truly free person is the one who makes a rational choice to follow these "rules of nature." In this instance, one's reason controls one's passions and not the other way around.

Epicureanism. Another less popular, practical philosophical movement in Rome, one that Seneca continually mentions in the *Moral Letters*, is named after its founder, Epicurus (341-270 BCE). Epicurus was a Greek who believed the sole goal of life was happiness through pleasure. He was convinced that a person's aim in life is to attain pleasure and avoid pain. To determine what is moral, the person considers what brings pleasure to his or her senses. Epicureanism seems to be a very individual, selfish philosophy. In fact, some Epicurean groups advocated cutting themselves off from other people and the state, and denounced marriage and kinship relationships. Some even valued friendship from a purely self-centered viewpoint.

While these attitudes led a number of Romans to indulge in the rampant pursuit of pleasure, Epicurus held very different ideas regarding pleasure and pain. First of all, he believed it was more important to avoid pain than to seek pleasure. He felt just being alive without problems was satisfactory on a physical level and that mental pleasure was more satisfying than physical pleasure. Likewise, mental pain was more acute than physical pain. In this same vein, spiritual satisfaction makes life enjoyable for old people who have lost the capacity for intense physical pleasure. He also taught that fear of death is groundless because at death we simply cease to be; therefore, we cannot be punished in future worlds. Nevertheless, adherence to the right philosophy and belief in God are the underpinnings of a satisfying life. Although technically speaking anything is permissible, in practice Epicurus advocated an austere way of life centered on friendship and kindness and moderation of one's appetites. Because Epicureanism accepted women and slaves as equal

---

SENECA, ST. PAUL, AND CHRISTIANITY

Perhaps because of Seneca's beliefs in a God within each person as well as a universal human brotherhood and equity among human beings, his views were seen as compatible with Christianity. Pronouncements scattered throughout his writings resemble Christian scripture. In fact, some early Christian thinkers saw his beliefs as comparable to their own. He, for example, advised viewing slaves as fellow humans when others still viewed them as property. This was a notion gaining momentum but still quite radical at the time. The new Christian religion expressed belief in a brotherhood of man and emphasized character, not the external trappings of this world. Another similarity lay in Christian beliefs and Seneca's statement about treating people as you would be treated. This parallel may account for the existence of some phony correspondence between Seneca and St. Paul, which was actually written after their lifetimes, in the Middle Ages. Although often attached to Seneca's *Letters*, the correspondence is clearly a forgery. While in reality the two men lived at the same time, there is no historical evidence that they ever met or corresponded. There is an interesting historical footnote in the fact that in 53 CE St. Paul is known to have encountered Seneca's older brother, Gallio, the proconsul of the southern Greek province of Achaea. The Christian New Testament's book of *Acts* 18:12-17 reports that the local Jewish community took Paul to court in a case over which, as proconsul at the time, Gallio presided. Seneca's brother decided in Paul's favor, and the meeting was over.

---

to everyone else and promoted happiness and the good life as preeminent goals, some Romans frowned on the movement.

Many of the tenets of Epicureanism and Stoicism overlap. This is evident in the numerous times Seneca quotes and/or refers to Epicurus in the *Letters*. Although Seneca often speaks of Epicurus as a rival, it is evident that he admires much of Epicurean thought. In fact in his philosophical essay "On the Happy Life," Seneca remarks that Epicureanism "has a bad name, is of ill repute, and yet undeservedly" (Seneca, *Moral Essays,* vol. 2, p. 131). But ultimately Epicureanism and Stoicism are at odds in their worldviews. The Epicurean is grounded in this world, seeking happiness or pleasure and self-contentment as primary goals. His or her focus is on the individual and denies the existence of a God concerned with human affairs. In contrast, the Stoic philosopher seeks not pleasure but adherence to reason and, consequently, freedom from slavish devotion to the passions. Believing in a God dwelling within each person, but not an afterlife, the Stoic seeks perfection by following the dictates of this God. The conviction is that these dictates are grounded in reason and the natural order, even when they call for the sacrifice of one's health or wealth.

Roman social elements. One of the most interesting aspects of the *Letters* is Seneca's commentary on social phenomena in ancient Rome. The modern reader can learn much about Roman life from Seneca's keen observations on gladiatorial games, the baths, and slavery, for example. Perhaps even more valuable are Seneca's conclusions regarding these activities, for he uses every opportunity to discuss what such observations teach us about how to exist in the world and how to live our lives.

The gladiatorial games exhibited in the Roman Coliseum fill him with moral outrage (Seneca, Letter 7). These spectacles staged in amphitheaters pitted armed men against each other in life-or-death contests. The men were condemned criminals, slaves, prisoners of war, or paid volunteers who fought to the death with swords, tridents, and other weapons. Sometimes women and dwarves were used as well. By Seneca's day, these "games" had become very popular free events that were often sponsored by the emperor. Seneca was particularly offended by the gladiatorial contests—in effect, executions—in which naked pairs of condemned men flailed away at each other with different weapons. Yet his letters move beyond these executions, using them as a vehicle to discuss his real subject. After carefully describing the scene, Seneca tells us how abhorrent to everyone these activities should be, but his key lesson is about how morally dangerous it is to follow the majority. "Lay these words to heart, Lucilius," he declares, "that you may scorn the pleasure which comes from the applause of the majority. Many men

praise you; but have you any reason for being pleased with yourself, if you are a person whom the many can understand? Your good qualities should face inwards" (Letter 7, p. 37).

There are many such lessons in the *Letters,* moral teachings that surface while discussing current customs, from the public baths to slavery. The Roman baths (Letter 56) were public bathing facilities provided by the emperors for the people. Often quite elaborate social gathering places, they could consist of a complex of buildings with many functions—changing rooms, hot and cold pools for bathing, a swimming pool, gymnasium, and exercise facilities. In Seneca's letter, he describes the goings-on in the baths over which he lives, as well as the continual noise associated with these activities, but his central point is that external noises ought not to disrupt the study of a man at peace with himself. In his letter on slavery (Letter 47), he turns to the subject of human interrelations. Slavery was a mainstay of the Roman Empire during Seneca's day. While population counts differ, one source estimates 5 million free inhabitants and 2-3 million slaves in Italy in 14 CE, totals that show how pervasive slavery was (Adkins and Adkins, p. 341). Slaves often came from being prisoners of war or children of slaves, and they were generally of the same race as their owners, although from foreign lands. Yet many of the middle- and upper-class Romans who kept slaves regarded them as mere property, as items to be bought, used, and sold. In keeping with this reality, Seneca's letter on slavery centers not on abolishing the practice of it (he himself owned slaves), but on treating one's slaves humanely. He, like the rest of Rome, accepts slavery as a fact of life. Romans owned slaves. Slave labor, to a large degree, kept their empire running and made it possible for a well-to-do few to be supported by the unfortunate many. Seneca's main concern is for the compassionate treatment of one's slaves, not as inhuman pieces of property but as fellow human beings.

The Letters in Focus

Contents summary. The *Moral Letters* consist of 124 letters from Seneca to his friend Lucilius, an administrator in Sicily at the time. It is unknown whether Lucilius was a historical person, a pseudonym, or a contrived addressee. Whether or not he wrote the *Moral Letters* to an actual friend, Seneca intended them for wider circulation. They are in fact short essays posing as letters and ranging from under one page (Letter 28) to 18 pages in length (Letter 90). Their titles are the invention of modern editors, not Seneca. While Seneca advises his friend about moral and ethical issues in the letters, they often begin with comments about everyday activities, such as the hardships of travel (Letter 57). Chief among Seneca's overall concerns is how to achieve wisdom and, therefore, virtue. In his view, this is the key to living the good life uninfluenced by one's surroundings. Prominent among his topics are attempts to answer questions such as, What is the good life? How should we choose to live our lives? What has meaning? Can we be self-sufficient? What is the nature of friendship?

Throughout the letters, Seneca quotes famous authors and then discusses their words. The Greek poet Homer, the Roman poet Virgil, and, oddly enough, his fellow philosopher and competitor Epicurus seem to be his favorites. Every letter begins "Greetings from Seneca to his friend Lucilius" and ends with a final "Farewell." As time passed, Seneca gave up offering Lucilius a "thought for today" in each letter, which he had promised him early in the correspondence. Many of these pithy sayings come from Epicurus, such as, "Whoever does not regard what he has as most ample wealth, is unhappy, though he be master of the whole world" or "The fool with all his other faults, has this also,—he is always getting ready to live" (Letter 13, p. 83). Up to about Letter 30, many of the missives center on such a wise saying, or at the very least it serves as a kind of gem to justify the existence of the letter.

A summary of three letters illuminates the whole series, since each letter aims at instructing Lucilius, Seneca—and the reader—on how to live the good life.

Letter 3, "On True and False Friendship." In this short letter Seneca discusses the nature of friendship, a subject of great importance to the Stoics because their belief in the brotherhood of humanity led to great value being placed on personal friendships. Seneca begins his letter by discussing the difference between polite usage of the term *friend,* on the one hand, and a true friendship, on the other hand. The advice he offers his friend Lucilius is to choose friends carefully but, once a friend has been chosen, to trust that person implicitly: "Indeed I would have you discuss everything with a friend"; once someone becomes a friend, "welcome him with all your heart and soul" (Letter 3, p. 11). Some people confide in everyone and some in no one, but Seneca sees both positions as extreme, for we should share

everything with a few intimate friends. This view is based on the Stoic notion that friends share mutual interests: what concerns my friend concerns me. The letter's moral lesson trumpets the importance of friendship in a productive life.

Letter 12, "On Old Age." Narratively speaking, not much takes place in Seneca's letter on old age. Seneca begins with a personal anecdote before

A SAMPLE OF SENECA'S TEACHINGS

"Virtue alone affords everlasting and peace-giving joy."
(Letter 27, "On the Good which Abides," p. 195)

"The place where one lives, however, can contribute little towards tranquility; it is the mind which must make everything agreeable to itself."
(Letter 55, "On Vatia's Villa," p. 371)

"The only harbor safe from the seething storms of this life is scorn of the future, a firm stand, a readiness to receive Fortune's missiles full in the breast, neither skulking or turning the back."
(Letter 104, "On Care of Health and Peace of Mind," p. 203)

"For nature does not bestow virtue; it is an art to become good."
(Letter 90, "On the Part Played by Philosophy in the Progress of Man," p. 429)

"It is with life as it is with a play,—it matters not how long the action is spun out, but how good the acting is."
(Letter 77, "On Taking One's Own Life," p. 181)

"To have whatever he wishes is in no man's power; it is in his power not to wish for what he has not, but cheerfully to employ what comes to him."
(Letter 123, "On the Conflict between Pleasure and Virtue," p. 425)

meditating on the larger meaning of growing old. He has been visiting his country home just outside Rome and is surprised to see it dilapidated, which the caretaker explains is due to the building's age. Seneca reflects on how he built the house himself. This and several similar events during his stay cause him to realize that he, too, is old. But old age is nothing to recoil from; we should relish old age. He goes on to observe that each of us should contemplate every day as our last because, young or old, we can't tell what Fortuna (fortune) has in store for us. However, if we live to the morrow we should happily accept that. Next, he observes that life is divided into parts—circles, each larger one encompassing a smaller circle. Then, after a historical anecdote about a friend (Pacuvius) who celebrates his own funeral every day because he knows he may die any day in a hostile land, Seneca quotes lines from the *Aeneid* (also in *Classical Literature and Its Times*), "I have lived; the course which Fortune set for me is finished" (Letter 12, p. 71). These stories seem to illustrate the truth of living every day as fully and honorably as possible: "And if God is pleased to grant another day, we should welcome it with glad hearts" (Letter 12, p. 71). He ends with the pithy quotation he promised Lucilius in each letter (this one attributed to Epicurus): "It is wrong to live under constraint; but no man is constrained to live under constraint" (Letter 12, p. 59).

Letter 47, "On Master and Slave." In this letter Seneca offers an opinion on slavery that is grounded in Stoic thought: all people are created equal. However, Seneca's view was in the minority; even some Stoics would have disagreed. While they espoused a brotherhood of humanity, many of them had not yet extended this idea to everyone, including slaves. Certainly the majority of the upper class would not have accepted the view that slaves belonged to this brotherhood, given the common notion of them as just property. Abolition, it should be noted, was never the issue. Most members of the upper class, whether Stoic or not, owned slaves and accepted the practice. Instead, the issue was whether to conceive of one's slaves as human beings or as mere merchandise. Seneca never advocates eliminating slavery; rather he stresses treating slaves well. People should do so, he says, because we are all equals and no one ever knows when he or she might become a slave. The only thing that separates humans is their character, not the external trappings of their lives. Consequently every human being should treat every other human being with courtesy and respect, no matter what the difference between their stations. In a statement fairly close to the Golden Rule, Seneca admonishes, "But this is the kernel of my advice: Treat your inferiors as you would be treated by your betters" (Letter 47, p. 307).

In this letter, as elsewhere, Seneca uses an existing social institution (slavery) as a vehicle to discuss a person's character and how one ought to live on a daily basis. Seneca's interest in slavery leads to a larger consideration; he ruminates on both how people should value character, not

social station, and how fortune controls us all. When commenting on the treatment of slaves, he proposes "to value them according to their character, not according to their duties. Each man acquires his character for himself, but accident assigns his duties" (Letter 47, p. 309). Of course, this advice is at the very core of Stoicism, which views one's character as created, while one's station in life is an accident: "So he is doubly a fool who values a man from his clothes or his rank, which is indeed only a robe that clothes us" (Letter 47, p. 311).

Roman rhetoric and the *Letters*. Roman writers studied rhetoric from an early age. They knew the five aspects of rhetoric well: invention, arrangement, style, memory, and delivery. The anonymous Latin text *Rhetorica ad Herennium,* written around 84 BCE, is the first text to discuss all five aspects and provides a view of what scholars have termed the "Roman rhetorical tradition," which existed for several hundred years. The text discusses the aspects with particular emphasis on style, describing 64 figures of speech a rhetorician might use (antithesis, metaphor, onomatopoeia, etc.). Seneca, who was strongly influenced by this rhetorical tradition, showed particular concern for style, as indicated by his *Letters*.

In the *Letters* Seneca's style is succinct and expressed in everyday language. Often he adopts a chatty, informal tone, whether the topic is crowds (Letter 7) or the attributes of the soul (Letter 113). Despite their casual style, the letters always employ rhetorical devices—sententia (epigrams), anaphora (repeating the same word at the beginning of a succeeding phrase or sentence), and repetitions of the same thought in seemingly endless variations. Seneca also worked tirelessly on the rhythms of Latin prose. These devices come together in Letter 12, on old age, and in Letter 34, when Seneca praises Lucilius for learning his lessons on life well:

> Fruits are most welcome when almost over; youth is most charming at its close; the last drink delights the toper—the glass which souses him and puts the finishing touch on his drunkenness.
> (Letter 12, p. 67)

> If the farmer is pleased when his tree develops so that it bears fruit, if the shepherd takes pleasure in the increase of his flocks, if every man regards his pupil as though he discerned in him his early manhood,—what, then, do you think are the feelings of those who have trained a mind and moulded a young idea, when they see it suddenly grown to maturity?
> (Letter 34, p. 242)

Both examples include an odd juxtaposition of several epigrams that reveal the same thoughts but use different images. In the first example, the epigrams are joined through parallel structure; the second example joins them by the repetition of *if*. What is not apparent in either example is Seneca's care with prose rhythms and cadences: "It was characteristic of Greek and Latin formal prose to be self-consciously rhythmical, and the effective use of prose-rhythm was seriously discussed by rhetorical theorists" (Costa in Seneca, *17 Letters*, p. 4). Because Seneca and other Silver Age (14-180 BCE) writers stressed style and rhythm so much, their work has been criticized both by their contemporaries and later critics as sacrificing substance to form.

Sources. The *Letters* are really a continuation of a classical tradition of introspection and meditation on the meaning of life. Plato, in his ***Apology*** (also in *Classical Literature and Its Times*), has Socrates tell the Athenian jury at his trial, "The unexamined life is not worth living" (Plato, pp. 71-72). Many sages after Socrates spoke and wrote about the profound importance of this concept. In the final analysis, the subject of Seneca's *Letters* is living with heightened awareness.

There is very little that is new in Seneca, but he gives existing ideas brilliant shape. For example, he certainly did not originate the Golden Rule (treat others as you would have them treat you in the same situation); however, he states a similar rule in his letters in elegant fashion. An eclectic work, the *Letters* borrows from Homer, Virgil, Epicurus, and other thinkers known to educated Romans. Consequently the *Letters* contain much that Seneca's fellow Romans would have found familiar; his great talent is to state the familiar in stunning language.

The epistolary sequence, the form of a series of letters, was not new to the Romans: there was already an existing tradition in the genre. Many people had written and published such a sequence, most notably Cicero (*Letters to Atticus* and others) and Horace (verse epistles). Demetrius even discussed it as an important form in his *On Style*. However, Seneca's series was unusual. Many cite his *Letters* as the beginning of a new form—the literary essay—because his sequence was different from any that had preceded it. Other epistolary sequences were either formal and serious, or they were informal but mundane. Seneca's *Letters* broke new ground by being informal yet full of meditative speculation, by exploring one serious subject or another in a conversational tone. This new form of literary essay was an important genre for future writers such as Michel Montaigne of France and Francis Bacon of England. Beginning with Bacon, many essayists have proclaimed their indebtedness to Seneca's *Letters*.

Reception and impact. Seneca was often criticized by people in his own and in later ages. They complained about his style and his life. In the first instance, the criticism centers on his seeming emphasis on form over substance. Caligula, for example, faulted his work for not being sufficiently unified and denounced him as a "mere textbook orator" (Caligula in Suetonius, p. 180). Quintilian, a teacher of rhetoric, took Seneca to task for trying too hard for epigrammatic brevity. Ever since these early reviews, critics have continued to discuss the relationship between form and content in Seneca's writings.

In attacking Seneca the man, critics of his own era focused on the disparity between what he espoused and how he himself lived. Seneca was tutor and advisor to one of the most immoral and depraved of Roman emperors—Nero. For his critics, this relationship tainted him. Furthermore, while Seneca preached that wealth was immaterial and one's station in life did not matter, his critics pointed out that he was the equivalent of a millionaire and lent money to others for a profit. They cited his vast estates, his income from vineyards, and his beautiful gardens superior to the emperor's as evidence that he was a hypocrite. Such criticisms have dogged his work to this day.

But other more approving voices have countered these critics by focusing on his works. What does it matter, they say, if Seneca was rich or curried favor with Nero? The important Seneca is the persona created in the *Letters*, a man who is mortal and vulnerable like the rest of us, who makes mistakes daily but wrestles with life to become a better man and live honorably. Herein lies Seneca's achievement and the importance of his *Moral Letters*.

—Larry S. Ferrario

For More Information

Adkins, Lesley, and Roy A. Adkins. *Handbook to Life in Ancient Rome*. New York: Facts on File, 1994.

Africa, Thomas W. *Rome of the Caesars*. New York: John Wiley, 1965.

Grant, Michael. *The World of Rome*. Cleveland: World Publishing, 1960.

Hoderich, Ted, ed. *The Oxford Companion to Philosophy*. New York: Oxford University Press, 1995.

Motto, Anna Lydia. *Seneca*. New York: Twayne, 1973.

————. *Seneca: Moral Epistles*. Chico, Calif.: Scholars Press, 1985.

Plato. *The Last Days of Socrates*. London: Penguin, 1980.

Seneca, Lucius Anneaeus. *Ad Lucilium Epistulae Morales* [Moral Letters to Lucilius]. 3 vols. Trans. Richard M. Gummere. London: William Heinemann, 1961.

————. *Letters from a Stoic*. Trans. Robin Campbell. Harmondsworth: Penguin, 1987.

————. *Moral Essays*. Vol. 2. Trans. John W. Basore. London: William Heinemann, 1958.

————. *17 Letters*. Trans. C. D. N. Costa. England: Aris & Phillips, 1988.

Sorenson, Villy. *Seneca: The Humanist at the Court of Nero*. Trans. W. Glyn Jons. Chicago: University of Chicago Press, 1984.

Suetonius. *The Twelve Caesars*. Trans. Robert Graves. New York: Penguin, 1989.

Tacitus. *The Annals of Imperial Rome*. Trans. Michael Grant. Baltimore: Penguin, 1966.

Odes

by
Horace

THE LITERARY WORK

A collection of poems in Latin that Horace arranged into books; three books (88 odes) published together as a group around 23 BCE, followed by a fourth book (15 odes) published around 13 BCE.

SYNOPSIS

The *Odes* deals with a range of topics, from a lover's difficulties in his relationships, through the local natural environment of central Italy, to subtle commentary about public issues and the fate of Rome in a sensitive, post-conflict period of the empire's history.

Born in 65 BCE to a modestly prosperous family, Quintus Horatius Flaccus, known to us as Horace, grew up during one of the most volatile eras in Rome's history and his own background reflected this. Horace's father, from the town of Venusia in the region of Apulia in southern Italy, had been enslaved for part of his life. Once freed, he achieved a reasonable level of prosperity as a businessman and thus gave his son a superior education at one of the better schools in Rome. Horace went to study at Athens as a young man, where he was recruited into the army of Brutus and Cassius, the assassins of Julius Caesar in 44 BCE. Surviving the defeat of the Republican cause at Philippi in 42 BCE, Horace returned to Rome where he obtained an administrative job and began to write poetry. The Roman poet Virgil, a near contemporary (he was five years older than Horace), introduced him to Maecenas, a wealthy aristocrat of Etruscan descent who already was an intimate political adviser to Octavian, the adopted son of Julius Caesar who would later become the emperor Augustus. Maecenas became Horace's friend and patron for 30 years, and through him, Horace was granted a country estate known as the Sabine Farm, about 30 miles outside Rome, where he lived and wrote for the rest of his life. Horace died in 8 BCE, leaving behind poetic works (the *Odes, Satires, Epodes, Epistles,* and *Art of Poetry*) that have influenced writers down to the present day. In Ode 11 of book 1, Horace coined one of his most famous lines—*carpe diem* ("seize the day"). Still well known after 2,000 years, the

expression is one of the finest examples of Horace's ability to craft a memorable phrase that is both elegantly appropriate in its poetic context and a clear echo of his common-sense philosophy. The *Odes* reveals a master poet who took the styles and traditions of Greek poetry to a new level in Latin literature, in the form of a subtle integration of the private and the public man.

Events in History at the Time of the Poems

From Republic to Empire. From the middle of the second century BCE the Roman Republic began to show signs of strain. The growth of Rome's foreign territories, the substantial deployments of major legions in far distant lands, and the ever increasing ambitions of military generals contending for political supremacy in Rome all contributed to this effect. By the time Horace was born (65 BCE) the battle for power had engulfed at least two generations of Romans. Vying for control were men such as Sulla, Marius, Pompey, Crassus, and Julius Caesar in struggles that had pitched Roman armies against each other across the Mediterranean world. In 44 BCE, shortly after being proclaimed dictator for life (*perpetuo*), Julius Caesar

---

FROM HORACE'S *ODES*—"SEIZE THE DAY"

Ask not . . . what end
the gods have allotted either to me or to you.
Nor consult the Babylonian tables. How much better
to patiently endure whatever comes . . .

. . . .

Even as we speak, envious Time is fleeting.
Seize the day: entrusting as little as possible to tomorrow.
(Horace, *Complete Odes*, book 1, Ode 11)

---

was assassinated. The political structure of Rome, it seems, was too unstable to guarantee anyone's future, even Caesar's.

Around this time, Horace, a young man of 20, traveled to Athens to study. The political domination of Greece by Rome was now more than a century old, but Athenians and other Greeks believed themselves to have cultural superiority over the Romans. This assumption provoked little opposition from Romans themselves—in fact, they largely agreed with it. In Rome itself, the fashion was for Greek-style decoration, design, and cultural models. The Greek cities of the eastern Mediterranean, especially Alexandria with its literary culture and Athens with its philosophical schools (including the Academy founded by Plato three centuries earlier), enjoyed high reputations. But though Athens was far from Rome (and Horace was there to study), Roman politics wielded a significant influence, especially on the young men of the city. When the assassins of Julius Caesar fled to Athens to find support for their efforts to restore the Republic, Horace was recruited into the army of Brutus and Cassius as a military tribune.

One of the rising stars in Roman political life was Octavian, a young military commander who

was a grandnephew and an adopted son of Julius Caesar. He proved to be calculating, ruthless, and sensitive to political dynamics. The so-called "Second Triumvirate"—a ruling coalition of three men including Octavian, Mark Antony, and Lepidus (who had been one of Caesar's lieutenants)—systemically murdered their political opponents, killing 300 senators as well as many others. Octavian determined that his most important objective was to neutralize Brutus and Cassius, the assassins of Caesar. To this end, he engineered, in alliance with Mark Antony, the defeat of the assassins' forces at the Battle of Philippi (42 BCE). Horace, an officer on the losing side, managed to survive the battlefield. He later joked in one of his odes that he threw away his shield and fled—an incident evocative of literary associations (the Greek poet Archilochus had made a similar assertion) rather than a statement of historical fact. The final defeat of Brutus and Cassius exposed the fragile alliance of the Second Triumvirate. Lepidus tried too late to turn himself into a more powerful presence by claiming authority over Sicily, but his troops deserted him, and he was disarmed. He escaped with his life intact, but lost his triumviral powers. After Lepidus's disgrace and failed conspiracy, rule of the empire became a struggle for power between two men, Octavian in Rome and Mark Antony in the East. In 41 BCE Antony attempted to control the empire from the eastern provinces by way of an alliance with Egypt and his marriage—he ultimately divorced his Roman wife—to Cleopatra, heiress to the Egyptian crown. The situation in Rome continued to be one of uncertainty and dread as society seemed once more to be held hostage to the power struggles of the military elite. In 31 BCE, the situation was resolved when Octavian's forces defeated Mark Antony's at the sea battle of Actium. One year later in Alexandria, Egypt, Antony and Cleopatra committed suicide. Their deaths left Octavian with no serious opponents. He returned to Rome and confronted the Senate with a new and radical state of affairs: no longer was a cluster of powerful military and political leaders at loggerheads, leading to waves of war, peace, and then war again; now, an undisputed victor had emerged. In subsequent years, Octavian endeavored to establish his supreme position according to traditional Republican models and political offices. In 27 BCE he formally accepted his powers from the Senate and took the name and title Augustus (most "revered" or "hallowed" one). He was, however, circumspect about displaying his new status and authority. Despite his unchallenged power, he made several strategic concessions to Rome's constitutional past and insisted that he was less an absolute ruler than *princeps* ("first citizen"), a title he adopted to show that he respected the rights of other Roman institutions and the tradition of senatorial power. However Augustus sought to represent or define the nature of his regime, Rome breathed a collective sigh of relief that the decades of turmoil and vicious, inconclusive struggle were finally over.

Patronage and poetry. The Rome that Horace had returned to in 42 BCE was one dominated by a new power structure—the uneasy 10-year joint rule of Mark Antony and Octavian. Patronage was still the key to social and professional security, and now the chain of favor and counter-favor went up a longer hierarchical ladder, ending with whoever headed the empire at that moment. To call this patronage corruption would not be accurate; it was closer to the tribal and clan loyalty structures still operative in areas of the world today.

Patronage was part of an aristocratic view of the world, a view that was linked to concepts of loyalty, duty, and reciprocal responsibility. Clients rendered services to a patron, someone higher up on the social scale. They, for example, voted for the patron, accompanied him each morning to the forum (the social and business center), or immortalized him in verse perhaps. In exchange, the patron provided clients with loans and free legal assistance or used his influence to help them secure a job, a plot of land, or some other asset.

In the Rome of Horace's day, the friendship and support of a senator, consul, or respected public figure could be of great use to a young man in any kind of career. For Horace, that was the kind of patronage he received from Virgil (an older and better connected fellow poet), from Maecenas (as noted, a close political adviser to Augustus), and even from Augustus himself. These types of patronage differed from one another, but all showed a willingness to support the creative artist, who in return dedicated some of his creative effort to promoting the social order or the patron, which is what made it possible for the support to be granted at all. Rome's most famous literary patron, Maecenas was actually patron to an entire literary circle, which included both Horace and Virgil. The two poets returned the favor by celebrating the political and social accomplishments of Augustus's regime in their verses. However, praise of the social order—in book 4 of Horace's *Odes,* for example—was not timid subservience to power. It

Horace. © Getty Images (formerly Archive Photos, Inc.).

could be, as in Horace's case, an opportunity for a poet to contemplate the social order, to consider (and indicate through poetry) the double-edged requirements of a strong state—strictness and generosity, politics and culture, prosperity and recognition of where the reach of prosperity ends. The poet could remind readers of harsh realities that entered into these requirements. Built into his role for a patron was a capacity to remind the patron of the nature of war, the meaning of loss and injury, the persistence of disappointment in political and personal affairs, and the certainty of impending death. The task for such a writer/social commentator was to achieve a balance between critique and celebration in an often dangerous political environment. Horace and his poet-colleagues had to be cautious in their use of historical and mythological allusions and poetic motifs.

Love, etc. The sexual structure of Roman society was in many ways divided. There was a great deal of power and respectability located in the family, which was very authoritarian and rigid, especially during the Republic, but that did not necessarily mean that its members were happy or emotionally fulfilled. Indeed, the amount of authority invested in the *paterfamilias*, the father, meant that a lot of tensions—emotional, social, sexual—could build up, and the more influential the family the nastier it could get. If the family was close to the political and military power struggles, violence within the family circle could transpire, as in Julius Caesar's case, when he was supplanted by his grandnephew Octavian.

Contracted to produce children and consolidate or improve family fortune, Roman marriages were generally arranged by family members, with little say given to the bride or groom when it came to selecting a marriage partner. Consequently marriages often lacked emotional depth or satisfaction, leaving women to fixate on other dimensions of family life, and many men and some women to seek sexual fulfillment elsewhere. Sexual morality was a matter of prudence, of being careful in one's selection of a sexual partner, rather than a matter of moral principle. For a man from the aristocratic class to have an affair with a woman of similar status could create personal problems for both, though such relationships did sometimes occur. It was safer for a man to have a liaison with a woman of a lower class who benefited materially. Forced sex with (male or female) house servants and the like was common, given that slaves were considered property.

In sexual relationships between men or between a man and a woman—the two types discussed in ancient literature—the same rules applied: prudence was valued; the social order should not be endangered by public misbehavior; family values should at least be outwardly maintained to guarantee the political stability of Roman society.

Within this context, poets and other writers kept up a vital tradition of love poetry and erotic allusion. The tradition of love poetry in Rome, as in ancient Greek society, is marked by two important factors: 1) the poems are as often about the irritating problems of human affections as about romantic celebration, and 2) the social context of the relationship (either existing or hoped-for) between the lovers could be as important as the feelings that the poet is expressing.

The Poems in Focus

Contents summary. The *Odes* of Horace comprise a total of 103 poems, 88 in books 1 to 3 (sometimes known as the *Carmina*, from the Latin word *carmen*, meaning "song") and 15 poems in the later book 4. The subjects range from the poet's thoughts on love, to his relationships and desires, to politics in Rome under Augustus, to human existence and the roles of various

deities, and finally to aspects of everyday life in his rural villa. Several poems are dedicated to Horace's close friend and patron, Maecenas. Others are dedicated to Caesar Augustus. Horace uses the ode, a long lyric poem of a serious nature written in calm, thoughtful, everyday language, to rove across many images and topics, often ending at a point unanticipated by the opening of the poem.

The public poems. The first book of Horace's *Odes* opens with a public dedication to his patron Maecenas, whose influence has brought Horace an ideal environment—his beloved farm—and the leisure to write. The poem also manages to tell us much about Horace himself. He describes the various manifestations of glory and success, from those of the Olympic winners "arriving at the goal / with wheels aflame and the noble palm of victory" (*Complete Odes*, 1.1) to those of farmers, hunters, and soldiers. The poetic speaker then says "Place me, then, among the lyric poets / with my head in the heavens; I shall touch the stars" (*Complete Odes*, 1.1). By suggesting that he, Horace, is destined for longer-lasting glory and immortality as a poet, he implicitly praises Maecenas for his good judgment in becoming his patron.

Later in the penultimate ode of book 1, Horace turns to the suicide of Cleopatra. Like other Romans, he was both repelled and fascinated by the Egyptian queen. She exuded a blend of feminine subtlety and political ambition that made her a dangerous presence. Yet for a time, she threatened to become a Roman power, along with her consort and ally, Mark Antony. On the heels of their crushing defeat at Actium (31 BCE) and their suicides in Egypt a year later, Horace composed a rich and complex ode (1.37) that shifts from an exuberant jubilation to thoughtful admiration, from a public celebration in Rome to a private act in Alexandria.

The ode begins with a double literary allusion. Horace's opening cry, "Now we must drink," translates the first words of a poem by the sixth-century BCE Greek poet, Alcaeus, one of Horace's favorite lyric models. But the initial word "Now" also looks back to one of Horace's own epodes, which he composed shortly after the battle at Actium, when Antony and Cleopatra escaped and the outcome was still unclear. (Horace began his career with 17 epodes, brief poems written in a bold, forceful tone and usually in couplets whose second line was shorter than the first.) Epode 9, the one being recalled, starts with a question to Maecenas, "When shall I drink the Caecuban wine with you?" The epode closes on a note of anxiety and uncertainty. But by the later Cleopatra ode, Antony and Cleopatra are dead, the threat has been eliminated, and this earlier question can be answered triumphantly, with a resounding call to celebrate. In earlier days, explains the poet,

> it would have been wrong to bring forth
> our Caecuban wine from the cellars of
> our ancestors, while a demented
> queen
> was plotting to destroy the
> capitol.
> (*Complete Odes*, 1.37)

The poem celebrates—exults in, even—the defeat and death of the Egyptian queen, but then unexpectedly adjusts its tone, portraying her as a complex personality, who in the end does not quake with fear, flee in cowardice, or allow herself to be paraded in ignominy down the streets of Rome as a war trophy. Rather she nobly, courageously, as portrayed by the poem, takes her fate into her own hands. She grows fiercer as she faces death, bravely surveying the ruins of her palace, boldly grasping the poisonous snakes and bringing them to her breast to fell herself with their dark venom. "So in premeditated death / fiercer yet she became, / Scorning to be led off in triumph [the victory procession of a Roman general] . . . / She, no longer a queen / but a woman unyielding, unhumbled" (*Complete Odes*, 1.37). First spotlighting Cleopatra as a public figure, the ode ends on not the queen but the private woman, who gains her own triumph through suicide. The ode takes a much-hated figure and celebrates her act of defiance, revealing the attitude of the poet to be as complex as his subject.

In Ode 1 of the second book, a poem addressed to Gaius Asinius Pollio, who was undertaking to write a history of the recent civil wars, Horace expresses a thought that occupied, perhaps even haunted, him: the meaning of the wars and struggle for power within a ruling family that plagued Rome for several generations. Pollio, who had been a close ally and friend of Julius Caesar and later Mark Antony, was also a well-known literary figure in Rome, who gave the city its first public library. Horace begins on an ominous note:

> The civil discord that began during the
> consulship
> of Metellus; the causes, the blunders, the
> phases

of those wars; the play of fortune;
of alliances of leaders boding ill.
> (*Complete Odes*, 2.1)

The poet implies that Pollio is in some personal danger due to the sensitive themes he touches on in his history. He, like Horace, fought on the side of the losers, and here he alerts his friend to take heed, as he himself does. Horace meditates on war and violence, forces that he is afraid might be too powerful to contain. He asks later in the poem, "What field is not fertilized with Latin blood? . . .

HORACE AND THE UNEXPECTED

Unexpected changes occur within Horace's poems. A casual evocation of everyday experience can give way immediately to a philosophical observation, after which the gods of Roman mythology make an appearance, or perhaps the shades of Horace's Greek poetic forbears. Ode 13 of book 2, for example, opens with the poet directing his hostility toward a tree on his farm that has nearly fallen on him: "Whoever first planted you, o tree, surely / did so on an ill-omened day, / and with a sacrilegious hand / reared you up for the destruction of posterity / and the shame of this village" (*Complete Odes*, 2.13). This leads the speaker into a meditation on the peculiar nature of fear, the fact that, so often, people fear the wrong thing or do not realize that others suffer the same fears; the speaker moves to the misdirected fears of sailors and the unknown fates that lurk ahead of them. Finally the poem takes a turn into the realm of death and the afterlife, as Horace realizes he has narrowly escaped a final trip to the underworld, where the spirits of Alcaeus and Sappho, two Greek poets of an earlier age, recite their songs. With this, the poem returns full circle to Horace's initial anger at the evil-intentioned tree, and recommends calming down and thinking about the big picture: nothing happened to hurt anyone.

---

what beach is not bathed in our blood?" (*Complete Odes*, 2.1). The poem refers to two muses, or goddesses of intellectual and artistic pursuits, the first being Clio, the stern, tragic muse of history. In conclusion, the poet invokes his own muse, Euterpe, the muse of lyric poetry, encouraging her to avoid such martial, political themes.

The ode begins as a public, political poem but, as Horace's work often does, retreats from that arena at the end. The respect for Pollio and his historical writing is genuine, but at the close

Horace asserts other literary values, those of his own poetry. Moreover, the assertion is not made apologetically, but rather almost forcefully. There is a deliberate shift here from the public discourse of history to the more individual voice of poetry.

A similar movement occurs among the so-called Roman Odes in book 3 (Odes 1-6). Addressed to Caesar Augustus, one of these odes (Ode 3.3) is a wide-ranging set of verses that invokes the image of a just ruler (Augustus) who resists the shallow desires of the mob and thus achieves immortal status. Augustus is seen in immortal company, which includes the goddess Juno, who describes her fury at the city of Troy, destroyed several centuries earlier and memorialized in Homer's ***Iliad*** (also in *Classical Literature and Its Times*):

> And so long as a wide ocean
> Fiercely divides Troy and Rome,
>   let the exiles reign in happiness
> Wheresoever they may please
>
> . . . .
>
>   And resplendently
> the Capitol shall stand, and warlike Rome
> dictate terms to the vanquished.
>   (*Complete Odes*, 3.3)

The poem argues for a connection between the ruins of Troy and the power of Rome hundreds of years later. The image of a mistaken attempt, on the part of Roman armies, to rebuild Troy dominates the later part of the poem, and seems to be a projection of a fear on the poet's part: that Rome will also become no more than ruins one day. At the end of the poem, Horace once again chides himself for allowing his muse to be carried away by themes that are inappropriately dramatic or political. To invoke the gods, says Horace, to engage in prophecy—such tasks are not well suited to his poetic talents.

Poems of love and everyday life. As noted, in Roman love poetry, the social context of a love relationship (either existing or hoped-for) could be as important as the feelings expressed. This is well illustrated by Ode 23 of book 1, in which the poet appeals to an unduly coy and reticent young woman named Chloë. He first reassures her that she has no need to fear him—he is not a wild animal—then finishes on a different note from the standard lover's pursuit:

> Stop clinging to your mother.
>   You have reached marriageable age:
>   the proper age:
>   the time for love.
>   (*Complete Odes*, 1.23)

The poet is not so enamored of the young woman that he is going to waste his time. His close reveals an impatience, a brusqueness almost; now the coyness and reticence he dealt with gently at the outset are condemned as socially inappropriate. Chloë is the beloved, but she needs to start acting like a young woman on the marriage market, not like a girl in a love story, desired by all. The force of the last stanza of the ode almost makes it an anti-love poem: as discussed above, in Rome social stability counts for more than sexual attraction, and Chloë needs to understand this.

Horace was a local patriot when it came to the produce of rural Italy. One of many odes that mention the everyday enjoyment of food and drink is Ode 27 of book 1, addressed to Horace's guests at dinner. He begins by disapproving of some primitive habits:

> Hurling wine cups made for joyous use
> is only fit for Thracians. Away with
>   that barbaric custom! Let us keep our
>   modest
> Bacchus far from all such bloody
>   quarrels.
>   (*Complete Odes*, 1.27)

Treating wine badly is not permitted in Horace's company. Wine is often a central image in the *Odes*, representing hospitality, as in Ode 29 of book 3, in which Horace announces that all is prepared for Maecenas's visit.

> Maecenas, descendant of Etruscan kings,
> an amphora of mellow wine not yet poured
>   has been waiting for you at my house
>   along with roses and balsam distilled
> for your hair. Delay no more!
>   (*Complete Odes*, 3.29)

The offerings of the host are not luxurious, but they are locally produced, thoughtful, and exactly what the exhausted guest will need. The poem reflects a familiar type of dinner invitation. In fact, such poetic dinner invitations were so common in Rome, notes one scholar, they became "a minor literary genre" (Shelton, p. 80).

Wine is, for Horace, also a diplomatic tool, helping to resolve disputes and produce a mellow atmosphere. Civilized gatherings make it possible to leave behind the strains and pressures of public life. Along with such gatherings, short vacations, often in villas outside the city, provided escapes for the Roman establishment. The Sabine Farm was just such a retreat for Horace, a place of natural grace, full of sunlight, trees, and vines, and an attractive setting for many of his poems of everyday life. In the concluding

The Meeting of Anthony and Cleopatra, 41 B.C., by Sir Lawrence Alma-Tadema, 1883. © Christie's Images/Corbis

poem of book 1, for example, Horace expresses a willingness to accept the ordinary, the non-special. The key motif in the poem is an instruction to his servant boy to stop straining himself to put together a garland from some difficult-to-find late summer rose: "Simple myrtle / is sufficient. I care not that you anxiously / add more" (*Complete Odes*, 1.38). In what one could read as a mature judgment by Horace on living and writing poetry, as well as advice for a young servant, to "anxiously add more," as far as he is concerned, can be as bad as adding nothing at all.

Roman attitudes to Cleopatra. The first century BCE was wracked by Roman civil wars (88-82 BCE, 49-45 BCE, and 44-30 BCE). With the resolution of these wars came the transition from republican to imperial rule, and relief from years of strife. For many Romans, the empire's new ruler, Caesar Augustus, stood for stability and order. It was a reputation he had gained by defeating some formidable enemies, including Antony and Antony's political and romantic ally, the Egyptian ruler of the Ptolemaic dynasty Cleopatra VII, whose figure towers over the late first century BCE.

This was not the only time that the Egyptian queen had played a major role in Roman affairs. A few years before, in her early twenties, while sitting on an insecure Egyptian throne, Cleopa-

tra became Julius Caesar's lover. Caesar found in her a useful, wealthy, and attractive ally in his ambitions to lead a military campaign in the East and to avenge an earlier Roman defeat at the hands of the Parthians. Shortly after he left Egypt, Cleopatra bore a son, whose paternity she publicly proclaimed by the name Caesarion ("Little Caesar"). Caesar himself never acknowledged the child, although he invited Cleopatra and her son to Rome. It was after Caesar's assassination in 44 BCE that Cleopatra allied herself to Mark Antony, selecting him as her new road to power. Together they strove to rule Rome, but the attempt led only to their own suicides.

Cleopatra was vilified by the poets of Rome and by its society in general. She was the daughter of the Egyptian king (Ptolemy XII), part of a family that was of Macedonian Greek descent and that had ruled Egypt since the death of Alexander the Great in the late fourth century BCE. Cleopatra shrewdly engaged in relationships with great Roman generals to her benefit, gaining territory (Crete, Cyprus, Palestine) from them in exchange for her financial aid to them. She became the first ruler in her line to speak the native language of the Egyptians, which may have had much to do with her success in Egypt. Winning the support of the Egyptians, Cleopatra developed an image among them as loving mother of her country. But in Rome, where she was hated, she attained a contrary image as the "whore queen," an unnaturally militant woman, given to drunkenness, immoral liaisons, and the abuse of political power (Wyke, p. 207). The Romans, their writers included, saw her as nothing short of a monstrosity, a mannish woman who unmanned her lovers (Wyke, p. 227). Using the Eastern image of royal luxury against her, Rome pictured her as wholly wicked. But her suicide interfered. Normally after a conquest, a Roman general jubilantly led the enemy and the enemy's children in triumphant procession through Rome. But Cleopatra's suicide, by the poisonous bite of the asp, say the ancient accounts, denied Augustus that pleasure. Defiantly, by her manner of death, Cleopatra reclaimed her dignity and authority—a perspective that countered the stereotype and that Horace's ode manages to convey.

In the ode, Horace reveals an ability to consider an imperial event in personal as well as historical terms. To make her defeat the central topic of an ode is very close to centering it on Cleopatra herself. The poet realizes that Rome has been both afraid of and fascinated by Cleopatra's ability to draw two leading Roman generals into a personal and political alliance just a few years apart. Her ambitions and conquests made her a disconcerting mix of sexual adventuress and political demagogue to the Romans, an image that was probably augmented by her suicide. As Horace's ode suggests, the way Cleopatra died must have only enhanced the romance and mystery surrounding her.

Behind the Roman understanding or misunderstanding of Cleopatra lay a cultural clash between a Roman worldview that vested political and social authority in its males and the Egyptian tradition of "empowering royal women" to some degree (Wyke, p. 201). Rome's male-only approach clashed with the possibility of female rule in Egypt (though the female always ruled in tandem with a male), a practice that seemed irrational and primitive to Romans of the day. Associated with the Greeks and the Egyptians, Cleopatra was maligned and hated as a foreigner. Horace's ode capitalizes on these attitudes, portraying her as a monster at the start but then transforming her into something quite different as she chooses suicide over the indignity of being paraded through Rome in defeat. In the ode, her final act appears worthy of the noble Roman, not a woman or a foreigner. How much this poem contributed to Rome's fascination with Cleopatra, or to the legendary figure she became is unknown. But certainly Ho-

race's multisided look at her death fits with the mystery that surrounds her. In the end, the true character of the young queen remains elusive; and the question of whether Caesar and Antony used her in their bid for power or whether it happened more the other way around will likely never be completely resolved.

Sources and literary context. The term "ode" comes from the Greek word for song, *aoidē*. It is sometimes described as a lyric poem in stanza form. Originally the ode was meant for performance by a chorus and began as a commissioned work composed in praise of some person or event. This is the key element in the so-called Pindaric odes, the poems credited to the Greek poet Pindar (522-448? BCE). The word was brought by the Roman writers into Latin poetry and was disseminated over the centuries into many European languages in an almost unchanged form.

Pindar wrote poems on commission to honor aristocratic leaders and to extol the winners at the various Greek sporting festivals, the Olympic Games among them. The development of the ode in Greece was also marked by a different kind of poem, a more personal meditation on love and individual feeling. This second form was identified with the female poet Sappho, whose *Poems* survive mostly in fragments (also in *Classical Literature and Its Times*). Sappho also invented for lyric poetry a new stanzaic form, consisting of 3 lines of 11 syllables followed by a fourth and final line of 5 syllables. Fittingly, this form became known as the Sapphic stanza. Together, these two models, that of Pindar and that of Sappho, established a dual tradition in the history of the ode—public and private—that Horace inherited and developed.

Horace was conscious of the double-edged nature of the ode. For him, it was an original and personal poem, but one that needed an object or addressee. It dealt with actual relationships rather than just inner feelings, politics and the dynamics of leadership in Roman society, and the poet's real-world surroundings.

Horace's collection of odes is remarkable for its diversity of ancient meters. In fact, the first nine poems of book 1 each display a different Greek meter adapted to Latin verse. Among his favorite meters are those that he borrowed from the Greek lyric poets Sappho and Alcaeus, who composed their various poems in stanzas (four lines in a fixed scheme of short and long syllables).

In subject matter several of Horace's most famous poems resemble the large-scale, public odes of Pindar, as in the second ode of book 1,

ARS POETICA

~

Horace is the author of one of the most famous and influential critical works in Western civilization, *Ars Poetica*, or *The Art of Poetry*. In this long essay, probably written late in his life, Horace lists many of the traps and faults that the aspiring writer should avoid at all costs and declares that training and skill must complement inspiration if the poet is going to do any good work at all.

Horace was especially dismissive of people who think that poetry will come to them simply because they have feelings, as if nothing else were needed. People who are not good at sports, or at playing music, normally stay out of the ballpark or avoid playing an instrument in public, but "the man who knows nothing about poetry has the audacity to write it" (Horace in *Classical Literary Criticism*, p. 109).

which closes with a prayer to the god Mercury, who, Horace exclaims in the ode, has assumed the guise of the young Caesar on earth:

> O may you return as late as possible to the
>   skies,
> and joyously remain among the people of
>   Quirinus [a state god],
> though Roman vices anger you, may you never
>   in an untimely blast
> be borne away. Here rather amidst your great
>   triumphs,
> here may you choose to be called Father and
>   Prince
> nor permit the Medes to raid us with impunity,
>   You, Leader, Caesar.
>   (*Complete Odes*, 1.2)

The devotion to Augustus is here both a matter of the public good—the preservation of Italy and the empire from attack by the outside world (represented by the Medes, a people related the Persians)—and a personal statement of affection and respect.

The Greek culture and poetic tradition that Horace picked up during his student days in Athens became a vital part of his literary work. The style of such writers as Sappho, Pindar, and Alcaeus appealed to him both for the mixture of public and private concerns, and for the way in which the "real world" can step aside to reveal the world of mythology and legend.

Reception and impact. Beyond realizing his own personal vision of the poetic art, Horace's work was produced partly, as we know, for the pleasure of his friend and patron Maecenas, and at times Caesar Augustus. No doubt other readers were also important to Horace, particularly

fellow writers like the highly regarded Virgil. However, we have little evidence of how his odes were generally received beyond the Roman establishment, although his ability to generate slogan-like phrases and lines might well have given him a reputation among ordinary Romans who would otherwise have had limited taste for his writings. To take one example, the persistence of the famous line in Ode 2, book 3 ("dulce et decorum est pro patria mori," or "it is sweet and appropriate to die for one's country" (*Complete Odes*, 3.2) suggests a certain level of popularity, as inscriptions of this epigraph have turned up on Roman funerary architecture. Horace himself claims in his later poetry that his odes did not achieve the acclaim he desired. It may be a telling confirmation of this claim that the elegy writers of the day (Ovid, for example) made no mention of Horace, but then neither did he mention them.

Horace's modern reception is much easier to document. He was rediscovered during the Renaissance, and his poetry became a model for aspiring verse-makers, especially in England, where there was a strong interest in exploring the ode—as conceived by both Pindar and Horace. The interweaving of personal and public issues was an attractive dimension of the ode as a poetic genre, particularly for writers in situations such as that in which Horace found himself: a volatile but exciting era with both dangers and promise.

One of the most expert and powerful examples of the English ode is Andrew Marvell's 1651 poem "Horatian Ode on Cromwell's Return from Ireland." In this text, the poet is both an admirer of, and somewhat intimidated by, Oliver Cromwell, the leader of the English Puritan revolution. The poem is about Cromwell at the moment of his return to England from Ireland after having crushed the Catholic, royalist rebellion there. Marvell's attitude to Cromwell, who overthrew the Stuart monarchy and had the king executed, matches that of Horace's to Augustus: a fear-inspiring military leader who just might be the right man to make sure that the national community survives intact into the future.

The Romantic poet John Keats was the major English practitioner of the ode in the early nineteenth century. He conceived "Ode to a Nightingale," "Ode on a Grecian Urn," "Ode to Psyche," and others, all over a nine-month period in 1819. Although neither Keats nor Marvell were part of a culture in which poets were regularly commissioned by individuals to write odes celebrating or memorializing people or events, it is clear from Keats's titles that something of that older dynamic haunts the modern ode.

In the twentieth century, there have been several famous odes in English and American poetry, including Allen Tate's "Ode to the Confederate Dead" and Robert Lowell's "For the Union Dead," two poems that meditate on the Civil War and its meaning for both the American nation and the poets themselves.

—Martin Griffin

For More Information

Armstrong, David. *Horace*. New Haven, Conn.: Yale University Press, 1989.

Cantor, Norman F. *Antiquity: The Civilization of the Ancient World*. New York: HarperCollins, 2003.

Classical Literary Criticism. Trans. Penelope Murray and T. S. Dorsch. London: Penguin, 2000.

Fraenkel, Eduard. *Horace*. Oxford: Clarendon Press, 1957.

Heath-Stubbs, John. *The Ode*. London: Oxford University Press, 1969.

Horace. *The Complete Odes and Satires of Horace*. Trans. Sidney Alexander. Princeton, N.J.: Princeton University Press, 1999.

Kebric, Robert B. *Roman People*. New York: McGraw-Hill, 2005.

Shelton, Jo-Ann. *As the Romans Did: A Sourcebook in Roman Social History*. New York: Oxford University Press, 1998.

Wyke, Maria. *The Roman Mistress: Ancient and Modern Representations*. New York: Oxford University Press, 2002.

Odyssey

by
Homer

Homer is one of the most romantic and most debated figures in the history of Western literature. The ancients identified him as the author of the **Iliad** as well as the *Odyssey*, two major epics of ancient Greece (also in *Classical Literature and Its Times*). Although he is popularly believed to have been a blind man who lived on the west coast of Asia Minor, scholars have questioned whether one poet composed both works and even if Homer ever existed. Today many classicists agree that the *Iliad* was indeed composed by a single male author, but whether he was a blind storyteller named Homer is another matter. While most agree that one author also composed the *Odyssey,* debate continues over whether the same man composed both epics. The author of the *Odyssey* seems to have worked from an in-depth knowledge of the *Iliad*. Without solid evidence to the contrary, most scholars fall into step with ancient Greek tradition in naming Homer the author of both epics. The more one researches the Homeric epics, the more one realizes that other details about the poems are fraught with uncertainty as well. There is little consensus among scholars regarding when Homer composed them. According to Herodotus, the Greek historian of the fifth century BCE, Homer produced the epics about 850 BCE, but most modern critics locate him between 750 and 700 BCE. In any case, there is no dispute over the wealth of oral tradition that gave rise to both epics or the importance of their impact on the Greeks and Western civilization in general. Of the two, the *Odyssey* reveals more about the domestic life, and much about the beliefs and values of some of the earliest Greeks.

LITERARY WORK

An epic poem set around 1200 BCE in the Mediterranean region; composed in Greek c. 725 BCE.

SYNOPSIS

As he wanders back from the Trojan War, Odysseus encounters a fantastic array of monsters, heroes, and gods, before encountering daunting threats at home.

Events in History at the Time of the Epic

Layers of history in the *Odyssey*. The *Odyssey* centers on prevailing Greek values, such as hospitality and the sanctity of marriage, rather than on events that transpired in a historical time period. In fact, while the events in the epic take place during the Mycenaean Age (1600-1200 BCE), the narrative details show that it actually interweaves layers of time up to the composition of the epic, from the Mycenaean Age through the Dark Age (1150-750 BCE) to the Greek Renaissance (750-700 BCE). There are seeming anachronisms in the *Odyssey* that bear witness to the centuries over which it evolved. In Homer's accounts of death, the bodies are cremated rather than buried in the beehive-shaped tombs characteristic of the Mycenaean period. Though his weapons are mostly made of bronze, many of the tools are iron, a popular metal of the later Dark

Homer. © Araldo de Luca/Corbis

ter"), followed by an army commander, then a high-status group of perhaps priests and military officers. Next came lesser officials and maybe some wealthy merchants and traders. Underneath was the mass of commoners, who lived in rural villages and labored as farmers, herders, and artisans. At the bottom toiled slaves, generally captives from foreign lands. Agamemnon is called a *wanax* in the *Odyssey*. Odysseus, whose own society seems somewhat unsophisticated, is not. If such a hierarchy existed in his land, he could be seen as the equivalent of a *wanax,* but this would demand drawing strict parallels between the legendary and real worlds, an impossible task since Homer mixes time periods.

Greek religious life appears to have depended more on the proper performance of rituals than anything else. Sacrifices, which involved the ritual slaying of an animal (generally a cow or sheep) in the name of a god, were the strongest element of worship. It is because Odysseus has sacrificed more to the gods than any other man that he wins the support of the king of the gods, Zeus, in his struggles to return home to Ithaca, a small rugged isle that the ancients identified with the land known today as Ithaca, located off the west coast of Greece in the Ionian Sea.

The late Bronze Age was a time of aggressive expansion for the Mycenaean Greeks. Fighting for territory, their top military men—their high-status warriors—rode chariots, or lightly wooded horse-drawn vehicles, to the front, then may have fought from the chariots or dismounted to do battle. Back home in their kingdoms, large walled cities dotted the landscape. The major cities had time-honored names— Mycenae, Thebes, and Pylos. Apparently they were the key dwelling places of the civilization's kings, whose palaces and citadels towered over their communities. The kings made certain that the region's food supply was secure and provided a basic framework of law and order. When they were not serving in the army or working at the palace in exchange for benefits, the men tended to their farming and their livestock. The women meanwhile spent most of their time spinning, weaving, cooking, and child rearing. A simple system of writing emerged—the Linear B script—only to disappear when the large cities were destroyed shortly after 1200 BCE. Archeologists speculate that a series of local disputes as well as climate changes and possibly earthquakes led to the fall of the cities and ushered in the Dark Age.

Age. Even Homer's own time finds its way into the story; a surge of real exploration begun shortly before the epic was composed recalls the wanderings of Odysseus.

The larger period of world history in which Mycenaean civilization thrived was the late Bronze Age, which takes its name from the metal that people used for their weapons and household tools. Much of what we know about the civilization itself comes from Linear B tablets, that is, tablets containing writing in Linear B script, a pre-alphabetic script that consists of roughly 90 signs, each of which stands for a syllable. Large numbers of Linear B tablets were discovered by archaeologists in ruins from the cities of Pylos (at the "palace of Nestor" ruins) and Knossos. The evidence indicates that Greek civilization during the late Bronze Age was highly sophisticated; kings lived in opulent palaces and commissioned artists to produce carefully wrought ceramics, mosaics, and metalwork. There existed well-built roads and a highly developed trading system linking Greece to the Near East, northern Africa, and Italy. Society at its most developed was arranged in a hierarchy. At the top stood the *wanax* (the word refers to the king, but may mean "lord" or "mas-

Backdrop of the Trojan War—Odysseus's ploy. At the time of the Trojan War, the Greeks were not a unified state but a collection of settlements. Due in large part to Homer's works, the war came to be viewed as a defining moment in Greek history. Homer's epics were performed publicly for centuries, becoming known to most inhabitants of these settlements, and developing into a standard by which all other works and values were measured.

The stories that made up the epics were not new to the Greeks. Homer's original audiences would have known the details of the Trojan War, which called Odysseus away from his native Ithaca. They would have come to the story armed with information from popular legends portraying Odysseus as a fighter in the Trojan War. From these same legends, they knew that Odysseus left the war as one of its greatest heroes, largely because of his crafty ploy of building the wooden horse, the trick that finally helped the Greeks win the painstaking ten-year war.

Legend has it that the Trojan War began with the Judgment of Paris. Insulted at not being invited to a banquet, the goddess of discord, Eris, sought to cause trouble among the gods. She threw a golden apple labeled *For the Fairest* into the banquet hall. Zeus, knowing better than to bear responsibility for deciding which of the goddesses deserved the apple, called for the decision to be made by a mortal named Paris, the prince of Troy. Paris had to choose among Aphrodite, Hera, and Athena. Each of the goddesses sought to bribe him for his favor, and Aphrodite's bribe—to reward Paris with the most beautiful mortal woman—worked. He chose Aphrodite. Now it was time for her to keep her end of the bargain. The problem was that the most beautiful woman in the world, Helen, was already married to a Greek king, Menelaus, of Sparta.

According to some accounts Paris kidnapped Helen; according to others, he seduced her. Either way, she was taken back to Troy and the enraged Menelaus assembled a huge fleet of Greek warriors, enlisting Odysseus in the effort. The Greeks initiated a ten-year siege against Troy, winning only after they enacted Odysseus's plan to trick the Trojans by building a huge wooden horse, filling its hollow belly with armed Greek warriors, and then pretending to sail away, as if defeated. The Trojans did not know what to make of this lone horse outside their walls, but they eventually dragged the horse inside the city. Under cover of night, the hidden Greeks streamed out of the horse, opened the gates for their fellow warriors (who had sailed back into the harbor), and sacked Troy. Again, all this would have been known to Homer's first audience.

In the *Odyssey* readers encounter Odysseus in the tenth year of his return voyage from Troy, that is, 20 years after leaving home. He departs from the battlegrounds of Troy with several ships still intact, but loses them all (and the men in them) during his adventurous journey home; in fact, he loses all the men on his own ship too. The *Odyssey* contains a scene in which a singer relates the story of Troy's destruction and the slaughter that took place there. Hearing the story, Odysseus weeps, perhaps over wartime memories, perhaps because he laments his long absence from home and separation from family and friends.

Monsters and gods. Greek mythology accounted for both benevolent and malevolent forces in the ancient world. By Homer's day, many of the monsters and gods within the *Odyssey* had a rich oral history that existed outside Homeric epics and, as with legends of the Trojan War, was well known to the average Greek audience. *Rhapsodes*, people who professionally recited epic poetry by Homer and others in ancient Greece, told stories involving various kinds of supernatural figures that make appearances in the *Odyssey*.

The two main gods in the *Odyssey*, Athena and Poseidon, were familiar mythological figures. Athena, goddess not only of war and wisdom but also of arts and crafts, united the traditional roles of male and female. According to myth, Athena was born from the head of Zeus, the supreme ruler of the gods, and thereafter she remained his favorite. In statues, paintings, and other renderings, Athena is frequently represented as an armed warrior. The city of Athens honored her as its protector, and she gained distinction as a goddess who often came to the aid of humans. Athena served as helpmate and mentor to various Greeks, including Odysseus, his son Telemachus, and other impressive mortals, like Perseus (who beheaded Medusa) and Bellerophon (who harnessed the winged horse Pegasus).

Poseidon, god of the sea, was thought to be Zeus's brother. Also the god of earthquakes and a tamer of horses, Poseidon could be both enemy and friend to man. It was said that he gave humans the first horse, but he was also dubbed "Earth-shaker" because of his tempestuous nature and his responsibility for earthquakes. He sided with the Greeks in the Trojan War but then developed a grudge against Odysseus, after he blinded the god's son, Polyphemus. Poseidon becomes Odysseus's primary antagonist. It is his curse that prolongs Odysseus's return and causes

In one adventure, Odysseus withstands the call of the Sirens, whose singing leads ships to destruction. Detail from mosaic tile work. © Vanni Archives/Corbis. Reproduced by permission.

such suffering. Odysseus has to somehow find his way back into the god's good graces to reach home. When the story begins, Poseidon has already cursed the hero.

The monsters in the *Odyssey* also had a rich oral history. Polyphemus is a Cyclops, a one-eyed giant who dwells with others of his kind who raise sheep and goats on a distant island (later thought of as Sicily). In Homer's epic, Polyphemus is a ruthless cannibal who traps Odysseus and his men in a cave and eats several of them alive. Later poets describe the giant falling madly in love with the sea nymph Galatea, who in some stories taunts him and in others respects him for being a son of the sea god, Poseidon. In the verse of one of these poets (Ovid), Polyphemus again behaves ruthlessly, crushing a rival for Galatea's affections with a rock. The murder does the monster little good, however; in none of the stories does he win her love.

According to Greek myth, Scylla, the horrible six-headed monster in the *Odyssey*, was once a beautiful nymph. Glaucus—a fisherman who had become half-man, half-fish—fell in love with her, but she would not have him. He appealed for help to Circe, the enchantress, who fell in love with Glaucus and wanted him for herself. Still smitten with Scylla, however, he would not

be swayed. Circe, driven by jealousy, poisoned Scylla, turning her into a monster with 12 dog-like legs, six necks topped by fierce dogs' heads, and three rows of teeth. Miserable, Scylla retreated into a cave (which tradition locates between Sicily and Italy in the Straits of Messina) and sought her revenge on passing sailors, whom she devoured, one for each of her six heads.

When sailors encounter Scylla in a narrow channel of water they must avoid a whirlpool on the opposite side created by the female sea monster Charybdis. The sailors face two equally threatening alternatives. Some scholars have theorized that Scylla and Charybdis represented actual nautical dangers: deadly countercurrents off the Strait of Messina (on the Sicilian side) may have been the inspiration for Charybdis, and Scylla may have been a huge squid of 3,000 years ago that inhabited the dangerously jagged rocks on the other side of the Strait, or perhaps she was simply the rocks themselves.

The Epic in Focus

Plot summary. Divided into 24 books, the story takes place during the tenth year of Odysseus's journey home from the Trojan War. Odysseus has been living on an island with the sea nymph,

Calypso, for most of the ten years. The delay causes tremendous despair among loved ones at home, who think Odysseus dead. At the root of the delay is Poseidon, the sea god, who is punishing Odysseus for blinding his one-eyed son, a Cyclops named Polyphemus. When the poem opens, the gods are deliberating over his fate. Poseidon, reports Zeus, wants to continue the punishment, but Athena adamantly supports this homesick warrior. Ruling in her favor, Zeus orders Calypso to send Odysseus home.

The first four books feature Telemachus, the only son of Odysseus. Now close to 20 years old, Telemachus has not seen his father since infancy. Currently he and his mother, Penelope, are suffering from an onslaught of suitors who want to wed her. Previously, in hopes of Odysseus's return, she craftily delayed them by saying she would remarry once she finished weaving a shroud for her father-in-law. She proceeded to shrewdly spend her days weaving and her nights undoing all the progress. But her deception has been discovered and the pressure to choose a new husband has grown. Since Odysseus's absence, the suitors have been feasting at Odysseus's home and otherwise abusing the family's hospitality (hospitality being one of the highest Greek values, whether serving a relative or a stranger). Into this unhappy environment comes Athena disguised as Odysseus's friend Mentes. In keeping with Greek hospitality, "Mentes" is welcomed into Odysseus's house. Disguised as this family friend, Athena directs Telemachus to leave in search of information about his father: "Come now, listen closely. Take my words to heart" (Homer, *Odyssey*, book 1, line 312). She later takes the form of Mentor, one of Odysseus's comrades in the Trojan War, and guides Telemachus as he ventures forth to seek news of his father, setting out for the homes of Nestor and Menelaus—two kings who fought with Odysseus in the Trojan War.

There is a break in the action as the narrative shifts away from Odysseus's family onto the hero himself. Book 5 centers on the hero in his current quarters. Odysseus is living with Calypso, the sea nymph, feeling miserably homesick, sitting out by the beach on a headland, "wrenching his heart with sobs and groans and anguish, / gazing out over the barren sea through blinding tears" (*Odyssey*, 5.94–95). Obeying Zeus, Calypso sends the mournful Odysseus home on a raft. Poseidon, still angry with Odysseus, causes the raft to be destroyed and Odysseus ends up with the Phaeacians, who, also in keeping with the high value placed on hospitality, invite

Odysseus to stay and dine with them even before they know his name. Odysseus recounts his entire journey up to his stay with Calypso, establishing a reputation for himself through story.

He tells of rescuing his men from the Lotus Eaters (who make people forget about home), escaping Polyphemus (the man-eating Cyclops), being attacked by the Laistrygones (giants who ate some of Odysseus's men and pummeled their fleet with boulders), spending a year in the bed of Circe (a sorceress who at first turned his men into swine), and many other fantastic adventures. Each provides a new lens through which to view Odysseus the hero; he is by turns proud, bold, crafty, reverent, and stalwart. Just before Odysseus reaches Calypso's island, his band lands on the island of the Sun god. Circe has cautioned him to refrain from killing the Sun god's cattle, but despite his warnings, his men sacrifice and then eat the cattle. Zeus punishes the wrongdoers by sending a thunderbolt to smash this last ship in Odysseus's fleet. Only he survives.

The Phaeacians—a kindly if boastful seafaring people—sympathize with Odysseus after learning his story. Not only has it been 20 years since he has been home, but he is now making his way there alone, bereft of all the men and ships he lost along the way. Finally, with the aid of the Phaeacians, Odysseus reaches Ithaca. With Athena's help, he disguises himself as an old beggar to rid his house of the menacing suitors who are vying for his wife's hand and his fortune. Athena lifts his disguise when Odysseus reunites with his grown son, Telamachus, who has returned from his own journey for information about his father a more mature and knowledgeable young man. The son and father join forces. Back in his beggarly disguise, Odysseus makes his way into the palace. When the "beggar" arrives, the suitors ridicule the newcomer. Believing Odysseus to be dead, they then compete for Penelope in the contest of the bow. She promises that whoever can string Odysseus's mighty bow and shoot an arrow through a dozen axes (probably through the ring on an ax handle used to hang it on a wall) will be the one to marry her. All of them fail, but then the beggar stuns them all by achieving the feat. Next Odysseus removes his disguise and shoots an arrow in the ringleader's throat, then threatens the rest of the suitors: "Now life or death—your choice—fight me or flee / if you hope to escape your sudden bloody doom! / I doubt one man in the lot will save his skin!" (*Odyssey*, 22.69-71). Athena and two loyal servants help Odysseus and Telemachus finish off the suitors. Next, father and son have the female servants who were sleeping with the suitors clean up the bloody mess before hanging these faithless servants too.

Having reclaimed his palace, Odysseus reveals himself to Penelope. In a touching recognition scene, the long-suffering beauty bursts into tears after so many years of hoping for his return in vain. Penelope rushes to Odysseus, throwing her arms around his neck. Weeping, the warrior holds "the wife / he love[s], the soul of loyalty, in his arms at last" (*Odyssey*, 23.260-261). The morning after, the families of the slaughtered suitors gather to wreak revenge on Odysseus and Telemachus. Fighting erupts, but Athena, again in disguise, appears to force a truce: "Hold back, you men of Ithaca, back from brutal war! / break off—shed no more blood—make peace at once!" (*Odyssey*, 24.531-532). With these words, the goddess restores harmony and brings the action to a peaceful close.

Greeks and the afterlife. One of the greatest adventures that Odysseus recounts to the Phaeacians is his trip to the underworld, from which mortals rarely return in Greek mythology. The underworld was often referred to as Hades, after the Greek god of death who ruled over it along with his bride, Persephone. Odysseus meets with several spirits there, including that of the blind prophet Tiresias, from whom Odysseus receives assurances that he will reach Ithaca and rid the palace of the suitors.

In Hades, Odysseus seeks to converse with the dead spirits. He sacrifices a lamb and a ewe, whose blood gives the shades the strength to talk. Odysseus speaks with Elpenor, one of his men who recently died. The spirit asks Odysseus for a proper burial, a wish he promises to fulfill upon his return to the land of the living. Odysseus speaks in turn with his mother, Tiresias, and various Greek heroes. His mother's speech reveals what the ancients thought happened to a human being after death:

> Sinews no longer bind the flesh and bones
>   together—
> the fire in all its fury burns the body down to
>   ashes
> once life slips from the white bones, and the
>   spirit,
> rustling, flitters away . . . flown like a dream.
>   (*Odyssey*, 11.250-252)

The spirits of all people, whether good or evil in life, wind up in Hades, according to the tales of Homer.

In the *Odyssey*, the underworld is a bleak and shadowy place. Even the names of waterways in Hades are sorrowful—Flood of Grief, River of Fire, River of Tears, and Stream of Hate (*Odyssey*, 10.563-564). Homer's grim portrayal of the afterlife is reinforced through the words of the famous veteran of the Trojan War, the Greek hero Achilles, who remarks, "I'd rather slave on earth for another man—some dirt-poor tenant farmer who scrapes to keep alive—than rule down here over all the breathless dead" (*Odyssey*, 11.556-558).

Since no glory was promised in the afterlife, Greeks sought to be remembered by their great deeds in life. Heroes and would-be heroes spent their whole lives striving for *kleos* (remembered fame). This desire helps explain Odysseus's refusal of Calypso's offer of immortality. If he were to accept, not only would he never see his family again but he would lose the opportunity to perform a greater record of heroic deeds by which to be remembered.

Odysseus's desire to remain mortal coincides with the fate that has been decided for him by the immortal gods. His return to Ithaca, "that year spun out by the gods when he should reach his home" is preordained, "though not even there would he be free of trials, / even among his loved ones" (*Odyssey*, 1.20–22). The idea of fate is complicated within the *Odyssey* by Zeus's insistence that the gods alone are not to blame for what happens to human beings. Instead, human beings bring misery on themselves: "Ah how shameless—the way these mortals blame the gods. / From us alone, they say, come all their miseries, yes, / but they themselves, with their own reckless ways, / compound their pains beyond their proper share" (*Odyssey*, 1.37-40). It is through this combined idea of fate and free will that heroes find the opportunity to build *kleos*. The gods may control their ultimate fortunes, but the heroes are free to decide what to do with the time and the obstacles they are given.

It is probably the desire for *kleos* that prompts Odysseus to reveal his real name to the Cyclops Polyphemus, after slyly tricking him into believing that Odysseus's name is "Nobody." Odysseus outsmarts the Cyclops, plunging a stake in his single eye, whereupon the monster cries for help:

> Hearing his cries, [the other Cyclops]
>   lumbered up from every side
> and hulking around his cavern, asked what
>   ailed him:
> "What Polyphemus, what in the world's the
>   trouble?

... surely no one's trying to kill you now by
    fraud or force!"
  "*Nobody*, friends" ...
  "*Nobody's* killing me now by fraud and not
    by force!"
"*If* you're alone" ...
and nobody's trying to overpower you now

. . . .

it must be a plague sent here by mighty Zeus
and there's no escape from that.
You'd better pray to your father, Lord
    Poseidon."

                   (*Odyssey*, 9.450-460)

With this the other Cyclops lumber off and Odysseus and his men make their escape. As they take to the sea, Odysseus brazenly taunts the still powerful but now eyeless brute: "Cyclops—if any man on the face of the earth should ask you who blinded you, shamed you so—say Odysseus, raider of cities, he gouged out your eye, Laertes' son who makes his home in Ithaca!" (*Odyssey*, 9.558-561).

In the short run, when Odysseus divulges his real name, he harms himself and puts his crew in danger, for the revelation allows Poseidon to punish Odysseus for blinding Polyphemus, and the curse leads to shipwreck and a prolonged journey home. In the long run, though, the adventure adds to Odysseus's *kleos*. He recounts the adventure along with others to the Phaeacians, thereby establishing and spreading his fame. It is through *kleos* that Odysseus seeks immortality. To gain such a reputation, to have one's name preserved on the lips of men, is the ultimate goal of the ancient Greek hero.

Gender roles. While Greeks viewed marriage as a vital and respected institution, a double standard existed when it came to fidelity. Women were expected to be unquestionably monogamous while men could have numerous affairs. Although Penelope's story serves as a backdrop to the adventures of her husband, her fidelity is highlighted as one of the central values to be taken from the *Odyssey*. To emphasize her faithfulness, Homer parallels her story with those of the legendary Helen—whose faithlessness led to the Trojan War—and of Helen's sister, Clytemnestra. Clytemnestra was well known in oral tradition for having an affair with her husband's cousin while Agamemnon, her husband, fought the Trojan War (Sophocles would later dramatize her treachery in **Oresteia**, also in *Classical Literature and Its Times*). Agamemnon survives the war only to be murdered by his wife upon his return. In the *Odyssey*, as if to punctuate the importance of female loyalty, Homer shares Agamemnon's thoughts from the underworld:

Agamemnon's ghost cried out. "Son of old
    Laertes—
mastermind—what a fine, faithful wife you
    won!
What good sense resided in your Penelope

. . . .

A far cry from the daughter of Tyndareus,
    Clytemnestra—
what outrage she committed, killing the man
    she married once!"

                 (*Odyssey*, 24.211-220)

Clytemnestra is condemned for her actions. But no mention is made of the female slaves with whom Agamemnon had relations during the war, one of whom he claimed to value more than his wife. Similarly, although Penelope's loyalty is commended, Odysseus is not blamed for the seven years he spent living with the nymph Calypso and the nearly one year that he shared a bed with the goddess Circe.

Although double standards clearly exist, the women portrayed in the *Odyssey* are neither incompetent nor powerless. Both Odysseus and Agamemnon leave their wives in charge of their separate kingdoms during the Trojan War. In Odysseus's absence, Penelope shows wit and intelligence in the stratagems she devises to avoid marriage. But clearly men are meant to be in charge. Odysseus will not sleep with Circe, the powerful enchantress, until he has exerted control over her. Similarly order is not restored in Ithaca until his return; the suitors have been growing ever more disrespectful and Penelope cannot contain the situation without him. Her still maturing son cannot contain it either, although he does gain more authority over Penelope as the story progresses. Early in the tale, Telemachus begins to exert control as head of the household in his father's absence, issuing directions: "Mother, / go back to your quarters. Tend to your own tasks, / . . . As for giving orders, / men will see to that, but most of all: / I hold the reins of power in this house" (*Odyssey*, 1.410-413). Penelope, though surprised by her son's newfound maturity, obeys without question despite her older age.

One of the only places where women appear to wield significant power is Scheria, the land of the Phaeacians, the ideal society, to which Odysseus recounts much of his story. Odysseus is advised to pay homage first to the queen, Arete: "If only the queen will take you to her heart, / then there's hope that you will see your loved ones, / reach your own grand house, your native land at last" (*Odyssey*, 6.343-345). While Arete rules alongside her husband, she clearly possesses political clout of her own. Calypso and Circe wield authority in their magical lands, but both appear less powerful than Odysseus, since he overpowers Circe and rejects Calypso's pleadings to stay by her side.

Sources and literary context. Literary Greek seems to start with Homer. He belonged to a mainly oral culture, in which people received most of their information by word of mouth: "In Homer the oral tradition which went back to Mycenaean times reached its culmination and its end. . . . Centuries of history have gone into the making of . . . [the] *Odyssey*" (Ehrenberg, p. 10).

It is generally believed that the *Odyssey* existed first as stories that were sung by generations of oral poets, traveling men who performed for entertainment. These singers relied on memory to recount their tales, but felt free to improvise in response to their audiences—thus, the assertion that centuries of history went into the making of the epic. The singers also used a number of repeated formulas to aid them in their musical storytelling. Epithets, descriptive words or phrases attached to a character's name, such as "bright-eyed goddess" and "Dawn with her rose-red fingers," which can be found throughout the *Odyssey*, were among the primary formulas.

Besides the *Iliad* and the *Odyssey*, there were probably other epic poems telling other parts of the Trojan War story. These were the forerunners of the Epic Cycle, a later collection of poems that, together with the *Iliad* and the *Odyssey*, told a continuous history of the Trojan War from the wedding of Achilles' parents (the mortal Peleus and the goddess Thetis) to the death of Odysseus. After the *Odyssey* comes the *Telegony*, which can be thought of as a sequel, for it treats Odysseus's later travels and military adventures, including his demise. These last two works in the cycle center on Odysseus, moving from the tale of the Greek hero's return home to his final adventures.

Events in History at the Time the Epic Was Composed

The Greek Renaissance. Traces of Homer's own era can be found within the *Odyssey*. First, Odysseus's adventures can be seen as mirroring the expansionist slant of Greece during the Greek Renaissance, the resurgence of cultural and social activity that began around 750 BCE, shortly before Homer's day. Odysseus is an experienced sailor who provides detailed observations of the people and geography of every land he visits, as

sailors in Homer's age would. Many scholars further believe that Odysseus's travels led him through Sicily and Italy, two main sites of Greek colonization in the eighth century BCE.

The political structure of Odysseus's Ithaca mirrors the evolving *polis* or city-state of the Greek Renaissance. In real life, this was the period in which the *polis* emerged as one small village grew into one another and as society became stratified, or more distinctly stratified. Those people in control of the land within and around the city walls began to concentrate their power. Since kings and royal families were no longer a feature of these societies, powerful landowners emerged as a new aristocracy. The towns in which they lived gained importance. Gradually a new type of community formed, wherein citizens were ruled by a class of noble landowners. The emergence of this new noble class may have inspired the reappearance of tales such as the *Odyssey*, which depict the exploits and problems of wealthy leaders. In all probability, the noble class liked to trace its ancestry to the same legendary heroes that Homer features in his tales.

Reception and impact. The *Odyssey* became the first Greek text to be translated for use by Roman schoolboys, and its fame continues unabated. For the Greeks, Homer's *Iliad* and *Odyssey* became primary sources for the mythology and legend that dominated much of their artistic culture. At least one Greek, however, remained torn about the value of Homer's work: some 300 years after the *Odyssey* was composed, Plato accuses Homer of telling unpleasant tales about the gods, heroes, and underworld.

Plato has positive comments about Homer as well. In **The Republic**, Plato called Homer "the most poetic and first of the tragic poets" (Plato, 606e; also in *Classical Literature and Its Times*). More specifically, he praised Homer for presenting images of self-control in *Odysseus*, particularly when the hero, in a moment of rage, wants to slay all the suitors single handedly rather than wait for aid. He wisely restrains himself, saying, "Endure, my heart, you have suffered more shameful things than this" (*Odyssey*, 20.18). His declaration indicates his growth, since at times on the long journey he has been a victim of his own lack of self-control, giving in to emotional reactions without considering the consequences.

In the fifth century BCE, the Greek historian Herodotus credited Homer with having "made" the great gods and heroes who people his compositions (*poet* in fact comes from the Greek for "to make"). It was a tribute Homer shared

THE *ODYSSEY* INSPIRES EDNA ST. VINCENT MILLAY (1892-1950)

An Ancient Gesture

I thought, as I wiped my eyes on the corner of my apron:
Penelope did this too.
And more than once: you can't keep weaving all day
And undoing it all through the night;
Your arms get tired, and the back of your neck gets tight;
And along towards the morning, when you think it will never be light,
And your husband has been gone, and you don't know where, for years,
Suddenly you burst into tears;
There is simply nothing else to do.
And I thought, as I wiped my eyes on the corner of my apron:
This is an ancient gesture, authentic, antique,
In the very best tradition, classic, Greek:
Ulysses did this too,
But only as a gesture, a gesture which implied
To the assembled throng that he was much too moved to speak.
He learned it from Penelope . . .
Penelope, who really cried.

(Millay)

with Hesiod, whom Herodotus credited as well (see Hesiod's **Theogony,** also in *Classical Literature and Its Times*). Herodotus singled out Homer as the finest transmitter of the Heroic Age in ancient Greece. The historian refers here to the fifth-century BCE belief in a prior age that was peopled by a race of larger, stronger, braver, and comelier looking men and women. In *Poetics* (fourth century BCE), the philosopher Aristotle praises Homer for his uniquely creative accomplishments. The philosopher praises Homer for developing a unified plot—that of Odysseus's homecoming—and recounting multiple episodes of this single plot instead of recounting all the actions and experiences of a hero, whether they are connected to that storyline or not.

Throughout the years, the Homeric epics have become two of the most influential works of Western literature. The *Odyssey*, in particular, has captivated many notable writers. Enchanted by the characters and themes surrounding Odysseus's journey, writers from Alfred Lord Tennyson to John Keats to Edna St. Vincent Millay to Eudora Welty to Margaret Atwood, have penned poems and short stories exploring the work from various perspectives.

Homer's epics have served as a blueprint for later epics, such as Virgil's *Aeneid* and Milton's *Paradise Lost*. The *Odyssey* would become the model for the archetypal hero's journey (Odysseus) as well as the archetypal themes of coming-of-age (Telemachus) and the human search for one's identity, all of which are continually explored in modern works. It is precisely these themes that James Joyce drew on in writing his masterpiece *Ulysses* (a name that is the Latin equivalent of the Greek Odysseus). Likewise, Charles Frazier drew on Homer's epic to write *Cold Mountain*, which features a journey like that of Odysseus, placed against the backdrop of the American Civil War. Thanks no doubt to its dual focus on self-development and social relations in a setting more ancient than Classical Greece, the *Odyssey* continues to inspire audiences as a rare lens into one of humanity's earliest societies and timeless humanity.

—Christina Nation

For More Information

Blundell, Sue. *Women in Ancient Greece.* Cambridge, Mass.: Harvard University Press, 1995.

Burstein, Stanley M., Walter Donlan, Sarah B. Pomeroy, and Jennifer Tolbert Roberts. *Ancient Greece: A Political, Social, and Cultural History*. Oxford: Oxford University Press, 1999.

Ehrenberg, Victor. *From Solon to Socrates: Greek History and Civilization during the Sixth and Fifth Centuries BCE*. London: Methuen, 1973.

Eickhoff, R. L. *The Odyssey*. New York: Tom Doherty Associates, 2001.

Higgins, Reynold. *Minoan and Mycenaean Art*. New York: Oxford University Press, 1981.

Homer. *Odyssey*. Trans. Robert Fagles. New York: Penguin, 1996.

Lacey, W. K. *The Family in Classical Greece*. London: Thames and Hudson, 1968.

Millay, Edna St. Vincent. "An Ancient Gesture." PoemHunter.com. http://www.poemhunter.com/p/m/poem.asp?poet=6999&poem=156241.

Plato. *The Republic*. Trans. G. M. A. Grube. Indianapolis: Hackett, 1974.

Pomeroy, Sarah B. *Goddesses, Whores, Wives, and Slaves: Women in Classical Antiquity*. New York: Shocken, 1975.

Powell, Barry B. *Homer*. Oxford: Blackwell, 2004.

On the Crown

by
Demosthenes

The Athenian orator Demosthenes (386-322 BCE) is generally considered the most accomplished public speaker of the ancient Greek world. When he was seven years old his father died, leaving Demosthenes' substantial inheritance in the hands of the boy's guardians, who expropriated and mismanaged the money. After an intensive study of law and rhetoric, Demosthenes successfully sued his guardians when he was 20, winning back what was left of his inheritance. Entering Athenian public life in the mid-350s BCE, Demosthenes became a leading political figure in Athens from the 340s until his death. He is best known for his staunch opposition to the Macedonian king Philip II, the architect of Macedon's rise to dominance over the Greek city-states during this period. Demosthenes' opposition can be charted in the *Philippics*, a series of four speeches against Philip that Demosthenes made between 351 and 341 BCE, as well as in many of his other surviving speeches. Demosthenes' call for the Greeks to resist Philip was to no avail; in 338 BCE Philip shattered Greek power in the battle of Chaeronea and subjugated most of the Greek city-states. A participant in the battle, Demosthenes was accused of running away by his enemies. The charge seems unlikely to be true, since his fellow Athenians chose Demosthenes to deliver the official eulogy honoring those who died at Chaeronea. When Philip was succeeded by his son Alexander the Great in 336 BCE, Demosthenes continued to call for the Greeks to resist Macedonian rule. Widely viewed as Demosthenes' masterpiece, *On the Crown* summarizes the long, unsuccessful campaign to

THE LITERARY WORK

A speech written in Greek and delivered in Athens in August 330 BCE.

SYNOPSIS

Demosthenes defends his career as a champion of Athenian independence.

preserve Greek freedom and offers a defense of his leading role in this effort.

Events in History at the Time of the Speech

Classical Greece. In the early fifth century BCE, Greece defeated two invasions by the mighty Persian Empire. The victory was celebrated by Greek poets and chronicled by the first Greek historian, Herodotus, in his **Histories** (also in *Classical Literature and Its Times*). Its effect widespread, the victory accelerated the flowering of Greece's already growing confidence and cultural vitality. Over the next 150 years, an age that modern historians refer to as Greece's Classical period, many of Western civilization's distinctive intellectual traditions emerged in Greek civilization, including philosophy, science, Western medicine, drama, history, and political science.

The basic political unit of Greek life in the Classical period was the *polis,* or independent city-state. Before the Persian Wars, Sparta was

Demosthenes. © Araldo de Luca/Corbis

the leading city-state, but other prominent ones included Athens, Thebes, Corinth, and Argos. Most city-states had oligarchic governments, in which an aristocratic elite held the reigns of power. The major exception was the democratic government of Athens. After the war, given its central role in the defeat of Persia, Athens challenged Sparta's position as leader.

With its powerful navy, Athens now rose to dominate the Greek city-states along the coast of the Aegean Sea, as well as on the many islands the Greeks had settled. These city-states, after starting out as Athens' "allies" in the struggle to preserve Greek "freedom" from Persian rule, quickly became part of an Athenian empire. In *On the Crown* Demosthenes assumes that his Athenian audience looks back with nostalgia and pride on the defeat of Persia and the imperial age that followed it. He plays to these sentiments in justifying his longstanding opposition to the more recent Macedonian campaign to conquer Greece. "The Athenians of that day," he declares at one point, "did not search for a statesman or a commander who should help them to a servile security: they did not ask to live, unless they could live as free men" (Demosthenes, *On the Crown*, section 205).

The power of Athens' rival, Sparta, was meanwhile land-based and reliant on an old network of alliances among mainland city-states. During the rest of the fifth century BCE, the Greek world was wracked by the clash between the competing powers of Athens and Sparta, and their respective networks of alliances. The struggle culminated in the Peloponnesian War between Athens and Sparta, which lasted from 431 to 404 BCE and was chronicled by the Greek historian Thucydides in his *Peloponnesian War* (also in *Classical Literature and Its Times*). This long and bitter conflict embroiled the entire Greek world and ended only when Sparta allied itself with Persia. Using Persian gold to fund a navy of its own, Sparta finally prevailed by sea, destroying the Athenian navy at the battle of Aegospotami in 404 BCE. Athens surrendered unconditionally, its empire was dissolved, and its democracy was replaced by a pro-Spartan oligarchy.

Modern historians sometimes refer to the next several decades as the Spartan *hegemony* (a Greek word meaning "supreme leadership"), the period in which Sparta dominated Greece after winning the Peloponnesian War. Yet Sparta by no means went unchallenged during this period. In Athens, democratic government quickly reasserted itself, and although it was no longer an imperial power, Athens rapidly resumed a place among the major Greek city-states. From 395 to 386 BCE, in the so-called Corinthian War, Athens led a Persian-backed alliance of other city-states (Corinth, Thebes, and Argos) against Sparta. Only when Persia switched sides once again did Sparta regain dominance with Persian help, in the Peace of Antalcidas (386 BCE; also called the King's Peace, because the Persian king essentially dictated its terms). Sparta soon attempted to exert more direct control, installing a garrison of soldiers in Thebes in 382 BCE, effectively occupying the city.

In 379 BCE, Thebes, under its gifted commanders Epaminondas and Pelopidas, liberated itself from Spartan occupation. With Athenian help, the Thebans overthrew the Spartan-backed Theban government and expelled the Spartan garrison. Thebes adopted a democratic government, and over the next several years Athens and Thebes again became allies against Sparta. At the same time, Athens founded a new network of alliances, the Second Athenian Confederacy.

In 371 BCE Epaminondas and the Thebans shattered the myth of Spartan military invincibility by destroying the Spartan army at the battle of

ATHENIAN DEMOCRACY

Athenian democracy differed from modern democracy in two important ways. First, it was direct rather than representative—that is, voters generally made decisions directly, rather than through elected representatives. Second, it always excluded three significant segments of the population from public life: women, slaves, and foreign-born residents of Athens. It did include *all* adult male citizens of Athens, regardless of fortune or titles, but participation was limited to just this group.

The roots of Athenian democracy went back to the early sixth century BCE, when Athens, like other city-states, had a form of popular Assembly (*ekklesia*). However, Athenian democracy's other basic institutions date from 508 BCE, when the Athenian reformer Cleisthenes completely reorganized Athens' political structure. Cleisthenes divided Attica into 139 *demoi*, or demes, geographical districts whose populations were distributed among ten *phylai*, or tribes. He also established a governing council of 500—the *boule*—made up of 50 citizens chosen by lot from each of the 10 tribes, with a certain number from each deme. There was a committee in charge of the *boule* that had the right to summons the Assembly.

In 461 BCE the democratic politician Ephialtes and his protégé Pericles introduced further changes that brought Athenian democracy to its final form. Ephialtes stripped an earlier, aristocratic government body—the Council of Areopagus—of various political powers. Pericles (c. 495-429 BCE), who dominated Athenian politics from the 460s until his death in 429 BCE, introduced another important innovation: paying the citizens who served on the all-important juries called *dikasteria*. Only male citizens over 30 could serve as jurors. Juries for each case were chosen by lot from a pool of perhaps 6,000 men and varied in size, depending on the nature of the case. Historians believe that Demosthenes delivered his speech *On the Crown* to a jury of at least 501 Athenian citizens.

Leuctra. As the aftermath of the battle made clear, Leuctra decisively ended the Spartan hegemony. Sparta never recovered its old position of dominance. Instead, Thebes now enjoyed its own period of ascendancy under the capable leadership of Epaminondas. However, the Theban alliance with Athens soon fell apart, as Athens and Sparta now found common cause against Thebes. The Theban hegemony ended after Epaminondas' death in the inconclusive battle of Mantinea in 362 BCE.

By about 360 BCE, mutual jealousy had ensured that whatever city-state rose to prominence would immediately be targeted by an alliance of the others. Moreover, a century of constant warfare had left the most powerful Greek city-states exhausted. Sparta was crippled, while Thebes and Athens both headed weak confederacies in which they were strongly disliked by their supposed allies. Into this situation stepped Philip II on his

ascension to the throne of Macedon in 359 BCE. "The disposition of the Greeks towards one another," Demosthenes observes of Philip in *On the Crown*, "was already vicious and quarrelsome; and he made it worse" (*On the Crown*, section 61).

The rise of Macedon. The northern kingdom of Macedon had no city-states. It was ruled by kings whose legitimacy came partly from descent and partly from acceptance by a circle of powerful nobles. Though Greek in ethnicity, the Macedonians were remote from the vibrant and sophisticated city-states further south. This led most of their Greeks to look down on the Macedonians as rustic near-barbarians. Yet the kings and nobles of Macedon liked to see themselves as part of the Greek cultural mainstream. The Macedonian kings imported Greek culture to their capital of Pella, and the kingdom's aristocrats took part in such all-Greek institutions as the Olympic Games.

Philip II was the younger brother of the Macedonian king Perdiccas. He had spent his formative years in Thebes, during the height of the Theban hegemony, as a hostage so the Macedonians would cooperate with Theban policy. In Thebes, he had a celebrated tutor in Greek political and military affairs—the renowned Epaminondas. When King Perdiccas was killed in battle in 359 BCE, Philip, still in his twenties, took over as regent for his infant nephew, and then managed to assume the throne for himself.

THE GREEK WORLD IN TRANSITION

Modern historians have defined the age in which Demosthenes lived as one of transition between the Classical and Hellenistic periods in Greek civilization. Greece's Classical period began with its repulsion of two successive invasions by the Persian Empire in 490 and 480 BCE. It ended with the death of Alexander the Great in 323 BCE and the spread of Greek ("Hellenistic") culture in the wake of Alexander's conquests. During the Classical period, the basic Greek political unit was the independent city-state, or *polis* (pl. *poleis*). In the Hellenistic period, the basic political unit would be the larger kingdom. By subjugating the Greek city-states, Alexander's father, Philip II of Macedon (c. 382-336 BCE), set the stage for the establishment of the larger kingdoms that characterized the Hellenistic period. Demosthenes, Philip's great Athenian opponent, has been seen by posterity as the determined defender of the independent city-state in this losing battle. His life spanned the twilight of the Classical period.

Macedon hardly seemed to be in a promising position when Philip became regent; it was under threat from hostile peoples to the north, such as the Illyrians (against whom Perdiccas had been killed fighting). But Philip paid off these enemies, gaining time to build up a formidable army. He then marched out and defeated them, starting in 358 BCE. As soon as he could, Philip also went on the offensive against Athens for control of Thrace, the area directly east of Macedon. Thrace's biggest prize was the strategically vital city of Amphipolis, which had long been coveted by Athens in its drive to become an empire. At the time, Athens was distracted by the so-called Social War (357-355 BCE), in which its allies revolted against Athenian domination. In 357 BCE Philip captured Amphipolis, although the Athenians continued to contest control of the city.

While engaged in a decade-long struggle with Athens over Amphipolis, Philip seized another opportunity to involve himself in Greek affairs. The Third Sacred War (355-346 BCE) pitted Thebes and the allied area of Thessaly (in central Greece) against Phocis, an Athenian ally. Having suffered several defeats by the Phocians in the early years of the war, Thebes and Thessaly invited Philip to intervene on their behalf. Philip defeated Phocis, but by the end of the war he controlled Thessaly and appeared poised to threaten nearby Thebes as well. At the same time (346 BCE) Philip wrested Amphipolis from Athenian control once and for all. His greatly expanded territory now stretched north to the Danube River, east to Thrace, and southward well into central Greece itself, including Thessaly.

Athenian policy toward Philip was cautious, even after the loss of Amphipolis and other territory. The famous orator Isocrates (436-338 BCE) counseled that the real enemy was Persia and that Philip offered the best hope of unifying Greece against it. Demosthenes disagreed. Starting with his first *Philippic*, probably delivered in 351 BCE, he had argued instead that Philip was the greater threat: "Surely it is obvious that he will not stop, unless someone stops him," Demosthenes had insisted then (Demosthenes, *First Philippic*, section 43). To stop Philip, Demosthenes proposed a detailed plan for strong military action, but the Assembly had voted it down, as it would continue to do with his other, similar proposals.

In 349 BCE Demosthenes delivered three more speeches against Philip called the *Olynthiacs*. They take their name from the northern Greek city of Olynthus, not far from Amphipolis, which requested a formal alliance with Athens to defend against Philip's aggression. Demosthenes advised the Athenians to send two strong forces to aid the Olynthians and at the same time to attack Philip. His advice was only partly heeded: Athens sent a group of mercenaries (not citizens, as Demosthenes had demanded) to defend Olynthus, and to little avail. The next year Philip captured Olynthus, shocking the Athenians by selling its inhabitants into slavery and destroying the city itself.

In 346 BCE Demosthenes represented Athens in negotiations with Philip that resulted in the Peace of Philocrates (346-340 BCE). While the peace lasted, the Macedonian king and Athens engaged in further diplomatic maneuvers. Each side sought to win allies among the remaining independent city-states for the coming struggle,

RHETORIC IN ATHENIAN PUBLIC LIFE

Whether made in the Assembly, the Council of 500, or the juries, every important public decision in Athens was decided by a vote. This meant that skill in rhetoric, or the art of oratory (public speaking), became highly prized in Athenian life. The goal of rhetoric was persuasion, and by the fourth century it had become a highly technical area of knowledge, with complex rules and sophisticated methods for swaying the opinions of listeners. Despite all the legal cases in Athenian public life, Athens had no lawyers at this time. Private individuals were expected to handle their own legal business and make their own speeches. However, a professional rhetorician might be hired to write the speech. Demosthenes made his living writing speeches for others until the mid-350s BCE, when he began delivering his own speeches, thus launching his career in democratic politics. Athenian trials were overseen by the city's main public magistrates (*archons*), who acted merely as administrators, not as judges. The jurors made all the decisions and did all the interpreting of the law (which modern courts leave to judges). Thus, emotional appeals generally carried more weight than technical legal arguments.

Athens lacked anything resembling a public prosecutor. All legal actions had to be brought by private individuals against other private individuals. When laws were broken, the offenders thus went unpunished unless a private citizen took them to court. By the same token, private individuals could sue political leaders for their public actions. In the fourth century BCE, the most common charge on which such political lawsuits were based was that of making an "unconstitutional proposal." This charge formed the immediate context of the trial in which Demosthenes delivered his speech *On the Crown*, although the accused party was not Demosthenes but his political ally Ctesiphon.

which now appeared inevitable. Demosthenes, meanwhile, continued to denounce Philip at home.

In 340 BCE Philip ended the diplomatic stalemate by attacking and besieging Perinthus and Byzantium, two important ports that Athens relied on for regular shipments of grain from the Black Sea region. The Athenian navy successfully defended both ports, however. The following year Philip marched south into Greece itself, capturing the city of Amphissa in 338 BCE. Led by Demosthenes, Athens marshaled the other city-states, including Thebes. In 338 BCE the two sides met in battle at Chaeronea, north of Thebes.

As Demosthenes points out in *On the Crown*, the battle of Chaeronea was closely fought, and Philip's victory was anything but a foregone conclusion. But in the end Philip won, and his victory shattered the remaining resistance. Philip now controlled most of Greece. Yet he wisely left the Greeks alone for the moment—he had made his point, and if he wished, could always impose

his will militarily. Instead, he began preparations for a major invasion of Persia.

The proposal that Demosthenes be awarded a crown. Two years after Philip's victory at Chaeronea, in 336 BCE, Demosthenes' political ally Ctesiphon proposed that the Council of 500 put a motion before the Assembly that, if passed, would award Demosthenes a golden crown (a merit award that was given in Athens) in recognition of his service to the Athenian people. The Council approved the proposal. However, before it could be put to a final vote in the Assembly, Demosthenes' long-time rival Aeschines charged Ctesiphon with making an "unconstitutional proposal" in suggesting that Demosthenes be awarded the crown. Such a charge was a common way of attacking a political opponent; if convicted, Ctesiphon would be liable to a sentence of exile.

Several times in the late 340s BCE Demosthenes had charged Aeschines, also a prominent Athenian orator and politician, with promoting Philip's plans to dominate the Greek world and with accepting bribes from Philip. Both men had together represented Athens in negotiations with Philip, almost always disagreeing sharply over the best course of action. By 336 BCE, when Ctesiphon made his proposal about Demosthenes' crown, Philip's control appeared less burdensome to most Greeks than Demosthenes had predicted. Accordingly, Aeschines thought the time was ripe to strike at Demosthenes through Ctesiphon. Yet just a few weeks after Aeschines made his accusation against Ctesiphon, Philip was dead, assassinated by a disgruntled Macedonian. As the Greek world was thrown into turmoil once again, Aeschines decided to wait and see how things turned out.

Philip's son Alexander (356-323 BCE), a boy barely out of his teens and an unknown quantity to the Greeks, became king of Macedon. Rebellions immediately broke out in the Greek city-states, but Alexander the Great turned out to be even more formidable an opponent than his father. He made a lightning march south into Greece with his army and intimidated the city-states into submission. However, when rumors of Alexander's death reached Greece in 335 BCE, Thebes revolted—only to be crushed by Alexander, who swiftly appeared with his army and made an example of Thebes by utterly destroying the city. Demosthenes had aided the rebels and narrowly escaped being executed for it.

Alexander now carried out his father's planned campaign against Persia. Leading an invasion force eastward, he defeated the Persian king Darius III twice, at Issus in 333 BCE and at Gaugamela in 331 BCE. Assuming the title "king of Persia" as well as "king of the Greeks," Alexander continued his campaign of conquest by marching further east. During all this time, Aeschines had held back from prosecuting his case against Ctesiphon and, by extension, Demosthenes. For his part, Demosthenes had counted on Persia to defeat Alexander. However, his hope of a Persian victory was now permanently dashed. With Persia's final defeat at Gaugamela, Aeschines judged that Demosthenes was once more vulnerable to attack, and shortly after the battle he again took up the case. By this time the Athenian assembly had awarded Demosthenes the crown, but this did not stop Aeschines from resuming the attack.

Aeschines attacks Demosthenes. In his speech *Against Ctesiphon*, delivered (historians believe) to a jury of at least 501 Athenian citizens in the summer of 330 BCE, Aeschines summarized Demosthenes' career in the most unfavorable light possible. His main purpose was to demonstrate that Demosthenes did not deserve the award of the crown, and in order to do so, he accused Demosthenes of numerous offenses against Athenian law, most seriously, the offense of taking bribes from Philip. In fact, central to both sides of the case was the argument by each man (Aeschines and Demosthenes) that his opponent had advanced Macedonian interests and accepted bribes from Philip.

Aeschines also made two technical charges against Ctesiphon: 1) Ctesiphon proposed that the city honor Demosthenes with a crown even though the city had not yet put Demosthenes through a final review or accounting of his services; 2) According to law, the crown needed to be awarded in the Senate or the Assembly, but, as Ctesiphon wanted, it had been awarded to Demosthenes in Athens' main theater. Both of these charges were probably true. But more important in the end was whether a jury would convict Ctesiphon for such minor infractions, when everyone in Athens knew that Demosthenes was the real target in the whole case. In August, as a witness for the defense, Demosthenes delivered a response to Aeschines' accusations.

The Speech in Focus

Contents summary. Demosthenes' response answers all the major points made by Aeschines' case *Against Ctesiphon*, but not in the order in which Aeschines presented them. In his accusations, Aeschines had made several arguments based on legal technicalities before criticizing Demosthenes' overall career. Demosthenes says at the outset that in reply he will follow his own order. This allows him to remind the jurors about his long and distinguished public service before he briefly addresses the legal technicalities that his side is accused of violating. Both sides know the main issue is Demosthenes' record of service, not these legal technicalities.

Throughout the speech, Demosthenes addresses his audience as if it comprised the entire people of Athens, rather than a relatively small body of jurors. The speech is divided into 324 sections, each taking about a third of a page in most modern translations. In addition, Demosthenes read into evidence some 38 documents during the course of the speech, which do not appear to have survived. Modern scholars agree that the documents appearing in the surviving manuscripts were all forged later.

In his attack on Demosthenes, Aeschines broke the orator's career down into four periods: 1) before 346 BCE; 2) from 346 to 340 BCE; 3) from 340 to the battle of Chaeronea in 338 BCE; 4) after 338 BCE. Demosthenes addresses the first three periods in turn. He essentially passes over events after the battle of Chaeronea. These three parts constitute the longest portions of the speech, and they can be seen as providing its chronological backbone. Between them he more briefly addresses other subjects outside this time-ordered framework. Often through the speech he also shifts between narrative and argument, at the same time interspersing flights of stirring rhetoric with passages of more matter-of-fact language.

A brief introduction reminds the jurors of their oaths and of the importance of upholding the laws. Demosthenes then protests Aeschines' charges against his private life (as distinct from those against his public career), urging the jurors to rely on their own personal knowledge about Demosthenes rather than believe Aeschines' "abusive aspersion" (*On the Crown*, section 10).

The next few sections introduce Demosthenes' discussion of his public career. Here he takes advantage of his rival's long delay in bringing the case to trial, and of the fact that Aeschines has brought charges not against Demosthenes himself, but only against Ctesiphon:

> If he ever saw me committing crimes against the commonwealth, especially such frightful crimes as he described just now so dramatically, his duty was to avail himself of the legal penalties as soon as they were committed, impeaching me, and so putting me on trial before the people. . . . Had he so acted . . . his denunciations would have been consistent with his conduct; but in fact he has deserted the path of right and justice . . . and then, after a long interval, he . . . stands on a false pretense, denouncing me, but indicting Ctesiphon.
>
> (*On the Crown*, section 15)

"It is a fair inference," Demosthenes continues, "that all his accusations are equally dishonest and untruthful" (*On the Crown*, section 17).

Demosthenes proceeds to discuss the first phase of his career, from the mid-350s to 346 BCE. This discussion centers on the Third Sacred War (355-46 BCE; see above), in which Philip intervened on the side of Thebes against Athens' ally, Phocis. Here as elsewhere, Demosthenes accuses Aeschines of accepting bribes from Philip in order to manipulate Athenian public opinion and thus influence Athenian policy towards Macedon. Characterizing Aeschines as a crooked and scheming agent of Macedonian interests right up to the time of the trial, Demosthenes de-

rides him as "Philip's hireling of yesterday, and Alexander's hireling of today" (*On the Crown*, section 52).

After a brief consideration of the actual indictment against Ctesiphon, that the proposal to award Demosthenes the crown was illegal, Demosthenes moves on to the second phase of his public life (346-340 BCE). He stresses that numerous cities (such as Perinthus and Byzantium, the ports that Athens defended against Philip in 340 BCE) voted to award ceremonial

---

PARALLEL PASSAGES FROM AESCHINES AND DEMOSTHENES

As Aeschines knew, Demosthenes regarded the Athenian alliance with Thebes as one of his proudest achievements. In his speech *Against Ctesiphon*, Aeschines attempts to deny credit to Demosthenes for persuading Athens to make the alliance, arguing that the need for it had been plain to all:

> You [the Athenians] went out and were on the point of marching into Thebes under arms, horse, and foot, before Demosthenes had moved one single syllable about an alliance. What brought you into Thebes was the crisis and fear and need of an alliance, not Demosthenes.
>
> (*Against Ctesiphon*, sections 140-141)

Compare Demosthenes' answering claims in *On the Crown*, where he argues that he alone persuaded the Athenians of the need for an alliance:

> The call of the crisis on that momentous day was . . . for the man who . . . had rightly fathomed the purposes and the desires of Philip; for anyone who had not grasped those purposes . . . was not the man to appreciate the needs of the hour. . . . On that day, then, the call was manifestly for me. I came forward and addressed you. . . . I, alone among your orators and politicians, did not desert the post of patriotism in the hour of peril.
>
> (*On the Crown*, sections 172-173)

---

crowns to Athens in honor of its role in defending them. Demosthenes himself takes credit for these awards: "Moreover all know that you have awarded crowns to many politicians; but no one can name any man—I mean any statesman or orator—except me, by whose exertions the city itself has been crowned" (*On the Crown*, section 94). He also reminds the jurors of a law that he successfully proposed under which the wealthy were made to pay more of the expenses for the Athenian navy, relieving the tax burden on the poor.

In several subsequent passages, Demosthenes refutes two minor charges against Ctesiphon, attacks Aeschines' own character and career, and charges him with deliberately provoking Philip's attack on Amphissa in 339-338 BCE. Aeschines, Demosthenes maintains, accused the Amphissans of cultivating sacred ground, a religious offense that allowed Philip to invade under the pretext of defending Greek religious law. Indeed, Demosthenes continues, Philip secretly paid Aeschines to make the false charge.

Demosthenes then reminds the jurors of his leadership in rallying Thebes and the other city-states to Athens' side after the fall of Amphissa. He briefly recreates for the jurors the speech he had earlier delivered to the Assembly, persuading them to send a diplomatic mission to Thebes with himself as main delegate.

Refusing to accept blame for the defeat at Chaeronea, Demosthenes challenges Aeschines to say what path Athens could have chosen that would have led to a better outcome:

> In those days you sat speechless at every assembly; I came forward and spoke. You had nothing to say then; very well,—show us our duty now. Tell me what plan I ought to have discovered. Tell me what favourable opportunity was lost to the state by my default. . . . You must not accuse me of crime because Philip happened to win the battle; for the event was in God's hands, not mine. Show me that I did not adopt, as far as human calculation could go, all the measures that were practicable, or that I did not carry them out with honesty and diligence. . . . Prove that, and then denounce me; but not till then.
>
> (*On the Crown*, sections 191-194)

Demosthenes then returns to his account of the events leading up to and including the battle of Chaeronea itself, praising the fighting prowess of the Athenians and their allies. In particular, Demosthenes argues, Athens was better off with allies than without them. He claims credit for negotiating Athens' main alliance against Philip, that with Thebes, as well as many other similar ones.

Demosthenes then renews his personal attack on Aeschines by comparing his own career with his rival's. He characterizes the man's family background as squalid, his education as nonexistent, his personal life as morally corrupt, his private career as trivial, his public career as self-serving, and his political stature as undistinguished. Aeschines has accused Demosthenes of artfulness at public speaking, and Demosthenes

admits it, but he also asserts that his artfulness has always been used to serve the public interest. He reminds the jurors that it was he who was chosen, not Aeschines, to deliver the official eulogy of those killed in battle at Chaeronea. Calling Aeschines and his cronies "profligates, sycophants, fiends incarnate," Demosthenes accuses them of having "pledged away their liberty in their cups, first to Philip, now to Alexander" (*On the Crown*, section 296).

In conclusion Demosthenes assails Aeschines with a series of rhetorical questions, demanding to know what accomplishments he has achieved, what public awards he has won, what policies of his have been put in place, what alliances he has created, what successful projects he has ever undertaken. Calling Aeschines an "incorrigible knave," Demosthenes further accuses him of refusing to contribute financially to Athens' defense even though he had inherited a fortune from his father-in-law (*On the Crown*, section 312). Aeschines has compared Demosthenes unfavorably with Athens' great leaders of the past. In response, Demosthenes accepts the comparison (with feigned modesty), but pointedly asserts that the jurors should really compare him not with the great heroes of another age, but with politicians of his own age—and especially with Aeschines and his friends. "I was powerless, I admit," he says, "but I was still the better patriot" (*On the Crown*, section 320). In a final prayer, Demosthenes hopes that the gods "implant even in them [his opponents] a better purpose and a better spirit" and "to us who remain grant speedy deliverance from the terrors that hang over our heads, and a salvation that may never fail" (*On the Crown*, section 324).

Democracy and the meaning of freedom. Near the end of *On the Crown*, Demosthenes repeats the now familiar accusation that, by aiding Philip, his opponent has betrayed the Greek ideal of freedom (*eleutheria*). Aeschines and his cronies, the orator charges, "have overthrown for ever that freedom and independence which to the Greeks of an earlier age were the very standard and canon of prosperity" (*On the Crown*, section 296). Demosthenes portrays himself, in contrast, as a "well-meaning citizen," which he defines as one who has "the honor and ascendancy of his country [*polis*]" as the "constant aim of his policy" (*On the Crown*, section 321).

The ideals of freedom and citizenship reflected in such passages are evidenced repeatedly in Greek history over the course of the Classical period. Yet to the modern sensibility at least, these ideals contain an element of contradiction, even paradox. Greek writers from Herodotus onward, for example, lauded the love of freedom that fired the Greek spirit of resistance to the Persian invasions in the early fifth century BCE. However, by the same token, their appetite for "honor and ascendancy" led the Greek city-states into endless warfare, leaving them exhausted and vulnerable by the time of Philip II. Furthermore, no polis could gain "honor and ascendancy" except at the expense of the "freedom and independence" of others. "Freedom" thus seems to have included the freedom of the powerful to oppress the less powerful.

In the ancient Greek world, modern scholars have suggested, concepts such as "freedom and independence" applied only to one's own polis—and indeed, only to a certain group (in Athens, adult males who were citizens) within the polis. In defending "freedom and independence," therefore, Demosthenes exalts Athens' right to dominate other city-states and, implicitly at least, upholds the exclusion of women, slaves, and others from basic civil rights.

Demosthenes represents the conventional view of such matters in the Greek world. That view did not go unquestioned. For example, Demosthenes' older contemporary Isocrates (see above) called for the Greek city-states to unify against a common enemy, Persia. Even more unusually, a fifth-century BCE Athenian writer named Antiphon (not to be confused with the better-known orator of the same name) had suggested that all people, Greek or not, were equal and deserved the same rights. Yet in the end the more conventional "polis-based" view of freedom that Demosthenes glorifies in *On the Crown* carried the day. As events had already made clear, however, it also carried the seeds of its own destruction at the hands of Philip II.

Sources and literary context. In general, Demosthenes' main source for *On the Crown* was his own career as Philip II's leading adversary in the Greek world. In the more immediate context, Demosthenes took many of his cues from Aeschines' speech *Against Ctesiphon*, the rebuttal of which was Demosthenes' foremost aim in delivering his speech.

Aeschines had accused Demosthenes of a number of crimes, including bribery, the same charge that Demosthenes repeatedly hurls against Aeschines. For example, he had argued that Demosthenes' push for an alliance against Philip between Athens and Thebes was motivated solely by hunger for bribes. At the same time, Aeschines had also portrayed Philip in sympathetic terms:

Philip did not despise the Greeks, and he was well aware (for he was not without understanding) that he was about to contend in a little fraction of a day for all that he possessed; for that reason he wished to make peace, and was on the point of sending envoys. The officials at Thebes also were frightened at the impending danger—naturally, for they had no run-away orator and deserter to advise them.... Now when Demosthenes saw that such was the situation, suspecting that the Boeotarchs [Theban officials] were about to conclude a separate peace and get gold from Philip without his being in it, and thinking that life was not worth living if he was to be left out of any act of bribery, he jumped up in the assembly....

(Aeschines, sections 148-49)

THE FAME OF DEMOSTHENES

Demosthenes' brilliance as a speaker gave rise to many colorful stories about him that may or may not be based on fact. Most famous, perhaps, is the description of how he overcame a speech defect as a young man in order to prevail in court. Here the first century CE biographer Plutarch describes Demosthenes' methods:

He corrected his lisp and his indistinct articulation by holding pebbles in his mouth while he recited long speeches, and he strengthened his voice by running or walking uphill discoursing as he went, and by reciting speeches or verses in a single breath. Besides this he kept a large mirror in his house and would stand in front of it while he went through his exercises in declamation.

(Plutarch, p. 197)

Demosthenes' death was no less dramatic than his life. In 322 BCE, eight years after delivering *On the Crown* and shortly after the death of Alexander the Great, Demosthenes took part in a failed Athenian revolt against Macedonian rule. Captured afterward by Macedonian soldiers, Demosthenes asked to be allowed to write a letter to his family. He killed himself by biting down on his pen, which he had earlier filled with poison instead of ink.

Only one other complete set of paired legal speeches (also by Demosthenes and Aeschines) survives from the Classical period, and so both sets constitute an important source of knowledge for modern scholars. Such speeches were customarily revised for publication. What form such publication took is uncertain, just as it is uncertain how closely the version that we have resembles the speech that Demosthenes actually gave.

The trial took place in a single day, and Demosthenes' rebuttal followed Aeschines' speech only a few minutes later. This legal setting must be kept in mind when assessing both speeches' literary and historical content. For example, the name-calling and personal invective in which both orators freely indulge was expected (and no doubt enjoyed) by the Athenian jurors. In addition, like many lawyers today, both speakers are more concerned with winning their cases than with truth or accuracy. As a consequence, while the speeches' value to modern historians is high, scholars have also noted the difficulty of ascertaining how reliable either orator's version of events actually is. Indeed, it has been observed that not only do Demosthenes' and Aeschines' accounts differ from each other in these two speeches, but in them both orators also contradict accounts of the same events that they give in other speeches. The rhetorical context demanded persuasion over accuracy, and rewarded gripping and dramatic claims over less colorful but more truthful ones.

Reception and impact. Owing to Demosthenes' supremely effective rhetoric in *On the Crown*, Aeschines lost his case against Ctesiphon, failing even to win the one-fifth of the votes necessary to prevent a fine for wrongful prosecution under Athenian law. Soon after the trial he left Athens, withdrawing to the Greek island of Rhodes, where he taught rhetoric. Shortly after Demosthenes' death, commentators were hailing him as the greatest orator of the ancient world and *On the Crown* as his greatest speech. The leading Roman authority on rhetoric, Quintilian (c. 30-

c. 100 CE), drew most heavily from *On the Crown* when illustrating Demosthenes' techniques in his book *Training in Oratory* (c. 90 CE).

As a masterful orator and defender of freedom, Demosthenes is often compared with the Roman politician and author Cicero (106-43 BCE), who idolized his Greek predecessor. The two were paired by the biographer Plutarch (c. 50-c. 120 CE) in his parallel lives of illustrious Greeks and Romans. Similarly, the Roman historian Tacitus wrote that "just as amongst the Attic [Athenian] orators the first place is awarded to Demosthenes . . . so at Rome, Cicero far outstripped the other speakers of his day" (Tacitus in Sharrock & Ash, p. 126).

—Colin Wells

For More Information

Aeschines. "Against Ctesiphon." In *The Speeches of Aeschines*. Cambridge, Mass.: Harvard University Press, 1919.

Boardman, John, et al. *The Oxford History of Greece and the Hellenistic World*. Oxford: Oxford University Press, 1986.

Demosthenes. *First Philippic*. In *Olynthiacs; Minor Public Speeches; Speech Against Leptines*. Loeb Series. Cambridge, Mass.: Harvard University Press, 1930.

———. *On the Crown*. In *Demosthenes II*. Cambridge, Mass.: Harvard University Press, 1926.

Hansen, Mogens Herman. *The Athenian Democracy in the Age of Demosthenes*. Trans. J. A. Crook. Oxford: Blackwell, 1991.

Plutarch. *The Age of Alexander: Nine Greek Lives by Plutarch*. Trans. Ian Scott-Kilvert. Harmondsworth: Penguin, 1973.

Sharrock, Alison, and Rhiannon Ash. *Fifty Key Classical Authors*. London: Routledge, 2002.

On the Nature of the Universe

by
Lucretius

T itus Lucretius Carus (c. 100-c. 55 BCE) was a Roman citizen, an aristocrat, and an enthusiastic follower of the Greek philosophic school known as Epicureanism. He was also an acquaintance of the Roman politician Gaius Memmius, to whom Lucretius dedicated *On the Nature of the Universe* (known in Latin as *De rerum natura*). Beyond these bare details, all of which have been inferred from the poem itself, nothing is known of Lucretius' life. A much later writer, the Christian apologist St. Jerome (c. 340-c. 420 CE), claimed that Lucretius committed suicide after being driven insane by a love potion. Jerome's assertions have been dismissed by most modern scholars, who note that the philosophical content of *On the Nature of the Universe* made Lucretius a natural target of the Christians during this time. Furthermore, Lucretius repeatedly urges his readers to embrace a life of rational self-discipline, advice that is wholly out of keeping with Jerome's picture of him as a love-crazed madman. Instead, modern commentators mostly agree that Lucretius was in fact what he presents himself as in the poem: an intelligent and educated Roman aristocrat who had found what he believed to be the solution to humankind's ills. The ills that Lucretius addresses in the poem are mostly universal in scope—ignorance, superstition, and fear of death. However, Lucretius also laments the violent unrest that plagued Roman society as it descended into the chaos of civil war.

THE LITERARY WORK

A poem set in the Roman world and written in Latin c. 60-55 BCE; published c. 55 BCE.

SYNOPSIS

Using the elevated language of epic poetry, Lucretius expounds the views of the Greek philosopher Epicurus (341-270 BCE).

Events in History at the Time of the Poem

The collapse of the Roman republic. By Lucretius' lifetime, Rome had endured decades of social and political upheaval. At the root of the problem lay the expansion of Roman power throughout the Mediterranean world, which had taken place over the previous century and a half. While territorial expansion brought great wealth to Rome, it also generated intense political rivalries over control of that wealth. Soon after Lucretius' death, these struggles would result in the fall of Rome's ancient republican system, which was based on a balance of power between the aristocratic Senate and the various popular assemblies. The republic would be replaced by an empire as one Roman aristocrat, Augustus (formerly known as Octavian), vanquished all rivals to bring Rome and its vast dominions under his sole control as emperor.

Although this long process had yet to reach its climax when Lucretius was alive, the struggles

Lucretius, illustration of a bust. © Archive Photos, Inc. Reprduced by permission.

that would result in the fall of the republic had already caused shocking civil warfare. In his poem, Lucretius repeatedly condemns the "greed and blind lust of status that drive pathetic men to overstep the bounds of right and may even turn them into accomplices or instruments of crime, struggling night and day with unstinted effort to scale the pinnacles of wealth. . . . So in their greed of gain they amass a fortune out of civil bloodshed; piling wealth upon wealth, they heap carnage on carnage" (Lucretius, *On the Nature of the Universe*, book 3, lines 59-71).

To find examples of such men, Lucretius had only to look around at members of the Roman aristocracy in his day. Roman governors routinely enriched themselves at the expense of the provinces they were sent out to govern, and military commanders lined their pockets through booty and the sale of prisoners into slavery. Along with wealth, Roman cultural values dictated that the most powerful men also craved the public honors that traditionally came with military conquest and great wealth. This is what Lucretius means by "blind lust of status."

Three such men dominated Roman politics in the 60s and 50s BCE, when Lucretius probably conceived and wrote the poem. They were Pom-

pey (106-48 BCE), Crassus (c. 112-53 BCE), and Julius Caesar (100-44 BCE), the granduncle and adoptive father of the future emperor Augustus. Like Lucretius, all three had grown up in the 80s BCE during Rome's first civil wars. At that time, rivalry between two powerful generals had led to the first instance of one Roman army fighting against another. The two rival generals were Marius (157-86 BCE), who represented the people, and Sulla (138-78 BCE), who represented the aristocracy. Their behavior, that is, the fighting between them, provided the precedent that Pompey, Crassus, and Caesar would follow.

By the 80s BCE, Marius and Sulla had both led Roman armies in successful wars of conquest against other states. In 88 BCE, Sulla was sent to command an army against a rebel king, Mithridates, in the eastern Mediterranean. The 70-year-old Marius came out of retirement, taking advantage of Sulla's absence to dominate Roman politics. Sulla returned from the east and marched on Rome. Marius and his supporters fled, but when Sulla turned back to the east, the popular Marius again took over. He declared Sulla an outlaw and murdered many of his aristocratic supporters in the Senate.

Marius died in 86 BCE, and his political heir, Cinna, continued to undermine the Senate in Rome. In 83 BCE, Sulla—having won the war against Mithridates in the east—returned to Rome. His army fought a year-long civil war against Marius' army, now commanded by Cinna. Sulla won this first civil war, then began a reign of terror in which he murdered not only his opponents, but also many of the wealthy whose property he wished to steal. Thousands perished throughout Italy. With the new wealth gained from "proscriptions" (citizens listed as outlaws, whose property was confiscated by the Roman state), Sulla rewarded his followers. He gave Rome a new constitution to restore stability and control by the Senate before he resigned.

But the damage had been done, and Sulla's constitution had less than the hoped-for impact. His rivalry with Marius had established the destructive pattern that Rome would follow over the next 50 years, until the establishment of the empire in 27 BCE. Military leaders—who acted more like warlords than generals—would use command of the army as a stepping stone to wealth and political power, vying to outdo each other in honors, riches, and influence.

Sulla died in 78 BCE, and soon afterward the Senate gave the young Pompey special powers in order to put down another revolt by Marius' followers. However, Pompey would soon show he had no special allegiance to the Senate. Forming an alliance with the wealthy senator Crassus, Pompey forced the Senate to abandon Sulla's constitution. During the 60s BCE, his foreign conquests in Rome's name—including a final victory over the still troublesome Mithridates—made him Rome's wealthiest, most powerful, and most popular figure.

As Pompey's power grew during these foreign campaigns, Crassus, remaining in Rome, began to fear that Pompey would no longer find the alliance necessary. Seeking a new ally, Crassus settled on Julius Caesar, an ambitious aristocrat who had nonetheless made a name for himself as a man of the people and a powerful public speaker.

When Pompey returned to Rome in 62 BCE, the Senate angered him by refusing him the public honors he felt he deserved. The following year, the Senate also angered Crassus by voting down a proposal that he had backed. The year after that, in 60 BCE, the Senate denied public honors to Julius Caesar, who was returning from a victorious campaign in Spain. Caesar then persuaded Pompey and Crassus to join together with him in a tense three-way alliance called the First Triumvirate (derived from the Latin for "three" and "men"). Though they looked on each other with suspicion, these potential rivals had one thing in common: their ambitions—and their "lust of status"—had been blocked by the Senate.

Many historians have seen the First Triumvirate as signaling the death of the republic, since it marked the effective end of the Senate as Rome's main governing body. It was clear at the time that the alliance could not last indefinitely and that Roman would again take up arms against Roman. Over the next several years, however, the alliance held together despite strong mutual antagonisms among its members. By the time it dissolved in the early 40s BCE, Lucretius would be dead, his poem having been written in the uneasy lull between one round of civil war and another.

Rome and the Hellenistic world. The growth of Roman power took place in three stages: in the Italian peninsula (c. 400 to c. 265 BCE); in the western Mediterranean (c. 265 to c. 200 BCE); and in the eastern Mediterranean (c. 200 to c. 50 BCE). In this third stage of Roman expansion, Romans came into close contact with the civilization dominant in the eastern Mediterranean, that of Greece.

The western Mediterranean was sparsely populated by non-literate tribal peoples whom the Romans would imitate the Greeks in calling "bar-

barians." In contrast, the more heavily settled eastern Mediterranean possessed great cities like Athens and Alexandria, and longstanding traditions of literature and learning based on Greek sources. Although many local peoples made up this patchwork of cultures, Greek civilization had been spread among their educated elites throughout the eastern Mediterranean and beyond by the conquests of Alexander the Great in the fourth century BCE, while Rome was busy consolidating its control of Italy. The Greeks referred to themselves as "Hellenes." Since Alexander's conquests spread their culture to many non-Greek peoples, the resulting Greek-based civilization is called "Hellenistic."

GAIUS MEMMIUS

The Memmius to whom Lucretius addresses *On the Nature of the Universe* was a member of the Roman aristocracy with an interest in Latin poetry and Greek literature. His personal life may have fallen short of the Epicurean ideal of restraint and self-discipline, which may be why Lucretius wished to convert him. Nothing is known of the relationship: they may have been friends, acquaintances, or near strangers. In 54 BCE Memmius was exiled after running a corrupt campaign in support of Julius Caesar. He was in Athens two years later when he engaged in a quarrel with the Epicureans there. It is thought that Lucretius was dead by the time the quarrel took place, but it suggests that Memmius did not take the poem's message to heart.

Into this Hellenistic world, which included Egypt, the Middle East, and Asia Minor, Rome expanded in the second century BCE. Just as it had transformed the other cultures exposed to it, Greek civilization now began to exert a profound influence on Roman culture, which was backward and unsophisticated by comparison. Eventually, Rome would become a conduit through which the Greek legacy was passed on to Western Europe. Lucretius himself was a pioneer in this process, which was still in its early stages during his lifetime.

The Mithridatic Wars, that is, the wars against Mithridates undertaken by Sulla and Pompey, proved to be a turning point. Mithridates (c. 128-63 BCE) was the last Hellenistic ruler to mount a serious challenge to Roman rule in the East. His large and powerful kingdom of Pontus in Asia

On the Nature of the Universe

GREEK PHILOSOPHY

Although Greek philosophy was a complex tapestry comprising many different strands of thought, by the first century BCE four main philosophical traditions had emerged. Each was associated with a Greek founder who had taught in Athens.

- **Academic philosophy** Founded by the Athenian philosopher Plato (c. 429-347 BCE), this tradition took its name from the "Academy," originally a grove of trees in Athens where Plato gathered with his students. Academic philosophy taught that the material world, the world detectable to human senses, is unreal. Each visible object corresponds to a nonmaterial "form" or "idea" of it, which represents true reality.
- **Peripatetic philosophy** Founded by Plato's student Aristotle (384-322 BCE), this tradition took its name from the covered walkway or *peripatos* where Aristotle taught at the school he founded in Athens (the school itself was called the Lyceum). In contrast to Academic philosophy, Peripatetic philosophy taught that the material world does indeed represent true reality.
- **Epicurean philosophy** This tradition was founded by Epicurus of Samos (341-270 BCE), who established a school in Athens c. 300 BCE. Epicurus taught that the only good in life is pleasure, by which he meant "peace of mind." Not all pleasure is good, only pleasure that is moderate and calm and that produces peace of mind. Excessive or immoderate pleasure is bad because it eventually leads to pain.
- **Stoic philosophy** Founded by Zeno of Citium (c. 335-c. 263 BCE), Stoicism took its name from the *stoa* or porch in Athens where Zeno taught his students. The Stoics saw a divine force everywhere, ordering everything. They taught that the good man maintains his philosophical self-possession in all circumstances, however dire or painful. The only duties of man are to avoid vice and practice virtue, which is based on knowledge.

Minor included important Greek cities, and in his campaigns against Rome he sought the support of Greeks in other cities, including Athens.

As a result of the Mithridatic Wars, starting in the 80s BCE large numbers of educated Greeks came to Rome. Some came as prisoners of war sold into slavery; others, as refugees. Some, too, were artists or intellectuals in search of a wealthy patron. Educated Greeks in Rome generally worked as teachers, scribes (slaves who copied literary works out by hand), or readers (slaves who read out loud to Roman aristocrats).

Thus, in the period in which Lucretius and his contemporaries were coming of age, Rome was exposed for the first time to Greek culture on a broad scale. One of the glories of Hellenistic civilization was Greek philosophy, literally "love of wisdom," which included what we consider science. Its undisputed capital was the city of Athens.

When Lucretius was a young man, each of the major Greek philosophies was represented in Rome by a well-known teacher who had come from Greece. For example, a popular and re-

spected Epicurean teacher named Phaedrus (c. 140-70 BCE) founded a school of Epicurean philosophy in Rome, probably sometime in the early 80s BCE. Lucretius' older contemporary, the Roman statesman, orator, and author Cicero (106-43 BCE), heard some of Phaedrus' lectures. Cicero reports that a large number of Romans were attracted to Epicureanism, and Phaedrus' teaching may have been partly responsible for the vogue that this philosophical tradition seems to have enjoyed in the late Roman republic. Although no evidence survives of any connection between Phaedrus and Lucretius, Phaedrus may have been the one who introduced Lucretius to the Epicurean ideas that Lucretius expounds so passionately in *On the Nature of the Universe*.

The Poem in Focus

Contents summary. *On the Nature of the Universe* survived into the Middle Ages in only one imperfect manuscript, on which all modern copies of the poem are based. The poem as we have it is clearly not complete, although scholars differ on how much might be missing, as well as on how much more work Lucretius may have had planned. They commonly suppose that the poet died just before completing a final draft and that the poem as we have it is substantially, if not totally, complete. The main reason for believing that the poem is nearly complete is that it is divided into six books of roughly equal length (ranging from about 1,100 lines to about 1,500 lines) and the reader is told that book 6 is the final one.

Thematically, the six books fall into three pairs:

- Books 1 and 2 explain physics and matter.
- Books 3 and 4 explain human psychology and sensory perception.
- Books 5 and 6 explain the history of life on earth and the origins of meteorological and geological phenomena.

Throughout the poem, it is important to bear in mind that the speaker is explaining not his own ideas, but those of Epicurus, whom he frequently praises. Lucretius' originality lies in how he translates the complex technicalities of Epicurean philosophy into poetic form.

Each book opens with a prologue or introduction. The longest of these is the prologue to book 1, which serves also as an introduction to the poem as a whole. The speaker begins by invoking the aid of Venus, the Roman goddess of love and the mother of Aeneas, Rome's mythical founder. He offers his dedication to the Roman politician Memmius, then concludes the prologue by praising Epicurus, the Greek philosopher who, the poet declares, first used reason to free humanity from the shackles of religious superstition:

> When human life lay grovelling in all men's sight, crushed to the earth under the dead weight of superstition whose grim features loured menacingly upon mortals from the four corners of the sky . . . a man of Greece was first to raise mortal eyes in defiance, first to stand erect and brave the challenge. . . . He ventured far out . . . voyaged in mind throughout infinity.
> (On the Nature of the Universe, 1.62-74)

From this mind's journey, the speaker continues, Epicurus returned with an understanding of how the universe works, of how nature is organized. "Therefore superstition in its turn lies crushed beneath his feet, and we by his triumph are lifted level with the skies" (On the Nature of the Universe, 1.78-79).

The rest of book 1 lays the cornerstones of Epicurean physics. Asserting that "nothing can be created out of nothing," the speaker begins to

address himself to the problem of "how things are created and occasioned without the aid of gods" (On the Nature of the Universe, 1.155-158). The universe, he declares, contains only matter and empty space, and all matter is made up of tiny indivisible particles called atoms. Before continuing, the speaker refutes the rival theories of other Greek philosophers about the universe's composition (for example, that all things in the universe are made up of one or two substances or that each type of thing has its own substance).

Book 2 focuses on the atoms themselves. Atoms are always in motion; the solidity of material objects is an illusion. There is a large but finite number of types of atoms, although the number of atoms is infinite. The qualities of all objects comes from the size and shape of the atoms comprising them. The atoms themselves, however, have no color, temperature, sound, taste, or smell. It is only their ever-changing combination with other atoms that makes it seem as if objects have these qualities.

Book 3 explains how atoms combine to form life. The prologue to this book introduces another fundamental Epicurean idea—that all evil in the world comes from the fear of death. The speaker explains that mind and spirit are material in nature, and are therefore comprised of atoms, like everything else. Their atoms are very small and loosely connected, with much empty space between them. The empty space, or void, allows the atoms to move. On death they drift apart like smoke. Since there is no afterlife, there is therefore no reason to fear death. Only by conquering fear of death can mortal beings be happy.

Book 4 describes sensory perception and how it influences the mind. By far the most space is given to explaining vision, which is described as a form of touch. Objects are visible because they give off a thin film of atoms, which strikes our eyes. Mental images are made up of even thinner films, which strike only the atoms of our minds. The last few hundred lines of book 4 deal with the effects of sex and love. While sex is pleasurable and leads to procreation, love disturbs the balance of reason and so ought to be avoided. Even if love is returned, it never brings satisfaction. The lover always craves more of his beloved's company, ignoring the business of his life and wasting his wealth on his beloved. If love is not returned, he is more miserable yet.

With book 5, the speaker moves to the larger scale of the universe, the earth, and human society as a whole. The world was formed not by the gods, says this book, but by the random coming together of atoms; it will end when the bonds between those atoms are dissolved. Plant and animal life arose from the heat and moisture of the earth. Since life was harder, early humans were stronger and more robust than modern ones. People emerged from savagery to civilization gradually, as social bonds provided protection from danger and experience gave rise to technology.

The final book, 6, covers natural wonders and is divided between atmospheric and terrestrial phenomena. The speaker focuses on events such as thunder, earthquakes, volcanoes, and floods that people have traditionally ascribed to the gods. Upholding his secular approach, he explains each one as arising ultimately from the movement of atoms. The book and the poem conclude abruptly with a graphic description of the plague at Athens in the fifth century BCE, based on a famous passage in the *Peloponnesian War,* by the Greek historian Thucydides (also in *Classical Literature and Its Times*).

Freedom from strife. Because it equates pleasure with good, Epicureanism has often been misunderstood as simple hedonism, or the unrestrained pursuit of sensual pleasures such as food, drink, and sex. Today, for example, the term "Epicurean" is used mainly to describe gourmet cooking—a usage that has nothing at all to do with the teachings of Epicurus. This same misunderstanding was also common in Lucretius' day, and Lucretius clearly hopes to set the record straight.

In the prologue to book 2, the speaker defines the highest pleasure according to Epicurean doctrine:

> But this is the greatest joy of all: to possess a quiet sanctuary, stoutly fortified by the teaching of the wise, and to gaze down from that elevation on others wandering aimlessly in search of a way of life, pitting their wits one against another, disputing for precedence, struggling night and day with unstinted effort to scale the pinnacles of wealth and power. O joyless hearts of men! O minds without vision! How dark and dangerous the life in which this tiny span is lived away! Do you not see that nature is barking for two things only, a body free from pain, a mind released from worry and fear for the enjoyment of pleasurable sensations?
>
> (*On the Nature of the Universe,* 2.7-19)

In other words, Epicurean doctrine defines pleasure negatively rather than positively, as the absence of something rather than its presence: pleasure is the absence of pain, care, and fear. Even wisdom is valuable primarily because it lets the wise remove themselves from "the strife of wits" that dominates the rest of humankind. Epicurean philosophy summed up this negative definition of pleasure with the Greek word *ataraxia*, "tranquility," or "freedom from strife."

The attractions of *ataraxia* to a poet living through an age of civil strife are obvious. In invoking the aid of Venus, the goddess of love, Lucretius transforms her into a symbol of peace as well. "Grant that this brutal business of war by sea and land may everywhere be lulled to rest," the speaker pleads with her in the prologue to book 1 (*On the Nature of the Universe*, 1.29-30). She can do so, he asserts, because of her seductive power over her lover Mars, the god of war: "as he lies outstretched . . . enfold him at rest in your hallowed bosom and whisper with those lips sweet words of prayer, beseeching for the people of Rome untroubled peace" (*On the Nature of the Universe*, 1.38-40).

Epicureanism was not the only Greek philosophy to emphasize tranquility as an important element of the good life. The writings of the Stoics also stress the ethical and moral desirability of *ataraxia*. Yet the Stoics drew the opposite conclusion from the Epicureans about how to achieve it. Whereas the Epicureans sought to avoid strife altogether, the Stoics sought to endure and ultimately to quell it. In Stoic philosophy, the pursuit of *ataraxia* calls for active engagement in public life, rather than withdrawal from it. Stoicism thus agreed with traditional aristocratic Roman values such as military duty and public service, and ultimately it would prove the most attractive of the Greek philosophies to the Roman upper classes. Even in Lucretius' own time, when Epicureanism enjoyed its brief surge of popularity at Rome, Lucretius' contemporary Cicero was writing in praise of the Stoics.

Sources and literary context. Lucretius drew on a wide range of philosophical and poetic sources in writing *On the Nature of the Universe*. Most important were the writings of Epicurus himself. Indeed, the title of the poem is a rough translation of the title of Epicurus' best known work, *Peri Physeos*, "On Nature," which has survived only in brief fragments. Another work of Epicurus, however, has survived: the "Letter to Herodotus," which shows close parallels with *On*

The Greek philosopher Epicurus; 1810 engraving by George Cooke. The Library of Congress. Reproduced by permission.

the Nature of the Universe. Modern scholars believe that this work may have been Lucretius' main source. Several of the more "scientific" passages of Lucretius' poem amount to loose translations of it. In other passages, Lucretius expands Epicurus' straightforward prose with vivid poetic images. This poetic quality comes through even in a prose translation of the Latin verses in Lucretius' poem:

From Epicurus' "Letter to Herodotus"

For all these, whether small or great, have been separated off from special conglomerations of atoms; and all things are again dissolved, some faster, some slower, some through the action of one set of causes, some through the action of another.

(Epicurus, p. 603)

From Lucretius' *On the Nature of the Universe*

It is natural, therefore, that everything should perish when it is thinned out by the ebbing out of matter and succumbs to blows from without. The food supply is no longer adequate for its aged frame, and the deadly bombardment of particles from without never pauses in the work of dissolution and subdual.

(*On the Nature of the Universe*, 2.1139-1145)

Epicurus wrote in prose and seems to have disparaged the arts, which puts Lucretius in the potentially uncomfortable position of writing a poem in which he passionately exalts the beliefs of a man who does not appear to have valued poetry. Still, although tension between poets and philosophers was already a common theme among ancient writers, a strong tradition of didactic or "teaching" poetry did exist in both Greek and Latin literature. A number of early Greek philosophers had even written their works in poetry. Lucretius singles out the Greek philosopher Empedocles (c. 490-c. 430 BCE) as second only to Epicurus in deserving praise; interestingly, Empedocles had written a philosophical poem called *Peri Physeos*, "On Nature." He viewed the world as balanced between the forces of Love and Strife. Although he was not an Epicurean, this idea clearly fits in with Epicureanism, and helped inspire Lucretius' own poetic vision.

POET OF PARADOX?

Critics have often noted that Lucretius' poem embraces a number of seeming contradictions. He is a poet writing about an unpoetic subject, a passionate advocate of a cause that denounces passion, and an apparently anti-religious thinker who invokes the aid of a goddess (Venus) in composing his poem. Some of these paradoxes can be partly resolved by closer consideration of the poet's goals. For example, Lucretius understands how dry his subject matter may seem. In a famous passage near the end of book 1, he writes that he wishes to sweeten his philosophy with poetry, just as doctors smear honey on the rims of cups that hold bitter medicine so children will drink it. Finally, epic poets traditionally ask for the aid of a goddess or muse, and in fact Lucretius never claims that the gods don't exist—merely that they don't have anything to do with the human world. Instead, they exist in an ideal state, free from all care about human activity.

The traditional verse form for didactic poetry was the dactylic hexameter, in which each line contains six long syllables. Hexameter was also the traditional form of epic poetry, and Lucretius' main poetic model was the early Latin poet Ennius (239-169 BCE), who aspired to be a Latin version of the Greek epic poet Homer (eighth century BCE). Sometimes called the father of Roman poetry, Ennius used hexameter for his narrative epic of Roman history, the *Annales*. Lucretius mentions Ennius by name as the first poet "destined to win renown among the nations of Italy" (*On the Nature of the Universe*, 1.117-119).

The influence of Ennius and epic poetry can be seen in Lucretius' fondness for compound words like *montivagus*, "mountain-wandering," or *fluctifragus*, "wave-smashing," as well as in such formulaic expressions as *caeli lucida templa*, "the shining temples of the sky" (a variant of Ennius' phrase *caeli caerula templa*, "the deep-blue temples of the sky"). Lucretius also uses obsolete Latin words and word forms from Ennius' era, much as a writer today might use words or expressions from Shakespeare or the King James Bible to evoke a sense of grandeur or majesty.

Lucretius' use of such techniques testifies to his desire to sound "old-fashioned," a literary approach that modern scholars refer to as *archaism*. His archaism sets him apart from other poets of his day, such as the younger Catullus (c. 84-54 BCE), who in his **Carmina** strove to sound fresh and new (also in *Classical Literature and Its Times*).

At the same time that he looks back, however, Lucretius also implicitly looks forward to a new age for Latin poetry. Still in its infancy as a literary language when Lucretius was writing, Latin lacked the breadth and flexibility necessary to explain complex philosophical ideas. Lucretius complains several times about "the poverty of our native tongue," saying that it has made his job more difficult (*On the Nature of the Universe*, 3.260). Like his archaism, such complaints fit Lucretius' poetic persona, which is that of an impassioned prophet struggling against the odds to bring the wisdom of the ages to an ignorant and troubled people.

Reception and impact. Little is known about Lucretius himself, and we don't know of any ancient Romans who were converted to Epicureanism by reading *On the Nature of the Universe*, his only work. Yet on the strength of this one poem, Lucretius remains one of the most respected and influential of all Latin poets. Cicero, the leading intellectual in the late Roman republic, was one of the first to recognize the poem's literary worth. In a letter to his brother, Quintus, who had himself apparently just referred to it in glowing terms, Cicero writes: "The poetry of Lucretius is, as you say in your letter, rich in brilliant genius, yet highly artistic" (Cicero in Smith, p. xi).

Cicero's letter, which reflects the traditional Roman distinction between inborn talent (genius) and technical skill (art), was written in February of 54 BCE. Lucretius is thought to have died perhaps a few months before the letter's date, near the end of the previous year.

Some two decades later, the poet universally recognized as Rome's greatest would pay a famous tribute to Lucretius. A boy of about 15 when Lucretius died, Virgil (70-19 BCE) was deeply influenced by the earlier poet's imagery and language. In his own didactic poem *Georgics* (30s BCE), Virgil applauds Lucretius for his achievement: "Lucky is he who can learn the roots of the universe, / Has mastered all his fears and fate's intransigence / And the hungry clamor of hell" (Virgil, *Georgics,* 2.490-492).

While Lucretius' poetry has always been admired by readers and emulated by poets, the poem's content has also served as our best surviving source for the thought of Epicurus. During the period in European history known as the Enlightenment (c. 1650-c. 1800 CE), scientists and intellectuals who exalted the power of reason regarded Lucretius as a hero. At the dawn of the Enlightenment, the French scientist Pierre Gassendi (1592-1655) revived Epicurean physics, especially the theory of atomism, making important contributions to the development of modern science. Gassendi listed Lucretius among his favorite authors. Since then, scientists have confirmed many of the same speculative ideas that Lucretius championed so forcefully more than two millennia ago.

—Colin Wells

For More Information

Boardman, John, et al. *The Oxford History of the Classical World: The Roman World.* Oxford: Oxford University Press, 1986.

Brown, P. Michael. *Lucretius: De Rerum Natura I.* Bristol, U.K.: Bristol Classical Press, 1984.

Epicurus. "Letter to Herodotus." In *Lives of the Eminent Philosophers,* by Diogenes Laertius. Vol. 2. Trans. R. D. Hicks. Cambridge, Mass.: Harvard University Press, 1950.

Kenney, E. J. *Lucretius.* Oxford: Clarendon Press, 1977.

Lucretius Carus, Titus. *De Rerum Natura III.* Ed. E. J. Kenney. Cambridge: Cambridge University Press, 1971.

———. *On the Nature of the Universe.* Trans. R. E. Latham. New York: Penguin, 1994.

Sharrock, Alison, and Rhiannon Ash. *Fifty Key Classical Authors.* London: Routledge, 2002.

Smith, Martin Ferguson. "Introduction." In *On the Nature of Things,* by Lucretius. Loeb series. Cambridge, Mass.: Harvard University Press, 2002.

Virgil. *The Eclogues; The Georgics.* Trans. C. Day Lewis. Oxford: Oxford University Press, 1983.

Oresteia

by
Aeschylus

The Athenian tragic dramatist Aeschylus (c. 525 BCE-c. 456 BCE) is thought to have been born in Eleusis, a town northwest of Athens, and to have written 70 to 90 plays. Of this large total, only seven or possibly six plays survive (some scholars now doubt Aeschylus' authorship of one play traditionally attributed to him, *Prometheus Bound*). Athenian tragedies were generally written and produced in trilogies in Aeschylus' day, though the practice appears to have afterwards died out. The *Oresteia* is the only of these trilogies by any author that has survived intact. In antiquity, these trilogies competed against one another. Altogether Aeschylus is credited with 13 first-place victories, his first in 484 BCE. After that, he dominated the field until his death. Of the six surviving plays securely attributed to Aeschylus, *Persians* was produced in 472 BCE, *Seven Against Thebes* in 467 BCE, *Suppliants* in 463 BCE, and the three plays of the *Oresteia*, for which Aeschylus won his thirteenth and last first-place prize, in 458 BCE. The *Oresteia* was Aeschylus' final production in Athens; shortly after it was produced, he moved to Syracuse in Sicily, where he died a year or two later. Appearing at the climax of the Athenian Empire, which emerged during Aeschylus' lifetime, the *Oresteia* ostensibly deals with events from Greece's mythical past. More subtly, the work celebrates Athens' new imperial status and democratic ideals; it also comments on related issues in contemporary Athenian politics.

THE LITERARY WORK

A trilogy of tragic dramas (*Agamemnon, The Libation Bearers, The Eumenides*) written in Greek and first produced in Athens, Greece, in 458 BCE.

SYNOPSIS

The trilogy depicts the murder of Agamemnon, king of Argos, by his wife Clytaemestra and her lover Aegisthus as well as the revenge killing of the murderers by Orestes (her son by Agamemnon) and Orestes' subsequent trial in Athens.

Events in History at the Time of the Plays

Epic poetry and the rise of Greek tragedy. Most classical tragic drama draws its subject matter from the mythic world of epic poetry. The characters and events in the *Oresteia* are adapted from a series of short epic poems, which in antiquity were sometimes attributed to Homer, sometimes to lesser-known poets. Direct influences, these poems concern the history of the descendants of Atreus, a mythical king of the ancient Greek city of Mycenae. More indirectly, Homer's **Iliad** and the **Odyssey**, which together comprise a foundation for all Greek literature, remain vital influences on Aeschylus' literary sensibilities (both also in *Classical Literature and Its Times*).

Aeschylus. © Araldo de Lyca/Corbis

The origins of tragedy itself remain shrouded in mystery—it may have originated in Athens, as some of the ancient authorities maintained, or elsewhere in Greece, as others stated. By the late sixth century BCE, roughly the time of Aeschylus' birth, it had taken hold in Athens and the surrounding territory of Attica. There early tragic plays were performed each spring as part of the City Dionysia, an important religious festival dedicated to Dionysus, the god of wine and revelry. In all likelihood, tragedy originated in performances staged as part of the ritual worship of this divinity by rural dwellers. Probably these rural dwellers brought their performances to the city when they came to sell their goods in the marketplace.

If its origins likely lie in Dionysian rites, tragedy's historical development in Athenian culture was definitively shaped by epic poetry. Later critics such as Plato and Aristotle, the fourth-century BCE Greek philosophers, regarded Homer as the first true tragedian; as Aeschylus himself put it, "We are all eating crumbs from the great table of Homer" (Aeschylus in Boardman, p. 151). From Homer, for example, came the grand themes with which tragedy would always be concerned, especially the *hubris* or overreaching pride of the tragic hero, along with the fate the gods have reserved as a punishment for it. In tragedy, as in epic, that divine justice can often span generations.

In the *Oresteia*, for example, the fates of Agamemnon and his children have been predetermined by an original offense on the part of Atreus, Agamemnon's father. Atreus had killed the children of his brother Thyestes and then served them to Thyestes at a banquet, driving Thyestes mad. Atreus' blood guilt caused the gods to lay a curse on his descendants, collectively referred to as "the house of Atreus." This curse, like other basic plot elements, would already have been familiar to Aeschylus' audience from Homeric epic. The crowd's enjoyment came from seeing these familiar elements worked out in a fresh way over the course of the trilogy.

The evolution of Athenian democracy. Tragedy was a highly popular form of entertainment, and it seems hardly accidental that its development in Athens parallels the rise and expansion of democratic institutions there. A case in point is Aeschylus' play *Suppliants* (463 BCE), which shows concern for the democratic issue of accountability to the people. According to one historian, the way the play's King Pelasgus replies to refugees who seek asylum in his city is indicative of the progressive empowerment of the common people in the 460s BCE.

> You are not suppliants at my own hearth;
> If the city in common incurs pollution,
> In common let the people work a cure.
> But I would make no promises until
> I share with all the citizens.
> (Aeschylus in Davies, pp. 71-72)

Just over 40 years earlier, in 508 BCE, the democratic reformer Cleisthenes introduced a new system of government in Athens. The system was based on the *boule*, a council of 500 male citizens. Before Cleisthenes, the most important political institution had been the elite council of the Areopagus, the oldest body of magistrates, which represented the aristocratic upper class. It was this body that Cleisthenes partly replaced with the more democratically chosen council of the 500. Possibly modeled on systems in use elsewhere (though this remains unclear), Cleisthenes' reform divided the populace of Attica into 139 districts, or *demoi* (demes), then further apportioned the population of the demes among 10 tribes, or *phylai*. The council was made up of 50 representatives chosen by lot from each tribe. In effect, the reform transferred loyalties from the family to the deme, establishing a society based on citizenship rather than kinship.

Cleisthenes also broadened the powers of the popular assembly, or *ekklesia*, which had existed since at least the early sixth century BCE. Under Cleisthenes' reforms, the council's main function was to prepare business for the assembly, which now became the main governing body of Athens. The assembly met several times a month, and any citizen—that is, any Athenian male over the age of 20—had the right to speak and vote there. As with the other organs of government, women, slaves, and foreigners were excluded from participation. While the total number of free male citizens is estimated to have been about 30,000, only around 6,000 could attend the assembly at any one time, owing to the space available at the meeting site (called the Pnyx). The assembly made most major policy decisions and appointed legislators from among its members to write new laws. Athenian democracy thus differed from modern democracies in being direct rather than representative.

Citizens could challenge the laws in court and could also sue political and military leaders for misconduct. Such suits were decided in law courts called *dikasteria*, in which the juries were composed of citizens chosen by lot. A board of nine magistrates, called *archons*, summoned the councils, oversaw the law courts, and supervised the many regularly scheduled religious festivals (including the City Dionysia, at which the tragedies were performed).

Athenian democracy was supported by many of the same ideological principles familiar to democratic societies today. The highest ideal was freedom (*eleutheria*), which included the right to political participation and the right to live according to one's own desires within the law. It also included *parrhesia*, or freedom of speech, which protected a citizen's right to public speech in the assembly as well as his right to speak freely in private. Again, these rights were accorded not to all, but only to free adult males who were citizens of Athens.

An especially important component of freedom was legal equality, the idea that all citizens were equal before the law. More than anything else, Athenians viewed their democracy as embodying the rule of law. In *Agamemnon*, Clytaemestra's crime overturns the established order. It is reestablished only at the climax of the final play, *The Eumenides*, when the goddess Athena herself, special protector to the city of Athens, delivers the deciding judgment, which acquits Orestes. Athena's decision lifts the curse on the house of Atreus and represents the tri-

umph of the rule of law over the forces of chaos. The trilogy begins with the "chaos" of intra-familial bloodshed rooted in two conflicting but morally defensible points of view. But from this beginning, it builds slowly to an explicit celebration of the newer ideal of the rule of law. In doing so, the trilogy points the way forward in time to the fully democratic Athens familiar to Aeschylus' audience.

The reforms of Ephialtes. After Cleisthenes, the next major changes to the Athenian system came in 462 BCE, just a few years before the *Oresteia* was produced. Initiated by the Athenian democratic leader Ephialtes, these reforms are essential to the trilogy's immediate political context.

ATHENIAN TRAGEDY IN PERFORMANCE

The staging of tragic plays probably began in Athens in the late sixth century BCE, during Aeschylus' young adulthood. In addition to the innovation of the stage itself, this period saw the development of other conventions that grew common as dramatic performances became popular in other cities. In subsequent legend, the sixth-century inventor of tragedy was the Athenian Thespis, from whose name we get the English word "Thespian," or actor. Many modern scholars, however, doubt that Thespis existed. The earliest form of performance may have involved just the chorus, a group of actors meant to represent a single character. Individual actors were then added: Aeschylus himself is credited with increasing the number of actors from one to two, and with reducing the role of the chorus. The actors used large masks, and performances were highly stylized.

While Cleisthenes' reforms had limited its powers, the Areopagus continued to exist and to exercise broad and vaguely defined political powers. For example, the Areopagus could hear complaints brought by one citizen against another for harming the state, and could try to punish the defendant. Scholars also believe the Areopagus had the power to hold investigations (*euthynai*) into the official conduct of magistrates.

In 462 Ephialtes brought a motion before the assembly to strip the Areopagus of these and other powers. The motion passed into law, leaving the Areopagus with only one real power: jurisdiction over murder trials. By curtailing the

ATHENS AND THE PERSIAN WARS

The Athenian Empire emerged directly from Athens' role, earlier in the fifth century BCE, in defeating two invasions of Greece by the mighty Persian Empire. Called the Persian Wars, these conflicts, in 490 and 480-79 BCE, set the stage for Athens' rise to power. Before them, Sparta had been the acknowledged leader of the Greek city-states. But because Athens took the lead in repelling both Persian invasions, it emerged with enhanced prestige and authority after them, challenging Sparta's traditional claims to leadership. As a soldier-citizen of democratic Athens, Aeschylus himself took part in both wars. He is reported to have fought with particular bravery at the battle of Marathon in 490 BCE, when Athenian soldiers, together with a contingent from nearby Plataea, boldly attacked and overwhelmed a much larger Persian force that had landed on the plain of Marathon near Athens. This crucial victory turned back the invading force, and Aeschylus' conspicuous role in it may have been his proudest achievement. His funerary epitaph records not his dramatic achievements, though they were highly lauded, but simply that he fought with distinction at Marathon. Ten years later Aeschylus is also thought to have fought at Salamis, where Athens led the Greeks in repelling an even larger second Persian invasion. Their decisive naval battle forms the backdrop for his play *Persians* (472 BCE), which—with startling sympathy for the Persians—portrays their defeated king Xerxes and his mother, Atossa, as tragic figures.

broad authority of the Areopagus, Ephialtes brought Athenian democracy to its fullest realization. Shortly after his reforms were passed, Ephialtes was assassinated. His supporters accused his political enemies, the embittered aristocratic "oligarchs," of the crime. (The term stems from "oligarchy," or "rule by few," and refers to the more conservative political system based on the traditional power of the aristocracy.)

These events were still fresh when Aeschylus produced the *Oresteia*. In *The Eumenides*, the Areopagus is the setting for Orestes' murder trial, which is depicted in such a way as to suggest that its jurisdiction over homicide cases constituted the Areopagus' original and therefore rightful function. Aeschylus, critics have concluded, thus indirectly implies his support for Ephialtes' reform.

Democracy and empire. Athens' foreign policy and the management of its empire were closely linked with developments in the Athenian political system. While critics have seen Aeschylus' endorsement of the democrats' domestic agenda as subtle and indirect, they regard the foreign policy message of the *Oresteia* as more overt and unequivocal. Aeschylus is seen as clearly supporting the aggressive anti-Spartan foreign policy associated with Ephialtes and other democratic leaders.

Among these others was Pericles (c. 495-429 BCE); Ephialtes' protégé and successor, Pericles would become the best-known Athenian statesman of his age.

Athens' empire, built up by its victories in the Persian Wars (490 and 480-79 BCE), was based on the powerful Athenian navy and consisted of most of the islands and coastline of the Aegean Sea. By contrast, Sparta, a land-based power, dominated much of the mainland, especially the Peloponnesus, the broad, leaf-shaped peninsula comprising southern Greece, where Sparta itself was located. In the years after the Persian Wars, tensions gradually rose between Athens and Sparta. Their ideologies contrasted sharply; while Sparta's political system was authoritarian and oligarchic, Athens' was open and democratic. (By the 430s BCE, as the Athenian historian Thucydides writes, the entire Greek world would be divided into two hostile camps. On one side stood Athens and its largely democratic subjects in the empire; on the other, stood Sparta with its mostly oligarchic allies in the Peloponnesus and elsewhere. This polarization was still in its beginning stages when the *Oresteia* was produced.)

Ephialtes, the democratic reformer, had a major opponent in Athenian politics named Cimon.

Peloponnesian War, this conflict lasted from 460 to 446 BCE and eventually brought Athens into direct but inconclusive conflict with Sparta. Again, critics have noted repeated expressions of support for the democrats' aggressive policies in *The Eumenides*. They also observe that Aeschylus often seems to promote foreign aggression as a healing influence at home, a way to alleviate the sort of domestic tensions that had resulted in Ephialtes' mysterious death, by assassination, his supporters believed. At one point in the *Oresteia,* the goddess urges the Athenian jurors not to "engraft among my citizens that spirit of war / that turns their battle fury in upon themselves. / No, let our wars range outward" (*The Eumenides*, lines 862-864). Elsewhere, too, the Chorus prays that "Civil War / fattening on men's ruin shall / not thunder in our city. Let / not the dry dust that drinks / the black blood of citizens / through passion for revenge / and bloodshed for bloodshed / be given our state to prey upon" (*The Eumenides*, lines 975-983). As one scholar observes, such "clear allusions to matters of a highly topical nature" are "quite unparalleled in anything else we know of Greek tragedy" (Sommerstein, p. 30).

The Plays in Focus

Plot summaries. The trilogy follows the family of Agamemnon, king of Argos, after his return from the Trojan War. In *Agamemnon*, the king is murdered by his wife Clytaemestra and his cousin Aegisthus, whom Clytaemestra has taken as a lover in Agamemnon's absence. In *The Libation Bearers*, Orestes—Agamemnon and Clytaemestra's son—is aided by his sister Electra in avenging their father by killing Clytaemestra and Aegisthus. In *The Eumenides*, Orestes is pursued for his crime by the Erinyes, or Furies, terrible creatures who enforce cosmic justice in Greek mythology, before the case is finally resolved in the law court of Athens.

Agamemnon. The first play is set in Argos, at the palace of Agamemnon, just after the fall of Troy at the hands of the Greeks. News comes of the Greek victory, and of Agamemnon's imminent return. The Chorus of Argive Elders enters and delivers a long speech recounting events preceding the war. The Trojan prince Paris had seduced Helen, Clytaemestra's sister and the wife of Agamemnon's brother Menelaus, king of Sparta, prompting the Greek expedition against Troy. The expedition was to be led by Agamemnon, senior king among the Greeks. But the Greeks had inadvertently angered Artemis, the goddess of the

Roman statue of Orestes and Electra. © Mimo Jodice/Corbis.

A conservative leader, Cimon, who dominated Athenian politics during much of the 460s BCE, pursued a policy of friendship towards Sparta. In c. 460 BCE, when Spartan actions gravely offended the Athenian populace, Cimon was exiled. This provided the opportunity for Ephialtes to push through his reform of the Areopagus. Under the leadership of the anti-Spartan politician Ephialtes, the Athenian assembly also signed an alliance with Sparta's enemy, Argos.

Aeschylus gives a prominent place to this still new alliance in the *Oresteia*. In *The Eumenides,* the Athenian jurors are promised on three separate occasions that if they vote to acquit Orestes, Athens will win "all the Argive host [army] to stand her staunch companion for the rest of time" (Aeschylus, *The Eumenides* in *Oresteia*, lines 290-291). In his commentary on *The Eumenides*, Alan Sommerstein notes that not everyone in the audience would have shared Aeschylus' partisan support for the anti-Spartan policy of the democrats: "It is taken for granted [in the play] that the alliance is a great and unmixed blessing for Athens; a proposition with which not all Athenians would necessarily have agreed" (Sommerstein, p. 30).

Shortly after the alliance, Pericles and the democratic leadership embroiled Athens in war against Sparta's ally Corinth. Called the First

KEY CHARACTERS IN THE *ORESTEIA*'S STORYLINE

Along with the characters who appear onstage in the *Oresteia*, there are a couple of offstage characters who do not appear but who have important roles in the background story.

Onstage Characters

Aegisthus: Lover of Clytaemestra; son of Thyestes, thus also Agamemnon's cousin.

Agamemnon: King of Argos; leader of the Greek army.

Apollo: A god of reason and order who protects Orestes.

The Argive Elders: The old men of Argos, loyal to Agamemnon, who make up the Chorus of *Agamemnon*.

Athena: A goddess of war and wisdom; patron of Athens.

Cassandra: A princess of Troy and a prophetess, taken as a war prize by Agamemnon.

Clytaemestra: Queen of Argos; wife of Agamemnon.

Electra: Daughter of Agamemnon and Clytaemestra; Orestes' sister.

The Erinyes: The Furies—ancient, savage, and implacable creatures who doggedly pursue all those who transgress the laws of nature. They form the Chorus of *The Eumenides*.

The Libation Bearers: Foreign serving women who form the Chorus of *The Libation Bearers*.

Orestes: Son of Agamemnon and Clytaemestra; Electra's brother.

Pylades: Orestes' friend.

Background Characters

Atreus: Agamemnon's father; Atreus murdered the children of his brother Thyestes (only Aegisthus survived).

Iphigenaia: Daughter of Agamemnon and Clytaemestra, whom Apollo ordered Agamemnon to sacrifice so that the Greeks might sail against Troy.

Thyestes: Atreus' brother; Aegisthus' father. Thyestes seduced Atreus' wife, beginning the chain of revenge that curses the family.

hunt, who had sent strong winds that kept the Greek fleet penned in the harbor at Aulis. Speaking through the priest Calchas, Apollo had ordered Agamemnon to placate Artemis by sacrificing Iphigenaia—Agamemnon and Clytaemestra's daughter—in order that the fleet might sail.

At first Agamemnon had been torn between his obligation as senior king (to lead the fleet) and his obligation as a father (to protect his daughter). Hardening himself as the other Greek leaders pressed him to do whatever was necessary, he had chosen to obey his obligation as senior king:

> But when necessity's yoke was put upon him
> he changed, and from the heart the breath
>   came bitter
> and sacrilegious, utterly infidel. . . .

> . . . . He endured then
> to sacrifice his daughter
> to stay the strength of war waged for a
>   woman,
> first offering for the ships' sake.
> Her supplications and her cries of father
> were nothing, nor the child's lamentation
> to kings impassioned for battle.
>   (*Agamemnon* in *Oresteia*, lines 217-220,
>   223-230)

Clytaemestra has entered as the Chorus speaks, and she now confirms the news that the Greeks have captured Troy. In further descriptive speeches, Clytaemestra and the Chorus express unease about the future. A herald announces Agamemnon's return, describing the hardship of war and the violence perpetrated by the Greek forces in capturing Troy. Angered by the violence, the gods sent a storm that wrecked much of the returning fleet.

Agamemnon arrives in a chariot with the Trojan princess Cassandra, whom he has taken as a war prize and who possesses powers of prophecy. Clytaemestra greets Agamemnon stiffly, offering an unconvincing excuse for the absence of their son, Orestes. She orders her servants to spread a luxurious purple carpet between the chariot and the palace door for Agamemnon to walk on; Agamemnon objects briefly to the unseemly extravagance of the gesture. They argue, Agamemnon noting that Clytaemestra's "lust for conflict is not woman-like" (*Agamemnon*, line 940). The two enter the palace. Bothered by a vague but persistent fear, the Chorus remains with Cassandra. Clytaemestra returns and with open hostility to the younger woman orders Cassandra to enter the palace.

After Clytaemestra exits, Cassandra (whose fate is to foretell the future accurately but never to be understood) steps down from the chariot. She now foretells a "new and huge stroke / of atrocity" that Clytaemestra "plans within the house," but the Chorus responds that it "can make nothing of these prophesies" (*Agamemnon*, lines 1101-1102, 1105). In a long conversation with the Chorus, Cassandra becomes more and more agitated, eventually saying plainly that she and Agamemnon are both to be killed. The Chorus still does not seem to understand. Cassandra enters the palace hopelessly.

As the Chorus wonders aloud how long the curse on the house of Atreus will continue, Agamemnon is heard to cry out twice from inside the palace that he has been mortally wounded. The Chorus falls into disarray, each member speaking paired lines, a reflection of the confusion. The palace doors open to reveal the dead bodies of Agamemnon and Cassandra. Clytaemestra emerges and announces that she has avenged the sacrifice of her daughter Iphigenaia. The Chorus laments, but Clytaemestra rejects the Chorus's accusations:

> Can you claim I have done this?
> Speak of me never
> more as the wife of Agamemnon.
> In the shadow of this corpse's queen
> the old stark avenger
> of Atreus for his revel of hate
> struck down this man,
> last blood for the slaughtered children.
> (*Agamemnon*, lines 1497-1504)

Aegisthus enters with an armed bodyguard and reveals his complicity in the murders, which he calls "just punishment" (*Agamemnon*, line 1611). Clytaemestra calls for reconciliation, but Aegisthus and the Chorus of Argive Elders profess undying hatred of each other. As the play ends, the Chorus looks forward to the day when "God's guiding hand brings Orestes home again" (*Agamemnon*, line 1666).

The Libation Bearers. The second play is also set in Argos, but several years later. Aegisthus and Clytaemestra are now ruling as king and queen. The play opens at the tomb of Agamemnon, as Orestes and his friend Pylades enter dressed as travelers. Having just returned to Argos, Orestes comes to mourn at his father's grave. He puts a lock of hair on the tomb and stands aside with Pylades. Electra, his sister, enters with a chorus of foreign serving women. At Clytaemestra's request, Electra has brought them to help her pour out a libation (ritual offering of ceremonial liquid) at Agamemnon's tomb. Clytaemestra has been tormented by nightmares and hopes the libation will placate Agamemnon's hostile spirit, which she holds responsible for her dreams. As Electra makes the libation, she notices the lock of hair and recognizes it as Orestes'. They reunite joyfully. Professing hatred for their mother, Electra hopes that Orestes' "strength of hand" will "win your father's house again" (*The Libation Bearers* in *Oresteia*, line 237).

They invoke the dead king's spirit to help them gain revenge, which they then plan out. Posing as a traveler, Orestes will go to the palace and seek entry as a suppliant, since custom dictates that Aegisthus and Clytaemestra must offer sanctuary to anyone seeking it. Having lulled them with false news of his own death, Orestes will then kill them both. The scene shifts to outside the palace doors, as Orestes and Pylades arrive to carry out the plan. Clytaemestra welcomes them, not recognizing Orestes, and graciously offers them every possible hospitality. They go inside. Orestes' childhood nurse enters briefly, saddened by the news of Orestes' death, but the Chorus hints to her that Orestes may not be gone after all. The Chorus then prays to Zeus "that those who struggle hard to see / temperate things done in the house win their aim / in full" (*The Libation Bearers*, lines 785-787).

Aegisthus enters briefly and states his intention to interrogate the visitor regarding Orestes' death. He goes inside the palace, and shortly afterward a cry is heard. One of Aegisthus' followers then emerges with the news of his murder. With Pylades, Orestes then reveals himself to Clytaemestra before the palace doors. They argue, and Clytaemestra realizes his intention:

> Clytaemestra: I think, child, that you mean to
>   kill your mother.
> Orestes: No.
> It will be you who kill yourself. It will not be I.
> Clytaemestra: Take care. Your mother's curse,
>   like dogs,
> will drag you down.
> Orestes: How shall I escape my father's curse,
>   if I fail here?
>
> (*The Libation Bearers*, lines 922-945)

Orestes and Pylades take Clytaemestra inside the palace. The Chorus hopes out loud that the chain of bloodshed has reached an end as the doors open to reveal Orestes. He stands over the bodies of Clytaemestra and Aegisthus. Justifying his act, Orestes says that the priest of Apollo has declared him guiltless in exacting his rightful revenge. Yet he cries out as the Furies, visible only to him, arrive to plague him relentlessly for the murder of his mother. Overcome by madness, he flees in panic. Where will it end, the Chorus wonders, as the play closes.

The Eumenides. The third play opens outside the shrine of Apollo at Delphi. A priestess enters and invokes all the gods, old and new, who have dwelled on the site since the beginning of time. She goes into the temple but immediately comes out again, terrified by the sight inside—a blood-stained Orestes crouches there, surrounded by the exhausted and now sleeping Furies. Next to Orestes stand Apollo and Hermes (the messenger god). Since it was he who made Orestes kill Clytaemestra, says Apollo, he will never give Orestes up to the Furies. Apollo sends Orestes to Athens, with Hermes as an escort. The Furies sleep on, until awoken by the ghost of Clytaemestra, who vanishes as they stir. Enraged to find their prey gone, they are driven away by Apollo, who informs them that he has sent Orestes to seek sanctuary with Athena in Athens. He tells them to go too, and to plead their case before her.

The scene changes to Athens, before the temple of Athena on the steep central hill known as the Acropolis. Orestes enters and bows down in supplication at the feet of Athena's statue. A chorus enters, made up of the Furies. They see Orestes and chant a magical spell in the form of a long ode or song, meant to "bind" him in their power (*The Eumenides* in *Oresteia*, line 306). Informing the audience about the powers of the Furies, the ode also reveals them to be an ancient authority; their powers go back to a time before the birth of Athena,

Apollo, and the other Olympian gods. Speaking of the Furies as a collective unit, the song concludes:

> Is there a man who does not fear
> this, does not shrink to hear
> how my place has been ordained,
> granted and given by destiny
> and god, absolute? Privilege
> primeval yet is mine, nor am I without place
> though it be underneath the ground
> and in no sunlight and in gloom that I must
>   stand.
>
> (*The Eumenides*, lines 389-396)

Athena enters in full armor, and the Furies and Orestes both agree to submit to her judgment. She goes to summon her best citizens to act as a jury. In another ode, the Chorus affirms its role of protecting the world from anarchy, since all order would dissolve if crimes such as murder were allowed to go unpunished. "There are times when fear is good," the Furies maintain. "There is / advantage / in the wisdom won from pain" (*The Eumenides*, lines 517, 519-521). Athena reenters with 12 Athenian citizens and a herald, who assembles the jurors. They are sworn in as the founding members of the council of the Areopagus, the oldest body of magistrates, representatives of the upper class.

The trial begins, with the Furies acting as prosecutors and Apollo acting for the defense. Orestes is the first witness. He admits killing Clytaemestra, but claims he was compelled to do so by Apollo, and that Clytaemestra herself was guilty of murdering Agamemnon, a far worse crime. Apollo himself then testifies that he was acting strictly according to the wishes of Zeus, ruler of the Olympian gods. Next Apollo offers several more dubious arguments on Orestes' behalf. He claims, for example, that a mother is not really of the same blood as a child, whose blood comes from the father. At one point he also urges the jurors to disregard their oath. The jurors vote in equal numbers for each side, but Athena has already announced that in event of a tie she will vote to acquit. Referring to her own origins (she was said to have sprung fully armored from Zeus' head), she claims that since she has no mother herself, she is always on the side of the male.

Orestes rejoices and, free to go, he leaves with Apollo. The Furies remain, embittered, and Athena attempts to soothe them by offering them an honored place upon the Acropolis, where they will be worshipped forever by the grateful Athenians. At length the Furies are won over, and pronounce their blessings on the city.

CLYTAEMESTRA

Clytaemestra may constitute the greatest threat to the male social order of any woman in Greek tragedy. Unlike the dangerous title character of Euripides' **Medea** (also in *Classical Literature and Its Times*), Clytaemestra is Greek. Yet she in no way feels hindered by the male-centered values of the Greeks, intimating as much when she addresses the (male) Chorus:

> You try me out as if I were a woman and vain;
> but my heart is not fluttered as I speak before you.
> You know it. You can praise or blame me as you wish;
> it is all one to me. That man is Agamemnon, my husband;
> he is dead; the work of this right hand
> that struck in strength of righteousness. And that is that.
> (*Agamemnon,* lines 1401-1406)

Clytaemestra not only refuses to accept the customary treatment shown to women; she also lays claim to the right of revenge, which traditionally belongs to men. Further still, she proclaims that killing her husband and his Trojan concubine gives her sexual pleasure: "He lies there; and she who swanlike cried / aloud her lyric mortal lamentation out / is laid against his fond heart, and to me has given / a delicate excitement to my bed's delight" (*Agamemnon,* lines 1444-1447). Clytaemestra even partially usurps Agamemnon's place as lord of Argos, insofar as she declares Aegisthus and herself to be co-rulers of the city. On the other hand, she is an adulterous wife who aids in the dispossession and murder of her husband, and her role as such underscores the threat that a woman could conceivably pose to the man of the house should she grow dissatisfied with him.

Old and new in conflict. In *The Libation Bearers,* as Orestes and Electra plan their revenge, Orestes declares: "Warstrength will collide with warstrength; right with right" (*The Libation Bearers,* line 461). Orestes thus tacitly recognizes the justice of Clytaemestra's vengeance on Agamemnon but presses his conflicting right to exact vengeance of his own. Throughout the trilogy, indeed, Aeschylus carefully balances the claims of both sides, making it clear that Clytaemestra has legitimate motives for her murder of Agamemnon. Far from a story of right against wrong, the *Oresteia* explores the clash of conflicting justices, of "right with right." This balance, which is highly characteristic of Athenian tragedy as a whole, comprises the main theme of the *Oresteia.*

The clash of "right with right" in the *Oresteia* has immediate relevance to the contemporary Athenian political scene after the assassination of Ephialtes in 462 BCE. This political scene entailed a conflict between old and new. Old laws, embodied by the Areopagus, stood in conflict with the new laws promoted by the reformers who oversaw the broadening of Athenian democracy during Aeschylus' lifetime. It is this clash between old and new laws that makes the trilogy relevant to its contemporary political context. Inherent in the play as well is an even older clash between the Areopagus and the earlier system of kin-based revenge, symbolized by the Furies, the spirits of punishment who pitilessly avenged crimes done to kinsmen, especially the crime of murder within a family. Aeschylus was first to introduce the Furies onstage, giving them a ghoulish appearance as bloodied, decomposing corpses, meant to terrify the audience as well as Orestes. They personified both the irrational, impulsive desire for revenge and the guilt associated with shedding a kinsman's blood. The Furies—whom Greek mythology considers more ancient than even the Olympians—represent the uncompromising power of blood relationsip that demands a death for a death and must in the world of law accommodate itself to a new order.

Sources and literary context. Although characters and events treated in the *Oresteia* also figure in Homer's epics, there are differences: in Homer's tales, Agamemnon is king not of Argos but of Mycenae, and it is not Clytaemestra who murders Agamemnon but her lover, Aegisthus, in whose territory Agamemnon lands after being shipwrecked during the voyage home. The Homeric poems emerged from a larger body of oral poems that modern scholars call the epic cycle. In antiquity these poems were sometimes attributed to Homer, sometimes to other poets.

FROM FURIES TO KINDLY ONES

The term *Eumenides*, "Kindly Ones," was likely put in place as the title of the *Oresteia*'s third play by later commentators. Scholars suspect that in Aeschylus' time the individual plays may have gone untitled, and that the name *Eumenides*, which was later commonly applied to the Furies, came into use only after Aeschylus wrote the *Oresteia*. The word *Eumenides* does not appear in the text of the trilogy itself; Aeschylus instead uses the older name Erinyes, "Furies." Still, the name *Eumenides* accurately reflects the transformation of the Furies that Athena brings about at the end of the trilogy, from harsh, implacable deities to the benevolent goddesses who offer blessings on Athens in the trilogy's closing lines.

They dealt with much of the same subject matter, such as the Trojan War and the subsequent fate of the heroes who fought it. None of these poems survives except in brief fragments put into written form by later poets than Homer, but from the cycle comes many of the basic details in the well-known story of the house of Atreus: the original crime of Atreus, the seduction of Helen, the marshaling of the Greek army by Agamemnon, and the anger of Artemis and the resulting sacrifice of Iphigenaia. Two of the later poets were Stesichorus (c. 630-565 BCE) and Pindar (c. 520-post 446 BCE, perhaps 438 BCE). Pindar composed a poem (*Pythian* 11) in which the murders of both Cassandra and Agamemenon are attributed to Clytaemestra (contrary to the Homeric version, in which Agamemnon's death is credited to Aegisthus). Stesichorus' *Oresteia*, an epic poem in two books, is thought to have been the specific inspiration for Aeschylus' trilogy. Stesichorus is also regarded as the first to show the Furies pursuing Orestes for his crime and the

first to bring in Apollo as the son's defender.

If the *Oresteia* is unusual in the degree to which it alludes to contemporary political events in Athens, it is by no means alone in doing so. In general, tragedy provided a means for such comment, leaving the audience to make the connections between situations in the play and the circumstances of the day. Aeschylus is the earliest tragic dramatist whose work survives, and so it is difficult to tell how much he followed his predecessors in making such allusions, and how much he acted as an innovator. All of Aeschylus' surviving plays contain a high degree of political thematic content, but none more explicit than that in the *Oresteia*, and especially in *The Eumenides*.

Reception and impact. While no specific contemporary reactions to the *Oresteia* have survived, clearly the work was extraordinarily successful from the start. First, as noted above, the *Oresteia* won Aeschylus his thirteenth and final award for best tragic trilogy at the City Dionysia in 458 BCE. It has been suggested that that the *Oresteia* established the later commonly attested identification of the Furies with the Semnai, Athens' "grave goddesses." If correct, this suggests that the *Oresteia* found a wide, appreciative, and long-term audience, one willing to take as authoritative Aeschylus' modifications to the traditions upon which he drew. Among that audience would have been the young Euripides (c. 485-c. 406 BCE), the third of the three great Athenian tragic dramatists, whose later play *Orestes* (408 BCE) was heavily influenced by the *Oresteia*.

In his influential book of literary criticism *The Poetics*, the fourth-century BCE critic Aristotle took Sophocles' *Oedipus the King* (one of **The Theban Plays,** also in *Classical Literature and Its Times*) as the greatest of all tragic dramas. However, more than one modern critic has disagreed, reserving that place for *Agamemnon* (which, at nearly 1700 lines, is the longest of the trilogy's plays by about one-third). These observers point to *Agamemnon*'s combination of simple action and extraordinarily rich imagery, which in their eyes give this play a power unrivalled by anything else ever brought to the stage.

—Colin Wells

For More Information

Aeschylus. *Oresteia.* Trans. Richmond Lattimore. Chicago: University of Chicago Press, 1953.

Boardman, John, et al. *The Oxford History of the Classical World: The Roman World.* Oxford: Oxford University Press, 1986.

Davies, J. K. *Democracy and Classical Greece*. Atlantic Highlands, N.J.: Humanities Press, 1978.

Denniston, John Dewar, and Denys Page, eds. *Agamemnon*. Oxford: Oxford University Press, 1957.

Dover, K. J. "The Political Aspect of Aeschylus' *Eumenides.*" *Journal of Hellenic Studies* 77 (1957): 230-37.

Easterling, P. E. ed. *The Cambridge Companion to Greek Tragedy*. Cambridge: Cambridge University Press, 1997.

Garvie, A. F., ed. *Choephoroi* [The Libation Bearers]. Oxford: Oxford University Press, 1986.

Goldhill, Simon. *Aeschylus: The Oresteia*. Cambridge: Cambridge University Press, 1992.

Lloyd-Jones, Hugh. *The Justice of Zeus*. Berkeley: University of California Press, 1983.

Macleod, C. W. "Politics and the *Oresteia.*" *Journal of Hellenic Studies* 102 (1982): 124-44.

Meier, Christian. *The Political Art of Greek Tragedy*. Baltimore, Md.: Johns Hopkins University Press, 1993.

Sommerstein, Alan H., ed. *Eumenides*. Cambridge: Cambridge University Press, 1989.

Parallel Lives

by
Plutarch

Plutarch was born about 47 CE to a wealthy family in Chaeronea, a provincial town in central Greece in the region of Boeotia. He did his advanced schooling in Athens, a city that would remain dear to his heart throughout his life, studying rhetoric, physics, and philosophy, as well as Greek and Latin literature. To cap his education, Plutarch traveled widely through Greece and Rome, meeting the Roman emperor Hadrian and other key figures along the way. He also visited Egypt and Asia Minor (Turkey) before returning to his beloved hometown and settling down to become a teacher and public servant. In about 68 CE, Plutarch married Timoxena and went on to father five children (four sons and a daughter)—only two of whom would outlive him. The now settled Plutarch went about his daily life, meanwhile maintaining ties with key figures in the Greco-Roman world, which won him a position from Hadrian. The emperor made Plutarch a procurator of Greece, an official whose duties included overseeing tax revenues. From his other connections, Plutarch received invitations to lecture on philosophy and ethics throughout Italy. Gradually he built a large and enthusiastic following, benefiting from the pro-Greek cultural climate that existed in Rome during his day. About 99 CE, Plutarch returned to Greece and began serving in various civic positions, most notably that of head priest at Delphi, the country's principal shrine. It is probably during this period that he wrote his two main bodies of works: the *Parallel Lives* and the *Moralia*, a catch-all title designating 60 or so writings on subjects ranging

THE LITERARY WORK

A collection of 23 pairs of biographical sketches (each matching the life of one Greek with one Roman man) and 4 single lives; written in Greek in the early 100s CE.

SYNOPSIS

The biographies illustrate the personal qualities of great figures of Greece and Rome, focusing on their actions. Plutarch groups every two figures according to his view of some basis for psychological comparison.

from religion to philosophy, ethics, politics, psychology, and education. Plutarch died about 120 CE, leaving behind a collection of paired biographies that seems to have met with immediate success and that became his enduring monument. Among its most exemplary pairs is that of Alexander the Great and Julius Caesar, who reached the pinnacle of individual achievement in the Greek and Roman worlds, respectively. Their importance to the collection is evidenced not least by the fact that the account of Alexander is twice as long as any of the other lives; Caesar's is only slightly shorter. The remaining pairs feature other statesmen and conquerors. Plutarch documents the feats and failings of these real-life figures to tell the story of Greco-Roman civilization and to enlighten the reader morally. In the process, he conveys thoughts on the quest for honor by

Medieval woodcut of Plutarch. © Bettmann/Corbis.

individual Greeks and Romans, and bequeaths to posterity a set of heroic portraits that has shaped conceptions of these individuals from antiquity to the present.

Events in History at the Time the Biographies Take Place

*Note: The history related to Alexander and Caesar is pertinent to many of the other lives in Plutarch's collection. An asterisk following the first use of a name indicates that Plutarch has written a sketch for this figure in his collection.

Greece's saga—from the Athenian Empire to Alexander the Great. Considered the greatest of all the ancient Greek and Roman generals, Alexander* (356-323 BCE) took the throne in 336 BCE, going on to dominate the Greeks, conquer the Persians, occupy Palestine, Egypt, and Phoenicia, and penetrate into northwestern India. When he first came to power in 336 BCE, the Greek city-states were already in decline. Athens, a center of Greek values, had reached the height of power in the age of Pericles* (461-429 BCE), more than a century before Alexander's rise. Philosophy, architecture, literature, and democracy had flourished then, becoming the foundation for a rich cultural legacy that would influence Alexander and the course of Western history itself.

Although Alexander was born in Macedon, a kingdom to the north of the Greek city-states, his kingdom was a center for Greek artists and scholars. Athens in particular wielded great influence on Alexander, in part because of its high status in the Greek world and in part because Alexander's tutor, Aristotle, had lived at Athens for many years, becoming a keen observer of its politics and culture. A century before Alexander was born, during the 400s BCE, Athens had seen the growth of robust democratic institutions, especially in the age of Pericles. A consummate politician, Pericles increased the degree of democracy in Athens. He added greater citizen oversight to government and heightened citizen control of the judicial system. Meanwhile, his own authority increased as he won repeated re-election to the office of *strategos* (military commander endowed with civil powers), a position of tremendous influence in Athens's machinery of government.

Yet Athens began to weaken during the fifth century, primarily because of two sets of wars. The first, the Persian Wars (490 BCE-479 BCE), began as Persian reprisal against the Greek city-states for encouraging the Greek-speaking cities of Asia Minor to revolt against their Persian overlords. The famous victories of the Greeks at Marathon (490 BCE) and Salamis (480 BCE) repelled the Persian assault, which, though aimed at all Greece, had been directed especially at Athens. It aptly, then, was an Athenian-led victory, which owed particular thanks to the *strategos* Themistocles*. The victory may well have preserved the very possibility of Greek civilization. The invasion of 480 BCE, during which Athens was burned, would inspire Alexander to claim that, in waging war against the Persian ruler Darius III in the 330s BCE, he was really avenging the Persian destruction of Athens' temples more than a century before his time.

The second conflict feeding into Athenian power in the fifth century was the Peloponnesian War, an armed contest between the city-states of Athens and Sparta for supremacy of Greece (431 BCE-404 BCE). The 27-year war ended in the destruction of the Athenian Empire. Complicating matters were the pronounced cultural differences between the two powers: Athens was democratic, urban, imperialist, and culturally experimental; Sparta, on the other hand, was aristocratic, agrarian, and culturally conservative.

The surrender of Athens in 404 BCE to the Spartan general Lysander* spelled the end of its empire. For the time being, government by democracy gave way to government by oligarchy (although Athens would manage to reestablish its democracy quickly). Sparta dominated much of Greece until 371 BCE, when its king Agesilaus*, till then a prudent monarch, needlessly provoked a war with Thebes because of a personal grudge. Contrary to all expectation, the Thebans, under the generalships of Epaminondas* and Pelopidas*, crushed Sparta in battle. Although Agesilaus' leadership saved the city itself from capture, Sparta's power was squashed forever. There followed a period of Theban hegemony that came to an end with the rise of another power, Macedon, led by Alexander's father, Philip II (whose kingdom comprised a substantial portion of the Balkan Peninsula to the north of the great cities of Greece). As Plutarch's life of Alexander makes clear, among Alexander's first acts was the continuation of his father's campaigns in Greece; these were followed by the eastward extension of his empire and his eventual transformation into a tyrant. Making an outward show of his status, Alexander donned the trappings of Persian as well as Macedonian royal attire. During his lifetime, some regions proclaimed him to be divine. People considered him a direct son of the Greek god Zeus. In contrast to Plutarch, who ascribed the death of Alexander to fever, a number of Alexander's contemporaries blamed his demise on poison.

From the Roman Republic to Caesar's empire—Rome's saga. Living twice as long as Alexander, Julius Caesar* (100-44 BCE) achieved his victories during one of the most troubled times in all of Roman history. Time and again, he led his troops to victory, extending Roman rule over all of Gaul (including modern-day France) and over the low countries (Netherlands, Belgium, and Luxembourg). The specter of civil war haunted Rome throughout Caesar's lifetime and beyond. He began his political career in the aftermath of civil war and attained absolute power in the state through victory in civil war. His assassination led to a series of further civil wars, first between his supporters and his assassins, then between his supporters.

Class conflict tore at the fabric of the Roman Republic, and violence spread into domestic politics. Two brothers, Tiberius Sempronius Gracchus* and Gaius Gracchus* (known together as the Gracchi), proposed reforms on behalf of the people. In 133 BCE Tiberius Gracchus, a tribune (one of the officials elected to protect the lives and property of the people) proposed to divide public lands among the landless. He met with vigorous opposition from some wealthy senators, who made a practice of illegally farming those lands to supplement the profits from their own holdings. Tensions escalated. Well aware of the solid opposition, Tiberius tried to circumvent the Senate and was murdered, along with 300 followers. His younger brother, Gaius Gracchus, who served as tribune in 123-22 BCE, carried on the struggle for reform. He stabilized the price of grain and lobbied to extend the right to vote to Rome's Italian allies (which would finally be granted in 88 BCE, after a bloody civil war between Rome and its allies). So great was the resistance of the conservative senators to Gaius that they characterized the struggle as a battle for the preservation of the Republic and authorized Rome's army to defend the state. In the conflict that followed, Gaius committed suicide and as many as 3,000 of his followers were killed. Thus was "the use of violence in domestic politics legitimized by official decree" (Mackay, p. 42). It was during the Gracchus brothers' terms as tribunes that murder was introduced into Roman politics as a strategic tactic.

Against the background of this violence emerged Marius*, a brilliant general who lacked the customary aristocratic credentials for leadership. Marius overcame this obstacle by building support among the commoners, courting the very political constituencies cultivated by the Gracchi brothers. Marius transformed the Roman army into a professional, all-volunteer force, creating a new breed of soldier who had no farm or work to which he needed to return and so could fight year round and for longer terms of service. Allegiance in this kind of army, however, shifted from the state to one's general—the leader who ensured his soldiers' fortunes. Marius' changes to the army and the politics of the Gracchi brothers gave rise to populist leaders, statesmen, and generals who aligned themselves more with the people than the Senate. Marius and his nephew-in-law Julius Caesar were two such leaders. Aligned with the Senate, others—like Sulla* (Marius' protégé and later rival)—were conservatives. But in either case, ambitious generals of all stripes now had political power bases in the armies that they led, a situation that made civil war an inevitable method for resolving political disputes.

Sulla, after a bloody purge of Rome's elite, orchestrated his own appointment to an unlimited term as dictator in 82 BCE. Once securely in power, he worked to restore stability. He even resigned his extraordinary official powers after three years. Unfortunately Sulla's methods of acquiring power had greater consequence than anything he did once he had it. After him, politician-generals such as Caesar, Pompey* (Sulla's protégé), and a host of lesser lights would use their wealth and military might to interfere directly in the politics of Rome. The electoral system soon became mired in a climate of scandal, violence, and bribery, giving rise to the uneasy triumvirate of Crassus*, Pompey, and Caesar, and, after the death of Crassus, to civil war between Pompey and Caesar. When Caesar emerged triumphant, he gave little thought to restoring the Republic but instead began to adopt the symbols of monarchy. This self-promotion had the same alienating effect on the Romans as Alexander had on his people when assuming the trappings of an Eastern potentate. Following Sulla's precedent, Caesar arranged to be appointed dictator-for-life (44 BCE), only to be assassinated by a band of senators led by Brutus* and Cassius.

A LOST COMPARISON?

~

Scholars face the perplexing problem of incomplete works in those that have survived from antiquity, *Parallel Lives* included. "There is good reason," says one scholar, "to think that the end of the [life of] Alexander and the start of the [life of] Caesar are lost. The text of Caesar's life seems to begin in mid-sentence" and "gives no treatment to Caesar's family or boyhood" (Duff, p. 254). Likewise, Plutarch may have written a brief comparison for this pair that is lost. Here are lines from another comparison for two of his lives, those of the Greek public speaker Demosthenes and his Roman counterpart, Cicero:

"For Demosthenes oratory was without all embellishment and jesting. . . . Whereas . . . in his love of laughing away serious arguments in judicial cases by jests and facetious remarks . . . [Cicero] paid too little regard to what was decent. . . . The power of persuading and governing the people did, indeed, equally belong to both.

(Plutarch, *Parallel Lives*, pp. 1070-1071)

The Biographies in Focus

Contents overview. Plutarch's *Parallel Lives* includes 23 pairs of biographical sketches, one Greek matched with one Roman in order to draw implicit comparisons and to extract lessons for moral improvement by example. Usually the Greek sketch precedes the Roman one, and the

two are followed by a brief comparison. Four of the pairs, however, include just the biographies without Plutarch's comparison, perhaps because, though it once existed, it has been lost. Forging new ground, the biographies center not only on the man in action but also on his mind and soul. Great figures from Greek and Roman history reveal themselves through a focus on human character tested under the pressure of major historical events and made manifest in everyday incidents. Before launching into the life of Alexander, Plutarch cautions the reader to bear in mind that he aims not to write a detailed history but a life story that promotes the discovery of virtue or vice in men and that reveals their characters. History, he says, is a "faithful mirror in which I observe these great men in order that I may seek to model my own life on their virtues" (Plutarch in Flacelière, p. 359). Since space prohibits a detailed summary for all the lives, featured here are Alexander and Caesar—the most famous military heroes of Greece and Rome. Although Plutarch pairs the two together, no comparison of them by him survives.

The Lives That Plutarch Pairs and Their Common Characteristics

Each pair below lists the Greek hero before the Roman. In parentheses after the names are the centuries in which the heroes scored their principal achievements. All centuries are BCE.

1. **Theseus** (fourteenth/thirteenth century) & **Romulus** (eighth century)
   Mythical heroes; the founders of their cities.
2. **Lycurgus** (eighth century or earlier) & **Numa** (eighth/seventh century)
   Also mythical; wise kings who established the important social customs of their respective peoples.
3. **Solon** (sixth century) & **Publicola** (sixth century)
   Statesmen who made peace between a stubborn aristocracy and an embittered peasantry.
4. **Themistocles** (fifth century) & **Camillus** (fourth century)
   Each saved his country from invasion yet was forced to endure exile. *There is no comparison for this pair.*
5. **Aristides** (fifth century) & **Cato the Elder** (third/second century)
   Famously moral public figures who revered tradition.
6. **Cimon** (fifth century) & **Lucullus** (first century)
   Both died before the unraveling of their countries; in different ways, both benefited Greece.

7. **Pericles** (fifth century) & **Fabius Maximus** (third/second century):

> Each was a canny military and political leader whose superior strategic ability averted wartime disaster (in Athens, only temporarily).

8. **Nicias** (fifth century) & **Crassus** (first century)

> Each was killed while leading the most disastrous military expedition in his country's history.

9. **Alcibiades** (fifth century) & **Coriolanus** (fifth century)

> Each had a noble but ill-governed nature; both took reprisal against domestic adversaries to the point of waging war on their own cities.

10. **Lysander** (fifth/fourth century) & **Sulla** (second/first century)

> Brilliant, pitiless military commanders in whom the extremes of good and bad coexisted starkly.

11. **Agesilaus** (fifth/fourth century) & **Pompey** (first century)

> Success gave way to disaster late in life for both men. Agesilaus recovered to save Sparta from its enemy Thebes; Pompey could not save the Roman Republic from Caesar.

12. **Epaminondas** (fourth century) & **Scipio Africanus** (third/second century)

> Two generals who defeated hitherto invincible foes: for Epaminondas, the foe was Sparta; for Scipio, Hannibal. *Both of these lives are lost.*

13. **Pelopidas** (fourth century) & **Marcellus** (third century)

> Each fell in battle as one of his country's greatest generals, but despite many impressive victories, neither actually conquered his country's primary foe.

14. **Dion** (fourth century) & **Brutus** (first century)

> Each man overthrew a dictator whom he knew personally: Dion overthrew Dionysius II of Syracuse; Brutus, Julius Caesar.

15. **Timoleon** (fourth century) & **Aemilius Paulus** (second century)

> Timoleon rescued Sicily from an invasion by Carthage; Aemilius conquered Macedon. Both are depicted as incorruptible.

16. **Demosthenes** (fourth century) & **Cicero** (first century)

> Each was a famous orator who foresaw the major threat to his city but was unable to stop it: for Athens, the threat was domination by Macedon; for Rome, the rise of totalitarian rule.

17. **Alexander** (Macedon, fourth century) & **Julius Caesar** (first century)

> Conquerors of extraordinary achievement, each died without fulfilling his ambitions. *There is no comparison for this pair.*

18. **Eumenes** (fourth century) & **Sertorius** (first century)

> Both overcame exile to lead victorious armies composed of foreign troops; each met his end through treachery.

19. **Phocion** (fourth century) & **Cato the Younger** (first century)

> Political figures held up even in their own times as models of incorruptible morality. *There is no comparison for this pair.*

20. **Demetrius** (fourth/third century) & **Antony** (first century)

> Would-be conquerors whose personal failings defeated their aspirations; this pair complements the other "negative" pair of Pyrrhus and Marius.

21. **Pyrrhus** (second century) & **Gaius Marius** (second/first century)

> Ambitious leaders whose natural greatness of character was perverted by bad influences. *There is no comparison for this pair.*

22. **Agis and Cleomenes** (third century) & **Tiberius and Gaius Gracchus** (second century)

> Two sets of brothers; each pair sought to reapportion wealth in their society more equitably.

23. **Philopoemen** (third/second century) & **Flamininus** (third/second century)

> Rivals in the period of Greece's decline and Rome's rise; the only pair in which Greeks and Romans interact.

Alexander. Plutarch begins this sketch by noting a series of supernatural events surrounding the hero's birth: omens, dreams, and signs that point to his future greatness. Much in Plutarch is unverifiable and some is fanciful. To his credit, however, he frequently signals that he is on uncertain ground by repeating the tags, "it is said" or "some say."

Plutarch covers little of Alexander's boyhood, offering instead a series of keen psychological observations that portray the hero's character. We are told, for example, that Alexander is not given to sensual pleasures and that from very early on, the desire to achieve great things is his driving passion. So intense is his "love of glory" that he resents his father's military achievements. The son "would tell his companions that his father would . . . leave him and them no opportunities

Alexander and Darius in the Battle of Issus, from a Roman mosaic. Reprinted from Charlotte M. Yonge, *A Pictorial History of the World's Greatest Nations,* Vol. 1. New York: Selmar Hess, 1882.

of performing great and illustrious actions" (*Lives*, p. 803). Philip arranges for Alexander to take tutorials with the philosopher Aristotle. The result is an education in fine works of literature as well as morals, ethics, politics, and rhetoric. Plutarch emphasizes Alexander's love of learning. The young man goes so far as to keep his edition of Homer's *Iliad* (also in *Classical Literature and Its Times*), the "casket copy"—a copy including Aristotle's notes—under his pillow, where he also stows his dagger.

Alexander quarrels with his father on many occasions, particularly over Philip's extramarital affairs. Eventually these affairs prove ruinous, "the troubles that began in the women's chambers spreading, so to say, to the whole kingdom" (*Lives*, p. 806). Resenting her husband's infidelity, his wife, Olympias, has someone slay Philip with a knife. This ensures Alexander's succession, which was threatened by his father's polygamous marriage to a Cleopatra (who precedes the famous queen of Egypt of this same name by some 300 years).

At the age of 20, Alexander inherits a kingdom "beset on all sides with great dangers and rancorous enemies" (*Lives*, p. 808). Alexander rejects his advisors' pleas for caution and presses campaigns first against the rebellious tribes to the north and east of Macedon, and then against

the people of Thebes, who have risen up against him in revolt (*Lives*, p. 808). Seeking to make an example of the Thebans to all Greece, Alexander surrounds the city with his armies. The Thebans stand at his mercy yet dare, says Plutarch, to demand that Alexander surrender to them. Earlier he had offered them amnesty but now he razes the city, then sells 30,000 Thebans into slavery and has another 6,000 killed by the sword, sparing from death only the priests, the descendants of the poet Pindar, and those who did not want to revolt. These are harsh punishments, says Plutarch, which Alexander will regret (indeed, he later attempts to make amends with the conquered Thebans). Alexander is likened to a lion whose fierce manner grows docile once his rage has subsided. After conquering Thebes, he is undisputed master of the Greece he reveres so deeply.

Plutarch devotes a good deal of the life to Alexander's conflict with Darius III, king of Persia. Darius' empire, the largest and wealthiest on earth, reaches from Asia Minor to India and from Egypt to present-day Russia. As always, Plutarch is more interested in what a particular battle reveals about Alexander's character than in the campaigns themselves. A good example is Alexander's first confrontation with Darius at the Granicus River (northern gateway to Turkey) in

334 BCE. Darius has assembled a vast army to defend his lands from Alexander, with the river imposing a barrier to the Macedonian warrior's southward advance. Because he realizes the psychological significance of the encounter, Alexander ignores the advice of his counselors to retreat and orders his 34,000 or so troops across the river toward the Persians' well-fortified positions. With Alexander diverting attention by leading the cavalry charge himself, his men ford the river and penetrate Persian territory, delivering a key blow to the larger Persian forces, whose losses Plutarch estimates at upwards of 20,000. Over the next several years, Alexander's Macedonian armies maintain dominance, but Darius himself continues to elude Alexander.

In narrating Alexander's several exploits in this period, Plutarch emphasizes both the aura of great fortune that surrounds the hero and his powerful imagination, as when he manages to cut the famous Gordian knot, which had so far stumped all who tried to untie it. Legend had it that whoever could undo the knot would reign over Asia. Although Alexander cut the knot instead of untying it, he considered himself the one who had finally undone it (his "feat" would develop into a saying—"to cut the Gordian Knot"—meaning to take drastic action to solve a problem). Plutarch observes the kindness shown by Alexander to Darius' wife and daughters when they are captured after the Persians lose the battle of Issus and Darius escapes. Alexander protects the female captives from harm and permits them to bury their dead so that they seem "rather lodged in some temple . . . than in the camp of the enemy" (*Lives*, p. 816). The wife, reports Plutarch, is accounted the most beautiful princess alive, yet Alexander refrains from intimate relations with her or her daughters. Plutarch uses the incident to highlight the importance of self-mastery, seen as a key facet of Alexander's ethical core. The king controls his lust instead of ravaging his enemy, putting into practice the common ancient philosophy that to rule others, one first has to rule oneself.

Alexander next marches southward along the eastern coast of the Mediterranean Sea, capturing cities along the way. He founds the city of Alexandria in Egypt, a site chosen on the basis of a dream in which the poet Homer speaks to Alexander about Pharos, a Greek island that lies across from the site. But first Alexander must finish off Darius, so he turns inland for his final confrontation with the Persians. The showdown gives rise to another revealing anecdote. When

Darius offers to avoid war by dividing the kingdom, one of Alexander's generals, Parmenio, says if it were up to him, he would take the deal. "So would I," retorts Alexander, "if I were Parmenio" (*Lives*, p. 822).

A climactic battle ensues between the Macedonians and the Persians in 331 BCE at Gaugamela, near Mosul in present-day Iraq. Once more, the odds are against Alexander. While ancient estimates are often inflated, Plutarch's sources say Darius had amassed a Persian force of one million men. Again ignoring his advisors, Alexander refuses to "steal" the victory by attacking at night. Despite the poor odds, he crushes Darius' army.

Plutarch's attention to Alexander's generosity early in his military career works nicely to set up the later portions of the narrative, in which Plutarch attributes Alexander's decline to a series of crippling character defects. Principal among these are overweening pride and intractable stubbornness. In the already-described battle at Granicus, Alexander insists on following his own instincts, even when his trusted military aides think otherwise, and his stubborn insistence pays off. Yet this same trait prompts him to surround himself with flatterers and to reject those who fail to applaud his decisions; he turns away even close associates, such as Aristotle.

When Plutarch narrates Alexander's famous march to India, he connects his increasingly ruthless behavior toward his close advisors to larger questions of his effectiveness as a military leader. Of particular importance here are the consequences resulting from setbacks at the River Ganges, where Alexander's forces face the daunting task of fording the wide river while a huge army awaits them on the opposite banks. Nothing Alexander says spurs his men forward, so he broods in his tent and declares petulantly that if the soldiers do not cross the river, he owes them "no thanks" for any previous service (*Lives*, p. 845). What is worse, Alexander miscalculates the journey back, once again by failing to listen to the sound advice of his men. The results are disastrous: withering attacks, a plethora of diseases, scorching heat, and dwindling rations reduce Alexander's army by three-fourths.

Alexander returns to Persia but fails to realize his dreams of additional conquests and the creation of a mighty Greco-Persian culture. Increasingly obsessed with ill omens and superstitious fears, he grows moody and pessimistic. He is deeply affected by the death of a close friend and male lover, Hephaestion. Alexander mourns the loss for several days, then turns to unbridled revelry. Stricken quite suddenly by a fever, he himself dies within ten days, a few months shy of his thirty-third birthday. Plutarch's tone makes clear that, great though he was, Alexander failed to live up to his early promise because he did not fulfill the Greek ideals of self-knowledge and self-discipline.

Caesar. Plutarch's portrait of Caesar begins with the hero's early career. Because he has family ties to Marius, Sulla's rival, Caesar is marked for death by Sulla. Caesar escapes, fleeing Rome only to be taken prisoner by pirates. They threaten him and demand a ransom for his return, yet Caesar nonchalantly flouts his captors, composing poems, engaging in saucy wordplay, and paying no mind to his dire predicament. Once his ransom has been duly paid, Caesar exacts a brutal revenge; capturing the pirates, he crucifies them. The episode reveals Caesar's overpowering sense of dignity, his iron self-control, and, above all, his capacity for ruthlessness against enemies.

Like Alexander, Caesar is more than simply a man of action; he is a well-rounded individual, who acquires an education in philosophy, rhetoric, and oratory. Indeed, his teacher is Apollonius, instructor to the great orator Cicero. Caesar's skills in public speaking portend his future political success. On the strength of them, he builds a large and enthusiastic public following, winning popular support by his easy and friendly, though carefully orchestrated, manner. He spends great sums of money, throws lavish parties, sponsors large gladiatorial contests, and curries favor with important figures in Roman society—and all these tactics are instrumental to his rapid rise.

Caesar rises into Rome's highest offices. He wins a close contest for the position of Pontifex Maximus, or high priest, and, through hard lobbying, gains a consulship. But his greatest achievements are military triumphs, which Plutarch narrates in great detail. Caesar's power grows, and he makes speeches in the Senate that antagonize the aristocracy, especially Cato the Younger, a champion of the republican government who sees Caesar's ambitions as a threat to its survival. Yet Caesar's exploits on the battlefield win the undying admiration of his soldiers. In less than ten years, estimates Plutarch, Caesar conquers several hundred cities and fights more than 3 million men. His campaigns in Spain and Gaul cement his reputation as a military leader and enrich him, as he takes the booty that comes with conquest (see ***Commentaries on the Gallic***

War, also in *Classical Literature and Its Times*). His troops wonder at the hardships he endures with them, and he shares his plunder with them, knowing it is their principal reward and realizing it can cinch their loyalty to him. Caesar's love of honor and his passion to distinguish himself spur him onward. Ambitious to achieve more, he compares himself unfavorably to Alexander: "Do you think . . . I have not just cause to weep, when I consider that Alexander at my age had conquered so many nations?" (*Lives*, p. 861). Here, as elsewhere in the *Lives*, Plutarch uses the first sketch in a pair to establish patterns taken up in the second one.

Plutarch stirringly narrates Caesar's campaigns in Gaul and Europe, observing how he leads his men across the Rhine River, becomes the first to sail in the Atlantic Ocean with an army, and ventures into the far reaches of the civilized world to do battle in Britain. The greatest of Caesar's military deeds is his capture of the most prized city, Rome itself. Allowing his ambition to overpower his reason, he wavers but then risks battle for control of Rome: Caesar's cunning and mastery of human psychology—much like Alexander before him—allows him to prevail against Pompey, a better-equipped foe.

As Plutarch tells it, Caesar's force has been reduced to only 300 cavalry and 5,000 footsoldiers by the time he advances against Pompey. But the small force works to his advantage, for his plan depends on speed, not power: "what was wanted was to make this first step suddenly, and so to astound his enemies with the boldness of it" (*Lives*, p. 874). Using surprise to his advantage, he arrives at the Rubicon, the river separating Italy from his own domain of Gaul, pauses to reflect on his actions, then boldly crosses the boundary.

The plan works to perfection. Afraid of civil war, the citizens of Rome panic and stream out of the city, including senators and other officials. Pompey escapes too. At first, Caesar gives chase, but then, victory assured, turns back toward Rome, having in 60 days without bloodshed "made himself master of all Italy" (*Lives*, p. 876). Later Caesar and his lieutenant Antony pursue Pompey and defeat him at the battle of Pharsalus in Thessaly (central Greece). Pompey's flight to Egypt, where he is later murdered, gives Plutarch the chance to narrate Caesar's Egyptian adventures, including, briefly, his affair with Cleopatra.

Plutarch turns to Caesar's further military adventures as he fights Pompey's sons in Asia, Africa, and Spain. Ever ambitious, notes Plutarch, Caesar yearns for further glory, as if he "might outdo his past actions by his future" (*Lives*, p. 887). Among his many achievements, he reforms the calendar, a feat of great "scientific ingenuity," adds an approving Plutarch, regularizing the year to 365 days, with an extra day added every fourth year (*Lives*, p. 888).

Around this time, Caesar begins to make many enemies. Some are offended by his lordly disdain of Senate traditions, others by prophecies that he will be made king. While Plutarch does not make explicit any moral lessons here, the implication is clear, especially for Plutarch's first readers, who would have known well how Caesar's story ends: the same vaulting ambition that drives him forward will be the cause of his downfall at the hands of enemies. He fails to temper his passion for honor with reason.

It is passion, not reason, that drives Caesar to celebrate his victory over Pompey's sons in a triumphal procession through Rome, thereby upsetting its citizens. They watch, their minds heavy with the thought that these sons are no enemies of Rome but the offspring of a great patriot. As the famous conspiracy against him mounts, Caesar grows suspicious, fearing ominous signs, such as the soothsayer's warning to beware the Ides of March, and his wife Calpurnia's dream of holding him "butchered in her arms" (*Lives*, p. 891). Nevertheless, he ventures forth to the Senate, urged on by one of the conspirators. They "were ready," said this conspirator, "to vote unanimously that [Caesar] should be declared king of all the provinces out of Italy. . . . But if he was possessed so far as to think this day unfortunate, yet it were more decent to go himself . . . to adjourn [the Senate] in his own person" (*Lives*, p. 891). Persuaded, Caesar proceeds to the meeting place, a building formerly dedicated to the public by his old rival, Pompey. Soon after Caesar appears, the assassins crowd around and cut him down with their daggers and swords. "Something of a supernatural influence," muses Plutarch, "guided the action," for a bloodied Caesar fell "at the foot of the pedestal on which Pompey's statue stood . . . so that Pompey himself seemed to have presided . . . over the revenge done upon his adversary" (*Lives*, pp. 892-93).

Plutarch and subjective biography. As he states at the beginning of his life of Alexander, Plutarch is interested not in "histories, but lives," for the reason that "the most glorious exploits do not always furnish us with the clearest discoveries of virtue or vice in men" (*Lives*, p. 801). In his life of Alexander, this means forfeiting a strictly fac-

tual and sequential approach for one that will, through the experience of reading, instill virtue in his audience (Duff, p. 55). Plutarch generally does not, however, insert moral judgments but leaves them for readers to glean, expecting them to identify the praiseworthy as well as blameworthy. By way of examples, his writing attempts to foster self-restraint, the rule of reason over passion and the exercise of basic virtues—compassion, kindness, generosity of spirit, and calmness.

Other writers of the day show a concern for the morally enlightening effects that history can have on readers, for example, Tacitus in his ***Annals of Imperial Rome*** (also in *Classical Literature and Its Times*). In focusing on the character of the men he profiles, Plutarch promotes this moral enlightenment. He compares himself to a portrait painter who finds in the telling detail a sign of the "souls of men," a larger truth about human nature that transcends "weighty matters and great battles" (*Lives*, p. 801).

A good example of the technique of the telling detail occurs early in the life of Alexander, when Plutarch illustrates Alexander's conflicts with his father, Philip. Plutarch tells the memorable story of Bucephalus, a magnificent but unmanageable horse offered for sale to Philip. Just at the point that Philip's attendants are ready to despair of ever mounting Bucephalus, Alexander proclaims that he will tame the horse. His father ridicules his son for speaking so rashly but then Alexander masters the animal without "striking or spurring him," instead using soft words and gestures (*Lives*, p. 805). Impressed by the strength of his son's will, the father resolves thereafter to deal with Alexander by persuasion rather than command. Instead of focusing on Alexander's willfulness, Plutarch portrays his hero as a sympathetic problem solver who understands other minds, which is a key trait of the military leader as Plutarch understands it. Beyond this one biography, the incident shows how Plutarch highlights a trait of a hero's life, which he sees as instrumental to the hero's success and as worthy of emulation.

Plutarch also brings character traits to the fore when he has one mind meet another in his biographies. He notes that after Alexander invaded Persia, although many wise men came to pay homage to the general, the philosopher Diogenes did not. He never so much as stirred "out of the suburb called the Cranium, where Alexander found him lying along in the sun" (*Lives*, p. 810). Does the philosopher need anything? Alexander wondered, whereupon Diogenes saucily replied, "I would have you stand [away] from between me and the sun" (*Lives*, p. 810). Instead of being offended, Alexander admired Diogenes for taking "so little notice of him" (*Lives*, p. 810). "If he were not Alexander," quips the mighty general, "he would choose to be Diogenes" (*Lives*, p. 810). This moment is open to several readings, which Plutarch, in typical fashion, leaves unsettled. A straightforward reading would focus on Alexander's generosity of spirit and self-deprecation. But another reading might stress this as a moment in which the man of action comes up against a force he cannot defeat, the man of philosophic contemplation, with the wider implication that while the armies of the Greek city-states have been overcome, their philosophic legacy is not so easily destroyed. In the account of this meeting, Plutarch emphasizes at this point how necessary it is for Alexander to remain a man of action. Ultimately, as the biography later shows, he is pulled down by his lack of self-knowledge, a preoccupation for many philosophers, a general pursuit in Rome, and one of the purposes of Plutarch's project. His *Parallel Lives* aims to aid readers in their own self-knowledge.

In Plutarch's portrait of Caesar as well, we are meant to see not just a great warrior but, more importantly, a human being struggling to understand himself and his place in the world he is shaping. A superb example of this interest in the hero's self-questioning can be seen in Plutarch's account of Caesar at the Rubicon. Although the *Life* depicts Caesar as having a well-formulated plan, the narrative slows down to convey his indecision as he ponders the enormity of his actions. When he reaches the Rubicon, the river marking the boundary between his province of Gaul and Italy, he pauses, wavering as he considers "the greatness of the enterprise," for his crossing threatens to touch off another civil war (*Lives*, p. 874). While Caesar deliberates, "computing how many calamities his passing that river would bring upon mankind," the fate of the Roman Republic is held in suspense and time seems to stand still, until he decides to cross the river and coins the famous phrase "The die is cast," an expression that has come to mean "taking an irreversible step" (*Lives*, p. 874). What matters in this episode is the complex psychological state of the hero. We see Caesar weighing in his mind the risks and rewards of his next step, and through this process we see also the moral lesson, in which Caesar chooses passion over reason, desire for glory over the preservation of the Republic, choices that ultimately lead to his fateful encounter with his assassins in the Senate.

In his last desperate moments, Caesar shifts his body to avoid the dagger thrusts of the conspirators. He falls, Plutarch notes, at the foot of a statue of his archrival, "so that Pompey himself seemed to have presided, as it were, over the revenge done upon his adversary, who lay here at his feet" (*Lives*, p. 893). Although the Alexander-Caesar pair lacks the comparison by Plutarch that exists for most other pairs, this last image suggests that Caesar, like Alexander, let himself be driven by ambition and that he, like his predecessor, was brought down by an excess of the very trait that had brought him his greatest success.

Sources and literary context. Plutarch's text is quite informative about his sources. In his life of Alexander alone, he names 24 of them. Although modest about his knowledge of Latin, Plutarch shows a wide familiarity with Greek and Roman authors. For the Roman leaders Cicero and Caesar, Plutarch drew on their own writings as well as other Latin sources. Underlying his understanding of virtues was training in Greek ethics and values. Plutarch viewed people as neither wholly good, nor wholly evil. In his view, those endowed with great natural ability were capable of great vice as well as great virtue.

With respect to the genre in which he was writing, "There is no specific model for Roman biographers, or for Plutarch himself, only a range of Greek biographical writing with quite different purposes and forms" (Mellor, p. 133). The fourth century BCE Greek author Xenophon wrote *The Education of Cyrus*, or *Cyropedia*, a largely fictional biographical study of Cyrus the Great, founder of the Persian Empire, as well as a short biography of the Spartan king Agesilaus that provides not a complex view of the man but one of pure praise. The Roman biographer Cornelius Nepos (c. 100-c. 24 BCE), a forerunner of Plutarch, sketched the lives of illustrious Romans, Greeks, and other non-Romans—these are the earliest biographies that have come down to us. Most of his work, however, has been lost, and those sketches that survive are very brief, often inaccurate, and again lacking in the psychological complexity characteristic of Plutarch. More specifically, Quitus Curtius Rufus (first or early second century CE) wrote a biography of Alexander but it too does not deal with the complex man, instead concentrating on vivid presentation of the dramatic events. With respect to Julius Caesar, Plutarch's Roman contemporary Suetonius (c. 70-130 CE) included a profile in his **Lives of the Twelve Caesars** (also in *Classical Literature and Its Times*). Suetonius uses a careful mixture of anecdote and public record to produce in the reader a sense of almost voyeuristic access into the subject, and avoids the sense of reasoned analysis of character and psychology found in Plutarch. Furthermore, Suetonius focuses to a greater extent on character defect (including sexual "excesses"); for Plutarch, however, even where his great men give cause for regret, greatness is the constant theme.

Events in History at the Time the Biographies Were Written

Greece under the Roman Empire. In the pairing of its heroes, the *Parallel Lives* draws a comparison between Greece, a great civilization from the past, and Rome, which expanded into a preeminent empire and was now enjoying a period of strong, stable government. Plutarch's beloved Greece had already been part of the Roman Empire for more than 250 years, but Greece remained a worldly, cosmopolitan center even in captivity. Chaeronea, Plutarch's hometown, while unimportant politically, was close to Delphi, site of the famous shrine or oracle of the god Apollo. The location enabled Plutarch to meet a steady stream of visitors from all over the Greek world and beyond.

The Greek elite, including Plutarch, benefited enormously from the prosperity and stability afforded by the Roman Empire and from the tendencies of emperors like Hadrian to indulge "his love for Greek art, sculpture and rhetoric (Goodman, p. 155). But there were disadvantages too. The Romans of Plutarch's era welcomed Greek architecture, literature, and philosophy into its fold, developing something of a passion for all things classically Greek. However, Roman writers had stereotyped later Greeks of their own empire as deceitful, unmanly, overindulgent, untrustworthy, and dishonorable. Their culture should be emulated; their personality traits disparaged. The fervent admiration for the Greek cultural legacy, however, made it possible for many Greek intellectuals of Plutarch's day to thrive, as Romans imported artists and philosophers to "glorify [Rome as] the new hub of the civilized world" (Gianakaris, p. 26). Also, by this time Greeks were being called to serve as officials in the Roman Empire, as Plutarch's personal experience shows.

The pairing of Greek and Roman figures for comparison and ethical instruction afforded Plutarch a perfect platform for placing one culture alongside the other in ways that enabled moral evaluation on the part of the reader. In less sub-

tle hands, it would have been easy to structure the portraits to paint the Romans in a consistently bad light by juxtaposing them against always noble Greeks. But Plutarch is remarkably fair-minded in his treatments, suggesting that he saw the cultures of Greece and Rome on equal terms, without prejudice or bias. Virtue and vice, he seems to have believed, are "no respecters of nationality" (Easterling and Knox, p. 668).

SHAKESPEARE AND PLUTARCH

Shakespeare relied extensively on Plutarch for background to his Roman plays: *Antony and Cleopatra, Coriolanus, Timon of Athens,* and *Julius Caesar.* His source was Thomas North's 1579 English translation of an earlier French version of a rendition in Latin of Plutarch's Greek, and thus quite a distance from the original. From North, Shakespeare lifted not just plots, themes, and characters but also some of the actual wording. In Shakespeare's *Julius Caesar* (first performed in 1599) several well-known aspects come directly from Plutarch. Examples are the prophecy to Caesar to beware the Ides of March, Calpurnia's dream of Caesar's butchered body, and Caesar's worry about what the "pale, lean fellows, meaning Cassius and Brutus" intend to do (*Lives*, p. 890). In Shakespeare's play, this worry turns into "Yond Cassius has a lean and hungry look" (Shakespeare, *Julius Caesar,* 1.2.194).

Impact. For the classicist J. A. K. Thomson, "It is hardly an exaggeration to say that at least up to the nineteenth century the picture of ancient Greece and Rome in the modern mind was the picture painted by [Plutarch]" (Gianakaris, p. 11). Indeed the *Lives* have shaped not only the modern world's assumptions about their subjects, but also our conceptions of who the important figures were and also what a biography should be. A measure of Plutarch's fame in the years immediately following his death may be found in the North African writer Apuleius' Latin novel ***The Golden Ass*** (also in *Classical Literature and Its Times*), in which the ethnically Greek narrator, anxious to show his scholarly pedigree, informs the reader he is descended from Plutarch. In antiquity the *Lives* served as a resource for schools of rhetoric, which used the dilemmas of the great as subject matter for oratorical exercises. A Greek text of the *Lives* was published in Italy in 1517 and a French version by Jacques Amyot in 1559.

Parallel Lives

Plutarch's *Moralia*—his treatises on superstition, the control of anger, and friends and flatterers, among other subjects—had a lasting impact on the French essayist Michel de Montaigne, as did the *Lives*. From the *Lives*, Montaigne borrowed Plutarch's subjective approach to human character and the interest in virtue. In Britain, Thomas North translated the *Lives* in 1579, which William Shakespeare consulted when writing his Roman plays. The *Lives* (as published in 1683-86, with a life of Plutarch by John Dryden) had a decisive impact on the development of British biography by James Boswell, Samuel Johnson, Lytton Strachey, and others (see Duff, pp. 3-5). In the United States, one of Plutarch's most fervent admirers was the nineteenth-century essayist and transcendentalist philosopher Ralph Waldo Emerson, who knew Plutarch's writings directly as well as through his beloved Montaigne.

Plutarch's tailoring of facts to his moral purposes and his lack of concern for strict chronology did not endear him to nineteenth-century historians. However, his reputation has of late undergone a "sea-change," largely as a result of new approaches to ancient history and the writing of historical narrative, which emphasize the creative role of the historian and the "process of writing itself as interpretation" (Duff, p. 8). Most recently, scholars have viewed Plutarch's work with renewed respect due to fresh insights into his purposes and strategies.

—Robert D. Aguirre

For More Information

Bullough, Geoffrey. *Narrative and Dramatic Sources of Shakespeare.* 8 vols. London: Routledge and Kegan Paul, 1957-75.

Duff, Tim. *Plutarch's "Lives": Exploring Virtue and Vice.* Oxford: Clarendon Press, 1999.

Easterling, P. E., and B. M. W. Knox, eds. *The Cambridge History of Classical Literature I: Greek Literature.* Cambridge: Cambridge University Press, 1985.

Flacelière, Robert. *A Literary History of Greece.* Trans. Douglas Garman. Chicago: Aldine, 1964.

Gianakaris, C. J. *Plutarch.* Twayne's World Authors Series. New York: Twayne, 1970.

Goodman, Martin. *The Roman World: 44 BC-AD 180.* London: Routledge, 1997.

Lamberton, Robert. *Plutarch.* New Haven, Conn.: Yale University Press, 2001.

Mackay, Christopher S. "The Republic." In *Cambridge Illustrated History of the Roman World.* Ed. Greg Woolf. Cambridge: Cambridge University Press, 2003.

Mellor, Ronald. *The Roman Historians.* London: Routledge, 1999.

Plutarch. *The Lives of the Noble Grecians and Romans.* [*Parallel Lives*]. Trans. several hands, attributed to John Dryden. Rev. Arthur Hugh Clough. New York: Modern Library, 1992.

Shakespeare, William. *Julius Caesar.* Ed. David Daniell. The Arden Shakespeare Series. Walton-on-Thames, Surrey, U.K.: Thomas Nelson, 1998.

Swain, Simon. *Hellenism and Empire: Language, Classicism, and Power in the Greek World AD 50-250.* Oxford: Clarendon Press, 1996.

The Peloponnesian War

by
Thucydides

Thucydides (c. 455-c. 400 BCE) was born into an aristocratic Athenian family during the period of Athenian expansion that followed the Persian Wars (490 and 480-79 BCE). Historians believe that he was related through his father to Miltiades, the general who in 490 BCE had led the Athenians to victory at the battle of Marathon in the first of those wars. Thucydides' father was Olorus, which is a Thracian name, and through him Thucydides is thought to have inherited property in Thrace, the northern region to the east of Macedonia. This is probably why in 424 BCE, during the Peloponnesian War, Thucydides was elected an Athenian general and assigned to protect the Thracian city of Amphipolis, which was subject to Athens. When a surprise attack by Sparta resulted in the city's capture, Thucydides was dismissed from his command and exiled from Athens. As he tells us dryly, this left him more time to work on his history of the Peloponnesian War, which he had begun shortly after the fighting broke out. The history breaks off abruptly in its coverage of the year 411 BCE. Because Thucydides refers several times to Athens' final defeat, he must have lived past the war's end in 404 BCE. Historians believe that he died shortly thereafter, still working on the history that would forever link his name with the war and with a pivotal development in the writing of histories.

Events in History at the Time of the Essay

The Athenian Empire. Although the city-state of Sparta was the traditional leader of the ancient

THE LITERARY WORK

A historical essay in eight books, written in Greek c. 430-400 BCE.

SYNOPSIS

Thucydides recounts the Peloponnesian War (431-404 BCE), which was fought between Athens and Sparta but ultimately involved the entire Greek world, resulting in the defeat of Athens and dissolution of its empire.

Greek world, in the early fifth century BCE, Athens took the lead in defending Greece against the mighty Persian Empire. Twice, in 490 and 480 BCE, the Persians launched large invasions of mainland Greece from the far western extent of their empire, the Aegean coast of Asia Minor, today's Turkey. Both of these Persian expeditions were defeated largely through the efforts of Athens, whose role in the Persian Wars led to the foundation of an Athenian empire that challenged Sparta's leadership. Early in *The Peloponnesian War*, Thucydides asserts that Sparta's fear of the growth of Athens' empire after the Persian Wars was the main reason for the outbreak of hostilities between the two powers.

As conceived by the Athenian statesman and general Themistocles, Athens' defensive strategy in the second Persian War had centered on its strong navy, which was the core of the combined fleet formed by the Greek city-states. A decisive sea victory at Salamis in 480 BCE was matched by a land victory the following year near Athens

Illustration of Thucydides. The Library of Congress.
Reprinted by permission.

Greeks most often called themselves Hellenes, their land Hellas, and their civilization Hellenic.

Athens offered its allies in the Delian League the option of donating either tribute payments or ships, men, and arms. Most contributed money, which led to the growth of Athens' navy and left the allies comparatively weaker. Even before the treasury was moved to Athens (c. 454 BCE), the league evolved into an Athenian empire, with Athens growing ever harsher in its dominance of the Greek city-states that were its supposed allies. Athens' treatment of its subject city-states is a central concern of *The Peloponnesian War*, which repeatedly explores the moral implications of imperial power.

As Thucydides stresses, Athens' power relied on the formidable Athenian navy and its dominance of the sea. From its subject city-states, situated almost entirely in coastal areas and islands, Athens derived not only tribute money but also goods, including food, all of which arrived by sea. In the early 470s, Themistocles, the main architect of Athenian naval power, spurred Athens to rebuild the city's fortified walls, which the Persians had destroyed. Later, from 461 to 456 BCE, Athens built a new set of fortified walls, which connected the city to its main port, Piraeus, about four miles away. These so-called Long Walls made Athens virtually impregnable to any force besieging the city by land. About 200 yards apart, the walls furthermore provided an area of refuge to the people who lived in the countryside surrounding Athens.

In his account of the half-century between the Persian Wars and the outbreak of the Peloponnesian War, Thucydides states that the construction of the Long Walls contributed heavily to Spartan suspicion of Athenian intentions. While the Athenians claimed the walls were built to defend their city against another Persian attack, by 461 BCE such an attack was clearly unlikely. Sparta, whose power came from its strength on land, correctly saw the walls as a means of securing Athens as much against Sparta as against Persia.

Thus, by the middle of the fifth century BCE, the Greek world had divided itself into two mutually hostile spheres of influence. The Athenian Empire, made up of allies who sent annual tribute payments to Athens, often under threat of force, spanned most of the Greek cities of the Aegean coastline and nearly all the Greek islands in the Aegean Sea. Meanwhile, Sparta, through its continued leadership of the older network of alliances, retained dominance of the mainland. By the 460s BCE, however, Athens was attempting to expand its influence there as well.

at Plataea. The Athenians again distinguished themselves in battle, and then led the Greek alliance that chased the retreating Persians back across the Aegean to Asia Minor.

There the Greek cities of Ionia—as the Greeks called Asia Minor's Aegean coast—had been under Persian rule since the 540s BCE. In the early 470s BCE, having defeated the two attempts to extend Persian power into mainland Greece, the Athenians supported their Ionian allies in mounting a revolt against the Persian occupiers. It was not the first time they had done so, but the earlier revolt had failed. Under Athenian leadership, the Ionian Greeks now succeeded in freeing themselves of Persian rule, and the Persians mostly withdrew into the interior of Asia Minor.

Historians refer to the Athenian-led anti-Persian alliance as the Delian League, because its treasury was first located on the island of Delos (later it would be moved to Athens). The more traditional network of alliances that remained under Spartan leadership is the Peloponnesian League. Thucydides himself refers to the two groups not as leagues but simply as "the Athenians and their allies" or "the Peloponnesians and their allies." (The term *Peloponnesian* comes from the Peloponnesus peninsula, the bottom part of mainland Greece, where Sparta and some of its major allies were located.) As for their larger culture, the ancient

The "First Peloponnesian War." Primary among Sparta's mainland allies was the powerful city-state of Corinth, which lay on the southwestern edge of the narrow isthmus separating the Peloponnesus from the rest of mainland Greece. In 460 BCE Corinth went to war over a boundary dispute with its neighbor Megara, another Spartan ally, located between Corinth and Athens. When Sparta refused a Megarian appeal for help, the Megarians turned to Athens, which sided with them and entered the war against Corinth. "It was chiefly because of this," notes Thucydides, "that the Corinthians conceived such a bitter hatred of the Athenians" (Thucydides, *The Peloponnesian War*, book 1, chapter 103). As the Athenians must have known it might, their support of Megara upset the tenuous balance of power. Sparta, obliged to help its ally Corinth, soon came into direct conflict with Athens.

Called the First Peloponnesian War, this round of hostilities lasted on and off for more than 15 years and included Athenian military expeditions as far away as Egypt and Sicily. It ended inconclusively in 446 BCE, after Megara returned to the Spartan alliance. Peace negotiations only just barely averted an all-out battle between the Athenians and a Spartan force that had invaded Attica, the southwest portion of central Greece in which Athens sat (an area of about 1,000 square miles, or 2,500 square kilometers). Though the ensuing treaty declared a "Thirty Years' Peace" between Athens and Sparta, suspicion and hostility remained strong on both sides.

The outbreak of the Peloponnesian War. In 433 Athens intervened in a bitter dispute between Corinth and the former Corinthian colony of Corcyra, deeply offending the Corinthians by forming a defensive alliance with Corcyra. Tensions rose the following year, when Corinth struck back by assisting a city-state, Potidaea, that had revolted against the Athenian Empire. At about the same time, the Athenian assembly passed an economic sanction known as the Megarian Decree, which banned Megarians from all harbors in the Athenian Empire and from the marketplace in Athens itself. This trade embargo against a major Peloponnesian commercial power threatened serious economic consequences for Sparta and its allies. Soon afterward, Thucydides reports, the Spartans issued an ultimatum, threatening war unless Athens revoked the decree.

The Athenian leader responsible for the Megarian Decree was Pericles (c. 495-429 BCE), an unusually gifted statesman who dominated

Athenian politics from the 460s until his death in the second year of the war. As a general, Pericles had led Athenian forces in numerous campaigns during the First Peloponnesian War, and he may also have been responsible for the construction of the Long Walls in the early years of that war. As a political leader, Pericles promoted the agenda of the democratic reformers who had progressively limited the power of the aristocrats over Athens since the late sixth century BCE.

ATHENS AND SPARTA: A STUDY IN CONTRASTS

Thucydides makes the differences between Athens and Sparta a major theme in his *Peloponnesian War*. Athens had begun experimenting with democracy in the sixth century BCE, with the democratic reforms of the Athenian statesman Cleisthenes (c. 570-508 BCE). These measures were strengthened after the Persian Wars first by Ephialtes and then by Ephialtes' protégé Pericles, who plays a central role in Thucydides' history. By the outbreak of the Peloponnesian War, all of Athens' male citizens could vote and were eligible for public office. In contrast, Sparta had evolved a rigidly militaristic and authoritarian system, in no small part because of its need to maintain the pacification of the Helots, the inhabitants of Sparta's neighbor Messenia, which Sparta had conquered and enslaved between c. 735 and c. 715 BCE.

In many ways, the Peloponnesian War was a conflict of the ideologies behind the actions of the two city-states, a point that Thucydides stresses in his history. Athens supported democratic factions in its subject city-states; Sparta generally supported the more traditional oligarchic or aristocratic factions. Thucydides also speaks of a divergence in the overall character of the two city-states, contrasting Athens' drive and energy with Sparta's hesitancy and stolidity. To Thucydides, Pericles epitomizes the best "Athenian" traits. Only when it produced leaders (such as Brasidas) with "Athenian" intelligence and boldness could Sparta hope to triumph over Athens.

Praising Pericles for his intelligence, dynamism, and foresight, Thucydides' history notes that "in his leadership of the state he invariably opposed Sparta, allowing no concessions and urging Athens on to war" (*The Peloponnesian War*, 1.27). Pericles' confidence rested on the naval superiority of Athens and on its fortifications, which together, he argued, would allow the Athenians to outlast any force that might besiege the city by land. His arguments, as Thucydides relays them, unfold in fine style. Athens' democratic institutions fostered a culture that rewarded public speaking, and the speeches that Thucydides puts in Pericles' mouth are among the best-known examples of this art, called rhetoric by the Greeks. Swayed by Pericles' powerful rhetoric, the Athenian assembly adopted his strategy and refused to give way to Spartan demands.

MILESTONES ON THE ROAD TO WAR

- **470s BCE** Athens rebuilds its fortified walls.
- **465 BCE** Athens besieges the rebellious island of Thasos, angering Sparta, which had concluded a secret pact with Thasos. Sparta is prevented from aiding the island when an earthquake in the Peloponnesus causes the Helots to revolt. The Athenian expedition to Thasos, says Thucydides, signifies the first open quarrel between Athens and Sparta.
- **461-56 BCE** Athens builds the fortified "Long Walls" linking the city to its port, Piraeus.
- **460-446 BCE** Athens and Sparta, with their allies, fight the "First Peloponnesian War."
- **440 BCE** Athens crushes rebels on the island of Samos.
- **433 BCE** Athens angers Corinth by interfering in Corcyra.
- **432** Athens besieges Potidaea and issues the Megarian Decree, prompting a Spartan ultimatum.

The Peloponnesian War. Hostilities began in the spring of 431 BCE, with a large Peloponnesian force marching into Attica under the Spartan king Archidamus. The invaders ravaged the deserted countryside for about a month before withdrawing. Attica's rural inhabitants took refuge behind the city's fortifications, as Pericles had planned. For the next decade, this basic pattern of temporary Spartan invasion and Athenian withdrawal continued. Historians call this first phase of the conflict the "Archidamian War" (after the Spartan king) or, less commonly, the "Ten Years War," since it lasted until 421 BCE. At that point the two sides, exhausted by the seemingly fruitless fighting, negotiated a fragile peace, the Peace of Nicias.

By that time, however, Pericles was dead. The plague had struck Athens in 430-426 BCE, and he died within a year of its onset, probably from the epidemic. Thucydides himself caught the disease,

which killed off about a quarter of the city's population. Thankfully, he recovered, going on to write a description of the disease that remains one of the best-known passages in *The Peloponnesian War*.

The leader who dominated Athenian politics after Pericles was Cleon, whom Thucydides characterizes as an unscrupulous demagogue. Despite Pericles' death and the losses caused by the plague, under Cleon, the Athenians enjoyed some notable successes in the Ten Years War. They recaptured Potidaea, won several naval battles, and crushed another rebellion on the large island of Lesbos. In 425 BCE the Athenians gained a valuable foothold in the Peloponnesus at Pylos, near Messenia. They established a garrison there in hopes of encouraging a revolt by the Helots, the enslaved inhabitants of Messenia upon whose forced labor Spartan society completely depended.

This threat drove the Spartans to sue for peace in 424 BCE, but the warlike Cleon persuaded the Athenians to turn down the offer. Several Spartan victories followed, including the capture of the important Athenian subject city of Amphipolis, for which Thucydides was blamed. Only then did the Athenians open the negotiations that resulted in the Peace of Nicias (421-413 BCE), which called for both sides to return all territory gained during the fighting.

Technically, the peace lasted eight years, but in fact military operations continued sporadically throughout. Cleon had fallen in 422 in the fighting over Amphipolis, and Athens was now dominated by two new leaders: Alcibiades, the brilliant but unstable young ward of Pericles, and Nicias, who had helped negotiate the peace that bears his name. Soon after the peace was signed, at Alcibiades' instigation Athens undermined it by plotting against Sparta with the Peloponnesian city-states of Argos, Elis, and Mantinea. In 418 BCE, however, Sparta defeated this confederation at Mantinea. Two years later, in 416 BCE, Athens conquered the small island of Melos, a Spartan ally that had refused to join the Delian League. In one of the war's darkest episodes, Athens executed nearly all of Melos' men and sold the women and children into slavery.

Though the peace was still technically in force, shortly after the massacre at Melos, Athens undertook the most extensive operation of the entire war: a massive expedition to Sicily in 415 BCE. A large and prosperous island off the southern Italian peninsula, Sicily was home at the time to numerous settlements that Greeks and others had founded. The expedition from Athens was in response to a request from the small city of

Segesta. It appealed for help against the larger city of Syracuse, which Athens feared might ally itself with Sparta. Promoted by the eager Alcibiades and opposed by the cautious Nicias, the Sicilian expedition was placed under the dual command of these two incompatible leaders. "Certainly," writes Thucydides of its ceremonious launching from Athens, "this expedition . . . was . . . the most costly and the finest-looking force of Hellenic troops that up to that time had ever come from a single city" (*The Peloponnesian War*, 6.31).

Shortly after embarking with the expedition, Alcibiades was recalled to Athens to face charges of religious impiety. He was subsequently exiled from Athens, and Nicias was left to lead an expedition he had opposed from the start. Under his indecisive command, and despite large reinforcements, in 413 BCE the huge and costly expedition was defeated and destroyed. A disaster of almost unimaginable proportions, the loss left the Athenians strategically weakened and psychologically demoralized.

Alcibiades, meanwhile, went over to Sparta. On his advice, the Spartans established a garrison deep within Attica itself, at Decelea, posing a new and constant threat to Athens and Athenian territory. Sparta also formed an alliance with Persia. With virtually its entire fleet destroyed in Sicily, Athens now seemed on the verge of collapse. In 411 BCE political unrest within Athens led to the overthrow of the democracy there and the installation of an oligarchic government, the Council of the Four Hundred. Revolts broke out throughout the Athenian Empire.

Yet somehow Athens managed to hang on for another seven years. The oligarchic government was overthrown within the year, and democracy was restored. At the same time a new Athenian fleet won a string of naval victories in the northeastern Aegean, starting with the battle of Cynossema in 411 BCE, the last event covered by Thucydides. However, Persian funds and the skilled leadership of the Spartan naval commander Lysander eventually negated the Athenian recovery. Although Athens won one last sea victory at Arginusae in 406 BCE, in the following year its fleet was caught by surprise and destroyed at Aegospotami, in the northeast Aegean. In 404 BCE Athens, under siege now by land and sea, surrendered unconditionally, and Sparta installed a puppet government. Sparta, the dominant military power, had gained control of the Greek world—only now it was a world shattered by decades of bitter warfare.

The Essay in Focus

Contents summary. In contrast to Herodotus, who filled his history of the Persian Wars with entertaining anecdotes and digressions, Thucydides stays narrowly focused on war and politics throughout the essay. Also unlike his predecessor, Thucydides chose as his main subject events not of the distant past but of his own times. As he explains in the essay's opening lines,

> Thucydides the Athenian wrote the history of the war fought between Athens and Sparta, beginning the account at the very outbreak of the war, in the belief that it was going to be a great war and more worth writing about than any of those which had taken place in the past. My belief was based on the fact that the two sides were at the height of their power and preparedness.
>
> (*The Peloponnesian War*, 1.1)

The essay's division into eight books, or sections, was made by later commentators, not by Thucydides himself. For convenience, later scholars also assigned descriptive names to the best-known passages, which are generally capitalized.

The first such passage, the Archaeology, appears at the beginning of Book 1, after the opening lines cited above. A summary of earlier Greek history, it is offered in support of Thucydides' contention that the Peloponnesian War was larger and more momentous than any earlier war, and also stresses the importance of sea power. In a brief Preface, Thucydides then describes his methods and notes the "real reason for the war," which was "the growth of Athenian power and the fear which this caused in Sparta" (*The Peloponnesian War*, 1.23). He recounts several of the war's immediate causes, such as the quarrel between Corinth and Corcyra and the revolt at Potidaea. Portraying a diplomatic summit at Sparta, Thucydides presents speeches by Spartan, Corinthian, and Athenian representatives, followed by Sparta's declaration of war. The important passage known as the Pentecontaetia ("Fifty-Year-Period") fills in the war's deeper background, tracing the rise of the Athenian Empire in the roughly five decades between the Persian Wars and the outbreak of the Peloponnesian War. There are digressions about the Athenian statesman Themistocles and the Spartan commander Pausanias (heroes of the Persian Wars who were afterwards accused of intriguing with Persia). Clearly the Persians are involved in the deepening hostility between Athens and Sparta. Book 1 closes with Pericles' first War Speech, giving reasons why Athens should be confident in going to war with Sparta.

Book 2 takes up the outbreak of the fighting, narrating an attack on Plataea, an Athenian ally, by a raiding party from Sparta's ally Thebes, and going on to describe the first Spartan invasion of Attica and the first year of the war. A public funeral in Athens for those killed in the fighting provides the occasion for one of the essay's most quoted passages, the Funeral Oration of Pericles. Calling Athens "an education to Greece," the orator celebrates the glories of Athenian democracy:

> Our constitution is called a democracy because power is in the hands not of a minority but of the whole people. When it is a question of settling private disputes, everyone is equal before the law; when it is a question of putting one person before another in positions of public responsibility, what counts is not membership of a particular class, but the actual ability which the man possesses. No one . . . is kept in political obscurity because of poverty. . . . Here each individual is interested not just in his own affairs but in the affairs of the state as well . . . this is a peculiarity of ours: we do not say that a man who takes no interest in politics is a man who minds his own business; we say that he has no business here at all.
>
> (*The Peloponnesian War*, 2.37)

Many of Pericles' points about Athens are quickly undercut, however, by the account of the plague that breaks out in the crowded city in 430 BCE. Claiming countless lives, the epidemic causes "unprecedented lawlessness" in Athens as its citizens selfishly disregard the city's laws and customs in their fear (*The Peloponnesian War*, 2.53). Before himself falling ill, Pericles delivers his Last Speech, an attempt to stiffen the Athenians' resolve. After reporting the statesman's death, Thucydides offers Pericles' Obituary, in which he praises Pericles' foresight and leadership. He also endorses Pericles' strategy, asserting that final defeat came only because later Athenian leaders departed from it, because the city itself fell into civil strife, and because the Persians decided to fund a Spartan naval fleet. Book 2 closes with the naval victories of the Athenian commander Phormio.

Book 3 opens with Athens crushing the revolt in the city of Mytilene on the island of Lesbos. Then comes the dramatic Mytilenean Debate, in which the Athenian demagogue Cleon calls for putting the rebels to death while his opponent Diodotus calls for leniency. Cleon carries the day and a ship is sent with the order to execute the rebels, but at the last minute the Athenian

assembly changes its mind and a second ship is sent to overtake the first. The order is thus countermanded. A corresponding Plataean Debate occurs when Thebes (Sparta's ally) captures Plataea (Athens' ally); the debate ends less happily though; this time more than 200 Plataeans are put to death.

There follows one of the most difficult and celebrated passages in the work, as Thucydides analyzes the Civil Strife (*stasis*) in Corcyra between the democratic allies of Athens and the oligarchic allies of Sparta. Calling war "a stern teacher," Thucydides describes how similar partisan strife infected other cities, leading to a breakdown in public order and the twisting of language itself:

> To fit in with the change of events, words, too, had to change their meanings. What used to be described as a thoughtless act of aggression was now regarded as the courage one would expect to find in a party member; to think of the future and wait was merely another way of saying one was a coward; any idea of moderation was just an attempt to disguise one's unmanly character; ability to understand a question from all sides meant that one was totally unfitted for action.
>
> (*The Peloponnesian War*, 3.82)

Remarkably, Thucydides' own language here seems to break down, becoming jumbled in a way that mimics the meaning.

Book 4 covers the Athenians' success at Pylos in the Peloponnesus in 424 BCE, various campaigns on the Greek mainland, and the capture of Amphipolis by the brilliant Spartan general Brasidas. Book 5 opens with the subsequent battle around Amphipolis, in which both Cleon and Brasidas are killed, and then describes the negotiations resulting in the Peace of Nicias. Next come the Peloponnesian intrigues of Alcibiades, culminating in the Spartan victory at Mantinea in 418 BCE. The book closes with the Melian Dialogue, a bleakly cynical discussion in dialogue form. The implacable Athenians converse with the hapless representatives of Melos (the small island that had refused to join the Delian League), who argue unsuccessfully that it would be in Athens' own best interests to spare them.

Books 6 and 7 are devoted almost entirely to the Sicilian Expedition, a detailed, highly polished account ending in a final nighttime sea battle at Syracuse in which the Athenian fleet is destroyed. Book 7 also includes the fortification of Decelea, the permanent garrison in Attica that the Spartans established on Alcibiades' advice.

Book 8 begins with the Athenians' stunned reaction to the expedition's fate, then moves east to cover revolts against Athens on the large islands of Lesbos, Chios, and Samos. Thucydides also describes the beginnings of Persia's intervention on the side of Sparta, which will ultimately prove a decisive factor in Athens' defeat. But the bulk of Book 8 is given over to the oligarchic coup of 411 BCE in Athens, whereby the Council of the Four Hundred comes to power before being replaced by the more democratic Council of the Five Thousand. Book 8 breaks off abruptly after narrating Athens' naval victory at Cynossema in 411 BCE.

The historian as objective observer. Early in *The Peloponnesian War*, Thucydides assures readers that he has taken great trouble over the accuracy of his information: "either I was present myself at the events which I have described or else I heard of them from eye-witnesses whose reports I have checked with as much thoroughness as possible" (*The Peloponnesian War*, 1.22). He furthermore has not, continues Thucydides, embellished the facts in order to make his account more entertaining:

> And it may well be that my history will seem less easy to read because of the absence in it of a romantic element. It will be enough for me, however, if these words of mine are judged useful by those who want to understand clearly the events which happened in the past and which (human nature being what it is) will, at some time or other and in much the same ways, be repeated in the future. My work is not a piece of writing designed to meet the taste of an immediate public, but was done to last forever.
> (*The Peloponnesian War*, 1.22)

With this disparaging reference to "a romantic element," Thucydides apparently intends to differentiate himself sharply from his illustrious predecessor Herodotus. Herodotus' account of the Persian Wars is replete with what can fairly be described as romance, adventure, and fable. Herodotus himself is said to have read parts of his account aloud to appreciative crowds in Athens shortly before Thucydides began his own work, which may be what provoked Thucydides' slighting allusion to "the taste of an immediate public." Indeed, immediately preceding the passage quoted above, Thucydides has ostentatiously corrected several errors that occur in Herodotus' text, without ever naming Herodotus. In the same breath Thucydides decries those storytellers (*logographoi*) "who are less interested in telling the truth than in catching the attention of their public, whose authorities cannot be checked, and whose subject matter is mostly lost

in the unreliable streams of mythology" (*The Peloponnesian War*, 1.21). Then, as if to hammer the point home, right after asserting that his work is meant to stand forever, Thucydides argues that the Persian Wars (Herodotus' subject, lost in the mists of time) are anyway less significant than the Peloponnesian War (Thucydides' subject, observed and recorded as it unfolded).

Thucydides also seems to go out of his way to avoid the word with which Herodotus had described his own endeavor—*historia*, or "inquiry." This is the word that has entered English as "history." Though the modern translator uses it in several of the quotations cited in this article, Thucydides in the original Greek does not. In the essay's opening lines, for example, he uses a phrase that might better be translated as he "wrote up the war" (*synegrapse ton polemon*) than he "wrote the history of the war." It is important to understand that "history" did not yet exist as a well-defined literary and intellectual discipline.

As Greek commentators began to define the study of history over the next century or so, Thucydides would come to be regarded as its second practitioner, after Herodotus. Yet Thucydides seems to wish to portray himself as more of an innovator than a follower, conspicuously departing from Herodotus in both subject matter and style. Instead of the irretrievable past, Thucydides analyzes contemporary events; instead of giving broad cultural and geographical information on Greece and its neighbors, Thucydides limits himself strictly to Greek politics and warfare; and instead of openly seeking to entertain his readers, Thucydides adopts an authorial pose of dispassionate objectivity.

Sources and literary context. As Thucydides tells us early in *The Peloponnesian War*, his main source of information was his own experience, backed by that of other eyewitnesses on whom he relied for knowledge of events that he himself did not see firsthand. In Book 5, he explains, "I lived through the whole of it [the war], being of an age to understand what was happening, and I put my mind to the subject so as to get an accurate view of it" (*The Peloponnesian War*, 5.26). After being exiled from Athens for his role in the loss of Amphipolis, he was in an especially good position to see "what was being done on both sides, particularly on the Peloponnesian side" (*The Peloponnesian War*, 5.26). Modern scholars take this to mean that Thucydides had good sources among the Spartans and their allies as well as among the Athenians and theirs. One scholar, Simon Hornblower, suggests that Thucydides

TRUE OR NOT EXACTLY?—THE SPEECHES

Despite Thucydides' self-conscious attempts to distance himself from Herodotus on points of method and style, the general ways in which he follows the earlier writer must ultimately be counted as more telling. Like Herodotus, Thucydides regularly puts direct speech in the mouths of his characters, usually in the form of a public address. Probably no aspect of his history has aroused more interest on the part of modern scholars than these highly elaborate speeches, whose linguistic difficulty marks them off from the more straightforward narrative bulk of the work. From a historical standpoint, the biggest questions that modern scholars have about the speeches involve their veracity. How true are they to what was actually said? Indeed, can they always be taken to represent a real speech that someone actually made? In Book 1, Thucydides himself comments on the speeches, but his much discussed remarks offer only limited help:

> In this history I have made use of set speeches some of which were delivered just before and others during the war. I have found it difficult to remember the precise words used in the speeches which I listened to myself and my various informants have experienced the same difficulty; so my method has been, while keeping as closely as possible to the sense of the words that were actually used, to make the speakers say what, in my opinion, was called for by each situation.
>
> (*The Peloponnesian War*, 1.22)

In other words, Thucydides either paraphrased the actual speakers or else he simply made up what he thought they ought to have said. Nowhere does he attempt to indicate which method he might be employing with any speech in particular. The result has been vigorous debate that promises to remain unresolved.

also had access to military reports written by commanders in the field to their superiors at home. Hornblower speculates that Thucydides' famously terse, impersonal literary style stems from his own experience writing such reports.

As indicated, Thucydides' predecessor Herodotus (c. 484-c. 430 BCE) had recorded the epic struggle between the smaller, disunited Greek city-states and the vast Persian Empire during the Persian Wars. Herodotus' account, *The Histories* (also in *Classical Literature in Its Times*), was the first sustained attempt at a rational rather than a religious explanation of past events, and it earned Herodotus the epithet "The Father of History." But, although he explains historical events in human terms, Herodotus still depicts divine powers as guiding the broad outlines of human history. Thucydides, however, takes Herodotus' newborn rational approach a step further by leaving the will of the gods out of his work entirely. While he disparages Herodotus, modern scholars have concluded that Thucydides relied on the earlier

writer both for specific information as well as for a general model. Thucydides also slights the Greek "storytellers," or *logographoi*, declaring that his evidence for Greece's early past is better than that of "the poets, who exaggerate the importance of their themes" (*The Peloponnesian War*, 1.21). Yet according to modern scholars, he relies on the poets for some of his historic information as well as for broader inspiration. The only poet Thucydides mentions by name is Homer (c. 750 BCE), credited with writing the *Iliad* and the *Odyssey*, the epics regarded as the foundation of Greek literature (also in *Classical Literature and Its Times*). Though scholarly opinion on the matter is divided, other genres of the time may have influenced Thucydides too, including rhetoric, Greek tragedy, and, in his descriptions of the plague, the medical writings that are attributed to his contemporary, Hippocrates of Cos (c. 470-c. 400 BCE).

With one exception, Thucydides (unlike Herodotus) makes no specific mention of other contemporary prose writers or thinkers. That exception is Hellanicus of Lesbos (c. 480-c. 400 BCE), a longer-lived contemporary of Herodotus whom Thucydides briefly mentions as having written a work about Attica. Hellanicus pioneered a genre that arose at around the same time as Herodotus and Thucydides were writing, and whose practitioners are called Atthidographers, after *Atthis*, the title ascribed to Hellanicus' work about Attica. These writers wrote chronicles of particular places, going back to mythical times and often focusing on fable and legend. While they dealt with the past, their works lacked the thematic unity and sustained analytical quality that Herodotus and Thucydides brought to their subjects. Thucydides mentions Hellanicus only to say that his coverage of Athenian history in the period between the Persian Wars and Peloponnesian War is scanty, and that he is inaccurate in his dates. Again, some modern scholars have suggested that Thucydides nevertheless used Hellanicus for sections such as the Pentecontaetia. In some places, too, scholars have seen Thucydides as correcting Hellanicus' mistakes, especially in regard to chronology. Thucydides adopts his own system of dating the events in the war by year (for example, the ninth year of the war), dividing each year into two campaigning seasons, winter and summer.

Publication and impact. While Herodotus had written his history to be read aloud to an audience, by Thucydides' time Greece had progressed in its transition from an oral to a literate culture. Various clues in the text—not least Thucydides' claim that his work is "meant to last forever" (*The Peloponnesian War*, 1.22)—make it fairly clear that Thucydides is writing for individual readers. Little is known, however, about how the unfinished work found its way into the hands of its first readers.

On the other hand, the work is known to have had a profound impact on early readers, not from any direct comments but from the other historians who soon followed in Thucydides' wake. These historians took up the account of the Peloponnesian War where he left off. The best of them, known as the Oxyrhynchus historian, wrote a continuation that unfortunately survives only in fragments of papyrus. Another historian, Xenophon, does Thucydides the honor of beginning his continuation of Thucydides with the words, "Some days later . . ." (Xenophon, p. 53). Born around the time the Peloponnesian War broke out, Xenophon is sometimes credited with having helped publish Thucydides' work.

Thucydides' severe, self-consciously rational approach has always impressed readers, and later ancient historians tended to take him, rather than Herodotus, as their model. Modern consensus holds that no other ancient historian came close to matching the insight, painstaking accuracy, and analytical ability of Thucydides. His reputation has been such that as late as the nineteenth century, a number of professional historians looked to him as the paragon of the scientific historian. By the end of the twentieth century, however, no longer so obsessed with being "scientific," historians had begun to question the pose of cold objectivity in his work. These historians have explored what they see as the often unexpectedly powerful emotional intensity of Thucydides, which he artfully and deliberately enhances with his terse, matter-of-fact delivery.

—Colin Wells

For More Information

Boardman, John, et al. *Greece and the Hellenistic World*. Oxford: Oxford University Press, 1986.

Connor, W. Robert. *Thucydides*. Princeton: Princeton University Press, 1984.

Cornford, F. M. *Thucydides Mythistoricus*. London: Routledge & Kegan Paul, 1965.

Gomme, A. W., A. Andrewes, and K. J. Dover. *A Historical Commentary on Thucydides*. 5 Vols. Oxford: Clarendon, 1945-81.

Hornblower, Simon. *Thucydides*. Baltimore: Johns Hopkins University Press, 1987.

Kagan, Donald. *The Peloponnesian War*. New York: Viking, 2003.

Meiggs, Russell. *The Athenian Empire*. Oxford: Clarendon, 1972.

Thucydides. *The Peloponnesian War*. Trans. Rex Warner. New York: Penguin, 1972.

Xenophon. *A History of My Times*. Trans. Rex Warner. New York: Penguin, 1966.

The Persian Expedition

by
Xenophon

THE LITERARY WORK

A nonfiction narrative set in Greece and Persia in 401-399 BCE; written in Greek c. 370 BCE and commonly known as the *Anabasis* (Journey Upcountry).

SYNOPSIS

Cyrus the Younger, a son of the deceased Persian king Darius II, hires a large contingent of Greek mercenary soldiers (the "Ten Thousand") to help him wrest the throne from his older brother, Artaxerxes II. When Cyrus is killed in battle, the Greeks undertake a dangerous march through more than 1,000 miles of hostile territory back to Greece.

Xenophon (c. 430-c. 350 BCE), an Athenian aristocrat, was born in Athens near the beginning of the Peloponnesian War, Athens' long, disastrous conflict with Sparta (431-404 BCE). Reportedly very handsome, he grew up to become a student of the philosopher Socrates and to serve in the Athenian cavalry during this war. After Athens lost, Xenophon left the city for political reasons. He capitalized on his cavalry experience by joining, in 401 BCE, the expeditionary force of Greek mercenaries hired by Cyrus the Younger to help overthrow his older brother Artaxerxes II, the king of Persia. Xenophon emerged as one of the expedition's leaders, which made him famous after the soldiers' return to Greece. He proceeded to serve Sparta, or more exactly the Spartan king Agesilaus, on campaigns in Greece. Exiled from Athens, he was rewarded by Agesilaus with a comfortable estate at Scillus, in northern Greece. After Spartan power was shattered by Thebes in 371 BCE, Xenophon was forced to move to Corinth, where he may have written *The Persian Expedition*. A cultivated man of conservative political views, Xenophon was a remarkably versatile author who would remain widely read in later periods. His surviving works include a history of his times (*Hellenica*), two books about Socrates (*Memorabilia* and *Apology*), and treatises on such diverse subjects as economics, estate management, hunting, and horsemanship. However, *The Persian Expedition* has always been his most popular work. Prized for its action-packed narrative, the work offers valuable insights into Greek warfare and customs, as well as Greek attitudes toward other cultures.

Events in History at the Time the Narrative Takes Place

Greece and Persia in the fifth century BCE. Greece's complex relationship with the vast Persian Empire, its powerful neighbor to the east, played a central role in the development of Greek civilization throughout the Classical period of Greek history (480-323 BCE). Indeed, Greece's Classical period of history started and ended in confrontation with Persia. The period began with

Illustration of Xenophon the soldier. © The Bettmann Archive. Reproduced by permission.

two Persian invasions of Greece (490 and 480 BCE) that saw the Greeks emerge victorious and that sparked a newly self-confident expansion of Greek culture. And the period ended a century and a half later with the death of the conqueror Alexander the Great (356-323 BCE), who had realized the longstanding dream of conquering Persia in Greece's name. The Greek incursion that Xenophon chronicles in *The Persian Expedition* stands in the exact middle of this timespan and has been seen as planting the seed that Alexander brought to fruition.

The Persian Empire had been founded in the mid-sixth century BCE by Cyrus the Great (ruled 559-530 BCE). Among other conquests, Cyrus incorporated Greek cities of Ionia (coastal Asia Minor) into Persia's growing domains. In 499 BCE, with the help of Athens, the Ionian Greeks revolted against Persian rule. Within six years Darius I (ruled 522-486 BCE) had crushed the Ionian revolt, and four years later he launched the first Persian invasion of mainland Greece, intending to punish Athens for aiding the rebels. Instead, the Athenians defeated the larger Persian force at the battle of Marathon (490 BCE). Ten years after that, Darius' son and successor, Xerxes, himself accompanied a far greater Persian invasion force. Whereas Darius had meant merely to punish Athens, Xerxes aimed to occupy Greece and turn it into a Persian province. Putting aside their differences, the Greek city-states united under Spartan leadership and defeated this invasion in several battles, including a naval engagement at Salamis (480 BCE), in which the Athenian navy destroyed the Persian fleet. The Athenians then chased the retreating Persians back across the Aegean Sea, winning several more battles and in time freeing the Ionian city-states from Persian rule.

The Persian Wars were followed by a long power struggle between the two leading Greek city-states, Sparta and Athens. From 431 to 404 BCE, these two rivals fought the Peloponnesian War, which embroiled most of Greece on one side or the other. At first it seemed like an even match. Both sides had many allies. Sparta, with a large and disciplined army, dominated on the mainland, while Athens, with its formidable navy, ruled the islands and coastal areas. For two decades, neither side could prevail.

At some point, probably in the early 410s, Athens made what turned out to be a fatal mistake: the Athenians aided two Persian satraps (governors) of western Asia Minor, who had rebelled against the Persian king Darius II (ruled 423-404 BCE). Angered by the participation of the Athenians in this failed revolt, Darius II decided to punish them by supporting Sparta. In drawn-out negotiations, the Spartan and Persian representatives struck a deal. Persia would make large payments of cash to Sparta, while Sparta would recognize Persia's rule over the Ionian Greek city-states. The Persian funds enabled Sparta to build a navy that could challenge the Athenian fleet, breaking the deadlock in Sparta's favor.

Athens surrendered in 404 BCE, ending the war and ushering in a period known as the Spartan hegemony, in which Sparta dominated the Greek world. The events that Xenophon describes in *The Persian Expedition* took place near the beginning of the Spartan hegemony; the narrative itself was probably written around the time it ended in 371 BCE.

Cyrus, Tissaphernes, and Artaxerxes II. One of Darius II's main representatives in Persia's initial dealings with Sparta was the regional governor Tissaphernes, who was satrap of southwestern Asia Minor. Tissaphernes offered Sparta less support than Darius wished, thereby angering Darius. In 407 BCE Darius removed Tissaphernes and appointed instead Darius' own second son Cyrus (called Cyrus the Younger to distinguish him from Cyrus the Great) as satrap of southwestern Asia Minor. Darius II also made Cyrus the supreme commander of all Persian forces in Asia Minor. Thus, Cyrus, who was a close friend of the Spartan naval commander Lysimachus, became responsible for supplying the crucial aid to Sparta. Tissaphernes, meanwhile, whose authority Darius II had curtailed in Cyrus' favor, resented the new governor. If the long-term relationship between Persia and Greece comprises the general background of *The Persian Expedition*, the enmity between Cyrus and Tissaphernes—who continued as a satrap of lands further east—provides the specific context in which the story begins to unfold.

Cyrus had won his influential appointment partly at the behest of his mother, the powerful Persian queen Parysatis. Cyrus, her favorite son, had an older brother. When Darius II died in 404 BCE, this older brother inherited the throne as Artaxerxes II.

In the opening pages of *The Persian Expedition*, Xenophon recounts what happened next:

> When Artaxerxes was established on the throne, Tissaphernes maligned Cyrus to his brother and accused him of plotting against him. Artaxerxes believed the story and arrested Cyrus with the intention of putting him to death; but his mother by her entreaties secured his life and his recall to his province. Still, after the danger and disgrace from which he had escaped, Cyrus took measures to ensure that he should never again be in his brother's power; instead, if he could manage it, he would become king in his brother's place.
>
> (Xenophon, *The Persian Expedition*, book 1, chapter 1)

In assessing his situation, Cyrus thus found himself in a position characterized by strong ties to the Spartans, good reasons to challenge his brother, and—perhaps most important—a large pool of experienced Greek soldiers on hand, men who needed a way to support themselves now that the Spartans had emerged victorious.

In the spring of 401 BCE, Cyrus put out the word to his Greek friends that he was looking for mercenary soldiers to make up an army, although he kept his intention of overthrowing his brother a secret for the time being. Cyrus also hired a number of Greeks to recruit and lead the force, one of whom was a Theban named Proxenus. It was Proxenus who invited his friend Xenophon to join the mercenaries.

Warfare in Greek society. Warfare was considered an honorable pursuit by the Greeks, who placed high social value on individual military prowess. This is clearly reflected in the earliest Greek literature, Homer's ***Iliad*** and ***Odyssey*** (also in *Classical Literature and Its Times*). Epic poems, the two works celebrate the deeds of great warriors such as Achilles and Odysseus in the Greeks' legendary war against Troy. Originally oral, these epics are thought to have first been put in written form in the eighth century BCE. Greek society changed profoundly over the next few centuries. By Xenophon's time, Greek warfare had evolved, too—although some aspects of war had remained remarkably similar to those described by Homer.

Scholars believe that Homer describes Greek warfare as it existed around the year 700 BCE (although the poems purport to recount a far earlier time). By the late fifth century BCE, Homeric

fighting techniques had been not so much replaced as refined and supplemented. For example, Homer's heroes fight on foot, with spears and shields, just as most soldiers still did in Xenophon's time. Horses were used in Homeric epic for transportation rather than as fighting platforms. Once on the battlefield, the aristocratic warrior would dismount and fight on his two feet. Xenophon, a foot soldier, uses his horse in precisely this way in *The Persian Expedition*. He was part of the infantry, though wealthier than most. Unlike the relatively rich Xenophon, infantrymen of his day generally traveled on foot. While foot soldiers still comprised the bulk of a Greek land force, cavalry—mounted soldiers who fought from horseback—had emerged to

RELIGION IN GREEK WARFARE

One aspect of Greek warfare that emerges clearly from *The Persian Expedition* is the crucial place of religious ritual. Success in war was thought to reflect the favor of the gods, and Xenophon repeatedly shows the Greeks seeking to secure divine approval before a critical operation. They did so primarily by carrying out a sacrifice, in which an animal such as a goat or sheep was butchered and parts of it were burnt as an offering. The rest was eaten in a ceremonial feast. The sacrifice's success might be discerned by a soothsayer, who would examine the animal or its entrails, the appearance of which was thought to be an omen (sign) of divine approval or disapproval.

In one passage, Xenophon describes how the Greeks urgently needed to break camp and march out in search of food, but the sacrifices showed unfavorable omens. "The soldiers were upset at this," he writes, "since the provisions which they had brought with them were running short and there was no possibility of buying food in the neighborhood" (*The Persian Expedition*, 6.4). Despite their growing hunger, they stayed in camp for several days as repeated sacrifices continued to show unfavorable omens. When they finally marched out—still against the omens—Xenophon tells us that they took heavy casualties. In this passage and many others, Xenophon's narrative reflects his strong religious piety.

take on an important if still supplementary role. In contrast to foot soldiers, who were generally expected to supply their own equipment, a cavalryman's horses were supplied by the state. The usefulness of cavalry was limited in the ancient world, however, because stirrups, essential for truly effective horseback fighting, had not yet been invented.

The growth of the Greek city-state in the sixth and fifth centuries BCE meant that warfare became less "personal" and more "public." That is, from disputes between aristocratic warriors and their fellows, in which personal loyalties were paramount, wars changed into disputes between city-states, in which men fought largely as citizen soldiers in a spirit of public service.

Yet in some significant ways warfare remained more "personal" than in modern times. For example, in addition to supplying their own weapons and equipment, soldiers were also responsible for their own food and drink. While traveling on extended missions, most of their time was spent foraging, as *The Persian Expedition* vividly shows. An enemy would do its best to despoil the land of available crops. Above all, perhaps, commanders relied on the goodwill of soldiers, who might easily refuse orders they found objectionable. Discipline was very difficult to maintain, as Xenophon's account also demonstrates. At one point, Xenophon defends himself to the other commanders for

beating a disobedient soldier with the argument that in this case the soldier's disobedience endangered the whole army.

Historians have also noted a trend toward closer and closer formation in the deployment of infantry units, as the loose organization of Homeric epic gave way to the so-called hoplite phalanx. Heavily armed footsoldiers (called "hoplites") arranged themselves in close formation (the "phalanx"), using their shields to make a wall and thrusting rather than throwing their spears. Homeric heroes had both thrusted and thrown. The hoplite preference for thrusting resulted in their spears being longer and heavier. Sometimes swords were also carried for hand-to-hand combat, and groups of archers harassed the enemy from a distance.

The hoplite phalanx proved highly effective. It was in fact the fearsome charge of massed hoplites that had allowed the Greeks to prevail over a much larger Persian force at Marathon in 490 BCE. In general, battles in fifth century BCE Greece were fought largely by citizen hoplites. Citizen forces, however, were limited in their range and mobility. Most men, especially farmers, could not afford to spend much time away from their other obligations. Except in highly militarized Sparta, training for combat was for centuries nonexistent. By the fourth century BCE, however, these amateur citizen warriors were being replaced more and more by professionally trained full-time soldiers.

MAJOR FIGURES IN *THE PERSIAN EXPEDITION*

Agesilaus, king of Sparta Mentioned in passing in the narrative, Agesilaus will later become Xenophon's ally and protector.

Artaxerxes II, king of Persia Cyrus the Younger's older brother.

Chirisophus, a Spartan commander Chirisophus becomes the expedition's supreme leader. Although Xenophon presents himself as getting along well with Chirisophus, some modern scholars suggest that Xenophon minimizes the leadership of the Spartan commander while exaggerating his own contributions.

Clearchus, a second Spartan commander Clearchus is among the Greek leaders murdered by the Persians after the battle of Cunaxa.

Cyrus the Younger, a Persian prince Cyrus the Younger hires the Greek soldiers of Xenophon's narrative.

Darius II, king of Persia Darius is the father of Cyrus the Younger and Artaxerxes II.

Parysatis, the wife of Darius II Parysatis is the mother of Cyrus the Younger and Artaxerxes.

Pharnabazus, Persian satrap (governor) Pharnabazus wields authority over northwestern Asia Minor.

Proxenus, a Theban commander Proxenus invites Xenophon to accompany the expedition.

Thibron, a Spartan commander Arriving after the expedition returns, Thibron hires the soldiers to make war on Persian forces in Asia Minor.

Tissaphernes, a second Persian satrap A governor in Asia Minor and a rival of Cyrus the Younger, Tissaphernes pursues the Greek soldiers after Cyrus' death.

Xenophon An Athenian gentleman who accompanies the expedition, and the author of *The Persian Expedition*. His initial status—was he a soldier or an observer at first?—is unclear.

Often such soldiers hired themselves out as mercenaries to the city-state that was the highest bidder. At the same time, lighter armed, more mobile troops called "peltasts" were superseding the heavier, less mobile hoplites. Peltast shields were lighter and smaller, allowing denser formation in the phalanx (the name "peltast" came from the light-weight wicker or leather shield, the pelta). By the end of the Classical period, the highly trained professional peltast phalanx had emerged as the force that would allow Alexander the Great to conquer much of the known world, including the Persian Empire.

While Xenophon's "Ten Thousand" are hardly the first mercenaries in Greek history, they were the first mercenary force large enough to take on the entire army of another state by themselves. And although their number included both hoplites and peltasts, their mission deep into hostile territory clearly demonstrated the advantages of traveling light and striking from afar. Historians have thus seen *The Persian Expedition* as reflecting a critical stage in the transition from hoplite to peltast, and from amateur to professional, that marked the Greek soldier's evolution during the Classical period.

The Narrative in Focus

Contents summary. Although Xenophon himself was present during many of the events he describes in *The Persian Expedition*, he tells the story in the third person. Even when referring to himself—which, as commentators note, he does frequently and flatteringly—he does so in the third person, as "Xenophon" rather than "I." Nowhere does he explicitly say that he is the author of the work, although his increasing prominence in the narrative might suggest it to the reader. At the beginning, the story is about Cyrus and his Greek mercenaries; by the end, it is primarily about Xenophon. The narrative is conventionally divided into 9 books (actually sections), each with 5-10 chapters (subsections).

The story opens with a summary of the circumstances that led Cyrus to attempt to overthrow his older brother, Artaxerxes II, the reigning king of Persia (explained above). Cyrus begins gathering an army of Greek mercenaries. He conceals his true motives from both Artaxerxes and the Greek soldiers themselves, under the pretext of making war on Tissaphernes, Cyrus' Persian rival, who was contesting Cyrus' control of Ionia. Among the Greek commanders who help Cyrus build up his army are Clearchus the Spartan and Proxenus the Theban (the Greek commanders are aware of Cyrus' real aims, which they help conceal from the soldiers). Cyrus gives each commander large sums of money to attract the best soldiers. After reporting to Cyrus at Sardis, the seat of Persian power in western Asia Minor, the Greek commanders and their troops set out with Cyrus on the long march into Persia. They number 11,000 hoplites and 2,000 peltasts, 13,000 in all.

Meanwhile, Tissaphernes warns Artaxerxes that Cyrus is marching against him, and Artaxerxes begins preparing his own army for battle. By the time they reach Tarsus, near the Syrian border, the soldiers suspect that they are really marching against the Persian king and threaten to mutiny. Clearchus and Cyrus (who raises the soldiers' pay) deftly defuse their complaints, without addressing their suspicions. Soon afterward the expedition is joined by Chirisophus, a junior Spartan commander who will later take a leading role. Only when they reach the city of Thapsacus, on the Euphrates River, does Cyrus openly reveal to the Greeks that they are marching against his brother, the king. The soldiers react angrily, but most are assuaged when Cyrus promises them a bonus worth about four months' pay.

By now the Greeks are crossing "Arabia," as they call the vast desert of today's Syria and Iraq. Cyrus and the Greek commanders deal with several disciplinary problems during the harsh desert crossing. The army makes it across the desert and begins marching through Babylonia. Artaxerxes, aided by Tissaphernes, has gathered his forces, which are far larger than Cyrus' army, even though the Greeks are now supplemented by some Persian troops loyal to Cyrus. When Artaxerxes retreats instead of giving battle, Cyrus becomes less cautious and moves forward quickly. At the town of Cunaxa (the exact site of Cunaxa remains controversial), Artaxerxes turns to attack. Although the Greeks break through the opposing Persian lines in many places, Cyrus himself is killed in the fighting.

Believing they have won the battle, the Greeks do not learn that Cyrus is dead until the next morning. At first amazed, they quickly grow despondent. The king sends heralds to negotiate with the Greek commanders, and the two sides agree to a temporary truce, to remain in force as long as the Greeks stay where they are. Clearchus and Tissaphernes then sign a treaty that promises the Greeks safe conduct through Persian territory; in exchange, the Greeks agree to buy their provisions rather than plunder the land, and to march as though they are "in a friendly country" (*The Persian Expedition*, 2.3).

The Greeks head north, to the southern shore of the Black Sea, setting out for the Greek colonies there. After several weeks' march, they arrive at the river Zapatas (today's Greater Zab), a tributary of the Tigris River. Followed by a large Persian force, the Greeks are tense and suspect that the Persians mean to attack. Tissaphernes allays their suspicions, making a show of friendship toward Clearchus and inviting him and the other Greek leaders to dinner. Tissaphernes' friendliness, however, is part of a ruse. Once he has the Greek commanders in his tent, he arrests them and soon afterward the king has them executed.

The Greeks are now thrown into turmoil and depression. Surrounded by the enemy, they have lost most of their best leaders, including Clearchus and Proxenus. They are still at least 500 miles from Trapezus, the nearest Greek city on the Black Sea. To get there, they face rugged, mountainous terrain, wide rivers, and hostile peoples. First, though, they must avoid destruction by the Persians.

That night Xenophon assists in gathering the remaining Greek officers. As they meet, he urges them to rise to the occasion:

> I think that first of all you could do a great service to the army by appointing generals and captains as quickly as possible to take the places of those whom we have lost. For where there is no one in control nothing useful or distinguished can ever get done. This is roughly true of all departments of life, and is entirely true where soldiering is concerned. Here it is discipline that makes one feel safe, while lack of discipline has destroyed many people before now.
>
> (*The Persian Expedition*, 3.1)

He advises the officers to call a meeting of the whole army, to let the soldiers know that the commanders have been replaced and to raise their morale. "You are well aware," he continues, "that it is not numbers or strength that bring the victories in war. No, it is when one side goes against the enemy with the gods' gift of a stronger morale that their enemies, as a rule, cannot withstand them" (*The Persian Expedition*, 3.1). After this stirring speech, Xenophon's recommendations are followed; he himself is chosen as one of the new commanders.

At the general meeting that follows, the new commanders address the soldiers. Xenophon gives several lengthy speeches, encouraging the troops and making tactical suggestions that are immediately adopted. For example, he advises traveling in a hollow square formation, with baggage carriers, servants, and others inside, protected by hoplites making up the square. He also suggests that they burn their wagons and tents and get rid of other inessentials, "only keeping what we have for the purpose of fighting and eating or drinking" (*The Persian Expedition*, 3.2). Chirisophus the Spartan, who has also been chosen as a commander, backs Xenophon's suggestions. On Xenophon's further advice, the experienced Chirisophus is chosen to lead the hoplite square, while Xenophon himself, as one of the youngest, is put in charge of the rear.

On this basis, the Greeks begin the journey, modifying the formation somewhat as circumstances demand but generally sticking to the basic square. They improvise weapons and tactics as they go, adapting to the changing terrain and varying peoples whom they meet along the way. Lacking cavalry and archers, at first they are harried by mounted Persian bowmen. In response, the Greeks create a small cavalry force using some of the baggage horses; they also deploy foot soldiers with slings, or leather pouches that they whirl to shoot small lead balls against the enemy. Resourcefully, they also pick up the Persians' spent arrows and make bows to shoot the arrows back. Tissaphernes follows the Greeks with a large army, and the two sides skirmish continually. Both sides send out advance parties to capture summits and other high ground over the route that the Greeks will take, and they fight several pitched battles.

Evading Tissaphernes once and for all, the Greeks cross into the rugged land of the Carduchi, a warlike people who have repelled Persian attempts to conquer them. It takes the Greeks seven days to battle their way through the land of the Carduchi, days of constant warfare in which they "had suffered more than they had suffered in all their engagements with the King and Tissaphernes" (*The Persian Expedition*, 4.3).

Still under attack, they cross a large river into Armenia, a province of Persia. There they are pursued by a Persian army under Tiribazus, the governor of Armenia. They march through days of heavy snow, bitter cold, and mountainous terrain:

> It was a relief to the eyes against snow-blindness if one held something black in front of the eyes while marching; and it was a help to the feet if one kept on the move and never stopped still, and took off one's shoes at night. If one slept with one's shoes on, the straps sank into the flesh and the soles of the shoes froze to the feet.
> (*The Persian Expedition*, 4.5)

After weeks of hard winter marching, the Greeks emerge from mountainous Armenia, crossing through the lands of the Phasians, Taochi, Chalybes, and Scytheni. Finally from the summit of a high mountain, the men in front catch sight of the Black Sea and let out a shout. Xenophon and the others in the rear assume they are being attacked.

> So Xenophon mounted his horse and, taking Lycus and the cavalry with him, rode forward to give support, and, quite soon, they heard the soldiers shouting out "The sea! The sea!" and passing the word down the column. Then certainly they all began to run, the rearguard and all, and drove on the baggage animals and the horses at full speed; and when they had all got to the top, the soldiers, with tears in their eyes, embraced each other and their generals and captains.
> (*The Persian Expedition*, 4.7)

A few more days' march brings them to the Greek city of Trapezus on the Black Sea, where they celebrate their arrival in Greek fashion with religious sacrifices and athletic games. The entire force at this point amounts to roughly 10,000, which suggests a loss of about 3,000 troops.

Unable to secure ships to sail home, the expedition marches from Trapezus westward along the southern coast of the Black Sea, towards the region known as Paphlagonia. Along the way, the men stop at other Greek colonies, such as Cerasus, Cotyora, and Sinope. At Cotyora the men find enough ships to hold all of them so they continue by sea. When they arrive in Paphlagonia, the land is so attractive that Xenophon suggests settling there and establishing a colony, but most of the soldiers prefer to continue homeward.

From Paphlagonia they sail to Heraclea, another Greek colony. When the Heracleans shut the city's gates on the arriving expedition, the soldiers travel on but divide into three groups in hopes of having better luck securing food. Xenophon leads one of the groups. They have little success, being attacked by local peoples such as Bithynians and Phrygians, as well as by

---

GREEK COLONIZATION

Colonies such as those mentioned in *The Persian Expedition* constituted an important way in which Greeks expanded their presence in lands beyond Greece itself. Colonies were sent out from a "mother city" (*metropolis*), the purpose often being to secure fertile farmlands for the city's excess population and to establish profitable trade links. The Greeks had no qualms about driving native inhabitants (whom they called "barbarians") off the land, often enslaving them and selling them to other Greeks.

Xenophon, who proposed starting a colony in Paphlagonia with the men from the expedition, had earlier brought up the possibility of returning one day to Asia Minor with a colonizing group. In his speech to the soldiers after the new leaders were selected, he tells them: "So I think that it is right and reasonable for us to make it our first endeavor to reach our own folk in Greece and to demonstrate to the Greeks that their poverty is of their own choosing, since they might see people who have a wretched life in their own countries grow rich by coming out here" (*The Persian Expedition*, 3.2).

Persian forces under Pharnabazus, the Persian governor of northwestern Asia Minor. Reunited, the expedition then scores a victory over the Persians in a pitched battle. After this the Persians keep their distance, and the soldiers have less trouble finding food. They march on to Chrysopolis, and then cross the Bosporus to Byzantium, where the Spartan admiral Anaxibius has promised to pay them.

However, when they get to Byzantium, Anaxibius orders them out of the city without paying them, treating them as dangerous thugs. Enraged, the soldiers threaten to loot the place, but Xenophon calms them by warning them that if they loot Byzantium they will make enemies of

the Spartans. Seuthes, the king of a Thracian people called the Odrysians, then hires the soldiers. (Thrace, the region west of Byzantium, lay between that Greek city and northern Greece and was inhabited by Greeks as well as non-Greek peoples, such as the Odrysians.) They spend the winter serving under Seuthes in Thrace, with Xenophon in command.

Reversing its earlier pro-Persian policy, Sparta now sends word that it "had decided to fight Tissaphernes" (*The Persian Expedition*, 7.6). The Spartan admiral assigned to lead the fight is named Thibron, and he arrives in the spring of 399 BCE. As Xenophon bids the soldiers farewell, Thibron incorporates them into the army he is leading against Tissaphernes and Pharnabazus, the Persian governors of western Asia Minor.

Greeks and "barbarians." After Cyrus' death in the battle of Cunaxa, Xenophon eulogizes the Persian prince at some length before returning to his main narrative. "My own opinion," Xenophon writes of Cyrus, ". . . is that there has never been anyone, Greek or foreigner, more generally beloved. And an additional proof of this is in the fact that, although Cyrus was a subject, no one deserted him and went over to the King," meaning the Persian monarch (*The Persian Expedition*, 1.9).

In addition to illustrating Cyrus' popularity, this passage offers valuable insights into Greek attitudes toward the Persians and their absolutist monarchy. The word translated here as "foreigners" is the Greek word *barbaroi*, literally "barbarians," which for the Greeks meant anyone who did not speak Greek. (To Greek ears, other languages sounded like the barking of dogs). "Barbarian" did not necessarily imply uncivilized, as it does in English; certainly the Greeks recognized the Persians as a civilized people. Yet they did not recognize the Persians as their equals, as is shown by another term used in the passage above, the word translated as "subject." Here as elsewhere, Xenophon uses the Greek word *doulos*, literally "slave," to mean a subject of the Persian king. And since all Persians were subjects of the king, all Persians—even the noble Cyrus, whom Xenophon admires—were routinely referred to by the Greeks as slaves, or *douloi*.

As the narrative repeatedly makes clear, what separates Greeks from the Persians above all is that Greeks are free while Persians are not. A Persian subject demonstrated his absolute subservience to the king by performing the ritual known in Greek as *proskynesis*, "bowing down like a dog"—that is, prostrating oneself at the king's feet. Most Greeks were shocked by such displays, which they reserved for the gods. "For you worship no man as a master, but only the gods," Xenophon encourages the soldiers in his speech at the war council after the new leaders have been chosen. He furthermore urges the soldiers to live up to "the freedom of the cities in which you have been born and brought up" (*The Persian Expedition*, 3.2). As Xenophon portrays them, the Greeks elect their own officers, argue among themselves, attempt to persuade others, and make collective decisions.

"Barbarians" was a term also used for peoples other than the Persians, and in such cases it might indeed carry the additional meaning of "uncivilized." But this was not its primary meaning then. The most dramatic example is the tribe Xenophon calls the Mossynoeci. Although they allied themselves with the soldiers, their customs included having sexual intercourse in public, which shocked the Greeks. "Those who were on the expedition," Xenophon writes, "used to say that these people were the most barbarous and the furthest removed from Greek ways of all those with whom they came in contact" (*The Persian Expedition*, 5.4). So the Greeks saw the Persians as civilized and other groups as uncivilized but both sets as barbarians. Barbarism, in other words, did not refer to a lack of civilization but rather to non-Greekness. The "most barbarous" group was "the furthest removed from Greek ways."

In book 4 the expedition comes upon a "barbarian" tribe called the Macrones, whose language is unintelligible to the Greeks until one of the peltasts offers to act as interpreter. He tells Xenophon that he himself had been a slave in Athens, "and that he knew the language of these people. 'Indeed,' he went on, 'I think that this is my own country'" (*The Persian Expedition*, 4.8). Greeks routinely captured and enslaved "barbarians" like the Macrones. This man had likely either been enslaved as a child, or born as a slave to parents who still spoke their "barbarian" language. Hence he recognizes the language but not the place.

As a leading historian explains in commenting on this passage, "Because the Greeks in fact got their slaves from barbarian lands, they supposed that the barbarians were by nature slavish" (Cawkwell in Xenophon, p. 213, note 8). Along with the civilized Persians, such uncivilized barbarians were thought of by the Greeks in terms that ultimately contrast Greek freedom with barbarian slavishness. From the Greek per-

spective, at the heart of the "barbarian" lay not a lack of civilization, but a lack of freedom. Conversely, at the heart of what it meant to be Greek lay freedom itself.

Sources and literary context. Xenophon's main source for *The Persian Expedition* was his own experience as a member of the group. Scholars have speculated about whether he first recorded his experiences in the form of diaries or notes that he used later, when composing the work. Having such notes at hand would explain Xenophon's rather exact recounting of distances and times covered by the Greeks in their march homeward, which would hardly have been easy to remember several decades later, when he wrote the work.

Alternatively, it has been suggested that Xenophon used another source for such details: the history of Persia written by his contemporary, the Greek physician Ctesias, who served both Darius II and Artaxerxes. Ctesias was present at the battle of Cunaxa, but on the Persian side. Returning to Greece in 398 BCE, he wrote a history of Persia that included a description of the battle. Xenophon mentions Ctesias by name as a source for his description of Cyrus' death in *The Persian Expedition*. Perhaps the earlier work, which no longer survives, also provided Xenophon with a detailed description of Persian geography to supplement his memory in composing *The Persian Expedition*.

A different account of the expedition appears to have been written by one of the original generals, Sophaenetus of Stymphalus. While Sophaenetus' work itself is lost, it may have been used by another Greek historian, Ephorus (fourth century BCE), whose version of the expedition seems to have differed from Xenophon's in significant details. This interpretation is complicated by the fact that Ephorus' work also no longer exists. However, he is known to have been a major source for a much later historian, Diodorus Siculus (first century BCE), who described the expedition, and whose work we do have. Based on a chain of speculation back from Diodorus, scholars have argued that the account written by Sophaenetus gave Xenophon a far less prominent role than the one he enjoys in *The Persian Expedition*, and even that this other account disparaged Xenophon. This would have provided Xenophon with a strong motive to write his version. It would also help explain Xenophon's perhaps exaggerated prominence in that version, and his occasional tone of self-justification.

Events in History at the Time the Narrative Was Written

The Spartan hegemony. As noted above, the end of the Peloponnesian War in 404 BCE ushered in a period known as the Spartan hegemony, in which Sparta dominated Greece. ("Hegemony" comes from the Greek *hegemonia*, meaning "leadership" or "supremacy.") Persia, whose support had helped Sparta win the war, continued to play a central role in Greek affairs. At the same time, a growing pan-Hellenic (Greek unity) movement, espoused most notably by the Athenian orator Isocrates (436-338 BCE), urged the Greeks to unite in order to topple the Persian Empire once and for all. Supporters of this pan-Hellenic movement argued that the success of the Greek mercenaries against the Persian forces demonstrated Persian weakness. It was further argued that the Greeks should exploit that weakness more.

The arrival of the Spartan commander Thibron at the end of *The Persian Expedition* signaled a major change in relations. Sparta no longer tried to identify its interests with those of Persia. Like Sparta, the Ionian Greek cities of Asia Minor had supported Cyrus against Artaxerxes. After Cyrus' death the Ionian Greeks, fearing retaliation by Tissaphernes and Artaxerxes for their support of Cyrus, had appealed to Sparta for help. By sending Thibron "to fight Tissaphernes," Sparta utterly reversed itself, abandoning its earlier recognition of Persian rule in Asia Minor and instead backing the Ionians' ongoing bid for independence.

In 396 BCE, the Spartan king Agesilaus replaced Thibron as Sparta's top commander in Asia Minor. Xenophon forged a close alliance with Agesilaus, later writing a praiseful biography of him, the *Agesilaus*. Agesilaus' dynamic personality stamped itself on Spartan policy throughout the Spartan hegemony. While Agesilaus enjoyed initial success against the Persians in Asia Minor, Persia allied itself with Sparta's rivals at home in Greece. In the Corinthian War (395-386 BCE), a conflict among Greek city-states, Persia backed Thebes, Argos, Corinth, and a resurgent Athens against Sparta. The war was ended by the "King's Peace," in which Persia dictated terms to the now exhausted Greek city-states. Alarmed by signs of Athens' revival, Persia switched sides again and threw its support behind Sparta. The treaty essentially left Sparta in charge of Greece.

Agesilaus and Sparta treated the other city-states with high-handed arrogance, installing a garrison of Spartan soldiers in Thebes (382 BCE) and similarly attempting to occupy Athens (379 BCE). Thebes and Athens entered a new alliance against Sparta, and in 371 BCE the brilliant Theban generals Pelopidas and Epaminondas shattered Spartan power forever at the battle of Leuctra. Victorious, Thebes itself now embarked on a period of dominance known as the Theban hegemony (371-362 BCE).

Publication and impact. In the upheaval that followed the end of Spartan power, Xenophon—whose fortunes had been made by his alliance with Agesilaus and Sparta—was evicted from his estate at Scillus. There, not far from Sparta, he had lived the comfortable life of a country gentleman. Now, deprived of his former possessions, he was forced to move to Corinth, where he lived in relatively modest circumstances.

Scholars generally believe that it was around this time—the late 370s or early 360s BCE—that Xenophon wrote *The Persian Expedition*. An alternative theory proposes that the first part of the narrative was written soon after Xenophon moved to Scillus in 386 BCE, and that the second part, beginning with the passage from book 5 quoted above, was written later.

Whether or not Xenophon's *Anabasis* (as the work is called in Greek) was prompted by another written account of the expedition, his graceful style and stirring descriptions ensured that his narrative rapidly became the most widely read version. Its publication strengthened the case for Greek unity and, according to scholars, may have helped inspire the eventual conquest of Persia by Alexander the Great. The work remained popular in later times and, like Xenophon's other writings, won especially high regard from Roman authors. Once unquestioned, Xenophon's reputation for historical accuracy and reliability has been irreparably damaged by recent scholarship. Archeologists in the twentieth century discovered papyrus fragments of a lost historical work that indisputably invalidates many of Xenophon's formerly accepted claims. The unknown author, a fellow writer of Xenophon's day, is called "the Oxyrhynchus historian," after the Egyptian town where the fragments were found. Yet Xenophon's literary reputation has survived intact, owing in large part to the skillfully told narrative of *The Persian Expedition*.

—Colin Wells

For More Information

Boardman, John, et al., eds. *The Oxford History of the Classical World: Greece and the Hellen-*

istic World. Oxford: Oxford University Press, 1986.

Hornblower, Simon, and Antony Spawforth. *The Oxford Companion to Classical Civilization*. Oxford: Oxford University Press, 1998.

Sealey, Raphael. *A History of the Greek City States 700-338 B.C.* Berkeley: University of California Press, 1976.

Sharrock, Alison, and Rhiannon Ash. *Fifty Key Classical Authors*. London: Routledge, 2002.

Van Wees, Hans. *Greek Warfare*. London: Duckworth, 2004.

Xenophon. *The Persian Expedition*. Trans. Rex Warner. Introduction and notes by George Cawkwell. Harmondsworth, U.K.: Penguin, 1972.

Phaedra

by

Seneca (Lucius Annaeus Seneca)

Born around 3 BCE in Cordova, Spain, Lucius Annaeus Seneca was a son of Seneca the Elder, who devoted himself to educating his sons in the study of rhetoric. The younger Seneca was educated in Rome, where he studied rhetoric and philosophy and earned renown as an orator while still young. He rose from advocate (lawyer), to quaestor (a state official), and then to senator. In the first year of Emperor Claudius' reign (41-54 CE), Seneca was charged with committing adultery with Claudius' niece Julia Livilla. His death sentence was commuted to exile, and he spent the next eight years on Corsica. Recalled to Rome in 49 CE, Seneca served as tutor to Nero, Claudius' stepson and eventual successor. After Nero became emperor in 54 CE, Seneca remained his advisor, exerting what most believed to be a calming influence on the volatile young ruler. Around 62 CE, however, Seneca lost the emperor's favor and began to spend a great deal of time away from Rome. Three years later, implicated in a plot against Nero's life, Seneca was forced to commit suicide. His surviving body of work consists of numerous scholarly essays and at least eight tragic plays, including *The Trojan Women, Oedipus, Medea, The Mad Hercules, The Phoenician Women, Phaedra, Agamemnon,* and *Thyestes* The latter were all based on earlier Greek models, to which they have often been unfavorably compared. It is unclear whether Seneca's tragedies were ever performed or if Seneca just intended them to be read or recited before small private audiences. In any case, the tragedies would have a profound effect on dramatists in later eras. The works would also

THE LITERARY WORK

A tragic play set in Athens, Greece during an unspecified mythological time; published in Latin c. 54 CE.

SYNOPSIS

A woman conceives an incestuous passion for her stepson. When he rejects her, she falsely accuses him of rape, with dire consequences for the family.

further the fusion of ancient cultural ways in Seneca's own era. In his adaptation of *Phaedra*, the tragedy of a queen who struggles with her incestuous love for her stepson, Seneca adds some distinctively Roman touches to an age-old Greek legend.

Events in History at the Time of the Play

Phaedra and Hippolytus—the legend. Seneca's play presupposes extensive knowledge of classical Greek and Roman mythology, especially the legend of Phaedra and Hippolytus. Scholars contend that the legend originated at Troezen, a town in the northeast Peloponnese by the Saronic Gulf. While the town's most important local deity was Poseidon—the Greek god of the sea—Hippolytus grew into a popular cult figure there. Over time the legend spread, gaining wide

Seneca. The Library of Congress. Used by permission.

renown in the region with the help of dramatic retellings by two of the foremost tragedy writers of Classical Greece (Sophocles and Euripedes).

While particulars of the Phaedra myth vary, the basic plot remains constant. Hippolytus, the bastard son of King Theseus of Athens and Queen Hippolyta of the Amazons, leads a perfectly chaste life. He worships Artemis, goddess of the hunt, and he shuns all mortal women. Phaedra, Theseus' wife, falls in love with Hippolytus, possibly because Aphrodite, the goddess of love, wishes to punish him for his stubborn insistence on remaining chaste. Initially Phaedra struggles to conceal her incestuous passion for her stepson, but she finally confesses her love to Hippolytus. (In another version, she confesses to her nurse, who then informs Hippolytus.) Horrified, he rejects her. Phaedra, fearing that Hippolytus will denounce her to Theseus, takes matters into her own hands and accuses the young man of attempted rape. Theseus believes her story, curses his son, and calls upon Poseidon to punish Hippolytus with death. In response, Poseidon has a sea monster frighten Hippolytus' horses. Terror-stricken, they fling their master from his chariot and then drag him to his death. Subsequently either human or divine intervention, depending on the version of the tale, proves Hippolytus innocent of the attempted rape. A guilt-ridden Phaedra commits suicide. Bereft of

wife and son, and distressed by his own part in the tragedy, Theseus is overcome with remorse at having destroyed his son.

Dramatic treatments of the myth differ, especially with regard to the characterizations of Hippolytus and Phaedra. In Euripides' *Hippolytus* (c. 428 BCE), the young man is portrayed as morally self-righteous and arrogant; the lovesick Phaedra, as a formerly virtuous queen who becomes the instrument of Aphrodite's vengeance against Hippolytus. A complex character, she suffers an internal struggle between her passion for Hippolytus and her deep sense of modesty. Centuries later, Seneca presented an innocent Hippolytus and his own complex, morally ambiguous Phaedra. The gods, who are a physical presence in Euripides' play, do not appear in Seneca's version; their absence renders Phaedra's incestuous love for Hippolytus more the product of her sensual nature than the curse of a goddess. Yet if Seneca's Phaedra is more shameless and sensual about her forbidden passion, she is also a sympathetic character. Manipulated by her crafty nurse into accusing Hippolytus of rape, the queen grows so remorseful after his death that she is driven to honorable action. "I lied, and sin / Which I myself conceived in mad heart crazed / Falsely alleged. . . . / To the just sword my impious breast opens, / Blood pays the death-dues for a sinless man" (Seneca, *Phaedra,* Act 6, lines 1192-94, 1198-99).

Women and marriage in Classical Athens. The time in which Seneca's *Phaedra* takes place is unspecified. But the values reflected in the course of the play may be likened to those of fifth century BCE Greece, when its playwrights began to dramatize the legend. In this era, often called the Classical Age, Athenian women of good family continued to live under the guardianship of their fathers or other male relations until they reached marriageable age. Ideally a young teenage girl of 14 married a man of about 30, mainly to bear his children.

The bride's guardian and the groom usually arranged the match, which was based mostly on economic and political considerations rather than affection or even attraction. Arrangements were often made for blood relatives to marry, the aim being to consolidate family financial and property holdings. Among the elite, marriage became a means to promote political alliances. A girl was expected to marry the man chosen for her, even if she had never met him.

The birth of children to carry on the family line was the highest priority of a marriage. Once a bride had borne offspring, preferably sons, she had fulfilled her main marital obligation. Since the purpose of the children was to perpetuate the father's family line, they were considered his property and they remained in his house, even if the marriage dissolved because of death or divorce.

In Seneca's play, Phaedra reveals that her own marriage to Theseus is a political arrangement, intended to quell hostilities between Athens and her native island of Crete. Although the marriage has produced two sons, little love appears to exist between husband and wife, as was often the case in ancient Greek and Roman marriages. Phaedra laments to her nurse, "Why compel me, hostage to a hated house, / Married to my foe, to consume a life / In pain and tears?" (*Phaedra*, 2.89-91). Within this context, Phaedra's romantic yearnings for her stepson, who may have very well been close to her age, become more understandable, if no less transgressive.

Incest and the ancients. Phaedra's forbidden passion for her stepson, Hippolytus, remains the most controversial element of the myth. Throughout antiquity, sexual relations or marriage between close kin was mostly forbidden or condemned.

The criteria for incest varied from region to region, allowing for certain exceptions. For example, siblings who shared a father could marry in Athens; siblings who shared a mother could do so in Sparta. Marriages between full siblings could occur in Egypt when it was part of the Greek and then the Roman Empire, but they occurred only rarely, usually to preserve the ethnic identity of a small population. It is telling that the Greeks of Egypt found these marriages shocking and incestuous, despite their infrequency and their legality. Siblings who were related only by adoption could wed if one of them no longer lived under the legal authority of a *paterfamilias* (father or grandfather). During the reign of Emperor Claudius (41-54 CE), marriages between nieces and paternal uncles were permitted in Rome, a practice that would later be outlawed. Marriages between a man and his sisters' daughters, granddaughters, and great-granddaughters remained forbidden, as did marriages between men and their aunts.

Parent-child incest was universally condemned, a fact reflected in several myths, including those of Oedipus (see **The Theban Plays**, also in *Classical Literature and Its Times*). Even when the parent and child commit the sin unknowingly, disaster and divine retribution inevitably follow. Although Phaedra is not related by blood to Hippolytus, she is his stepmother by virtue of her marriage to Theseus, as her nurse forcibly reminds her

in Seneca's play: "Will you confound beds of father and son, / In impious womb take mongrel progeny?" (*Phaedra*, 2.171-172).

The Play in Focus

Plot summary. The play begins one morning in Athens as Hippolytus, the illegitimate son of King Theseus, prepares for a hunt with his comrades. Virile and handsome, Hippolytus scorns women and love, devoting himself instead to the worship of the virgin goddess Diana (Rome's equivalent of the Greek goddess Artemis).

THE LEGENDS OF THESEUS

The Phaedra and Hippolytus story is part of a larger cycle of myths about Theseus, a legendary king of Athens who is said to have ruled in the generation before the Trojan War. In his youth, Theseus had many adventures, including the slaying of the Minotaur, a monstrous creature—half-bull, half-man—born of an unnatural coupling between a wild bull and Queen Pasiphae of Crete. Her husband, King Minos, makes use of the monster. Demanding an annual tribute from Athens, he forces its citizens to send him seven youths and seven maidens each year to be devoured by the Minotaur. One year Theseus disguises himself as one of the youths and travels to Crete. With the help of Ariadne, Minos' eldest daughter, he finds his way into the maze in which the Minotaur is hidden and kills it. Theseus quickly flees Crete, taking Ariadne with him, but he abandons her on the isle of Naxos for reasons that vary from version to version. In another famous legend, Theseus travels to the land of the fierce women warriors known as Amazons and carries off their queen, alternately known as Hippolyta or Antiope. The queen bears him a son, Hippolytus. She dies, either in battle or by Theseus' own hands, after which Theseus marries Ariadne's younger sister, Phaedra. In Seneca's portrayal, Theseus is a mostly unsympathetic character; the play depicts him as a faithless, often cruel husband.

In the second act, Theseus' queen Phaedra and her nurse engage in a heated discussion about her incestuous love for Hippolytus. Phaedra argues that the absent Theseus is a neglectful, philandering husband and that she is only following her own nature by craving an illicit love. By way of explanation, she cites her mother's passion for a great bull, which led to the birth of the monstrous Minotaur. Even the nurse's argument that Hippolytus shuns women fails to sway Phaedra from her infatuation. Nonetheless, the nurse continues to exhort Phaedra to resist this illicit love and remain true to her husband. Phaedra finally yields to these pleas, resolving to commit suicide rather than to expose her love and stain her honor. Alarmed, the nurse reverses her previous stance and promises to approach Hippolytus on Phaedra's behalf.

THE PROBLEM OF EXCESS

The Greek word *sôphrosynê* can be translated variously as "common sense," "self-restraint," and most often, "temperance" or "moderation." The practice of these qualities was important to both Greek and Roman culture. According to the Greek historian Polybius, moderation was a Roman trait; famous Romans—from the orator Cicero, to the poet Horace, to Seneca himself in his ***Moral Letters*** (also in *Classical Literature and Its Times*)—counseled moderation as a virtue. In Seneca's *Phaedra*, although Phaedra and Hippolytus strive for *sôphrosynê*, each fails to exhibit moderation. Phaedra gives vent to an excess of passion, while at the opposite extreme, Hippolytus insists on remaining chaste. Yet, in Euripides' dramatization, Hippolytus credits himself with being *sôphrosynê*. A few times in the play, including on his deathbed, Hippolytus says with conviction that "there is no man more *sôphrône* than I" (Euripides in Skinner, p. 136).

The Chorus enters at this point to deliver a monologue on the destructive power of love. When the third act opens, the nurse reveals that the lovesick Phaedra has now taken to her bed, weeping and refusing all comfort. Moved by the queen's distress, the nurse prays to Diana to soften Hippolytus' heart and render him amenable to the love of women. When Hippolytus himself approaches Diana's shrine, the nurse tries to convince the youth to abandon his rural pursuits and embrace the pleasures of Venus (Rome's equivalent of the Greek goddess Aphrodite). Hippolytus resists, defending his austere way of life and reiterating his hatred of women: "I loathe them all, I dread, I shun, I curse them, / Be it reason, nature, or insensate rage, / I choose to hate them" (*Phaedra*, 3.566-567).

In the midst of their confrontation, Phaedra enters and swoons into Hippolytus' arms. Hoping for the best, the nurse draws aside, leaving them alone. Upon reviving, Phaedra tries to confess her love but Hippolytus repeatedly misunderstands her, believing she is pining for Theseus. When the truth of her passion finally emerges, Hippolytus recoils in disgust. At first he considers stabbing Phaedra, then flings away his sword as defiled by her touch and flees to the woods while Phaedra swoons again. Finding the queen unconscious, the nurse decides to conceal her charge's guilt and accuse Hippolytus of rape instead. Phaedra herself later makes this false accusation, echoing the deceit. The act concludes with another monologue from the Chorus, this one addressing the hazards of male beauty.

In the fourth act, Theseus, who was trapped in the realm of the dead until rescued by Hercules, returns to find his palace in an uproar. The nurse enters and tells the king that Phaedra means to commit suicide because of some unknown shame. Hurrying to the queen's side, Theseus finds her holding Hippolytus' sword and urges her to confess her sorrows. Phaedra tells Theseus that the bearer of the sword has raped her. Recognizing the blade as Hippolytus', a horrified Theseus calls upon Neptune (the Roman Poseidon) to destroy his son. The Chorus somberly laments the gods' indifference in letting the innocent suffer and the guilty go unpunished.

In the fifth act, a messenger arrives at Theseus' palace to reveal that Hippolytus is dead. He was torn to pieces when his chariot's horses fled at the sight of a monstrous bull from the sea. Hippolytus' companions enter with parts of his body, which they lay before Theseus. He weeps, despite his belief in his son's treachery; meanwhile, the Chorus comments upon the fickleness of fortune.

The sixth act begins as Phaedra enters, frantic with grief. On beholding Hippolytus' dismembered body, she breaks down completely, confesses her sinful love for her stepson and her lie about the rape, and stabs herself to death with Hippolytus' sword. A devastated Theseus laments his part in the family tragedy, then gives orders for the disposal of the dead. Hippolytus is to receive all ritual honors due his station, but Phaedra will be ignominiously buried: "This one— earth press deep upon her, / And soil lie heavy on her impious head" (*Phaedra*, 6.1279-1280).

Stepmothers in antiquity. *Phaedra* concerns a classically infamous literary character, that of the villainous stepmother. Greek literature has given rise to more than 20 legends that feature a stepmother's mistreatment of her stepchildren. The ancient Greek legend of the evil stepmother first gained popularity in the fifth century BCE and continued to attract audiences thereafter. In general, these stepmothers are an unsavory lot—they tend to be evil, self-centered, jealous, cunning, treacherous, and lacking in self-control. Often the stepmother's villainous plans fail and she is punished, either forced to flee or commit suicide. The typical literary stepmother is unequivocally evil while the other characters in these ancient legends are unequivocally good.

The legends fall into two main categories: 1) a jealous stepmother abuses or plots to kill her stepchildren, usually to make her own son the heir; and 2) the stepmother plots against her stepson because he has rejected her amorous advances. Neither storyline reflects real-life commonplaces in fifth-century BCE Athens. But the *possibility* of the amorous stepmother existed, since, as noted, young girls (aged 14) often married older men (aged 30). As in Phaedra's case, this meant that the stepmother was likely closer in age to her stepson than to her husband, which could lead to love, infatuation, or sexual tension. Yet, despite this danger, "there are virtually no stories involving lust on the part of a stepson" (Watson, p. 88). Instead, the legends feature (and condemn) the stepmother as the root of amorous desire, perhaps because the ancient Greeks and Romans considered women more subject to sexual passion than men. It was furthermore thought that if women acted on these impulses, disaster would follow.

Sources and literary context. By the fifth century BCE, the myth of Phaedra and Hippolytus had become well established enough to have inspired at least three Greek plays, one by Sophocles, entitled *Phaedra*, and two by Euripides, both entitled *Hippolytus*. Probably Seneca was familiar with all three, which today survive only in fragments or, in the case of one of Euripides' versions, not at all. Seneca may also have been influenced by lost dramatizations, such as the *Hippolytus* of Lycophron, a tragedy writer of about 280 BCE. Still another likely influence was Ovid's *Heroides* (Heroines, c. 5 BCE), a series of fictitious letters from mythological women to the lovers who have spurned or abandoned them. The fourth letter in the sequence is from Phaedra to Hippolytus, confessing her love and begging him to love her back.

I thought I should be able to resist
Temptation—does such strength of mind
 exist?

Vanquished but royal, I embrace your knees:
A lover overlooks the decencies,
And shame forsakes its standards of the field.
Forgive my frankness, heart of stone, and
 yield!

(Ovid, p. 46)

In Ovid's letter, Phaedra anticipates Hippolytus' surprise at the advances of his stepmother: ". . . but why should incest shock / You? Don't believe that pious poppycock; / Nowadays such scruples seem as old- / Fashioned as the fabled age of gold" (Ovid, p. 45).

Seneca's plays are often considered in the context of the Hellenization of Roman culture (its fusion with Greek ways). Roman artists and writers adopted or borrowed elements from Greek

FUNERAL RITES

Funeral customs varied throughout the classical world. At Athens, where Seneca's *Phaedra* takes place, funeral rites changed over time. Burial in stone-lined pits covered with wood or stone was customary in the eleventh century BCE, followed by cremations, with the ashes stored in urns, from 1000-750 BCE. Next came burial in earth-cut pit graves from 750-700 BCE and cremations within the graves themselves from 700-550 BCE. From 550 BCE onwards, people buried their dead either in stone coffins decorated with sculpture (sarcophagi) or in pit graves. In the Roman Empire of the first and second century CE, urn cremation was the most popular practice. Burial did not become customary until late in the second century CE. Seneca's play reflects these circumstances when Theseus orders that Hippolytus be cremated and Phaedra ignominiously buried in the earth.

art and literature, mixing Greek and Roman aesthetics, a practice that during Seneca's lifetime was on the rise. Seneca's age also valued experimentation, paradox, absurdity, exaggeration, wit, and artificiality. Authors of the era usually employed a colorful style, full of passionate speeches and dazzling rhetorical displays that constituted ends in themselves. While rich in rhetoric, Seneca's plays also exhibit an experimental flair. *Phaedra,* for example, takes audiences into the realm of the gruesome and sensational. While Euripides' version has Theseus view the maimed body of his dying son, Seneca's depicts the king trying to piece together the fragments of his son's mangled corpse: "His strong right hand goes here / Here put his left hand which controlled the reins / With skill; I recognize signs of his left side. / But how great the part still lacking our tears" (*Phaedra*, 6.1258-1261).

Events in History at the Time the Play Was Written

Greek culture in Roman life. The influence and then the predominance of Greek culture in Roman high society was a gradual, centuries-long process. Between 197 BCE and 146 BCE, Rome became a supreme force, extending its control over much of Alexander the Great's former empire, which included Egypt and Greece. The wealth and beauty of Greek civilization enraptured many Romans, leading to the spread of Greek (Hellenic) culture throughout the Roman world. So seductive did the Greek influence

---

CATO THE YOUNGER'S SUICIDE

Cato of Utica (95-46 BCE) was a firm believer in the cause of the Roman Republic (the idea that political power rested with the people). He strongly opposed Julius Caesar's drive to turn Rome into a dictatorship under his rule. When Cato realized that Caesar would conquer Rome, Cato took action. He attempted suicide—twice. The first time Cato stabbed himself with a sword, missing all his vital organs. He was found by his physician, stitched up, and saved. Regaining consciousness, with desperate resolve, Cato reattempted suicide, this time ripping out the stitches with his bare hands. Successful at last, Cato gained posthumous renown as a champion of the republic and an anti-imperial martyr.

---

prove that the Roman poet Horace declared "*Graecia capta ferum uictorem cepit* (Captured Greece captured her savage conqueror)" (Horace in Jones and Sidwell, p. 22; italics added).

Numerous aspects of Greek life were absorbed into Roman civilization over the next few centuries. The Greek and Roman pantheons of gods merged, Roman aristocrats adopted Greek dress and collected Greek art, and Roman architects designed buildings in the Greek style. Likewise, the literature of Greece greatly affected Roman writers, who adapted Greek legends and plays

for Roman audiences (see Plautus' *The Braggart Soldier* and Terence's *The Brothers*, both also in *Classical Literature and Its Times*).

Sometime after the first Punic War (264-241 BCE), Rome decided it ought to increase its intellectual achievements. In their wanderings, "young Roman soldiers came into contact with the flourishing Greek civilization" (Butler, p. 79). Spending lengthy periods in Sicily, an island that had been colonized by the Greeks in the eighth century BCE, the soldiers likely picked up some of the Greek language and attended the plays frequently staged there. With the encouragement of the soldiers, as well as the many Greek slaves in Rome, its writers were soon translating and adapting Greek plays into Latin. The first person to translate, adapt, and produce a Greek play in Latin was a Roman of Greek descent named Livius Andronicus (c. 284-204 BCE). Although much remains unknown about his life, he appears to have been a freed slave who worked as a tutor. The practice of adapting Greek plays for Roman audiences grew increasingly common after his initial effort. Theater became one more aspect of Roman life that was strongly influenced by Greek culture, which in the century after Seneca's *Phaedra* would predominate in Rome.

Rise of aristocratic suicide. During Seneca's lifetime the act of suicide was in vogue among the upper classes. Suicides increased between the time of Tiberius' ascension to the throne (14 CE) and Nero's death (48 CE). In his *Annals*, the Roman historian Tacitus reports 74 recorded suicides over 50 years, more than Livy reported for 500 years in his *From the Founding of the City* (both also in *Classical Literature and Its Times*). While modern society regards suicide as an intensely personal act, many ancient Romans saw it as an opportunity for self-staged display, a way to preserve one's honor or avoid shame. In Seneca's era, for example, people saw the self-inflicted death of Cato the Younger (95 BCE-46 BCE) as the pinnacle of moral acts—a "lesson learned by every school boy" (Hill, p. 179). Cato had held fast to his republican principles, opting for death rather than life without them.

Seneca admired Cato's suicide. Like Cato's, Seneca's suicide was a long, drawn-out affair. Gathering his friends around him, Seneca expounded on Nero's murderous cruelty before killing himself in a death scene that must have been agonizing to watch. First, Seneca made incisions in his arms. But the blood did not flow quickly enough, so he sliced the arteries and vessels in his legs as well. As the dark red liquid oozed out, Seneca dictated a lengthy discourse to his secretaries and then drank poison. But the poison appeared to have no great effect—nor did placing his lacerated body into a container of slightly heated water. Finally, after being lowered into a very hot bath, Seneca suffocated to death from the steam. The onlookers probably felt admiration, as well as pity, fear, and grief.

Often aristocrats opted for suicide knowing that Romans looked with favor on a member of the upper class who took his or her own life instead of being executed. The state dropped all legal action against those who were accused of wrongdoing once they had committed suicide. By contrast, if an accused received the death penalty at his trial, he would lose his right to Roman citizenship. His name could be erased from all records, his property and assets would be seized and given to the state, and he would be denied a Roman burial. These consequences brought shame not only on the convicted but also on his family. Suicide forestalled such a dishonorable end.

As Cato and Seneca demonstrated, suicide could also be a tool of political protest. The historian Tacitus reports that Seneca's final words, intended for public hearing, turned the spotlight on Nero's barbarous behavior: "Surely nobody was unaware that Nero was cruel! . . . After murdering his mother and brother, it only remained for him to kill his teacher and tutor" (Seneca, *Letters*, p. 243). Dying for one's convictions is often seen as martyrdom, "whereby the individual's willingness to die rather than renounce his or her ideals is held to be proof of the value of these ideals themselves" (Hill, p. 192). In Cato's and in Seneca's days, a well-staged suicide could serve as a powerful call for Senate opposition to imperial authority.

Performance and impact. Although it is unclear whether Seneca's plays were ever staged in his lifetime, a tradition of performing Latin plays began in the fifteenth century in the circle of Pomponius Laetus (1427-1497), a professor of Latin in Rome. Seneca's *Phaedra* appears to have been performed in 1490. A century later in England, two more productions were staged, the first at Westminster School in 1546, the second—under the alternate title of *Hippolytus*—by William Gager of Christ Church in 1591. No record survives of how these performances were received.

For many years, critics have compared Seneca's tragedies unfavorably with the Greek dramatists he imitated. His works have been dismissed as plays full of empty bombast, as constructs that lack emotional resonance and sincerity. Nonetheless, Senecan tragedy deeply influenced the works of later ages, passing down to the Renaissance such conventions as the five-act play, soliloquies and asides, and a Chorus that exited and re-entered as the tragedy unfolded. Seneca's vivid scenes of violence and horror found imitators too, in England's Thomas Kyd, Christopher Marlowe, and John Webster, among others. In France, Seneca's influence is evident in Jean Racine's *Phèdre* (1677), the play often held to be the French playwright's masterpiece. Like Seneca, Racine depicts the title character as a complex individual, focusing on her own guilt and horror over her love for Hippolytus.

—Pamela S. Loy and Lisa Granados

For More Information

Butler, James. *The Theatre and Drama of Greece and Rome*. San Francisco, Calif.: Chandler, 1972.

Casson, Lionel. *Everyday Life in Ancient Rome*. Baltimore, Md.: Johns Hopkins University Press, 1998.

Harrison, George W. M., ed. *Seneca in Performance*. London: Duckworth, 2000.

Hill, Timothy. *Ambitiosa Mors*. New York: Routledge, 2004.

Hornblower, Simon, and Antony Spawforth, eds. *The Oxford Companion to Classical Civilization*. Oxford: Oxford University Press, 1998.

Jones, Peter, and Keith Sidwell, eds. *The World of Rome*. Cambridge: Cambridge University Press, 1997.

Ovid. *Heroines*. Trans. Daryl Hine. New Haven, Conn.: Yale University Press, 1991.

Pomeroy, Sarah B. *Goddesses, Whores, Wives, and Slaves*. New York: Schocken Books, 1995.

Seneca. *Letters from a Stoic*. Trans. Robin Campbell. London: Penguin, 1969.

———. *Phaedra*. Trans. A. J. Boyle. Wolfeboro, N.H.: Francis Cairns, 1987.

Skinner, Marilyn. *Sexuality in Greek and Roman Culture*. Malden, Mass.: Blackwell, 2005.

Watson, Patricia. *Ancient Stepmothers*. New York: E. J. Brill, 1995.

Poems

by
Sappho

Sappho was born on the island of Lesbos, Greece, around 630 BCE, but little else about the poet's life is certain. Centuries after her death, writers generated biographies about her life, but these were based more on legend and speculation than on fact. The biographies claim that Sappho had several brothers, and also that she was married. However, only a brother and possibly a daughter, named Kleis, figure in her poems. Scholars place Sappho's death around 570 BCE. In her 60-year lifespan, she produced some remarkable lyric poetry, mostly for solo performance. It is unclear when Sappho began to compose her poems, most of which dealt with her love for other women. She also wrote a number of wedding songs, hymns to deities, and poems expressing personal concerns about, for example, the safety of her brother. At one time there apparently existed nine books (scrolls) of Sappho's poetry in Alexandria, Egypt, but these have been lost. Until the 1890s Sappho's extant work consisted of one complete poem (cited in full by the Greek historian Dionysius of Halicarnassus), one long fragment, and perhaps a hundred shorter fragments. Since then, archaeologists have recovered more fragments of varying length on scraps of papyrus and potsherds. Though few of her lyrics survive in complete form today, their candor, passion, and artistry inspired Plato to identify Sappho with the nine muses (goddesses of literature, music, dance, and the intellectual pursuits). The fragments that remain have given rise to endless speculation about her life, her art, and the extent to which the two intertwine.

THE LITERARY WORK

Lyric love poems, set mostly on the Greek island of Lesbos, around the seventh century BCE; written during the seventh century BCE, translated into English around the sixteenth century.

SYNOPSIS

A woman reflects upon the nature of love and passion, most notably in her relationships with other women and young girls.

Events in History at the Time of the Poems

Sappho—fact and legend. The incompleteness of Sappho's work and the scarcity of indisputable facts about her life have presented scholars with a never-ending array of challenges. Holt N. Parker writes that "Every age creates its own Sappho. . . . She is recreated in each age to serve the interests of all who appropriate her, whether friend or enemy" (Parker in Greene, *Re-Reading Sappho*, pp. 149-150). Legends about Sappho date from antiquity. Even then she inspired works of art and literature that presented her as an almost mythical or legendary figure. Not all the portrayals were flattering; at least one of the six classical comedies titled *Sappho* introduced the idea that she was a prostitute. Apparently most of these plays dealt with Sappho as a sen-

Illustration of Sappho. The Library of Congress. Reproduced by permission.

sual wanton, in constant pursuit of love and sexual gratification.

Throughout the ages, Sappho was associated with numerous male lovers, regardless of whether such relationships can be considered credible. The elegiac poet Hermesianax invented a romance between Sappho and the poet Anacreon (c. 570-485 BCE), whose lifespan was actually later than hers. Another Greek writer, Diphilus, linked Sappho with the poets Archilochus and Hipponax. Arguably, one of the most famous stories concerning Sappho's love life circulated around the fourth century BCE. She was said to have fallen in love with the handsome Phaon and thrown herself from a cliff on the island of Leucas when he did not return her affections. This tale inspired the Roman poet Ovid, who included in his *Heroides* (Heroines)—a series of fictional letters written by legendary women to their lovers—an epistle from Sappho to Phaon. Modern historians tend to discount this story, along with most of the accounts of Sappho's love affairs with men. However, Sappho was described as a lover of women only in post-classical times; it may be that assumptions about a real-life marriage and the many stories that circulated about her affairs with men hindered her early readers from perceiving the homoerotic subtext in her poems.

A more persuasive, though not conclusive, representation of Sappho has depicted her as a mentor to young, unmarried girls (*parthenoi*, or "virgins") from noble families on Lesbos. Proponents of this scenario argue that Sappho's group of students and companions might have received some ritualized instruction in music, poetry, and erotic love, intended to prepare these girls for their roles as adult, married women. Philostratus, the Greek orator, and Maximus of Tyre both believed that Sappho formed the center of a literary circle. Noting the eroticism in her poetry, Maximus compared her relationships with young girls to Socrates' relationships with young boys, in that sexual desire and intellectual influence became inextricably intertwined: "What Alcibiades and Charmides were to [Socrates], Gyrinna and Atthis and Anactoria were to [Sappho]" (Maximus in Reynolds, p. 73).

Although Ulrich von Wilamowitz-Moellendorf, a German scholar of the early twentieth century, tried to argue that Sappho only displayed interest in girls because she ran a school, later scholars and critics dismissed that theory. Holt N. Parker argues that there is no evidence to suggest that Sappho ever served as a "schoolmistress" or even as a mentor to the maidens of Lesbos; he also points out that there is no proof even in Sappho's poems to indicate that she was older than the women of whom she wrote. Rather, Parker writes,

> Sappho's society was a group of women tied by family, class, politics, and erotic love. Like any other association, it cooperated in ritual activities, cult practice, and informal social events. Her subjects, like those of the other lyric poets, were praising her group's friends, attacking its enemies, celebrating its loves, and offering songs for its banquets.
> (Parker in Greene, *Re-Reading Sappho*, p. 183)

In other words, Sappho did not need to be a teacher, mentor, or even a leader to influence the women in her community: she had only to be a gifted poet.

Lyric poetry. Sappho's work belongs to a tradition of Greek lyric poetry—so called because it was set to the music of the lyre, a harp-like stringed instrument—that flourished between 750-450 BCE. Lyric poetry was short, sung rather than recited, personal and introspective in nature, composed in a variety of meters, and focused on present rather than past concerns. Examples of lyric poems included epithalamia (wedding songs), paeans (brief hymns of praise or triumph), dirges (laments for the dead), and choral song and dance.

While the Greeks may not have made this distinction, modern scholars tend to consider choral and monodic (solo) works as separate divisions of lyric poetry. Choral poetry was performed—sung and danced—by a choir, most often for public occasions, like religious festivities and rituals. Typical subjects of choral poems included marriage, death, praise of the gods, and victory in war. Choral lyrics also tended to have more elaborate metrical schemes, unique to each poem. By contrast, monodic lyrics employed simpler metrical patterns, which were repeated from song to song. In addition, the dialect tended to be based on the poet's vernacular—or everyday—speech. Monodic lyric poetry dealt with such varied subjects as love, politics, war, wine, and even abuse of one's enemies, often distilling the poet's personal experiences through the medium of myth; the audience for such performances may have been correspondingly smaller and more intimate.

The brevity and intensely personal nature of Sappho's poems suggests that she composed mostly monodic lyrics. However, a few fragments seem to indicate that she composed choral lyrics as well, including a lament for the mythical youth Adonis (Fragment 140) and a longer song about the marriage between Troy's prince Hector and Andromache (Fragment 44). Sappho also invented for lyric poetry a new stanzaic form, consisting of 3 lines of 11 syllables followed by a fourth and final line of 5 syllables. Fittingly, this form became known as the Sapphic stanza.

Sexual standards. Within the classical world, same-sex relationships—especially between men—were generally deemed acceptable. Significantly, the ancient Greeks did not categorize sexual behavior solely on the basis of the participants' gender; instead, "they evaluated sexual acts according to the degree to which such acts either violated or conformed to norms of conduct deemed appropriate to individual sexual actors by reason of their gender, age, and social status" (Hornblower and Spawforth, p. 347). It was, for example, considered normal for a socially superior male to be the active partner and the socially inferior male to be the passive partner in the sexual act. On the other hand, the opposite scenario was potentially shaming for the male of greater social rank.

Sexual relationships between Greek men, as observed in classical Athens, tended to involve an adult male and a youth who had just emerged from boyhood. The former enacted the role of lover, the source of desire; the latter, the role of

beloved, the object of desire. Again, the beloved remained the passive recipient of his lover's attentions. It was important not to seem too welcoming during the sexual act, lest the beloved be identified as unmanly.

While examples of male homosexuality were widely documented, evidence for sexual relations between women remains sparse in antique sources. Around the first century CE, the Roman historian Plutarch claimed that in Sparta older women and young, unmarried girls shared friendships that were both sexual and educational, paralleling those

THE WORSHIP OF APHRODITE

Aphrodite, the Greek goddess of love, figures heavily in Sappho's poetry. She was born, according to one legend, from the severed genitals of Uranus; in another version, she was the daughter of the king god Zeus and Dione (a minor goddess). Emerging fully formed from the sea, Aphrodite was wafted to Cyprus, which became her island home. The ancient Greeks associated her with erotic passion, seductive charm, fertility, and deception. While there were cults dedicated to Aphrodite throughout Greece, she was primarily worshipped by women, as a woman's goddess. It has been suggested that Aphrodite became a strong presence on Lesbos, Sappho's homeland. Many of Sappho's songs mention the goddess, often calling on her to aid the poet in matters of the heart. In Sappho's only complete lyric, she exhorts Aphrodite to help her win the affections of an unresponsive girl; in a shorter fragment, Sappho laments, "Sweet mother, I can no longer work the loom. / Slender Aphrodite has made me fall in love with a boy" (Sappho, *Poems and Fragments,* Fragment 36).

observed between men and boys. However, most men appear to have been uncomfortable with the very idea of sexual relations between women, as if they deemed it unnatural. A passage in Artemidorus' *On the Interpretation of Dreams* (c. second century CE) reflects this squeamishness, predicting dire results from the sexual act between women, even if it occurs only in dreams. If in a dream, the work predicts, a woman is the passive sexual partner of another woman, "she will be divorced from her husband or become a widow" (Artemidorus in Lefkowitz and Fant, p. 176).

In any case, scholars maintain that Sappho's poems provide evidence of homoerotic desire among women. Some fragments even suggest that the sexual dynamic between females might not be vastly different from that existing between males. In one poem, Sappho seems to depict herself as the older, more dominant lover of a much younger girl: "I loved you once, Atthis, long ago. / You seemed like a child to me, little and graceless" (*Poems*, Fragment 49). In another, she recalls a tearful parting between herself and one of her favored companions: "Truly I wish I were dead. / She was weeping when she left

---

THE ISLAND OF LESBOS

Located near Asia Minor, Lesbos was the third largest Aegean island. Throughout antiquity, Lesbos was usually divided into five competing *poleis* (states): Mytilene, Methymna, Pyrrha, Antissa, and Eresus. Sappho herself is said to have come from Mytilene. Historian J. J. Winkler writes that little is known about the society and culture of classical Lesbos beyond a few general facts and rumors: "a culture of some luxury, at least for the wealthy; aristocratic families fighting each other for power; the typical sixth-century emergence of tyrannies (Myrsilos) and mediating law givers (Pittakos)" (Winkler in McClure, pp. 40-41). During Sappho's lifetime, Lesbos appears to have been a vulnerable territory, continually threatened by the superior military capabilities of the province of Lydia (now part of mainland Turkey). Lesbos' reputation as a place known for sensuality and varied sexual practices appears to date from at least the fifth century BCE; the Greek verb "lesbi[a]zein"—to act like one from Lesbos—denoted fellatio (oral sex) performed upon men by women (Hallett in Greene, *Reading Sappho*, p. 129). Moreover, the Roman poets Catullus (c. 84-54 BCE) and Martial (c. 36-101 CE) wrote of women called "Lesbia," who were highly skilled in the sensual arts.

---

me, / and said many things to me, and said this: / 'How much we have suffered, Sappho. / Truly, I don't want to leave you'" (*Poems*, Fragment 11).

Sappho's poetry perhaps reflects a wider phenomenon. The society of Lesbos, her birthplace, may have encouraged sexual freedom among its inhabitants, male and female. Historians have noted that, "in Greek literature generally, references to the women of Lesbos connoted unusually intense eroticism, both homosexual and heterosexual. Anacreon, writing in the generation after Sappho, complained that the girl from Lesbos

whom he desired "gapes after some other woman" (Pomeroy, p. 54). Thus, it was from the island of Lesbos that "lesbianism," the nineteenth-century term for female homosexuality, was derived.

The Poems in Focus

The contents. Sappho's lyrics include epithalamia (marriage songs), religious hymns, and even a few choral compositions. Like her contemporaries, Sappho draws heavily upon Greek myths and legends. Her hymns are addressed to Aphrodite, the goddess of love, and Hera, the goddess of heaven; her choral fragments refer to the death of Aphrodite's mortal lover, Adonis, and the marriage of Hector, the Trojan hero most familiar to audiences from Homer's *Iliad* (also in *Classical Literature and Its Times*). However, Sappho writes mainly about erotic love, especially between women. She herself is a prominent figure in her poems, expressing longing and desire for her female companions, whom she addresses by such names as Atthis and Anactoria. (The Lumbardo translation imposes a new order on the fragments; the original fragment number, if different, follows in parentheses.)

Fragment 1
Shimmering
iridescent
deathless Aphrodite,
child of Zeus, weaver of wiles,
I beg you,
do not crush my spirit with anguish, Lady,
but come to me now, if ever before
you heard my voice in the distance
and leaving your father's golden house
drove your chariot pulled by sparrows
swift and beautiful
over the black earth, their wings a blur
as they streaked down from heaven
across the bright sky—
and then you were with me, a smile
playing about your immortal lips
as you asked,
what is it this time?
why are you calling again?
and asked what my heart in its lovesick
    raving
most wanted to happen:
"Whom now
should I persuade to love you?
Who is wronging you Sappho?
She may run now, but she'll be chasing soon.
She may spurn gifts, but soon she'll be giving.
She may not love now, but soon she will,
willing or not."
Come to me again now, release me

from my agony, fulfill all
that my heart desires, and fight for me,
fight at my side,
Goddess.

In the preceding poem, believed to be her only complete lyric, Sappho appeals to Aphrodite to grant her heart's desire. The goddess replies to the poet's passionate supplication with an amused query that may suggest familiarity with Sappho's affairs: "Whom now / should I persuade to love you?" It is subsequently revealed that Sappho loves a woman who does not return her affections, but Aphrodite assures her that the object of her desire "may run now, but she'll be chasing soon. . . . / She may not love now, but soon she will, / willing or not." The goddess's supreme confidence in her power to make even the most reluctant fall in love contrasts sharply with Sappho's longing and uncertainty as she again exhorts Aphrodite to "fight at my side, Goddess."

Fragment 20 (originally numbered 31)

Look at him, just like a god,
the man sitting across from you,
whoever he is,
listening to your
close, sweet voice,
your irresistible laughter
And O yes,
it sets my heart racing—
one glance at you
and I can't get the words out,
my voice cracks
a thin flame runs under my skin,
my eyes go blind
my ears ring
a cold sweat pours down my body,
I tremble all over,
turn paler than grass
Look at me
just a shade from dead
But I must bear it, since a poor

The poem trails off here, remaining an incomplete fragment. The Greek critic Longinus quoted it at length in the first century CE as an example of "love's madness" (Longinus in Reynolds, p. 21). Right away the poem presents a tableau of thwarted erotic desire. Yearning after an unattainable woman and envying the man who claims the woman's attention instead, Sappho experiences the pains of unrequited love: "a thin flame runs under my skin, / my eyes go blind / my ears ring / a cold sweat pours down my body / I tremble all over" (*Poems*, Fragment 20). Intriguingly, her contradictory symptoms—simultaneously freezing and burning, for example—seem to anticipate

the extravagance of Petrarchan love poetry that would become all the rage more than a thousand years later.

Fragment 31 (originally numbered 16)

Some say an army on horseback,
some say on foot, and some say ships
are the most beautiful things
On this black earth,
but I say
It is whatever you love.
It's easy to show this. Just look
at Helen, beautiful herself
beyond everything human,
and she left
her perfect husband and went
sailing off to Troy
Without a thought for her child
Or her dear parents, led astray
lightly
reminding me of Anactoria
who is gone
and whose lovely walk
and bright
shimmering face
I would rather see
than all the chariots
and armed men in Lydia
but it cannot be
humans
pray to share
unexpectedly

More meditative in tone than the other two lyrics, the preceding fragment offers insight on how love confers beauty upon the beloved. Citing the myth of Helen of Troy, the woman to whom classical legend attributes the cause of the Trojan War, as an example of the importance of pursuing one's desires, Sappho reveals how this divinely beautiful queen abandoned husband, child, and family. She did so, says Sappho, "without a thought," for love of Paris, a Trojan prince. Turning from the mythic to the personal realm, Sappho wistfully recalls a lost companion—"Anactoria / who is gone" and whom she would rather see "than all the chariots / and armed men in Lydia." The fragment ends inconclusively, but Sappho apparently holds out little hope of being reunited with her beloved.

Women and relationships. Whether as goddesses, companions, mothers, and even children, women are the dominating presence in Sappho's work. By contrast, men are often absent or only implied to exist in her poems. There are no rapturous hymns in praise of a male lover's beauty, nor prayers in which Sappho urges

POETS ON SAPPHO

The numerous references to Sappho in the works of later poets attest to the enduring quality of her literary legacy. In the following passages, three poets, born generations and countries apart, pay tribute to her art. Nossis of Locri, writing around the fourth century BCE, boldly claims her place alongside Sappho as "one dear to the Muses." The nineteenth-century British poet Lord Byron (1788-1824) acknowledges Sappho's gifts even as he mischievously includes her among classical authors considered immoral by modern readers. And the American poet Amy Lowell (1874-1925) reflects upon Sappho's place within the relatively small community of women poets.

> If, stranger, you sail to Mytilene of the lovely dances
> to find inspiration in the flower of Sappho's graces
> tell them there that Locri has borne one dear to the Muses and to her;
> and know that my name is Nossis, and then go.
>
> (Nossis in Reynolds, p. 70)

> Ovid's a rake, as half his verses show him,
> Anacreon's morals are a still worse sample,
> Catullus scarcely had a decent poem,
> I don't think Sappho's Ode a good example,
> Although Longinus tells us there is no hymn
> Where the sublime soars forth on wings more ample.
>
> (Byron in Reynolds, p. 230)

> Taking us by and large, we're a queer lot
> We women who write poetry. And when you think
> How few of us there've been, it's queerer still . . .
> There's Sapho, now I wonder what was Sapho.
> I know a single slender thing about her:
> That, loving, she was like a burning birch-tree
> All tall and glittering fire, and that she wrote
> Like the same fire caught up to Heaven and held there,
> A frozen blaze before it broke and fell . . .
> And she is Sapho — Sapho — not Miss or Mrs,
> A leaping fire we call so for convenience . . .
>
> (Lowell in Reynolds, p. 313)

Aphrodite to help her win a man's heart. Indeed, in the famous Fragment 20 (or, originally, 31), quoted above, the speaker describes the man as her romantic rival for a girl's affection; he is not enviable in himself but because he enjoys the beloved's company. Men are presented more favorably in Sappho's epithalamia (marriage-songs)—"To what shall I compare you, dear bridegroom? / I shall compare you to a slender sapling" (*Poems*, Fragment 44). In Fragment 57, Sappho prays for her brother's safe return.

Nonetheless, the interest and enthusiasm in Sappho's poems are directed mainly toward women. Besides invocations to Aphrodite (worshipped mainly as a women's goddess), Sappho also reveals love for her daughter, Kleis, and a wide range of emotions concerning her female companions. Toward the absent Anactoria, mentioned in Fragment 31 (or, originally, 16), she expresses wistful longing; toward Atthis, who has abandoned her for another, she expresses reproach: "Atthis / you have come to hate the very thought of me, / And you run off to Andromeda" (*Poems,* Fragment 59). In another lyric, she reveals her delight in feminine beauty: "for when I look at you face to face / not even Hermione can compare, / and it is no slight to liken you / to golden Helen" (*Poems,* Fragment 33).

Unsurprisingly, Sappho's emphasis on women has fueled much of the debate over her sexuality. Even if the poems are not read biographically, though, one can argue that in antiquity relationships between women, whether romantic or platonic, could have deep emotional significance. Within classical society, the sexes were often separated, the men involved in public life, the women confined to the domestic sphere. Women who occupied the same household or lived in close proximity could develop solid friendships. Moreover, religious rituals and ceremonies in which only women were allowed to participate could also strengthen the bonds.

Additional evidence of female friendship and love can be found in the few examples of women's writing to survive antiquity. Besides Sappho's poetry, there was that of Erinna of Telos (c. 353 BCE), whose poem, *The Distaff,* laments the loss of her girlhood friend, Baucis, first to marriage, then to death: "Unhappy Baucis, these are my laments as I cry for you deeply, / these are your footprints resting in my heart, dear girl, / still warm, but what we once loved is now already ashes" (Erinna in Plant, p. 50). A stone tablet placed upon the grave of Biote, an Athenian woman who died in the late fifth century BCE, records a similar message of love and grief: "Because of your true and sweet friendship, your companion Euthylla placed this tablet on your grave, Biote, for she keeps your memory with her tears, and weeps for your lost youth" (Euthylla in Lefkowitz and Fant, p. 170).

Sources and literary context. Sappho's primary sources of inspiration appear to have been Greek mythology and her own life. Besides allusions to familiar legends such as the death of Adonis and the Trojan War, the poet refers several times to members of her own family. In Fragment 57, she prays for her brother's safe return, as previously noted, while in Fragment 30 she mentions her "beautiful child, graceful / as golden flowers, my precious Kleis." Sappho's chosen medium—monodic lyric poetry—is generally intimate and subjective. She draws on personal relationships, so many of the poet's readers study her works within the context of her firsthand experiences.

Sappho's poems evoke frequent comparison with those of her contemporaries Alcman (630 BCE) and Alcaeus (c. 620 BCE), who were also lyric poets. Alcaeus was from Lesbos as well; he and Sappho employed many of the same themes—love, passion, nature, and myth—and composed their works in the same Aeolic dialect. Sappho's lyrics are held to be distinctive because of their frankness, sensuality, and emotionalism, which exerted a powerful influence on later generations of poets who chose to write about love. Women writers of the Hellenistic Age (c. 336 BCE–14 CE) who may have been inspired by Sappho's work included Erinna, Moero, Anyte, and Nossis.

Impact. Perhaps the earliest surviving commentary on Sappho's poetry is the following epigram attributed to the Greek philosopher Plato (c. 427-348 BCE): "Some say there are nine Muses . . . but how careless, look again, . . . Sappho of Lesbos is the tenth" (Plato in Reynolds, p. 70). Another Greek writer, Meleager, writing around 100 BCE, described the body of Sappho's work as "little but all roses" (Meleager in Reynolds, p. 70). Dionysius of Halicarnassus and Longinus—whose critical writings helped preserve Fragments 1 and 31, respectively—rendered favorable judgments as well. In *On Literary Composition* (c. 30 BCE), Dionysius praised Sappho's language, comparing her sentences to "the onflow of a never-resting stream" (Dionysius in Powell, p. 42). Longinus expressed similar admiration for the poet's insight into emotional states in his treatise *On the Sublime:*

> Are you not amazed how at one and the same moment she seeks out soul, body, hearing, tongue, sight, complexion as though they had all left her and were external, and how in contradiction she both freezes and burns, is irrational and sane, is afraid and nearly dead, so that we observe in her not one single emotion but a concourse of emotions? All this of course happens to people in love. . . .
>
> (Longinus in Reynolds, p. 21)

More than 500 years after her death, Sappho's songs were still being performed, and women of the time were expected to be able to sing them. Later admirers of her work included the Roman poets Catullus, Horace, and Ovid.

Around the ninth century CE, Sappho's poetry virtually disappeared from the scene, leading some historians to speculate that zealous early Christians may have burned the papyrus scrolls containing her works. Fragments of her poems began to resurface—again, most often quoted in the works of later authors—during the European

Renaissance, especially after the recently invented printing press published editions of Dionysius' *On Literary Composition* and Longinus' *On the Sublime*. Over the centuries that followed, Sappho and her work attracted new generations of admirers, many as fascinated with the poet herself as with her songs. At various times Sappho has been represented as a learned lady, a seductive wanton, a literary role model, and even a prototype of the New Woman. Nor has the incompleteness of her work hindered admiration; rather, it has fostered a lasting fascination. Summing up the enduring appeal of Sappho and her poetry, Margaret Reynolds writes in *The Sappho Companion* that

> what we have of the work and what others have made up about her life suggests different qualities, much admired since the time of the Romantics: enthusiasm, passion, commitment. . . . As far as we can tell from the Fragments, Sappho was a dedicated poet; a wordsmith who could craft emotion and experience. She seduces still, and is used to seduce still, in fictions both heterosexual and homosexual.
>
> (Reynolds, p. 7)

—Pamela S. Loy

For More Information

Cantarella, Eva. *Pandora's Daughters*. Baltimore: Johns Hopkins University Press, 1987.

Greene, Ellen, ed. *Reading Sappho*. Berkeley: University of California Press, 1996.

——. *Re-Reading Sappho*. Berkeley: University of California Press, 1996.

Hornblower, Simon, and Antony Spawforth, eds. *The Oxford Companion to Classical Civilization*. Oxford: Oxford University Press, 1998.

Lefkowitz, Mary R., and Maureen B. Fant. *Women's Life in Greece and Rome*. Baltimore: Johns Hopkins University Press, 1992.

McClure, Laura, ed. *Sexuality and Gender in the Classical World*. Oxford: Blackwell, 2002.

Plant, I. M., ed. *Women Writers of Ancient Greece and Rome*. Norman: University of Oklahoma Press, 2004.

Pomeroy, Sarah B. *Goddesses, Whores, Wives, and Slaves*. New York: Schocken, 1995.

Powell, Jim, trans. *Sappho: A Garland*. New York: Farrar, Strauss, Giroux, 1993.

Reynolds, Margaret. *The Sappho Companion*. New York: Palgrave, 2000.

Sappho. *Poems and Fragments*. Trans. Stanley Lombardo. Indianapolis: Hackett, 2002.

Politics

by

Aristotle

Early in life Aristotle (384-322 BCE) was moved to a superb vantage point for the firsthand study of politics. He came from the small city-state of Stagira in northern Greece to the court of King Amyntas III of Macedon, arriving with his father, Nicomachus, who attended the king as court physician. At the age of 17, Aristotle traveled south to democratic Athens, where he studied with his teacher Plato for the next 20 years. When Plato died in 347 BC, Aristotle left Athens for the west coast of modern Turkey to join a small community of philosophers there. He was warmly received by the local ruler, Hermias of Atarneus, a supporter of scholars who gave his adopted daughter, Pythias, to Aristotle as a wife. Pythias bore a daughter and died soon after. At some later point Aristotle fell in love with Herpyllis, and she gave birth to his son, Nicomachus. When the threat of Persian aggression began to loom over Assos in 344, Aristotle wound his way back to Macedon and resided at the court of King Philip II, son of Amyntas. There he instructed the young Alexander, who would prove his greatness through the conquest of the Persian Empire. In 335, after his student had gained the throne as Alexander III, Aristotle returned to Athens and attracted students to study under him at the Lyceum, where he taught for 13 years and produced basic works on a staggering range of subjects. We have surviving treatises on physics, metaphysics, ethics, rhetoric, botany, and zoology, while Diogenes Laertius recorded a still greater quantity and range of works by Aristotle

THE LITERARY WORK

An analytic treatise in eight books, composed in Greek between 347 and 335 BCE.

SYNOPSIS

Aristotle examines the principles of government and analyzes the types of rule that exist in his day (democratic, oligarchic, aristocratic, monarchic, tyrannical, and mixed).

that have since been lost to time. Among Aristotle's interests were social and political organization, and it was during this time that his students are thought to have gathered information on the constitutions of 158 different Greek city-states. Aristotle drew upon these constitutions to inform his discussion of political theory but was stopped short before finishing the task. Getting caught up in the tumult that ensued after Alexander's death (323 BCE) and an Athenian revolt against Macedonian domination, Aristotle found it expedient to flee, lest the Athenians harm him because of his Macedonian connections. Rather than face charges contrived against him, he fled to the Greek city of Chalcis. Aristotle died there of a stomach ailment in 322 BCE, leaving behind a mass of insightful notes on constitutions and political theories, some of which were published as the *Politics* and have both guided and puzzled scholars ever since.

Events in History at the Time of the Essay

An unstable era. Aristotle is generally thought to have composed the *Politics* at intervals between the death of Plato in 347 BCE and his own death in 335 BCE. Both among and within states, this was a period of political instability as powers rose and fell in quick succession and revolutions put one form of government in place of another like so many strokes of an old Greek warship's flashing oars. It was a time of challenge to the very concept of the *polis* (an independent political entity, or city-state, consisting of an urban center with surrounding agricultural land). Coming to the fore during this era were viable alternatives to the polis: leagues, federations, kingdoms, and empires, configurations that dwarfed the polis in population and resources (Athens, the largest polis of all, did not number much more than 250,000 inhabitants, while most city-states were far smaller).

Looming large over the previous century was a Greek civil conflict that had pitted Athens against Sparta and had ended in the victory of the latter. But, in scoring the victory, Sparta had been brought to its knees. The civil conflict, called the Peloponnesian War, had left the city-state bloodied and battered after a 27-year slogging match (431-404 BCE). Rather than repeat an old mistake of withdrawing from the Aegean Sea and leaving a power vacuum, Sparta tried to rule an empire with a constitution ill-suited to the task, and ultimately ruined both its empire and its constitution. New challenges surfaced to Spartan domination of the Greek city-states. At the battle of Leuctra in 371 BCE, the Spartan army was devastated by a force from Thebes that had been trained by talented commanders such as Pelopidas and Epaminondas. The Thebans destabilized and crippled Sparta by detaching its important territory of Messenia and populating it with slaves that had been freed from Spartan control. But the Thebans were not satisfied with ending the domination of Sparta; rather they sought to replace its supremacy with their own. Not strong enough, they failed in the attempt, meanwhile driving the neighboring city-state of Phocis to the desperate measure of plundering a treasury at Delphi to hire mercenaries to defend itself. Almost overnight, the move transformed Phocis into an important power. Other aspiring powers waxed and waned like so many passing moons: the Dionysii in Sicily and southern Italy, Alexander of Pherae in central Greece, and Mausolus of Caria in southwest Turkey. Meanwhile, major foreign powers, such as Persia and Carthage, funded one Greek polis against another, or intervened directly to destabilize the balance of power. The polis was proving to be too small and too little inclined to search for fair and peaceful solutions that would promote security and stability. A contemporary observer of the fourth-century free-for-all must have wondered how order could be imposed on chaos. Some Greeks, like the orator Isocrates (436-338 BCE), tried to encourage the Greeks to cease making war on each other and join in a panhellenic attack on the rich and vulnerable territories of Persia. Despairing of persuading the citizens of the poleis (Greek city-states) to reconcile their differences, these voices began to look instead to kings and tyrants of rising nations, like Jason, Evagoras, and Philip, to bring peace to the Greek city-states by force.

In the end, this was accomplished. In 338 BCE, anarchy among the city-states of Greece was checked by the unlooked-for dominance of not a polis but of the kingdom of Macedon, whose supremacy promised new stability. The city-states were compelled to join and to cede control over their foreign policy to a new federation, the League of Corinth, which was in fact dominated by Macedonia. While the poleis retained a degree of autonomy, Philip II was the undisputed leader of their combined forces. These foundations were barely laid when they were shaken by the assassination of Philip in 336 BCE, and by major revolts against Alexander III, his son and successor. In quelling the uprising of 335 BCE, Alexander leveled the mighty polis of Thebes, massacring its men, and selling the surviving women and children into slavery. These tactics shocked the Greek world, not so much for their brutality (great poleis had done such things to lesser ones more than once), but because they proved the shape of power had been fundamentally altered. Henceforth kingdoms, not city-states, would dominate.

Alexander went on to transform the Greek world by a lightning conquest of the Persian Empire. He, a Macedonian, became king over lands extending to India, wielding a power held by no Greek before or since. The wealth he seized dwarfed a century's income of the richest city-state, and the peoples he ruled were legion. What place was there for a polis in such a world? Had the cosmos been reconfigured on new lines? Would Macedonia's dominance survive Alexander?

The answers to these questions were very much in doubt in 323 BCE, when Alexander died

Detail from *The School of Athens* (c. 1510-1512), by Raphael, illustrating Plato (left) and Aristotle (right).
© Bettmann/Corbis. Reproduced by permission.

of a fever in Babylon and the poleis of mainland Greece revolted against Antipater, their Macedonian governor. Known to history as the Lamian War, the revolt was initially successful, and there was no certainty that Alexander's generals could maintain their sway over either the Greek poleis or the Persian Empire. Ultimately the revolt would fail and Macedonia would reassert its authority. But on his deathbed in Chalcis, Aristotle could have had no certainty about what future political order would emerge—and no surety that order would emerge at all.

The problem of internal instability. The belligerents of the Peloponnesian War made clever use of propaganda. Athens fought for "democracy." Sparta fought for "freedom." What this meant in practice is that the Athenians tended to support democratic elements within the poleis under their sway (like Samos), and backed democratic factions in other poleis (in, for example, Corcyra [modern Corfu]) over which they wished to exert influence. The hope was that sharing a common form of government would encourage a common interest and strengthen an alliance. The Spartans, on the other hand, championed freedom from dominance by another polis (i.e., Athens) and supported poleis and factions that Aristotle, in his *Politics,* classified as oligarchies or republics. Hence the internal political shapes of smaller states were influenced by their alliance with one power or the other, and vice versa. When the Spartans finally emerged victorious, they planned to solidify their control over the Aegean by replacing politically incompatible governments (especially democracies) with more congenial ones (especially republics and oligarchies). To this end, they forced states to elect or appoint commissioners sympathetic to Sparta and its political ideals. Examples of such commissioners are the Thirty at Athens (many of whom were connected to Plato and Socrates, both anti-democratic philosophers) and the decarchies, or ruling bodies of ten military officers, set up by the Spartan admiral Lysander in the coastal poleis. This type of interference did not end with the Peloponnesian War, or with Sparta's domination. Powerful states continued to back political factions within smaller poleis, and the failure to establish order among the various city-states only aggravated problems within them.

Given all this instability, it was of vital and immediate interest to consider what forms of government were most enduring and resilient. It is this real-world interest that prompted Aristotle's research into the development of so many states. Again, the endeavor resulted in 158 treatises; of these, only one (the *Constitution of the Athenians*) survives. This same real-world interest also explains his consideration in the *Politics* of the merits of the most admired polities (i.e., Sparta, Crete, and Carthage) and the need to propose and develop forms that might prove more successful than the ill-fated poleis of the fourth century.

While the contents of the *Politics* are enlightening, there are some striking absences to consider, most notably Aristotle's failure to discuss leagues and federations. These came into being in the fourth century BCE, and were affected by the struggle for supremacy. Federal states were outlawed in the general peace of 387 BCE (which was all but dictated by Persia and Sparta). The Spartans used this treaty to justify their forcible dismantling of a confederacy known as the Olynthian League, and they waged a protracted war to undermine the status of Thebes as the dominant power among the poleis in the Boeotian federation. Towards the end of Aristotle's life, Greece would see the rise of the Aetolian League—a federal state that gave people of Aetolian ethnicity (the vast majority of whom did not live in poleis) an identical political status (*sumpoliteia*) and that gave an equal but not identical status (*isopoliteia*) to others. The league had an assembly that met a couple of times a year; its members voted on various matters and also established a representative council and a smaller executive committee. Aetolia played a significant role in the Lamian War, and its contribution to the anti-Macedonian alliance was critical.

Yet such political innovations do not occupy Aristotle's attention. Instead his focus remains on the traditional polis, perhaps following the lead of his old and honored teacher Plato. Was he wrong to do so? Perhaps not. While the international scene would henceforth be dominated by kingdoms and leagues, the poleis would continue to survive as semi-independent communities with their own cultural and civic identities, meanwhile preserving the full spectrum of constitutional forms for centuries to come.

The Essay in Focus

Contents overview. By later convention, the *Politics* is divided into eight sections, or books. There is no certainty as to its original structure, although it has been characterized as the compilation of at least three sets of lecture notes, composed at different times with somewhat different themes. Furthermore, the present order does not reflect a sequence from older to more recent material—books 7 and 8, for example, are probably older than books 4 through 6. It follows, then, that a reader should not expect the artful polish and unity of a continuous dialogue, but rather a series of terse, pointed, and thought-provoking essays. A general outline of these follows:

Contents summary. "We see, then, that every state is a sort of association, and every association is formed with a view to some good" (Aristotle, *Politics*, book 1, chapter 1, section 1). So Aristotle begins, and so he defines the essential problem of the entire work. For him, the state is a human construction that serves to complete the citizen by providing an environment to sustain one's physical and moral being. The state is both natural and indispensable to the preservation of humanity, even as the coming together of male and female is necessary for reproduction. More exactly, says Aristotle, the relationship of the "naturally ruling" with the "naturally ruled" (a less palatable claim to modern than to ancient taste, given its application to slavery) is necessary to preservation. But while the bonds of parent and child, husband and wife, and ruler and ruled are the foundation of a community, they are not sufficient in themselves. Thus, families combine to form a village, and villages, in turn, combine to form a polis, in which it is possible not only to live, but live well, in accordance with the proper disposition of human nature. Such a life is, for Aristotle, the highest good, and hence his problem and need to analyze and define the types of association and government that are conducive to attaining it.

The polis is natural, but since humans possess speech and reason, its laws are not derived from natural compulsions but deliberate decisions as to how to regulate and encourage a virtuous life in common. It follows (in book 2) that some decisions as to the organization of a state will be more conducive to the good life than others. With this in mind, Aristotle proceeds to examine the merits and flaws of a sampling of real and theoretical states. He begins with Plato's conception of an ideal republic—an ideal that was never adopted in the ancient world, although Plato did attempt to influence the tyrant Dionysius I of Syracuse to rule according to its principles. Aristotle finds a number of faults with Plato's conception, one being that Plato's idea of a city owning property and children in common will not resolve the tensions that arise from some owning more than others, for these tensions stem from basic human failings. Take away private property, says Aristotle, and people will find other objects of strife, such as honor. There is even a danger to doing so. Without separate property, society fails to cultivate a sense of responsibility, for people neglect things that they do not see as their own.

Aristotle finds a basis for his criticism in the real problems of even the most admired states of his day—Sparta, Crete, and Carthage. He indicts Sparta on a number of counts, including too much license for women (which, he says, undermines the polis's social strength) and too many lower-class participants in high office (in view, he explains, of the belief that they are particularly liable to bribery and corruption). But his most fundamental objection is that the Spartans have mistaken a part of virtue—virtue in war—for the whole, and so their state and their lives lack balance. Crete's form of government recalls the one in Sparta, but in debased form. Lastly, Carthage has some of the merits and stability of an aristocracy (in that those best able to rule are more likely to have the opportunity to do so) but since wealth factors into eligibility for office, it has the vices of a plutocracy (i.e., rule by the wealthy). Aristotle is more sympathetic to the great compromise of the Athenian statesman Solon; even though he allocated political privileges according to income, Solon conceived of the advantage of a proper mixture of aristocratic and democratic elements. This mixture, which Aristotle calls a *politeia* (variously translated as "polity" or "republic") is the best attainable (as opposed to theoretical) regime, since it adopts the finest and moderates the worst features of the two forms of government.

After contemplating the view of a polis from on high, Aristotle (in book 3) adopts a ground-level perspective to reflect on who should be considered a citizen. He concludes that it is not enough to be a free adult male born in the polis (women, children, slaves, and foreign residents were automatically excluded from participation in government). What leads him to this conclusion is the consideration that some regimes (a monarchy, for example, or an aristocracy) limit access to decision-making (Aristotle implicitly accepts such limitations—he is not, after all, advocating democracy). He thus defines a citizen as a person (he means a free adult male) who has some share in the judicial and executive part of government. The qualities of a good citizen are not always identical to those of any good man, since a citizen's qualities are good insofar as they benefit the polis. While a good man would not suffer to be ruled by another, a good citizen should know both how to rule and how to be ruled. These definitions lead us to paradoxes. For instance, can it be said that there were no good men in Macedonia or Persia, since both were ruled by a king? It is highly unlikely that Aristotle would have been so tactless as to apply such reasoning to Macedonia, given his personal experience in and ties to the kingdom.

Aristotle next considers the ways in which citizens rule and are ruled by looking at types of regimes. Properly, these are three: rule by a single person (monarchy), rule by a few, (aristocracy), and rule by the multitude (*politeia*, or republic). When these forms are debased, in that the rule is no longer for the common good but rather for the good of the ruling element, they turn into tyranny, oligarchy, and democracy. Criteria of wealth and the concept of justice divide oligarchy and democracy. Justice, in an oligarchy, is equity: in other words, proportionate inequality for unequal people; in a democracy, justice entails equality for all. The former is flawed because its standard of measurement is often wealth, the latter because it fails to recognize inherent inequalities (in intelligence, skill, artistic talent, athletic ability, beauty, and so forth). Since the polis aims to produce a good life, this dispute about justice is at the core of disputes about regimes. The solution is to leave the rule of the city not to one faction or another (e.g., the elite in an oligarchy, or the mob in a democracy) but to law. The law, however, only provides general principles, whereas a competent and virtuous individual or group can render specific responses to particular problems. For Aristotle, the individual or group making such responses must be determined once again by a sense of justice. If one person surpasses all others in virtue, then that individual should be king.

ARISTOTLE DEFINES *VIRTUE*

Aristotle creates a definition of *virtue* (*arete* in Greek) in his *Nicomachean Ethics* (2.6.15). Rejecting that it might be an emotion or a capacity, he argues instead that virtue is a habit or disposition in actions or emotions. Specifically, it is a disposition to choose the right thing, that is, the mean between extremes as determined by a prudent person. Courage, for instance, lies between the extremes of cowardice and recklessness. In Aristotle's view, a virtuous person would be disposed to choose a course of action between such extremes. It follows that a monarch of surpassing virtue, with this definition in mind, could make the best possible choices for the state.

If there is not a clear distinction in merit, then it is more fitting to have rule by an aristocracy or a republic. In the end, the good man does suffer himself to be ruled by another, at least when he dwells in a good city where justice and virtue are the criteria for both political rule and for self-rule.

Altogether Aristotle has identified six types of regime: three fundamental ones (monarchy, aristocracy, and republic) and their debased forms (tyranny, oligarchy, and democracy). Now (in book 4) he considers which is best and which is most practicable. He calls tyranny the worst of the deviant regimes. True aristocracy, rule by the finest few or very best, is a form that Aristotle seems to think is not possible. Moving to oligarchy and democracy, he notes that each is either ill or well suited to a polis depending on its social and economic composition. The primary division of interest is the rich and the poor; the regime reflects the balance of power between them. Some democracies, like that of the Athenians in its better moments, advocate equality to rich and poor alike and abide by the ultimate authority of rule of law. But other democracies substitute the will of the majority for law (in effect, abandoning a "constitution"). Likewise, some oligarchies recognize the supremacy of law (though they have property or familial requirements for holding office). But others substitute the will of the rich for the rule of law. It is apparent that the rule of law is of prime importance to a state: "He who commands that law should rule may thus be regarded as commanding [that] God and reason alone should rule; he who commands that a man should rule adds the character of the beast" (*Politics*, 3.11.4).

Rather than advocate a pure form (although he acknowledges the ideal of the virtuous king), Aristotle seeks to balance the virtues and imperfections of the various possibilities by contriving a composite form, including some elements from the rule by the many and some from rule by the best (an aristocracy). Aristotle calls this composite form a *politeia*, which leads to confusion, as this is the term that he also uses for rule by the many in the interests of the whole. Hence, later scholars, from Cicero to the founders of the United States of America and beyond, have redubbed the composite *politeia*, instead using the Latin name for this same form—the republic.

The republic can be contrived in various ways. People can establish it by incorporating or synthesizing laws from its two component forms (*politeia*, rule by the many, and aristocracy, rule by the best). Or people can aim for the mean between the two component forms. Either way, the republic secures its stability and virtue from the middle populace, those who are neither very rich nor very poor. They are a center of gravity, a virtuous mean between the vacillations of either side.

WOULD ARISTOTLE CALL AMERICA A DEMOCRACY?

Although today many refer to the United States as a democracy, Aristotle would consider it to be a republic. The essential distinction is the relationship of the people to the government. In a democracy, the citizens and the government are the same, and the general assembly of all citizens holds ultimate power. All citizens can and should actively participate in making laws, judgments, and policy. When officials are necessary for day-to-day tasks, they are selected by a lottery system that ensures that the powerful and influential have no more chance of holding office than the weak and inconsequential. In a republic, the citizens do not themselves participate in decisions, but are represented by elected officials. In some republics, like ancient Rome and medieval Florence, there were strong democratic elements. In Rome, citizen assemblies or their representatives could nullify (i.e., "veto," which is Latin for "I forbid") or make laws (through the plebiscite, a direct vote to accept or reject them). Other republics, like Renaissance Venice and modern America, give less power to the people, and more to officials, who are elected (e.g., the U.S. president, who exercises the veto) or appointed (e.g., the U.S. supreme court justices). For a Greek living in a democratic state, like Athens, the idea of electing somebody to represent you in politics would be analogous to electing somebody to work out for you at a gymnasium. The Athenian would think that a free citizen must himself participate, or he would not be a free citizen, just as those who wish to be fit must themselves exercise, or they would not be fit.

To those who would devise a regime, Aristotle recommends careful consideration of how one organizes its policymaking, official and judicial parts. In deliberating, a democratic regime might have its citizens make decisions in turns, all at once, or in response to an agenda proposed by officials. An oligarchic regime might open debate to only those who meet a property requirement or only those who hold office. Both democracies and oligarchies have recourse to officials. The types, nature, and number of offices, and the qualifications for the officeholders, will vary according to the polis's size and regime. What qualifications judges must have and how to select them must also be determined, as must the size and purview of the courts.

No sound political treatise in the fourth century BCE could neglect the role of revolution. In his fifth book, Aristotle not only examines the nature and causes of revolution, but also makes recommendations as to how to avoid it. The ultimate cause of revolution, says Aristotle, is factional conflict, which stems from differing ideas on justice and equality. As noted above, oligarchs hold that proportionate inequality (or equity) is just; democrats uphold equality. A balance between equity and equality, upheld by the middle class (literally, the ones in the middle, *hoi mesoi*), may make the polis relatively stable, but even then it is subject to other causes of strife. Human nature can be swayed to side with a faction by profit, honor, fear, contempt, and a perception of difference. Petty disagreements among the powerful may permeate and trouble the state. Also, gradual changes in demography (the size or composition of a population) can have a subtle effect on the balance, one that suddenly comes to the foreground in a crisis. If, for instance, more and more people move to a coastal city to take advantage of new opportunities in trade, the inland farmers may suddenly find that their interests are no longer regarded as important. Democracies are particularly vulnerable to demagogues and popular leaders, especially popular generals. Dionysius of Syracuse is one example. Such leaders can subvert a democracy into a tyranny. On the other hand, not a few oligarchies have fallen due to their unjust treatment of the multitude. Others have fallen because internal competition led to the dominance of a single oligarchic or popular leader. There are dangers inherent in oligarchies too. When the status of the oligarchs is based on property, gradual changes in the distribution of wealth can result in an outmoded hierarchy and consequent in-fighting. Aristocracies and their corrupted form, the oligarchy, are particularly liable to deviations from justice and resulting revolutions. Monarchy stands or falls on the character and behavior of the ruler, while tyrants often lose power when they alienate the people through cruel and depraved acts.

The essential remedy for these ills is adherence to and enforcement of the laws. The rulers should cultivate virtues and justice appropriate to the regime and instill them in the people. The needs of the poor must be heeded in an oligarchy; the property of the wealthy should be respected in a democracy. Kings must observe limits to their authority; tyrants must instill awe and forestall rivals. In any case, the middle class should not be neglected, since it provides stability.

Aristotle returns once more to democracy in book 6, considering its defining principles: freedom to live as one wants and equality based on membership rather than merit. Such values are not easily suited to rule by others but, if necessary, citizens can compromise on ruling and being ruled in turn. In a democracy, all citizens are eligible for office, but many elections are by means of a lottery, not by vote (as in a republic). Officials are paid, so that all can afford the time in office. The terms are brief, and a citizen can hold an office only once. Juries are made up of average citizens, and an assembly of all citizens has ultimate authority.

The essential character of a democracy depends on the population of the polis. Where farmers predominate, the democracy is soundest, since its citizens devote their time and effort to their crops rather than to assemblies. They do not seek out the honors of office and are content to leave these to others, so long as they can check their behavior through audits. Herdsmen are similar to farmers. Merchants and laborers are not as reliable as herdsmen or farmers, and are prone to meet more often because they reside in the city, leading to disturbance and instability. Thus, the character of the populace is important. It would be best to encourage the growth and prominence of a middle class, lest the more wayward crowds dominate. State income must be carefully managed—surpluses are dangerous when subject to the whims of demagogues; they should be administered judiciously and distributed to the poor, who might otherwise become desperate.

The guidelines for a democracy or a republic are applicable to an oligarchy—indeed the best of these resemble republics. Lower offices should be open to the less wealthy, higher offices to those few who can afford the public expenses attached to them (this not only limits the number who can hold the offices, but also relieves the officeholder of jealousy—since he will be paying an unenviable price for holding an office).

In books 7 and 8, generally agreed to be the earliest parts of the *Politics*, Aristotle speculates on the best regime imaginable without worrying about practicalities. His evaluation is naturally based on his idea of the best way of life—that is, a life of happiness derived from virtue. For Aristotle, the happiest polis acts most in accordance with justice, prudence, and wisdom, and the best regime is one whose citizens are able to practice such virtues. These "goods of the soul," the highest goods, are supplemented by care for the material needs of the citizen, those met by the provision of external goods and the goods of the body (e.g., food and shelter). Thus, not only are the good man and the good citizen one and the same. The contemplative nature of the philosophic life is also married to the active political life.

Aristotle does not neglect the physical structure of the ideal polis. The city is to be large enough to be self-sufficient, but not so large that it can no longer be well managed. It should not be too poor or too rich, but instead provide for a large middle class. Its territory must be large enough to supply its citizens with sufficient resources and the ability to live with leisure to enjoy life and develop virtue, but small enough to be defensible by its own population. It should be close enough to the sea to enjoy the fruits of trade, but its port should be far enough away so that foreign visitors and merchants can be controlled and regulated. In terms of climate, the city should be neither too cold nor too hot so it can possess the high spirit that Aristotle attributed to cooler climes and the love for thought and art he associated with warmer lands.

Its people will, of course, need food, shelter, and goods. But the production of necessities is not a job for freeborn citizens. Their needs will be met by laborers, artisans, farmers, and so on, both free people and slaves. Although these workers will live in the polis, they will not be a part of its political life. They have neither time nor temperament, explains Aristotle, for the development of rational minds. War and judgment, which require courage and wisdom, will be the realms of the citizens, who will rule and be ruled, in turn, since they are alike. This likeness must be reinforced through a communal education, similar to Sparta in that it instills virtue, different in that its conception of virtue is complete. Unlike Sparta, in which citizens train only for war, the citizens of Aristotle's polis will prepare themselves for a virtuous life in both war and peace. Marriage and childrearing will have to be regulated to guarantee a future of healthy, strong, and virtuous citizens.

In the final book of the *Politics*, Aristotle devises a program for educating the children of the ideal polis. As indicated, this education is communal, not private, and covers the same material for all, since it aims to achieve a single goal—the creation of a virtuous populace—for the city as a whole. The citizen exists not merely for himself, but as a part of the whole polis, whose importance supersedes his. The curriculum deals with both the students' bodies and their minds. To teach lessons necessary for the development of the free man, it neglects trades and crafts, since these are the duties of hirelings or slaves. Instead the curriculum focuses on gymnastics and music (which includes poetry by Homer and others) for young minds, followed by art and literature for more mature ones. Lessons are instilled first through habit, then through reason. They shape the citizen, endowing him with practical knowledge and the capacity to enjoy leisure in a proper manner.

In essence, a well-conceived polis is the proper context for what Aristotle considers to be the good life, which in turn is the proper goal for a human being. This context, developed so painstakingly by Aristotle over the course of eight books, is absolutely vital, for he says that a man who is "incapable of entering into an association, or so self-sufficient that he has no need to do so, is no part of a polis, so that he must be either a beast or a god" (*Politics*, 1.1.12). Aristotle is writing for neither beast nor god, but for humans, and shows them how they might realize their full potential by shaping their political and social environment.

Aristotle, kingship, and Alexander. Two candidates for the ideal regime compete in the *Politics*: a republic and a monarchy. On the basis of both this work and one of Aristotle's ethical treatises (*Nicomachean Ethics*), at least one scholar has identified monarchy as Aristotle's preferred form. The scholar (Hans Kelsen) points to explicit and implicit praises of it in both of Aristotle's works and argues that the shifting primacy of the two in the *Politics* is a product of his delicate position in the struggle between the Athenian polis and the Macedonian kingdom.

The argument for monarchy is not an easy one to make at the Lyceum in fourth-century Athens. Many leading Athenians, most notably, Demosthenes, presented an anti-Macedonian policy in the guise of a defense of liberty against the encroachments of a depraved king. The king of Macedon, they argued, has enslaved his own people, and aims to do the same to others. This was a criticism directed not only at King Philip, but at royalty in general. Indeed, the subjects of the Great King of Persia, even if they were nobles in charge of vast tracts of land, were often referred to as slaves (*douloi*). Alexander, the successor to the thrones of both Macedon and Persia, became a target of the same charge—and perhaps with more justification.

Philip and Alexander consciously worked to change the way Macedonian kings ruled. Previously, their authority was bound by tradition and by jealous defense of aristocratic prerogatives. Both Philip and Alexander sought to expand their authority by looking abroad to some Eastern conceptions of kings as divine (as in Egypt, where the pharaohs of old had been represented as the incarnation of the god Horus). Philip encouraged the blending of the heroic status of the dead (traditionally observed) with a heroic status of the living (decidedly unconventional), and was able to compel some degree of recognition of his family's special status, as indicated by a monument to his family within the sacred bounds of the sanctuary of the supreme god Zeus at Olympia (the site of the ancient Olympics, not to be confused with Mount Olympus, reputed home of the gods, which lay well to the north in Philip's territory). Alexander went much farther than his father. His coins depicted the famous Greek hero Herakles (Hercules) in his own image, promoting a sort of ruler cult, not only in foreign parts of the empire, but also back in Greece. He was no doubt encouraged in this by the fact that the Egyptians recognized him as their pharaoh and the Persians practiced the ritual of proskynesis (prostrating themselves before their king, probably by getting down on their hands and knees and kissing the ground between the hands). Such behavior had never been asked of the Greeks. In fact, Aristotle, like most Greeks of his day, would not have hesitated to refer to even very powerful Persians as slaves, because they normally prostrated themselves before their king. Part of Alexander's divine status was derived from a claim to be the son of Zeus-Ammon (an equation of Zeus with the Egyptian god Ammon). Some also recognized his claim that he deserved heroic (hence divine) status because of his *areté*, or excellence. While bizarre to many modern readers, this made a degree of sense in the fourth century BCE. The barrier between mortal and

HERAKLES (IN LATIN, *HERCULES*)

In Greek myth, Herakles was the son of Alkmene, a human woman, and Zeus, king of the gods. Considered the greatest of Greek heroes, Herakles is most famous for his 12 labors, the common theme of which was the deliverance of people from savage monsters that preyed on them. The most significant of these labors was his descent into the underworld to bring back Cerberus, a three-headed hound that guarded the realm of the dead. Not only did Herakles subdue the beast; he returned from the dead. His return, along with his later death and rise to Mount Olympus, home of the gods, gave him a special sort of immortality. It is said that this special state was granted at least partly because of his amazing and noble deeds, and the excellence (in Greek, *areté*) that he demonstrated in accomplishing them. In fact, Herakles epitomized the Greek fascination with excellence and the transcendental qualities they attached to it. It is no accident that his image (often identified by his lion-skin armor and a heavy club) appeared in many contexts, and was manipulated to many ends. In ancient comedy, he is cast as a stupendously strong but weak-minded glutton (e.g., Aristophanes' *Birds*); in ancient tragedy, as a man testing the limits of humanity (e.g., Euripides' *Madness of Herakles*). He also appears on Macedonian coins minted in Aristotle's day, where his figure recalls both the mythical pedigree of the Macedonian royal house (which traced its ancestry back to Herakles) and the ideal of excellence that the kings wished their people to associate with their rule. Similarly in his *Politics*, Aristotle argues for the primary and transcendent merit of kingship as a form of government if (and only if) the king surpasses all others in excellence, just as Herakles surpassed lesser mortals.

immortal was permeable at times. The myths of Herakles, for example, awarded divine status to this hero in return for his virtue and accomplishments, and certainly Alexander had surpassed Herakles's exploits in war.

But however great Alexander would appear in hindsight, he was not universally admired in his day. In effect, when a king grasped at authority beyond that permitted by tradition, he became a tyrant. How might Aristotle, a denizen of both the Macedonian court and the Athenian Lyceum, reconcile those two worlds? Aristotle's solution was found in the virtuous king:

> But if there is any one man so greatly distinguished in outstanding virtue [*areté*], or more than one but not enough to be able to make up a complete state, so that the virtue of all the rest and their political ability is not comparable with that of the men mentioned . . . it is no longer proper to count these exceptional men a part of the state; for they will be treated unjustly if deemed worthy of equal status, being so widely unequal in virtue and in their political ability: since such a man will naturally be as a god among men. . . . It remains therefore . . . for all to obey

such a man gladly, so that men of this sort may be kings in the poleis for all time.

> (*Politics*, 3.8.1,7)

Aristotle had already noted that different mixtures of democracy and aristocracy are appropriate to different circumstances. With the same recognition of the various possibilities in human nature, he now notes that men who are exceptional because of their excellence and virtue (*areté*) warrant exceptional treatment. If there is any doubt that Aristotle is referring to the kings of Macedon, it is dispelled when we read of rulers who "like [the mythical Athenian king] Codrus, have prevented the state from being enslaved in war" and who "like [the Persian king] Cyrus, have given their country freedom, or have settled or gained a territory, like the Lacedaemonian, *Macedonian*, and Molossian kings" (*Politics* 5.8.5; emphasis added).

Aristotle based his philosophy on a hard look at the real world. If, in the real world, Alexander had surpassed even the myth of Herakles, and burst the boundaries of the known world, how could he be contained in the confines of a republic?

Sources and literary context. The Archaic Age (c. 620-580 BCE) saw the founding of Greek colonies all around the Mediterranean region, each independent of its mother state (e.g., Syracuse, founded by Corinth, was from the start an independent polis). Self-governing, these colonies created their own constitutions, often adopting the form of government in the mother state but adapting it to meet local needs. The age also saw regime changes in the various city-states of Greece. Thus, Aristotle had real-life examples on which to draw. Also writers articulated political ideals in poetry and prose. Our earliest academic speculation on political forms harks back to the Greek historian Herodotus who in the 430s or early 420s BCE contrived a fictional scene in which Persian nobles debate the relative merits of democracy, aristocracy, and monarchy. Thucydides also gave considerable attention to the behavior and dynamics of various types of states, in his own narrative and in the speeches he attributed to historical figures (such as the Funeral Oration of Pericles in his essay **The Peloponnesian War,** also in *Classical Literature and Its Times*). But it was the fourth century that would give rise to the first treatises on the workings of the polis. While Plato concerned himself with theory, Xenophon concentrated on practice in a real polis.

Xenophon was the author not only of historical works like the **Persian Expedition** (also in *Classical Literature and Its Times*), but also of short technical treatises on hunting, horsemanship, and the like. He wrote advice to aspiring leaders, in sections of the *Memorabilia* (philosophical dialogues featuring Socrates) and especially in the *Education of Cyrus* (a handbook on rule and leadership). Xenophon was profoundly interested in Sparta, and wrote a biography of one of its kings, Agesilaus, with whom he was well acquainted. Also attributed to him (although the authorship is uncertain) is the *Constitution of the Lacedaemonians* (*Lacedemonian* was the ancient Greek name for Sparta), which tried to explain Sparta's role as the dominant power by focusing on its political and social structure. The introduction to this treatise made a groundbreaking connection: "It occurred to me one day that Sparta, though among the most thinly populated of states, was evidently the most powerful and most celebrated city in Greece; and I fell to wondering how this could have happened. But when I considered the institutions of the Spartans, I wondered no longer" (Xenophon, *Constitution of the Lacedaemonians*, 1.1). Here the author links a polis's political and social institutions to its civic greatness. In so doing, he points to a new

type of treatise, which others will develop in centuries to come. These others (among them, Aristotle's students) will compile information on many poleis so that their teacher can synthesize the material, draw general conclusions, and devise theories based on hard data—in other words, so that their teacher can write the *Politics.*

Aristotle's teacher, Plato, explored politics too, but his explorations concerned less earthy examples. Like Xenophon, Plato admired Sparta. He examined its customs and laws, assessed their merits and flaws, and devised an ideal but imaginary state, predicated on the virtue of justice, which he described in his **Republic** (also in *Classical Literature and Its Times*). Towards the end of his life, Plato revisited the problem of justice and virtue in the hypothetical founding of a new colony, and produced the *Laws.* Aristotle was intimately familiar with both works. He found himself in disagreement with some of Plato's premises and more concerned with realism and practicality. It is often argued that Aristotle began his *Politics* soon after Plato composed the *Laws* (in the 340s BCE); in any event, their influence on the *Politics* is everywhere visible in Aristotle's challenges to his teacher's tenets.

Finally, it would be remiss not to mention the connection between the *Nicomachean Ethics* and the *Politics.* In the former work, Aristotle sets the foundations for themes that will recur in the *Politics*, such as his conception of virtue and its development through habit and reason. Also discussed in his earlier work is the notion of a virtuous mean between two extremes, a foreshadowing of his assertion that the "middling elements" are the polis's source of stability. Finally, the *Ethics* ends with the promise of a discourse on their practical application in the polis, which is fulfilled in the *Politics.* This later work intends to help ensure that the ethical behavior set down in the *Ethics* is enforced in laws.

Publication and reception. Upon Aristotle's death in 322 BCE, the manuscript of the *Politics*, together with his other unpublished works, became the responsibility of Theophrastus, who succeeded Aristotle as head of the Lyceum. Theophrastus, in turn, willed his collection of manuscripts to an obscure individual by the name of Neleus, who brought it to Scepsis in Asia Minor (modern Turkey), where it languished hidden and forgotten until the first century BCE. While copies may have survived in major philosophic centers such as Athens, Alexandria, and Rhodes, these copies seem to have had little impact on the writers of the third and second centuries BCE. A critical edition finally emerged in the early first century BCE when, according to tradition, a wealthy scholar named Apellicon discovered the text, brought it back to Athens, and tried diligently to restore the neglected and damaged manuscript. Apellicon's library was seized by the Roman general Lucius Cornelius Sulla during his sack of Athens in 86 BCE, and brought to Rome, where it received a welcoming and attentive audience in such renowned figures as Cicero. The Roman writer Andronicus published a corrected edition, and a revival of interest in Aristotle in general, and the *Politics* in particular, ensued.

The subsequent influence of the *Politics* has been profound. It influenced John Locke and Thomas Jefferson, and echoes of Aristotle's voice can be heard in the language of the American Declaration of Independence. Even today, his ideas provide a foundation for debate on issues that he framed over two millennia ago.

—Frank Russell

For More Information

Adler, Mortimer. *Aristotle for Everybody: Difficult Thought Made Easy.* New York: Macmillan, 1978.

Aristotle. *Politics.* Trans. H. Rackham. Loeb Classical Library. Cambridge, Mass.: Harvard University Press, 1990.

Barker, Ernest. "The Life of Aristotle and the Composition and Structure of the Politics." *Classical Review* 45 (1931): 162-172.

Barnes, Jonathan, ed. *The Cambridge Companion to Aristotle.* Cambridge: Cambridge University Press, 1995.

Diogenes Laertius. *Lives of Eminent Philosophers.* Trans. R. Hicks. Loeb Classical Library. Cambridge, Mass.: Harvard University Press, 1972.

Jaeger, Werner. *Aristotle: Fundamentals of the History of His Development.* Trans. R. Robinson. Oxford: Clarendon Press, 1948.

Kelsen, Hans. "The Philosophy of Aristotle and the Hellenic-Macedonian Policy." *International Journal of Ethics* 48, no. 1 (1937): 1-64.

Kraut, Richard. *Aristotle: Political Philosophy.* Oxford: Oxford University Press, 2002.

Lord, Carnes. "The Character and Composition of Aristotle's Politics." *Political Theory* 9, no. 4 (1981): 459-478.

Mulgan, R. G. *Aristotle's Political Theory: An Introduction for Students of Political Theory.* Oxford: Clarendon Press, 1977.

Xenophon. *Constitution of the Lacedaemonians.* In *Scripta Minora.* Trans. E. C. Marchant. Loeb Classical Library. Cambridge, Mass.: Harvard University Press, 1984.

Yack, Bernard. *The Problems of a Political Animal: Community, Justice, and Conflict in Aristotelian Political Thought.* Berkeley: University of California Press, 1993.

The Republic

by
Cicero

A uthor, orator, philosopher, and statesman, Marcus Tullius Cicero (106-43 BCE)
holds a unique place in the history of
Rome. His voluminous writings have made the
age in which he lived better known to historians
than any other period of Roman history. But Cicero was also a participant in history itself, an
important player in the drama that unfolded as
Rome's ancient republican government crumbled
and power ultimately became concentrated in the
hands of an emperor, a single ruler with dicta-
torial powers over all. Cicero was born in the
town of Arpinum, near Rome, into a wealthy but
not an aristocratic family. Educated in Greece as
well as in Rome, he went on to make a name for
himself as a lawyer. In 66 BCE, Cicero entered
politics, supporting the Roman general and
politician Gnaius Pompeius, or Pompey. Three
years later, Cicero was elected to be one of
Rome's two consuls, the annually chosen chief
magistrates of the Roman government. As consul he won fame for crushing the Catilinarian
conspiracy, an attempt to take over the government by Cicero's former rival for the consulship,
Lucius Catilina. A staunch defender of republican values, Cicero went on to vocally oppose the
three-way alliance known as the First Triumvirate, among Pompey, Marcus Crassus, and Julius
Caesar. This triumvirate dominated Roman politics in the 50s BCE. Forced out of politics as a
consequence, Cicero devoted himself to writing.
It was during this period that he produced a
number of key writings, including *The Republic*.
Grounded in Greek political theory, *The Republic*

THE LITERARY WORK

A dialogue in six books set on a country estate
near Rome in 129 BCE; written in Latin and
published (as *De Republica*) c. 54-51 BCE.

SYNOPSIS

Cicero portrays the famed Roman general and
statesman Scipio Aemilianus (185-129 BCE)
discussing political theory with several
friends.

reflects Cicero's attempt to apply Greek ideas to
the Roman model in the interest of understanding the problems that afflicted the Roman political system and offering solutions that might help
save it.

Events in History at the Time
the Dialogue Takes Place

The stages of Roman expansion. Cicero lived
at a time when the Italian city-state of Rome was
finalizing its imperial control of the Mediterranean world. According to a tradition widely believed in Cicero's day, Rome had been founded
in 753 BCE. The long process by which it rose to
become an imperial superpower can be roughly
divided into three stages of expansion into different areas: the Italian peninsula (c. 400 to c.
265 BCE); the western Mediterranean (c. 265 to

THE ROMAN POLITICAL SYSTEM

The Roman republic was based on a balance of power between the aristocratic Senate and a variety of popular assemblies. The most important such assembly was the *comitia centuriata*, or "assembly of centuries." This body acted as a legislature, and it also elected the two yearly consuls—the republic's chief executive officers, who conducted Rome's foreign relations and commanded its armies. Holding the office of consul qualified a man to enter the Senate after his term expired, thus drawing into the body a number of non-aristocrats, such as Cicero. This type of inductee was called a *novus homo* or "new man." All legislation was subject to veto by any of the Tribunes of the Plebs, ten officers elected annually to guard the interests of the lower classes. In a time of crisis, with the approval of the Senate, a consul had the power to publicly nominate a dictator, who could make decisions that were not subject to the Tribune's veto. The dictator was named to accomplish a specific task—to command the army in putting down a rebellion, for example—and his term in office was limited to six months. The Senate, as indicated, played a key role in naming him. Until the late second century BCE, when Cicero's *Republic* is set, the senators, through their wealth and influence, generally exercised the upper hand in Roman politics.

c. 200 BCE); and the eastern Mediterranean (c. 200 to c. 50 BCE).

Understanding the first of these stages helps explain the careers of many "Roman" politicians and writers, including Cicero, who did not originally come from Rome itself. As smaller Italian towns like Cicero's hometown of Arpinum came under Roman control, their inhabitants were granted Roman citizenship. By the time *The Republic* is set, the late second century BCE, the sharing of Roman citizenship had helped weld the often distinctive loyalties of the Italian towns into a unified Roman identity. It also allowed promising and talented young men like Cicero to come to Rome and take part in politics and culture there. As a politician from a wealthy but not an aristocratic family, the first in his family to attain the position of consul, the Senate considered him a *novus homo*, or "new man"; he made the breakthrough for the rest of his family, who would henceforth be of Senatorial rank. This meant that he was the first of his family to attain the office of consul.

The second and third stages of Roman expansion relate directly to the historical and cultural background of the dialogue itself. The dialogue's main character, Scipio Aemilianus, came from a famous military family that had led the way in conquering Rome's foes. In the process of expanding into the eastern Mediterranean, Rome

had meanwhile encountered the Greek ideas on which *The Republic* would be based.

The Punic Wars. During its second stage of expansion, Rome was challenged primarily by the North African city-state of Carthage, a strong commercial and imperial power that dominated western Mediterranean areas such as Spain and North Africa. By defeating Carthage in three bitter wars fought over more than a century, Rome inherited Carthage's power in the western Mediterranean.

Carthage had originally been founded by the Phoenicians, a people from the area of today's Lebanon. Romans called them the *Poeni* or *Puni*, and so the three wars against Carthage are known as the Punic Wars:

The First Punic War (264-241 BCE) broke out because Rome's expansion in the Italian peninsula brought it into conflict with Carthage's dominance in Sicily and southern Italy. Rome won the war, seizing the islands of Sicily, Sardinia, and Corsica, its first overseas provinces. Carthage remained a strong power elsewhere in the west.

The Second Punic War (218-202 BCE) broke out after Rome began encroaching on Carthage's empire in Spain. The great Carthaginian general Hannibal marched from Spain into Italy, where his army defeated the Romans several times and threatened Rome for more than a decade. Rome appointed Publius Cornelius Scipio (237-183

BCE) to command its army in Spain. After winning against Carthaginian forces in Spain, Scipio crossed to North Africa in 204 BCE, threatening Carthage and forcing Hannibal to return and defend the city. Scipio then defeated Hannibal at the battle of Zama in 202, ending the war. Known as Scipio Africanus for the victory, this Scipio is the adoptive grandfather of Scipio Aemilianus, the main character in *The Republic*. Near the end of the dialogue, in the famous passage known as "The Dream of Scipio," Scipio Aemilianus describes a dream in which he converses with his grandfather's ghost.

The Third Punic War (149-146 BCE) resulted in Carthage's final destruction. Although by this time Rome's old foe was no longer a threat to Roman power, Scipio Aemilianus commanded a Roman army that conquered the city and razed it to the ground.

Rome consolidated its imperial growth in the western Mediterranean during the second century BCE. Most notably, from 154 to 133 BCE, Rome fought a series of wars in Spain against local rulers who resisted Roman rule. Increasingly brutal, these campaigns of conquest came to a climax in 134 BCE, when Scipio Aemilianus captured the pivotal fortress of Numantia, which—like Carthage a dozen years earlier—he utterly destroyed.

Rome and the Hellenistic world. Although Rome continued adding to its western empire, by the second century BCE much of its attention had turned to the eastern Mediterranean. In contrast with the backward and sparsely populated west, the culturally advanced eastern Mediterranean consisted of wealthy kingdoms and ancient, populous cities. Comprising many different ethnicities, the upper classes in these kingdoms were educated in ancient Greek literature and learning, which had been spread throughout the region by the conquests of Alexander the Great in the fourth century BCE. Since the Greeks referred to themselves as "Hellenes," this Greek-based civilization in the East is called "Hellenistic."

Also in contrast with the west, Rome's expansion into the Hellenistic world of the east occurred haphazardly. Instead of facing a single powerful rival such as Carthage, during the second century BCE Rome was drawn into a series of wars between the various Hellenistic kingdoms. The most troublesome kingdom was Macedon, which began expanding in the late third century under its aggressive king, Philip V (ruled 221-179 BCE). Typically, smaller powers would appeal to mighty Rome for help. Rome would sign a defensive alliance with them, and would then be embroiled in war when they were attacked. Between 215 and 168, Rome fought three such wars against Philip and his successors: the First Macedonian War (215-205 BCE); the Second Macedonian War (200-197 BCE); and the Third Macedonian War (172-168 BCE).

Despite such conflicts, Rome did not yet attempt to occupy areas of the eastern Mediterranean directly. Instead, Roman leaders at first preferred to let the Greeks and others rule themselves, establishing a patchwork of different sorts of relationships across the empire, from ally to direct ruler. Yet its new role of international policeman demanded that Rome exercise an increasingly harsh level of power. By the end of the Third Macedonian War, Rome was punishing the leaders of anti-Roman factions in the Greek cities.

The wars in the East exposed upper-class Romans to the glories of Greek civilization. One of the first was Scipio Aemilianus, whose father commanded the Roman army in the Third Macedonian War. As a young man serving under his father, Scipio won fame for his courage in the Battle of Pydna, which ended this third war in 168 BCE. Scipio's father had made sure that his sons were tutored by the best Greek teachers, and in the future many more upper-class Romans would follow his example. By Cicero's time, the prestige of Greek culture had become firmly established in Rome. The historical Scipio was well known as an early pioneer in this process, making him a logical choice as the main character in a dialogue based on Greek political thought.

Scipio Aemilianus and Tiberius Gracchus. By the late second century BCE, the immense wealth generated by Rome's imperial expansion had created strong social and political tensions in Rome. Enriched by income from the provinces, Roman aristocrats had amassed huge estates, often illegally, while the poor were driven off the land. In 133 BCE the aristocratic reformer Tiberius Sempronius Gracchus, elected as a tribune of the plebs, proposed a series of land reforms aimed at helping the poor. The move was upsetting to many in the Senate, who stood to lose large tracts of land that they had illegally acquired. When the Senate induced another tribune to veto the land-reform law, Tiberius Gracchus had that tribune illegally removed from office and the law was passed. Tiberius then ran for a second term as tribune but was killed amid the social disturbances that followed.

Scipio Aemilianus was Tiberius Gracchus's brother-in-law and his chief opponent in the Senate. Along with his reputation for integrity,

Scipio's role in opposing the Gracchan reforms made him a hero to the defenders of the Senate in Cicero's day and thus a perfect mouthpiece for the conservative republican views that Cicero espouses through him in the dialogue.

In other words, Cicero calls for "harmony between the orders," or peace between the different classes vying for power in Roman society (i.e., the Senate and the business class). In the dialogue, Cicero implies that, by causing strife between the orders, the land reforms of Tiberius Gracchus were the beginning of the problems that beset the republic in his own day. Modern historians instead tend to see the reforms as an attempt to address the complex set of inequities that were the real cause of Rome's troubles.

The Dialogue in Focus

Contents summary. Consisting of six sections, referred to as "books," Cicero's *Republic* has survived only in incomplete form. Much of what we have today, about one third of the original, comes from a single, badly damaged manuscript that was discovered in the Vatican library in 1820. Entire sections are missing from it. In addition, a number of brief passages have survived because they were quoted by later writers. Finally, the dialogue's best-known passage, "The Dream of Scipio," from the sixth and final book, was copied and widely read on its own. It has thus survived in a separate manuscript tradition.

SCIPIO'S CIRCLE OF FRIENDS

In addition to his political and military leadership, Scipio Aemilianus was also well known as a patron of Greek culture. Drawing on Cicero's portrait of Scipio in the dialogue and in other works, modern scholars have speculated that Scipio and his friends constituted a social circle through which elements of Greek culture were first passed to Rome.

Because the first 17 pages are missing from the Vatican manuscript, the modern reader begins the preface of the first book about two-thirds of the way through. Drawing on their study of the prefaces to Cicero's comparable works, scholars believe the missing pages contain the author's dedication, most likely to his brother Quintus, whom Cicero appears to address in the surviv-

ing portions of the work. Cicero's main goal in the preface is to establish that participating in politics is a good and rewarding activity for citizens to undertake, despite the arguments of some philosophers against it. (Debating the relative merits of an "active life" in public service and a "contemplative life" of philosophical study was a favorite pastime of ancient philosophers.)

Declaring his intention to present "a discussion of the state," Cicero introduces the dialogue as a conversation "that was once reported by Publius Rutilius Rufus to you [probably Cicero's brother] and me in our youth" and that covers the matter from every conceivable angle (Cicero, *The Republic*, book 1, lines 12-13). Rutilius Rufus was a historical figure, an older acquaintance of Cicero's, who as a young man had known the celebrated Scipio. He may well have reported such a conversation to Cicero and his brother when they were young, although it is equally possible that Cicero is simply making this claim as a way of lending verisimilitude to the work.

The dialogue itself is set during a winter holiday gathering of Scipio's "closest friends" at his country estate near Rome (*Republic*, 1.14). Along with Scipio himself, these friends comprise the dialogue's cast of characters. They include Quintus Tubero, Scipio's nephew; Lucius Furius Philus, a leading Roman politician and orator; Publius Rutilius Rufus, Cicero's purported source for the conversation; and Gaius Laelius, another leading politician and Scipio's closest friend. Several others are also present. By far the most prominent speaker is Scipio, but Laelius also contributes significantly to the discussion, and the others chime in frequently as well.

The dialogue proper begins in speculation about "a second sun" that has appeared over Rome (*Republic*, 1.15). Like eclipses, comets, and other such phenomena, this "second sun" was the subject of intense speculation. A reflection caused by ice crystals in the atmosphere, it was thought to have supernatural implications for events on earth. Laelius suggests that they confine the discussion to "more important things," such as the political turmoil that followed the reforms of Tiberius Gracchus a few years earlier, when Rome was divided into "two senates and almost two nations" (*Republic*, 1.30 and 1.31).

Laelius then asks Scipio what form of government he thinks is best. Scipio begins by defining the three basic sorts of constitutions as outlined according to traditional Greek political theory:

Monarchy ("rule by one"), in which power is held by a king or other supreme ruler
Aristocracy ("rule by the best"), in which power is held by a ruling class
Democracy ("rule by the people"), in which power is held by the people as a whole

None of these is perfect, Scipio continues, although each can provide adequate government "provided no forms of wickedness or greed find their way into it" (*Republic*, 1.42).

Each also has "a depraved version of itself" (*Republic*, 1.44). Thus monarchy can be corrupted into tyranny, aristocracy into oligarchy ("rule by the few"), and democracy into mob rule:

And so political power passes like a ball from one group to another. Tyrants snatch it from kings; aristocrats or the people wrest it from them; and from them it moves to oligarchic cliques or back to tyrants. The same type of constitution never retains power for long. That is why, though monarchy is, in my view, much the most desirable of the three primary forms, monarchy is itself surpassed by an even and judicious blend of the three forms at their best.
(*Republic*, 1.68-69)

Such a mixed constitution, Scipio concludes, is better able to withstand the pressures of instability—unless, he warns, "the politicians are deeply corrupt" (*Republic*, 1.69). He offers Rome as a positive model, asserting that "no form of government is comparable in its structure, its assignment of functions, or its discipline, to the one which our fathers have received from their forebears and handed down to us" (*Republic*, 1.33).

Though he prefers a mixed constitution above all, when pressed by Laelius to say which of the three forms of government he favors by itself, Scipio chooses monarchy.

SCIPIO: Recently, when we were at your villa in Formiae, I observed that you gave the staff instructions to take orders from one person only.
LAELIUS: Quite; my agent.
SCIPIO: What about your house in town? Do several people run your affairs?
LAELIUS: No indeed; just one.
SCIPIO: What of the whole establishment? Is anyone else in charge of it apart from you?
LAELIUS: Certainly not.
SCIPIO: So why don't you admit that in a state, too, the rule of one man is best, provided he is just?
LAELIUS: I'm almost persuaded to agree with you.

(*Republic*, 1.61)

In book 2, Scipio goes on to recount the historical development of Rome's republican consti-

tution. He begins by praising the city's legendary founder, Romulus, who acted as king but who also introduced aristocratic and democratic elements into his government. After Romulus's death, however, Rome's monarchy descended into tyranny, a process that culminated in the late sixth century BCE, with the despotic king Tarquinius Superbus. A period of aristocracy followed, in which Rome was ruled, responsibly at first, by the *decemviri* or "Ten Men." However, the decemvirate soon deteriorated into an oligarchic faction, "cruel and greedy in their domination over the people" (*Republic*, 2.63). At this point, several missing pages apparently bring the reader up to about 450 BCE, when Cicero believes that Rome's republican form of government had taken shape. About 15 pages are missing near the end of this book.

Book 3 begins with several missing pages in which it is thought that Cicero, writing in his own voice, argues that man is a rational animal and discusses connections between philosophy and politics. Further missing pages obscure what follows, reducing most of the surviving remainder of book 3 to opposing arguments by Philus and Laelius over the role of justice in the state. Assenting to a request that he take the less popular side, Philus agrees to argue against the importance of justice, a position that he doesn't actually hold. The primary job of the state, he asserts, is to promote the strength and security of its people, and giving weight to the interests of justice undermines this responsibility. Laelius (much of whose argument is lost) argues that justice is necessary to the state's legitimacy. Scipio then resumes his discussion of the three types of constitution, relating them to the original meaning of the Latin word *respublica*, literally "public thing." All three are republican in their uncorrupted forms, but Scipio concludes, with some reluctance, that only democracy can be considered a "public thing" in its corrupted form (mob rule).

Just a few pages survive of book 4 and book 5. The extant parts of book 4 discuss the education and training of youth, comparing Roman customs favorably with Greek ones. Scipio, for example, reflects on Roman modesty, objecting to the way that young Greek men exercise naked. Book 5's few surviving fragments concern the ideal statesman, whom Scipio compares with a farm manager, ship's captain, or doctor in applying expert knowledge from a variety of areas to the goal of guiding the state. The ideal statesman, he says, should possess a wide knowledge of law, a thorough education, sensitivity to public opinion, and a strong sense of honor.

Apart from a few isolated fragments, all that survives of the sixth and final book is the passage commonly known as "The Dream of Scipio," which runs to less than eight pages in most translations. It begins as Scipio recalls a visit he made in 149 BCE to Masinissa (c. 240-148 BCE), king of the North African kingdom of Numidia and a longtime ally of the Romans against Carthage. The old king entertained Scipio—who at that point was not yet the famed conqueror of Carthage and Numantia—with tales of his friendship with Scipio's grandfather, the great Scipio Africanus. That night Africanus appeared to Scipio in a dream.

"Don't be afraid, Scipio," Africanus tells Scipio in the dream: "Listen to me and remember what I say" (*Republic*, 6.10). Africanus first foretells Scipio's political and military career, including his destruction of Carthage and Numantia. Then Africanus predicts that in Scipio's 56th year—that is, in 129 BCE, the year in which the dialogue is set—Scipio will have to save Rome itself in a time of dire need: "you will be the one man on whom the country's safety depends," Africanus tells him (*Republic*, 6.12).

Africanus continues:

> Yet, to make you all the keener to defend the state. . . . I want you to know this: for everyone who has saved and served his country and helped it to grow, a sure place is set aside in heaven where he may enjoy a life of eternal bliss. To that supreme god who rules the universe nothing (or at least nothing that happens on earth) is more welcome than those companies and communities of people linked together by justice that are called states. Their rulers and saviours set out from this place [heaven], and to this they return.
>
> (*Republic*, 6.13)

Africanus takes Scipio to a great height, and they see the whole earth stretched out beneath them. Together they view the stars and planets, and listen to the music of the spheres. (According to ancient Greek cosmology, the earth was the center of the universe. As the planets, sun, and stars revolved around the earth, they were thought to make a beautiful, harmonious sound, the so-called "music of the spheres.") Africanus tells Scipio to keep in mind that although the body dies, the soul is immortal. Africanus explains that the souls of those who live selfishly are trapped on earth after the death of the body. The souls of those who have devoted themselves to serving their country fly upward more easily, because their connection to the lowly earth has already been weakened by their

higher purpose in life. Africanus then leaves, and Scipio awakens.

Cicero's analysis of Rome's problems. Writing in his own voice at the beginning of book 5, Cicero quotes from the *Annals*, an epic poem about Rome by the early Latin poet Ennius (239-169 BCE): "On ancient customs and old-fashioned men / the state of Rome stands firm" (*Republic*, 5.1). Cicero then goes on to ask rhetorically:

> What remains of those ancient customs on which he [Ennius] said the state of Rome stood firm? We see them so ruined by neglect that not only do they go unobserved, they are no longer known. And what shall I say of the men? It is the lack of such men that has led to the disappearance of those customs. . . . it is because of our own moral failings that we are left with the name of the Republic, having long since lost its substance.
>
> (*Republic*, 5.1-2)

In other words, Rome's problems came from a decline in morality as Romans strayed from the virtuous traditions of the past.

Cicero's solution was to call for a return to the traditions of selfless service that he thought distinguished Rome's glorious past from its corrupt present. Accordingly, as envisioned by Cicero, the ideal statesman is the man who "by the splendour of his mind and conduct" offers "himself as a mirror for his fellow-citizens" (*Republic*, 2.69). Such men had been common in Rome's past, Scipio argues in his summary of Roman history in book 2. Significantly, Scipio implies that the Roman constitution is best not because of how it organized the government, but because of the quality of the men who founded it. The flaw, Cicero clearly wishes his reader to conclude, was not with the system but with the leadership and the citizens.

Modern scholars have characterized Cicero's analysis of politics as personal rather than structural—that is, as having to do more with people than with institutions or ideology. They point to a number of factors of which Cicero could hardly have been unaware, but that he neglects to include in his picture of the Roman political scene. For example, he ignores the rising power of the business class, known as the *equites*. These merchants and manufacturers controlled a growing proportion of Rome's wealth but were largely excluded from politics, which remained the province of the aristocrats. Similarly, while he condemns Tiberius Gracchus for going against the constitution in pursuing his reforms, Cicero ignores instances in which his hero Scipio likewise advanced his own career by unconstitutional means.

Cicero was not alone in blaming individuals for problems that modern commentators would see as the failings of a system. His analysis actually represents the best thinking of his age, when political science was still in its infancy. At this stage, a politician either put himself first, in which case he was regarded as corrupt, or he put the state first, in which case he was viewed as noble. In early political theory, as in ancient politics, personal interest, not ideology, was the guiding force.

Sources and literary context. Cicero's main model for *The Republic* was the well-known dialogue of the same title by the Greek philosopher Plato (c. 429-347 BCE). In the lost part of his introduction, Cicero reportedly calls himself "a companion of Plato" (Cicero in Powell & Rudd, p. xvi, n. 20). Both dialogues focus on questions such as the ideal state and the nature of justice, and Cicero frequently quotes from Plato's *Republic* or alludes to Plato's ideas throughout his own *Republic*. Just as Plato followed his *Republic* with a companion dialogue called the *Laws*, so did Cicero compose his own *Laws* after completing his *Republic*.

Cicero drew not only on the work of Plato but also that of his student Aristotle (384-322 BCE). Plato and Aristotle were the first to articulate the picture of three forms of government, each with a corrupted version, which is so central to Cicero's analysis (see Plato's **Republic** and Aristotle's **Politics,** both also in *Classical Literature and Its Times*). By Cicero's day, this sixfold menu of political options had become a standard part of Greek political theory. Another important Platonic concept also makes up part of the dialogue's backdrop: the doctrine of forms that Plato developed in his own *Republic*. Plato believed that the material world of everyday existence was in fact unreal, and that true reality resided in invisible entities he called *ideai* or "ideas," often translated as "forms" in English. Every material object, from a person to a tree, represented a mere projection into our tangible world of a unique and immaterial "form." These intangible forms alone had truly real existence. Aristotle had rejected this notion. Although Cicero's characters allude to it in *The Republic*, they stop short of endorsing it, and it does not have the centrality in his *Republic* that it does in Plato's.

While Cicero does not agree with all of Plato's notions, he does embrace Plato's most influential idea of all—that of the immortal soul. This concept would find its way from Platonic philosophy into Christian theology starting about a century after Cicero's death, as would the idea of a heaven where the souls of the good dwell in eternal bliss. It is no accident that many of the fragments of Cicero's dialogue that survived as quotations did so because they were cited by Christian writers. Nor is it an accident that the manuscript was discovered in the library of the Vatican, power center of the Western Christian world.

The exception that proves the rule is "The Dream of Scipio," which was preserved not by a Christian writer, but by a fourth-century interpreter of Platonic philosophy, Macrobius. Along with Macrobius's commentary on it, "The Dream of Scipio" would become very popular during the highly religious Middle Ages, illustrating the common ground shared by Platonic and Christian beliefs. Cicero's dream is based loosely on a section known as the "Myth of Er" at the end of Plato's *Republic*, in which a soldier named Er comes back to life after being killed in battle and describes his experience of the afterlife.

Cicero relied on other sources as well, including the Greek historian Polybius, a contemporary and friend of Scipio's, who is mentioned several times in the dialogue. Polybius had described the Roman constitution and chronicled the expansion of Roman power into the Greek world.

Events in History at the Time the Dialogue Was Written

The fall of the Roman republic. The political problems that Cicero addresses in *The Republic*—as well as the ones he fails to address—were more apparent by Cicero's day than they had been almost 80 years earlier in Scipio's. The turbulence of the Gracchan era had resulted in assassination and violence, but not in civil war between two Roman armies. Tiberius's younger brother Gaius, a reformer as well, had been murdered in similar political violence in 123 BCE. After that, the Senate had managed to maintain its shaky grip on power for the moment, but by the 80s BCE, when Cicero was a young man, that grip was weakening. During that decade, a rivalry between two powerful generals, Marius (157-86 BCE) and Sulla (138-78 BCE), led to armed clashes between their supporters and also between their armies.

Marius, who came from Cicero's hometown of Arpinum, was a *novus homo* like Cicero, a successful general but a political outsider who was the first of his family to hold the rank of consul. Like the Gracchus brothers, he represented the interests of the people. After his death, his lieutenant, Cinna, carried on the war against Sulla's troops.

CICERO'S PLACE IN LITERARY HISTORY

Though Cicero played an important part in the political events of his day, his role in Western literary and intellectual history was more decisive. Cicero's writings fall into four main categories:

Speeches Cicero rewrote many of his courtroom speeches and political orations for publication; 58 of them survive in whole or in part (see *Cicero's Speeches*, also in *Classical Literature and Its Times*).

Rhetorical works In addition to practicing rhetoric (the art of oratory, or public speaking), Cicero also wrote instructional and theoretical books on the subject, based on Greek rhetorical theory, including *On Rhetoric* (55 BCE), *Brutus* (46 BCE), and *Orator* (46 BCE).

Philosophical works *The Republic* and its companion, *The Laws,* are Cicero's two major works of political philosophy. But he also wrote treatises on moral philosophy, favoring the ideas of the Stoics. Perhaps best known is *On the Offices* (44 BCE), in which he purports to explain Stoic philosophy to his son.

Letters Cicero's letters, dozens of which survive, comprise the single most important historical source for his life and times. They fall in two groups: "Letters to Friends," and "Letters to Atticus," Atticus being Cicero's lifelong friend Titus Pomponius Atticus.

Above all, Cicero organized Greek thought, conveying the ideas of the Greek philosophers, rhetoricians, and others in a form that was easily graspable for a Roman audience. His writings were the primary conduit through which Greek ideas passed to Rome, and as such they had a profound effect on the development of Roman and European civilization.

Meanwhile, Sulla, a Roman aristocrat, represented the interests of the aristocracy and the Senate. Sulla won the civil war and was appointed to the temporary office of dictator in 82 BCE. As a dictator, attempting to strengthen the Senate, Sulla murdered thousands of Marius's supporters throughout Italy. He retired from power in 79 BCE, leaving Rome with a new constitution designed to restore stability and Senatorial control.

Soon after Sulla's death the following year, the Senate gave Pompey (106-48 BCE), still only in his twenties, extraordinary power to crush another revolt by Marius's followers. However, Pompey then turned on his benefactors, forcing the Senate to abandon the Sullan constitution for a return to the status quo. During the 60s BCE, Pompey and his army won many victories over Rome's enemies abroad, making him Rome's most popular leader. Cicero allied himself with Pompey, possibly in the hope that Pompey would turn out to be an "ideal statesman" of the kind that Cicero would describe a few years later in *The Republic*.

If so, Cicero's hopes were in vain. It later became apparent that Pompey was motivated largely by self-interest and a thirst for power and recognition. So were the two other powerful aris-

tocrats with whom he allied himself in 60 BCE, Marcus Crassus (c. 112-53 BCE) and Julius Caesar (100-44 BCE). Together the three of them—Pompey, Crassus, and Caesar—formed the so-called First Triumvirate. Hostile to both, Cicero was bitterly disappointed by Pompey's decision. Indeed, he himself was invited to join the alliance but refused.

The First Triumvirate ended with Crassus's death in 53 BCE. At the time Caesar, perceived as a champion of the common people and an enemy of the Senate, was waging war in Rome's name in Gaul, to the north. He was a *popularis*. Pompey, a fair-weather champion of the aristocrats, resumed his opportunistic alliance with the now toothless Senate. The next year, in an unprecedented move aimed against Caesar, the Senate appointed Pompey as sole consul. Rome tensely awaited Caesar's return from his command in Gaul. It was around this time that Cicero completed *The Republic*, which some observers have seen as a final attempt to win Pompey over—to turn him into the selfless statesman that Cicero envisioned. Caesar returned and proved more than a match for Pompey and the Senate, defeating Pompey in battle in 48 BCE. Pompey fled to Egypt but was murdered there by one of his men, who hoped to curry favor with Caesar.

Decades of civil war still lay ahead for Rome. Having engineered his appointment as "dictator for life," Caesar was assassinated at the meeting place of the Senate (Pompey's Theater) in 44 BCE. Cicero, who applauded the assassins as saviors of the Republic, would himself die in the violence that followed. He delivered fiery speeches denouncing Caesar's lieutenant, Mark Antony, earning Antony's hatred. In 43 BCE Antony struck a deal with Caesar's adopted son and heir, Octavian, in which Octavian agreed to have Cicero assassinated.

Thereafter, the demise of the Republic became even more of a certainty. Civil war eventually resumed between Octavian and Antony, resulting in Antony's defeat in 31 BCE. Unopposed, Octavian emerged as Rome's first emperor, becoming known as Caesar Augustus.

Despite the years of war that followed the First Triumvirate, many historians look back to the alliance itself as signaling the fall of the Republic, because it marked the effective end of the Senate as Rome's main governing body. As Cicero himself may have suspected, his dialogue amounts to an epitaph for a dying political system.

Reception and impact. Cicero's *The Republic* was well received by the contemporary reading public, as a letter from his younger friend and student Marcus Rufus Caelius attests. "Your political books are doing splendidly with everyone," Caelius wrote in 51 BCE, shortly after Cicero began circulating the work (Caelius in Cicero, *Cicero: Select Letters,* p. 27). The dialogue continued to be widely read during the early Roman Empire.

As suggested above, the echoes of Plato in Cicero's dialogue made it popular among early Chris-

tian writers; their quotations from *The Republic* have provided many of the surviving fragments. These writers include Lactantius (c. 240-c. 320 CE) and St. Augustine (354-430 CE), whose works were themselves widely read in the Middle Ages.

Chief among the non-Christian authors who helped preserve interest in Cicero's *Republic* was the earlier mentioned Macrobius, whose popular commentary on "The Dream of Scipio" gave this passage a separate life of its own. Also the early-fourth-century literary compiler Nonius Marcellus reproduced excerpts of Cicero's writing that supplied many of the surviving fragments. Such second-hand access to the political thought of *The Republic* ensured that it remained influential, even before the manuscript containing a large portion of it came to light in 1820.

—Colin Wells

For More Information

Boardman, John, et al. *The Oxford History of the Classical World: The Roman World.* Oxford: Oxford University Press, 1986.

Cicero, Marcus Tullius. *Cicero: Select Letters.* Vol. 1. Ed. W. W. How. Oxford: Clarendon Press, 1925.

———. *The Republic and the Laws.* Trans. Niall Rudd. New York: Oxford University Press, 1998.

Crawford, Michael. *The Roman Republic.* Hassocks: Harvester Press, 1978.

Everitt, Anthony. *Cicero: The Life and Times of Rome's Greatest Politician.* New York: Random House, 2001.

Powell, Jonathan, and Niall Rudd. "Introduction." In *The Republic and the Laws,* by Cicero. Oxford: Oxford University Press, 2001.

Rawson, Elizabeth. *Cicero.* London: Allen Lane, 1975.

Republic

by
Plato

Plato was born in Athens c. 429 BCE to a wealthy and aristocratic family. Little is known about his youth. Diogenes Laertius, in his *Lives of Eminent Philosophers*, reports that at the age of 20, when Plato met Socrates, Plato was an aspiring tragedian. After conversing with Socrates, he burned his tragedies and devoted himself to philosophy. Ten years later, in 399 BCE, the philosophical tutelage was cut short when Socrates was tried, convicted, and executed on charges of impiety and corrupting the youth. But Socrates' influence over Plato endured. When he began to write philosophical dialogues, something Socrates never undertook, Plato made his teacher the protagonist of nearly all of them. The Platonic corpus comprises 35 such dialogues and 13 letters. Of the dialogues, 14 are regarded as spurious works, as not really by Plato. Though all the letters are penned as though by Plato, there is no scholarly agreement as to their authorship. In Athens c. 387 BCE, Plato founded a philosophical school, the Academy, which stands as the ancient precursor to the modern university. Aspiring young philosophers, including Aristotle, were enrolled at the Academy, which would remain in existence long after Plato's death in 347. In his lifetime, Plato exhibited a continuing interest in politics; his two longest dialogues, the *Republic* and the *Laws*, though quite different in approach, deal with the same fundamental problems of politics. By his own admission, he himself had youthful political ambitions. Plato's *Seventh Letter* describes these ambitions as being derailed by two momentous experiences: the cruel and oppressive rule of the oligarchy

---

THE LITERARY WORK

A philosophical dialogue set in the Piraeus, the port of Athens, Greece, c. 411 BCE; written in Greek sometime between 388 and 360 BCE.

SYNOPSIS

Socrates and the group with which he converses construct a "city in speech" in order to discover the meaning and value of justice.

---

known as the Thirty Tyrants, many of whom were his friends and relatives; and the execution of Socrates by the restored democracy (for Plato's portrayal of this trial, see his **Apology,** also in *Classical Literature and Its Times*). Plato's seventh letter also describes his failed attempt to instruct Dionysius II of Syracuse, the tyrant of Sicily. Contained in Plato's *Republic* is a long meditation on the possibility of an ideal city and the seemingly insurmountable obstacles to its achievement. One can see in this work a reflection of the failures in government that Plato witnessed in Athens as a youth, as well as his own failed attempt to influence the political situation in Syracuse as a mature adult.

Events in History at the Time the Dialogue Takes Place

The regime of the Four Hundred. Though when the *Republic* is set cannot be firmly established, most scholars agree that the conversation takes place c. 411 BCE (judging by the age of the participants, all of whom were actual historical figures). In that year, circumstances were bleak. Financially strapped and militarily weakened, the Athenians made a radical change to their regime. The democratic Assembly voted the democracy out of existence and set in motion a chain of events which led ultimately to the institution of an oligarchic regime, consisting of 400 rulers. In order to understand Athens's dire military and financial straits in 411, one must step back and reflect upon the emergence of the Athenian Empire and the set of decisions that threatened its existence.

The Persians had twice attempted to invade mainland Greece and both times been defeated by an alliance of Greek city-states. As the greatest military power in Greece at the time, the Spartans led the pan-Hellenic (pan-Greek) coalition. But the Athenians distinguished themselves in battle: first by nearly single-handedly defeating a much larger land army of Persians at Marathon in 490 BCE and second by spearheading an incredible Greek naval victory at Salamis ten years later in 480 BCE. On the strength of these accomplishments, and dissatisfaction with the Spartan leadership, Athens took the helm of a second alliance of Greek city-states, the Delian League, a naval coalition made up mostly of city-states on the Greek islands and on the coast of Asia Minor. Members assembled for meetings on the island of Delos, which housed the league's treasury.

The members of the Delian League supplied ships or made a monetary contribution for their joint military expeditions against Persia. The growth of the Delian League into an empire—the Athenian Empire, to be exact—was gradual but, after the Athenians moved the treasury to the acropolis in Athens (about 454 BCE) and forced its allies to pay a yearly tribute to Athens, its supremacy was clear.

It was only a matter of time before Athens's growing sphere of influence would come into conflict with that of Sparta. In **The Peloponnesian War,** his account of the conflict between Athens and Sparta, the historian Thucydides holds that "the growth of the power of Athens and the alarm which this inspired in Sparta made the war inevitable" (**The Peloponnesian War**, 1.23; also in *Classical Literature and Its Times*). The war (431-404 BCE) stood at a virtual stalemate until Athens made a strategic blunder by attempting an ambitious expansion of its empire during a temporary truce in 415 BCE. Athens decided to send a vast contingent of ships and land forces to gain dominion in Sicily by challenging the domination of Syracuse there. Massive amounts of equipment and provisions were required. But more remarkable than the size of the expedition was how much wealth it required to finance it. When the Athenian forces met with more resistance from the enemy than expected, they dispatched even more money and considerable reinforcements. Despite the magnitude of the Athenian force, the Syracusan military, with Spartan assistance, crushed the invading Athenians both on land and at sea. Athens lost almost all of its entire invading force—in the end, the Sicilian expedition turned out to be a complete disaster for Athens.

In 411 BCE, Athens, whose democratic Assembly had chosen to mount such a disastrous expedition, was persuaded to change its constitution. The Athenians considered their situation. Though now at a significant disadvantage, they were determined to continue the Peloponnesian War against Sparta and to maintain their empire in the Aegean Sea. According to Thucydides, the exiled Athenian general Alcibiades, who was a well-known associate of Socrates and who had defected to the Spartan side during the war, claimed to have a deal in place with the Persian ambassador: in exchange for much-needed financial assistance from the Persians and a military alliance with them, the Athenians would have to recall Alcibiades and change their constitution to an oligarchy. While Aristotle, in his *Constitution of Athens* (29), and Thucydides, in *The Peloponnesian War* (8.54), agree that the Athenian Assembly, though at first resistant, was finally persuaded to change the democratic constitution, they differ significantly in their portrayals of this dramatic decision. While Aristotle makes the process seem like a peaceful constitutional convention wherein a series of reforms were proposed and adopted, Thucydides showcases the attempt of the upper classes, those who would most benefit from an oligarchy, to intimidate and in some cases violently suppress any opposition to the change and to ensure that the oligarchy would be as radical as possible. Given this discrepancy, scholars differ on how to reconstruct accurately the chain of events that led to the regime of the Four Hundred. What is certain is that the initial capitulation of the democratic Assembly led to power being vested in a group of 400, thereby instituting an oligarchy in place of the democracy—the regime of the Four Hundred. This body would rule without the approval of the people; the Assembly was never summoned while

THE THIRTY TYRANTS

In 404 BCE, Athens finally lost the Peloponnesian War. The Spartan army occupied Athens, tore down its walls and instituted an oligarchic regime composed of thirty Athenian aristocrats, called "The Thirty"; its leader was Critias, an uncle of Plato and a one-time follower of Socrates. The regime became known as the "Thirty Tyrants" because of its cruel, oppressive rule and brutally violent tactics. The Thirty confiscated money and property as they saw fit and exiled or murdered many Athenian citizens, especially, but not exclusively, those who were suspected of being democratic sympathizers. One of their most notorious exploits was the forcible removal and mass execution of close to 300 men of the town of Eleusis so the Thirty would have a base of operations against the growing democratic resistance (Xenophon, *Hellenica*, 2.4). That resistance, led by Thrasybulus, had its own base in the Piraeus, the chief port of Athens, where the *Republic* is set. Ultimately the resistance succeeded and, in 403 BCE, reinstated the democracy. The restored democracy declared general amnesty for those who supported the Thirty, but not for the Thirty themselves or for those who committed murder on their behalf. Two victims of the tyrants were the brothers Polemarchus and Lysias, in whose house the *Republic* takes place. Both brothers had their property confiscated and were targeted for further persecution. While Lysias managed to escape, the Thirty took Polemarchus into custody and executed him. In the *Republic*, Lysias gives a vivid account of Polemarchus's arrest in a prosecution speech against Eratosthenes, the tyrant who imprisoned his brother.

it was in power. The soldiers in the Athenian fleet, who were patrolling the Aegean at the time and thus could not have attended the Assembly in order to vote against the constitutional change, refused to acknowledge the new government. Persian assistance never came and the oligarchs quickly made themselves unpopular and were deposed. After another set of Assemblies, a new, more inclusive oligarchy, consisting of 5,000 members, was instituted in place of the Four Hundred. Though Thucydides praises this regime as the best he had ever seen in Athens (*The Peloponnesian War*, 8.97), we know very little about it and it lasted a very short while. The democracy was restored after only a few months. It is just prior to the oligarchic revolution of 411, when democratic Athens is in the midst of a real-life debate about the best form of government, that Plato sets his *Republic*, a dialogue about the best constitution.

The Dialogue in Focus

Plot summary. In the *Republic*, Socrates discusses the meaning of justice with a group of men in the Piraeus: Glaucon and Adeimantus, who were Plato's brothers; Polemarchus and

Lysias, two wealthy resident aliens in whose home the dialogue takes place; and the sophist Thrasymachus, who in 411 had published a political pamphlet criticizing the existing democracy. Just as Socrates and Polemarchus are agreeing that justice implies that it is always wrong to harm another, Thrasymachus bursts into the conversation "like a wild beast" (Plato, *The Republic*, 336b). He introduces his propositions that "justice" is the advantage of the stronger and that injustice is more advantageous than justice. According to this logic, to be just is to follow the laws, which are set down by the powerful ruling class for their own advantage. The laws thus force others to act on behalf of the ruling class. It follows that injustice lies in freedom from the law and the pursuit of one's own advantage. The unjust man is better off because, shaking off the laws, he pursues his own interests, not those of others, and so is better off than those who follow the rules. Socrates attempts to refute these claims on the grounds that a true ruler will be unselfish and always care for his subjects; he argues that not only is justice itself superior to injustice with respect to virtue and wisdom, justice provides the only path to real happiness. Thrasymachus concedes, though unwillingly,

Socrates, Plato's speaker. © Gianni Dagli Orti/Corbis. Reproduced by permission.

but Socrates himself casts the conclusion into doubt by lamenting the fact that they had failed to define justice adequately.

In book 2, Glaucon and Adeimantus challenge Socrates to come up with better arguments that being just is naturally (regardless of consequences) more advantageous than being unjust. Glaucon sets up two ideals—a thoroughly just man who has the worst reputation for injustice and is despised by all who know him; and a thoroughly corrupt and unjust man who has the greatest reputation for justice and is honored by the city for it. Socrates' task is to prove that the just man in this case is still better off than the unjust man. In order to accomplish the task, which will take up the rest of the *Republic*, Socrates proposes an analogy between the just city and the just soul of an individual and suggests that they look for justice in the city, where it will be easier to see, so they may, by analogy, understand it in the individual soul (*Republic*, 368d).

In conceiving the ideal city, Socrates first takes up the education of the guardian, or soldier, class. In order to make guardians harsh to their enemies but gentle to their fellow citizens, Socrates proposes a balanced educational program of music and gymnastics. The gymnastics will train the body, making the guardians tough and hard; they will be impervious to harsh external conditions and to the lure of pleasure. The

musical education, which encompasses all of the fine arts (including poetry and its stories), will train the soul, preparing the guardians for rational argument and providing them with models of good moral conduct. In order to prepare the guardians for argument, all art forms will be strictly regulated so that they will only be exposed to art that exhibits, and thus encourages, harmony and order. The stories that are told to the guardians, especially those of Homer, will be strictly censored so that they never listen to any that encourage bad behavior by portraying any unjust actions of gods or heroes, who ought to be moral exemplars. Since a great deal of Greek poetry did in fact contain portrayals of gods and heroes engaging in unjust activities, Socrates' criteria for acceptable poetry will banish large swaths of the existing canon. The program of censorship amounts to a direct challenge to the independent authority of poets as moral educators. All active poets will be subject to strict government oversight so their poetry serves the goal of properly educating the guardians. Thus educated, the guardians will acquire the ideal mixture of gentleness and harshness for developing harmonious, well-ordered souls.

The finest of the guardians will comprise the ruling class. In order to determine who amongst the guardians is best suited to rule, they will be subjected to a series of tests—those who unwaveringly look to the benefit of the city even in the most adverse conditions will prove themselves worthy of ruling. To ensure the loyalty of the rulers and the citizenry as a whole, Socrates contrives a "noble lie" (*Republic*, 414c). The citizens will be told that they are all born from the earth, their mother, and so constitute a single family. Three classes of citizens are to be divided according to the metal mixed in their soul: gold for the rulers, silver for the soldiers, and bronze or iron for the farmers and craftsmen. The guardians will live a communal life, eating together in a mess hall "like soldiers in a camp"; they will possess no money, private property, or individual families (*Republic*, 416e).

In book 4, Socrates, having established the city in speech, investigates it to see where its virtues lie. Its wisdom consists in the knowledge of the rulers; its courage, in the spiritedness of the soldier class; its moderation, in the agreement of the whole city as to who should rule. Its justice resides in each class "doing its own work" or "minding its own business" (*Republic*, 433a). Drawing an analogy to the soul, the three classes of the city—rulers, soldiers and craftsmen—correspond to the rational, spirited, and desiring parts of the soul ("the spirited part" being the portion reserved for anger, honor, pride, and courage). Four virtues have been linked to the city—wisdom, courage, moderation, and justice. These four virtues likewise match up with the virtues of the soul. Like justice in the city, justice in the soul consists in each part of the soul minding its own business. Part of the business of the rational part, since it has knowledge, is to rule and control the spirited and desiring parts.

At the beginning of book 5, when Socrates is about to discuss four deficient types of regime and the souls that correspond to them, Polemarchus and Adeimantus challenge Socrates to defend certain aspects of his ideal city. He must fend off arguments against three radical proposals that are fundamental to his city: (1) that men and women are equal; (2) that the individual family unit be abolished and replaced by an enlarged sense of family including all citizens; (3) that philosophers should rule as kings. Socrates first argues that women and men must be treated as equals. Since they are different only with respect to physical strength and reproduction, women are equally capable of ruling and must be afforded the exact same education as men. Socrates defends the abolition of the family unit by arguing that, when particular familial bonds are eliminated and one cares for every other citizen equally, public and private interests will become identical. Since no one will be able to recognize his or her own child, the scope of paternal and maternal relationships will be expanded to include a whole generation of offspring rather than any individual member of it. Further, all children born in any given generation will consider each other siblings. The rulers, by virtue of their ability to calculate the mysterious "nuptial number," the mathematical basis of eugenics, or selective breeding for the benefit of the human race, will regulate the sexual relationships between men and women to produce the best children. After they have passed the age of procreation, men and women will be permitted to have sex with whomever they choose, excepting those whom they consider children.

Socrates claims that philosophers must rule the city as kings if this ideal city is ever to be approximated in reality. In order to rule perfectly, the philosopher must undertake the "greatest study" and come to know "the idea of the good," without which nothing else can be truly useful or beneficial (*Republic*, 505a). Socrates refuses to say what the idea of the good is, since he does not himself know, but he explains what the good *is*

like using three images: the sun, the divided line, and the allegory of the cave. First, just as the sun is responsible for our vision and the visibility of what is seen, the good is responsible for our knowledge and the intelligibility (or knowability) of what is known. Second, the divided line provides an account of what exists: Socrates draws a basic division between what is visible and what is intelligible. He then subdivides the visible into physical images and objects; the intelligible, into mathematical objects and forms. The line is ordered hierarchically: forms are most real on the divided line; physical images are least real. In book 7, Socrates' allegory of the cave illustrates the education necessary for the rulers to achieve knowledge of the idea of the good. Socrates portrays education as a liberation of the soul from slavery to images and as a turning of the soul towards the good. In the allegory, humans sit in the cave, chained to their seats and staring at a screen, onto which images are projected. The projected images are their whole world. When one of the prisoners is released, that person sees that what he or she has been taking for reality is actually only a set of projections made by other people. Having detected the source and nature of the images in the cave, the person is led up a harsh path out of the cave into the light. Once in the real world, the person can perceive the true reality and may after a long time look at the sun (the source of the real beings of the world, the forms and their intelligibility by people). After doing so, the person feels compelled to return to the cave to liberate others. Outside the cave, one is in the intelligible realm, the realm of knowable forms; the sun stands for the idea of the good, which provides both being and intelligibility to the forms. One can come to know the good: "in the knowable the last thing to be seen, and that with considerable effort, is the idea of the good; but once seen, it must be concluded that this is in fact the cause of all that is right and fair in everything . . . it [has] provided truth and intelligence" (*Republic,* 517b-c).

The extensive study that will accomplish this turning of the soul to knowledge of the good, Socrates claims, will consist of the following disciplines: philosophical arithmetic, plane geometry, solid geometry, astronomy, harmonics, and finally dialectic (the search by study and argumentation for the most real beings, the forms). The students who have made it this far—they are by now about 50 years old—will look to the good itself and employ it in order to rule the city justly.

In books 8 and 9, Socrates resumes the discussion of deficient regimes and souls. He takes them

THE MYTH OF ER

In the myth of Er, Socrates recounts the tale of a man named Er, who died in battle and 12 days later came back to life. Having observed what happens to souls in the afterlife, he recounts the story. After death, souls come to a demonic place with four holes, two in the earth and two in the heavens. A judge passes judgment on the soul, sending the unjust down under the earth to suffer tenfold for the suffering they caused while alive and sending the just up into heaven to enjoy tenfold rewards for good deeds done in life. After a thousand years of reward or punishment, all souls return to the demonic place to choose their next life (except for the worst tyrants and criminals who suffer eternally in the underworld). Each soul receives a numbered lot and, in order of the drawing, chooses its next life from among the lives available. The souls coming from heaven, forgetting what got them into heaven, tend to choose the life of a tyrant or other powerful sort, ensuring that next time they die, they will be sent down under the earth. Conversely, the souls coming up from under the earth, mindful of the mistakes of the earlier life, tend to choose more carefully and wind up with more just lives so that after death they will find themselves in the heavenly place. Thus, most souls are caught in an endless reincarnation cycle of virtuous and vicious lives. The myth emphasizes the importance of the ability to distinguish between the good life and the bad so that one will be able to recognize and choose a just life both while alive and later in the demonic place. Only philosophical inquiry, with its sustained reflection on the good life, will provide the human soul with the intellectual resources to make the right decision consistently and thus escape the cycle of virtue and vice that unphilosophical souls must endure. Included in Plato's myth are figures from the epics of Homer. Odysseus, stripped of his concern for honor, is Plato's hero: "By chance Odysseus' soul had drawn the last lot of all and went to choose; from memory of its former labors it had recovered from love of honor; it went around for a long time looking for the life of a private man who minds his own business; and with effort it found one lying somewhere neglected by the others" (*Republic*, 620c). Odysseus rejects the ethos of honor and fame characteristic of Homer's world and chooses instead a private life of quiet reflection, nurturing through philosophy his soul and thus minding his most important business.

up in the order of degeneration from the best regime. The timocratic state—governed on principles of honor and military glory—will love victory most of all, and the timocratic man will be dominated by the spirited part of his soul. The oligarchic regime will be ruled by the rich, and the oligarchic man will be ruled by the desiring part of his soul, though, being stingy, he will only seek to satisfy his necessary desires. The democratic regime is the most diverse and superficially attractive; a democracy makes everyone equal by granting freedom to all. In truth, the democratic man is also ruled by his desires. But he treats all desires, both necessary and unnecessary, as equally important; he looks, says the dialogue, to satisfy whichever one happens to strike him. A tyranny is ruled by the desires of one autocratic man; it is warlike and oppressive, violent both to its neighbors and its own citizens. The tyrannical man is ruled by the sadistic, lustful, and unlawful desires that most people encounter only in dreams. Just as the tyrannical regime enslaves and dishonors its best citizens— the philosophers who insist on thinking for themselves—so too the tyrannical man enslaves and dishonors the best part of his soul—his reason. The tyrant, the most unjust man, has the most disharmonious soul possible and is the most unhappy. At this point, Glaucon and Adeimantus are satisfied that Socrates has answered the objections they raised at the start of book 2. Glaucon observes at the end of book 9 that in order to become and remain harmonious in soul, the just man will not be politically engaged:

> "[The just man] won't be willing to mind the political things."
>
> "Yes, by the dog," [Socrates] said, "he will in his own city, very much so. However, perhaps he won't in his fatherland unless some divine chance coincidentally comes to pass."
>
> "I understand," [Glaucon] said. "You mean he will in the city whose foundation we have now gone through, the one that has its place in speeches, since I don't suppose it exists anywhere on earth."
>
> "But in heaven," [Socrates] said, "perhaps, a pattern is laid up for the man who wants to see and found a city within himself on the basis of what he sees. It doesn't make any difference whether it is or will be somewhere. For he would mind the things of this city alone, and of no other"
>
> (*Republic*, 592a-b)

Thus, the just man, instead of being a politically active citizen in his actual city, will fix his gaze on the ideal city in order to found a just regime in his soul.

In book 10, Socrates revises his earlier account of poetry in the ideal city. Poetry as a whole is banished on the grounds that it is mimetic, or imitative. Imitation, Socrates argues, contains no knowledge since it creates superficial images of a more complex preexisting reality. Imitation also harms the soul by gratifying, and thus fortifying, the part that desires. To finish off the argument, Socrates turns to the consequences of justice and argues that justice will not go unnoticed by one's fellow citizens nor unrewarded by the gods in this life. He then recounts the "Myth of Er" to show that justice is also advantageous in the afterlife because, in death, we are called to account for our actions in life.

The trial of Socrates. In 399 BCE, at the age of 70, Socrates stood trial for impiety and corrupting the youth. Plato dramatized this event in an earlier dialogue—the *Apology* (also in *Classical Literature and Its Times*). The work is called an *apology* because *apologia*, in Greek, refers to a legal defense speech; Socrates certainly does not apologize for anything. We have no way of knowing how accurately Plato was in his rendition of Socrates' speech, an important consideration to keep in mind, especially since another major writer, Xenophon, provides a markedly different account of the trial.

In Plato's version, Socrates mounts an elaborate defense not just of himself but of his philosophical

mission in life. Socrates relays how a friend consulted the oracle at Delphi to find out if there was anyone wiser than Socrates. When the oracle replied that no one was wiser, Socrates, realizing he himself was not wise, set out to discover the hidden meaning of the oracle's words. He went around interrogating those who claimed to be wise, only to discover that many of them did not possess wisdom after all. Socrates reasoned that the oracle must mean that "human wisdom is worth little or nothing" but that his *Socratic wisdom*, the knowledge that he was ignorant, was superior to misguidedly believing oneself to be wise. Socrates argues that by disabusing the Athenians of their pretensions to wisdom, he was performing an immensely valuable service. He was alerting them to the fact that they were fundamentally ignorant about the most important thing—what kind of life they should lead. Because they all falsely believed that they already knew the answer, they neither investigated nor paid attention to the matter. They neglected the attempt to educate themselves through philosophical inquiry. This neglect, Socrates argues, amounts to a failure to take care of their most important possession, their souls; it ignores a crucial implication of Socratic wisdom, that the "unexamined life is not worth living" (Plato, *Apology*, 38a). The jury did not agree. By a vote of 280 to 220, they convicted Socrates and, after he antagonized them by proposing free state-sponsored meals for himself as his "punishment," they sentenced him to death by an even wider margin. It was a misled jury, say some scholars, who condemned Socrates because of his relationships with two unsavory Athenians of the day: a traitor to the city (Alcibiades) and the leader of the Thirty Tyrants (Critias). In any case, in the *Republic*, Socrates offers a second, more elaborate defense of philosophy and the role of the philosopher in the city. Every political community shuns the philosopher as either useless or vicious. They are "useless"—not part of the horde clamoring for political power, philosophers are left unused by the establishment. There is no dearth of examples of Athens's enmity towards philosophers: Anaxagoras was exiled on charges of impiety; Socrates was executed; and Aristotle fled Athens a year before his death to escape being prosecuted for impiety. Socrates also argues that those who have great natures suited to philosophical inquiry become vicious when they abandon their philosophical training too soon and attempt to achieve political power. This explanation exonerates Socrates for the crimes of his one-time associates Alcibiades and Critias and accounts for why they became such notorious figures despite being the philosophical companions of Socrates. Philosophy and politics will be at odds, *The Republic* implies, until the "divine chance coincidentally comes to pass" and they converge in the ideal city (*Republic*, 592a).

Women and the education of youth in Athens. In the *Republic* Socrates proposes that women and men are intellectual equals and that, because of this, they should be treated as equals with respect to ruling the city. To understand how radical and shocking this proposal was, one must know the legal and social status of women in fifth-century Athens.

At no time in her life did an Athenian woman fail to have a protective male guardian, or *kyrios*. Her father played this role until she was married, at which point her husband assumed responsibility for her. If her husband chose to divorce her or if he died, her guardianship reverted back to her father and, if possible, a new husband was found. There were complex rules governing who was to become her guardian in case her father was dead but, in general, her closest living male relative, including her son if she had one, would take over her protection.

Athenian women did not possess functional citizenship rights: they could not attend or vote in the Assembly, or *ekklēsia;* they could not hold any political office or administrative position in government. Women were also not permitted to serve on juries. Not surprisingly, women possessed a diminished legal status as well. They could not prosecute cases on their own behalf, nor could they mount their own defense when prosecuted. Except in rare cases, women did not testify in court. Their names were not even mentioned; they were rather identified by their relationship to the legally relevant males—wife of, sister of, or daughter of. A woman's testimony, if it was required, could be delivered by her guardian on her behalf; oaths sworn by women at holy shrines were also admissible as evidence. In sum, male guardians stood up for women when it came to political or legal matters in ancient Athens.

Athenian women did play a crucial role in the transaction of wealth in the city, but they had little or no control over this role. In marrying off his daughter, an Athenian citizen was expected to send with her person a considerable dowry. This dowry would become the property of her husband and guardian although the woman retained a claim to it in case he divorced her, at

which point, it would revert back to her father. In cases where a father left no direct male descendants, his daughter inherited the estate but her control over it was nominal. A woman who thus became an heiress could be claimed in marriage by her father's closest male relative even if both of them were already married. Any property, including inherited property, associated with an Athenian woman would become the property of her guardian, which at least partly explains why the transfer of guardianship was so strictly regulated. After Pericles passed a law restricting citizenship to those with Athenian heritage on both their mother and father's side (451 BCE), having an Athenian wife became necessary for the bearing of legitimate heirs.

An Athenian woman's domain of authority and influence was the household, or *oikos*, the fundamental social unit of the city. Women were expected to manage the household slaves and to care for the children. Women also played key roles in events associated with family. At funerals, for example, women were the primary caretakers of the corpse.

Part of caring for the children was making sure they were properly educated. Customarily elementary instruction of boys was conducted in private tuition-based schools; girls for the most part were educated at home. The cost of education was fairly inexpensive, so a rudimentary level of schooling was widespread; however, since schooling was not mandatory, basic education was limited to those who were willing to educate their children and could afford to do so.

Primary school consisted of three programs of study: letters, music, and physical education. These were taught concurrently beginning sometime between the ages of five and seven. Physical education included both fitness training and coaching in the techniques of the various sports (in javelin throwing, discus throwing, wrestling, etc.). In their music instruction, students learned to play the lyre and sing the poetry of renowned lyric poets. The study of letters encompassed instruction in reading and arithmetic, with a concentration on the reading and memorization of poetry, especially that of Homer. In fifth-century Athens, poetic education was intended "as the basis of moral training, as providing examples of noble conduct to be emulated" (Beck, p. 117). The poets themselves were considered educators: in the *Republic*, Socrates claims that many people praise Homer as the poet who "educated Greece" (*Republic*, 606e).

Higher education was available in professional disciplines (like medicine), in purely intellectual pursuits (philosophy, mathematics, and science), and in rhetoric, which provided training for speaking persuasively in the law-courts and in the Assembly. The sophists were a group of traveling educators who charged high fees for courses in rhetoric and public speaking—they tended to train students intent on achieving political influence. In democratic Athens, the sophists had many clients since the ability to persuade your fellow citizens in public policy was tantamount to achieving political power. Plato's portrayal of the sophists in several of his dialogues, including his depiction of Thrasymachus in the *Republic*, is an attempt to refute the self-serving ethics they promoted through their style of teaching rhetoric. In his view, their teachings promoted ethical relativism, the idea that there is no right or wrong except by convention or agreement. What's good or right in a given culture or time period, according to this view, is so only because that is what the culture considers good or right. There is no such thing as independent moral truth, only moral conventions. For Plato, ethical relativism allows a man to act as he pleases in an amoral world, a world without any true right or wrong.

Sources and literary context. After Socrates was executed in 399 BCE, several of his followers began writing literature commemorating Socrates' life. This phenomenon was widespread enough for Aristotle, in the *Poetics*, to treat Socratic literature, *Sokratikoi logoi*, as an established literary genre. But only the Socratic literature of Plato and Xenophon still exists. The genre itself occupied a space between history and fiction, a precursor, one might argue, to contemporary historical fiction. It featured characters who were based on real historical figures, but the conversations they had were fictional. Casting Socrates in the role of the hero, the conversations typically portrayed him and a few companions discussing matters of ethical and philosophical import. How close they are to what Socrates really believed remains a matter of vigorous debate. The members of the Socratic circle were not the first to dramatize the figure of Socrates; the comic dramatist Aristophanes satirized Socrates by portraying him as a charlatan and the consummate sophist in his **Clouds** (also in *Classical Literature and Its Times*).

Scholars have for a long time noticed that the revolutionary social proposals of Plato's *Republic* bear remarkable similarities to those found in Aristophanes' *Assemblywomen*. In that comedy,

Plato conversing with a student. © Bettmann/Corbis. Reproduced by permission.

the Athenian women, disguised as men, enter the Assembly and vote to hand over all political power exclusively to the women. Praxagora, the leader of this group, institutes a monumental (and fanciful) governmental change: private property is to be held in common, all will eat their meals together, and the family unit will be abolished. As in the *Republic*, the parent-child relationship will be expanded to encompass whole generations, and all will live as if in "a single household" (Aristophanes, *Assemblywomen* in *Comoediae*, line 674; trans. F. Trivigno). The similarities are too extraordinary to assign to chance though scholars have not come to an agreement about the relationship between the two texts. Most agree that Plato's *Republic* probably did not predate Aristophanes' *Assemblywomen* and so rule out the possibility that Aristophanes is parodying Plato. Scholars, perhaps uncomfortable with the idea that something so serious and philosophically interesting could have had its origin in comedy, have been likewise reluctant to accept that Plato took up these proposals from Aristophanes. However, since in book 2 of his **Politics** (also in *Classical Literature and Its Times*), Aristotle asserts that Plato was the first to take

THE DIALOGUE FORM

Plato, unlike most other philosophers, dramatized his philosophical vision rather than divulging it in a treatise. Plato's own absence from the dialogues presents the reader with a set of interpretive problems unparalleled in the discourse of other philosophers. Why did Plato write dialogues? How does one discover the philosophical meaning of a dialogue? And even if the meaning can be discovered, how does one relate the dialogues to each other? The easiest solution would be to equate the views expressed by Socrates with the philosophical thought of Plato, but this solution poses several problems. It renders the dramatic context empty and meaningless, which suggests that Plato wasted his dramatic gifts gussying up the dialogues with dramatic details when he could have just as easily written a straightforward treatise. This solution also fails to address the fact that across several dialogues, Socrates makes incompatible, even contradictory, claims. Would Plato himself hold such contradictory attitudes? Another approach is to hold that the dramatic context and the views of characters in a dialogue comprise a meaningful whole. The dramatic presentation discourages passive reliance on authority for received wisdom and encourages an active intellectual role for readers, who are prompted to engage in their own philosophical pursuit. Scholars who favor this position, however, disagree over what the philosophical meaning of a dialogue is and even whether any philosophical content is intended at all. Others say that Plato held a unified view throughout his career and that the different dialogues represent different teaching strategies for advancing the same philosophical content. Still others argue that Plato's views changed over time, as shown by the various positions endorsed by different dialogues. Lastly, some interpreters argue that Plato has no systematic philosophy at all and that the dialogue form shows that he just wanted to provoke his readers into asking philosophical questions. In the *Republic,* he would be provoking them into focusing on such major philosophical issues as the nature of justice, the structure of the soul (or mind), the conditions for the possibility of knowledge, and the role of art in society.

these radical proposals seriously, probably Plato made serious what Aristophanes conceived as hilariously funny.

Events in History at the Time the Dialogue Was Written

The Athenian democracy. As noted, an oligarchy ruled Athens the year that the *Republic* takes place. The oligarchy interrupted several decades of rule by democracy, which was the system in effect when Plato wrote his *Republic*. The English word, *democracy*, comes from the Greek, *dēmokratia*, which literally means the rule (*kratos*) of the people (*dēmos*). Like modern democracy, the Athenian democracy valued liberty, equality, freedom of speech, and citizen participation. Pericles, in describing the Athenian character,

observed, "We do not say that a man who takes no interest in politics is a man who minds his own business; we say that he has no business at all" (Pericles in Thucydides, 2.40). Apart from these similarities, however, Athenian democracy differs in several fundamental ways from the modern version. While the latter depends on the election of representatives who, for a term of office, represent the political interests of their constituency, in Athens, any citizen over 20 could speak and vote in the Assembly (*ekklēsia*), the deliberative body that made nearly all of the important political decisions. The number of times the Assembly met increased gradually from 10 days a year in the early fifth century to 40 days a year in the fourth century. Any one of the 30,000-60,000 Athenian citizens could enter the Assembly on any day it met.

The daily administration of government affairs required about 1,200 magistrates, or public officials. A few positions were elected by the Assembly from the pool of citizens who possessed the relevant expertise (e.g., army generals). "The vast majority of Athenian magistrates were selected by lot; and, since almost all of them held offices that only lasted a year and could not be held by the same person again, the people had to choose 1100 persons in that manner every year" (Hansen, p. 230). Only those citizens over 30 who presented themselves for allotment were eligible, but the expectation was that every male citizen of Athens can and ought to engage in the affairs of the state.

The agenda of the Assembly was set by a committee of magistrates known as the Council of Five Hundred (*Boulē*). Any citizen, however, could offer an amendment or modification to a proposal. Debate in the Assembly entailed any number of participants making speeches for or against the proposal, some prepared, some extemporaneous. Though everyone had the right to speak, a small group of professionally trained orators generally dominated the discussion and greatly influenced decisions. In the fifth century, since the responsibilities of the Assembly were so wide-ranging, a citizen trained in persuasive argument could exert considerable influence over the Assembly. In the fourth century, after the fall of the Thirty, the restored democracy curtailed the Assembly's ability to pass laws though it retained full authority in foreign policy to pass decrees, elect generals, or declare war.

The Athenian jury system selected 6,000 jurors yearly from citizens who applied for service and were older than 30. The number of jurors at a trial was variable, but could amount to as many as 501 or more. In the fourth century, jurors might be selected to serve as legislators as well. To enact a new law, the Assembly would call for a board of 1,000 legislators, who were chosen by lot from the 6,000 jurors, to decide if the proposed amendment should become law.

There was no district attorney to represent the interests of the state and no defense lawyer to represent an individual's rights; in both civil and criminal proceedings, individual citizens served as prosecutors, and defendants had to defend themselves. In the courts, as in the Assembly, rhetorical virtuosity was highly prized. Any citizen could hire a speechwriter (Lysias, for example) to prepare an eloquent and persuasive speech, but the litigant had to deliver it himself. According to standard procedure, the prosecution and then the defense presented their evidence, interviewed their witnesses, and made their case. The jury voted without any deliberation, which, given the size of the juries, would have been next to impossible. No standard appeal process existed except in the rarest of cases. If a defendant was found guilty and no penalty was prescribed, both parties proposed a penalty, defended it, and then waited for the jurors to vote on the penalty.

The tyranny in Syracuse. It is unclear when Plato composed the *Republic*. The range of conjectures falls between the dates of Plato's first and last visits to Syracuse (388 BCE and 360 BCE). The relationship between the writing and these visits is no mere coincidence: scholars have long tried to firmly establish a relationship between the ideal city articulated in the *Republic* and the account Plato gives of his trips to Syracuse in his letters. Diogenes Laertius and Plutarch provide independent confirmation that Plato made three visits to Syracuse and that, in each case, his attempts to influence the Syracusan tyrant were spectacular public failures.

On Plato's first trip to Sicily, he made the acquaintance of Dion, the brother-in-law of the Syracusan tyrant, Dionysius I. Dion found in Plato an inspirational teacher of philosophy and Plato found in him a dedicated and gifted pupil. *The Seventh Letter* claims that Plato had come to Syracuse convinced that the problem of political justice could only be solved by the convergence of philosophy and power. In his *Life of Dion*, Plutarch reports that Dion, having been convinced by Plato of the desirability of having a philosopher-king, arranged for Plato to meet Dionysius I, hoping to ignite the spark of philosophy in the ruler of Syracuse. Dionysius I was a military strongman who had established his monarchy violently, made several attempts to subdue all of Sicily, and remained at war for most of his career. When the two met, Plato apparently offended him by arguing that tyrants, least of all, possess true courage. Insulted, Dionysius I arranged to have Plato, while on his journey back home, sold into slavery. Plato's friends ransomed him soon after.

Plato made a second trip to Syracuse on the invitation of Dionysius II, the son of the by-then-dead Dionysius I. The younger Dionysius, encouraged by Plato's former pupil Dion, was eager for philosophical training. For Plato, the attraction was the opportunity to put his political principles into practice. Upon arriving, he found the court "full of faction and malicious reports to the tyrant about Dion" (*Republic*,

1.329b). Soon after, Dionysius II exiled Dion for allegedly having plotted against the tyranny; he was accused of using philosophy to subdue and control the tyrant. Although the philosophical relationship never got very far, they parted on more or less friendly terms.

Though the court harbored considerable hostility towards Plato, Dionysius II persuaded him to return to Syracuse several years later. Plato was offered the opportunity to effect a reconciliation between the exiled Dion and Dionysius II and to instruct the latter philosophically. Despite Plato's efforts, Dionysius II steadfastly refused to attempt any reconciliation with Dion. Plato found that the king had been dabbling in philosophy, his head "full of half-understood doctrines" and was quite unwilling to endure the long, rigorous education required for the study of philosophy (Plato, *The Seventh Letter,* 340b). Plato fell out of favor with Dionysius II and lived as a virtual prisoner in Syracuse until some friends pleaded successfully that he be permitted to leave. Thus, the attempt to turn a real-life king into a philosopher-king, never got very far.

After Plato's failure, Dion deposed Dionysius II by seizing Syracuse when the former was away on a military campaign. As ruler, Dion tried to implement a Platonic system of government but lacked the support and resources to achieve it. His rule, beset with turmoil and infighting, lasted only briefly before he was assassinated. Plato's *Seventh Letter* is addressed to Dion's friends and associates, encouraging them to follow in his footsteps by trying, in a nonviolent way, to create "the best and most just constitution and system of laws" (*Republic,* 1.351c). Syracuse, plagued by social and political unrest, would not recover any semblance of stability for the next 20 years.

Reception and impact. The first major review of Plato's work was done by his student, Aristotle, in his *Metaphysics* and *Politics.* In the *Politics,* Aristotle argues that the regime of the *Republic* is excessively unified, harmonized to an unattainable and undesirable degree. He argues that once family relations are extended to the whole community, rather than having the desired effect of making everyone love each as his own, no one will love anyone as his own. As Aristotle sees it, the citizen's individual interests in his family and his property are good for the city as a whole because the state is naturally composed of a diversity of elements whose competing interests help the

community thrive. But, of course, Aristotle's rebuke of Plato depends on his interpretation of Plato's ideas, and many scholars have found this interpretation to be lacking.

It would be difficult to overstate the impact of the *Republic* or of Plato more generally on the history of Western philosophy. Plato set the stage for the discipline by asking and offering the first attempts to answer nearly all of its central questions (What exists? How is knowledge possible? Where do moral obligations come from?). These questions would become the foundational ones for the different branches of philosophy (metaphysics, epistemology, ethics, political philosophy and aesthetics). Modern interpretations have varied significantly on the meaning of the *Republic.* Some argue that the city that Plato envisions is a utopia and provides justification for a totalitarian government; both the Nazis and the Soviets found a justification for their regimes in Plato. On the other hand, many have seen in the *Republic* an indirect argument for democracy, since it is the most tolerant and congenial to philosophy. Still others have interpreted the *Republic* as encouraging indifference to politics. According to this interpretation, Plato shows us that political justice is impossible. Socrates makes the conditions for the perfectly just city unattainable by demanding that its rulers acquire a totally comprehensive wisdom in order to rule justly. Thus read, the *Republic* becomes an anti-political document, encouraging us to refrain from engaging in the politics of our city and to concentrate exclusively on the politics in our soul.

—Franco Trivigno

For More Information

Aristophanes. *Comoediae.* Ed. F. W. Hall and W. M. Geldart. 2 vols. Oxford: Oxford University Press, 1991.

Aristotle. *The Complete Works of Aristotle.* Ed. Jonathan Barnes. Princeton, N.J.: Princeton University Press, 1984.

Beck, Frederick A. G. *Greek Education: 450-350 B.C.* London: Methuen, 1964.

Diogenes Laertius. *Lives of Eminent Philosophers.* 2 Vols. Trans. R. D. Hicks. Cambridge, Mass.: Harvard University Press, 1925.

Edelstein, Ludwig. *Plato's Seventh Letter.* Leiden, The Netherlands: E. J. Brill, 1966.

Hansen, M. H. *The Athenian Democracy in the Age of Demosthenes.* Trans. J. A. Crook. Oxford: Blackwell, 1991.

Just, Roger. *Women in Athenian Law and Life.* London: Routledge, 1989.

Krenz, Peter. *The Thirty at Athens*. Ithaca, N.Y.: Cornell University Press, 1982.

Meiggs, Russell. *The Athenian Empire*. Oxford: Clarendon Press, 1972.

Plato. *Apology*. In *Four Texts on Socrates*. Trans. Thomas G. West and Grace Starry West. Ithaca, N.Y.: Cornell University Press, 1984.

———. *The Republic*. Trans. A. Bloom. New York: Basic Books, 1968.

Plutarch. *Lives*. 11 Vols. Trans. B. Perrin. Cambridge, Mass.: Harvard University Press, 1918.

Thucydides. *The Peloponnesian War*. Trans. R. Crawley. Rev. T. E. Wick. New York: Modern Library, 1982.

Xenophon. *Hellenica, Books 1-4*. Trans. Carleton L. Brownson. Cambridge, Mass.: Harvard University Press, 1918.

Roman Elegy

by
Tibullus and Propertius

lbius Tibullus was born sometime
between 55 and 48 BCE in the town of
Gabii or Pedum (20 miles east of Rome)
in the area of Latium near the Tiber River. Members of the equestrian or ancient Roman business
class, his family suffered in the land confiscations
of 41-40 BCE, which were conducted to reward
war veterans. Possibly while acquiring an education at Rome, Tibullus met the older poet Horace, who may have introduced him to the statesman and seasoned military man Marcus Valerius
Messalla Corvinus (c. 32 BCE). As a trusted advisor to the Roman emperor Augustus, Messalla
wielded great influence. He was also a devotee
of Roman literature. He quickly recognized
Tibullus' poetic talents, and the two forged an
enduring friendship. They forged a professional
relationship too—a literary circle developed
under Messalla's patronage, one centered on the
reportedly handsome young poet. Tibullus
proceeded to accompany Messalla on a military
campaign to Aquitania, part of Gaul (today's
France), and wrote a poem (27 BCE) in honor of
his patron's triumph there. Around this time
Tibullus also published his first book of elegiac
love poems, which is dominated by his affair with
a fickle, luxury-loving lady called Delia (whose
real name—if indeed she existed—may have
been Plania). After the campaign in Gaul, Tibullus ventured to the East with Messalla, only to
fall ill along the way and be left behind. A recovered Tibullus retired to his country estate on
the Italian peninsula. Horace says that at this
point Tibullus grew withdrawn and melancholy.

THE LITERARY WORKS

Poems set in the city of Rome or the Italian
countryside in the late first century BCE; first
published in Latin between 28 and 16 BCE.

SYNOPSIS

Written in a prescribed meter, the Roman
elegy is usually about a male speaker's
tempestuous love for an unattainable and
unfaithful woman. She is a woman of dubious
social standing, to whom he figuratively
enslaves himself.

He released a second book of poems (c. 19 BCE)
about a greedy courtesan referred to as Nemesis
("Avenging Goddess"), who again may be based
on a real woman or may be a female construct.
According to an epigram by Domitius Marsus,
Tibullus died in 19 BCE.

Sextus Propertius was born between 54 and
47 BCE to an aristocratic family in Asisium (modern-day Assisi) in the Italian region of Umbria.
Like Tibullus' family, Propertius lost land in the
confiscations carried out to compensate war veterans. The poet had a sad boyhood. His father
died shortly after the Perusine War of 41-40 BCE
(an unsuccessful revolt against the land confiscations). His mother proceeded to raise him for
a public career. To this end, she had him educated in law at Rome, but Propertius, supposedly

of a pale complexion and frail constitution, discovered he had poetic talents and turned instead to literary pursuits. He moved to Esquiline Hill (one of Rome's seven hills, on its eastern side), where he remained, only rarely leaving the city thereafter. In contrast to Tibullus' withdrawal, Propertius filled his days with urban social pleasures. He seems to have had an unhappy, passing fancy for a lady known as Lycinna before meeting Cynthia, on whom much of his poetry centers. It was Cynthia who inspired his debut book of poetry, *Cynthia Monobiblos* (29 or 28 BCE;

THE ELEGIAC METER

What makes a poem an elegy is its meter or rhythm. The elegiac meter consists of couplets (pairs of lines) made up of one six-beat line known as a hexameter followed by one five-beat line known as a pentameter. The five beats, more properly known as "feet," consist of two two-and-a half-foot measures. Each foot is a dactyl (long syllable followed by two short syllables) or sometimes a spondee (two long syllables).

Cynthia, the Single Volume). The book met with an overwhelmingly positive response, bringing Propertius to the attention of Gaius Cilnius Maecenas, a great literary patron and the chief cultural advisor to Emperor Augustus. There are no references in Propertius' poetry to any event after 16 BCE. The scope of his poetry is more diverse than that of Tibullus; his later books (3 and 4) include elegies on the current events of his day as well as on ancient or mythological matters. But along with Tibullus, Propertius is best remembered for developing a new form of poetry, one that features love as the sole experience that gives life meaning.

Events in History at the Time of the Poems

Octavian becomes Augustus. In 43 BCE, three key figures—Mark Antony, Octavian (the future emperor, who would be renamed Augustus), and Lepidus—formed the Second Triumvirate. This body of three rulers held absolute power for five years at a time (the first term would be renewed). All three had been supporters of Julius Caesar before he was assassinated by, among others, the statesmen Brutus and Cassius. After defeating

them at the Battle of Philippi in 42 BCE and forcing Lepidus to take an appointment in Africa, Antony and Octavian began to vie for sole power. Antony's family fought Octavian unsuccessfully in a bloody siege at Perusia while Antony was away in Egypt. But direct confrontation between the two was delayed by the Pact of Bundisium (40 BCE), which split the empire, giving Octavian the troubled west and Antony the rich east. To seal the bargain, Antony, whose first wife, Fulvia, had died, married Octavian's sister, Octavia. There was a period of cooperation, during which the two rulers negotiated a treaty (at Misenum near Naples) with Sextus Pompeius, who controlled Sicily and Sardinia and was blocking the importation of grain to Rome. Although Octavian and Antony solved this pressing problem together, their cooperation was short lived. Each of the two leaders wanted to consolidate his own separate powers and become the sole ruler of Rome's burgeoning empire.

Antony allied himself to the Egyptian queen Cleopatra VII. In so doing, he aimed to enlarge Rome's empire to include Egypt and in this way match an achievement of the earlier imperial leader Alexander the Great. Becoming personally as well as politically attached to Cleopatra, Antony conceived children with her (while still married to his Roman wife Fulvia). Meanwhile, in Rome, Octavian became embroiled in a scandal of his own when he divorced his wife, Scribonia, and married Livia Drusilla, a dignified, intelligent, beautiful woman who was six months pregnant at the time. His able general Agrippa put down some rebellions in Gaul and, with Antony and Lepidus, defeated Sextus Pompeius for good in 36 BCE. Making the most of his reputation as Julius Caesar's heir and adopted son, Octavian presented himself as a deserving descendant and took credit for the military victories, gaining recognition as the savior of the west. At the same time he instigated a fierce propaganda campaign against Antony and Cleopatra, portraying the queen as a threat to the Roman state and Antony as her puppet. Octavian brought the rivalry to a head in Rome by disclosing the contents of what was probably a forged document: in this document, Antony, in case of his death, named Cleopatra's son Caesarion the true heir of Julius Caesar. On the heels of this disclosure, Octavian stripped Antony of his right to command and declared war on Cleopatra. The Romans rallied behind Octavian—all Italy, he later glowed, volunteered their allegiance to him.

In 31 BCE, at Actium in Greece, Antony and Cleopatra assembled a massive but in reality ill-prepared force to fight Octavian's troops at sea. The battle was stunningly brief. A portion of Antony's troops fought and finally surrendered to Octavian, while Cleopatra and Antony escaped. A year later, when Octavian defeated their forces in the Egyptian city of Alexandria, Antony and Cleopatra committed suicide. Their deaths left Octavian in control not only of Rome but also of Egypt with all its wealth.

Returning to Rome in 29 BCE, Octavian celebrated a splendid triumph (honorary procession). Wisely he deferred any attempt to solidify his powers or define his true role in the government. Then, in 27 BCE, Octavian made a dramatic and shrewdly planned gesture: he resigned his powers and formally returned them to the Senate and people. A shocked and grateful Senate reacted by voting to give him control of the major provinces and by gracing him with many honors; it was at this point that they renamed him Augustus, which means "revered one" or "deserving of reverence." Twice more, in 23 and 19 BCE, Octavian redefined his relationship to the government, each time expanding his powers and eventually taking on the title *princeps* ("first or chief citizen") to mask what amounted to a monarchical role. After 500 years as a republic, Rome had shifted into one-man rule under an emperor, a type of regime that would endure in the West for almost 500 years.

The Augustan morality project. Once Octavian—renamed Augustus—had settled into his expanded powers in 19 BCE, he inaugurated a return to traditional religious and social values. He aimed to promote morality and civic pride and to connect his regime with the venerable past. Augustus wished to be remembered not only as a great ruler, but also as a shaper of social values. This goal was in part self-serving. Only the maintenance of the highest moral standards could justify increased Roman imperialism; world domination could then be touted as the "duty" of the morally superior. Augustus' moral-improvement project also justified his increasing personal control of government. To these ends, Augustus restored temples, revived rituals, and resurrected ancient religious offices. He also passed legislation to regulate marriage and promote families.

In large part, these laws were passed to combat a falling birth rate and an overall decline in morality. The absence of men, fighting for Rome in distant lands, may have encouraged unstable marriages and greater female independence.

Divorce grew more common among the upper classes. Also upper-class women began to act in a more assertive and sexually liberated manner than ever before. By conventional standards, women were supposed to exhibit the virtues of *pietas* (loyalty to traditional religion), *fides* (faithfulness in marriage—which was to continue even after a husband's death), and *puditicia* (modesty, especially irreproachable sexual conduct). The very fact that Roman women were being urged by the Augustan legislation to practice these virtues suggests that a considerable number had been violating them.

Augustus may have proposed some moral legislation in the previous decade, perhaps as early as 27 BCE. A poem by Propertius suggests that an earlier law compelling men and women to marry and have children had been passed but then rescinded. But probably Augustus was just testing the waters with these proposals, since no other ancient source mentions such a law. In any case, Propertius' poetry makes his attitude toward such legislation very clear:

> Cynthia delights, certainly, that the law has
>   been lifted,
> Those edicts we once cried so much over,
> Afraid they'd separate us.
>   (Propertius, *The Complete Elegies*, book 2,
>   poem 7, lines 1-3)

The subsequent "Julian" legislation concerning marriage and family was part of a cluster of laws put into effect the following decade, in 18 BCE. The next year Rome held the Secular Games, a traditional festival of games and sacrifices to celebrate the passage of 100 years and, in this instance, the birth of a new age, a moral renaissance. Addressed mainly to the ruling classes (the aristocracy and equestrian or business class), the Julian laws sought to have women make the most of their childbearing years. The laws made marriage mandatory for men aged 25 to 60 and for women aged 20 to 50. Divorced or widowed women had to remarry within six to twelve months, and fathers could not obstruct their children's marriages. Marriages between Romans and ex-slaves, otherwise known as freedmen or freedwomen, became permissible for all but senators' families, though prejudices no doubt continued to exist. Some laws tried to rein in extramarital affairs, while others encouraged women to raise a family—an endeavor that many doubtlessly saw as a civic duty. The government introduced incentives, such as tax relief for those with large families, while the unmarried and childless could not inherit or bequeath property. Interestingly, Horace, Virgil, and various other Roman writers, though unmarried and childless, were given some of the same privileges as a citizen with three children. The reasoning was that these writers' works extolled the social and moral responsibility that the laws aimed to instill.

The Julian laws, like much else during Augustus' reign, were experimental—they combined a return to the past with innovation. Augustus risked much in instituting them, for some actually went against revered traditions. Examples are the ideal of *univira* (that a woman should have only one husband and remain faithful to him even after his death) and the practice of *patria potestas* (that a father had complete control over his children, including the power to determine when and whom they married). The Julian laws therefore provoked a strong reaction. Only in 18 BCE, after the legislators made some concessions, such as prolonging the time allowed for remarriage after a husband's death, could these laws go into effect. And even then, they continued to meet with so much protest that further modifications had to be made in 9 CE.

Major conventions of the Roman love elegy. The history of the Latin elegy begins in the first century BCE, when a set of innovative poets turned away from traditional Roman norms to embrace the Greek culture associated with Alexandria, Egypt. The Alexandrian school seemed to these poets—known as the *neoterics,* or "new poets"—to provide a superior model for life as well as art. While almost every standard feature of Latin love elegy can be traced back to Greek models, the neoterics modified the Greek elements to create their own independent form. Indeed, elegy became the one genre in which the Romans could challenge the Greeks.

Early Roman love elegy was built around certain poetic conventions and motifs. The central convention was the figurative enslavement of the lover to the beloved, who behaved as a dominating mistress, controlling her paramour and the relationship, even though she was the poet's social inferior. Such a relationship reversed the normal pattern of male dominance and female submissiveness in Roman society and so implied a life of degradation and self-debasement on the part of the poet. In fact, nothing could have been more contrary to ancient ethics than a man enslaved by his passion for a woman. Traditionally women were considered not only inferior to men but also in need of taming and teaching. The Romans as well as the Greeks depicted women stereotypically—as unruly, spiteful, and/or treacherous. Although other, more positive images of women existed as well, this damaging one endured.

The poet's atypical kind of love affair was only one aspect of his resistance to established Roman values; he also rejected military duty and public service for a life of leisure (*otium*). Yet paradoxically, the poet employed the vocabulary and concepts of conventional Roman society to describe his unconventional relationship. He styled his liaison with his mistress a conjugal relationship, associating it with (or lamenting the absence of) traditional Roman ideals, such as modesty and fidelity. Similarly, while the poet repudiated military or civil service, Tibullus in particular often depicts the poet as "a soldier of love." The perils and vagaries of the love affair are equated with those of war.

Roman elegiac love poetry also had a didactic or instructive strain. The poet often assumed the role of a teacher of love, a *praeceptor amoris,* whose numerous, often failed experiences as a lover could help others. Thus the narrator of the love elegy, which is always written in the first person, has a dual role: the teacher is distinct from the naïve lover. While the teacher has acquired knowledge which benefits others, the lover continues to suffer and is even comic in his lack of know-how.

In love elegies, the poet's love affair is his whole life: love is his very reason for being. Also the beloved and poetry are typically identified with each other. Insofar as the poet's mistress is his inspiring Muse, and hence a construct as much as a real person, she is interchangeable with the body of his writings and represents his poetics as a whole.

Finally, a standard feature of the Roman erotic elegy is the construction of an ideal world alongside the real world of first-century BCE Rome. Tibullus uses the Italian countryside, in which he imagines living a peaceful, rustic existence with the beloved of his first book (Delia). Propertius, by contrast, brings into his poetry the world of mythology, in which he finds ideal parallel situations and characters.

The Poems in Focus

Contents summary—Tibullus. The two books of Tibullus' elegies contain 16 poems. An example taken from the first book, its second poem, is a mixture of conventional love elegy motifs and themes and images unique to the poet; it is also part of the cycle of poems that focuses on Delia. Cast in the form of a lament by the locked-out lover (called a *paraclausithyron*), the poem is set at a drinking party and shifts its focus several times before returning to the party. Included are some standard postures of the Roman love elegy; the elegy also expresses the poet's characteristic dream of love in the countryside.

The lament begins in line seven with a direct address, in the form of a curse, to the door that denies the poet access to his Delia: "Damn you, door!" (Tibullus in Raynor, book 1, poem 2, line 7). This lament may derive from a stock scene of Greek comedy in which, late at night, a drunken lover serenades his beloved through her bolted door. Many traditional elements of the Greek form are present here: the lover carries garlands, appeals to the weather, and tries to persuade the door or threatens it with violence. He also fears his beloved has been unfaithful but meets with nothing but the door's obstinate silence and cruel obstruction. A distinctly Roman feature is the treatment of the door as a divinity: here the poet-lover offers his door-deity not just standard prayers, but prayers combined with curses that he turns back upon his miserable self: "If I just said / Harsh things, may curses light on my own head" (Tibullus in Raynor, 1.2.11-12).

The poem moves from the convention of the lament to the standard elegiac posture of the *praeceptor amoris*, or teacher of love. Here, instead of taking on this role directly, the poet-lover sets up Venus, the goddess of love, as the teacher of amorous skills. In the guise of receiving his own lessons in the art of love, the poet-lover is able to turn his pitiful experiences into a handbook on illicit love affairs for his readers' benefit:

> Venus teaches sorties [love strategies] out of
>   bed,
> Teaches our footsteps soundlessly to pad,
> Or lovers to communicate by sighs.
>   (Tibullus in Raynor, 1.2.19-22)

The poet-lover can count on instruction in love from the goddess; he can also count on her protection even on the dark and dangerous streets of nighttime Rome. He will be the conventional sacred and protected lover; thanks to Venus, not even the elements can harm him:

> But Love protects me from the switch blade
>   knife . . .
> No frosty winter might can do me harm;
> Rain falls in torrents, but I'm safe and warm.
>   (Tibullus in Raynor, 1.2.25-28; 29-30)

From the reality of city life and the convention of the protected lover, follows a standard appeal to the supernatural. With the help of magic, the poet hopes to deceive his rival (a creation of the poem, not necessarily real). But a slave to his mistress, a soldier in the service of love, he does not ask to be freed from Delia's bondage or for the power to live without her. To him, life and love are inseparable:

> The sorceress claimed that she could cure me
>   too;
> Her charms and herbs could set me free—of
>   you . . .
> But what I prayed for was a love to share;
> Life without you would be bleak and bare.
>   (Tibullus in Raynor, 1.2.59-64)

From the realm of magic, Tibullus moves now to developing a contrast that recurs often in his poetry: the wealthy warrior versus the simple lover. Who would pursue war instead of love? Who would ravage the countryside rather than revel in its pastoral bliss? Only an iron-headed fool would choose war. A lover's service is to *Amor* (love), not *Roma* (Rome). (This infamous pun—*Amor* is *Roma* spelled backwards—was nothing short of a revolutionary assertion.) The typical warmonger is greedy; he plunders for material possessions, but the countryside lover needs little to be comfortable and content: "When we are intertwined in one embrace, / Sweet sleep on the bare ground is no disgrace" (Tibullus in Raynor, 1.2.73-74). Peace, not war, and the country, not the city, are Tibullus' distinctive refrains. While they betray nostalgia for the days before civil wars and land confiscations, the theme of peace also fits with the later Augustan times of the poet. In these later times, however, peace had become part of the machinery of political propaganda and was a condition that, in a burgeoning empire like Rome, required constant military surveillance.

The dream of a rustic, peaceful life in the country with Delia is not possible, for Delia is no country girl; rather she belongs strictly to the world of the city. The poet-lover must face this along with the fact that she has other lovers, even as he faces her unyielding door.

The poem comes full circle to its starting point and the ongoing drinking party. Now the poet-lover undercuts the seriousness of his plight with self-mockery. Let his amused drinking companion be warned: his time to suffer may come. The poet-speaker wishes his own lovesickness on his companion by using the image of the aged lover overwhelmed by Venus' powers. Like the lament, this is a stock image from comedy that helps to counter the gloomy strain of the lover's complaints: "But soon his wrinkled neck is in the yoke / He whistles senile ditties to the air" (Tibullus in Raynor, 1.2.90-91).

With a final prayer to the unpredictable goddess of love, Tibullus closes the elegy using a metaphor from country life: "Venus, I've always served you faithfully / Don't burn your harvest [i.e. do not deny me love] in your rage at me!" (Tibullus in Raynor 1.2.97-98).

Contents summary—Propertius. In his four books of elegiac poetry, Propertius reveals himself as intensely introspective. The initial poem of his first book begins with the name Cynthia: Cynthia the lover, the woman, the book; Cynthia the inspiration and the essence of his poetry and poetics. Next the poet plunges into the standard Latin elegiac motifs of being debased and dominated by a mistress, whether that mistress is a real woman, his poetry, or a combination of the two. Either way the poet-lover is dedicated to Cynthia and to poetry and the devotion is the equivalent of enslavement. The life this fixation breeds is at odds with a Roman value system based on military service, civic duty, and male dominance. Inner turmoil has resulted too: the lover has suffered madness as well as debasement since his heart was captured by Cynthia a year ago.

The poem is addressed to Propertius' friend and figurative counterpart, Tullus; he represents the outside world of politics and service, the world the poet himself has renounced for the private world of poetry and love. As in poetry by the earlier Alexandrian poet Callimachus, mythic examples and lessons follow. The myth here concerns the huntress Atalanta, who places seemingly insurmountable obstacles in her suitor's path. The most common version of the myth features a footrace in which the hero wins Atalanta by dropping golden apples in her path, which she stops to pick up. Propertius draws on a darker version of the myth, in which the suitor is more aggressive. In pursuing Atalanta, he must endure many trials and slay Hylaeus the centaur, a creature with the legs and body of a horse but the chest, arms, and head of a man:

> Milanion [the suitor], Tullus, by refusing no trial,
> Beat down harsh Atalanta's cruelty.
> Crazed, he would wander Parthenian caves,
> Head-on face hairy beasts . . .
> So prayers and feats prevail in love.
> (Propertius in Raynor, 1.1.9-12; 16)

The exact opposite of such a suitor, the poet-lover is the artless, dull victim of a sluggish love.

He "forgets" even to plod down old paths, such as the well-worn ones of traditional epic poetry; these he cannot follow because they do not allow him to express what he feels in his mad and enslaved condition.

Propertius now turns to the conventional appeal to magic and witches. Here, as in the poem by Tibullus, a sorceress has the ability to bring down heavenly bodies from the sky. This time the heavenly body is the moon, connected with the Italian huntress-goddess, Diana, who is associated with the mythical huntress Atalanta and with her real-world counterpart Cynthia. The poet-lover seeks magic to affect the woman he loves, which is no easy undertaking. The power to change her mind is tantamount to being able to rule rivers and move stars with a song from Colchis, the homeland of the legendary enchantress Medea.

But the poet's love, it turns out, is a disease and a form of helplessness that not even magic can cure. Ultimately he can find no relief from his passion for Cynthia, no satisfactory end to his obsession with her. Not even the magical powers of poetry can save his heart, for there is no respite from the slavery of love:

> Friends, you call me back too late—I've fallen:
> Seek help for an unsound heart . . .
> Against me our Venus wields sleepless nights
> And untiring Love never rests.
> (Propertius in Raynor 1.1.25-26; 34-5)

Propertius's poet-lover, like Tibullus', closes with a warning for those who think they may escape the shackles of passion. Better to remain with a comfortable sweetheart then fall victim to a frenzied love. One who fails to do so will surely suffer the same incurable pain, a torment that the poet's words have the (magical) power to elicit: "But, oh, the one my warnings touch too late— repeating my words will make him ache" (Propertius in Raynor, 1.1.37-38).

The beloved—fact or fiction? Roman elegiac love poetry was a contrivance, more a statement of ethics and poetics than a slice of life. While the poetry seems confessional, it is only artificially so, unlike the earlier elegies of Catullus, which contain more historical elements (see *Carmina*, also in *Classical Literature and Its Times*). Although Tibullus or Propertius may have drawn on personal experience, the woman and the situations presented are typical rather than individual. This is also true of the settings. The poet creates an urbane, "realistic" world (which he then counters with a purely dream or mythic world). This realistic world is derived from the lower strata of Roman society, the strata of freedmen and women, foreigners, and various colorful and marginal characters. While the higher-class poet may have had a mistress who came from these lower strata, he sings not about his personal beloved but about the amorous life in general. He is a poet first and a lover second; the characters and scenes he creates are mostly fictional. Poetry and its conventions are what shape the love affair, not vice versa.

In the case of Delia, Tibullus says that she has a man or *vir* (poem 1.2). The term frequently meant "husband," but could mean "boyfriend," although the poet also claims that Delia is an adulteress. He further informs us (poem 1.6) that she wore neither a headband nor the flowing *stola*, the traditional dress of the freeborn Roman matron (married women, widows, or divorcees were matrons and wore a long dress or *stola* to show that they were "untouchable"). Therefore, if Delia truly did exist and was married, she was in all likelihood a woman from the lower class.

About Cynthia we are told that she changes lovers every night. Descriptions of her appearance vary from poem to poem: in one poem (2.2) she is blonde, in another (2.12) she has dark eyes, while in still another poem (2.18), the poet tells her it is wrong to dye her hair. All that remains the same is that Cynthia possesses every attraction and causes her lover excessive suffering. The many changes in her physical appearance support the notion that Cynthia should be viewed not as a real woman (though she may have been based on one) but as a composite, a type, the convenient cause of the poet's wretched state. She serves as a poetic device; she is a literary fiction.

We do not have to look far, however, to find real women in first-century BCE Rome who resembled the given type—cultivated, beguiling, and sexually liberated. The Roman historian Sallust (86-35 BCE) writes about Sempronia, a noblewoman and the wife of Decimus Junius Brutus (consul 77 BCE), who had many affairs and supported Lucius Sergius Catilina, the notoriously depraved aristocratic politician, in his grand conspiracy against the Roman government in 64-62 BCE. Like Cynthia, Sempronia was a *docta puella* (learned girl); erudite, talented, charming, and daring as well as independent, Sallust describes her as seducing and dominating all her partners.

The non-love poems. Not all elegies were love poems. In a few of his poems, Tibullus repudiates war and denounces the wealth it brings. For example, his opening elegy takes a firm stand against the traditional Roman value system, which celebrates battle and its spoils. This same antiwar sentiment is even more vehemently expressed in the closing poem of his first book:

> Whoever first invented swords was more
> Than merely fierce, but feral [savage] to the
>   core!
> First battles and then warfare, genocide—
> A whole new way to death he opened wide.
>   (Tibullus in Raynor, 1.10.1-4)

THE ROMAN POETESS SULPICIA

Found in Tibullus' collection of manuscripts are six short love poems by a woman named Sulpicia. Sometimes called the "Little Love Letters of a Roman Woman," these are the only complete poems by a Roman poetess that have survived to the present day. Perhaps it is because the ancients considered female writings less worthy of preservation that only these poems and scattered fragments of works by other Roman women still exist. Sulpicia's cycle of six poems, one of which is translated into prose below, seems to describe a waning love affair.

> At last a love has come of such a kind that my shame, Gossip, would be greater if I kept it covered than if I laid it bare. Cythera [my muse], implored by my verses, brought that man to me and gave him into my embrace . . . my sin is a joy, though it's tiresome to keep a straight face for gossip's sake. Let it be said that I was a worthy woman, with a worthy man.
>   (Sulpicia in Lefkowitz and Fant, 3.13.1-4)

More than Tibullus, however, Propertius is known for bypassing the subject of love in order to treat current events or ancient or mythological matters. His poems encompass a far broader span of subjects than Tibullus' collection and some of them also convey antiwar sentiments. Two such poems (1.21 and 1.22) treat the Battle of Perusia; understanding them requires some knowledge of the infamous land confiscations and their historical context.

Even before the Battle of Philippi (42 BCE), at which Mark Antony and Octavian defeated the assassins of Julius Caesar, 18 Italian cities were designated for land confiscations. The confiscated lands would be redistributed to veterans as compensation for military service. Octavian was in charge of resettling not only his own veterans but also those of Mark Antony. The victims, who had their names posted on lists and their estates

confiscated to provide the needed land, were not paid in any way. It was during this same period that Sextus Pompeius, in control of the large islands of Sicily and Sardinia, blocked grain importation, leaving the countryside ravaged by famine. Thus impoverished and oppressed, the region was ripe for rebellion, and the slow pace of the veterans' resettlement only exacerbated matters. Mark Antony's brother, Lucius Antonius, a chief official in 41 BCE, became a rallying point for the disaffected and dispossessed in Etruria and Umbria, north of Rome. Lucius and Antony's wife Fulvia took advantage of the confiscations and Antony's absence in Egypt to maneuver against Octavian. Fulvia and Lucius urged the victims to resist the land redistribution in the name of liberty and established law.

Antony's brother occupied Rome with an army and marched north toward Etruria, hoping to link up with troops led by Antony's other supporters, but uncertain of Antony's wishes, these supporters hesitated to intervene. Meanwhile, in Egypt, Antony may have thought it best not to respond to the situation in Perusia so he could manipulate the outcome (whatever it might be) to his advantage. The siege wore on until the winter of 41/40 BCE, when Antony's soldiers and the Perusians were finally starved out. With horrific bloodshed, the city fell in the spring of 40 BCE and was handed over to Octavian's troops to pillage and burn. Octavian executed the Perusian senate and had all but one of the town councilors killed. But Antony's brother, Lucius, was spared along with his veterans, and Fulvia was allowed to escape to Athens. For his own part, Octavian had the satisfaction of controlling Italy. A few years later, Propertius, whose relative had apparently died in the siege, would conclude his first book with two short but disturbing poems (21 and 22) on the suffering in Perusia:

> You allowed my relative's limbs to go
>   abandoned,
> You cover the poor man's bones with no
>   earth
> Neighboring Umbria, below Perusia on the
>   plain bore me,
> Fertile Umbria, productive land.
>   (Propertius, *The Complete Elegies*, 1.22.7-10)

Sources and literary context. Like most Latin genres, the Roman love elegy derives from Greek precursors and is defined by and intimately connected with its poetic meter. The roots of elegy may reach back into the eighth-century BCE, where in Ionia, on the coast of Asia Minor, short poems in the elegiac meter (sometimes of an erotic nature) were sung over wine to the accompaniment of a flute. An *elegos* was properly a song of lament, but most of the earliest elegies we have are not laments; the elegiac couplet was instead an all-purpose meter, and an elegy was any poem written in elegiacs.

Our earliest extant elegies are from the middle of the seventh century BCE; the poets Archilochus of Paros and Callinus of Ephesus are both held to be the inventor of the form. Elegy of the erotic type, however, seems properly to have begun with another archaic Greek poet named Mimnermus, who wrote poems in the elegiac meter to express both his passion for a flute-playing girl, Nanno, and his grief at youth's passing. The resulting book of poetry, which he called *Nanno,* became the prototype for subsequent collections of both Greek and Latin love poetry named after the woman on whom they focus.

It was Antimachus of Colophon on the western coast of modern-day Turkey who set an important precedent when, around 400 BCE, he composed an elaborate elegy to console himself on the death of his beloved wife or mistress, Lyde, by relating the sorrowful love affairs of the heroes and gods from mythology. His innovation paved the way for the writers of elegy in Alexandria, the poet-scholars who combined romantic subjects with mythological learning.

Later writers of elegy include Callimachus (305-240 BCE) and Philetas (both of whom Propertius recognizes several times in his poetry). Callimachus from Cyrene was by far the most celebrated. The most well-known of his works was the *Aetia* (dealing with the origins of cities, games, religious forms), whose elegies, Propertius says, furnished the pattern for his own poems. Callimachus embodied the *doctus poeta* or "learned poet" of Alexandria, whose art was bound up with a command of obscure knowledge. Future poets, including the love elegists, would emulate his preference for the shorter poem over the traditionally lengthy epic. In his poetry, he adopts the stance of a teacher of love that future poets would assume.

The Roman neoteric poet Catullus (c. 84-54 BCE) stands out as the first ancient poet to describe in detail the progress of one deeply felt love affair, a practice imitated by his successors—Gallus, Tibullus, Propertius, and Ovid. Catullus, who instigated a literary revolution and a moral rebellion, wrote a long poem (number 68) that is considered the model Augustan love elegy. His successor, Cornelius Gallus (69-26 BCE)—only

ROMAN ELEGY AND ITS FOUR BASIC LOVE POETS

The late-first-century CE teacher of oratory and literary critic Quintilian said he counted four among the canon of love poets—Gallus, Tibullus, Propertius, and Ovid. The poet Cornelius Gallus established most of the conventions of the love elegy, Tibullus and Propertius developed and refined them, and Ovid exploited them to create a new, erotic poetry. First, Gallus transformed the beloved woman from an aristocrat who was the poet's social superior to a courtesan who was, by definition, his inferior. With this shift, the nature of the love affair changed from an adulterous liaison to a permissible, if not socially approved, relationship. Gallus' own beloved, whom he called Lycoris, was an ex-slave, a stage actress, and a formidable courtesan—the former mistress of both Brutus and Mark Antony. In Gallus' poetry can be found the beginnings of the standard elements of elegy: self-debasement, enslavement to a mistress who dominates both the lover and the relationship, defiance of Roman values, and the equation of poetry and love with life. By the time of Propertius and Tibullus, the beloved was becoming more symbolic and the creation of such poetry took on a game-like quality. Ovid continued to push the bounds of the convention, creating a persona who no longer styled himself as a slave to his beloved or contented himself with a single lover. Instead of adoring one lady, he vows devotion to the experience of love itself. In creating this persona, Ovid merges the knowing poet-narrator and the naïve poet-lover featured in the writings of Tibullus and Properitus into a savvy poet-narrator-lover.

a tiny fraction of whose work survives—seems to have given the Latin love elegy its distinctive character. Next came the poems of Tibullus and Propertius, followed by Ovid (43 BCE-17 CE), in whose hands the love elegy would undergo a major transformation.

Reception. Tibullus was apparently quite popular in antiquity, especially among his contemporaries, as evidenced by the comments of Horace, Domitius Marsus, and Ovid. A bit later, the critic Quintilian is straightforward in his praise of the poet's elegant and smooth style and in his preference for it over the writing of Propertius. In later antiquity, Ovid seems to have overshadowed Tibullus, while in the Middle Ages he was neglected for Propertius. In the 1300s, Petrarch brought a Tibullan manuscript found in France to Italy. While the poet's work was not immediately popular, in the early to mid-1400s the existing manuscripts were copied and Tibullus found fame again. His favor lasted into the nineteenth century when the German poet Goethe wrote his *Roman Elegies*, in part loosely based on Tibullus' poetry.

Like Tibullus, Propertius enjoyed immediate success with his *Cynthia Monobiblos*—a success that endured for a century. The popularity of the volume is attested by the discovery of verses inscribed on the walls at Pompeii, and it was still a favorite gift in the second half of the first century CE. From the end of antiquity (c. 400 BCE) until the middle of the twelfth century, Propertius seems to have gone underground; only a few, indirect allusions to his texts survive from this time. In the very early Renaissance, Petrarch was responsible for bringing a manuscript of Propertius from France to Italy; his poetry became increasingly popular thereafter. Goethe's *Roman Elegies* (1795) was influenced by the poems of both Propertius and Tibullus, and in the early twentieth century, the American poet Ezra Pound wrote his famous "Homage to Sextus Propertius" (1919) Since then, Propertius has enjoyed the greater popularity.

—Christine M. Maisto

For More Information

Cairns, Francis. *Tibullus: A Hellenistic Poet at Rome.* Cambridge: Cambridge University Press, 1979.
Galinsky, Karl. *Augustan Culture.* Princeton, N.J.: Princeton University Press, 1996.

Harrington, Karl Pomeroy, ed. *The Roman Elegiac Poets*. Norman: University of Oklahoma Press, 1968.

Lefkowitz, Mary R., and Maureen B. Fant. *Women's Life in Greece & Rome: A Source Book in Translation*. 2d ed. Baltimore, Md.: Johns Hopkins University Press, 1992.

Lyne, R. O. A. M. *The Latin Love Poets from Catullus to Horace*. Oxford: Clarendon, 1980.

Ovid. *The Love Poems*. Trans. A. D. Melville. Oxford: Oxford University Press, 1990.

Propertius, Sextus. *The Complete Elegies of Sextus Propertius*. Trans. Vincent Katz. Princeton, N.J.: Princeton University Press, 2004.

Raynor, Diane J., and William W. Batstone, eds. *Latin Lyric and Elegiac Poetry*. New York: Garland, 1995.

Tibullus. *Tibullus: Poems with the Tibullan Collection*. Trans. Philip Dunlop. Harmondsworth, England: Penguin, 1972.

Wyke, Maria. *The Roman Mistress*. Oxford: Oxford University Press, 2002.

Satires

by
Juvenal

Decimus Junius Juvenalis was born around 60 CE, at Aquinium near Rome. Little is known about his youth, family background, or education, although a fourth-century biography written by Lactantius claimed that Juvenal was the son of a freedman and that he practiced rhetoric for his own amusement until he was middle-aged. It is known that Juvenal spent time in Rome during the reign of Domitian (81-96 CE), who may have exiled Juvenal to Egypt, a country for which the satirist later shows contempt. In the course of his life, Juvenal experienced the rule of nine emperors, of whom many figure in his satires, though seldom to their advantage. Juvenal began publishing his writings around 100 CE, several years after Domitian's death. Savage, incisive, merciless, and sometimes sardonically funny, Juvenal's 16 satires—the last of which survives only as a fragment—were to influence many later writers, including Jonathan Swift and Samuel Johnson.

Events in History at the Time of the Satires

The reign of Domitian. Although Juvenal lived under several emperors, his cynical view of Roman rulers may stem mostly from the repressive regime of Emperor Domitian (r. 81-96 CE). The younger son of Emperor Vespasian and the brother of Emperor Titus, Domitian was a member of the Flavians, an equestrian (business-class) family that became increasingly prominent during the first century CE. His father, Vespasian, had

---

> ## THE LITERARY WORK
>
> Satirical poetry set within the Roman Empire during the first century CE; published in Latin as *Saturae* c. 100-127 CE.
>
> ## SYNOPSIS
>
> The satirist comments savagely upon what he perceives as the evils of his age, which range from corrupt social institutions to human vice in all its manifestations.

---

distinguished himself as a military commander before acceding to the imperial throne at the end of a turbulent period known as the Year of the Four Emperors. Within 18 months Rome had experienced four rulers, three of whom reigned ineffectually and met violent ends. The fourth, Vespasian, became emperor in late 69 CE and managed to restore order and stability to the state in the course of his ten-year reign. His eldest son, Titus, ruled only for two years (79-81 CE), but he carried on his father's policies.

Unlike Vespasian and Titus, Domitian had no military experience at the time of his accession; while his father and brother campaigned in the African provinces and Judaea, the young Domitian remained in Rome, studying rhetoric and literature. This tendency to be overshadowed continued during Vespasian's and Titus's reigns. Domitian was granted no important imperial position or office, though he held several honorary

Juvenal, engraving by Ambroise Tardieu.
© Corbis/Bettmann. Reproduced by permission.

consulships and priesthoods. Thus, he gained little official training for leadership.

Domitian nevertheless ruled moderately during the early years of his reign. Conscientious and diligent, he promoted religious festivals, erected public buildings, led military campaigns in the Rhine and the Danube areas of Germany, and raised army pay by a third, which fostered loyalty between him and the Roman troops. Domitian's regime was not, however, an unqualified success. Because of an economic depression, the value of Roman currency dropped dramatically and Domitian's numerous public works further strained the state's finances.

In the later years of his reign, Domitian became increasingly rigid in his policies. He had long been concerned with public morality and adherence to religious ritual. When three Vestal virgins broke their vows of chastity, Domitian sentenced all three to capital punishment and later had Cornelia, the chief Vestal, buried alive. No doubt this brutality lost supporters among the general population. The emperor's relations with the senatorial class meanwhile deteriorated too as he became more determined to rule as an absolute monarch. His arrogance eventually led him to take away the Senate's decision-making powers, and he grew ruthless in his efforts to suppress opposition, reviving treason trials, en-

couraging informers, and prosecuting members of the senatorial and equestrian orders whom he suspected of conspiring against him. At least a dozen former consuls were executed during Domitian's reign, mainly for dissent or alleged conspiracy against the emperor.

Ultimately, Domitian's fear of assassination became a self-fulfilling prophecy. His enemies in the Senate, members of the Praetorian Guard (his household troops), and his own wife, Domitia Longina, successfully carried out a plot against his life. The actual assassin was a steward attached to Domitian's niece's household, who on September 18, 96 CE fatally stabbed the emperor eight times. Juvenal's own loathing of Domitian is evident in his fourth satire, "Against a big fish," in which Domitian summons his terrified adherents, who live in fear of his cruel caprices, to his palace to discuss how a big fish given to him as a gift should be prepared. Juvenal concludes, "Would that to nonsense like this [Domitian] had given all his devotion. / Spared that savage caprice which took away from the city / Bright illustrious souls. . . . / Nobles he could kill. He was soaked in their blood, and no matter. / But when the common herd began to dread him, he perished" (Juvenal, *Satires*, Satire 4, lines 150-152; 153-154).

Patrons and clients. One aspect of Roman society mentioned frequently in Juvenal's satires is the patron-client relationship, which involved political and social connections. Dating from the time of the Roman Republic, patrons, usually of patrician (aristocratic) rank, would take clients—younger patricians or plebeians (commoners)—under their influence. Patrons would provide their clients with advice, money, and business opportunities in exchange for personal loyalty, political support, and other services intended to enhance the patrons' status. Clients could be freedmen (former slaves), businessmen, artists, or writers; indeed, patrons with political aspirations often chose to ally themselves with prominent writers, who received financial support and publishing opportunities in exchange for exercising their talents at their patron's behest.

A client had duties to his patron. These might include visiting the patron every morning to greet him formally, accompanying him to the Forum and to other places of business, and supporting him politically in the assembly. The ceremony associated with these daily rituals was as important as the actual performance of them; the more clients seen attending the patron, the greater status and prestige attributed to him. Faithful clients might be rewarded with handouts of coins or food for their morning efforts or, if they were of sufficiently high rank, with an invitation to dine with their patron. It is worth noting that the patron-client relationship operated at all levels of Roman society. Patrons themselves tended to be clients of their political and social superiors.

In his *Satires*, Juvenal frequently attacks the patron-client system, which he portrays as having deteriorated into a humiliatingly unequal relationship. Stingy patrons dole out meager rewards to obsequious clients who are too cowed to protest their treatment. In the fifth satire, Juvenal chides clients who futilely hope for a good meal from a patron when he keeps the best dishes for himself and gives them only scraps: "He's a wise man to treat you like this, for if you can stand it, / You can stand anything else, and, by God, I think that you ought to! / Some day you'll offer your shaved-oft heads [the mark of an ex-slave] to be slapped, and a flogging / Won't seem fearful at all" (*Satires*, 5.169-172).

The development of satire. Derived from the Latin term "lanx satura" (full plate, usually consisting of mixed fruits), satire is considered a uniquely Roman genre. The Roman critic Quintilian (c. 35-90s CE) boasted, "Satire, at any rate, is all our own" (Quintilian in Hornblower and Spawforth, p. 636). As its name suggests, satire was comprised of a mixture of elements, including parody, exaggeration, deflation, caricature, and invective. The use of satiric techniques varied from writer to writer.

Lucilius (c. 180-102 BCE) was usually considered the father of satire; he specialized in stringent criticism of his contemporaries and fixed the dactylic hexameter as the conventional meter for satire. He was also known for his earthy, sometimes coarse, conversational writing style. Although he reportedly composed some 30 books of satiric verse, only 1300 lines survive. Another popular form of satire, which mingled verse and prose, was associated with the Cynic philosopher Menippus of Gedara (c. third century BCE) and became known as Menippean satire. Both satirists had their admirers, adherents, and imitators.

Among the satirists who followed Lucilius's example most closely, Horace (65-8 BCE), Persius (34-62 CE), and Juvenal are perhaps the best known. Horace and Juvenal, however, put their own stamp on the genre as well. Using a less bitter tone than Lucilius and avoiding political themes, Horace created an urbane persona that gently mocked human foibles. By contrast, Juvenal's persona in his satires was an outraged

moralist, railing against the vices and corruption of his city and its denizens.

Associated with the relative freedom of the Roman Republic, satire became more hazardous to write after the establishment of imperial rule. In his opening satire, Juvenal vividly depicts the likely fate of satirists who offend cruel or capricious rulers; dare to name names and you become "a torch in a tunic / Standing where other men stand, victims, choking and smoking, / Till you fall, and your corpse makes a furrow across the arena" (*Satires*, 1.155-157). To write satire, Juvenal argues, requires more courage and audacity than it takes to rewrite ancient myths and plays.

FREEDMEN IN THE ROMAN EMPIRE

Some historians have speculated that Juvenal was the son of a freedman, a circumstance that might account for his extensive knowledge of the patron-client relationship, since freedmen automatically became clients of their former owners. As the term suggests, *freedmen*—and *freedwomen*—were emancipated slaves. In the Roman world freedmen could be granted manumission by their owners or could raise enough money to buy their freedom. Informal manumission (before friends) did not grant citizenship to freedmen, who were nonetheless protected by the praetor. Formal manumission, which took place before a magistrate, conferred citizenship as well as freedom upon the former slave. However, no freedman was eligible for political office, though if his children were born after his manumission, they qualified as free citizens who could hold political office. Even first generation freedmen could play a role in government, though. Emperor Claudius appointed several as his secretaries, and Caenis, a freedwoman of Claudius's mother Antonia, became Emperor Vespasian's long-term mistress, living with him until her death.

The Satires in Focus

The Sequence of Juvenal's Satires

Satire 1 "On his compulsion toward this form of writing"
Deals with why the poet has chosen to write satire.
Satire 2 "Against hypocritical queens"
Attacks homosexual men.
Satire 3 "Against the city of Rome"
Catalogues all the ills of Rome and the reasons one should abandon the city.

Satire 4 "Against a big fish"
Mocks fawning courtiers of the late Emperor Domitian.
Satire 5 "Against mean patrons"
Attacks stingy patrons and the clients who tolerate their abuse.
Satire 6 "Against women"
Presents a diatribe against women couched within an argument against marriage.
Satire 7 "On poets, pedagogues, and poverty"
Laments the straitened financial circumstances of poets and scholars.
Satire 8 "Against base nobles"
Argues that noble blood should be less important than worthy deeds.
Satire 9 "On the griefs of a career man"
Attacks pimps and informers.
Satire 10 "On the vanity of human wishes"
Dissects the folly of common human aspirations and dreams.
Satire 11 "With an invitation to dinner"
Criticizes extravagance at mealtimes, promising a simple repast served in peace as an alternative.
Satire 12 "On the near-shipwreck of a friend"
Celebrates a friend's narrow escape from death and attacks legacy hunters.
Satire 13 "For a defrauded friend"
Offers consolation to a friend who has been defrauded and enumerates the torments of a guilty conscience.
Satire 14 "On education in avarice"
Discusses the evils of avarice and the importance of setting a good example for one's children.
Satire 15 "On the atrocities of Egypt"
Attacks the customs of Egypt, especially an instance of cannibalism.
Satire 16 "On the prerogatives of the soldier"
Discusses the advantages enjoyed by Roman soldiers, who have started to trample upon civilians' rights; appears to be incomplete.

Overview. Juvenal's satires were apparently published in five books of varying length. The first book contains Satires 1-5; the second book, Satire 6 alone; the third book, Satires 7-9; the fourth book, Satires 10-12; and the fifth book, Satires 13-16. The angry, ranting tone of the first two books, which deal mainly with issues related to Roman men and women, differs from the more detached, ironical tone of the last three books. The transformation is detectable in the following set of the few satires this writing describes in further detail. While Juvenal's speaker remains cynical throughout, the difference in tone may suggest a degree of internal growth in the narrator; he has perhaps gained a measure of control over the ungoverned anger of his earlier self.

Satire 1. The first satire, "On his compulsion toward this form of writing," begins with an at-

tack on the mediocre poets of his day as Juvenal's speaker asks, "Must I be listening always, and not pay them back?" (*Satires*, 1.1). The speaker bemoans not only the quality but also the quantity of doggerel produced by these hack writers, whose works continue to recycle old epic themes and subjects. Taking the satirist Lucilius for his model, the speaker declares his own intention of writing satire, especially in light of the many vices plaguing his society, asking, "What human being / Has such iron control of himself in this city of evil / As to hold his tongue" (*Satires*, 1.29-31).

According to the speaker, immorality flourishes in Rome in the shape of greedy lawyers, backstabbing informers, ambitious lackeys, and countless other malefactors. The speaker asks, "Do things like these not rate the midnight oil of a Horace? / Should I not bring them to light?" (*Satires*, 1.51-52). In this age of vice and folly, the speaker maintains, satire practically writes itself. A mere observer could fill notebooks with verses about the crimes and misdeeds that occur in Rome on a daily basis, from forgery to poisoning.

The speaker goes on to depict a humiliating scene of the city's poor clients lining up to receive a grudging pittance from their wealthy patrons. While the poor must scrounge for food and fuel, the patron gluts himself at lavish banquets, gobbling up the price of an estate at one sitting. The speaker predicts no improvement over the present injustices, predicting that future ages will practice the same vices.

The writer of satire should be aware of the risks he is taking in speaking out against the evils of his time. Ancient myths and legends are far safer subjects about which to write, exciting neither anger nor distress. "But when Lucilius roars and draws the sword in his anger, / Then the listener's mind, cold with its guilty knowledge, / Reddens and sweats; hence tears and wrath. You'd best think it over; / Once the helmet is on, it is much too late to be sorry" (*Satires*, 1.165-168). The satire concludes with the speaker's declaration, "Let's see what can be done about less fortunate mortals, / Those whose ashes lie by the great roads out of the city" (*Satires*, 1.170-171).

Satire 3. The third satire, "Against the city of Rome," begins with a framing narrative about the poet's friend Umbricius, who is leaving Rome to settle "in the ghost town of Cumae" (*Satires*, 3.2). While waiting for his goods to be loaded onto a wagon, Umbricius launches into a lengthy monologue about the many evils plaguing his native city.

According to Umbricius, Rome is no longer a place for an honest man, who is doomed to idleness and poverty if he remains there. Thus, Umbricius plans to settle where he can enjoy his declining years in peace, abandoning Rome to the wealthy and corrupt who wield all the power in the city. Rome itself has become a city of detestable foreigners, more welcoming to flattering, fawning Greeks, whose manners and customs have beguiled the patrons of the city and have become the fashion. Unable to compete, native Romans find themselves slandered by the Greeks and subsequently dismissed from their patron's service.

Umbricius declares that Romans' faithful service is not valued, that only wealth matters. Poor men are mocked for their shabby clothes and prevented from advancing socially through marriage or employment. The rising cost of living and the pressure of trying to keep up with one's neighbors drive poor men further into debt.

In addition, Rome offers terrible living conditions in the form of dilapidated houses with cracked walls and ruined beams. When a fire erupts, the poor man finds himself without help or possessions, while a rich man whose home burns receives financial and emotional support from his many friends to replace what he has lost. It is far better, Umbricius insists, to live in the country, where decent housing is cheap and plentiful.

Umbricius goes on to condemn Rome's lack of tranquility and high crime level. Only the rich can sleep in peace and make their way in cushioned litters through crowded streets without fear of getting jostled or trampled (the litter being a couch mounted on poles and used to carry or transport someone). The streets themselves are full of hazards, especially at night; drunkards, hoodlums, and thieves lurk in the shadows to assault the poor and unwary passers-by, while burglars scheme to break into citizens' houses. Most of the iron and steel in Rome are used to forge chains for criminals, rather than to make hoes and ploughshares.

Bringing his tirade to a close, Umbricius announces that he must be on his way. He declares that he will gladly come to visit his friend should the latter desert Rome for the Aquino and even promises to listen to his friend's satirical verses.

Satire 10. "On the vanity of human wishes," one of Juvenal's more famous satires, begins with this solemn observation: "In all the lands that reach from Gibraltar to the Euphrates / Few indeed are the men who can tell a curse from a blessing. . . . / In peace, in war, in both, we ask for the things that will hurt us" (*Satires*, 10.1-2, 9). Instead of

trusting the gods' judgment, petitioners pray for the blessings of eloquence, physical strength, and wealth, which too often turn out to have unpleasant consequences.

Wealth is most often prayed for. But rich men live in continual fear of their lives, often becoming the target of envious rivals or poisoners. Poor men, by contrast, venture forth at night without dreading attacks by robbers. The laughing philosopher Democritus and the weeping philosopher Heraclitus both deplored the craving for riches; their wisdom should set an example for all.

Political power likewise brings about ruin. The once-mighty Sejanus, leader of the palace military guard, lost the favor of Emperor Tiberius, fell from his high position, and was dragged as a disgraced prisoner through the streets of Rome. The fickle Roman populace shows no loyalty to former favorites, caring only for bread and entertainment. High rank and ambition have been the downfall not only of Sejanus but of Crassus, Pompey, and even Caesar himself. "Few are the kings who descend without wounds or murder to Pluto. / Few tyrants die a dry death" (*Satires*, 10.114-115).

Verbal eloquence can also be a two-edged sword. Budding scholars may pray for the talents of Demosthenes and Cicero, two famed orators. But both were undone by their talents. Cicero died at the hands of Mark Antony's soldiers who cut off his head and hands. Demosthenes lived an ill-starred life and died miserably as well.

Military glory similarly proves to be a hollow aspiration. Taken away from the battlefield, what are spoils of war but a motley collection of battered weapons, arms, and demoralized captives? Hannibal's military ambitions eventually brought ruin to his native Carthage, Alexander the Great died young, and King Xerxes of Persia suffered a great defeat, losing all but one of his ships, at the Battle of Salamis.

Many pray for a long life, but "a long old age is full of continual evils" (*Satires*, 10.190). The elderly lose their looks, their vigor, their teeth, their hearing, their sense of taste, and their ability to perform sexually. Worse, they suffer from a succession of illnesses and injuries, eventually growing senile and unable to care for themselves. Meanwhile, those who retain their mental faculties into old age must endure the deaths of their siblings, spouses, and children. Who would be like the ancient kings Nestor or Priam, whose sons predeceased them? Moreover, Priam lived to see his kingdom destroyed before he himself was slaughtered. Many men, including Marius and Pompey, survived long enough to be conquered, exiled, or imprisoned. An early death would have spared them these indignities.

Fond mothers pray to Venus to grant beauty to their sons and daughters. But men prey upon beautiful girls, while handsome boys are seldom virtuous. Beauty often leads to corruption and vice; even handsome men who resist temptation, like Bellerophon and Hippolytus, may find themselves the target of lustful, predatory women (for more on Hippolytus, see **Phaedra,** also in *Classical Literature and Its Times*).

What should one pray for? The speaker advises readers to respect the wisdom of the gods and allow them to choose what blessings to bestow upon their supplicants. Meanwhile,

> Pray for a healthy mind in a healthy body, a
>   spirit
> Unafraid of death, but reconciled to it, and able
> To bear up, to endure whatever troubles
>   afflict it,
> Free from hate and desire . . .
> I show you what you can give to yourself:
>   only through virtue
> Lies the certain road to a life that is blessed
>   and tranquil.
>   (*Satires*, 10.358-361, 363-364)

The virtue of simplicity. Although Juvenal offers little in the way of solutions to Rome's many evils, it would be inaccurate to say that he is pessimistic about or indifferent to every aspect of the human condition. Indeed, one may contend that his outrage reflects the magnitude of his concern for the welfare of Rome. There are things that Juvenal clearly values, including true friendship and simple pleasures (a good meal, a long soak in the baths), the latter best enjoyed in moderation: "Isn't pleasure / All the more keen in our lives the less we're inclined to repeat it?" (*Satires*, 11.207-208).

The need for moderation and simplicity is a recurring theme throughout Juvenal's satires. He deplores extravagance in all forms, whether in food, clothing, expenditures, or customs, and seems to ascribe much of it to foreigners who have taken up residence in Rome and made it somehow less Roman. In Satire 3, the speaker Umbricius declares, "Citizens, I can't stand a Greekized Rome. Yet what portion / Of the dregs of our own town comes from Achaia [Greece] only? / Into the Tiber pours the silt, the mud of Orontes, / Bringing its bauble and brawl, its dissonant harps and its timbrels" (*Satires*, 3.61-64). Umbricius goes on to argue that "Long before now, all poor Roman descendants of Romans /

Ought to have marched out of the town in one determined migration" and taken up quieter, simpler lives in the country (*Satires*, 3.163-164).

When extending a dinner invitation to his friend Persicus, Juvenal describes a plain, wholesome meal that is meant to contrast with the wasteful extravagance and opulent decor of most Roman banquets. He promises "things we can't get in a market," such as "the fattest kid in the flock, and the tenderest," "fresh eggs . . . warm from the nest," "Syrian bergamot pears" and "fragrant sweet-smelling apples . . . perfectly ripened" (*Satires*, 11.65-74). He maintains that "Such a meal would have pleased our luxury-loving senate / In the good old days" when everything was "perfectly simple, / Furniture, household, food" (*Satires*, 11.76-77, 98-99).

Although readers might question whether "the good old days" Juvenal describes so nostalgically ever truly existed, modesty and simplicity, along with frugality, piety, and chastity, were qualities that many Romans prized. The Emperor Augustus, for example, was often praised for his own modest lifestyle: he furnished his palace simply, ate moderately, and wore unremarkable clothes when at home. Simplicity and moderation were also characteristic of the reigns of Vespasian and Titus, two of Augustus's more respected successors, who ruled during Juvenal's lifetime.

Sources and literary context. Juvenal drew mainly upon his experiences in Rome and upon the city's long history. Frequent references are made to past incidents and scandals, such as the fall of Sejanus and the affairs of Empress Messalina, as well as to more recent events, like the tyranny of the late Emperor Domitian and the deterioration of the patron-client relationship.

While Juvenal's personal observations provide the meat of his satires, he was also writing within an established tradition of satire inherited from Lucilius, Horace, and Persius. In his first satire, Juvenal even refers to Lucilius and Horace, announcing that he will follow "on the drill ground / Where Lucilius drove the wheels of his chariot" (*Satires*, 1.20-21). In style, however, Juvenal followed Horace's example, adopting a refined, almost conversational tone that becomes more detached in the later satires. Cynicism, pessimism, vivid pictorial imagery, and biting invective characterize Juvenal's work; he seldom offers constructive criticism or proposes solutions while railing against vice, folly, and corrupt institutions.

Impact. While Juvenal is said to have enjoyed moderate success as a writer during his lifetime, his satires were seldom read for two centuries after his death. Towards the end of the fourth century, however, interest in Juvenal's work revived. Between the fourth and fifth centuries, the reading public in Italy, Gaul, Spain, Africa, and the Greek-speaking East continued to enjoy his *Satires*. In the West and the East, Juvenal was included among the classical writers studied in the school curricula of the time.

During the period known as the Dark Ages Juvenal's work fell into obscurity again, but manuscripts of his writings, which had survived from late antiquity, were rediscovered and copied by the end of the eighth century. Later medieval and Renaissance scholars also found Juvenal a subject worthy of study, as a moralist and as an example of a classical poet. Between 1470 and 1500 there were at least 50 known printings of Juvenal's work. Later satirists, such as John Dryden, Jonathan Swift, and Samuel Johnson, admired Juvenal and were influenced by him to some degree. Johnson, in particular, based two of his own famous works, *London* and *On the Vanity of Human Wishes*, on Satires 3 and 10 from Juvenal's corpus.

—Pamela S. Loy

For More Information

Anderson, William S. *Essays on Roman Satire*. Princeton, N.J.: Princeton University Press, 1982.

Boardman, John, Jasper Griffin, and Oswyn Murray, eds. *The Oxford History of the Roman World*. Oxford: Oxford University Press, 2001.

Coffey, Michael. *Roman Satire*. London: Methuen, 1976.

Courtney, E. *Commentary on the Satires of Juvenal*. London: Athlone Press, 1980.

Freudenburg, Kirk. *Satires of Rome*. Cambridge: Cambridge University Press, 2001.

Grant, Michael. *The Roman Emperors*. New York: Charles Scribner's Sons, 1985.

Highet, Gilbert. *Juvenal the Satirist: A Study*. Oxford: Oxford University Press, 1954.

Hornblower, Simon, and Antony Spawforth, eds. *The Oxford Companion to Classical Civilization*. Oxford: Oxford University Press, 1998.

Juvenal. *The Satires of Juvenal*. Trans. Rolfe Humphries. Bloomington: Indiana University Press, 1958.

Knoche, Ulrich. *Roman Satire*. Trans. Edwin S. Ramage. Bloomington: Indiana University Press, 1975.

Satyricon

by
Petronius

The *Satyricon* is the sole surviving work of an author referred to as Petronius Arbiter. The title (in Latin, *Satyrica* or *Libri Satyricon*) may be referring to *satura*, a culinary term for "mixed dish" that gave rise to *satire,* the name of a literary form devoted to exposing hypocrites and the socially pretentious. Using ridicule to bring into focus human vice and folly, satire was developed by the Romans into a genre whose typical work contained diverse subjects and sometimes diverse literary forms (i.e., was a "mixed dish"). Petronius's title may also be referring to satyr, the Greek mythological figure given to sexual excess and dissolute behavior, phenomena that figure prominently in the novel. As with the meaning of the title, there is uncertainty about the length and overall storyline of the original *Satyricon.* Only fragments of the original survive, painstakingly ordered by generations of scholars. The longest and most famous sequence that remains intact is the account of a bizarre dinner party thrown by a fabulously wealthy and extravagant ex-slave named Trimalchio.

There is some debate over the author's identity, but many suppose him to be the same Petronius described by the second-century CE historian Tacitus in his **Annals of Imperial Rome** (also in *Classical Literature and Its Times*). This Petronius was an aristocrat, a government official, and a man intimate with the emperor Nero's social set. According to Tacitus, Petronius was the emperor's authority on what was and was not fashionable in Roman society. Coincidentally or not, the *Satyricon* (especially its most famous section, the

---

THE LITERARY WORK

A novel set in southern Italy during the midfirst century CE; written in Latin and published in the 60s CE.

SYNOPSIS

Four companions—conceited, amoral, and impoverished—become enmeshed in a series of outlandish, often perverse adventures.

---

above-mentioned dinner of Trimalchio) is shot through with such sensibilities. In 65 CE a failed attempt on Nero's life (the Pisonian conspiracy) resulted in the deaths of over 100 prominent Roman aristocrats. The Petronius described by Tacitus was among those ordered to commit suicide, which he did in 66. Composed in the politically tense years just prior to this suicide, the *Satyricon* is a sophisticated and lurid tale of amoral, opportunistic characters racing through the seamy underside of mid-first century Italian society.

Events in History at the Time the Novel Takes Place

Emperor Nero and his court. The emperor Nero, under whose reign (54-68 CE) Petronius wrote the *Satyricon*, was originally named Lucius Domitius Ahenobarbus. He was the son of Agrippina and Gnaeus Domitius Ahenobarbus (who,

Satyricon

Illustration of Petronius. © Hulton Getty/Liaison Agency. Reproduced by permission.

according to some, was the heir of a noble family known for its cruelty and violence as well as its military victories). There is a tale that Agrippina consulted an astrologer about her son's future; when he informed her that the boy would become emperor but would also kill his mother, she responded, "Let him kill [me], so long as he rules" (Tacitus, *Annals,* book 14, chapter 9). When her husband died, Agrippina insured her and her son's fortune by marrying the next emperor, her uncle Claudius. Although Claudius already had a son, Britannicus, the emperor adopted Lucius Domitius as a second son, then favored him over Britannicus. The favored stepson took a new name, Claudius Nero, becoming known simply as Nero. In 54 CE, Nero's adoptive father was fatally poisoned, probably by Agrippina. Nero became emperor and, shortly thereafter, Britannicus, his potential rival, was also poisoned. In spite of these dark beginnings, Nero's reign was well received for several years. He was beloved by the people and coexisted peacefully with the Senate. In the early 60s CE, however, for reasons that remain somewhat obscure, this governmental harmony began to deteriorate.

Nero was an enthusiastic patron of the arts, as indicated by the successes of writers of the era. It is unknown to what extent, if at all, he en-

couraged Petronius to write the *Satyricon*. But in any case Petronius is known to have been one of the brilliant literary talents that flourished under Nero's reign. Three other major writers of the era are Persius, Seneca the Younger, and Lucan (Seneca's nephew). Seneca, who served as Nero's tutor and political advisor, produced philosophical and poetic writings that Petronius parodies in his novel. Lucan wrote an epic poem entitled *The Civil War*, which Petronius also parodies (*Satyrica*, chapters 119-124, pp. 118-128). It is possible that literature may have flourished under Nero partly as a way for ambitious aristocrats to attract the emperor's attention. If so, Petronius's allusions to the works of Seneca and Lucan may be part of the competition for court favor. Since both had fallen from favor by the early 60s CE, Petronius's parodies of their works may have struck with particular force.

Nero himself indulged in public display, an endeavor that every emperor had to master. He became particularly infamous for his activities in the theater and amphitheater alike. Turning himself into the spectacle, Nero performed tragic roles onstage and drove chariots through the amphitheater. His antics endeared him to the masses but horrified Rome's aristocratic elite. What must have been at least partly a public relations stunt to win the affections of common citizens was taken by the elite as evidence of a decadent emperor's bottomless capacity for vice. Whether they were scandalized by this capacity or frightened by his popularity with the public is open to question.

Nero's unpopularity with the Senate finally led to a conspiracy to take his life in 65 CE. As noted, the conspiracy failed, and the emperor retaliated, blaming Petronius for treachery, or perhaps some other offense, and forcing him, among others, to commit suicide. Two years later Rome finally turned on Nero. Revolts in the western provinces in 68 CE encouraged the Senate to avenge itself both in respect to those who died by Nero's order and in outrage at his disregard for traditional mores in the conduct of his office. The Senate declared Nero a public enemy and he fled into hiding, then committed suicide himself. After Nero's rule came the Year of the Four Emperors, a period that saw the return of bloody civil war to the Roman world as three would-be emperors attempted to rule Rome, assuming power in quick succession until a fourth contestant, Vespasian, seized and successfully retained control. The death of Nero had brought to an end the Julio-Claudian dynasty that began with Augustus.

From slave to freedman in Nero's Rome. The main surviving episode in *Satyricon* centers on an ex-slave, Trimalchio. Ex-slaves were commonly known as "freedmen" or "freedwomen" (in contrast to Roman citizens who had always been free and were known as "free men" or "free women"). How possible was it for slaves to win their freedom? In ancient Rome, a slaveowner could free a slave whenever the owner wished. Some slaves bought their freedom by paying the owner the price for which they had been purchased, though amassing enough money was prohibitive for most. Often a male slaveowner would free his slaves to display his wealth, power, or generosity. Many slaves were freed in the will of their owner (who thus kept possession of them until his death). Upon manumission, a freedman shaved his head, according to one ancient source, after the practice of sea travelers who survived storms and then, after returning home, shaved their heads and dedicated their hair to the gods. Similar to these travelers, the freedmen had escaped the "storm of slavery." With freedom came legal rights and privileges—citizenship and the right to contract a marriage and produce legitimate offspring, children who were "fully" free citizens. "Halfway" citizens themselves, the freedmen could not run for public office.

While there is insufficient information to ascertain the number of freedmen and freedwomen in ancient Rome, historical evidence suggests that by this era their population had grown quite large. The former status of a dead person was noted on his or her tombstone. A survey of 1,000 tombstones in the city of Rome revealed that three times as many belonged to freedmen as to the freeborn. Publius Cornelius Sulla, a general of the early first century BCE, is reported to himself have freed 10,000 slaves; the fire brigade in the city of Rome, numbering 7,000 at its creation in 6 CE, consisted entirely of freedmen; in the same period, under the emperor Augustus, a law was introduced that forbade a master from freeing more than 100 slaves in his will—perhaps indicating a concern that too many freedmen were entering the population or too many heirs were being deprived of their human "property."

Owners who freed their slaves did not lose all rights to their services; in fact, it was not uncommon for a former master to retain his ex-slaves in his employ. Insofar as freedom was considered a show of kindness on the part of the master, freedmen were bound to their former master by "obligations of gratitude." It was legally their duty to be at his and his family's service for as long as he lived. The type of service a freedman was obligated to supply to his former master would be negotiated before manumission, then confirmed by taking an oath. An ex-master could punish an "ungrateful" freedman by having him "lightly" whipped or fined, or even by revoking his freedom (a rarely exercised option). The Roman jurist Ulpian wrote that a judge "should not endure the slave of yesterday, who today is free,

FROM TACITUS'S BIOGRAPHICAL SKETCH OF PETRONIUS

In C. Petronius' case some brief background must be given. . . . He was considered . . . a man of educated luxuriousness. Nevertheless, as proconsul of Bithynia and later as consul, he showed himself vigorous and equal to business. Then, recoiling into vice, or by imitations of vice, he was enlisted by Nero among a few of his establishment as the arbiter of elegance, inasmuch as he thought that nothing was attractive or had the soft feeling of affluence except what Petronius had approved for him.

(Tacitus, *Annals*, book 16, chapter 18)

to complain that his master has spoken abusively to him, or struck him lightly, or criticized him" (Joshel, p. 34). During Nero's reign, the Senate even entertained a law to revoke the manumission of ungrateful freedmen; perhaps realizing that the sheer number of freedmen in all levels of society would make such a law both unpopular and disruptive, Nero returned the proposal to the Senate with the recommendation (which, of course, could not be ignored) that the Senate instead handle the issue on a case-by-case basis.

Emperors often placed their own freedmen in important posts in the empire. An emperor's ex-slaves might supervise the collection of taxes or oversee provincial governors. Rome's first emperor, Augustus, used his ex-slaves to staff his administration, as other Roman officials had before him. Rome's fourth emperor, Claudius, Nero's adoptive father, went much further, making an ex-slave, Narcissus, his private secretary and then giving the freedman a prominent voice in government, much to the disgruntlement of the Roman aristocracy. After Claudius died, Narcissus retained power, and the next emperor, Nero, could not roll back this power, at least not immediately. Narcissus remained a potent force for several years, while his brother Felix served as a particularly brutal governor of Palestine. As these examples suggest, freedmen were a diverse group:

> Freedmen . . . were not a class, all poorer or wealthier than the freeborn. Moreover, the freedman of an ordinary tailor must be distinguished from the emperor's freedman, who held a high post in the imperial bureaucracy. Freedmen's relations with patrons, too, varied: some were working in their shops; others had no living patron, no obligations to the patron's heir, or were themselves their master's heir.
>
> (Joshel, pp. 34-35)

Dining and other forms of decadence. The surviving fragments of the *Satyricon* treat diverse aspects of Roman social life in Petronius's day. Feasting was a topic of both contemporary relevance and traditional concern. According to a common view of Roman history, all the wealth flowing from imperial conquests eroded the stern discipline and virtue of early Rome, nurturing greed and a taste for decadence. Greater wealth led to more opportunities for showy display. The ancient historian Livy (59 BCE–17 CE) complains that the cook, the least important slave of the earlier Roman household, was in his day the most important slave. At great expense, cooks prepared rare, exotic dishes, extending not just to their taste but also to their visual appeal. And more than food was on display.

Elite dining included a vast array of entertainment, including dancers, jugglers, acrobats, poets, musicians, and/or entire acting companies. The entertainments reflected a host's wealth, social status, and degree of cultural refinement, as well as his estimation of the guests in attendance. A host would not, for example, offer a feast accompanied by jugglers and acrobats to guests accustomed to refined music and poetry readings. The whole experience of hosting a dinner—the preparation and display of food and wine, the entertainers, and so forth—became critical to the competition for social approval. The elite (and would-be elite) dined in a spirit of rivalry.

In the low status that it accorded to the entertainers themselves, the elite (however unconsciously hypocritical it might have been) adhered to a double standard: to engage in providing pleasure to others was considered dishonorable, but to employ the entertainers was acceptable. These "entertainers" ranged from food vendors on the street, to cooks, and especially to prostitutes, actors, and gladiators (people who used their bodies to provide pleasure

to others). While society thought it fine to avail oneself of their services, excessive reliance on them was frowned upon. Indulgence of appetite was an area about which the elite showed particular anxiety. The man who was immoderate at the table, it was thought, might easily be sexually immoderate as well. The belief was that raw appetites were linked to one another; to indulge in any of them was to betray an effeminate lack of self-control that could extend to them all.

Emperors were not spared this scrutiny. If the ancient historical accounts can be believed, Nero exceeded all norms of indulgence—in sex, in feasting, and in other pursuits. A hostile bias in the ancient sources may be partly responsible for the portrait of Nero's monstrous excesses. But in any case, a balance had to be struck in such activities, and as emperor, Nero did not strike it.

Socially acceptable sexual conduct might include, for a man, sex with a woman outside marriage, provided she was a slave or prostitute (so as not to violate the household of the man to whom a free woman belonged, either as wife or daughter). A man could have sex with another man, provided he was the "active" participant, the one who penetrates the body of the other party and thus displays his virility. To become the passive party, or worse yet to enjoy and habitually seek it out, was a disgrace, an adaptation of the male body to female behavior. Since eating is a passive pleasure, to indulge in feasting excessively could be taken to imply an interest in other passive pleasures.

The Novel in Focus

Plot summary. The main characters of the *Satyricon* are a trio of young men. Two, Encolpius and Ascyltos, are perhaps in their twenties; the third, Giton, is about 16. He is at first the teenage lover of Encolpius but switches to having an affair with their companion Ascyltos. These three are eventually joined by an aged and lascivious self-styled poet.

The *Satyricon* opens as the narrator Encolpius expresses his contempt for the state of rhetoric. In his eyes, it has grown stale and silly on an unhealthy diet of unrealistic themes prescribed by the schoolmasters. Encolpius addresses this opinion to just such a teacher of rhetoric, who sadly agrees with the bleak assessment. The teacher blames parents. If schoolmasters refuse to teach what parents misguidedly wish their children to learn, their schools will be empty. To underscore this truth, he launches into a poem on the theme of rhetoric's decline, from its glorious Greek origins and Roman apex to its present decay. Encolpius departs, then reunites with his teenage lover, Giton, and with Ascyltos, his partner in misadventures. Ascyltos, it so happens, has designs on Giton himself. In the following fragment, the three barely escape a series of close calls.

There appears a priestess of the god Priapus (the guardian spirit of sheep and goats, known for his lust). The priestess, whose name is Quartilla, has encountered Encolpius in the past; he interrupted some sacred rites being conducted in honor of Priapus. She dispatches a slave to announce her arrival to the surprised young men, who are assured she comes not to blame or punish. When Quartilla herself arrives, she weeps profusely and informs the youths that after Encolpius disrupted the rites being conducted in honor of Priapus, she fell ill. A cure was revealed to her in her dreams, along with the instruction that she seek out those responsible and carry out the cure in their company. She further begs them to keep to themselves the secret goings-on they witnessed in Priapus's shrine. They readily assure her of their full cooperation as well as their pious silence. Quartilla cheers up and informs them that it is good they agreed, because otherwise a lynch mob would have shown up at their door to avenge her dishonor. As it happens, the cure takes the form of a raucous, free-for-all sexual orgy.

The next episode features a grand dinner party thrown by the well-known freedman Trimalchio, who is a businessman and a gourmet. Encolpius, Ascyltos, and Giton have all been invited. While mingling with the other guests, Encolpius spots an old man with a shaven head, the badge of the freedman. The man in question is none other than their host, Trimalchio. Dressed in a red tunic, he seems to be playing a game of catch with a circle of long-haired slave boys. It is a strange version of catch. He makes no effort to retrieve the balls that he fails to catch. Instead a slave stands by with a steady supply of new ones at the ready. Also strange is the method of keeping score. Instead of counting successful catches and returned throws, the scorekeeping slave counts the number of balls dropped.

Our narrator passes a mural decorated with scenes from Trimalchio's own life:

> It depicted a slave market complete with price tags. Trimalchio himself was in the picture; his hair is long and in his hand he grips the wand of [the god] Mercury. [The goddess] Minerva

leads the way as our hero enters Rome. A painstaking artist had carefully portrayed the whole course of his career, complete with captions: how he first learned to keep the books and then was put in charge of the cash. In the last scene . . . Fortuna is at his side carrying her burgeoning cornucopia, as the three Fates spin the golden threads.
> (Petronius, *Satyrica*, chapter 29, p. 25)

The mural follows Trimalchio from his sale at the slave market to his entry into Rome. Pictured is his climb up the social ladder—guided by Mercury (god of profit and commerce) and Minerva (goddess of wisdom)—to the present peak of his career, which finds him at the side of the goddess Fortune while the Fates spin out the allotments of his prosperous life in golden thread. As our threesome proceeds, Encolpius notices that on the doorposts of the entrance to the dining room there are rods and axes affixed to the bronze prow of a ship (traditional symbol of a naval victory). The fixture bears an inscription citing Trimalchio's membership in a public religious order open to freedmen: "Presented to C. Pompeius Trimalchio, Priest of the College of Augustus, by Cinnamus the Steward" (*Satyrica*, chapter 30, p. 26). The rods and axes are the official emblem of public executive authority; they symbolize the powers of corporal and capital punishment (the rods stand for beating; the axes, for execution). It was not out of bounds for a priest of the College of Augustus to display these symbols, but since he normally would not have either of these powers, it is a rather melodramatic gesture. Exaggerating the showiness of the fixture to a ridiculous extent is the grandiose addition of a ship's prow, which likely refers to the fortune Trimalchio made in the import-export business. Later, during the dinner, a slave brings out statuettes of Trimalchio's household gods—Gain, Luck, and Profit. While it is appropriate for each household to have its own particular gods to watch over it, Trimalchio's set of domestic deities is comically absurd, and therefore entirely appropriate to him. Every sort of extravagance is in evidence at the feast. Trimalchio's entrance into the dining room and all other events at the feast, including the arrival of each course, is announced by music. Guests are treated to pedicures while they wait (whether they want them or not), and with musical accompaniment.

Trimalchio is carried into the dining room on a litter. He wears on his fingers one gold-plated ring and another of a solid gold decorated with iron studs; gold rings were the mark of the equestrians or businessmen (Rome's second wealthiest class, after the senators). Tucked about his neck is a napkin with a purple stripe, a badge of distinction usually found on a senator's toga. Trimalchio is a mass of conflicting pretensions to any and all status symbols in Roman society.

When 100-year-old wine is brought into the room, Trimalchio makes the melancholy observation that a bottle of wine outlives a human being. This grim note is followed by a slave who produces a silver skeleton with hinged joints that he throws about on the floor as the guests watch its limbs fall in different patterns. As usual, Trimalchio sums up the moment with some bad impromptu verse:

> Alas! Poor us! We all add up to squat;
>   once Hades gets his hooks in, that's the lot;
>   so live while it's your turn, 'cause then it's not.
>   (*Satyrica*, chapter 34, p. 31)

Encolpius turns to one of his table companions and inquires after the identity of a very conspicuous woman moving about the dining room. Her name is Fortunata. She is Trimalchio's wife, and she thoroughly dominates him. Aside from being hot-tempered, she is as frugal as he is extravagant and knows far better than her husband what he owns and how much. As Encolpius is listening to this news, Trimalchio offers his guests a personal interpretation of a course of food that has just been brought in, 12 separate dishes arranged according to the signs of the zodiac. Taurus (bull) is represented by a rump roast; Libra (balance), by a set of scales with a cheese tart on one side; and so forth. Next Trimalchio gives a crass and cynical account of different psychological types born under the astrological signs, their major characteristics and preferred professions: "Whoever is born under the Ram has many flocks, lots of wool, a shameless mug, a hard head, and a horny noggin. Under this sign are born many scholars and other boneheads" (*Satyrica*, chapter 39, p. 34). The audience applauds wildly for their host's impromptu performance, as for all his speeches.

Soon after, Trimalchio departs for the bathroom and the focus shifts to the conversation of the freedmen guests, his social milieu. The language takes on a more rural, earthy tone as the freedmen gossip about who is making a profit, who is losing money, and who is dishonest. Trimalchio returns, announcing to everyone that lately he has been constipated, but for the moment a mixture of pomegranate rind and pinesap boiled in vinegar has done the trick. He then encourages his guests to fart right in the dining room, for comfort and good health are more important than restrictive social conventions. If not expelled from the body, he warns his guests, gas vapors will go straight to the brain and could even kill a person. The guests once again applaud, this time saluting his advanced ideas about health versus social custom.

Next Trimalchio demonstrates his knowledge of art to the assembled, recounting the origin of Corinthian bronze. He wildly misinforms everyone, saying that after sacking Troy, the leader Hannibal (who was not a Greek at Troy c. 1200 BCE but Rome's enemy at Carthage a thousand years later) melted down all the different metals in the city to produce a unique bronze alloy, called Corinthian. Trimalchio blithely confuses Carthage, Rome's most famous enemy, with Troy, site of the most famous war in Greco-Roman literature. The blunder demonstrates his ignorance, of classical culture, and, by implication, that of the class he represents. Trimalchio happily makes it all up as he goes along, mixing things together the way he mixes senatorial stripes and equestrian rings on his own body.

After more bizarre food, poor poetry, and assorted mishaps, the host once again turns his attention to the temporary existence of man, and of himself in particular. He asks a freedman acquaintance whom he has hired to build his tomb how the work is coming, listing all sorts of details he wants included on it. Next Trimalchio recites his epitaph, breaking into tears at the thought of it. As if on cue, his wife, the freedman responsible for his tomb, and all of his slaves break into tears too. Encolpius, Ascyltos, and Giton try to make their escape but are foiled and so must watch as Trimalchio stages his own funeral to see how everyone will mourn him when he dies. He orders trumpets to be sounded. The local fire brigade mistakes the trumpet blast for an alarm signal and, bursting in on the proceedings, throws water over everything. Amid the mayhem, Encolpius and his companions seize their chance and escape.

In the next episode, Encolpius and his friends fall in with a hypocritical, immoral old hack, a poet named Eumolpus, who joins the group. From him we hear two extended poems and some short verse, along with reports of sexually indecent incidents the poet has heard of or experienced. Prominent among these is the story of "The Widow of Ephesus," a tale Eumolpus alleges to be true. The widow in question was a singularly virtuous matron whose husband had just died. So devoted was she that she locked herself in the mausoleum in which her husband's body was entombed, intending to die there. A soldier nearby guarding the crosses on which several criminals had been crucified noticed that the tomb was occupied. Investigating, he discovered the young widow and her maid. He encourages first the maid to refrain from grief and then, with her assistance, exhorts the widow to accept food and drink. Eventually the widow relents and allows the soldier to visit her in the tomb. Acceptance of food and drink is followed by acceptance of sex with the soldier in the tomb, next to the corpse of her husband. The maid speaks on the soldier's behalf, quoting to the widow the advice that Dido's sister Anna gives to Dido in Virgil's *Aeneid* (also in *Classical Literature and Its Times*)—to accept the stranger Aeneas into her embrace. Dido, a tragic figure, abandons her oath of devotion to her dead husband, only to be abandoned by her new love. Not so for the widow. While sexually engaged with the widow in the tomb, the soldier, of course, cannot do his duty of guarding the bodies of the crucified criminals. The parents of one of them grabs the chance to take down his body. The missing corpse will reveal the soldier's dereliction of duty, the penalty for which is death. As the soldier prepares for this fate, the widow encourages him not to throw away his life needlessly. She has a plan. Since her husband is already dead, she proposes they hang him on the cross in place of the criminal's stolen corpse. The soldier agrees, avoids death, and there the story ends.

After many twists, turns, and near-disasters, the foursome approaches the southern Italian city of Croton, where they hatch a plan: Eumolpus will pose as a wealthy landholder from Africa, in poor health and grief-stricken at the premature death of his son. The conspirators expect the greedy people of the area to shower a wealthy but sick old man with gifts so that he will include them in his will. The ruse proves too tempting for local legacy hunters to resist. The con men are showered with gifts and illicit sexual favors. The plot closes on a gruesome note. Eumolpus's will, which he reads to the legacy hunters, stipulates that inheriting his money is contingent upon eating his dead flesh. Cannibalism, he explains, is revered in many cultures and should not give them cause for hesitation. At this point our copy of the original text breaks off abruptly.

Roman widows and the "Widow of Ephesus." The story of the "Widow of Ephesus" is told as evidence of female inconstancy. No background information is given for the widow of the story. Ephesus was a predominantly Greek city in Asia Minor, which in Petronius's day was a province of the Roman Empire. But whatever her ethnic and cultural background, the writer's Roman audience would have judged the widow's character by their standards. Her initial impulse, to remain with her dead husband inside his tomb, though extreme, exemplifies a decision that was entirely commendable from the Roman standpoint. The *univira* ("one-husband woman") was a stereotype in Roman society, who, through devotion to the memory of her deceased husband, did not seek remarriage after his death and was revered in aristocratic circles. To some degree, this may have been because the *univira* was by no means the norm. Although not entirely approved of, divorce and remarriage were common among upper-class Romans of the mid-first century CE; earlier legislation, under Augustus, had furthermore demanded remarriage after the death of a spouse. The true sting in this tale is less the tremendous disrespect the widow heaps upon her husband's corpse than the mockery she makes of the *univira,* by beginning as a paragon of virtue and then behaving in a way that ridicules the very notion of such a wife. When Dido, the tragic heroine of Virgil's *Aeneid,* to whom Petronius irreverently connects the widow, abandons her commitment to the memory of her first husband, she pays for it by failing to find happiness. Her new lover, the hero Aeneas, abandons her, and Dido takes her own life. When she briefly reappears in the Underworld, she is walking with her husband; in death, she reclaims her former virtue.

> At length she flung away from [Aeneas] and fled,
> His enemy still, into the shadowy grove
> Where he whose bride she once had been, Sychaeus,
> Joined in her sorrows and returned her love.
> Aeneas still gazed after her in tears,
> Shaken by her ill fate and pitying her.
> (Virgil, *Aeneid*, book 6, p. 176)

In contrast, Petronius's widow simply tosses off her virtue along with the memory of her husband and ends up thoroughly content.

Sources and literary context. The *Satyricon* is so unlike any other surviving Greek or Roman literature that scholars have often felt that it must

Written shortly after 385 BCE by Plato, the pupil of Socrates judged even in antiquity as the most literarily accomplished interpreter of Socratic wisdom, the *Symposium* is the account of a dinner party attended by Socrates in the year 416 BCE. The occasion is the celebration of the recent victory of the tragic playwright Agathon at the competition among playwrights in the festival of Dionysus, god of wine and tragic poetry. It is decided that each of the five celebrants, including the comic playwright Aristophanes, will deliver a speech on *philia*, which may be translated as "love," either carnal or otherwise, but also means friendship. The dialogue's examples of interpersonal, sexual love are between men. Important to an appreciation of the *Symposium* is an understanding of the positive social role a sexual and emotional liaison between an adult male and an adolescent male was understood to play. The adult would gain erotic satisfaction, while the youth would gain a mentor and ally, as well as a positive role model. When the youth reached full maturity, identified by the growth of his beard, the relationship as such would end. Erotic *philia* would give way to the *philia* of friendship. Socrates argued that the actual object of a person's love is whatever motivates it. If one's love is motivated by erotic concerns, as Agathon's speech reveals him to be, then it is the erotic that one truly loves, not the body or its owner. In keeping with this idea, Socrates advocates not the sexual love of young men's bodies for one's own pleasure, but rather the love of ideas which will make young men beautiful in soul.

be a continuation of or a response to some earlier literary genre or trend that has not survived. It has been argued in this vein that Petronius is parodying earlier Greek novelists. The surviving examples of that genre, however, appear to postdate Petronius, with one possible exception, *Chaereas and Callirhoe* by Chariton. And there is a strong case for dating his work after Petronius's as well.

While the literary tradition that produced Petronius's *Satyricon*, if such ever existed, remains very much an open question, it can certainly be said that he draws on well-known literature, weaving in humorous references to both Greek and Roman literature from across the full spectrum of genres. "The Dinner of Trimalchio" draws in particular on the eighth poem in Horace's second book of satires, "The Dinner of Nasidienus," and on Plato's dialogue on the subjects of love and beauty, the *Symposium*. When Trimalchio excuses himself during dinner to answer a call of nature, five freedmen guests each deliver a speech, recalling the five speakers of Plato's *Symposium*. In addition to highly specific verbal echoes of the *Symposium*, Petronius's freedmen recall and, of course, ridicule the positions of Plato's speakers: "Each group has its nostalgic defender of religious

tradition . . . each has its cynical advocate of moral indifference . . . and each has its pedantic purveyor of pseudo-scientific medical wisdom" (Bodel, p. 40). Such intricate use of the literary tradition is only part of the novel's allusive repertoire. Petronius also uses literary classics in a more explicitly comic vein by having his characters liken their petty and ignoble shenanigans to the momentous circumstances and lofty events of tragedy and epic. When, for instance, Encolpius is trying to hide Giton from his sometime companion Ascyltos by having him cling to the underside of his bed, he compares the situation to the episode in Homer's **Odyssey** in which Odysseus eludes the Cyclops by clinging to the underbelly of the monster's giant sheep (also in *Classical Literature and Its Times*). Petronius, like his second-century successor Apuleius, draws on the Greek "Milesian Tale" (see **The Golden Ass**, also in *Classical Literature and Its Times*). This was a notoriously lurid, highly popular form of reading entertainment. Petronius adapts the form most famously in "The Widow of Ephesus," the tale told by Encolpius, Petronius's poet of dubious merit. The lurid nature of this tale, culminating in sex between a soldier and a widow in her husband's tomb and the substitution of the dead husband's corpse for the body of a crucified criminal, is refined by a subtle literary sensibility shown in the allusions made to the lofty epic the *Aeneid*. It is a mark of Petronius's style that the text interweaves the lowest scurrility and crudeness with the keenest literary sophistication.

Publication and impact. Classical antiquity barely acknowledges Petronius's *Satyricon*. The exception to this silence is the fourth-century scholar Macrobius, who dismisses the novel as mere entertainment devoid of educational value. This near-total silence may mean that the novel was not widely circulated. In fact, while some clerical scholars of the later middle ages seem to have had access to as much of the text as we have today, Petronius's work did not become broadly accessible to literate society until the appearance of a succession of published editions beginning in the late fifteenth century.

The earliest surviving manuscript of the *Satyricon* dates from the ninth century CE and consists of short excerpts largely free of obscene material. Over time these fragments were filled out with material found in other manuscripts of the work. Apparently the earliest manuscript was censored to make Petronius's subject matter as morally praiseworthy as his literary style was. Medieval anthologies, compiled for the moral improvement of their readers, included a number of excerpts from Petronius's *Satyricon*, which were then used to create this cleaned-up version of the novel. While the first printed edition of the *Satyricon*, produced in Milan in the early 1480s, relied entirely on the purified edition, the suppressed fragments resurfaced with the discovery of another manuscript tradition in the 1500s. A manuscript of just the Trimalchio episode was discovered in 1650 and printed in 1664. A scholarly edition of the complete and uncensored surviving text of the novel was compiled and published in 1709.

Petronius's presence has been felt in the fiction of the twentieth century. The American novelist F. Scott Fitzgerald's *The Great Gatsby,* which features a dinner party, is in many ways a Jazz Age adaptation of the Trimalchio episode. (In fact, *Trimalchio* was the title of an earlier version of Fitzgerald's novel.) James Joyce refers directly to an episode from the *Satyricon* ("The Widow of Ephesus") in his novel *Ulysses.* "The Widow of Ephesus" was also adapted for the London stage in 1959 by British playwright Christopher Fry in an acclaimed production entitled *A Phoenix Too Frequent.* Finally, the Italian director Federico Fellini has adapted the *Satyricon* into film, though he uses it more as a point of departure and inspiration for his own complex and fascinating tale than an end in itself. An intense and challenging spectacle, Fellini's cinematic *Satyricon* is at first glance quite different from the novel in respect to storyline; its fidelity is to be found rather in its kaleidoscopic recreation of the bewildering, labyrinthine world through which Petronius's characters roam.

—Seán Easton

For More Information

Bodel, John. "The *Cena Trimalchionis.*" In *Latin Fiction*. Ed. Heinz Hoffman. London: Routledge, 1999.

Courtney, Edward. *A Companion to Petronius.* Oxford: Oxford University Press, 2001.

Hallett, Judith P., and Marilyn B. Skinner, eds. *Roman Sexualities.* Princeton, N.J.: Princeton University Press, 1997.

Hopkins, Keith. *Conquerors and Slaves: Sociological Studies in Roman History.* Vol. 1. Cambridge: Cambridge University Press, 1978.

Joshel, Sandra R. *Work, Identity, and Legal Status at Rome: A Study of the Occupational Inscriptions.* Norman: University of Oklahoma Press, 1992.

Petronius. *Satyrica.* Trans. R. Bracht Branham and Daniel Kinney. Berkeley: University of California Press, 1997.

Plato. *Symposium.* Trans. Alexander Nehamas and Paul Woodruff. Indianapolis, Ind.: Hackett, 1989.

Rosati, Gianpiero. "Trimalchio on Stage." In *Oxford Readings in the Roman Novel.* Ed. S. J. Harrison. Oxford: Oxford University Press, 1999.

Scullard, H. H. *From the Gracchi to Nero: A History of Rome from 133 BC to AD 68.* London: Methuen, 1959.

Sullivan, J. P. *Literature and Politics in the Age of Nero.* Ithaca, N.Y.: Cornell University Press, 1985.

Tacitus. *Annals.* Trans. A. J. Woodman. Indianapolis, Ind.: Hackett, 2004.

Virgil. *Aeneid.* Trans. Robert Fitzgerald. New York: Vintage, 1990.

The Theban Plays

by
Sophocles

Sophocles was born at Colonus, just a mile outside Athens, in the year 496 BCE. The son of a wealthy family, he was raised with every possible educational and social advantage. At age 16 he made his debut in the theater by performing in a chorus that celebrated an Athenian victory (at Salamis), and soon afterward he began composing original poems and songs. Sophocles entered his first dramatic competition at the age of 28, where he took the top prize over Aeschylus, who was then considered the reigning master of tragedy. Apart from his dramatic interests, Sophocles was quite civic minded; he held a variety of political and military offices in his lifetime. These included a term as president of Athens' imperial treasury, one as an official of a religious organization, and appointments to various embassies. His military service included two generalships, one under Pericles and one under Nicias. Sophocles' long life of 90 years spanned the Peloponnesian War and Athens' corresponding rise and fall as a great empire. Unlike his fellow playwrights Aeschylus and Euripides, who often travelled to the courts of foreign kings and died abroad, Sophocles only left Athens in the service of the city and died at home. He is credited with the writing of 123 plays, only seven of which have survived intact. Of these, the Theban plays are widely considered perfectly structured dramatic masterpieces. Like Sophocles' other tragedies, they question the unrelenting forces of fate that frustrate humanity's best laid plans, and the justness of a cosmos that allows individuals and cities to experience undeserved reversals of fortune.

THE LITERARY WORKS

Plays set in Thebes during the thirteenth century BCE; written in Greek in the early 400s BCE—*Antigone* c. 442 BCE (or, some argue, the 430s BCE), *Oedipus the King* probably 10 to 15 years later, and *Oedipus at Colonus* c. 405 BCE.

SYNOPSIS

In *Oedipus the King*, the mighty ruler of Thebes falls into staggering misfortune and misery. In *Oedipus at Colonus*, after wandering in exile for years, the former king is vindicated by the gods just before death, but his children go on to suffer a tragic fate in *Antigone*.

Events in History at the Time the Plays Take Place

The ancient city of Thebes. The myth of the House of Oedipus, upon which Sophocles' plays are based, takes place in Thebes in the thirteenth century bce. At the time, Thebes was the dominant city of Boeotia (central Greece), located in that region's eastern part. The city had its own acropolis, or fortress, which stood on a plateau overlooking the lower city, with portions of the rivers Dirce and Ismenus on either side.

Thebes had an especially rich mythology. It was said to have been founded by Cadmus, who

Sophocles. © Archivo Iconographico, S.A./Corbis.
Reproduced by permission.

arrived there from Phoenicia. According to the myth, he used dragon's teeth to sow a harvest of splendid warriors, several of which were said to be the ancestors of the Theban aristocracy. The plays take place during the Bronze Age, at which time Thebes rivaled Mycenae as the dominant city in all of Greece. Thebes' success during this period is attributed to the richness of its soil and its geographic location, which gave the city access to a variety of routes between Attica (Athens' region) and central Greece. Archaeological evidence indicates, however, that by the end of the Bronze Age, the center of the city had been "sacked, burned, and abandoned," and Thebes never regained its former glory (Grant, p. 643). Sophocles may have intended the setting to have particular resonance for his audience, who saw fifth-century Thebes as a frequent military enemy of Athens.

The Plays in Focus

Plot summaries. *The Theban Plays* are not considered a trilogy because they were not written or produced at the same time, in the way Aeschylus' *Oresteia* was (also in *Classical Literature and Its Times*). Sophocles wrote the plays over some 40-odd years, and the chronological order of

their writing does not correspond to the sequential order of the stories. He wrote *Antigone* first, then *Oedipus the King*, and *Oedipus at Colonus* last. While many translations present the plays in sequential order, a few scholars argue that the plays should be presented in chronological order, so that each may be approached as an independent unit, as Sophocles intended.

Oedipus the King. As the play opens, Oedipus is talking to a priest who represents a group of Theban citizens begging for relief from a terrible plague. Trying to console them, Oedipus says he has already dispatched his brother-in-law, Creon, to ask the Oracle at Delphi how the city might be saved. Creon returns with the oracle's pronouncement, which is that Thebes is suffering because the murderer of its former king, Laius, lives within its walls unpunished. Oedipus curses the killer and vows to save the city by searching him out and bringing him to justice. As Oedipus turns to go into the palace, the Chorus begins to chant a prayer for Thebes and its recovery but ominously worries about the effects of this investigation into the past. Oedipus is advised to send for Tiresias, the blind prophet, since "anyone searching for the truth . . . might learn it from the prophet, clear as day" (Sophocles, *Oedipus the King,* lines 324-325). Under questioning, Tiresias refuses to say much. He hints that he knows some awful truth but keeps insisting that it is better for everyone if he does not reveal it. His reticence proves too much for Oedipus to bear, and the king explodes in fury, accusing Tiresias of conspiring with Creon in a plot to overthrow him. After being pushed to the limits of his patience, Tiresias finally foretells a very dark prophecy indeed:

> Blind who now has eyes, beggar who now is
> rich, he will grope his way toward a foreign soil,
> a stick tapping before him step by step.
> Revealed at last, brother and father both to the
> children he embraces, to his mother son and
> husband both—he sowed the loins his father
> sowed, he spilled his father's blood!
>
> (*Oedipus the King,* lines 517-523)

Later, when Creon meets with the king to try to defend himself against the charge of treason leveled at him by Oedipus, he begs his brother-in-law not to jump to conclusions but to carefully consider the facts of the case. Oedipus refuses to believe Creon and announces that he does not want Creon merely banished, but dead. The Chorus begs Oedipus to reconsider, and Creon warns him that "sullen in yielding, brutal

RIDDLES AND THE SPHINX

Stories, statues, and pictures of the sphinx existed in ancient Greece, Egypt, Assyria, and Phoenicia. A mythological creature, its name stems from a Greek word meaning "squeezer," and its gender in Greek mythology seems to have been female. The sphinx referred to in Sophocles' *Oedipus* was believed to have lived on a high rock outside Thebes. Greeks pictured the sphinx as a winged creature with the body of a lion and the head of a woman. As was common in many versions of the myth of the sphinx, she posed a particular danger to men, whom she carried off and devoured if they were not able to answer her riddle correctly. As Oedipus was passing the sphinx on his way to Thebes, he was able to solve the riddle, thereby causing her to hurl herself off the rock in anger and plunge to her death. Although not repeated verbatim in the play, the riddle that the sphinx supposedly asked was, "What has one voice and walks with four feet in the morning, two feet in the afternoon, and three feet in the evening?" The correct answer was "man, who crawls as a baby, walks erect as an adult, and needs a cane in his twilight years." Oedipus himself can be seen as the subject of the riddle, for, according to some, though he is a young man, he must use a cane due to an injury he suffered as an infant on Mount Cithaeron (Segal, pp. 36-37).

The sphinx is not the only supernatural element in the play. Much of the drama in the play is brought about by an "oracle," a term used by the ancient Greeks to refer to a shrine where people would come and pray to the gods for guidance. The gods were thought to communicate through select individuals known as priests, or prophets, who could reveal the will of the gods and predict the future. Sophocles presents an interesting juxtaposition between the riddle of the sphinx, which Oedipus can solve, and the riddles of the oracles, which are not as easy for him to decipher. When Oedipus questions the prophet Tiresias, instead of answers, the prophet supplies "riddles, murk and darkness" (*Oedipus the King*, line 500). Tiresias taunts Oedipus, saying, "Ah, but aren't you the best man alive at solving riddles?" and at the end of his prophecy challenges him to "go in and reflect on that, solve that" (*Oedipus the King*, lines 501, 523). The irony is that Oedipus ultimately discovers the truth and solves the mystery of his identity but, in so doing, brings about his own downfall and destruction.

in your rage—you will go too far. It's perfect justice: natures like yours are hardest on themselves" (*Oedipus the King*, lines 746-749).

At this point, Jocasta the queen, who has come to make peace between her brother Creon and her husband, Oedipus, insists on being told what has happened. Upon hearing that the source of the controversy was Tiresias' prophecy, Jocasta seeks to console her husband by relating to him a years-old prophecy that never came to pass. Apparently Laius, Jocasta's first husband and former Theban King, had been told that he would suffer his death at the hands of his own son. Tortured by this prophecy, Laius and Jocasta gave their infant son to a servant, who tied his ankles and left him to die of exposure on the side of a mountain. And as Jocasta reminds Oedipus, Laius was actually killed years later, not by his son, but by "strangers, thieves, at a place where three roads meet" (*Oedipus the King*, lines 789-790).

Oedipus, startled, questions his wife about the precise location and time of Laius' murder, also asking her for a physical description of the slain king. Hearing that there was one witness to the crime, a shepherd, Oedipus asks that he be sent for and pours out his fears to his wife. He recounts to her how he traveled to Delphi from his native Corinth in order to consult the oracle regarding his parentage after being called a foundling at a party. Instead of answering his

ATTITUDES TOWARD INCEST IN ANCIENT GREECE

Sources agree that although attitudes toward sexual practices were quite liberal in ancient Greece, this freedom existed only for males. Married men were expected to keep their wives happy enough so that they would produce and rear as many healthy children as possible. As long as this was accomplished, the men were free to engage in sexual relations outside marriage, including consorting with female prostitutes known as courtesans, and engaging in relationships (often emotional as well as sexual) with young boys.

Liberal attitudes to men's sexual practices did not extend to incest. Sexual relationships between parents and their children, such as the one between Oedipus and his mother Jocasta, were strictly forbidden (although the ancient Greeks did not consider relations with more distant relatives incest; cousins could marry). Other literary references to incest portrayed the incestuous unions as resulting in the birth of hideous monsters such as the sphinx (Hesiod's *Theogony*), or depicted incest as a deplorable practice accepted only by barbarians or "non-Greeks" (in Euripides' *Andromache*). Plato's *Republic* provides additional insight into what the ancient Greek attitudes toward incest were. In his famous treatise on the most ideal organization of the state, Plato introduces the idea of communism of women and children. Private families will be abolished, as men and women will simply pair off according to lots that they draw for the sake of procreation. But precautions are taken to insure that this does not result in incestuous relations (for example, individuals who are conceived the same year will all consider each other siblings, and will not be paired off by the state). Once "individuals are beyond the age of procreation," according to Plato, they are "left to have intercourse with whomsoever they wish, except with a daughter, a mother, the children of their daughters, and the ancestors of their mother, a son, a father, the children of their sons" and so on (Plato, p. 140).

question about his parents, the oracle informed Oedipus that he would one day kill his father and sleep with his mother. Assuming that the people who raised him, King Polybus and his wife Merope, were his biological parents, Oedipus fled Corinth for Thebes to insure that this awful prophecy would never come to pass. On his way, he encountered a group of men traveling by wagon who haughtily tried to force him off the road, and in his anger, Oedipus killed all of them. Oedipus recalls that this occurred at Phocis, where the three roads meet, exactly where Laius was killed. As the audience has already been informed, after killing Laius, Oedipus proceeded to Thebes, stopping just outside the city to destroy the sphinx, an awful creature who was terrorizing the Thebans. For this courageous act, they rewarded him with the hand in marriage of their newly widowed queen and with the position of king.

Oedipus holds out one hope, however . . . according to the eyewitness who reported the murder, it was thieves who killed the king, and since "one can't equal many," Oedipus could not have been the killer (*Oedipus the King,* line 934). He begs Jocasta to send for the shepherd immediately, to confirm that it was several men who killed Laius.

While they await the shepherd's arrival, a messenger arrives with the news that King Polybus is dead and that the people of Corinth want to make Oedipus their king. Oedipus is actually relieved to hear that the man he believed to be his father is dead, so tormented was he by the oracle's prediction that he would kill his own father. Jocasta is relieved too and points out to Oedipus that the first part of the prophecy that he so feared turned out to be "nothing, worthless" (*Oedipus the King,* line 1064). Jocasta urges him to forget the second part as well, claiming that many men have dreamed of sharing their mother's bed, but that it means nothing. Oedipus, however, feels that as long as his erstwhile mother, Queen Merope lives, he still must live

OEDIPUS' PUNISHMENT

The messenger's description of Oedipus' self-blinding can aptly be described as gruesome, as the audience is told how Oedipus plunges the pins into his eyes again and again, while "at each stroke blood spurts from the roots, splashing his beard, a swirl of it, nerves and clots—black hail of blood pulsing, gushing down" (*Oedipus the King,* lines 1412-1414).

The vivid description features a punishment quite unparalleled in the Greek literary tradition. Moreover, Athenian laws do not indicate that such a punishment was the norm in Sophocles' time. In fact, the laws regarding homicide allow for the perpetrator to be exiled or, if a surviving relative of the victim agreed, pardoned altogether. Previous versions of the Oedipus story had ended on a much different note. In Homer's *Iliad,* for example, Oedipus dies on the battlefield, and in the *Odyssey,* he continues his rule of Thebes. Even Aeschylus' version in *Seven Against Thebes,* which ends with Oedipus' self-blinding, is quite different, in that the king is portrayed as one possessed by madness. Sophocles' Oedipus is fully sane and aware of what he is doing. The theatrical blinding serves two purposes in Sophocles' play. First, it attests to Oedipus' free will and freedom of choice, a key issue for Sophocles. Second, it demonstrates a heroic element in Oedipus' character, his courage to endure extraordinary pain and suffering.

in fear of the second part of the prophecy coming to pass. The messenger, upon hearing this exchange and wishing to put his mind at ease once and for all, reveals to Oedipus that he was an abandoned infant, a foundling. The messenger turns out to be a shepherd, who rescued Oedipus as an infant and gave him to Polybus and his wife, a childless couple who were desperate for a baby of their own. When Oedipus asks the shepherd for more details about where and how he was found, the man replies that it was not he, but another shepherd who actually discovered the infant, with his ankles fastened, left to die on the side of Mount Cithaeron. Frantic, Oedipus asks if this second shepherd still lives and where he can be found, and is told by his advisor that the man is already on his way to the palace. The second shepherd and the eyewitness to Laius' murder are one and the same.

Jocasta, coming to realize Oedipus' true identity, begs him to "stop—in the name of god, if you love your own life, call off this search!" (*Oedipus the King,* line 1162). But Oedipus refuses to listen, insisting that he "must know it all, must see the truth at last" (*Oedipus the King,* lines 1168-1169). Jocasta, shrieking, yells at Oedipus that he is doomed and then runs from the palace. The second shepherd finally arrives and admits that he disobeyed Laius, who gave orders to have the

baby killed because of the awful prophecy he had received. Taking pity on the infant boy, the shepherd gave him away, hoping his new caretaker would take him far away from Thebes and give the baby another life. Oedipus did have the chance for a new life in Corinth, but in an ironic twist, for which Sophocles is famous, his consultation with the Oracle at Delphi as a young man actually brought him back to Thebes, which resulted in the oracle's prophecy coming to pass. Oedipus, crying out that he is "revealed at last," rushes through the doors (*Oedipus the King,* line 1308). After the Chorus sings a song about the cruel nature of fate, a messenger enters to relate the news of Jocasta's suicide and describes Oedipus' frenzied grief and guilt at the sight of her hanging in the noose. The messenger relays a graphic account Of Oedipus' self-inflicted punishment, the gouging out of his own eyes with Jocasta's brooches.

Next we see Oedipus, a blind man being led by attendants, cursing himself and his fate and begging Creon, the new Theban king, for banishment from the city. Creon says that he has sent a messenger to the Oracle at Delphi in order to discover what the gods wish him to do.

Taking pity on Oedipus, Creon sends for his two daughters, Antigone and Ismene. After a tearful goodbye and the extraction of a promise

PREDESTINATION V. FREE WILL

Astaple notion in Greek tragedy is the belief that all human actions are guided or determined by "fate." This unseen force may refer to the gods and their plans or to some other unfathomable workings of the universe, but to refuse to submit to it was considered *hubris,* a sin of pride and arrogance. Sophocles' treatment of fate presents an interesting contrast to that of other playwrights in his day. Some scholars argue that in the plays of Aeschylus, the characters seem compelled to act in certain ways as a result of the gods' power and influence. Aeschylus creates an Oedipus who blinds himself because a divine spirit or *daimon* drove him to it (Segal, pp. 54, 134). In Sophocles' drama, all the characters are portrayed as having the freedom to act. At each stage of *Oedipus the King,* the characters make choices. True, the choices end up making the gods' prophecy come to pass; still they are, in Sophocles' view, to some degree a function of man's free will, of his own passions and desires. It is because Oedipus, for example, lets his temper get the better of him at the crossroads that he kills an entire wagonful of people, fulfilling the first part of the prophecy.

Likewise, Oedipus' tragic downfall from a heroic king to a blind and exiled beggar is a function of his own action. Contrary to advice from Tiresias and Jocasta, who at several points urge caution, restraint, and the abandonment of his investigation into the past, Oedipus relentlessly forges ahead, a man of action fixated on solving this old mystery. Of course, Oedipus has noble motives; he begins his quest for the killer out of civic mindedness, to purge Thebes of its guilt and the resultant plague. Moreover, there is something admirable and heroic about his single-minded pursuit of the truth at any cost. Nonetheless, had Oedipus chosen to simply let the matter rest, his sins would never have been discovered and his life could have continued undisturbed. After his self-blinding, Oedipus laments his actions: "I've stripped myself," he admits. "I gave the command myself" (*Oedipus the King,* p. 243).

from Creon that he will look after Oedipus' sons, Oedipus is led away by the guards. The play closes with his fate being left uncertain.

Oedipus at Colonus. The second play in the saga occurs some years after Oedipus' exile from Thebes. Antigone and Oedipus are wandering; exhausted, they sit at a grove to rest. A man appears and orders them to leave the spot, for it is holy ground and guarded by divinities known as the furies. Upon hearing this, Oedipus declares that this is his "refuge," "the sign, the pact that seals my fate," and that he will never leave this spot (Sophocles, *Oedipus at Colonus,* lines 53, 55). He is informed by the stranger that this spot is part of the rich lands called Colonus, after the horseman who is their founding father, and that they are part of Athens, under King Theseus' rule. Oedipus begs the man to dispatch a messenger so that the king may come and speak to him. In Oedipus' ensuing speech, the importance of this resting place is revealed:

When the god cried out those lifelong prophecies of doom he spoke of this as well, my promised rest after hard years weathered— I will reach my goal, he said, my haven where I find the grounds of the awesome goddesses and make their home my home. There I will round the last turn in the torment of my life: a blessing to the hosts I live among, a disaster to those who drove me out!
(*Oedipus at Colonus,* lines 105-116)

Next the Chorus happens upon Oedipus. They immediately try to expel him when they discover that he is the infamous, "wretched, suffering Oedipus" (*Oedipus at Colonus,* line 237). Antigone intervenes on his behalf, and Oedipus makes the first of several self-defense speeches, pointing out to the Chorus that he knew nothing of his actions, so how could he be called "guilty, how by nature?" (*Oedipus at Colonus,* line 289).

Antigone's sister Ismene arrives to warn Oedipus that his sons, Eteocles and Polyneices, are feuding. Polyneices was driven out of Thebes to Argos by Creon and Eteocles, and is now planning an attack on Thebes. Creon is also aware of the prophecy and is coming to bring Oedipus back to Thebes in order to insure victory for his side. Oedipus rails at this, remembering that when he had first learned of his transgressions, he wanted public execution, or at the very least, exile. Once he calmed down, however, he wanted to be allowed to remain in Thebes. But Creon marched Oedipus out of the city, and Oedipus' own sons refused to help him: "For want of one small word from those two princes I was rooted out, a beggar, an outcast, fugitive forever" (*Oedipus at Colonus*, lines 495-497). The Chorus, whose members have now become sympathetic toward Oedipus, urge him to pour out his story. With their prodding, he recounts his sins, stressing again that he is "innocent! Pure in the eyes of the law," since he committed the crimes of patricide and incest "blind, unknowing" (*Oedipus at Colonus*, lines 615, 617).

Next Theseus appears. He is wary of Oedipus at first, but then agrees to grant him protection and to allow Oedipus to carry out his last wish. Theseus leaves just prior to Creon's arrival. Although he pities Oedipus at first, Creon becomes enraged when Oedipus refuses to return to Thebes and accuses Creon of "brazen gall" and "brutality" (*Oedipus at Colonus*, lines 865, 883). Creon takes Ismene and Antigone captive. And he is about to lay hands on Oedipus when Theseus returns and dispatches troops to save Oedipus' daughters from Creon's attempted kidnapping. Oedipus speaks again in his own defense, referring to his "unwilling crimes" and claiming that he was led on by the gods (*Oedipus at Colonus*, line 1102).

The next person who comes to visit Oedipus is his son Polyneices. After expressing pity at his father's haggard appearance, the son appeals to his father for help in the war against Thebes. In reply, Oedipus reminds his son of his disloyalty years before and places a curse upon him: "You'll fall first, red with your brother's blood and he stained with yours—equals, twins in blood" (*Oedipus at Colonus*, lines 155-156). While Antigone tries to dissuade her brother from going to war and rushing out to his death, Polyneices says it is his duty to meet his fate, even if that fate is the end of his life. Before departing, he asks his sisters to make sure that he receives a proper burial.

Antigone Strewing Dust on the Body of Her Brother, by late-nineteenth-century British painter, Victor J. Robertson. © George Steiner, 1984. All rights reserved. Reproduced by permission of The Mansell Collection Limited, London.

Suddenly a storm breaks out; there are loud explosions of thunder and lightning. Knowing from the prophecy that this heralds his death, Oedipus cries out for Theseus, who arrives at his side shortly. Oedipus imparts his blessing to the king, and then Hermes and Persephone, the godly escort of the dead and queen of the dead, appear to him. He follows them accompanied by his daughters and Theseus. During their absence, the Chorus prays for Oedipus.

A messenger appears to announce that Oedipus has passed away; after being attended to by his daughters, anointed with spring water, and dressed in fine robes, he was called by the gods to move further on, where only Theseus accompanied him to witness the mystery. A moment later, when the others came upon him, Theseus was standing alone, with "his hands spread out against his face as if some terrible wonder flashed before his eyes and he could not bear to look" (*Oedipus at Colonus*, lines 1873-1875). Antigone and Ismene are in mourning for their father. As the play closes, they plan to return to Thebes and try to stop the impending deadly battles between their brothers.

Antigone. Again, although this play is last in the saga, *Antigone* was written first. Some critics argue that Sophocles introduces a theme in it that comes to full fruition in the two Oedipus plays, written years later. This is the notion that an individual believes he or she is acting justly but is actually guilty of breaking divine law, not intentionally but because of ignorance of it.

The play begins right after Oedipus' death and the death of his two sons, who have killed each other in battle just as their father foretold. Creon, the new king, has issued a decree that Polyneices cannot receive a proper burial but his carcass must rather be left exposed, for animals to feed on. Creon feels justified in his action because Polyneices is a traitor, the worst of men, guilty of betraying his state in a grab for power. But the lack of proper mourning and burial rituals is a terrible sin against the gods, so, although Ismene is too afraid to get involved, Antigone resolves to give her brother a proper burial. She will ignore the civil law of the political world that her uncle represents and follow what she believes to be a higher authority, divine law.

Despite the fact that Creon has posted someone to guard the body, Antigone manages to bury her brother in secret. When the guard comes to tell Creon what has happened, he is furious and accuses the guard of succumbing to bribery and burying the enemy himself. Like Creon, who was unjustly accused of treason in *Oedipus the King*, the guard maintains his innocence and resents Creon's accusations. The guards soon discover that Antigone is guilty of burying the corpse. When Creon questions her, Antigone claims that the edict of Creon, "a mere mortal," cannot override "the great unwritten, unshakable traditions" of the gods (Sophocles, *Antigone*, lines 504-505). Creon responds by sentencing Antigone to death; if she loves the dead so much, he says, she should go to Hades herself to be with them. Ismene intervenes on her sister's behalf, reminding Creon that Antigone is the betrothed of his own son, Haemon. This does not sway Creon in the least. Next Haemon himself comes to plead for Antigone's release, hinting that public opinion is turning against Creon. Father and son argue, and Creon mandates that Antigone will die by being left to starve in a hollow cave. As Antigone is led away to the cave, she sings a dirge in her own honor, asserting once again that she was right to respect both the family bond and divine law over political law.

The prophet Tiresias enters and tells Creon that the city of Thebes is suffering because of his stubbornness. Creon has sent a blight upon Thebes, in much the same way Oedipus had in

the first play: "The public altars and sacred baths are fouled, one and all, by birds and dogs with carrion torn from the corpse, the doom struck son of Oedipus! And so the gods are deaf to our prayers, they spurn the offerings in our hands, the flame of holy flesh" (*Antigone*, lines 1124-1128). Tiresias urges Creon to reconsider, as Ismene and Haemon had, but Creon flies into a rage, and accuses the prophet of treason. Finally Tiresias warns Creon that soon he will have to sacrifice his own child to atone for these corpses. This frightens Creon, and he hurries off to release Antigone. Soon Creon's wife Eurydice receives shocking news. A messenger informs her that upon entering Antigone's tomb, he and his companions found her dead. She had committed suicide by fashioning a noose from her own clothing and hanging herself. Haemon was there with her, crying in pain, but when Creon asked him to come out of the tomb, Haemon rushed at his father with his sword, and when he missed, turned the sword on himself. He died embracing Antigone, as his blood covered her white cheek. Creon returns to the palace with Haemon's body, but his suffering does not end here. He is told by a messenger that his wife, Eurydice, has killed herself. With her dying breath, the messenger informs Creon, she "called down torments on your head—you killed her sons" (*Antigone,* lines 1430-1431). Creon, claiming that he now is nothing, begs to be sent away, but the Chorus reminds him that no human can escape his fate and reminds the audience that happiness depends on wisdom.

Prophecy, the gods, and divine law. The writings of the ancient historians, particularly Herodotus (c. 484-c. 424 BCE; see **The Histories,** also in *Classical Literature and Its Times*) indicate that oracles played a major role in Greek political and military affairs. As the means, it was believed, through which the gods make their will known to humans, oracles were routinely consulted. Statesmen and governments sought out oracles prior to any major policy decision, and individuals traveled to consult with them on questions of a smaller scale as well.

The Oracle at Delphi plays a prominent role in all three plays, as does the prophet Tiresias, whose sometimes ambiguous messages are meant to warn individuals that they are straying from the will of the gods. In *Oedipus the King*, Oedipus has a less-than-pious attitude toward religion. Haughtily he states to the citizens of Thebes, "You pray to the gods? Let me grant your prayers. Come, listen to me—" (*Oedipus the King*,

THE ORACLE AT DELPHI

Delphi was a village located on Mount Parnassus on the northern side of the Gulf of Corinth. It owed its fame to the fact that it was home to the most renowned temple of Apollo. Through ancient Greek history, the Oracle at Delphi was the most respected of the oracles. People traveled far to consult it—not just Greeks but others from Egypt, Asia Minor, and Italy. Their donations to the city of Delphi contributed to the region's booming economy. The Greek city-states made frequent and generous contributions, and many of them (including Athens, Thebes, Syracuse, and Siphnos) established small buildings at Delphi where they placed offerings to Apollo, god of prophecy. The belief was that Apollo spoke through the oracle, using a priestess named Pythia as his mouthpiece. The priestess engaged in mysterious rituals (which included sacrifice, ceremonial bathing, and the inhalation of vapors) prior to answering a supplicant's question, and her predictions were often phrased in a very vague and general way. This encouraged misinterpretation. The most famous example is that of Croseus, the king of Lydia, who in 550 BC asked the oracle if he should attack Persia. The response came back that if Croseus crossed a river, he would indeed destroy a great empire. Confident in his impending victory, he proceeded into battle only to have all of his forces decimated. When he accused the oracle's prophecy of being false, Pythia replied that her prediction had proven true. Croseus had, in fact, destroyed a great empire . . . his own.

Plutarch (c. 46-c. 120), a high priest of the temple, is one of several ancients who said that the Pythia's state was induced by vapors, or gases, which erupted from a chasm at the site and inspired the trance in which she was possessed by the gods. When subsequent investigations failed to find a chasm or any other geological feature that would produce vapors, the ancients were discredited and other explanations were sought for her trance-like state (including a self-induced trance via potassium cyanide from laurel leaves that were chewed during the ritual). Scientific discovery, however, has proven the ancients right. A team of scientists found fault lines at the site of the oracle and confirmed that in the waters of a spring nearby there were gases with narcotic/euphoric effects, gases such as ethane, methane, and ethylene. The emissions (produced by the bituminous limestone) resemble the vapors described by Plutarch and explain the Pythia's "trance." In the words of these later scientists, "Our research has confirmed the validity of the ancient sources in virtually every detail" (de Boer, p. 710).

line 245). Throughout the play Oedipus and Jocasta question and challenge the veracity of the oracles, while the Chorus warns that "They are dying, the old oracles sent to Laius, now our masters strike them off the rolls. Nowhere Apollo's golden glory now—the gods, the gods go down" (*Oedipus the King*, lines 995-997). Of course, by the end of the play, Oedipus is chastened, as the divine prophecy indeed comes to pass. As the saga proceeds, in *Oedipus at Colonus*, we see an Oedipus with a different attitude toward divine prophecy. He struggles to insure that his death

and burial are in accordance with divine will. Finally, in *Antigone*, Creon ultimately comes to see that he ignored divine will at his own peril, much like Oedipus in the first play.

At the time Sophocles made the notion of divine law and its revelation to mortals such significant themes in *The Theban Plays* there was an intellectual revolution of sorts going on in Athens. The famous philosopher Socrates (c. 470-399 BCE) was engaging in a rationalist critique of many things, especially Athens' religious tradition. Also other "philosophers," known as the sophists, who prided themselves on being able to win any argument, were subjecting conventional beliefs and practices to increased scrutiny. These intellectual forces, along with the suspicion aroused by charlatans trying to pass themselves off as prophets for hire, began to make the Athenians wary of even the most time-honored oracles. The questions surrounding the notion of prophecy—whether or not the gods existed, whether they were the creators and caretakers of an orderly cosmos, and whether they made their will known through oracles—were very controversial in Sophocles' day. If divine knowledge and foreknowledge were discredited, the entire religious tradition would be thrown into doubt. How could the gods exist yet not know the future?

Sources and literary context. The source for Sophocles' plays was the storehouse of myths and legends that circulated among the ancient Greeks. The story of Oedipus, like that of other myths, was already well known to the Athenians and had been treated by other playwrights prior to Sophocles. Thus, the audience was familiar with the characters and the basic plot. What the playwright offered was a new perspective and a fresh presentation of the myth. He may also have offered an original twist; some scholars argue that Oedipus' end at Athens is Sophocles' invention.

Sophocles' dramas, including *Oedipus the King,* were innovative for their time. Among his legacies to the world of drama are the various technical improvements Sophocles made to the theater, which were well received by the ancient Greeks. These included the enlargement of the chorus and the addition of painted scenery. By far the most significant improvement was the addition of a third actor to drama. This crucial development in the history of the theater greatly enlarged dramatic possibilities.

Events in History at the Time the Plays Were Written

Athenian theater in Sophocles' day. Sophocles' dramas and those of his fellow playwrights were performed at festivals for the god Dionysus. They took place twice a year, in the spring and winter, and lasted several days. Plays began as simple religious rituals, wherein the Chorus presented songs. In the year 534 BCE the poet Thespis introduced an actor (*hypokrites,* meaning answerer or interpreter), who could deliver speeches of his own and interact with the Chorus. State holidays,

these festivals included religious rites such as prayer and the sacrifice of a goat or lamb. Attendance was not an optional matter; it was considered an important civic responsibility.

The ancient Athenians mixed religious and civic affairs. The state, in fact, subsidized performances by giving citizens the money to purchase their tickets, after obliging wealthy citizens to make contributions that would finance the performances. In addition to the important religious rites, there were political components to the festivals, such as the presentation of children orphaned by war and brought up at Athens' expense, or the display of silver tribute paid to Athens. The state bestowed various honors and distinctions on individuals during the festival. And in keeping with Athens' democratic principles, the state opened the festivals to all citizens. Some scholars say women, though not considered citizens, could attend; certainly slaves were excluded. Even those in jail were granted bail to attend. Three playwrights presented their plays on three consecutive days and won either first, second, or third prize. Athens' democratic structure was evident in the way in which the competition was organized. The citizenry at large selected ten judges to decide which plays would be awarded prizes, and the judges, it seems, took their cues from the reactions of the audience. So theater in Sophocles' Athens is imbued with a political significance: "Drama was special to Athens as an intrinsic and key institution of the *democratic* city of the later fifth century. . . . Audiences sat through the day from first light on, expected to reflect and concentrate, as part of their role as citizens of Athens" (Beard, p. 88). In the case of *The Theban Plays,* the performance might cause audiences to reflect on the reliability of prophecy and its appropriate role in society, or on the ideal ruler.

The Peloponnesian War and the plague. Athenians in the fifth century BCE had witnessed their city's ascension to economic, military, intellectual, and social dominance in Greece under the leadership of the controversial but talented statesman Pericles. During Sophocles' lifetime, however, Athens' fortune would change dramatically. War broke out with Sparta in 431 BCE, sometime before the staging of *Oedipus the King,* and it continued for almost three decades. Sophocles, who did not live to witness the defeat of his beloved Athens by Sparta, was probably writing *Oedipus at Colonus* during the last days of the war. It ended very shortly after his death. Initially Athens was the most powerful of the city-states, but by the debut of *Oedipus the King*, the war had begun to take a grim toll. Athenians had gathered together behind the walls of the city during an invasion by Sparta and war refugees had poured into Athens from outlying areas, such as Attica, resulting in tremendous overcrowding. When the plague broke out, the conditions behind the walls of the city encouraged it to spread very quickly. Lasting for several years, the disease claimed a quarter of Athens' population. How appropriate, then, that the first scene of *Oedipus the King* consists of Oedipus comforting citizens who have come to him for relief from the terrible sickness that holds their city in its deathly grip!

> Our city—look around you, see with your own eyes—our ship pitches wildly, cannot lift her head from the depths, the red waves of death. . . . Thebes is dying. A blight on the fresh crops and the rich pastures, cattle sicken and die, and the women die in labor, children stillborn, and the plague, the fiery god of fever hurls down on the city, his lightning slashing through us . . . plague in all its vengeance, devastating the house of Cadmus!
>
> (*Oedipus the King*, lines 27-37)

The ancient historian Thucydides describes Athens' suffering during the plague in very similar terms:

> Not many days after their [refugees] arrival in Attica the plague first began to show itself among the Athenians. . . . A pestilence of such extent and mortality was nowhere remembered. Neither were the physicians at first of any service . . . but they died themselves . . . ; nor did any human art succeed any better. Supplications in the temples, divinations, and so forth were found equally futile, till the overwhelming nature of the disaster at last put a stop to them altogether.
>
> (Thycidides, p. 94)

Sophocles obviously also had the war on his mind while writing *Oedipus at Colonus*. Oedipus was exiled by Thebes, and his final resting place turns out to be in Athens, under the rule of King Theseus, who receives Oedipus and allows him to die in fulfillment of the prophecy. When Theseus asks Oedipus if this action will cause conflict between the cities, Oedipus assures him that should there ever be trouble between Athens and Thebes, the Athenians, by accepting Oedipus' body, will insure their victory.

At this time Thebes was in fact an enemy of Athens. The Peloponnesian War began when Thebes attacked Platea in 431 BCE. Platea was the only Greek city that helped Athens during the

Battle of Marathon, and now Athens rushed to Platea's defense. Sparta rose up to protect its ally—Thebes—and the war began, with all the Greek city-states choosing sides. By the time Sophocles was writing *Oedipus at Colonus*, Athenian fortunes had dwindled and Athens' defeat was imminent. By the time the play was performed, Athens had admitted defeat and accepted the peace terms offered by Sparta. The great walls of Athens were torn down and the Athenian Empire

EVIDENCE OF THE ATHENIAN PLAGUE

A mass grave was discovered in Athens in 1995 during excavations prior to construction of a subway station. The mass grave was located near the surface, and skeletons were found helter-skelter, with no soil between them. The team who excavated the site found cheap, unadorned burial vessels. The members of the team could tell the bodies had been piled into the pit within a day or two. All the evidence suggested a panicky mass burial, the result, perhaps, of a plague. They dated the grave to 430-426 BCE, which is consistent with the dates of the plague Athens suffered during the Peloponnesian War.

dissolved. Thebes and Corinth wanted nothing less than the total destruction of Athens, but Sparta, fearing the void in power this would cause, opted instead for the installation of a dictatorship known as the Thirty Tyrants.

The question of tyranny. Other translations of the title "Oedipus the King" include "Oedipus Tyrannus," or "Oedipus the Tyrant." According to most scholars, the term *tyrant* was at first almost interchangeable with *king* and did not have the negative sense in Sophocles' day that it would start to acquire near the end of the 400s BCE. Still, there has been vigorous debate about whether or not Oedipus is a tyrant in the negative sense of the term, that is, whether he is a harsh, overbearing, oppressive ruler. Some argue that he epitomizes the Athenian ideal of the Golden Age. Oedipus is intelligent, confident, courageous, energetic, and assertive, all qualities lauded by Pericles in a speech recounted in Thucydides' history *The Peloponnesian War* (also in *Classical Literature and Its Times*). Known as the Funeral Oration because its occasion is a memorial service for those men who died in the first year of battle, Pericles recounts these virtues as qualities that Athens and the Athenians possess in comparison to their enemy, Sparta. According to one view, Oedipus as portrayed by Sophocles is the fulfillment of Pericles' idealized vision. Others disagree. They point to Oedipus' frequent outbursts of temper, his seeming inability to moderate his emotions, and his relentless suspicion of those around him (bordering on paranoia) as evidence that Sophocles intended to portray him as a tyrant. In fact, at one point the Chorus, usually quite favorable toward Oedipus, chides him with a warning:

> Pride breeds the tyrant—violent pride, gorging, crammed to bursting with all that is overripe and rich with ruin—clawing up to the heights, headlong pride crashes down the abyss—sheer doom! No footing helps, all foothold lost and gone.
>
> (*Oedipus the King,* lines 963-969)

There is no debate about another character. Although Sophocles' Creon opens the play *Antigone* with an eloquent and temperate speech about the importance of citizen loyalty, he quickly deteriorates into a tyrant as his niece refuses to accede to his will. He disregards the advice of the prophet Tiresias and of his own family, and he blasphemously dismisses the gods in his unwillingness to be defeated by a woman. "No woman," Creon fumes, "is going to lord it over me" (*Antigone,* p. 86). The ultimate expression of his tyrannical bent comes when his son Haemon says the citizens of Thebes are turning against Creon and siding with Antigone. A defiant Creon asks, "Is Thebes about to tell me how to rule? . . . Am I to rule this land for others—or myself?" (*Antigone,* lines 821, 823). When Haemon reminds him that the city is not "owned" by one man alone, Creon responds by asserting "The city is the king's—that's the law" (*Antigone,* lines 824-825).

Even if we assume that through Oedipus and Creon, Sophocles intended to warn others about the dangers of tyrannical rule, it is uncertain whom he might have regarded as the real-life tyrant. One possible interpretation is that the tyrant represents the city of Athens itself, which at the height of its power ruled its "allies" quite ruthlessly. The alliance among the various Greek city-states that united against Persia, their common enemy, was called the Delian League. Over time, the League was criticized as existing simply for other city-states to funnel tribute money to Athens. Also Athens violently and brutally quashed revolts in city-states that clamored for more independence and refused to pay Athens, such as Melos and Mytilene. Another possibility is that the tyrant represents the city of Sparta, the

closed, militaristic, autocratic regime with which Athens was at war.

More likely, however, is that the tyrant represents Pericles, who came to power as general of Athens in 460 BCE and ruled for 29 years. Many were critical of his use of power. Thucydides wrote that although Pericles' Athens was a democracy in name, it was in effect ruled by one man. And while there is no doubt that Pericles ruled during Athens' Golden Age and conducted an unprecedented amount of public building projects on a grand scale (such as all of the structures of the Acropolis, including the Parthenon), questions were raised regarding the source of the funds. It was no secret that the tribute paid by other states was used by Pericles to fund not only building projects, but public plays and other amusements, and that some of the public funds were even dispersed to the poorer citizens. Several critics went so far as to call this embezzlement, arguing that Athens' allies meant for the funds to be used for the common defense of the Greeks against the Persians. Indeed, a public charge was brought against Pericles accusing him of misappropriation of public funds, and the citizens passed a decree stating that he would have to give a full accounting to a jury. Pericles was even removed from power because of the public distrust, but then quickly reinstated because of panic over the war against Sparta.

Once the war started, Pericles' popularity began to decline. Pericles had urged the Assembly to declare war on Sparta, claiming Athens would win because of its superior intelligence and planning. Pericles ordered walls to be built around the city to protect the road to Piraeus, Athens' port. He argued that Athenians should abandon all surrounding land and prepare for a long siege within the city's walls. His strategy for defeating Sparta consisted of avoiding land battles in favor of fighting at sea, since the Athenian naval fleet was invincible. Pericles' plan for the defeat of Sparta seemed to have accounted for everything; in addition to a huge fleet of ships, Athens boasted 13,000 infantrymen, 1,200 cavalry, and 16,000 reserves. At first everything went according to Pericles' plan. Early in the war, the Athenians were so confident that Pericles' main problem was restraining them from starting land battles, which were not part of his strategy. But there was one thing that Pericles could not foresee: the plague, carried to Athens on the grain boats, which arrived to feed the city. The disease spread like wildfire through the overcrowded city.

Clearly Pericles shares some traits with Sophocles' Creon and Oedipus. Despite the fact that both fictional characters are dedicated kings who

THE OEDIPUS COMPLEX

A famous modern reference to the play *Oedipus the King* is its use as the cornerstone of psychoanalytic theory by Sigmund Freud in the early 1900s. According to Freud, childhood and family relationships are driven primarily by the sexual urges of children for their parents. In the "Oedipus complex," the young boy and his parents form an erotic triangle in which the child feels hostility toward his father and erotic desire for his mother. (The young girl's equivalent, taken from the myth of Agamemnon and Clytemnestra, is called the "Electra complex.")

ultimately have the best interests of the city at heart, their arrogance causes them to ignore other opinions and plans, and ultimately leads to their downfall. Scholar Donald Kagan has made a similar argument about Pericles himself, claiming that it was the general's superhuman confidence and the hubris of his inordinate faith in reason that played an important part in not only his own downfall, but also that of Athens.

Reception and impact. Sophocles' drama was praised by audiences in his own day. Out of the 120 plays that he authored, 96 won prizes at festivals. While *Oedipus the King* only won second prize at the festival in which it was performed, posterity has proven a more favorable judge. About a century after the debut of *Oedipus the King*, Aristotle's *Poetics* repeatedly referred to the play as a masterpiece of tragedy and cited it as a model for all playwrights to follow. Athens had two leading institutions of learning, the Academy and the Lyceum; their headmasters both agreed that Sophocles' work surpassed that of his contemporaries Aeschylus and Euripides, singling out *Oedipus the King* as the finest of Sophocles' plays. Later, under Roman rule, *Oedipus the King* reappeared in versions written and/or produced by Julius Caesar, Nero, and Seneca. Thereafter, the works of the tragedians seem to have faded from popularity until the 1500s, when the manuscripts of Greek tragedies began circulating again in Italy. Of these manuscripts, Sophocles' were the first to be reprinted.

Antigone has been one of Sophocles' most popular plays. By the fourth century bce, some 60 years after Sophocles' death, it was already considered a classic. In fact, the statesman Demosthenes had a court clerk publicly read Creon's speech on the responsibilities and loyalties of the citizen. Two famous modern adaptations of the play are Jean Anouilh's in Paris in 1944 and Bertolt Brecht's in Switzerland in 1945. In the first, *Antigone* is meant to represent the French resistance to the Nazi occupation; in the second, *Antigone* symbolizes the hope of a German resistance rising up against Hitler, a resistance that never actually occurred.

—Despina Korovessis

For More Information

Axarlis, Nikos. "Plague Victims Found: Mass Burial in Athens." *Archaeology*, April 15, 1998. http://www.archaeology.org/online/news/keram eikos.html.

Beard, Mary, and John Henderson. *Classics: A Very Short Introduction.* Oxford: Oxford University Press, 1995.

Bower, Bruce. *The Oedipus Complex: A Theory under Fire.* In *Readings on Sophocles.* Ed. Don Nardo. San Diego: Greenhaven, 1997.

De Boer, J. Z., J. R. Hale, and J. Chanton. "New Evidence for the Geological Origins of the Ancient Delphic Oracle (Greece)." *Geology* 29, no. 8 (August 2001): 707-710.

Demand, Nancy. *Birth, Death, and Motherhood in Classical Greece.* Baltimore: Johns Hopkins University Press, 1994.

Grant, Michael. *A Guide to the Ancient World: A Dictionary of Classical Place Names.* New York: Barnes & Noble, 1986.

Kagan, Donald. *Pericles of Athens and the Birth of Democracy.* New York: Free Press, 1991.

Plato. *The Republic of Plato.* Trans. Alan Bloom. New York: Basic, 1968.

Segal, Charles. *Oedipus Tyrannus: Tragic Heroism and the Limits of Knowledge.* Oxford: Oxford University Press, 2001.

Sophocles. *The Three Theban Plays: Antigone, Oedipus the King, Oedipus at Colonus.* Trans. Robert Fagles. New York: Penguin, 1982.

Thucydides. *History of the Peloponnesian War.* Trans. Richard Crawley. London: Orion, 1993.

Theogony ("Birth of the Gods")

by
Hesiod

Hesiod (c. 700 BCE) was born in Askra, a small farming village in Boeotia, a district of central Greece. Askra lay in the shadow of Mount Helikon, commonly known as home of the Muses, nine goddesses who inspire music, song, and poetry. After the death of their father, Hesiod and his brother Perses inherited the holdings equally. However, Perses squandered his inheritance and soon tried to obtain his brother's share by bribing area magistrates and bringing him to trial; the outcome of the suit is not known. At some point Hesiod apparently traveled to Chalkis, the chief city of the Greek island of Euboea, where he competed and by his own account placed first in a poetry contest in honor of Amphidamas, a king of Chalkis; he may have recited his *Theogony* during the contest. Little else is known about Hesiod; nearly all details of his life are derived from his own poems. As with Homer, who lived during approximately the same time, no contemporary account of Hesiod survives, leading scholars to speculate on whether he was a historical person. Some contend that "Hesiod" should be viewed as a fictive character created by the poems' actual author for literary reasons. Others suggest that "Hesiod," or "the sender of the voice," may be nothing more than a cult figure around whom a local guild of poets arose. According to these scholars, the guild incorporated the figurehead "Hesiod" into the body of poems circulating among themselves. In any case, the poet who wrote the *Theogony* records part of his autobiography in another surviving work ascribed to him, *Works and Days*, a

THE LITERARY WORK

An epic poem set in a mythological time and place; composed in Greek between the late eighth and mid-seventh centuries BCE.

SYNOPSIS

This account of the origin and descent of the gods of Greece describes the beginnings of the universe and a violent pattern of divine intergenerational strife.

didactic poem mainly about farming. His *Theogony* describes events leading to the kingship of Zeus and the reign of associated gods on Mount Olympos (or *Olympus*—in this discussion, the Greek spellings conform to the system used in the *Theogony* cited and listed in the bibliography). Recounting a vivid, often violent story of divine succession, this foundational Greek epic may have stemmed from myths of the Near East.

Events in History at the Time of the Poem

From an oral to a literate culture—Greece in flux. The works of Hesiod and Homer are the earliest surviving Greek texts, which means there are no other texts in the language with which to compare them. Moreover, the period of their composition, somewhere between 750 and 650

BCE, is the seminal era in which elite societies acquired writing as a cultural resource, beginning to shift out of their status as a wholly oral culture. Around this time, the Greeks experienced increased contact with Semitic peoples in the Levant (eastern Mediterranean region), particularly in Phoenicia (a collection of city-states in today's Syria and Lebanon). The contact was inspired by trade of goods, but cultural exchange occurred too. Around this time the Greek alphabet, an adaptation of the Phoenician script, first appeared in the form of abcederies (texts that teach the alphabet) and on engraved works of art. Writing subsequently spread throughout the Greek world, preserving public records and bestowing a fixed form upon poems and legends that had existed for generations as oral literature.

THE ORAL POET'S TECHNICAL TRICKS

Unlike written compositions, oral literature exhibits distinctive patterns and behaviors that would have facilitated recitation, such as repeated terms and phrases. Readers of the **Iliad** or the **Odyssey** (both also in *Classical Literature and Its Times*) will recognize such formulae as "grey-eyed Athena," "swift-footed Achilles" or "Hector of the shining helm." The *Theogony* employs similar formulae: in the poem's opening lines, Hesiod refers to "owl-eyed Athena," "Poseidon earth-embracer, earth-shaker," and "glancing Aphrodite" (Hesiod, *Theogony*, lines 13, 15, 17). An oral poet builds up an enormous repertoire of these formulae so that he can recite a long poem fluidly while maintaining the meter or rhythm of the poem. This formulaic system also helps make it possible for the same poem to be recited repeatedly, with little substantial variation. Through these repeated recitations, oral poems could be handed down over many generations. Several song cycles developed around various legends, such as that of the Trojan War, which inspired the *Iliad* and at least three other long poems.

However, since Hesiod's poems (and Homer's for that matter) appear during the transitional period from orality to literacy, it is difficult to determine how these works were composed. A talented rhapsode (or "stitcher of songs," a term for a reciter of oral poems) named Hesiod could have arranged assorted traditional material about the origins of the universe and the gods and given

it a definitive form that someone eventually recorded. It is equally likely that the same poem could have circulated orally for many generations and could have been transcribed many years later. With the question of authorship undetermined, it is unclear how much of the material originates with a poet named Hesiod and how much belongs to an oral tradition. Though the answer may forever remain hidden, Hesiod is nonetheless credited with imposing a rational order onto the body of Greek myth.

Expansion and colonization. Between 1200 and 900 BCE Greece seems to have been in a period of relative stagnation. Magnificent palace centers had existed at Pylos, Tiryns, Athens, and Thebes during the Mycenaean period (c. 1600-1200 BCE), but these were destroyed around 1200 BCE. Thereafter, the population of mainland Greece dwindled, and its arts appear to have declined. Relatively little survives in the archaeological record of this period, which is referred to as the Dark Age.

However, around 900 BCE the situation changed. The population began to grow steadily, fresh settlements arose, and trade expanded. Moreover, a power vacuum developed in the larger Mediterranean region around the middle of the eighth century BCE. Egypt and Phoenicia, formerly the dominant states in the region, both suffered declines, and no rival power emerged to threaten Greece's commercial and political development.

Between 730 and 580 BCE Greece underwent a period of major expansion, much of it through colonization. To support their growing population, several Greek cities encouraged private exploration and settlement of the central and eastern Mediterranean area. By the time the movement ended, the number of Greek cities had approximately doubled. Southern Italy alone had grown so densely colonized that it became known as *Magna Graecia* or "Great Greece."

One consequence of colonization was a rise in trade, which brought Greece increasingly into contact with other cultures, especially the Near Eastern civilizations of Syria and Phoenicia. In the process, Greeks were exposed to such innovations as coinage, the alphabet, the so-called Orientalizing pottery style, and eastern customs and myths, all of which were to leave a lasting impression on their own developing culture. Historians contend that creation myths of the Near East may have shaped Hesiod's *Theogony*; however, it is not known whether Hesiod acquired knowledge of such myths directly—through his own experience—or indirectly, through their influence on Greek literary tradition, which the poet inherited.

Influence of Near Eastern myths. The ancient Near East extended eastward from the Mediterranean Sea towards and beyond the Persian Gulf, including such peoples as the Assyrians, Babylonians, Hittites, Israelites, and Phoenicians. The Greeks encountered Near Eastern cultures sometime in the Bronze Age, which stretched from roughly the third millennium to the first millennium BCE. The Near Eastern cultures could have had a pronounced impact about the middle of this period, during the Minoan-Mycenaean ages (c. 1600-1200 BCE) and/or after, especially during the late Archaic period (c. 630-480 BCE).

If a native Greek tradition of theogony (that is, of origins or birth of the gods) existed, it was most likely subjected to Near Eastern influences during the Minoan-Mycenaean era. In any case, there appears to be little doubt that connections exist between Greek and Near Eastern accounts of the origin of the gods. The Hittite myth, *Kingship in Heaven,* and the Akkadian-Babylonian epic *Enuma Elish* ("When on High") are often cited as the two most likely influences on the Greek theogonic tradition. Recorded some 500 years before Hesiod's tale, the *Kingship in Heaven,* which survives only in part, tells of Alalu, who rules as king of the gods for nine years, before being overthrown by Anu (Sky)—a cupbearer in the divine court. Anu rules the heavens for nine years himself until his own cupbearer, Kumarbi, a descendant of the original ruler Alalu, deposes and then castrates him by biting off and swallowing his genitals. Kumarbi becomes pregnant by this act, then gives birth on his own to three divine descendants: the storm god, Heshub; his attendant, Tasmisu; and the river Aranzaha (the Tigris). At one point, Kumarbi, who plans to eat one of his children, is given a stone to swallow instead. He gags on the stone and spits it out, after which it becomes an object of cult worship. When the storm god emerges from Kumarbi's body, he is supposed to defeat Kumarbi and reign in his stead, though the text becomes unreadable at this juncture.

Enuma Elish, probably composed some 300 years before Hesiod's tale, tells of the union between primal waters. Apsu (Father of All), the sweet underground water, and Tiamat (Mother of All), the salty sea, join together to conceive the first four gods: Lahmu and Lahamum, followed by Anshar and Kishar. This last pair's son, Anu (Sky), sires Ea, chief of the gods. Each genera-

tion surpasses the prior generation in strength, culminating in Ea, who is superior not only in strength but also in wisdom. Great dissension arises between the generations of the gods, whose number increases over time to 600. Over Tiamat's protests, Apsu plots to destroy the younger generations because of the disturbance they create within Tiamat's body. Learning of Apsu's plan, Ea kills him and assumes the divine throne. He then begets a son, Marduk, a giant with four eyes and four ears.

THE POLIS: HUMAN AND DIVINE

During the mid-eighth century BCE, rural communities began to band together in political unity to form individual city-states or *poleis*. These *poleis* were built around the concept of the *demos*, which refers to a body of citizens, encompassing both a land and its people. The most important political bodies in the *demos* were the council of elders and the assembly of men of fighting age, which approved or vetoed measures put before the state. These institutions, common and essential to every Greek *polis*, would, centuries later, become the foundation not only for Athenian democracy but also for other forms of government. In Hesiod's *Theogony*, the realm that the gods inhabit under Zeus and the customs they obey reflect the basic organization and structure of a real-life Greek *polis*. Zeus comes to power after a long period of intergenerational strife between the gods. Each father is violently overthrown by his youngest son, with aid from the mother. Only Zeus can end this cycle by achieving political consensus. Unlike his predecessors, Ouranus and Kronos, Zeus does not resort to violence; rather, he is elected to his position by the gods who are his peers. Lastly, once in power, he apportions the various realms and spheres of influence that the gods will enjoy: he himself will control the sky, while his brothers Poseidon and Hades will control the sea and the underworld, respectively.

Seeking to avenge Apsu's death, Tiamat enlists the aid of Mother Hubur, the goddess who forms all things. She creates eleven monstrous children to combat Ea's line. Choosing an older deity, Qingu, to command them, Tiamat assembles her forces. Ea and Anu try to fight Tiamat but are unsuccessful. Marduk steps forward to lead the charge, but offers his services on the condition that all the assembled deities proclaim him to be supreme ruler. Marduk defeats and kills Tiamat, cutting her body in half to create heaven and earth. Now established as ruler of the gods, Marduk marks out the year and the months, divides the 600 deities into two equal parties to occupy the heaven and the lower world, and creates mankind from the blood of Qingu, whom he has also defeated and slain. The epic concludes with the construction of a great temple to Marduk in Babylon and a celebratory banquet at which the gods recite Marduk's 50 honorific names.

Hesiod's *Theogony* suggests the influence of many elements from creation and succession myths of the Near East, including unions between earth and sky; unusual conceptions and births of divine offspring; and violent intergenerational struggles among deities, involving murder, castration, and cannibalism. The similarities between *Enuma Elish* and the *Theogony* may reflect an indirect influence of the former on the latter (*Enuma Elish* may have influenced Hittite storytelling, which then influenced the *Theogony*). Or both works may have been influenced by a Canaanite story, brought from Palestine to the regions of Mesopotamia (by a people known as the Amorites) and Greece (by the Phoenicians). In fact, both the Hittites and the Phoenicians may have introduced versions of Canaanite myth to the Greeks.

The Poem in Focus

Overview. Although the *Theogony* combines several disparate elements, such as myths, genealogies, and hymns of praise, it is perhaps best defined as an extended family tree. The poem traces the lineage of two divine families of gods and goddesses over the course of three generations, cataloguing not only their marriages and births but their bitter conflicts with one another. Only after years of warfare does a stable pantheon of gods emerge, headed by Zeus. At times the narrative is broken up by digressions or expansions on specific points, such as the origin or significance of an individual deity. For example, Hesiod breaks off his account of the succession struggles between the generation of the Titans and the generation of the Olympians to sing a hymn to Hekate, a fairly minor goddess. Other digressions mention the exploits of certain Greek heroes, like Herakles (also known as Hercules) and Perseus.

Plot summary. The poem begins with a traditional invocation to the Muses, who hold a particular significance for the poet. According to Hes-

iod, the Muses visited him while he was tending his sheep at the foot of Mount Helikon, gave him the gift of song, and bade him to sing about the Olympian gods. However, since all song begins and ends with the Muses, Hesiod first sings a hymn to these daughters of Zeus, whose songs celebrate the order of the universe: first the primeval generation of gods (Mother Earth [Gaia] and Father Sky [Ouranos]), next the race of the Titans, and lastly Zeus and his Olympic brethren and mankind. Hesiod stresses the beauty of the Muses' songs and the harmony it brings to their father Zeus' realm of Olympos. He elaborates on their birth to Mnemosyne (Memory) and Zeus, asking their aid in the execution of his song. At this point Hesiod begins to narrate his theogony—which literally means "the origin and descent of the gods."

The world begins with the spontaneous emergence of four deities: Chaos, Gaia (Earth), Eros (Desire), and Tartaros (Underworld; more exactly, *Tartaros* named the deepest region of the Underworld). The first two deities begin to reproduce separately: Chaos bears Erebos (Darkness) and Nyx (Night), who together produce Light and Day, while Gaia gives birth to Ouranus (Sky) as her male consort, as well as tall mountains, glens, wooded haunts, and Pontos, the sea. Gaia also conceives offspring with Tartaros and Ouranus. By the former, she bears the monster Typhoeus near the end of the poem; by the latter, Gaia bears Okeanos (Ocean) and several other Titans, including Themis, Mnemosyne, Iapetos, Koios, Rhea, and Kronos. Lastly, Gaia and Ouranos beget two sets of bestial divinities: the three Kyklopes (Cyclopes)—Brontes (Thunderer), Steropes (Lightner), Arges (Bright)—and the hundred-armed monsters Kottos, Briareos and Gyges.

All these children hate their father, as does Gaia, because Ouranus, fearing his own overthrow, forces them back into her womb to prevent their birth. In retaliation Gaia makes a large iron sickle, which she gives to her youngest Titan son Kronos, who castrates his father. Absorbing her consort's blood, Gaia bears the Giants and the Erinyes (Spirits of Vengeance); meanwhile, Ouranos' severed genitals land in seafoam, from which Aphrodite is born, with the deities Himeros (Passion) and Eros (Desire) as attendants at her birth. She becomes the goddess of erotic love and sexual pleasure. The defeated Ouranos reproaches his Titan sons for their wickedness and predicts that they too will suffer retribution for conspiring against him.

Hesiod concludes his narrative of the first generation by listing the many descendants of Nyx (Night), who, like Gaia, has conceived various forces and deities on her own (without male participation). Nyx's children include Moros (Doom), Thanatos (Death), Hypnos (Sleep), Oneirai (Dreams), Momos (Blame), Oizyos (Pain), the Moirai (Fates), and the Erinyes (Furies, three winged goddesses who punish wrongdoers for unavenged crimes). Some of Nyx's children, such as Nemesis (Righteous Anger) and Eris (Strife), prove especially troublesome to mortal men. Eris continues Nyx's destructive line by bearing Sorrow, Famine, Wars, Murders, Slaughters, Feuds, Lies, Dysnomia (Lawlessness), Madness, and Oath (which causes destruction when broken).

Hesiod then lists the descendants of Gaia's son Pontos, which include sea deities, like Nereus (the Old Man of the Sea), his siblings Phorkys and Keto, and hybrid monsters like the Gorgons. The poet relates the story of Medusa, one of the three Gorgons, who lives at the limit of the world. Unlike her sisters, Stheno and Euryale, Medusa was mortal and the focus of several myths. Poseidon mates with her, the Greek hero Perseus later cuts off her head, and the winged horse Pegasus springs fully formed from her blood. Phorkys and Keto, from whom the Gorgons were descended, beget other monsters: the Graiai (the Gray Sisters); the half-woman, half-snake goddess Echidna; and the giant serpent that guards the golden apples of the Hesperides (maidens who also guard the apple tree). With Typhoeus, Echnida bears a monstrous brood, including Orthos, the two-headed hound of the giant Geryoneus; Cerberus, the fifty-headed watchdog of the Underworld; the Hydra, a many-headed serpent; and Chimaira, a monster described as a lion in front, a goat in the middle, and a snake behind. Brief allusions are made to the Greek heroes 1) Bellerophon, who slew the Chimaira, and 2) Herakles, who vanquished Geryoneus, the Hydra, and finally the Nemeian lion (a beast that, along with the Sphinx, came from the union of Chimaira and Orthos).

Retracing his steps, Hesiod recounts the offspring of the other older Titans, paying close attention to the river nymph Styx, daughter of Okeanos and his sister Tethys. It is to Styx that Zeus will grant the honor of being the binding oath by which the gods must swear. Hesiod then digresses from his main narrative to offer a hymn in praise of Hekate. The daughter of the Titans Perses and Asteria, Hekate has the special power to grant wealth and fortune (later she would be associated with the souls of the dead and identified as a deity who sent ghosts and demons into the world at night). Her hymn directly precedes the birth of the Olympians and Zeus,

marking the end of the Titans' primordial past and foreshadowing Zeus' emergence as leader of the Olympian gods.

Having succeeded Ouranos as ruler of the sky, Kronos unites with his sister Rhea to produce Hestia, Demeter, Hera, Hades, Poseidon, and

First Three Generations of Gods

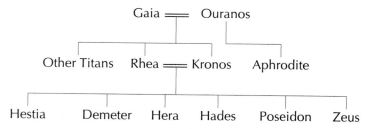

Zeus. As each child is born, Kronos swallows them whole, to prevent the kingship of the gods from passing to another generation. Rhea turns to Ouranos and Gaia for help; they send her to Crete just as she is to give birth to Zeus, and when he is born, Gaia nurses him in a hidden cave. To fool Kronos, they give him a heavy stone wrapped in swaddling clothes, which he swallows, believing it to be his son.

Once Zeus matures, Gaia tricks Kronos into disgorging his children. The stone, the last thing he swallowed, comes out first, followed by Zeus' brothers and sisters. Zeus frees the Kyklopes, whom Ouranos had imprisoned in Tartaros; in return, they grant him thunder and lightning as his own weapons. The reign of Kronos ends and that of Zeus begins.

Zeus subsequently undergoes a series of tests that will establish his right to rule. First he deals with his Titan rivals (the sons of Iapetos and Klymene, Okeanos' daughter). Zeus strikes one Titan, Menoitios, with a thunderbolt as punishment for arrogance; Zeus sentences another possible rival, Atlas, to hold up the heavens on his shoulders. At an assembly of gods and men, Prometheus, the slyest of the Titans, attempts to trick Zeus into accepting the inferior portion of a sacrificial ox for himself. Hesiod locates in this deceit the origin of how Greeks of his own era conducted their sacrificial ritual: the community shared the edible portions of the animal as a meal and burned the inedible parts as an offering to the gods, puzzlingly sacrificing the less desirable parts until one understands that the practice derives from this attempt of Prometheus to deceive Zeus, who, of course, sees through the trick. (It was for just such explanations that the ancient Greeks looked to Hesiod and other talebearers.)

The Consorts of Zeus and the Children They Conceived with Him

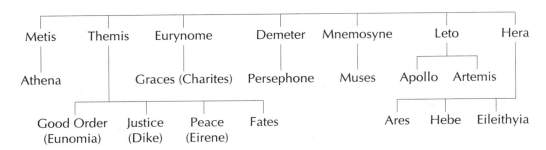

This inferior portion is the bare bones of the beast, covered in white fat; the meat, hidden under the skin of the ox's stomach, Prometheus attempts to reserve for mortal men. As punishment for this treachery, Zeus withholds from Man the gift of fire. Prometheus steals fire from the heavens and delivers it to Man, for which offense Zeus chains him to a column and sends an eagle to tear out his liver each day, until Herakles later releases Prometheus.

Meanwhile, Zeus punishes Man by ordering the creation of the first woman, out of earth. Each of the gods assists in making the woman, whom Zeus presents to Man as a cunning gift. The race of women proves to be man's bane, consuming his wealth through their fondness for luxury. However, the man who avoids women, fares no better: without women, no one will tend to him in old age and his estate will fall to kinsmen. Even the man who takes a good wife will experience both good and evil, while the man who takes a bad wife will experience only misery.

For ten long years the Olympians (the children of Kronos and Rhea) battle the Titans (the children of Ouranos and Gaia) for control of the universe. On Gaia's advice, Zeus frees the "Hundred-Arms" (Briareos, Gyges, and Kottos), whom Ouranos had bound beneath the earth in fear of their power and shape. Fortifying his new allies with nectar and ambrosia, Zeus wins their loyalty and persuades them to fight on the Olympians' side against the Titans.

With the aid of the Hundred-Arms and Zeus' thunderbolts and lightning, the Olympians triumph over the Titans, who are subsequently imprisoned in Tartaros, below the earth. Hesiod embarks upon a lengthy description of the Underworld, which is apparently so deep that, if one were to drop an anvil from the earth, it would take ten days to reach its destination. The Titans are confined within these gloomy depths, surrounded by a brazen moat and three layers of

night, guarded by the Hundred-Arms who are posted at the gates of this inescapable prison.

Other denizens of Tartaros include Atlas, who supports the sky on his head and shoulders; Nyx (Night) and Hemera (Day), who never inhabit their house at the same time; Nyx's children, Hypnos and Thanatos; and most prominently, Hades and his wife Persephone. The hound Cerberus guards the gates of the Underworld (which is sometimes called Hades after its ruler). The multi-headed hound fawns upon those who enter but never lets them leave, eating those who make the attempt.

The River Styx, by whom the gods take oaths, also dwells within the Underworld, in her own house. When dissension arises among the gods, Zeus sends Iris (the messenger of the gods) to fetch a vase of Styx's water; if any god swears falsely while pouring libations with this water, he is denied sustenance, lapsing into a coma for a full year. Upon awakening, he is exiled from the other gods for another nine years and may not rejoin them on Olympos (the mountain where the Olympian gods lived) until the tenth year.

Hesiod resumes his narrative of Zeus' trials. After the Titans' defeat, Gaia mates with Tartaros and conceives the monstrous Typhoeus, from whose shoulders sprout one hundred snakeheads. After a fierce battle that makes Olympos itself tremble, Zeus subdues Typhoeus with his thunderbolts and hurls him down into wide Tartaros.

Supported by his fellow Olympians and by Gaia, Zeus assumes his position as uncontested ruler of the immortals. After dividing the divine honors between the various gods, Zeus turns to the business of marriage and procreation. He takes seven consorts, siring offspring on each. His first consort, Metis (Cunning) conceives Athena, goddess of wisdom, but Zeus, on Ouranos and Gaia's advice, swallows Metis before she can give birth, successfully forestalling the prophecy that her second child, a son, would overthrow him. The pregnant Metis (Cunning) now lives inside Zeus and is his constant counselor, advising him in good and evil.

Zeus' second consort, Themis (Divine Right) produces the triplets Eunomia (Lawfulness), Dike (Justice), and Eirene (Peace), and the three Fates, Klotho (Spinner), Lachesis (Allotter), and Atropos (Unbending). Klotho spins the thread of life, Lachesis measures it, and Atropos cuts it. Zeus and Eurynome produce the three Graces (Aglaia, Euphrosyne, and Thalia), personifications of the grace and beauty that make life pleasurable. With Demeter, Zeus sires Hades' wife Persephone. With Mnemosyne, Zeus fathers the nine Muses. And with Leto, he sires the twins Apollo and Diana. Lastly he takes his sister Hera as wife, a union that produces Ares, the god of war, Hebe the goddess of youth, and Eileithyia, goddess of childbirth. Metis' daughter Athena, goddess of war, finally springs fully-grown from Zeus' head. On her own, Hera, enraged by Zeus' usurping the female's role in childbirth, bears a son named Hephaistos, a gifted craftsman but physically deformed and lame.

The births of various other gods are then reported as well as the line of various heroes conceived from unions between goddesses and mortal men. The poem concludes as it began, with an invocation to the Muses, but one that possibly signals the introduction of a new subject: the race of women. However, the *Catalogue of Women* is now considered to have been written considerably later than Hesiod's poem.

Procreation, succession, and inheritance. Of the various recurring themes and patterns in Hesiod's poem, the most prominent is intergenerational conflict. Each successive king of the gods attempts to retain his power by suppressing his children, and each is overthrown by the youngest son, with aid from the mother. Ouranos succumbs to Kronos, who succumbs to Zeus. In keeping with this pattern, prophecies alert Zeus to potential instability and threats during his reign. But, thanks to wise counsel, as well as his own superior powers, Zeus is able to avoid the fates of his father and grandfather.

Significantly, each divine ruler tries to maintain his supremacy by interfering in the process of procreation, the primary goal of marriage and sexual union. Ouranos forces his Titan offspring to hide within "a dark hole of Gaia," their mother, not letting them emerge into the light (*Theogony*, line 158). Kronos, Ouranos' successor, attempts to dispose of his children, the future Olympians, even more drastically: by swallowing the infants whole as they emerge from the womb of their mother, Rhea. Even Zeus puts his first wife, Metis, "down in his belly," after he learns that she will otherwise bear him a son "proud of heart, king of gods and men" with the powers to rival Zeus' own kingship (*Theogony*, line 890).

The gods' preoccupation with succession may have been another theme that Hesiod inherited from Near Eastern creation myths. In any case, elements from various myths—local and imported, ancient and more recent, from Hesiod's point of view—were absorbed into *Theogony*. The

---

LOCAL DEITIES

In the *Theogony* Hesiod transforms the gods into "national" or universal figures. The Greek gods as we know them (like Zeus, the king of the gods and god of lightning) were not so known to Hesiod's contemporaries. They began as local gods and goddesses. Each god existed as an incarnation tied to a specific place—for example, Delian Apollo (Apollo of Delos). These incarnations were distinct from others, such as Pythian Apollo (Apollo of Delphi, presided over by a priestess called the Pythia). They furthermore inspired legends and myths particular to their area of worship. The tales would often differ depending on the surroundings, with various stories attached to the Delian Apollo and the Pythian Apollo, for example. Each incarnation of the god oversaw specific rites, practices, and activities, and each city cultivated its particular incarnation of a chosen deity. As unique city-states arose across Greece, temples to particular gods sprang up across the Greek landscape.

Greek world's adoption of Hesiod's and Homer's versions of the pantheon appears to have coincided with the Greeks' growing sense of their own identity as Greeks, the realization that they shared their language, customs, religion, and general heritage. This phenomenon, known as Panhellenism (all-Greece), became widespread during the eighth century BCE and led to the establishment of religious festivals in which worshippers throughout the Greek world were invited to participate. Additionally, Panhellenic centers of worship were founded at such sites as Olympia (for Zeus and Hera) and Delos (for Apollo and Artemis). Perhaps the most striking development of Panhellenism was the inauguration of the Olympic games, athletic contests held every four years at the festival of Zeus at Olympia in the northwest Peloponnese, the large peninsula of southern mainland Greece. Introduced in 776 BCE, the Olympian games eventually attracted competitors and spectators from all over the Greek world. The main religious ceremony was the sacrifice of 100 bulls (called a hecatomb) on a great altar devoted to Zeus.

Sources and literary context. Hesiod's works, along with Homer's, are among the first and earliest literary compositions of classical antiquity. Therefore, it is both unclear how much of the *Theogony* is Hesiod's own creation and difficult to identify sources on which he drew. However, like Homer, Hesiod appears to have inherited a rich oral tradition that included material on the origin and descent of the gods. This tradition may hark back to Indo-European myths, Minoan-Mycenaean civilization and its relations with Eastern cultures, the development of Boeotia, and even Boeotian contacts with the Near East. For his account of the succession struggles between the divine rulers, Hesiod may have drawn upon a particular Asian myth that also influenced the already-mentioned Hittite myth *Kingship of Heaven* and the Babylonian creation epic *Enuma Elish*.

As a work, Hesiod's poem is classified as a theogony (the origin of the gods) and a cosmogony (the origin of the world). It has also been viewed as didactic literature, because its intent is to instruct the reader—in this case, about the formation of the world and the rise of the Olympian gods. While theogonies may have existed in Greece before Hesiod's poem was composed, these would have been oral compositions and thus have not survived. For the Greeks of classical antiquity, Hesiod's *Theogony* soon became the most widely accepted version of how the world began and the standard by which later theogonies were judged.

Impact. While no contemporary record of the response to Hesiod's works survives, his poems seem to have become famous within a few generations of his death. Indeed, the number of didactic and genealogical poems posthumously attributed to Hesiod may be a testament to his prominence throughout the Panhellenic world.

As one of the earliest written compositions, *Theogony* and Hesiod's other famous poem, *Works and Days*, survived as Alexandrian papyrus scrolls, some of which dated from the third century BCE. Later, the *Theogony* was preserved, in total or in part, in an estimated 69 manuscripts from the medieval and Renaissance periods. Hesiod's complete works were published in Venice during the late fifteenth century.

Although other poems on the origin of gods and the world were composed throughout classical Greece, none supplanted the *Theogony* as an account of how the earth, the heavens, and the reigning deities came into existence. Along with Homer, Hesiod is said to have shaped the Greeks' perceptions of their gods as powerful but flawed beings, who possessed recognizable, even human failings. The philosopher-poet Xenophanes of Colophon (c. 565-470 BCE) wrote that "Homer and Hesiod have attributed to the gods everything that is held discreditable among men—thieving, adultery, deceiving one another" (Xenophanes in West, p. xx). The Greek historian Herodotus more sweepingly declared, "It was [Homer and Hesiod] who constructed a divine genealogy for the Greeks and who gave the gods their titles, allocated their powers and privileges to them, and indicated their forms" (Herodotus in West, p. xx). Subsequent generations of Greek literature have testified to the accuracy of Herodotus' pronouncement and the enduring nature of these poets' works. The gods of Olympos, their exploits and dominions, their natures and proclivities—which are on display in almost all of Greek tragedy, comedy, lyric, philosophy, history, and epic—can be said to have their origins in Homer's epics and Hesiod's didactic poems.

—Ian Halbert and Pamela S. Loy

For More Information

Burkert, W. *Greek Religion*. Oxford: Basil Blackwell, 1985.

Clay, Jenny Strauss. *Hesiod's Cosmos*. Cambridge: Cambridge University Press, 2003.

Easterling, P. E., and B. M. W. Knox. *The Cambridge History of Classical Literature*. Vol. 1. Cambridge: Cambridge University Press, 1985.

Garland, Robert. *Daily Life of the Ancient Greeks*. Westport, Conn.: Greenwood Press, 1998.

Hesiod. *Hesiod's Theogony*. Trans. Richard S. Caldwell. Newburyport, Mass.: Focus Classical Library, 1987.

Hornblower, Simon, and Antony Spawforth, eds. *The Oxford Companion to Classical Civilization*. Oxford: Oxford University Press, 1998.

Lamberton, R. *Hesiod*. New Haven, Conn.: Yale University Press, 1988.

Lovin, R. W., and F. E. Reynolds, eds. *Cosmogony and Ethical Order*. Chicago: University of Chicago Press, 1985.

Luce, T. J. *Ancient Writers*. Vol. 1. New York: Scribner's, 1982.

Martin, Thomas R. *Ancient Greece*. New Haven, Conn.: Yale University Press, 1996.

Pucci, P. *Hesiod and the Language of Poetry*. Baltimore, Md.: Johns Hopkins University Press, 1977.

West, M. L. *Hesiod: Theogony and Works and Days*. Oxford: Oxford University Press, 1988.

The Twelve Caesars

by
Suetonius

Gaius Suetonius Tranquilus was born around 70 CE into a family of the equestrian or wealthy business class. The family probably came from Hippo Regius (near Annaba in Algeria), but their origin remains uncertain. Although few facts are known about Suetonius's early life, it is believed that he taught literature at Rome for a time and practiced law as well. Later he served on the staff of Pliny the Younger, who was governor of Bithynia-Pontus (northern Asia Minor). Apparently Suetonius also worked as a secretary to the Roman emperor Hadrian (117-138 CE) but was dismissed around 122 CE, reportedly because of disrespectful behavior towards the empress Sabina. Yet Pliny describes Suetonius as a quiet, studious man devoted mainly to writing and scholarship. His works, composed mostly during the second century CE, include *The Twelve Caesars, Royal Biographies, Lives of Famous Whores, Roman Masters and Customs, The Roman Year, Illustrious Writers*, and *Offices of State*. The majority of these writings no longer exist. Only *The Twelve Caesars*, for which Suetonius is best known, has survived almost wholly intact. Combining a rational assessment of each ruler's achievements with intriguing details of his private life, *The Twelve Caesars* remains a highly accessible and readable work today.

Events in History at the Time of the Biographies

From republic to empire. Distrusting the rule of a single monarch, the ancient Romans established

---

THE LITERARY WORK

A group of biographies, set within the Roman Empire between 85 BCE and 96 CE; composed in Latin during the second century CE.

SYNOPSIS

The reigns and characters of 12 Roman rulers, from Julius Caesar to Domitian, are explored in detail.

---

a republican government that endured for centuries. Their constitution divided power between two elected officials (called consuls), an advisory body called the Senate, and a popular Assembly, the latter consisting of all adult male citizens. The consuls (there were two) commanded the army, fulfilled all sacred and sacrificial functions, and often served as judges and generals. The Senate served as the lawmaking council. The Assembly approved or rejected whatever laws were proposed and elected the magistrates—the officials who performed judicial, administrative, and priestly duties. There were three tiers of lesser magistrates: in ascending order, quaestors, aediles, and praetors. Quaestors were in charge of financial duties; aediles, of public works and festivities. Praetors served as judges. There were also the tribunes, officials charged with protecting the lives and property of the people. Tribunes had no administrative responsibilities but, like all magistrates, could propose laws to the Assembly. Moreover, they had the unique power to veto any legislation. They did not, however, serve in the Senate.

Engraving of Suetonius. The Bettmann Archive.
Reproduced by permission.

On the other hand, all other magistrates were members of the Senate, in which they could propose and debate legislative measures. The Senate had begun with little power but grew into a greater force than the Assembly of the People. It fixed elections and controlled access to the magistracies, or political offices. Over time, the Roman republic became more of an oligarchy; wealthy, aristocratic landowners, known as *patricians* (from "patres" or fathers) dominated the Senate, Assembly, and consulships.

By the first century BCE, Rome had established itself as the dominant force throughout the Mediterranean, acquiring huge amounts of wealth and territory through conquest. The age-old republican system was proving inadequate in handling the growing empire's needs. Meanwhile, the ruling classes grew wealthier, a new middle class emerged and thrived, and the poor grew poorer.

Magistrates who were appointed to govern Rome's foreign provinces established their own power bases, aided by the military forces assigned to support their authority. Ambitious Romans therefore sought rich provincial appointments abroad, rather than within Rome itself. The character of the Roman army also changed, as citizen soldiers were replaced by professionals whose first loyalty was to their individual commanders rather than the state.

The meteoric rise to power of Gaius Julius Caesar (100-44 BCE) provides a striking counterpoint to the decline of the Roman republic. The son of a patrician family, Caesar had emerged as a force to be reckoned with, thanks to his display of military acumen, political shrewdness, personal charm, and ruthlessness towards enemies. His achievements, chronicled in his autobiographical writings and in the biographical accounts of Suetonius, Plutarch, and Cassius Dio, included the conquest of Gaul, which extended Rome's imperial domain as far as the Atlantic Ocean, and the first Roman invasion of Britain (see ***Commentaries on the Gallic War,*** also in *Classical Literature and Its Times*). From 49 to 48 BCE, Caesar waged a civil war that resulted in the defeat of his chief rival Gnaeus Pompeius Magnus (Pompey) and that turned Caesar into the undisputed leader of the Roman world.

In 47 BCE Caesar was proclaimed dictator-for-life by the Senate, a move that dealt a death-blow to the already faltering republic. Not all senators, however, approved of the honors being lavished upon Caesar; many resented his supremacy and feared that the republic would be replaced by a monarchy. Led by Caesar's friend Marcus Brutus, a band of republican conspirators stabbed Caesar to death at a meeting of the Senate, on the Ides of March (mid-month), 44 BCE. Ironically, the assassination led not to the restoration of the republic but to another series of civil wars that confirmed the fall of the republic and the rule of an emperor. Ultimately they ushered in the imperial rule of Caesar's adopted son Augustus and his successors. He and his successors added the name "Caesar" to their own, transforming it into a title for the reigning emperor.

The Julio-Claudian dynasty. Although Julius Caesar founded the dynasty that was to rule Rome for nearly a century, his successor Augustus is actually considered the first of the Julio-Claudian emperors. After Caesar's assassination, Augustus—then called Octavian—traveled to Rome with a band of followers to claim his inheritance. Seeking to avenge his predecessor's murder, Octavian formed an uneasy alliance with Marcus Antonius (Mark Antony), Caesar's main supporter who had defeated his assassins Brutus and Cassius.

Antony and Octavian proceeded to fight for control over the empire for the next 10 years. Rivals, they made untrustworthy allies. Antony compounded this political offense by his liaison with the Egyptian queen Cleopatra, for whom he had deserted his own wife, Octavian's sister, Octavia. After Octavian's forces defeated Antony conclusively at the Battle of Actium (31 BCE), Antony and Cleopatra committed suicide (30 BCE). It was at this juncture that Octavian, like Caesar before him, was recognized as the undisputed master of the Roman Empire.

In 27 BCE, after serving as consul for several consecutive terms, Octavian proposed to resign all his offices and restore the republic. But most of the senators protested that Rome could not survive without his rule (their objections were probably orchestrated by Octavian). He therefore agreed to remain in power, functioning as proconsul over provinces in Gaul, Spain, Syria, and Egypt. He also continued to control Rome. As commander-in-chief of the Roman army, Octavian retained the rights to declare war and to negotiate treaties. He at this time took the name *Augustus*, by which he was thereafter known. By 23 BCE, Augustus was "princeps" (first man) of Rome, emperor in all but name, a position that he held until his death in 14 CE.

Augustus's 44-year reign introduced a long era of peace and prosperity, known as the Pax Romana (Roman Peace). His achievements included reorganizing the army, creating a permanent navy, and extending his empire northward to the natural boundaries of the Rhine and Danube rivers in Germany. Roads were constructed to link Augustus's imperial domain. New temples, libraries, and theaters were built, often of marble instead of common clay bricks. Finally Augustus provided the empire with a centralized administration and a uniform system of law.

Lacking a son, Augustus chose several potential heirs among his male relatives; unfortunately all of these predeceased him or proved unfit to rule. Finally, Augustus designated his stepson Tiberius Claudius Nero as his successor. The eldest son of Augustus's wife Livia by her first husband, Tiberius was a capable general who had given many years of service to the empire; he acceded to the throne in 14 CE at age 55. Well established in the government, he encountered little opposition when he assumed his new position. He ruled prudently, following many of his stepfather's precedents; he exercised a defensive foreign policy, bolstered the empire's frontiers, and, by practicing economy, left the empire wealthy at his death in 37 CE. But Tiberius's reign was marred by bitter family conflicts and a distrustful relationship with the senatorial aristocracy. In 26 CE he left Rome and governed from the isle of Capri for the rest of his life. Worst of all, Tiberius fell under the influence of an ambitious adviser, the Praetorian commander Lucius Aelianus Sejanus, for several years. Hoping to seize the throne for himself, Sejanus encouraged Tiberius's paranoid suspicions and harsh persecutions of suspected enemies. Finally, warned by his sister-in-law of Sejanus's intended treachery against Gaius, the emperor's chosen successor, Tiberius denounced his former friend in a letter addressed to the Senate. Sejanus was tried and executed in 31 CE.

HAIL, CAESAR!

The names of Roman citizens generally had three components, though additional names could be added. The first name would be the personal name, the second the gens or clan, the third the particular branch of that clan. Thus, the given name of the ruler known to the modern world as Julius Caesar was actually Gaius, and he belonged to the Caesars' branch of the Julian clan. However, it was the name "Caesar" ("hairy") that became the most important, used to denote not only a family but also the highest position of power in Rome. Even the emperors who were not related to the Julio-Claudian dynasty were hailed as "Caesar" upon their accession to the throne. The terms "Kaiser" and "Tsar," formerly used for rulers of Germany and Russia, are derived from "Caesar."

Tiberius's nephew, Gaius Julius Caesar Germanicus (also known as Caligula or "Little Boot") succeeded his uncle in 37 CE. According to Suetonius, whose profile is the earliest surviving source for Caligula's life, the reign of this emperor began well. Gaius's father Germanicus had been popular with the Romans, who were thus disposed to regard his son favorably. Gaius pardoned many prisoners who had been persecuted under Tiberius, reduced some taxes, distributed gifts, and held lavish games and public spectacles. But after recovering from a grave illness in the first year of his reign, he exhibited alarmingly erratic behavior. Convinced that he was a living god, he demanded to be worshipped as one, even to the point of insisting that his statue be displayed in synagogues in the East. Also Gaius turned against the Senate, spent funds lavishly, launched several unsuccessful military campaigns, threatened to make his favorite horse, Incitatus, a consul, and revived treason trials to

Augustus, considered the first ruler of the Julio-Claudian dynasty. Prima Porta statue located in the Vatican museums. The Library of Congress. Reproduced by permission.

eliminate anyone whom he perceived as a threat to his authority. His behavior in private, says Suetonius, was also depraved: Caligula committed incest with his three sisters and demanded sexual intercourse from respectable married women of Rome (the accusation cannot be verified or denied, due to the dearth of ancient sources on Caligula's life). Unable to otherwise check their emperor's absolute powers, several senators and Praetorian guards assassinated Caligula in 41 CE.

Gaius's unlikely successor was his lame, elderly uncle Claudius, younger brother of Germanicus. Considered feeble-minded by most of his family, Claudius proved to be a competent, if inconsistent, ruler. He introduced several social reforms, including an administrative bureaucracy structured around his freedmen (former slaves granted their liberty) and built some significant public works: aqueducts in Rome, roads in the provinces, and a harbor at Ostia. He also conducted a successful foreign policy, acquiring Mauretania and Thrace for the empire and conquering Britain, which became a Roman province. Unfortunately Claudius's relationship with the senatorial aristocracy was troubled and he married unwisely several times. Messalina, his much-younger third wife, had numerous affairs; she was executed after marrying her lover Gaius Silius (when Claudius was absent from Rome) and trying to make her new "husband" emperor. Claudius's fourth wife, Agrippina, was his own niece; he legalized the marriage with a special decree. She schemed successfully to make a son she had earlier, Lucius Domitius Ahenobarbus (Nero), the imperial heir over Claudius's son, Britannicus, then is popularly supposed to have killed Claudius by feeding him a dish of poisoned mushrooms.

At 17, Nero was the youngest emperor to date. His ambitious mother Agrippina sought to govern through him, which alarmed Nero's adherents. Her influence began to wane within a year of Nero's accession; after the sudden death of Claudius's son Britannicus—Nero allegedly had him poisoned—Agrippina was transferred to a separate residence at the emperor's command, never regaining her influence. By the time she was murdered, on Nero's orders, she had made herself so hated that few regretted her demise. Guided by his tutor Lucius Annaeus Seneca and the praetorian prefect Sextus Afranius Burrus, Nero governed soundly for a time, taking steps to improve public order, guard against forgery, and reform treasury procedure. In 62 CE, however, Burrus died, from poisoning perhaps by Nero, and Seneca retired from the court. Nero meanwhile fell under the influence of Gaius Ofonius Tigellinus, who encouraged the emperor's worst excesses. Nero divorced and killed his first empress, seduced his second empress away from her husband and later kicked her to death, and became increasingly obsessed with artistic pursuits at the expense of governing the state. His relations with the senatorial class deteriorated rapidly, and several conspiracies against his life were formed, though none came to fruition. In March 68 CE Julius Vindex, governor of Lugdunese Gaul, raised a rebellion against Nero, which received the support of Servius Sulpicius Galba, governor of Spain. Although Vindex lost, the triumphant Roman legions stopped accepting Nero's authority. After the Senate declared him a public enemy and ordered him flogged to death, Nero fled to his villa and stabbed himself to death in the throat.

The Year of Four Emperors. Nero's suicide in June 68 CE ended the Julio-Claudian dynasty and initiated a period of political upheaval. From 68-69 CE, several ambitious Romans vied to become emperor in his stead in a period that became known as the Year of the Four Emperors.

Control over the troops was a pivotal factor for any claimant to the imperial throne. The Roman army did not exist as a coherent entity; rather, some 30 legions, consisting of about 150,000 men, were scattered throughout the empire, which stretched from Britain in the west to Armenia in the east and encompassed parts of Africa and Germany as well. After Nero's death, Servius Sulpicius Galba (r. July 68-January 69 CE), the 73-year-old governor of Spain, received the support of the Spanish legions, the Senate, and the praetorian guardsmen in Rome in his imperial bid. He served as emperor for about six months, alienating many of his supporters through a mixture of rigidity and stinginess before being murdered.

The Senate recognized Nero's friend Otho as Rome's new emperor. Otho's reign lasted only the first few months of 69 CE, however. As ordered by their commander Aulus Vitellius, who himself had been one of Nero's favorites, the empire's German legions marched on Rome to engage Otho's army. Although Otho's forces triumphed in three initial skirmishes, they were heavily defeated at Bedriacum. Disheartened by the setback, Otho chose not to continue to fight but to commit suicide. Three days later, the troops in Rome swore allegiance to Vitellius, as did the Senate. Vitellius himself arrived in Rome in July 69 CE and became the third emperor in a year.

Vitellius's reign prospered no better than that of Galba or Otho. He ruled ineffectually, more interested in feasting and drinking than in governing his empire. In the East, a faction arose in support of Titus Flavius Vespasianus (Vespasian), governor of Judaea, as a candidate for emperor. Joined by others, the Flavian army marched towards Rome. After one of Vitellius's generals was defeated, Vitellius tried to abdicate in exchange for his life and a million gold pieces. Although the enemy (represented by Vespasian's brother, Flavius Sabinus) accepted, Vitellius's supporters would not let him abdicate and fighting broke out in the Capitol. Pieces of burning wood were put to use along with other weapons, and soon the Capitol was ablaze. Many Flavians perished in the fire and one of their leaders (the same Flavius Sabinus) was captured and treacherously slain. But the Flavian army soon overran the city, hunted down a fleeing Vitellius, and killed him in turn. On December 21, 69 CE, the Senate confirmed Vespasian's accession to the throne, bringing the tumultuous Year of the Four Emperors to a close.

The Flavians. After witnessing the lurid crimes of the later Julio-Claudians and the ineptitude of

Vespasian, first ruler of the Flavian dynasty. The Library of Congress. Reproduced by permission.

the emperors that succeeded them, Rome was sorely in need of stable, practical rulers. Two of the three Flavian emperors fulfilled that need. Compared to their aristocratic predecessors, the Flavians were lowborn, only of equestrian rank. Emperor Vespasian's father had been a tax collector, but Vespasian and his older brother Sabinus had found opportunities for advancement, especially in the military. As a young man, Vespasian had joined the army and served in the Balkans. Later, during Caligula's reign, Vespasian became quaestor, then aedile. He later attracted the patronage of a prominent official (named Narcissus), which gained him entry into court circles, and won distinction as the commander of a legion in the invasion of Britain.

During Nero's reign, Vespasian's fortunes declined. In 63 CE he was made governor of Africa, an appointment that held little prestige, and his circumstances worsened on his return to Rome when he was seen to fall asleep at one of the emperor's recitals. He was recalled from retirement in February 67 CE, however, and appointed governor of Judaea, with three legions under his command and the task of suppressing the First Jewish Revolt (see *The Jewish War,* also in *Classical Literature and Its Times*). By the following year, Vespasian had subdued most of the region, but Nero's death drew his attention back to Rome again. After the chaotic

Year of the Four Emperors ran its course, Vespasian emerged as Rome's new ruler.

Vespasian ruled with a firm hand and an eye to practical matters. Knowing that Rome needed to be restored physically and financially, he ordered the rebuilding of the burned Capitol and Temple of Jupiter and then raised the taxation rates to replenish the state's depleted treasury. He also completed the construction of several public works, especially the Colosseum. Throughout his reign, he retained close ties with the army, to whose loyalty he knew he owed his new position, yet continued to maintain a high standard of military discipline. Vespasian ensured that imperial power remained in the hands of the Flavians; the plan was for his elder son and designated successor, Titus, to be perceived as his colleague in important matters of state, the better to ensure a smooth transition when Titus himself acceded to the throne. By the time Vespasian died in 79 CE, the empire was once again solvent and stable, its treasury full, its army disciplined, and its frontiers no longer vulnerable to attacks from invaders.

Like Vespasian, Titus was a capable military leader; on his accession, he proved to be a competent emperor as well. He retained most of his father's economic and political practices but cultivated a milder, more liberal image. He made generous provisions for areas stricken with disaster, such as the eruption of Mount Vesuvius in 79 CE and the outbreak of fire and plague in Rome the following year. Titus's promising reign was cut short by his sudden death in 81 CE; his younger brother Domitian succeeded him.

Unlike Vespasian and Titus, Domitian lacked military experience; as a youth, he remained in Rome, studying rhetoric and literature while his father and brother campaigned in the African provinces and Judaea. Domitian was similarly overshadowed when Vespasian became emperor; he held several honorary consulships and priesthoods but no important imperial position or office. His prominence did not increase significantly during Titus's reign, though Titus chose no other heir. Upon his own accession in 81 CE, Domitian ruled moderately, but his administration was not wholly successful. Rome suffered an economic depression that resulted in the heavy devaluation of its currency; Domitian's attempts to reconstruct and embellish the city by erecting many new buildings did not improve the state's finances. In the later years of his reign, he revealed a rigid, even cruel streak. He alienated the entire ruling class by attempting to govern as an absolute monarch, withdrawing all of the Senate's decision-making powers. Fearing assassination, he became suspicious to the point of paranoia, reviving treason trials and executing members of the senatorial and equestrian orders whom he suspected of plotting his downfall. Ironically Domitian's actions made his assassination almost inevitable. A plot was hatched among his enemies in the Senate, members of the Praetorian Guard, and Domitian's own wife Domitia Longina. Acting on the conspirators' orders, Stephanus, a steward attached to Domitian's niece's household, fatally stabbed the emperor eight times on September 18, 96 CE.

The Biography in Focus

Contents overview. In *The Twelve Caesars*, Suetonius takes a thematic rather than a strictly chronological approach to profile the first dozen emperors of Rome. After discussing each Caesar's ancestry and early life and career, he recounts the emperor's accomplishments as ruler and describes the man's personal characteristics, however unusual they may be. The biographical sketch finishes with a description of the Caesar's death. The sketch may deal with military experience, administrative abilities, or some other thematic aspect of life, depending on the Caesar. In the process, the sketch conveys much of the information relayed in the historical discussion above and furthermore imparts a positive or negative picture of the particular man. To back up general statements about the various Caesars, the sketches include personal anecdotes—some racy, some of questionable truth. Each chapter ends not only with an account of the Caesar's demise but also of the omens that presaged his death. Although there are variations within the chapters, Suetonius maintains this same basic organization throughout the biographies.

Contents summaries—one to twelve. *Julius Caesar* (r. 47-44 BCE). Julius is the first of the Caesars and Suetonius covers his early career—military and political—in meticulous detail. He discusses Caesar's terms in public offices (as quaestor, aedile, and consul), his involvement in political intrigues and alliances, and his military campaigns that culminated in the deaths or defeats of his more powerful enemies and led to his becoming undisputed dictator of Rome. Caesar's achievements as dictator include introducing the Julian calendar and increasing the yearly quota of senators, priests, and magistrates. On the personal side, Suetonius emphasizes Caesar's ruthlessness (captured by pirates as a young man, he carries out his threat to later crucify them in return). The account also documents Caesar's extravagant liaisons with other women, especially the Egyptian queen, Cleopatra, who bore him an illegitimate son, Caesarion. Finally, it makes specific mention of Caesar's growing arrogance and its effect on the senatorial class. Alienating many of them, observes Suetonius, this haughty air of self-importance led to his eventual murder during the Ides of March, 44 BCE, after which Caesar was deified or raised to the stature of a god.

Augustus (r. 27 BCE-14 CE). Suetonius first discusses the history and accomplishments of Augustus's paternal relatives, the Octavii, in favorable terms. Augustus was the son of Julius Caesar's niece, Atia, and Gaius Octavius the Younger. His father died when Augustus was four. (In fact, the boy at first also went by the name Gaius Octavius, then by the name Octavian and finally by Augustus, meaning someone who is majestic or venerable.) Suetonius then relates Augustus's adoption as Caesar's heir, his accession to power after Caesar's assassination, and his successful struggle to maintain his position and authority. In describing Augustus's long, peaceful reign, Suetonius emphasizes his construction or restoration of numerous public works in Rome, his revival of obsolescent rites and appointments, and his implementation of laws to encourage marriage and discourage adultery. Augustus's positive character traits are emphasized: his modest demeanor, personal frugality and his loyalty to friends and family. (His palace was simply furnished and he preferred not to wear showy clothing.) The sexually immoral behavior of several relatives saddened and offended Augustus, who confined his promiscuous daughter Julia to a prison island for five years and refused to see or forgive her thereafter. Succumbing to a feverish chill in 14 CE, Augustus died. He was posthumously deified, as Caesar had been.

Tiberius (r. 14-37 CE). A discussion of the Claudians, whose family became connected to the Julians by marriage, narrows into an account of Augustus's stepson and successor Tiberius. Suetonius describes Tiberius's military successes, his political career, his ill-fated marriage to Augustus's daughter Julia (at the emperor's command), and his strange decision to quit public life while emperor and retire to the island of Rhodes, leaving the Roman official Sejanus to run the empire. The decision angered Augustus,

though he and Tiberius were later reconciled. Throughout the chapter, Suetonius compares Tiberius unfavorably to Augustus, though he acknowledges that Tiberius initially ruled with modesty and discretion, vetoing bills for the dedication of temples to his future elevation to the status of a god and refusing to adopt the inherited title "Augustus." The biography also credits Tiberius with abolishing foreign cults in Rome, trying to enforce public morality, and fortifying the realm against outlaws by decreasing the distance between military posts. However, Suetonius dwells at length on Tiberius's debaucheries or his preoccupation with his own sensual pleasures in later years, especially after the emperor left Rome for Capraea (Capri): Tiberius reportedly set up a residence furnished with pornographic pictures and statues, where sexual extravagances of all kinds—including oral sex and sex with children—were practiced for his pleasure. Disgusted by Tiberius's dissolute habits, Romans greeted the news of his death—from a fever at age 77—with jubilation.

Gaius Caligula (r. 37-41 CE). Suetonius briefly recounts the virtues of the military leader Germanicus, Tiberius's nephew and Caligula's father. Germanicus's early death was a devastating blow to the Roman people, who had hoped he would be their next emperor. Gaius, Germanicus's youngest son, was brought up among army troops, who adopted him as a mascot and gave him the nickname Caligula ("little boot," from "caliga," the term for the heavy, hobnailed sandal of the Roman soldier). According to Suetonius, young Gaius exhibited brutal and vicious tendencies, which were encouraged by Tiberius. When Gaius succeeded Tiberius, many hoped he would prove to be as noble as his father. Suetonius concedes that the new emperor recalled exiles, dismissed all pending criminal charges, allowed previously suppressed works of history to be published anew, and completed the construction of several unfinished buildings started by Tiberius, including the Temple of Augustus and Pompey's Theater. However, Suetonius focuses more extensively on Gaius "the Monster," who had incestuous relations with his sisters, proclaimed himself a living god, and ordered the deaths of several relatives, including a young cousin whom Tiberius had designated as joint heir to the imperial throne (Suetonius, *The Twelve Caesars*, p. 163). Cruel and given to indulging his whims, Gaius would have trials by torture executed in his presence while he was eating or otherwise entertaining himself. After

Gaius's assassination by his own imperial guards, two books containing the names and addresses of men whom he planned to kill were later found among his papers.

Claudius (r. 41-54 CE). Claudius was born to Antonia the Younger, Marc Antony's daughter, and to Drusus, a son of Livia's not by Augustus but by her first husband. Drusus, an accomplished military leader and a devotee to republicanism, died when his son Claudius was still an infant. Suetonius recounts Claudius's sickly childhood, the low opinion in which his family held him, and his sheltered youth, spent largely in scholarship. Ignored by the emperors Augustus and Tiberius, Claudius was brought more into the public eye by his nephew Gaius (Caligula), partly to be made the butt of jokes. Found hiding behind a curtain after Gaius's assassination, Claudius was hailed as emperor by the Guards who committed the murder. Suetonius assesses Claudius as an inconsistent ruler who made both prudent and foolish decisions; during one hearing a Greek lawyer was said to have lost his temper and publicly called the emperor "a stupid old idiot" (*Caesars*, p. 195). Claudius's conquest of Britain and construction of public works are listed among his positive accomplishments. Suetonius casts a less favorable light on Claudius's personal life, depicting him as dominated by the whims of his wives, especially the promiscuous Messalina and the scheming Agrippina. The latter, his own niece, was rumored to have poisoned Claudius to benefit her son Nero. Claudius was given a lavish funeral and posthumously deified.

Nero (r. 54-68 CE). Suetonius traces Nero's family back to the Ahenobarbi, many of whom were arrogant, vicious, and cruel. After relating the particulars of Nero's parentage, youth, adoption as an imperial heir, and accession to the throne, the biography focuses on the ways Nero perpetuated the worst tendencies of his ancestors. The biographer acknowledges Nero's more positive accomplishments, lowering taxes, awarding money to the commons, settling annual salaries on impoverished senators, and introducing a new form of architecture to the city. However, as with Gaius, Suetonius concentrates on Nero's crimes, especially the murders of his stepbrother Britannicus, his two empresses (Octavia and Poppaea), and his mother (Agrippina), for whom he nursed an incestuous passion. Nero's colossal vanity is also emphasized: convinced he was a brilliant singer and musician, Nero forbade Roman audiences from leaving the theater while he was performing. According to one anecdote, Nero set fire to one of the poorer areas of Rome itself, then donned a tragedian's costume and sang *The Sack of Ilium* while witnessing the city's conflagration. Despite his monstrous qualities, the Nero of Suetonius's biography proves incapable of coping with threats to his authority, such as the revolts in Gaul and Spain. His suicide, which ended the Julio-Claudian imperial dynasty, caused "widespread general rejoicing throughout Rome," although Suetonius reports that some people revered the late emperor's memory to the point of pretending he was alive and would return to defeat his enemies (*Caesars*, p. 246).

Galba (r. 68-69 CE). Servius Sulpicius Galba, from an ancient aristocratic family, succeeded Nero as emperor. According to one story, the Emperor Augustus told young Galba that he would taste a little of the imperial power too. Suetonius details Galba's political and military career, especially his appointments to foreign provinces during the reigns of Claudius and Nero. Also described is Galba's involvement in the Gallic revolts against Nero, which led to Galba's emergence as emperor of Rome. After his accession, however, Galba alienated many of his supporters, becoming unpopular especially with the army after he went back on his word and denied the military a promised bonus. Suetonius depicts Galba as stingy, greedy, and cruel, with no real understanding of how to rule the state. Heavily influenced by three corrupt, incompetent officials, Galba "was far less consistent in his behaviour—at one time meaner and more bitter, at another more wasteful and indulgent" (*Caesars*, p. 254). The biographer implies that Galba's fall from power and assassination were inevitable, owing to the emperor's unwise decisions and the unfavorable omens attending most of his short reign.

Otho (r. 69 CE). Marcus Salvius Otho was also descended from an ancient, distinguished family. Suetonius recounts how the ambitious, calculating Otho insinuated himself into the favor of Emperor Nero and the possibly scandalous nature of their friendship (an inappropriate homosexual relationship). Nero married his mistress Poppaea Sabina to Otho, only to annul the marriage, reclaim Poppaea, and exile Otho to Lusitanian Spain for ten years, where the latter served as governor. To revenge himself on Nero, Otho joined Galba's rebellion and supported the new regime, but was shocked when Galba later adopted the inconsequential nobleman Piso as his heir. Believing that his best chance for survival lay in becoming Emperor himself, Otho mounted a successful coup against Galba and acceded hastily to the throne. Suetonius offers little insight into Otho's short reign, focusing instead on his ill-fated attempt to defend his throne and his decision to commit suicide after his forces were defeated at Bedriacum.

Vitellius (r. 69 CE). While the origins of Aulus Vitellius's family were unclear, Suetonius writes that Vitellius himself had acquired a reputation "for every sort of vice," though this did not prevent him from becoming a fixture at the courts of Caligula, Claudius, and Nero (*Caesars*, p. 269). The biographer recounts the events of Vitellius's political career leading up to his appointment to the governorship of Lower Germany and his subsequent, successful campaign to become emperor, with the support of the German legions. As with Galba and Otho, a largely negative account of Vitellius's reign follows. Suetonius identifies Vitellius's ruling vices as "extravagance and cruelty," mentioning that he drank heavily and banqueted up to four times a day (*Caesars*, p. 273). Vitellius habitually commissioned luxurious courses for his banquets; one favored dish, named "Shield of Minerva the Protectress of the City," included such exotic ingredients as pike-livers, pheasant-brains, peacock-brains, and flamingo-tongues. Suetonius also describes Vitellius as a vicious enemy, who "would kill or torture anyone at all on the slightest pretext, not excluding noblemen who had been his fellow-students or friends" (*Caesars*, p. 274). His incompetence as a ruler, combined with his mishandling of peaceful negotiations with the rival Flavian faction, sealed his fate: Vitellius was captured and killed when the Flavian army entered Rome.

Vespasian (r. 69-79 CE). Suetonius credits Vespasian, the younger son of an obscure but well-to-do family, with restoring stable government to Rome. Vespasian's distinguished military career is discussed in detail, as are his fluctuating fortunes in imperial service: he prospers during Claudius's reign, loses favor under Nero, but later proves an effective governor of Judaea. Backed by the Roman legions in Moesia, an unopposed Vespasian becomes emperor following the deaths of Galba, Otho, and Vitellius. Suetonius offers a mainly positive account of Vespasian's reign, emphasizing his control over the army, his restoration and construction of public works, and his reform of the senatorial and equestrian orders. (The equestrians by this time consisted of an assorted group of leading men of the empire.) Even Vespasian's flaws—stinginess and a low, earthy sense of humor—are rendered almost affectionately. In one anecdote, Vespasian's son Titus complains about the emperor's taxing the public urinals, only to have his father point out that the coins resulting from the tax did not smell bad, despite their origin. Described as modest and lenient, Vespasian lived simply, conducting most of his imperial business in the morning. Fatally stricken with fever in the ninth year of his reign, Vespasian joked on his deathbed that he felt himself turning into a god. He was deified posthumously.

Titus (r. 79-81 CE). Suetonius paints a flattering portrait of Vespasian's elder son and successor Titus as well. As a child, Titus exhibited considerable intelligence, grace, and charm, excelling in languages, music, and feats of arms. As a young man, Titus proved himself to be a capable military leader in Germany, Britain, and Judaea, and, after Vespasian's accession, to also be a trusted colleague of his father. Suetonius mentions that some Romans initially feared Titus would prove wildly immoral and cruel: he had a former consul stabbed to death in his own dining room and he conceived an improper passion for Queen Berenice of Judaea. On becoming emperor, however, Titus mended his ways, broke with Berenice, banished informers, and gave every indication of being a benevolent ruler. After only two years as emperor, however, Titus died abruptly of fever. Ironically, his early demise enhanced his reputation among his subjects, who "began speaking of him, now that he was dead, with greater thankfulness and praise than they had ever used when he was alive and among them" (*Caesars*, p. 298). Titus too was deified after his death.

Domitian (r. 81-96 CE). Vespasian's younger son, Domitian, succeeded Titus. During Vitellius's reign, Domitian had narrowly escaped death beside his uncle Sabinus when Vitellius's followers set fire to the Capitol. Suetonius's assessment of Domitian is mainly negative: he notes that Domitian lacked military experience and never held any major position of authority during Vespasian's reign. Also the biographer portrays Domitian as continually plotting, secretly or openly, against Titus. Suetonius concedes that, as a ruler, Domitian was a conscientious dispenser of justice; he took a rigorous stance on improving public morality, even to the point of sentencing several Vestal Virgins to death for unchastity. However, Suetonius emphasizes Domitian's cruel streak, observing that "he prefaced all his most savage sentences with the same speech about mercy: indeed this lenient preamble soon became a recognized sign that something dreadful was on the way" (*Caesars*, p. 307). According to the biographer, Domitian eventually became so feared and hated that his friends and servants plotted to murder him, with his own wife's connivance. A household steward, Stephanus, stabbed Domitian to death, losing his own life in the struggle. The Roman Senate denounced their dead emperor's memory and decreed that all records of his reign should be obliterated.

Omens and auguries. One striking feature of *The Twelve Caesars* is Suetonius's detailed account of the various supernatural omens associated with each Caesar's reign. Whether favorable or unfavorable, plausible or incredible, auguries and prophecies seem to have been inescapable phenomena in the lives of Roman rulers.

Arguably, the most famous of these prophecies concerns Julius Caesar, who was warned by the augur Spurinna that he would face grave danger no later than the Ides of March (the middle of March). Several signs appeared to underscore the warning: a bird, known as the King Bird, was torn to pieces by a flock of other birds on the day before the Ides; Caesar's last dream was that he was soaring above the clouds and then shaking hands with Jupiter; and Caesar's wife Calpurnia dreamed that a gable ornament, one of the honors bestowed upon Caesar by the Senate, collapsed and that she held her husband's dying body in her arms. Despite these auspices, Caesar proceeded to the Senate without hesitation on the fateful day. Encountering Spurinna on the way, he derided the augur as a false prophet, announcing that the Ides of March had come. Spurinna countered, "Yes, they have come . . . but they have not yet gone" (Spurinna in Suetonius, p. 30). Ironically, someone had earlier handed Caesar a note warning him of the plot against his life, but Caesar only added it unread to the sheaf of petitions he was already carrying. Moments after Caesar entered the Senate's Assembly Hall, located at Pompey's Theater complex, the conspirators fell upon him and stabbed him to death.

Caesar's successors had similar, if less dramatic, experiences. Comets with fiery tails, presaging deaths, appeared in the sky shortly before the demises of Emperors Claudius and Vespasian. A noted physiognomist observed Claudius's son Britannicus and Vespasian's son Titus as boys, and revealed that the former would never succeed his father but the latter would succeed *his*.

Astrologists predicted the very hour, day, year, and manner of Domitian's death, all of which were fulfilled. While it is possible to interpret Domitian's end, at least, as a self-fulfilling prophecy—reportedly, he became crueler and more despotic as the fateful day approached—Suetonius's inclusion of such omens emphasizes the trust many Romans placed in augury and the supernatural.

Augurs were, in fact, a recognized and accepted element in Roman religious life. From the inception of the republic, there had been two religious colleges: the *pontifices*, headed by the *pontifex maximus* (chief priest) and the *augures*. The former concerned themselves with sacrifices to the gods, the latter with determining the will of the gods, often through observing the behavior of sacred animals, usually birds. It was considered foolhardy and unwise to ignore auguries, however much the petitioner might wish to do so. During the first Punic War (264-241 BCE), the Roman naval commander Publius Claudius Pulcher reportedly ignored an inauspicious sign: the sacred chickens refused several times to eat their corn, which would mean that any battle launched that day would go against the Romans. Infuriated, Pulcher had the chickens thrown overboard and initiated an attack on the Carthaginians that resulted in the almost total destruction of the Roman fleet.

As unlikely as some auguries seemed, they could be made to serve a practical purpose. Signs that appeared to herald a victory in battle or the accession of a stable ruler after a period of chaos—as with Claudius after Gaius's reign of terror or Vespasian after the Year of the Four Emperors—could lend hope and inspiration to disheartened, fearful Romans.

Sources and literary context. Although the Julio-Claudian and Flavian rulers were long dead by the time *The Twelve Caesars* was written, Suetonius had access to the imperial archives, which contained letters and public and private records, during some part of the biography's composition. It is often speculated that Suetonius's dismissal from court occurred after only the first two books—on Julius Caesar and Augustus—were complete, as subsequent installments were less detailed. Nonetheless, other written sources were available to Suetonius, such as Tacitus's *Histories* (c. 109-110 CE), Plutarch's *Lives of Galba and Otho* (c. 96 CE), and Pliny the Elder's *Continuation of the History of Aufidius Bassus* (c. 79 CE). Suetonius seldom cites his sources directly, but he quotes from the works of Claudius Pollio twice and Cremutius Cordus once. He also echoes the Emperor Augustus's own *Acts.*

Along with the writings of Tacitus and the much later Greek historian Dio Cassius, Suetonius's biographies remain one of the few extant literary sources for imperial Rome. While Tacitus is sometimes considered the superior historian, Suetonius is credited with providing a more personal view of his subject. The simplicity of Suetonius's style and his employment of vivid details have also made him accessible to generations of readers.

Events in History at the Time the Biographies Were Written

The development of Latin biography. *The Twelve Caesars* marks a shift from history to biography among scholars and fashionable readers. The works of Tacitus, especially his *Histories* and *Annals,* were considered unsurpassed, a circumstance of which Suetonius would most likely have been aware. Consequently, Suetonius may have chosen a different approach to his material, one that focused more on the personal characteristics and private lives of his subjects.

Since so few biographical works from Classical Rome have survived, it is difficult to assess Suetonius's exact placement within the literary traditions in which he worked. However, it can be noted that earlier writings on the lives of emperors or other prominent persons tended to be eulogistic in tone. Writing perhaps half a century after Domitian's death, Suetonius could present a more objective view of his subject without fear of persecution. Consequently, he juxtaposes his account of each Caesar's achievements as ruler with detailed descriptions, illustrated by many anecdotes, of his private life. Suetonius thus creates a series of compelling character portraits, which, if not always wholly accurate, still present a more balanced view of the Caesars than had existed previously.

Impact. As one of the few surviving accounts of imperial Rome, *The Twelve Caesars* was read, studied, and imitated by successive generations. Suetonius's work provided a model for Einhard's *Charlemagne,* written in the nineteenth century, and a source for Petrarch's *Lives of the Illustrious Romans* in the fourteenth century. More recently, the British novelist and poet Robert Graves drew heavily upon *The Twelve Caesars* as a basis for his famous historical novel *I, Claudius.* Graves, who also penned a modern English translation of *The Twelve Caesars,* wrote that "The younger Pliny . . . wrote that the more he knew of Suetonius, the greater his affection for him grew. I have had the same experience" (*Caesars,* p. 10).

—Pamela S. Loy

The Twelve Caesars

EVALUATING THE EMPERORS

While *The Twelve Caesars* maintains a greater degree of objectivity than earlier biographical writings, Suetonius does not entirely refrain from expressing his own opinion on his chosen subject. His accounts of the more notorious emperors—Gaius, Nero, and Domitian—are occasionally scathing. There is a perfunctory quality to his description of their positive accomplishments while emperor; whereas, when he describes their faults and follies, his tone is condemnatory. One-third of the way through his chapter on Gaius, Suetonius writes, "So much for the Emperor; the rest of this history must deal with the Monster" (*Caesars,* p. 163). By contrast, the chapters dealing with Augustus, Vespasian, and Titus are more flattering in tone: the virtues of these rulers are presented as outweighing their flaws. One can infer from individual chapters in his work that Suetonius approves most of the emperors who are competent administrators, courageous without being reckless, modest, scrupulous, and capable of controlling their appetites and passions.

For More Information

Boardman, John, Jasper Griffin, and Oswyn Murray, eds. *The Oxford History of the Roman World.* Oxford: Oxford University Press, 2001.

Dorey, T. A., ed. *Latin Biography.* New York: Basic Books, 1967.

Grant, Michael. *The Roman Emperors.* New York: Charles Scribner's Sons, 1985.

Hornblower, Simon, and Antony Spawforth, eds. *The Oxford Companion to Classical Civilization.* Oxford: Oxford University Press, 1998.

Jones, Brian, and Robert Milns. *Suetonius: The Flavian Emperors.* Bristol: Bristol Classical Press, 2002.

Jones, Peter, and Keith Sidwell, eds. *The World of Rome.* Cambridge: Cambridge University Press, 1997.

Massie, Allan. *The Caesars.* London: Secker & Warbeck, 1983.

Suetonius. *The Twelve Caesars.* Trans. Robert Graves. Harmondsworth, England: Penguin, 1989.

Wallace-Hadrill, Andrew. *Suetonius.* London: Duckworth, 1995.

Index

F

G

H